Dictionary of Literary Biography • Volume Sixty-two

Elizabethan Dramatists

Dictionary of Literary Biography

Documentary Series

Yearbooks

Concise Series

Dictionary of Literary Biography • Volume Sixty-two

Elizabethan Dramatists

Edited by
Fredson Bowers
University of Virginia

A Bruccoli Clark Layman Book
Gale Research Company • Book Tower • Detroit, Michigan 48226

Manufactured by Edwards Brothers, Inc.
Ann Arbor, Michigan
Printed in the United States of America

Library of Congress Cataloging-in-Publication Data

Elizabethan dramatists.

(Dictionary of literary biography; v. 62)
"A Bruccoli Clark Layman book."
Includes index.
1. English drama—Early modern and Elizabethan, 1500-1600—History and criticism. 2. English drama—Early modern and Elizabethan, 1500-1600—Bio-bibliography. 3. Dramatists, English—Early modern, 1500-1700—Biography—Dictionaries. I. Bowers, Fredson Thayer. II. Series.
PR651.E48   1987   822'.3'09 [B]   87-19779
ISBN 0-8103-1740-0

Contents

Plan of the Series

. . . Almost the most prodigious asset of a country, and perhaps its most precious possession, is its native literary product—when that product is fine and noble and enduring.

Mark Twain*

The advisory board, the editors, and the publisher of the *Dictionary of Literary Biography* are joined in endorsing Mark Twain's declaration. The literature of a nation provides an inexhaustible resource of permanent worth. We intend to make literature and its creators better understood and more accessible to students and the reading public, while satisfying the standards of teachers and scholars.

To meet these requirements, *literary biography* has been construed in terms of the author's achievement. The most important thing about a writer is his writing. Accordingly, the entries in *DLB* are career biographies, tracing the development of the author's canon and the evolution of his reputation.

The purpose of *DLB* is not only to provide reliable information in a convenient format but also to place the figures in the larger perspective of literary history and to offer appraisals of their accomplishments by qualified scholars.

The publication plan for *DLB* resulted from two years of preparation. The project was proposed to Bruccoli Clark by Frederick G. Ruffner, president of the Gale Research Company in November 1975. After specimen entries were prepared and typeset, an advisory board was formed to refine the entry format and develop the series rationale. In meetings held during 1976, the publisher, series editors, and advisory board approved the scheme for a comprehensive biographical dictionary of persons who contributed to North American literature. Editorial work on the first volume began in January 1977, and it was published in 1978.

In order to make *DLB* more than a reference tool and to compile volumes that individually have claim to status as literary history, it was decided to organize volumes by topic, period, or genre. Each of these freestanding volumes provides a biographical-bibliographical guide and overview for a particular area of literature. We are convinced that this organization—as opposed to a single alphabet method—constitutes a valuable innovation in the presentation of reference material. The volume plan necessarily requires many decisions for the placement and treatment of authors who might properly be included in two or three volumes. In some instances a major figure will be included in separate volumes, but with different entries emphasizing the aspect of his career appropriate to each volume. Ernest Hemingway, for example, is represented in *American Writers in Paris, 1920-1939* by an entry focusing on his expatriate apprenticeship; he is also in *American Novelists, 1910-1945* with an entry surveying his entire career. Each volume includes a cumulative index of subject authors and articles. Comprehensive indexes to the entire series are planned.

With volume ten in 1982 it was decided to enlarge the scope of *DLB*. By the end of 1986 twenty-one volumes treating British literature had been published, and volumes for Commonwealth and Modern European literature were in progress. The series has been further augmented by the *DLB Yearbooks* (since 1981) which update published entries and add new entries to keep the *DLB* current with contemporary activity. There have also been *DLB Documentary Series* volumes which provide biographical and critical source materials for figures whose work is judged to have particular interest for students. One of these companion volumes is entirely devoted to Tennessee Williams.

We define literature as the *intellectual commerce of a nation:* not merely as belles lettres but as that ample and complex process by which ideas are generated, shaped, and transmitted. *DLB* entries are not limited to "creative writers" but extend to other figures who in their time and in their way influenced the mind of a people. Thus the series encompasses historians, journalists, publishers, and screenwriters. By this means readers of *DLB* may be aided to perceive literature not as cult scripture in the keeping of intellec-

---

*From an unpublished section of Mark Twain's autobiography, copyright © by the Mark Twain Company.

tual high priests but firmly positioned at the center of a nation's life.

DLB includes the major writers appropriate to each volume and those standing in the ranks immediately behind them. Scholarly and critical counsel has been sought in deciding which minor figures to include and how full their entries should be. Wherever possible, useful references are made to figures who do not warrant separate entries.

Each *DLB* volume has a volume editor responsible for planning the volume, selecting the figures for inclusion, and assigning the entries. Volume editors are also responsible for preparing, where appropriate, appendices surveying the major periodicals and literary and intellectual movements for their volumes, as well as lists of further readings. Work on the series as a whole is coordinated at the Bruccoli Clark Layman editorial center in Columbia, South Carolina, where the editorial staff is responsible for accuracy of the published volumes.

One feature that distinguishes *DLB* is the illustration policy–its concern with the iconography of literature. Just as an author is influenced by his surroundings, so is the reader's understanding of the author enhanced by a knowledge of his environment. Therefore *DLB* volumes include not only drawings, paintings, and photographs of authors, often depicting them at various stages in their careers, but also illustrations of their families and places where they lived. Title pages are regularly reproduced in facsimile along with dust jackets for modern authors. The dust jackets are a special feature of *DLB* because they often document better than anything else the way in which an author's work was perceived in its own time. Specimens of the writers' manuscripts are included when feasible.

Samuel Johnson rightly decreed that "The chief glory of every people arises from its authors." The purpose of the *Dictionary of Literary Biography* is to compile literary history in the surest way available to us–by accurate and comprehensive treatment of the lives and work of those who contributed to it.

The *DLB* Advisory Board

Foreword

The Renaissance in England reached its full flowering in the reign of Queen Elizabeth I (1558-1603). By common consent the drama of the Elizabethan period (in which we loosely include the reigns of James I and Charles I) up to the Closing of the Theaters by the Commonwealth in 1642 produced the period's greatest literature, which has not been surpassed since its day. Yet a paradox intrudes itself here, for at the time plays were not thought of as "literature," which was taken to be of higher seriousness and value. Indeed, when in 1616 Ben Jonson collected his plays under the title of *Works,* a name reserved for proper literature, there was a certain amount of sniggering at his presumption. Under few circumstances were plays even thought of as an art form. Instead they were generally taken as providing a simple and unintellectual form of amusement, something on the order of a commercial moving picture of today, except that in Elizabethan days plays were not considered to be entirely suitable for a respectable moral person to view or to read. More sermons were printed than any other type of book. It was a commonplace of the drama's opponents that tragedies encouraged great crimes, and comedy gave countenance to and even taught various forms of knavery and immorality.

One factor in this view was the general dislike of the puritanical city fathers of the City of London, who succeeded in banishing the outdoor playhouses to the suburbs where they flourished among the taverns and houses of ill-repute, what would now be called the "red-light district." Moreover, the city authorities gave to the actors the general status of rogues and vagabonds and thus forced them to seek the protection of some great lord, or even of the King or Queen, who accepted them as servants and thus gave them a legal being. In addition to their moral disapprobation the aldermen of London had a practical reason for disliking the crowds that thronged the playhouses. Not only did the throngs occasionally provoke riots, especially when apprentices went on a rampage in celebration of some event, but more particularly the congregation of large crowds increased the danger of the plague, which was always present during these years. Indeed, the theaters were automatically banned whenever the weekly deaths from the plague rose

above a certain number, often being closed in the summer but occasionally for many other months. In such times the out-of-work actors were likely to tour the provinces, where they traveled from town to town, acting in whatever places could be used as makeshift stages, for otherwise they would starve.

The typical Elizabethan theater was an outdoor building, open to the sky, holding several thousand people. The groundlings—the poorer sort—stood in the pit before the stage through the whole performance. The more prosperous bourgeoisie and the gentry sat in higher-priced galleries that surrounded the thrust-out stage on three sides, whereas a few select noblemen, or aspirants to public attention, could rent the Lords' Rooms, set above and to the side of the stage. Sometimes spectators were permitted to sit on stools on the very stage itself. From at least 1576, however, the choristers of the Chapel and of Paul's were permitted to act plays in Blackfriars, a building turned into an indoor theater in a district removed from the City's jurisdiction. Boy actors always took the female parts on the Elizabethan stage, but these all-boy companies became so popular after their regular establishment at Blackfriars after Michaelmas 1600 as to give rise to the well-known discussion between Hamlet and Rosencrantz about the "little eyases" who have displaced the adult companies in public esteem. About 1607-1608 the adult companies invaded these so-called private theaters and took them over for their own use, acting both here and in their larger public open-air theaters, in part according to the season.

Plays in the public theaters were acted in daylight without intermission. Much to their advantage, such plays were designed to appeal to the whole spectrum of the London populace from the highest to the lowest. The private indoor theater, on the other hand, exacted a stiff entrance fee and was attended almost exclusively by the gentry and nobility. Two or three brief intermissions were provided with music for entertainment.

Some plays were acted both outdoors and indoors, just as Shakespeare's company used both the public Globe and the private Blackfriars theaters. But a more or less separate repertoire began to develop according to the tastes of the different audiences for which each theater was designed, a split not always with happy effects for the drama. Plays for the public theaters might sometimes be written down to the lowest level of the populace, yet ordinarily they chose a middle course, and thus their appeal was universal from apprentice to lord and has remained so to the present day. The indoor theaters, on the other hand, fostered a clique audience, which enjoyed in-plays aimed at their special group, plays that at one time were especially satirical of individuals and at all times were likely to be highly artificial in plotting and characterization, as we find in Beaumont and Fletcher's popular plays aimed at the upper classes. The seeds of the decadence that was to overtake the theater in Caroline times were being sown.

The Court, always in need of amusement, had patronized and protected the theater from the beginning, and if plays like Thomas Edwards's or John Lyly's were written especially for it, the result at the time was an increase in sophistication for which the popular drama was badly in need. During Shakepeare's day both Elizabeth and James ordered the theater's best plays to be presented at Court, but under Charles increasingly a court coterie of dramatists sprang up who aimed their plays at the relatively idle fashionable court audience and

lost touch with the popular theater and its life blood in their effort to please the King and his courtiers. Such plays were determinedly artificial and mannered and, unfortunately, began to influence the public stage. The elaborate and costly masques, given exclusively at court for royal entertainment on feast days and state occasions, represent a special genre. For the delectation of the vulgar some of the dramatists began to insert masquelike scenes in their plays purely for entertainment value and with little dramatic motivation.

One reason for the preeminence of the Elizabethan drama at its height was its native tradition that was able to overcome attempts to imitate the frigid classicism of the continental European drama, especially the French. This popular tradition was established early. English drama began as little dialogues, or tropes, inserted in the Latin Mass on such church festivals as Easter and Christmas. It rapidly outgrew the church and came under the civic protection of the trade guilds, so that in the fifteenth and early-sixteenth centuries citizens acted cycles or series of little plays each of which dramatized some one event in the whole biblical history of mankind from Creation to the Day of Judgment. These so-called miracle or mystery plays

Part of Mathias Merian's View of London *in about 1600 showing the playhouses of Bankside, outside the jurisdiction of the London city fathers: the Swan (number 39), the Beargarden (number 38), and the first Globe (number 37) with the Rose between it and the river. The Globe and the Swan are shown too close to the river and the Rose is located incorrectly (from J. L. Gottfried's* Neuwe Archontologia Cosmica, *1638).*

A performance of a miracle play on a pageant wagon

were acted on scaffolds but also on top of pageant wagons that were drawn from station to station in the streets to repeat the performance before a fresh group of townspeople, followed by the next wagon, and so on. Devout as these plays were in their subject matter, some of them made sturdy attempts at realistic characterization. Moreover, in certain plays the course of realistic true-to-life narrative began to edge out the pious sentiments and formal religious presentation. The Cain and Abel story, as elaborated, rang true to real life in its portrait of surly anger and jealousy. Abraham and Isaac acquired true pathos verging on tragedy. Secular events intruded. For instance, in *The Second Shep-* *herds' Play* most of the action is taken up with the sheep-stealing activities and ultimate detection of a rascal named Mak until such time as the angelic voices announce the birth of Jesus to the shepherds. Noah was given a shrewish wife who refused to leave her gossips to enter the ark and had to be carried in by force after belaboring her husband unmercifully.

Occasional allegorical characters made their appearance in these miracle plays, but it was only when the popular drama fell into the hands of groups of itinerant actors that it became secularized, even in allegorical terms, in what came to be known as the morality play. Here the allegorical

Virtues and Vices took over the dramatized conflict for the soul of Mankind, a conflict that increasingly was developed in terms of real-life incidents and problems as in the best of this type, the well-known *Everyman*. In another development that attracted the popular audience, emphasis began to be placed on crude comedy, focused in the person of a character known as the Vice. Starting as an evil tempter of man, the Vice bit by bit grew into a trickster, with more merriment than evil in his makeup, and the basic plot of man's temptation, fall, and forgiveness began to treat more subjects, like methods of education, or satires on manners, with the moral emphasis considerably subdued.

The turn in the drama's development came when in the universities, in the schools for training the professions like the Inns of Court, in the households of noblemen, and especially in the royal court the demand for entertainment called in a new kind of professional dramatist, like John Heywood for instance, playwrights who first writing for amateur performances soon turned to providing plays for touring bands of actors playing in inn yards, a structure that had a profound effect on the later Elizabethan theater. The rising tide of demand for entertainment brought in as actors for the court under Henry VIII, and then for the public under Elizabeth, the chorister Children of the Chapel Royal for whom Lyly wrote. The training ground was prepared for dramatists who would mix the popular with the courtly tradition for a wider audience in London and the provinces, and the true form of the drama was born as both writing for the stage and acting became profitable occupations that attracted university graduates like Greene, Peele, and Marlowe, whose plays were acted not only in inn yards but in newly built theaters for professional acting companies.

The most convenient division for the forms of drama in its final development is that of History, Comedy, and Tragedy, the categories adopted in Shakespeare's First Folio of 1623.

History plays were early popular, in some small part because their events provided ready-made plots that carried the aura of truth but chiefly because dramatized English history appealed to the patriotic fervor before and after the Armada years and the skirmishes on the Continent in which England took part against its traditional enemies France and Spain. As an art, history had been slow to develop in Elizabethan times and confined itself mainly to chronicles, that is, to recording with little comment or interpretation the main public events of each year, in chronological order, intermixing political and military actions of importance with trivial accounts of natural wonders, storms, monstrous births, and particularly sensational murders. The usual early history play, known as a chronicle-history, narrated its active subjects with little more order than the chronicles and with very small recognition of the cause and effect of the tides of history, the interaction of royal supremacy with the commons, the constant conflict of king and nobles for power. Such plays, as most commonly read now in Shakespeare's *Henry VI* trilogy, made little effort to shape action into an artistic plot with a beginning, a middle, and an end. In something of a dead-end situation, romantic comedy was tried in order to piece out an historical background, as in Greene's *Scottish History of James IV*. To Marlowe in his two-part *Tamburlaine* goes the credit of first forcing scattered historical events into some sort of meaningful pattern. In the later *Edward II* he was the first to attempt to analyze history in terms of personalities, of characterization, and the opposing political forces of king, barons, and commons. In his *Richard III* Shakespeare learned from Marlowe's *Tamburlaine* the unifying force that could be given to history by concentrating on a powerful dominant character who controlled the action. In his *Richard II* he learned from Marlowe the anatomy of weakness and the disease that overtook a kingdom governed by a willful king more concerned with his own private emotions and pleasures than with the national welfare. The apotheosis, the high point of the chronicle-history, came with Shakespeare's *Henry V*, but before that he had unified history as dramatic action and as dramatic fiction into a play in which the characters as individuals and as historical figures merged into one, and the dramatic story line became more important than the historical events. This was the celebrated first part of *Henry IV* in which history and comedy form a single strand. In such plays as *Julius Caesar* and *Antony and Cleopatra*, or *Macbeth*, the union is so perfect that the history can no longer be felt as an independent action. Character and historical events are swept up into the purest form of tragedy.

Elizabethan comedy separated itself, at least for a time, into three recognizable groups. There is romantic comedy as in Greene's *Friar Bacon and Friar Bungay*, Dekker's *Old Fortunatus*, Shakespeare's *As You Like It* and *Twelfth Night*. Ben Jonson formulated the comedy of humours in *Every Man in His Humour*, and in his masterpieces *Volpone* and *The Alchemist* he combined these humours with an intrigue plot to create the ultimate in this form of comedy. In some part stemming from Jonson's an-

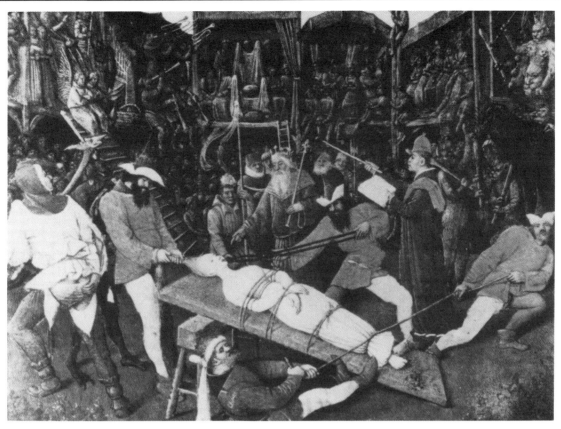

The torture of St. Apollonia in a miracle play. This miniature by Jean Fouquet is the only known medieval illustration of the action in such a play (from Les Heures d'Etienne Chevalier, *circa 1460; by permission of the Musée Condé, Chantilly).*

tiromantic comic theories, comedies of bourgeois London life were popular, like Dekker and Webster's *Westward Ho!*, Middleton's *Michaelmas Term*, or Jonson, Chapman, and Marston's *Eastward Ho!* Indeed, these became the prevailing form of comedy for some years when dramatists found it difficult to emulate Shakespeare's romantic comedy and could only merge it into a new form of tragicomedy as in Beaumont and Fletcher's *Philaster*. Comedies of manners, in the later sense of the reaction between personality and social codes, were always present in Shakespeare but did not usurp the main plot line. Some few comedies of manners like Fletcher's *Wild-Goose Chase* anticipate what was to develop fully in the Restoration, although Shirley's *Lady of Pleasure* can also be considered as a forerunner.

The clever slave of the Roman comedy of Plautus and Terence gave rise to Brainworm in Jonson's *Every Man in His Humour* and to countless other Elizabethan servants who were more quick-witted than their masters and who amused the audience and kept the plot rolling by manipulating their superiors. But a more far-reaching influence helped to shape the form and attitude of Elizabethan comedy. In a broad sense this was the doctrine of decorum. If we dig beneath the surface manifestation of decorum as form, such as whether in tragedy violent action must be narrated, not performed—a matter of far more moment to the French than to the English, who ignored it—we may see that decorum is associated with character first, and only then with plot, which is the summation of actions appropriate for given characters and not a force independent of character. Decorum was the moving principle of Roman comedy and (though in a less obvious manner) was strongly operative in Senecan Roman tragedy. According to the principle of decorum established in Roman comedy, an old man is supposed to be appreciative of his own wisdom derived from experience but often hardened into formulas of conduct, and thus he will not value the instincts and opinions of youth. He is suspicious but easily deceived, inclined to be loquacious, overly careful of family position and wealth, conservative, and is opposed to all change.

A young man is supposed to be ardent, generous, brave, ruled in his actions more by his emotions than by his reason, and so on. This decorum was not only personal but was also applied to the various conditions of mankind. A merchant was supposed to be prudent, cautious, peaceable; a soldier, valiant, quarrelsome, honorable. The characters of all trades and professions thus became codified. It was as indecorous for a merchant to swagger like a bravo as for a swineherd to possess a refined sensibility. If an opposite to the system was exhibited for satirical purposes, as in the person of the braggart soldier, it was usually made clear that the person was, in fact, no soldier but a pretender to military life.

When in *The Defense of Poesy* Sir Philip Sidney remarked that "comedy is an imitation of the common errors of our life," he was enunciating perhaps the strongest theme of the doctrine of decorum, which reserved comedy for low or middle actions in private bourgeois life beneath the level of greatness; and tragedy for the important affairs of great men, whose private actions must always have public repercussions. (It is clear how romantic comedy broke with this tradition and created a decorum of its own which had no relation to the classical formulas.) Especially under the influence of Ben Jonson, it was held in comedy that actions of private men were to concern the common errors of ordinary life, for Jonson the moralist was fixed in his purpose that comedy was the agent of reform and by exposing abuses should warn the audience against being deceived by similar deceptions or falling into similar irrational ways of thought and action (humours). This moral purpose never left the comedy of ordinary life during the Elizabethan period, for indeed it constituted one of the arguments that the stage did not teach vice by its exhibition of faulty actions but instead exposed these by showing their invariable lack of success as a warning to the audience. That this stance became more lip service than conviction among the dramatists does not affect the general attitude.

Although decorum was a fixed principle in the portrayal of Virtues and Vices in the early morality play, as the popular drama became more secularized and the moral intent more ostensible than real, the degeneration of the morality play's initial high seriousness was accompanied inevitably by degeneration in the consistency of word and action in the characters if the entertainment of the audience was thereby served. That ambiguous figure of the Vice may be something of an example, for a dramatist grappling with new material did not always draw a clear line between mischievousness and deadly corruption aimed at the damnation of the soul, or even between firmly held virtue and formal priggishness.

When the morality play finally surrendered to pure comedy, the principle of decorum imposed a much-needed discipline on the new dramatists, especially the more learned. Ready to hand from Roman comedy was a whole parade of stock figures with characteristics already formulated and tested for dramatic effect. When the Roman comedy was consciously imitated, the transition was a natural one of clever slave to Merygreke in *Ralph Roister Doister* or Diccon in *Gammer Gurton's Needle,* classicized Vices with their fangs drawn in an English setting. A more extreme application and extension of decorum may be observed even in such a potpourri as Greene's *Friar Bacon and Friar Bungay* where social classes are carefully distinguished, as in the calculated wooing of Margaret by Lacy, Earl of Lincoln, and the court paid her by Lambert and Serlsby, mere country gentlemen of her own class. We also see decorum relied on as a substitute for dramatic explanation of action. Lacy's cruel (and, to modern sensibility, meaningless) testing of Margaret's constancy is never motivated. Obviously, Greene did not feel it necessary to explain the reasons for the trick to an audience accustomed to the whims of the great ones. It would seem obvious, according to Greene, that Lacy's action must be suitable for a nobleman in his position. Dekker's *Patient Grissill* has a similar but more highly developed theme.

Whenever plot is predominant, characters are likely to sink into types, of course. Type characters abounded on the English stage, even encouraged in part by the automatic application of a watered-down Jonsonian theory of humours, or overriding passions and tendencies of thought governing action; but it is one of the glories of the Elizabethan drama that there was a constant pressure to break through these standardized molds of form. Decorum and type formulas are usually associated with an emphasis on manners, or a picture of ways of life as represented in the adjustment of character to social position and customs, and the problems that arise when individuality acts to change the rules of the game. The comedy of manners is usually associated with high life, but it need not be; as in Jonson, occupation can take the place of social position in the seesaw of conflict—for the bourgeoisie and even low-life characters have their manners as well as their betters. Yet it was a distinctive manifestation of the Elizabethan delight in individuality

The inn yard at the White Hart, Southwark, where plays were performed on a temporary platform

instead of formulas that led Ben Jonson to give at least as much attention to the eccentricities of human nature in their humours as he did to the characteristics of social types. The distinction is already drawn in *Every Man in His Humour*. The elder Knowell is the ever-careful father of classical comedy, a figure of complete decorum for his age and station. Brainworm is a slightly modified clever slave. But Cob can scarcely be called a characteristic water drawer; Bobadill breaks the bounds of the formal braggart soldier by the inclusion of many other characteristics; and Justice Clements's private amusement in the power of his office is not typical of Justices of the Peace, as Thomas Cash's inbuilt faithfulness is, in contrast, typical of the careful journeyman. Kitely is interesting because in type he is a merchant but in humour he is an irrationally jealous man. The shell of decorum of occupation is broken, and manners are considerably broadened, by packing into him personal attributes that have little or nothing to do with the attributes of his profession. His comic actions may be judged according to ideas of decorum, of what was suitable

for a jealous man to do or say; but these have little connection with the more formal concept of decorous action and words suitable for a merchant. Jonson interchanges one concept for the other, back and forth; but only in a single occasion in this play does he make dramatic use of a conflict between them, as when Kitely cannot bear to leave his merchandise unattended while he pursues what he regards as his faithless wife.

In sum, although in various of their manifestations the humours that dominated Elizabethan comedy reinforced the theory of decorum in manners, as in the model comedy *Eastward Ho!*, nevertheless the seeds of character interest that drove humours away from types and toward unique portraits of individualized fixations substituted another rationale to displace classical decorum with Elizabethan variety: the rationale of inner faithfulness to a coherent individual in his own terms. The terrible picture of Harry Dampit in Middleton's *A Trick to Catch the Old One* goes far beyond any contribution that the theory of decorum ever made to the type of a usurer. Correspondingly, the

The first Globe theater, which burned to the ground on 29 June 1613 (from J. C. Visscher's View of London, *1616)*

great dramatic character of Sir Giles Overreach in Massinger's *A New Way to Pay Old Debts* is faithful to an internal rationale that transcends the usurer of stage tradition. The tendency of Elizabethan comedy, thus, was to free itself from the limitation of formal type decorum as a dramatic principle, and to substitute inner coherence in its own terms of observation, a rationale that placed decorum on a raised level of truth to nature unknown in its classical antecedents except in the most general terms.

On the other hand, some argument may be made for the reverse operation in tragedy. Few Elizabethan dramatists except Shakespeare were affected by the Aristotelian concept of the protag-

onist of moderate virtue who yet has some unsuspected flaw through which tragedy strikes and so enforces the justice of the fatal ending. Instead, the red glare of Seneca's villains enraptured most playwrights. Shakespeare could create a unique villain in Macbeth, who was as little Senecan as he was Aristotelian. Working more within the standard Elizabethan tradition, Webster could yet transcend convention not only by the imaginative power of his realistic portraits of vice but also by his ability to intermingle humanity in such persons as Bosola, Brachiano, and Vittoria.

In 1615 one of the puritanical opponents of the stage, J. Greene, in his *Refutation of the Apology for Actors,* tried to instill repugnance in his readers by a description of the vices of tragedy: "The *Trage-dies* discourseth of lamentable fortunes, extreme affects, horrible villainies, rapines, murthers, spoils, tyrannies, and the like." And a little later he is more specific: "The matter of *Tragedies* is haughtiness, arrogancy, ambition, pride, injury, anger, wrath, envy, hatred, contention, warre, murther, cruelty, rapine, incest, . . . rebellions, treasons, killing, . . . treachery, villany, &c., and all kinds of heroyck evils whatsoever." To such diatribes the actors could only respond that though their tragedies did portray the evil deeds of evil men; yet these criminals always came to a bad end, and thus the cause of virtue was served by showing the inevitable defeat of vice. Yet it could not be concealed that "all kinds of heroyck evils whatsoever" performed by appropriate villains was what the Elizabethans took over as the action and character that fulfilled tragic decorum. The popular Elizabethan villain play stemmed directly from this narrowing of the matter of tragedy from Shakespeare's huge canvas of tragically flawed good men to the appropriate deeds of great villains. This limited tragic concept led to a limited number of plot formulas and to a stiffening of the formulas of characterization that contrasts with the freedom with which character and plot were exploited in Shakespearean tragedy.

The explanation for this paradox is not far to seek. The common association of tragedy with the exhibition of vicious character in action could thrill the audience with horror, but despite the actors' protestations it could scarcely purge in the manner that comedy proposed for its end. Members of the audience could perhaps see something of themselves and their own experiences on the comic stage and thereby be led to a self-consciousness that was the prerequisite for reform; but the ability to identify with blackest villainy was strictly limited, as Aristotle had long before observed. The Elizabethan comic dramatists had found in Plautus and Terence a strict formula for comedy which they proceeded to broaden and make meaningful by a strong infusion of variety, and its peculiar order of truth, that followed on sympathetic, or at least intimate, observation of real life. The Elizabethan tragic dramatists found in Seneca a formula that was as rigid in its springs of action as the Roman comedy, though less formal in the organization of the plot line and its details. However, the Senecan desertion of the Aristotelian balanced principle in protagonist and plot forced the Elizabethan tragic dramatists away from the realities of observation and into a world of imagination

where their fantasies could not match in artistic validity the lively curiosity about the differences in human nature which alone could break the writers loose from the limitations of formal tragic decorum in character and plot, if we define classical not as Greek (the Greek drama being largely unknown to the Elizabethans) but as Senecan.

Indeed, the Elizabethan tragedians tended to impose a formula on themselves, with the result that the usual Elizabethan villain is likely to be more rigidly typed than his Senecan prototypes. In this process the extraordinary Elizabethan preoccupation with Machiavellism stifled much individuality in character portrayal and channeled villainous motivation into a relatively few standard patterns. (Not all dramatists were capable of the larger view held by Marston in *The Malcontent* of Italian villainy.) It follows that interest in individual character gives place to an emphasis on conventionally motivated startling action. For instance, we know little of the original Marlovian concept of the latter half of *The Jew of Malta*, but the noteworthy degeneration of character when the attention is diverted to intrigue in the plot is either a symptom of an inherent flaw caused by a catering to Machiavel or—perhaps as likely—the effect of the imposition of degenerate Caroline dramatic values on the revision of an old play.

The pernicious influence of Machiavellism was far-reaching. It led to the association of tragic passion exclusively with ambition, lust, envy, hatred, vice, and thus with the establishment of the villain as the protagonist of the usual Elizabethan tragedy, Shakespeare apart. It also led to an action based mainly on intrigue. The Elizabethans were thoroughly horrified with what they had heard of Machiavelli's *The Prince*. They did not understand its cool analysis of the facts of life among the Italian petty tyrants but took its objectivity for approval of every kind of breaking of faith, conscienceless action, and the free use of murder as a political weapon. The lurid stories told in histories of Italy, and the sometimes equally lurid tales in the Italian *novelle* only confirmed an initial anti-Catholic distrust of Italy as the land of poisoners, lust, hypocrisy, and bloodshed. In all this mixture of truth and fantasy the Elizabethans could bring little of their own observation or experience in common humanity to bear. The thrill of an alien villainy rampant in an alien civilization took the place of identification with tragic action and protagonist.

As the period wore on, the absoluteness of formulary Machiavellian villainy blotted out the subtler earlier attempts at portraying the essentially

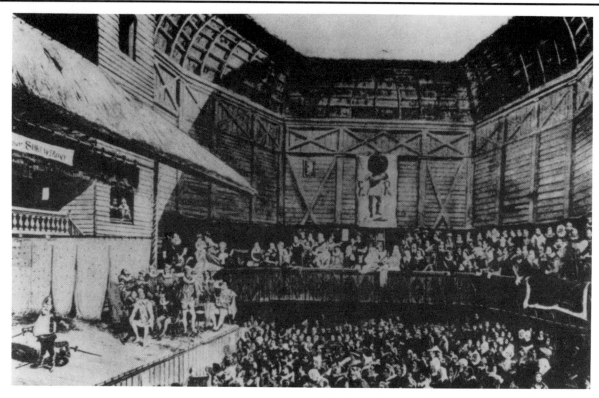

The interior of the first Globe theater. The groundlings stood in the pit and more-prosperous theatergoers sat in the gallery, in the lords' rooms, and on the stage itself.

good man like Hamlet or Othello and the balance of pity and fear that accompanied his expiatory downfall. When tragic catharsis, at the heart of the Aristotelian principle of decorum, was pushed aside by the coarser shock effects of horror and amazement, the reign of terror that passed for tragic decorum of character and action on the imagined Senecan stage completed its conquest of the minor Elizabethan tragic dramatist.

As the drama passed the first quarter of the seventeenth century, comedy remained lively though growing farther away from the Shakespearean romantic ideal and tending either toward tragicomedy or the continued studies of middle-class life, with emphasis on intrigue beginning to take the place of humours. Following Fletcher, some tendency may be observed, as in Shirley's *Lady of Pleasure,* for comedy to study the manners of the upper classes instead of the bourgeoisie or the lower orders. When Shakespeare grew somewhat out of fashion, Beaumont and Fletcher usurped the greater popularity. Not only in his unaided works but also in his frequent association with Massinger, Field, Rowley, and Shirley either as collaborators or revisers, Fletcher was a major force in the deterioration of the ethical seriousness of the

earlier drama and its attempts to hold the mirror up to nature whether in realistic or idealistic contexts. Although to the Jacobean and Caroline audiences Beaumont and Fletcher's characters reflected accurately the manners and sentiments that they fancied were—or should have been— their ideals, the present day thinks differently. We now recognize the coarseness of moral fiber characteristic of their plays; the complete artificiality and extravagance of sentiment held by the heroes of their tragicomedies and tragedies like *Philaster, The Maid's Tragedy, A Wife for a Month, A King and No King,* or *The Loyal Subject;* the fawning adulation lavished on the monarchical principle stemming from the divine right of kings; the sudden and unmotivated changes in character according to the arbitrary demands of the plot, including the abrupt repentance of evil characters; the constant sexuality of theme and outlook, the titillations of incestuous passion that turns out to be legitimate after all— this essentially cheap sensationalism helped lead to the decline of the drama. On the other hand, some of Fletcher's comedies can hold their own today, and without question he had a true comic gift for plotting and characterization. It is the essential falseness of his tragicomedies of court life and their basic sentimentality and extravagance that led his imitators astray and without question fostered, ultimately, the peculiar genre of Restoration heroic tragedy.

A few dramatists were fascinated by plots based on abnormal psychology, even though the theme had always been latent in the earlier portraits of Italian ducal villains out of Machiavelli and the histories. John Ford's *'Tis Pity She's a Whore* offers a powerful picture of incestuous love until the play collapses in the Grand Guignol extravagances of the catastrophe. Ford's *The Broken Heart* attempts a study of thwarted love in a complex web of platonic conventions. The most extraordinary psychological probing of situation and character appears in Middleton and Rowley's *The Changeling,*

which paints unsparingly the degeneration of a woman fatally caught up in an abnormal, even diseased, sexual passion that had started in disgust and in physical as well as psychic repugnance.

The latter days of the drama could not equal the energy, the variety, and the delight found in the Renaissance spirit of the earlier plays, reaching its height, of course, in the unique poetic drama of Shakespeare. The need to stimulate an increasingly jaded audience by sensationalism in tragedy, regardless of consistency of theme and characterization, and by increasing the sexual charge in comedy, led to a marked decline in the ethical seriousness of the dramatic form in the hands of minor playwrights. Major dramatists like Middleton, Massinger, and Shirley, on the other hand, did

The second Globe theater (incorrectly labeled "Beere bayting h"), built on the site of the first, was opened in late spring 1614 (from Wenceslaus Hollar's "Long View" of London, engraved in 1644 and published in 1647)

succeed in maintaining some semblance of a higher aim in tragedy and tragicomedy and of social criticism in comedy by their very professionalism operating through authentic literary talent. The drama brought to a close by the Commonwealth inhibition had grown tired and had declined from its earlier height, but it was cut off while it still shone, even though palely, with the reflected glow from its great period of most astonishing Renaissance vigor and magnificence.

—Fredson Bowers

DLB 62: Elizabethan Dramatists is a companion to *DLB 58: Jacobean and Caroline Dramatists.* Because many dramatists whose careers began during the reign of Elizabeth I (1558-1603) continued writing during the reign of James I (1603-1625) and in some cases into the reign of Charles I (1625-1649) as well, there are playwrights in each volume who might justifiably have been included in the other.

At the beginning of each entry in these volumes there are lists of an author's play productions and books. Because records for the period are incomplete, the productions listed under the first rubric are the first known performances of plays, and the dates and locations of these productions are sometimes matters of conjecture based on the best available evidence. Many of the texts for plays written in the period are no longer in existence, though some of these plays are mentioned in contemporary documents. If the author of the entry has evidence that a lost play was produced, it is listed under play productions. The reader should be aware that many of these playwrights may have written or helped to write other plays that are unknown to modern scholars or that remain unattributed or misattributed.

Many plays were published anonymously or were erroneously attributed by their first publishers, and the authorship of some is still unresolved. Attributions of the plays listed under both play productions and books are based on the contributors' assessments of most recent scholarship and are not necessarily the same as authors' names listed on title pages of plays' first editions.

Under the play productions rubrics and in the body of the text these entries refer to plays by the titles by which they are now most commonly known, employing modern spellings. Under the books rubrics, while titles are frequently shortened, the spellings of the first printings of surviving books are transcribed as they appear on the original title pages, with the following exceptions: long *s* is transcribed *s*, and for books printed after 1601 *u* and *v* and *i* and *j* are sometimes transcribed according to modern usage ("have" and "use" for "haue" and "vse," "joy" and "filii" for "ioy" and "filij," for example). Imprints are listed as they appear on title pages, but, in cases where a printer, publisher, or bookseller is known but not printed on the title page, the name is added. The authorities for the publication information in this volume are *A Short-Title Catalogue of Books Printed in England, Scotland, & Ireland and of English Books Printed Abroad 1475-1640,* compiled by A. W. Pollard and G. R. Redgrave, second edition, revised and enlarged, begun by W. A. Jackson and F. S. Ferguson, completed by Katharine F. Pantzer (2 volumes, 1976, 1986); and A *Short-Title Catalogue of Books Printed in England, Scotland, Ireland, Wales and British America and of English Books Printed In Other Countries, 1641-1700,* compiled by Donald Wing, revised and enlarged edition (3 volumes, 1972-   ).

At the end of listings of first editions, under the subheading "Editions," authors of entries have listed the most authoritative later texts of the subjects' works. Quotations in this volume are drawn from these editions.

A general bibliography of works relating to the authors in both these *DLB* volumes is included in this volume.

Acknowledgments

This book was produced by Bruccoli Clark Layman, Inc. Karen L. Rood, senior editor for the *Dictionary of Literary Biography* series, was the in-house editor.

Copyediting supervisor is Patricia Coate. Production coordinator is Kimberly Casey. Typesetting supervisor is Laura Ingram. Lucia Tarbox and Michael Senecal are editorial associates. The production staff includes Rowena Betts, Charles Brower, Mary S. Dye, Charles Egleston, Gabrielle Elliott, Sarah A. Estes, Kathleen M. Flanagan, Joyce Fowler, Cynthia Hallman, Judith K. Ingle, Maria Ling, Warren McInnis, Kathy S. Merlette, Sheri Neal, Joycelyn R. Smith, and Elizabeth York. Jean W. Ross is permissions editor. Joseph Caldwell, photography editor, and Joseph Matthew Bruccoli did photographic copy work for the volume.

Walter W. Ross and Rhonda Marshall did the library research with the assistance of the staff at the Thomas Cooper Library of the University of South Carolina: Lynn Barron, Daniel Boice, Donna Breese, Kathy Eckman, Gary Geer, Cathie Gottlieb, David L. Haggard, Jens Holley, Dennis Isbell, Marcia Martin, Jean Rhyne, Beverley Steele, Ellen Tillett, and Virginia Weathers.

Special thanks are due to Tom Lange of the Henry E. Huntington Library and Art Gallery and Charles Mann of the Pennsylvania State University Library for their help in providing illustrations.

Dictionary of Literary Biography • Volume Sixty-two

Elizabethan Dramatists

Dictionary of Literary Biography

George Chapman

(1559 or 1560-12 May 1634)

Gordon Braden
University of Virginia

PLAY PRODUCTIONS: *The Blind Beggar of Alexandria*, London, Rose theater, 12 February 1596;

A Humorous Day's Mirth, London, Rose theater, 11 May 1597;

The Fount of New Fortunes (or *The Ill of a Woman*), London, Rose theater, 1598;

All Fools but the Fool (or *The World Runs on Wheels*, possibly a first version of *All Fools*), London, Rose theater, 1599;

The Four Kings, London, Rose theater, 1599;

A Pastoral Tragedy (possibly unfinished), London, Rose theater, 1599;

All Fools, London, Blackfriars theater, 1601;

May Day, London, Blackfriars theater, 1601-1602;

Sir Giles Goosecap, London, Blackfriars theater, 1602;

The Gentleman Usher, London, Blackfriars theater, 1602-1603;

The Old Joiner of Aldgate, London, St. Paul's theater, February 1603;

Bussy D'Ambois, London, St. Paul's theater, 1604;

Monsieur D'Olive, London, Blackfriars theater, 1604-1605;

The Widow's Tears, London, Blackfriars theater, 1604-1605;

Eastward Ho, by Chapman, Ben Jonson, and John Marston, London, Blackfriars theater, 1605;

The Conspiracy and Tragedy of Charles Duke of Byron, London, Blackfriars theater, 1607-1608;

The Revenge of Bussy D'Ambois, London, Whitefriars theater, 1610-1611;

Masque of the Middle Temple and Lincoln's Inn, Westminster, Whitehall Palace, 15 February 1613;

The Tragedy of Chabot Admiral of France, date and theatrical history uncertain;

Caesar and Pompey, date uncertain, possibly never performed.

BOOKS: Σκιὰ νύκτος. *The Shadow of Night: Containing Two Poeticall Hymnes* (London: Printed by R. Field for W. Ponsonby, 1594);

Ouids Banquet of Sence. A Coronet for His Mistresse Philosophie, and His Amorous Zodiacke. With a Translation of a Latine Coppie, Written by a Fryer, Anno Dom. 1400 (London: Printed by J. Roberts for R. Smith, 1595);

Hero and Leander, parts 1 and 2 by Christopher Marlowe, parts 3-6 by Chapman (London: Printed by F. Kingston for P. Linley, 1598);

Seaven Bookes of the Iliades, translated by Chapman from books 1-2, 7-11 of Homer's *Iliad* (London: Printed by J. Windet, 1598);

Achilles Shield, translated by Chapman from book 18 of Homer's *Iliad* (London: Printed by J. Windet, 1598);

The Blinde Begger of Alexandria (London: Printed by J. Roberts for W. Jones, 1598);

A Pleasant Comedy Entituled: An Humerous Dayes Myrth (London: Printed by V. Syms, 1599);

Al Fooles (London: Printed by G. Eld for T. Thorpe, 1605);

Eastward Hoe, by Chapman, Ben Jonson, and John Marston (London: Printed by G. Eld for W. Aspley, 1605);

The Gentleman Usher (London: Printed by V. Simmes for T. Thorppe, 1606);

Monsieur D'Olive (London: Printed by T. Creede for W. Holmes, 1606);

Sir Gyles Goosecappe Knight (London: Printed by J. Windet for E. Blunt, 1606);

Bussy D'Ambois (London: Printed by Eliot's Court Press for W. Aspley, 1607);

The Conspiracie, and Tragedie of Charles Duke of Byron (London: Printed by G. Eld for T. Thorppe, sold by L. Lisle, 1608);

Homer Prince of Poets, translated by Chapman from books 1-12 of Homer's *Iliad* (London: Printed by H. Lownes for S. Macham, 1609?);

Euthymiæ Raptus: Or The Teares of Peace (London: Printed by H. Lownes for R. Bonian & H. Walley, 1609);

The Iliads of Homer, translated by Chapman from all twenty-four books of Homer's *Iliad* (London: Printed by R. Field for N. Butter, 1611);

May-day (London: Printed by W. Stansby for J. Browne, 1611);

An Epicede or Funerall Song: On the Death, of Henry Prince of Wales (London: Printed by T. Snodham for J. Budge, 1612);

Petrarchs Seven Penitentiall Psalms, Paraphrastically Translated: With Other Philosophicall Poems (London: Printed by R. Field for M. Selman, 1612);

The Widdowes Teares (London: Printed by W. Stansby for J. Browne, 1612);

The Memorable Maske of the Middle Temple, and Lyncolns Inne (London: Printed by G. Eld for G. Norton, 1613);

The Revenge of Bussy D'Ambois (London: Printed by T. Snodham, sold by J. Helme, 1613);

Andromeda Liberata. Or the Nuptials of Perseus and Andromeda (London: Printed by Eliot's Court Press for L. L'Isle, 1614);

A Free and Offenceles Justification, of a Lately Publisht and Most Maliciously Misinterpreted Poeme: Entituled Andromeda Liberata (London: Printed by Eliot's Court Press for L. L'Isle, 1614);

Eugenia: Or True Nobilities Trance; For the Death, of William Lord Russel (London, 1614);

Homer's Odysses, translated by Chapman from books 1-12 of Homer's *Odyssey* (London: Printed by R. Field for N. Butter, 1614?); enlarged, with books 13-24 added (London: Printed by R. Field & W. Jaggard for N. Butter, 1615?);

The Whole Works of Homer; in His Iliads, and Odysses, translated by Chapman (London: Printed by R. Field & W. Jaggard for N. Butter, 1616);

The Divine Poem of Musaeus, translated by Chapman (London: Printed by I. Jaggard, 1616);

The Georgicks of Hesiod, translated by Chapman (London: Printed by H. Lownes for M. Partrich, 1618);

Two Wise Men and All the Rest Fooles (London, 1619);

Pro Vere, Autumni Lachrymæ. Inscribed to the Memorie of Sir Horatio Vere (London: Printed by B. Alsop for T. Walkley, 1622);

The Crowne of All Homers Worckes: Batrachomyomachia. His Hymn's and Epigrams, translated by Chapman (London: Printed by Eliot's Court Press for J. Bill, 1624?);

A Justification of a Strange Action of Nero; In Burying One of the Cast Hayres of His Mistresse Poppæa. Also The Fifth Satyre of Juvenall (London: Printed by T. Harper, 1629);

The Warres of Pompey and Caesar (London: Printed by T. Harper, sold by G. Emondson & T. Alchorne, 1631);

The Tragedie of Chabot Admirall of France, by Chapman, revised by James Shirley (London: Printed by T. Cotes for A. Crooke & W. Cooke, 1639).

Editions: *The Plays and Poems of George Chapman*, 2 volumes, edited by Thomas Marc Parrott (London: Routledge / New York: Dutton, 1910-1913);

The Poems of George Chapman, edited by Phyllis Bartlett (New York: Modern Language Association / London: Oxford University Press, 1941);

Chapman's Homer, 2 volumes, edited by Allardyce Nicoll, revised edition (Princeton: Princeton University Press, 1967).

George Chapman was the most intellectually ambitious of the English Renaissance dramatists, the one with the highest claims for the philosophical dignity and importance of his work. His nearest rival was his friend and sometime collaborator Ben Jonson; and, like Jonson, he based much of his claim to seriousness on his study and use of the wisdom of classical antiquity, with much overt display of scholarship. Praise of humanist learning and scorn for the

onely, all things knows." Other sketchy evidence from his early years has him at the Inner Temple, in the service of Sir Ralph Sadler, borrowing money from a London usurer and trying his luck as a soldier in the Low Countries. It is poetry that finally gave this life direction and visibility when in 1594, at age thirty-five, he published *The Shadow of Night*, a combatively vatic bid to establish its author as an Elizabethan laureate. In that volume's "Hymnus in Noctem" he announces:

> like fierce bolts, well rammd with heate & cold
> In Ioues Artillerie; my words vnfold,
> To breake the labyrinth of euerie eare,
> And make ech frighted soule come forth and heare.

The work consists of two Orphic hymns, to Night and to Cynthia. Their densely metaphorical texture of esoteric mythography and philosophical abstraction–and knotty and evasive syntax–became Chapman's lifelong staple. In his introduction to *Achilles Shield* (1598) he calls it "my farre-fetcht and, as it were, beyond-sea manner of writing"; it is a style darker than that of any other Elizabethan poet except possibly Fulke Greville. The obstacles were at least intentional, defiantly so: "I rest as resolute as *Seneca*," he writes in the dedication of *The Shadow of Night*, "satisfying my selfe if but a few, if one, or if none like it." And the stylistic difficulty answers to the overriding conceit of the "Hymnus in Noctem," which is a rejection of the light of common day, "with whoredome soked quite," that Chapman associates with the normal ugly round of human life. Seeing clearly only excites our lower appetites; darkness baffles them and gives the melancholic intellectual the opening for nobler ambitions:

> since the eyes most quicke and dangerous vse,
> Enflames the heart, and learnes the soule abuse
> ....
>
> All you possess with indepressed spirits,
> Indu'd with nimble, and aspiring wits,
> Come consecrate with me, to sacred Night
> Your whole endeuours, and detest the light.

The "Hymnus in Cynthiam" follows with a celebration of the moon goddess who shines within the night. Her crucial attribute is a ravishing chastity:

> The purenesse of thy neuer-tainted life,
> Scorning the subiect title of a wife,

Ouids Banquet of SENCE.

A Coronet for his Miftreffe Philofophie, and his amorous Zodiacke.

VVith a tranflation of a Latine coppie, written by a Fryer, Anno Dom. 1400.

Quis legat hæc ? Nemo Hercule Nemo, vel duo vel nemo : Perfius.

AT LONDON.
Printed by I. R. for Richard Smith.
Anno Dom. 1595.

Title page for the 1595 quarto edition of Chapman's second book (Folger Shakespeare Library)

> Thy bodie not composed in thy birth,
> Of such condensed matter as the earth
> ....
>
> Commit most willing rapes on all our harts.

These rapes are made sublime by their unfulfillment. The centerpiece of the poem is Cynthia's creation of an unending erotic chase in which the nymph Euthymia, charged to tame "the cares and toyles of earth," changes shape into panther and boar as she is pursued by hunters and dogs; they are still at it when Cynthia dissolves things at the approach of dawn. Like a Petrarchan mistress, she is all-powerful in her inaccessibility. That power is political as well, since Cynthia is, inevitably, Elizabeth:

> Then set thy Christall, and Imperiall throne,
> (Girt in thy chast, and neuer-loosing zone)

Gainst Europs Sunne directly opposit,
And giue him darknesse, that doth threat thy light.

The symbolism here has been most fully explicated by Raymond B. Waddington. The sun is specifically Elizabeth's suitor François, Duke of Alençon, in a warning against the last of her prospective marriages. More generally the poem affirms a connection between the cult of the virgin queen and England's rising power, the growth of what Chapman repeatedly calls an empire. Individual self-restraint translates into expansive control of the rest of the world: a *pax imperii* both inward and outward.

This mixture of hermeticism and politics was meant to speak to and for a highly placed coterie. Chapman's poems are the principal evidence for an elite School of Night that may be the object of satire in Shakespeare's *Love's Labor's Lost;* they are definitely related in some fashion to Chapman's involvement in the intellectual circle attached to Sir Walter Raleigh (which also included Matthew Roydon and Thomas Harriot). They are also attempts to start a kind of poetic career that the age made especially enticing and prestigious; an updated mode of classical mythic narrative was the means by which more than one poet strove to secure aristocratic patronage. The immediate stimulus may have been Shakespeare, whose *Venus and Adonis,* appearing in 1593 with a dedication to the Earl of Southampton, is often construed as his attempt to leave the stage. Chapman possibly intervened in that attempt with some intimacy; he is a credible candidate for the rival poet of Shakespeare's sonnets. It is in any case evident that the literary effort which Shakespeare effectively abandoned after *The Rape of Lucrece* (1594), Chapman pursued with competitive fervor for the rest of his working life, until it constituted one major strand of his career.

Two of Chapman's best-known poems ring complex changes on the Ovidian heritage that is the ground for most of the mythic verse of the 1590s. *Ovid's Banquet of Sense* (1595) offers a fable about the biographical origins of Ovid's own poetic inspiration. His fictional love Corinna is actually the Emperor's daughter Julia, whose song while bathing he overhears one day: "Whereat his wit, assumed fierye wings, / Soring aboue the temper of his soule." Hearing is followed by the other senses as he by stages smells, sees, kisses, and touches her, in what he experiences as an intellectual progression as well: "The sence is giuen vs to excite the minde." With his hand fi-

HERO AND LEANDER:

Begun by *Christopher Marloe*; and *finished by* George Chapman.

Vt Nectar, Ingenium.

At London,
Printed by *Felix Kingston,* for *Paule Linley,* and are to be solde in Paules Church-yard, at the signe of the Blacke-beare.
1598.

Title page for the 1598 quarto edition of Marlowe and Chapman's version of the story of legendary lovers. Chapman divided Marlowe's erotic poem, which was published earlier that year, into two sestiads and added four sections whose moral tone contrasts sharply with that of Marlowe's poem (British Library).

nally on her naked breast, he finds his literary purpose clear:

Sweete touch the engine that loues bow doth bend,
The sence wherewith he feeles him deified,
The obiect whereto all his actions tend,
In all his blindenes his most pleasing guide,
    For thy sake will I write the Art of loue.

We might take this as a bold program for artistic sensuality, but that would be badly out of key with both the rest of Chapman's poetry and the poem's specific context in the 1595 quarto, where it is preceded by a characteristic defense of "obscurity"—"with that darknes wil J still labour to be shadowed"—and followed by a brief but morally explicit sequence of intellectual love sonnets "for his mistress Philosophy":

> Muses that sing loues sensuall Emperie
>
> ....
>
> Abiure those ioyes, abhor their memory,
> And let my loue the honord subiect be
> Of loue, and honors compleate historie.

Context makes the title poem seem less a celebration of Ovidian poetry than an ironic exposure of its corrupt roots.

This agon becomes clearer in Chapman's revisionary continuation of the most powerfully sexual example of the genre. Christopher Marlowe's *Hero and Leander* ends with the lovers' memorably mutual loss of virginity, and, despite an appended "Desunt nonnulla," the first printed edition (1598) may well constitute a complete poem. The second edition of the same year, however, divides Marlowe's text into two semi-epic "Sestiads" and then adds four more by Chapman to bring the story to its traditional tragic conclusion in an untraditionally moral spirit. Chapman sends his own "strangely-intellectuall fire" for inspiration to Marlowe—"whose liuing subiect stood / Vp to the chin in the Pyerean flood"–but only after affirming that he is taking on a different and more august theme:

> More harsh (at lest more hard) more graue and hie
> Our subiect runs, and our sterne *Muse* must flie.
> Loues edge is taken off. . . .

Leander, at the height of erotic reverie, is visited by the goddess Ceremony, who "sharply did reproue / *Leanders* bluntnes in his violent loue; / Tolde him how poore was substance without rites." Hero, alone at Sestos, suffers anguished swerves of guilt and rationalization and is denounced by her mistress Venus for perverting her religious office: "Now minion to thy fate be trew, / Though not to me, indure what this portends; / Begin where lightnes will, in shame it ends." Hero witnesses the creation, out of her own sacrifice, of the goddess Eronusis–Dissimulation–to whom Venus gives new power over human love: "since then / Neuer was any trust in maides nor men." The poet retains his sympathy for the lovers themselves and graces their death with an unprecedented Ovidian metamorphosis into goldfinches; but he also insists, to a new degree, on the serious burden to what in his dedication he calls "so trifeling a subiect."

A more obviously important task was al-

ready to hand. In 1598 Chapman published translations of two sections of the *Iliad*. The Homeric epics had never been translated into English before, nor, even among humanists, did they have the unique authority that is now their lot; "soule-blind Scalliger," as Chapman calls one sixteenth-century scholar, was not wholly eccentric in finding Virgil the superior poet. Chapman's sustained project for the rest of his career was the complete translation of the Homeric corpus and the promulgating of an attendant conviction of Homer's unexcelled poetic primacy. A version of the entire first half of the *Iliads* (as Chapman referred to it) appeared in 1609, the complete poem in 1611, the complete *Odysses* by 1615, and a combined edition in 1616. When, circa 1624, Chapman added the hymns and other apocrypha in *The Crown of All Homer's Works*, he announced, "The Worke that I was borne to doe is done."

From the first, the project suited Chapman in its proud exclusivity: "You are not every bodie," he tells his reader in his introduction to *Achilles Shield*, "nor is it more empaire to an honest and absolute man's sufficiencie to have few friendes than to an Homericall Poeme to have few commenders." But the personal appeal of the task came to reach even deeper; it engaged Chapman's whole conception of learning as exemplary self-fashioning, the key to "mans true Empire": "to direct / Reason in such an Art, as that it can / Turne blood to soule, and make both, one calme man." So he puts it in *Euthymiæ Raptus*, an allegorical sequel to *The Shadow of Night* published in 1609; the argument of the new poem depends from a famous opening in which Chapman is visited by the spirit of Homer himself:

> I am (sayd hee) that spirit *Elysian*,
> That (in thy natiue ayre; and on the hill
> Next *Hitchins* left hand) did thy bosome fill,
> With such a flood of soule . . .
>
> ....
>
>   . . . thou didst inherit
> My true sense (for the time then) in my spirit;
> And I, inuisiblie, went prompting thee,
> To those fayre Greenes, where thou didst english me.

For his major learned enterprise Chapman claimed the authority not of patient scholarship but of subjective ghostly infusion. The scholarship is in fact notoriously vulnerable; Chapman's Greek seems to have been weak, and he was heavily dependent–more than he admitted–on the Latin version in Jean de Sponde's edition (1583). But Chapman was convinced that he had impor-

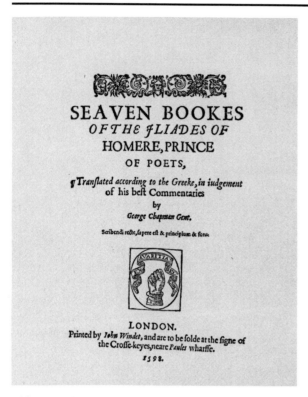

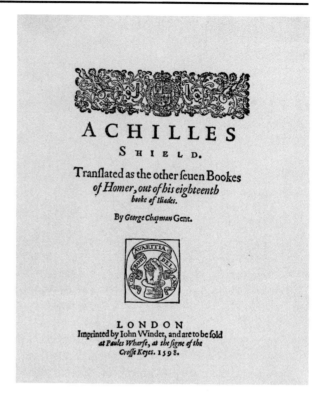

Title pages for the 1598 quarto editions of the first English translations of sections from the Homeric epics. These versions of books 1-2 and 7-11 (left) and part of book 18 (right) of the Iliad *were the beginning of Chapman's lifelong mission, the translation of all Homer's works (Anderson Galleries, sale number 2077, 20-21 May 1926).*

tant leverage denied to his predecessors; after completing the *Iliads*, he proclaimed in his commentary on book one: "I dissent from all other Translators and Interpreters that ever assaid exposition of this miraculous Poeme, especially where the divine rapture is most exempt from capacitie in Grammarians meerely and Grammaticall Criticks, and where the inward sense or soule of the sacred Muse is onely within eye-shot of a Poeticall spirit's inspection." A promise to write a "Poeme of the mysteries / Reveal'd in Homer," made in the introductory poem to the *Iliads*, was never fulfilled, but it is clear enough from the translation and commentary what Chapman was seeing. Working through the second epic clinched his intuition. The introduction to the *Odysses* provides a well-known formulation: "the first word of his *Iliads* is μῆνιν *wrath;* the first word of his *Odysses,* ἄνδρα, *Man*—contracting in either word his each worke's Proposition. In one, Predominant Perturbation; in the other, over-ruling Wisedome; in one, the Bodie's fervour and fashion of outward Fortitude to all possible height of Heroicall Action; in the other, the Mind's inward, constant and unconquerd Empire, unbroken, unalterd with any most insolent and tyrannous infliction." Read through, the Ho-

meric epics offer an allegory of the progress of the soul toward mental autarky.

This reading indisputably skews the translation, often in remarkably overt ways. Chapman's not unreasonable defense of his right to "periphrasis or circumlocution" does not prepare us for his extensive amplifications, intruded glosses, and wholly original additions. The result, in addition to local vagaries of interpretation, is a pervasive slanting of everything toward a moralistic intonation that no longer seems authentically Homeric. But Chapman's foreconceit also supplied him with the fire and conviction that have given the translation its staying power. Some moments in the *Odysses* are especially fine:

I have of old bene usde to cuffes and blowes;
My minde is hardn'd, having borne the throwes
Of many a soure event in waves and wars,
Where knockes and buffets are no Forreinars.
And this same harmefull belly by no meane
The greatest Abstinent can ever weane:
Men suffer much Bane by the Bellie's rage,
For whose sake Ships in all their equipage
Are arm'd and set out to th'untamed Seas,
Their bulkes full-fraught with ils to enemies.

A commanding poem in its own right, in which Chapman's esoteric vehemence is for once tightened across a strong narrative frame, the collected Homer has become what Chapman expected it to be, the centerpiece of his reputation.

The part of his life which this achievement crowned, however, was a difficult and ultimately unsatisfying time; the history of Chapman's career as a narrative poet is also an exemplum, more detailed than Shakespeare's, of the dangers and discontents of the search for aristocratic support. As the dedicatee of his first Homer volumes, Chapman had chosen the Earl of Essex, "renown'de Achilles": an incautious decision, from which, perhaps luckily, nothing seems to have come. The whole project lapsed, and Chapman published no nondramatic poetry for more than a decade. In 1600 he was imprisoned–not for the last time–for debt. About then he appears to have been courting a well-placed widow; we have one letter, written from jail, asking for £5. The episode seems finally to have brought only bitterness: "I wishe not the ende of your lyfe, but I muche repent me of the begynnynge of our acquaintance." Good fortune came with the accession of James in 1603, when Chapman was given a position ("sewer-in-ordinary") in the household of the young Prince Henry, whose cultural ambitions made the early Jacobean years a bright time for the arts. Henry undertook sponsorship of the Homer project, pledging £300 and a pension on its completion. But Henry's death in 1612 was, for Chapman as for others, a disaster. James, unsympathetic to many of his elder son's plans, did not honor a deathbed request that the promises to Chapman be kept. A passionate *Epicede* on the dead prince is angrily despairing: "Men had better dye / Than out-liue free times; slaues to Policie." In a dedicatory epistle to an appropriately unknown Henry Jones, Chapman forswears further courtship of the powerful: "I will neuer more dare, to looke vp to any greatnesse, but resoluing the little rest of my poore life to obscuritie, and the shadow of his death; prepare euer hereafter, for the light of heauen."

That vow was not immediately kept. In 1613 Chapman supplied a masque for the marriage of Princess Elizabeth to the Elector Palatine; Jonson's praise of Chapman's abilities in this line suggests that there may have been others. The next year saw the publication of *Eugenia*, a lengthy elegy on William, Lord Russell, celebrated both for a "true Noblesse" whose defini-

tion is the main task of the poem–"A man, all Center is, all stay, all minde"–and for his bequest of it to his surviving son, the poem's addressee. More important, that year Chapman also published *Andromeda Liberata*, an allegorical poem on the wedding of Robert Carr, a royal favorite newly created Earl of Somerset, who by then had become Chapman's second real patron. Somerset's marriage to the former Countess of Essex is celebrated as a moral triumph over "*The monstrous beast, the rauenous Multitude,*" which will ever envy "*truth of excellence.*" But fortune's smile was deceitful. The scandal surrounding the Countess's divorce from her first husband was not to be so easily sponged off; it spread to include charges of murder that eventually consigned Somerset and his wife to imprisonment and enduring disgrace. *Andromeda Liberata* itself apparently managed to offend both sides; it was Chapman's last major original poem. He stayed loyal to Somerset even as doing so ceased to be expedient, dedicating to him both the *Odysses* and *The Crown of All Homer's Works*, but then he himself faded into virtual invisibility until his death on 12 May 1634.

It may well have been no more than the spottiness of these efforts that kept Chapman writing plays. The public stage, even the indoor stage for which Chapman did most of his work, was unquestionably the lesser dignity; and Chapman did not fight Jonson's fight to change that prejudice. In a dedicatory sonnet to *All Fools*–suspect in its provenance, but authentic in its sentiment–he dismisses one of his plays as an inconsequential sideline to his real work:

> I am most loth to passe your sight
> with any such light marke of vanitie,
> Being markt with Age for Aimes of greater weight,
> and drownd in darke Death–vshering melancholy.

Criticism has tended to sanction that contrast in a slightly different form; since Charles Lamb (1808) it has been a commonplace that Chapman's imagination was too solipsistic for true theater: "Dramatic imitation was not his talent. He could not go out of himself, as Shakespeare could shift at pleasure, to inform and animate other existences." Nevertheless, Chapman was, from the start, a notably successful playwright in a city not short on theatrical talent. *The Blind Beggar of Alexandria*, his earliest surviving play, had a recorded first run of twenty-two performances, greater than all but three of the contemporary works

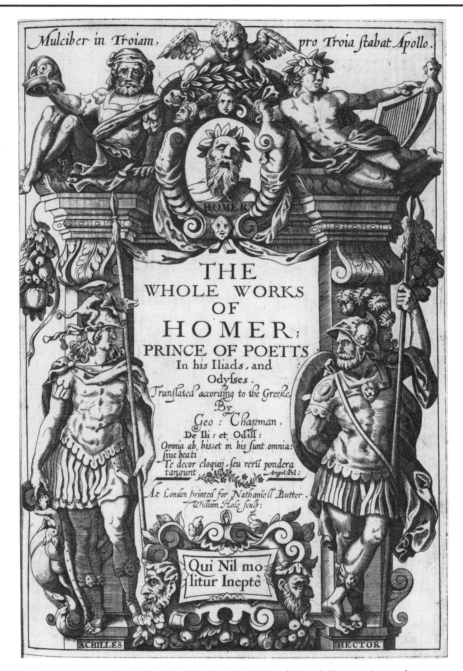

Title page engraved by William Hole for the 1616 folio edition of Chapman's complete translations of the Iliad *and the* Odyssey *(Henry E. Huntington Library and Art Gallery)*

cited by Philip Henslowe in his famous diary. Chapman also seems to have been fairly well paid; one year's work for Henslowe brought him £28 10s, and he sold a later play (the lost *Old Joiner of Aldgate*, produced in 1603) for an impressive 20 marks (more than £13). As early as 1598 Francis Meres—not known as an original thinker—listed Chapman among the best writers for both tragedy and comedy. After his death, printers saw fit to publish as his at least three plays—*The*

Ball (1639; probably by James Shirley), *Alphonsus, Emperor of Germany* (1654), and *The Revenge for Honor* (1654)—that he almost certainly did not write: such was his continuing marketability as a dramatist, while the handsome Homer folios sat unsold.

The means by which that marketability was achieved were not uniformly respectable; *The Blind Beggar of Alexandria* in particular (produced in 1596) has been dealt with harshly by critics as

Title page engraved by W. Pass for the 1624(?) folio edition of Homeric apocrypha, the last of Chapman's translations from the Greek (Maggs Bros., catalogue number 826, December 1954). When he completed this volume, Chapman, who is portrayed at the bottom of the title page, proclaimed: "The Worke that I was borne to doe is done."

an especially shameless exercise in crowd pleasing. No one involved seems to have had much respect for the text; the version published in 1598 is so mutilated that the main plot is almost unintelligible, and no other edition was forthcoming. The underplot that survives is an utterly amoral sexual farce, perhaps the most maniacally systematic disguise plot on the Elizabethan stage: "The joys of many I in one enjoy." The title character, Irus, dispenses spiritual advice to the women of Alexandria, and then—being in truth neither blind nor a beggar—pretends to be the suitors he prophesies. Marrying two women, he then seduces each in the guise of the other's husband, so that he succeeds in, as he puts it, cuckolding himself, twice. In yet another identity, he is Cleanthes, object of the Queen's lust; by the end both Queen and King are gone, false deaths are reported for Cleanthes's other personae, and Cleanthes, having gotten away with everything, has become King of Egypt. Yet the very shamelessness of this all makes it a paradigm for something more important, the capacity of the individual to dominate his world through versatile self-creation. Irus does not forget his resemblance to Chapman's own secular saint—"Homer was blind, yet could he best discern / The shapes of everything, and so may I"—and his progress from that starting point to untrammeled imperial power resonates with some of the deepest concerns of Chapman's poetry. The play's complex machinery of role-playing and manipulation is in effect a way of giving those concerns dramatic form: holding all at an efficient distance, the hero rises by being in the world but not of it. The theater, even the low comic theater, thus has a place for Chapman's great theme; and indeed, it provides opportunities for exploring that theme that are arguably more various, surprising, and compelling than does the seemingly more congenial mode of didactic epic. As the disreputable vehicle of a noble tenor, Irus is already more interesting than any figure in the much more fully articulated poems.

A line of descent runs from Irus through the subtler plays to follow. The complicated plot of *A Humorous Day's Mirth* (produced 1597; published 1599) revolves around the adroit mischief of the quick-thinking courtier Lemot. His name reflects his capacity for the kind of patter and fast talk of which Chapman reveals himself a master ("Well hit, Monsieur *Verbum!*"). Lemot is keenly aware of the edge he has over the more ponderous minds that surround him and lives for the regal joy of sizing people up; he will, he announces early, preside over the day to come "like an old king in an old-fashion play. . . . thus will I sit, as it were, and point out all my humourous companions." Such knowledge leads to action; the main business of the play is Lemot's response to several related displays of jealousy and possessiveness. His interlocking lies and tricks bring everyone together for an explosive show in Verone's ordinary; when the smoke clears, the relevant characters have made public fools of themselves, peace has been restored to the marriages, and the old man's daughter has been paired with a more appropriate mate. Lemot improves on Irus in being able to handle a more fully devel-

oped set of characters and also in the curious self-lessness of his motives. When he has almost succeeded in seducing the puritanical young wife, he quite deliberately aborts by biting her lip: "Oh, barbarous cannibal! Now I perceive / Thou wilt make me a mocking stock to all the world!" Lemot aims not at sexual conquest but at a goal that is simultaneously his own anarchic fun and her moral instruction: "Away, repent, amend your life; you have discredited your religion for ever!"

What is to hand is of course humors comedy, for whose creation Chapman is often given credit (the terminology is already there in *The Blind Beggar of Alexandria,* and Jonson's *Every Man in His Humour* was not performed until 1598). In this Elizabethan mutation of classical Roman comedy, the tricky servant becomes what Millar MacLure calls a Hermes-figure, a psychopomp whose comic talents lead the unsociably impassioned out into the open air. But in Chapman's play sociability is not quite the inclusive value that it is for other playwrights. The most widely advertised "humorous" character is the melancholic Dowsecer, who would rather read Cicero than beget an heir:

> What can seem strange to him on earthly things,
> To whom the whole course of eternity,
> And the round compass of the world is known?

Even the observers who had come expecting entertainment find his scorn "a holy fury, not a frenzy"; it indeed wins him a woman's love. He is Chapman's private visionary; and even when, as the genre demands, he is cured of his misogyny, he becomes if anything more abstracted:

> The excellent disposer of the mind
> Shines in thy beauty, and thou hast not changed
> My soul to sense, but sense unto my soul.

Another dramatist might be making fun; but Chapman reserves real mockery for the court dolt's attempt to pull off the same act later on and ends by awarding Dowsecer a caduceus, "Mercury's rod."

There is no Dowsecer in *All Fools.* The character Valerio briefly sounds like one—"So Love, fair shining in the inward man . . ."—but people know him too well: "Th'art known in ordinaries, and tobacco-shops, / Trusted in taverns and in vaulting houses." He turns out to be more than a bit of a show-off—"My spirit longs to swagger"—and takes his lumps for it; he is also one of the most ar-

Inigo Jones's design for the costume of an Indian torchbearer in Chapman's Masque
of the Middle Temple and Lincoln's Inn, *produced in 1613 at the festivities for
the marriage of Princess Elizabeth and Frederick, Elector of Palatine (Stephen Orgel
and Roy Strong,* Inigo Jones, *1973)*

ticulate voices for the play's leveling ethos:

> Nay, never shun it to be call'd a gull;
> For I see all the world is but a gull,
> One man gull to another in all kinds.

It is both a maturer play than *A Humorous Day's Mirth* and more comprehensively comic in its vision. Chapman apparently wrote it for Henslowe in 1599, but the 1605 quarto places it at Blackfriars, Chapman's main theatrical home after 1601, and may well give a revised text. (A lost play, *All Fools but the Fool* or *The World Runs on Wheels*, produced in 1599, may be the first version.) The plot is a skillful adaptation of Terence's *Heauton Timoroumenos*, with some help from *Adelphoe:* Valerio and his friend Fortunio contrive secret courtships and marriages not only under the very eyes of their disapproving fathers but, by grace of an intricate set of deceptions, with their fathers' active encouragement. Chapman adds, to serve as his main conspirator, Valerio's scholarly younger brother Rinaldo, who, indifferent to love, talks of his business rather like a playwright: "you shall see to what a perfect shape / I'll bring this rude plot, which blind Chance (the ape / Of counsel and advice) hath brought forth blind." And later: "My fortune is to win renown by gulling." Rinaldo, far more than Valerio, is Chapman's authorial surrogate and here fits his dramatic genre with definitive snugness. The genre rounds itself off, however, when Rinaldo himself is gulled by, of all people, the comic husband in a humors subplot, who tricks him into a misstep that exposes everything. Valerio had in fact called that shot–"A bachelor to a cuckold is a gull, / All to a poet, or a poet to himself "–and he ends the play with a virtuoso oration at the Half Moon Tavern on "the horned age" of all-encompassing cuckoldry that has succeeded the golden, silver, brass, iron, leaden, and wooden ages. The mood is less cynical than festive, a disciplining of the aspiration for merely individual dignity to make possible Chapman's most cheerfully communal conclusion.

May Day is similar if rougher in spirit. Though published in 1611, it is sprinkled with echoes of a number of plays (including *Hamlet*) that were being performed 1599-1601 and is probably not much later itself. The plotting is based on Alessandro Piccolomini's *Alessandro* (circa 1545), a popular *comedia erudita* in the Terentian mode; Chapman cuts back on the sexual intrigue involving a pair of cross-dressed lovers but follows Piccolomini closely in choreographing the aging Lorenzo's unintentionally intersecting attempts to marry his daughter to "an old clown" rather than to the young scholar she loves and to seduce the wife of the local *miles gloriosus*. Chapman takes from his source the *servus dolosus* who tricks Lorenzo into disguising himself as a chimney sweep ("by consideration that Jove for his love took on him the shape of a bull, which is far worse than a chimney-sweeper"); characteristically, he adds another, higher-born intriguer, Lorenzo's nephew Lodovico, who is Chapman's most vigorously racy specimen of the breed: " 'Sdeath, if any wench should offer to keep possession of my heart against my will, I'd fire her out with sack and sugar, or smoke her out with tobacco like a hornet, or purge for her, for love is but a humour; one way or other I would vent her, that's infallible." Chapman also considerably amplifies the role of the soldier Quintiliano to make him not just a braggart but also, in a series of tangential but vivid episodes, a highly successful coney catcher himself, as well as an impressive theorist of social climbing: "be impudent enough, for that's your chief virtue of society. . . . there's no prescription for gentility but good clothes and impudence." By the end, both Lodovico and Quintiliano have added their humiliations to Lorenzo's: Lodovico when he lets himself be lured by some spectacularly deceptive sexual bait ("How was I gull'd! Hand, hide thyself for shame, / And henceforth have an eye before thy fingers!"); Quintiliano when he thinks, and cannot disprove, that he has been cuckolded by a *senex*.

Still, even as he takes his rogues down a peg, Chapman keeps an important empathy with them. We may draw a significant contrast with *Eastward Ho*, his collaboration with Jonson and John Marston performed and published in 1605. The play is primarily well known for its Scots jokes (probably Marston's) that offended the Scots-born King James and his court; they landed Chapman and Jonson briefly in prison (and may, according to one reading of the dates, have ended Chapman's career as a writer of comedies) but are only incidental to far more extensive mockery of the London middle class. The play was apparently meant both to capitalize on the popularity of Thomas Dekker and John Webster's *Westward Ho* (produced 1604) and to give the city-comedy genre a moral backbone. Critical consensus assigns Chapman primary responsibility for the subplot of the middle acts, where a title-wielding con artist pauses in his flight with the

Page from the diary of theater impresario Philip Henslowe listing receipts from productions of The Blind Beggar of Alexandria *on 12, 16, 19, 22, and 26 February 1596 (1595 according to the calendar then in use)*
(MSS VII, l. 14ᵛ; by permission of Dulwich College, London)

money of his socially ambitious city wife to fancy the young bride of an aging usurer. Chapman adapts from a novella of Masuccio di Salerno the ruse whereby the old husband is tricked into abetting the elopement under the impression that someone else's wife is meant. In Masuccio the lovers escape; in *Eastward Ho* all plans are spoiled by a sudden tempest that throws everyone together at Cuckold's Haven. What follows is vigorous and funny, but not the party with which *All Fools* and *May Day* end. The conclusion, probably by Jonson, is stern in tone–"Now London, look about, / And in this moral see thy glass run out"– and the light throughout on the intriguer and his accomplices is more uniformly satirical than is otherwise the case with Chapman. Chapman surely consented to that intonation, but it is still significant that, on his own, he did not use comedy to bring even the most discreditable individualism so sharply to heel.

By the time of *Eastward Ho* Chapman had been experimenting with comic form in remarkable ways, in order to accommodate his own people more fully. In *Sir Giles Goosecap* (which may be dated circa 1602 by contemporary allusions) Dowsecer is back as the moody and impoverished scholar Clarence. He is indeed one of the main reasons for attributing the play to Chapman. It was published anonymously in 1606 and 1636, but the attribution is now secure; there are too many signatures in the text:

> Divine Eugenia bears the ocular form
> Of music and of Reason, and presents
> The soul exempt from flesh in flesh inflam'd:
> Who must not love her then that loves his soul?

Eugenia would later be the name of Chapman's personification of true nobility; here she is Clarence's female mirror, "A dame of learning, and of life exempt / From all the idle fancies of her sex." A rich widow slow to come out of mourning, she eventually finds in Clarence, as Clarence does in her, a cure for melancholy that does not compromise the high values behind it. Getting the two solitaries together requires the work of a high-minded intriguer, Momford; his actions are those of an ennobled Pandarus, and the story indeed is based in some detail on that of Troilus and Cressida. Chapman in effect recasts the first three books of Chaucer's poem as a Neoplatonic allegory of intellectual self-transcendence that clearly represents one of his own supreme fantasies: "knowledge is the bond, / The seal, and crown of our united minds." Hopes raised by Chapman's own courtship–of a rich widow–are very possibly involved.

None of this engages the play's title character, who figures only in tangential scenes of sociable foolishness in which–as Thomas Marc Parrot puts it in his edition of Chapman's *Comedies*– "there is nothing that can be called a plot, and a curious absence even of incidents." Goosecap and his fellows are ostensibly suitors to Eugenia and her female companions, but they keep out of the way of the real story and spend their time mostly just showing their stuff: "Be caparisons odious, Sir Cut.? What, like flowers?" "O ass! They be odorous." "A botts o' that stinking word, 'odorous'; I can never hit on't." The structural cleavage here is so drastic that it looks almost like part of the allegory, though we might also take it as a symbolic moment in theatrical history: in the con-

THE BLINDE
begger of Alexan-
dria, moſt pleaſantly diſcourſing his variable humours
in diſguiſed ſhapes full of
conceite and pleaſure.

As it hath beene ſundry times
publickly acted in London.
by the right honorable the Earle
of Nottingham, Lord high Admirall his ſeruantes.

By George Chapman: Gentleman.

Imprinted at London for William
Iones, dwelling at the ſigne of the
Gun, neere Holburne Conduict,
1598.

Title page for the 1598 quarto edition of Chapman's first surviving play, first produced on 12 February 1596 and performed twenty-two times by 1 April 1597 (Bodleian Library, Oxford)

trast of main plot and subplot, humors comedy
faces off a new mode of tragicomic romance.

Chapman's most substantial contribution to
this genre is *The Gentleman Usher* (published in
1606, probably produced 1602-1603). Its Italian
court is populated with a number of conspicuous
fools (one of whom is even called "Sir Giles
Goosecap"), and Chapman's scorn is especially evident in his portrait of the unlettered and grace-
less courtier Medice. But most of the mockery is
subsumed within an air of festivity and display—
there are two masques in the opening acts—and
the leisurely paced love story of Vincentio and
Margaret. She is also desired by Vincentio's father, Duke Alphonso, so the young people must
court secretly. Vincentio recruits as a go-between
Bassiolo, the gentleman usher in Margaret's
house, using a bait of princely fellowship that the
servant finds irresistible: "Use not my lordship,
nor yet call me lord, / Nor my whole name,
Vincentio, but Vince." Bassiolo—the gull as
intriguer—jumps into his matchmaking task with
memorably maladroit enthusiasm:

> if she turn her back,
> Use you that action you would do before,
> And court her thus:
> "Lady, your back part is as fair to me
> As is your fore-part."

The lovers already know their course, though,
which they ratify with grave improvisation:

> may not we now
> Our contract make, and marry before heaven?
> ....
> . . . Are outward rites
> More virtuous than the very substance is
> Of holy nuptials solemniz'd within?
> Or shall laws made to curb the common world,
> That would not be contain'd in form without them,
> Hurt them that are a law unto themselves?

Comedy balances against sentiment flushed with
heroism; up to a point it is the sweetest of
Chapman's works.

Things swiftly and shockingly change in the
fourth act, when the lovers are discovered.
Medice, at Alphonso's incitement, seriously
wounds Vincentio; Margaret, thinking him dead,
disfigures her face in revenge. Swerving toward
unexpectedly brutal tragedy, the love story acquires new weight and force. And even as it
swerves back, it keeps those depths through the
sense of having been touched by a power beyond

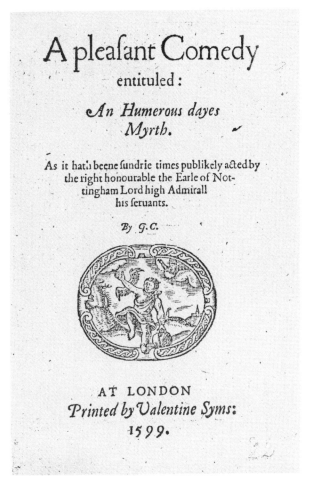

A pleasant Comedy
entituled:

*An Humerous dayes
Myrth.*

As it hath beene sundrie times publikely acted by
the right honourable the Earle of Nottingham Lord high Admirall
his seruants.

By *G.C.*

AT LONDON
Printed by Valentine Syms:
1599.

*Title page for the 1599 quarto edition of Chapman's second
surviving play, first produced on 11 May 1597 and performed eleven times before the London theaters were closed by
authorities at the end of July (British Library)*

the ordinarily human. The courtier Strozza, who
until the fourth act is an appealing but apparently minor character, is shot with an arrow by
Medice's henchmen. Told by his doctor that it cannot be removed, he first rages in pain and threatens suicide; his wife urges instead a Christian
stoicism:

> 'tis said afflictions bring to God,
> Because they make us like him, drinking up
> Joys that deform us with the lusts of sense,
> And turn our general being into soul.

Her advice succeeds more than she expects; in a
turn taken from the records of Neoplatonic medicine, Strozza comes back from his torment an inspired visionary:

> Humility hath rais'd me to the stars;
> In which (as in a sort of crystal globes)
> I sit and see things hid from human sight.

He accurately prophesies his own miraculous recovery and becomes the presiding genius of the play's happy ending. His physician cures both lovers. He himself brings Alphonso to repent and bless their marriage, and Medice to confess his low birth and real name, Mendice. Strozza's rise to benign dominance both completes the tragicomic pattern and sets a high-water mark of achievement for Chapman's dramatic heroes.

As those heroes proliferate on the Jacobean stage, their valences become more complicated. *Monsieur D'Olive* (published 1606, usually dated 1604-1605) is informed by the same cleft that structures *Sir Giles Goosecap*, but to less straightforward effect. The main plot again concerns two figures of withdrawn obsessiveness: the Earl of St. Anne, who keeps his dead wife's body preserved in his chambers; and the virtuous Marcellina, who, in disgust at her husband's unfounded jealousy, has hidden in her room, curtained her windows, and vowed never again to see "the common pandress light." In taking these stands, they bring the extremity of Chapman's poetry into the theater to more troubled effect than is the case with Clarence and Eugenia. St. Anne's example sets a standard of ascetic courage—"To leave the world and all his pleasures, all his friends and honours, as all were nothing"—that inspires unexceptionable admiration: "When I observ'd his constancy in love /.../ I grew in love, even with his very mind." Marcellina is herself an acknowledged Neoplatonic paragon who is only putting into practice what the "Hymnus in Noctem" preaches. Yet the pathology of both characters is still monstrous and unmistakable, and curing them is the task of the play. Their psychic physician Vandome, on the other hand, himself prompts mixed responses. He is Marcellina's Platonic lover, whose worship even her husband now realizes is exemplary in its tact; but in treating his patients he becomes one of Chapman's most Machiavellian manipulators, with flashes of cruel gleefulness: "I'll play a little with his fantasy." With his mistress he is especially rough, provoking her to accusations of rudeness and insolence; his final strategy is, Iago-like, to taunt her with false evidence of her husband's infidelity until, against all her own principles, she loses control: "a feign'd device / To kindle fury in her frozen breast." When the device works, Vandome's succeeding disclaimer is unnervingly brusque: "all was but a shoeing-horn to draw you hither; now show yourselves women, and say nothing." All these moves have their reasons, but they give the happy ending something of the dissonance of a Shakespearean problem play.

The title character circumambulates this story to no practical effect. He is chosen by the Duke to petition the King concerning St. Anne, but things there never get going; the ponderous pointlessness of his "great ambassage" seems to be topical satire of early Jacobean diplomacy, all hype and no substance. D'Olive himself, who receives the assignment because of his reputation for cleverness, is a portrait of the new courtier as fast-talking fraud: "the perfect model of an impudent upstart, the compound of a poet and a lawyer." But he also talks too much like Chapman himself to be merely a joke: "As I am, I possess myself, I enjoy my liberty, my learning, my wit; as for wealth and honour let 'em go." His elevation is, among other things, a fable of cloistered virtue finally recognized: "As though Achilles could hide himself under a woman's clothes; was he not discovered at first?" And the mood surrounding him is not notably satiric; his wit is genuinely appreciated and leavening—he is given an oration on tobacco that includes what MacLure calls "easily the finest piece of rhetoric in Chapman's comedy"—and even after his failure and gulling, the Duke stands by him: "reserve yourself, I pray, / Till fitter times.... / follow us to Court." Brought onto the great stage, retired individuality can find itself lit from any number of directions at once.

The Widow's Tears (which was published in 1612, but probably performed about the same time as *Monsieur D'Olive*) is much more single-minded. It is Chapman's only comedy organized around a specific satiric thesis: woman's constancy, as manifested in the vows of widows not to receive new love, is a fraud. That proposition is demonstrated twice—first by "the late governor's admired widow, the rich and haughty Countess Eudora," who is persuaded to marry the former page of her dead husband; second by the happily married Cynthia, whose husband Lysander decides to test her with a false report of his own death. The second demonstration becomes a redaction of Petronius's story of the Ephesian matron when Lysander returns disguised as a soldier and manages (like Irus) to cuckold himself—indeed, in his own tomb, where Cynthia has taken up a vigil. His disillusion is vehement: "O I could tear myself into atoms.... Is't possible there should be such a latitude in the sphere of this sex, to entertain such an extension of mischief and not turn devil?" The play has often

Thy vain dependence, and convert my duty
And sacrifices of my sweetest thoughts
To a more noble deity, sole friend to worth,
And patroness of all good spirits, Confidence.

Confidence is "the third blind deity," an allegorical newcomer but decisively dominant over not only Fortune but also Love. Tharsalio's courtship strategy is presumption and insult, which, with the help of some carefully planted reports of his sexual prowess, he rightly calculates Eudora will find uncontrollably arousing. He would seem to have read the penultimate chapter of Machiavelli's *The Prince;* he does brag of having been to Italy, whose air "hath refined my senses, and made me see with clear eyes." Indeed, he seems to find the confirmation of such insight at least as exciting as actual sexual and social gains; when he witnesses Cynthia's seduction, he becomes ecstatic, "dances and sings," entranced

Title page for the 1605 quarto edition of what may be a revised version of the lost Chapman play All Fools but the Fool *or* The World Runs on Wheels, *which was produced at the Rose theater in 1599, two years before* All Fools *was presented at Blackfriars (Boston Public Library)*

Title page for the 1611 quarto edition of the play for which Chapman drew on the popular sixteenth-century Italian comedy Alessandro *by Alessandro Piccolomini (Maggs Bros., catalogue number 493, 1927)*

been linked to Chapman's bitterness in the wake of his own courtship; the narrow ferocity of its theme does suggest an unusually personal investment.

What gives the play its real integrity, though, is not its thesis but its main character. Tharsalio, Lysander's brother, is the suitor who wins Eudora, the source of Lysander's doubts about Cynthia, and the stage manager of most of the action. He is also the articulate exponent of a theory of Renaissance individualism in its most abrasively simple guise:

> thou that lad'st
> Th'unworthy ass with gold, while worth and merit
> Serve thee for nought, weak Fortune, I renounce

with his own prophetic soul: "By heaven, I wonder, now I see't in act, / My brain could ever dream of such a thought. / And yet 'tis true." His joy is to have everyone's number, and within the play there is no denying that he does. No comeuppance awaits him; not since Irus has a Chapmanian intriguer come to so complete a fulfillment. It is if anything the sheer fact of that success, the authority of his knowingness, that makes him seem, in the midst of all his fun, naggingly odious: "I marvel what man, what woman, what name, what action, doth his tongue glide over, but it leaves a slime upon't?"

Risking such sharp ambivalence comes close to moving beyond comedy. In his unpalatability, Tharsalio threatens not to belong to the society which he dominates and offers a negative image of that discrepancy between genius and the world on which Chapman insists so often in his poetry. And the author of *The Widow's Tears* had already shifted most of his theatrical attention to the genre in which, as it were, those negative and positive images superimpose, to a stereoscopic effect that, in the judgment of most critics, yielded Chapman's greatest art. It unquestionably yielded his most famous play: his earliest datable tragedy, but a fully formed and original one that was to set the direction for the rest of his dramatic career.

Bussy D'Ambois was printed in 1607–anonymously, though Chapman's name appears in the Stationers' Register. A second edition appeared in 1641, "being much corrected and amended by the author before his death"; it is the source of the only major textual problem in Chapman's oeuvre, with most editors accepting the revised version, but with some–notably Nicholas Brooke–arguing that it is only partly Chapman's doing. The original version has been dated as early as 1598, but consensus now centers on 1604. The story, like that of all but one of Chapman's surviving tragedies, is taken from recent French history–so recent, in fact, that no written source has been found for it. Louis de Clermont d'Amboise, Seigneur de Bussy, in the service of Alençon, was murdered in 1579, at the age of thirty, while attempting an assignation with the wife of the Comte de Monsoreau (Chapman's Montsurry). He seems to have been famous mainly as a compulsive duelist and troublemaker in the court of Henry III; his death was connived by both his King and his master, glad to be rid of him. Chapman starts the play by making him an ascetic philosopher:

> Fortune, not Reason, rules the state of things,
> Reward goes backwards, Honour on his head;
> Who is not poor, is monstrous; only Need
> Gives form and worth to every human seed.

So Bussy is solus, down at the heels and without a place at court. When the Monsieur (Alençon) offers him money and advancement, though, he accepts with casual indifference and is, in one reading of the situation, seduced and corrupted by the allure of what he pretends to despise. Yet Bussy himself never comes to such an assessment, and the real challenge Chapman takes up in the play is to dramatize Bussy's subsequent career not as the rejection but as the application of his stoic primitivism. Indeed, Bussy sounds if anything more like Seneca when he justifies a particularly lethal duel to the King:

> Let me be king myself (as man was made)
> ....
> Who to himself is law, no law doth need,
> Offends no law, and is a king indeed.

Bussy's quarrelsomeness, in other words, is what a philosophical conviction of personal independence becomes as it moves into the social sphere. It is also his great resource in that sphere; the King is convinced, sees Bussy as "A man so good, that only would uphold / Man in his native noblesse," and offers him a trusted place as resident satirist: "flatterers are kites / That check at sparrows; thou shalt be my eagle."

There are other voices to be heard from, including that of Bussy's own patron:

> to feed
> The ravenous wolf of thy most cannibal valour
> (Rather than not employ it) thou wouldst turn
> Hackster to any whore.

Bussy's career is still that of an amoral rakehell; and we see, as he himself apparently does not, that he is digging his own grave. His seduction of the countess Tamyra is an especially treacherous success. Chapman does not make the affair unduly sordid, but he has no philosophical dignity to give it; and by galling the Monsieur, whose advances Tamyra had virtuously rejected, it becomes the key to a united conspiracy against Bussy. Yet even as two of the conspirators contemplate Bussy's imminent fall, they see it signifying something other than welcome retribution; just

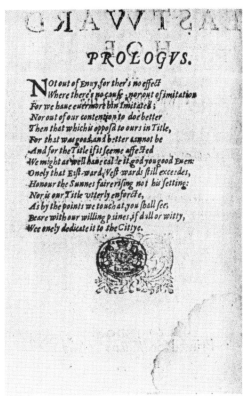

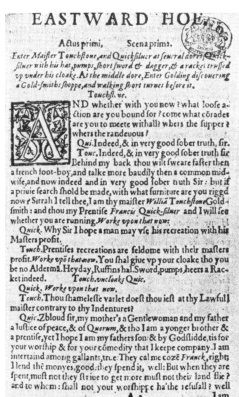

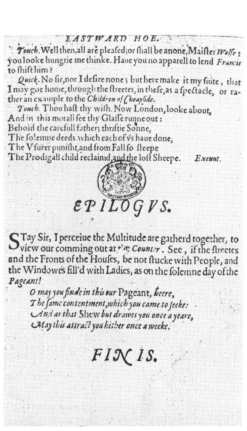

Title page, prologue, and first and last pages of text from the 1605 quarto edition of the play whose jokes about the Scots offended James I and led to the brief imprisonment of Chapman and Ben Jonson. The play referred to in the prologue is Westward Ho, *a popular play by Thomas Dekker and John Webster that had been produced in 1604 (British Library).*

as hollow trees survive the storm, but solid ones are uprooted,

> So this whole man
> (That will not wind with every crooked way,
> Trod by the servile world) shall reel and fall
> Before the frantic puffs of blind-born chance,
> That pipes through empty men, and makes them
> dance.

He owes his end neither to fate as such nor to some contingent tragic flaw, but to the very nature of his strength and greatness; he is one of the prime examples of what Eugene M. Waith calls "the Herculean hero," whose self-destructiveness is inseparable from his grandeur. Dying, Bussy is once again proudly autarkic:

> The equal thought I bear of life and death
> Shall make me faint on no side; I am up;
> Here like a Roman statue I will stand
> Till death hath made me marble.

It is an effect meant to awe its audience—"Oh, my fame, / Live in despite of murther"—and supernatural means are used to assure us that it does: "Farewell, brave relics of a complete man, / Look up and see thy spirit made a star; / Join flames with Hercules. . . . "

But that is still not all there is to be said. If Chapman's other tragedies lack the bravura of *Bussy D'Ambois*, that is partly because they probe more soberly and searchingly the paradoxes that fire it. Those are recognizably the paradoxes in which Chapman's own creative work was ensnared; the aspiring spirit's very freedom is in fact implicated in a higher authority that both raises and checks. Bussy himself comes close to finessing such an awareness; but within a few years, Chapman retells his story with very different balances. *The Conspiracy and Tragedy of Charles Duke of Byron*—two plays printed and apparently planned together—draws, with some detailed help from Edward Grimeston's *History* (1607), on even more recent French politics: the treason and execution in 1602 of Henry IV's most ambitious courtier. The currency of the events—Henry was still very much alive and King—made them risky material and indeed caused trouble. The French ambassador had three of the actors arrested in 1608 over a scene between the King's wife and his mistress; the censor excised it from the quarto published later the same year—leaving a conspicuous hole in act two of the *Tragedy*—and also apparently objected to an appearance by Elizabeth I in act four of the *Conspiracy*, which was converted

into awkward reportage. The play was reprinted in 1625—the only play of Chapman's republished in his lifetime—but the cuts were never restored. What we have nevertheless preserves the serious touchiness of Chapman's subject. His chosen hero was often compared, both in life and in the play, to Essex: two symbolically dangerous figures of aristocratic resentment against the new centralized monarchies of Western Europe. With the Byron plays, Chapman comes, probably inevitably, to the Renaissance tragedy of state, in which two of his ideals, the empire of the self and that of the world, come into sharp conflict.

Chapman's Byron has many points in common with Bussy:

> There is no danger to a man that knows
> What life and death is; there's not any law
> Exceeds his knowledge; neither is it lawful
> That he should stoop to any other law.
> He goes before them, and commands them all,
> That to himself is a law rational.

He is Herculean in his *virtù*—"Fortune to him was Juno to Alcides"—and like Achilles in the quickness and pride of his temper. But he also sets his sights notably higher than Bussy does. There is no Tamyra in his story—"his blood is not voluptuous, / Nor much inclined to women"—and his political goals are spacious and grandly expressed:

> We must reform and have a new creation
> Of state and government, and on our Chaos
> Will I sit brooding up another world.

Bussy's energy and philosophy are here set toward more obviously deserving ends. Yet Chapman if anything accords Byron less sympathy and even less dignity than he does Bussy. Within the action of the play, Byron is clearly the dupe of his less high-minded coconspirators, who pick him out and manipulate him with a good deal of cunning, while Henry is Chapman's most admiring portrait of monarchy: grave, wise, and—up to a point—exceptionally patient and forgiving. The *Conspiracy* ends with Henry's acceptance of Byron's seemingly decisive repentance:

> 'Tis all acknowledg'd, and, though all too late,
> Here the short madness of my anger ends:
> If ever I did good I lock'd it safe
> In you, th'impregnable defence of goodness.

Neither Byron nor the audience is allowed to for-

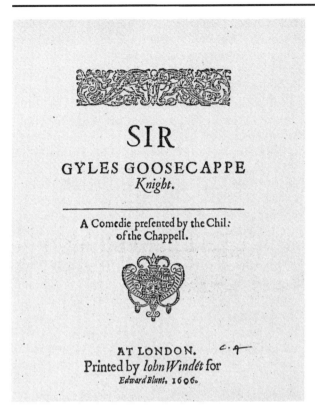

Title page for the 1606 quarto edition of a play that has been attributed to Chapman, in part because of the similarity of its character Clarence to Dowsecer in A Humorous Day's Mirth *and to Chapman himself (Anderson Galleries, sale number 1405, 4-5 March 1919)*

get that it was Henry who gave Byron his proud title; the technical term is, of course, "created." In the *Tragedy*, though, Byron resumes his plots without comment, while baldly protesting his innocence as Henry again offers to pardon him if he will confess. As the circle of justice closes on him, he becomes more and more erratic; the play's powerful last act, based closely on Grimeston, dramatizes a vertiginous series of swings among terror, arrogance, rage, and despair as Byron finally realizes that Henry does not, after all, consider him indispensable: "He alters every minute: what a vapour / The strongest mind is to a storm of crosses!" In defying his King he has destroyed the real basis for his strength and integrity.

The image of royalty appreciably darkens, however, in *The Revenge of Bussy D'Ambois* (printed in 1613, probably produced 1610-1611). A sequel to *Bussy D'Ambois* had surely not been planned originally; the one Chapman wrote is almost wholly unhistorical, full of imaginary characters and events, and inconsistent with its predecessor on numerous points. In particular, Henry III, benign and generous in *Bussy*

D'Ambois, becomes sinister and Machiavellian: "Treachery for kings is truest loyalty; / Nor is to bear the name of treachery, / But grave, deep policy." With such values enthroned at the top, the world in which Chapman's hero must make his way becomes appreciably more perilous. The hero himself is significantly more upright. Clermont D'Ambois, Bussy's invented brother (his name apparently plucked from Bussy's own run of titles), is Chapman's most elaborately dramatized philosopher: "Holding all learning but an art to live well, / And showing he hath learn'd it in his life." In him, stoic antinomianism is disciplined into its more principled, inward form: "He that to nought aspires, doth nothing need; / Who breaks no law is subject to no king." As philosophical doctrine, this is correct and stable in a way in which Bussy and Byron never are.

Yet that rectitude has problematic consequences. Clermont's tendency toward sententious passivity is not an obvious dramatic strength; much is heard from him, but he does almost nothing for most of the play, despite a call from his brother's ghost to kill Montsurry. The result bears a strong resemblance to *Hamlet*, though Clermont is more clearheaded about his reasons for not acting. We cannot, he asserts in a profession of orthodox stoic doctrine,

> call it virtue that proceeds
> From vicious fury. I repent that ever
> (By any instigation in th' appearance
> My brother's spirit made, as I imagin'd)
> That e'er I yielded to revenge his murther.
> ....
> . . . never private cause
> Should take on it the part of public laws.

When summoned again by the ghost in act five, though, Clermont does take revenge, in a way that almost seems to satisfy his scruples; the justness and manliness of his action even wins Montsurry's own forgiveness: "if now I die, / Sit joy and all good on thy victory!" Yet the dilemma suddenly reasserts itself in crueler form. Chapman has complemented his debasement of Henry by giving Clermont a patron, the Duke of Guise, to whom he professes extraordinarily intense gratitude and loyalty; and on that compromise to his apathy he is caught. Fast upon the killing of Montsurry comes news of Guise's murder at the King's order—an act which strikes Clermont even harder than the death of his brother—"Shall I live, and he / Dead, that alone gave means of life to me?"—but which he knows with total certainty

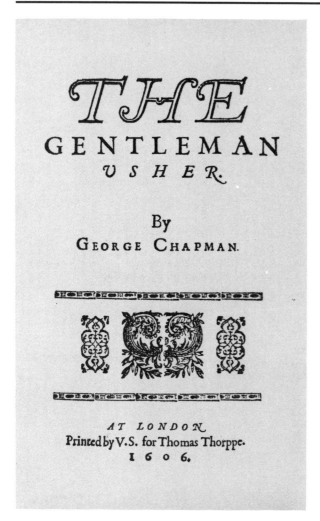

Title page for the 1606 quarto edition of a play that probably dates from 1602-1603 (Chapin Library, Williams College)

that he cannot avenge: "There's no disputing with the acts of kings, / Revenge is impious on their sacred persons." Trapped between the conflicting imperatives of clientage and royal authority, he sees no alternative but suicide: "I come, my lord! Clermont, thy creature, comes."

In his last French tragedy, Chapman sets out a similar ordeal in which King and patron are the same man. *The Tragedy of Chabot Admiral of France* was published in 1639, with a joint ascription to Chapman and Shirley; an unusual lucidity and balance in the language testify to Shirley's hand, probably as a belated reviser, but there is little doubt about Chapman's fundamental responsibility for the play's conception and design. It has proved difficult to date; Norma Dobie Solve argued that it was Chapman's dramatic allegory of the Somerset affair and so was probably composed 1621-1624, but Albert H. Tricomi now fa-

vors a date close to that of *The Revenge of Bussy D'Ambois*. The plot is taken from Estienne Pasquier's account of events in the reign of Francis, "first of that imperial name." Chabot, an exemplary royal servant, finds himself crowded by the rise of a new favorite, Montmorency. His enemies seize on his only exploitable failing, a quick-tempered righteousness: "in the heart hath anger his wisest seat, / And gainst unjust suits such brave anger fires him." The King is brought to sign an unworthy bill that Chabot is sure to reject, indeed that he tears to pieces. Francis forcefully reminds Chabot of his indebtedness–"Is your will so strong / Now against mine, your power being so weak / Before my favour gave them both their forces?"–only to be met with steely independence: "You merit not of me for benefits, / More than myself of you for services." The King is appalled, and authorizes his Chancellor, a schemer in Montmorency's faction, to investigate Chabot's affairs, on the expectation that something illegal will turn up. There is almost nothing to be found, but the Chancellor pushes through a show trial and bullies the judges into a death sentence: "You that so late did right and conscience boast, / Heaven's mercy now implore, the King's is lost."

The King in fact intends to show mercy, in order to make his earlier point more effectively:

> I joy
> This boldness is condemn'd, that I may pardon,
> And therein get some ground in his opinion,
> By so much bounty as saves his life.

But when the pardon is offered, Chabot remains obstinate: "You cannot pardon me, sir . . . / It is a word carries too much relation / To an offence, of which I am not guilty." This time his intransigence works for him. The King, startled, investigates and discovers the true nature of the trial and the Chancellor's behavior; Chabot is quickly exonerated and the Chancellor convicted and harshly sentenced. This turn of events finally softens Chabot and wins from him the profession of dependence that Francis wants:

> I have found
> A glorious harvest in your favour, sir;
> And by this overflow of royal grace,
> All my deserts are shadows, and fly from me.

Yet the experience has also ruined him; he is dying as he says this–broken, we are told, by his awareness of Francis's part in his troubles:

Some apprehension of the King's unkindness,
By giving up his person and his offices
To the law's gripe and search, is ground of his
Sad change; the greatest souls are thus oft wounded.

A royal visit and the granting of several petitions–including a pardon for the Chancellor–cannot heal the wound. The dependence was there all along and has proved mortal–though, in a final twist, death is a last, unanswerable move in the power play: "He has a victory in's death," the King concedes; "this world / Deserv'd him not."

That verdict, in more openly aggressive form, glosses Chapman's one other surviving tragedy, which may be either his earliest or his last. *Caesar and Pompey* was published in 1631, and tradition has tended to follow the publication sched-

Title page for the 1606 quarto edition of the play whose title character is "the perfect model of an impudent upstart, the compound of a poet and a lawyer" (Victoria and Albert Museum)

Title page for the 1612 quarto edition of a play that probably dates from 1604-1605 (British Library)

ule and date it late. Chapman himself, however, wrote of finding it surprisingly good for something "written so long hence"; and Bellamont, a character in Dekker and Webster's *Northward Ho* (1605-1606) evidently based on Chapman, is said to have produced a play on the subject. (Chapman claimed that his own play had never been performed, though a 1653 reprint says it was acted at Blackfriars.) It is easy to imagine Chapman either leaving the Rome so popular with other dramatists for a French territory that he could make uniquely his own or coming to Rome at the end of his career as though discovering the natural landscape for his imperial themes. The fierce simplicity of his own Roman play might similarly be either the narrowness of a beginner or the achieved clarity of a master. The play's pattern is in either case one of Chapman's basic fables, in which the individual's revenge against the world that masters him is, in the person of the Stoic Cato, wholly intentional, controlled, and virtuous.

Cato is the central figure even though he is

missing from the middle of the play, during which the title conflict comes to its climax at Pharsalia. Chapman makes neither of the principals hero or villain. Pompey defends the right side but is clearly no less ambitious than Caesar and unimpressively erratic in his leadership. Caesar's ambition has more grandeur–"I, that have ransack'd all the world for worth / To form in man the image of the gods"–but he is Machiavellian and ruthless in its pursuit. Chapman's sympathies tip only with Pompey's reaction to his defeat. His "philosophress" wife Cornelia welcomes him back as a hero, and they celebrate the spiritual growth that loss has made possible:

> let us still be good,
> And we shall still be great; and greater far
> In every solid grace than when the tumour
> And bile of rotten observation swell'd us.

"Miraculous standing in a fall so great!" exclaims an admiring ally; "Would Caesar knew, sir, how you conquer'd him / In your conviction!" To which:

> 'Tis enough for me
> That Pompey knows it. I will stand no more
> On others' legs, nor build one joy without me.

"O Pompey, Pompey," cries his wife, "never 'Great' till now!"

Pompey has, in other words, come to Cato's state; and the rest of the play's conclusion is given over to Cato's more deliberate and complete declaration of personal autonomy through suicide. He defends that action as the logical extension of the principle of self-control:

> is not our free soul infus'd
> To every body in her absolute end
> To rule that body? In which absolute rule
> Is she not absolutely empress of it?
> And being empress, may she not dispose
> It, and the life of it, at her just pleasure?

He knows, moreover, that Caesar will spare his life–we have already witnessed the pardoning of Brutus–and Cato is determined to resist the domineering subtext of that apparent generosity: "My fame affirm my life receiv'd from him! / I'll rather make a beast my second father." His suicide is in effect a refusal to let Caesar be his patron: "Come Caesar, quickly now, or lose your

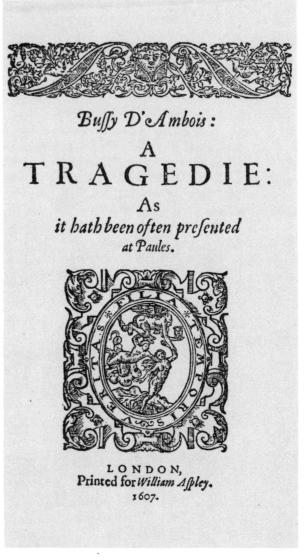

Bussy D'Ambois:
A
TRAGEDIE:
As
*it hath been often presented
at Paules.*

LONDON,
Printed for *William Aspley.*
1607.

Title page for the 1607 quarto edition of the tragedy for which Chapman drew on the true story of Louis de Clermont d'Amboise, Seigneur de Bussy, who was murdered in 1579 while attempting an assignation with the wife of the Comte de Monsoreau

vassal." The spite is accurately calculated; Caesar indeed finds his victory hollow:

> All my late conquest, and my life's whole acts,
> Most crown'd, most beautified, are blasted all
> With thy grave life's expiring in their scorn.
> ....
> O Cato, I envy thy death, since thou
> Envied'st my glory to preserve thy life.

Rising to this lucidly triumphant act of self-destruction, Cato's spirit flourishes with an almost Christian confidence in the immortality of the soul:

that our souls in reason are immortal
Their natural and proper objects prove;
Which immortality and knowledge are.
....
Since 'twere absurd to have her set an object
Which possibly she never can aspire.

In the reasoned conviction that the universe bears no such absurdity, he goes to "see the gods' state, and the stars."

Bibliography:

Terence P. Logan, "George Chapman," in *The New Intellectuals,* edited by Logan and Denzell P. Smith (Lincoln: University of Nebraska Press, 1977), pp. 117-170.

References:

Nicholas Brooke, Introduction to *Bussy D'Ambois,* edited by Brooke (London: Methuen, 1964);

Charles Lamb, *Specimens of English Dramatic Poets, Who Lived about the Time of Shakespeare* (London: Longman, Hurst, Rees & Orme, 1808);

Millar MacLure, *George Chapman: A Critical Study* (Toronto: University of Toronto Press, 1966);

Norma Dobie Solve, *Stuart Politics in Chapman's Tragedy of Chabot* (Ann Arbor: University of Michigan, 1926);

Albert H. Tricomi, "The Dates of the Plays of George Chapman," *English Literary Renaissance,* 12 (Spring 1982): 242-266;

Raymond B. Waddington, *The Mind's Empire: Myth and Narrative Form in George Chapman's Narrative Poems* (Baltimore: Johns Hopkins University Press, 1974);

Eugene M. Waith, *The Herculean Hero in Marlowe, Chapman, Shakespeare, and Dryden* (New York: Columbia University Press, 1962).

Papers:

A handful of letters very possibly by Chapman are transcribed in a manuscript now at the Folger Shakespeare Library (MS V. a. 321); the manuscript has been edited by A. R. Braunmuller as *A Seventeenth-Century Letter-Book* (Newark: University of Delaware Press, 1983).

Samuel Daniel
(1562 or 1563-October 1619)

James L. Harner
Bowling Green State University

PLAY PRODUCTIONS: *The Vision of the Twelve Goddesses*, Hampton, Hampton Court Palace, 8 January 1604;

Philotas, London, at Court, 3 January 1605;

The Queen's Arcadia, Christ Church, Oxford, 30 August 1605;

Tethys' Festival, Westminster, Whitehall Palace, 5 June 1610;

Hymen's Triumph, London, Somerset House, 2 February 1614.

BOOKS: *The Worthy Tract of Paulus Jouius, Contayning a Discourse of Rare Inuentions, Called Imprese* (London: Printed by G. Robinson for Simon Waterson, 1585);

Delia. Contayning Certayne Sonnets: With the Complaint of Rosamond (London: Printed by J. Charlewood for Simon Waterson, 1592);

Delia and Rosamond Augmented. Cleopatra (London: Printed by J. Roberts & E. Allde for Simon Waterson, 1594);

The First Fowre Bookes of the Ciuile Warres betweene the Two Houses of Lancaster and Yorke (London: Printed by P. Short for Simon Waterson, 1595);

The Poeticall Essayes of Sam. Danyel (London: Printed by P. Short for Simon Waterson, 1599)–comprises books 1-5 of *The Civil Wars*, the first revision of *Cleopatra*, *Musophilus*, and *Letter from Octavia*;

A Panegyrike Congratulatorie to the Kings Maiestie. Also Certaine Epistles (London: Printed by V. Simmes for E. Blount, 1603); republished with *A Defence of Ryme* (London: Printed by V. Simmes for E. Blount, 1603);

The Vision of the 12. Goddesses (London: Printed by T. Creede for Simon Waterson, 1604);

Certaine Small Poems Lately Printed: With the Tragedie of Philotas (London: Printed by G. Eld for Simon Waterson, 1605);

A Funerall Poeme uppon the Death of the Late Noble Earle of Devonshyre (London, 1606);

The Queenes Arcadia (London: Printed by G. Eld for Simon Waterson, 1606);

Certaine Small Workes (London: Printed by J. Windet for Simon Waterson, 1607)–includes *The Queen's Arcadia*, the second revision of *Cleopatra*, and the revised version of *Philotas;*

The Tragedie of Philotas (London: Printed by Melch. Bradwood for Edw. Blount, 1607);

The Civile Wares betweene the Howses of Lancaster and Yorke Corrected and Continued (London: Printed by H. Lownes for Simon Waterson, 1609);

Tethys' Festival, in *The Order and Solemnitie of the Creation of the High and Mightie Prince Henrie* (London: Printed by W. Stansby for John Budge, 1610);

The First Part of the Historie of England (London: Printed by N. Okes, 1612);

Hymens Triumph (London: Printed by J. Legat for Francis Constable, 1615);

The Collection of the Historie of England (London: Printed by N. Okes, 1618);

The Whole Workes of Samuel Daniel (London: Printed by Nicholas Okes for Simon Waterson, 1623).

Editions: *The Complete Works in Verse and Prose of Samuel Daniel*, 5 volumes, edited by Alexander B. Grosart (London: Privately printed, 1885-1896);

The Tragedy of Philotas, edited by Laurence Michel, Yale Studies in English, 110 (New Haven: Yale University Press, 1949; revised and enlarged edition, Hamden, Conn.: Archon, 1970);

The Tragedie of Cleopatra, in *Narrative and Dramatic Sources of Shakespeare*, volume 5, edited by Geoffrey Bullough (London: Routledge & Kegan Paul/New York: Columbia University Press, 1964), pp. 406-449;

The Vision of the Twelve Goddesses, edited by Joan Rees, in *A Book of Masques: In Honour of Allardyce Nicoll* (Cambridge: Cambridge University Press, 1967), pp. 18-42;

Title page, with portrait of Samuel Daniel, for the 1609 quarto edition of the history Daniel began in about 1594 (Henry E. Huntington Library and Art Gallery)

Tethys' Festival, in *Inigo Jones: The Theatre of the Stuart Court,* by Stephen Orgel and Roy Strong, volume 1 (London: Sotheby Parke Bernet, 1973), pp. 191-201.

Though admired as a lyric poet and historian, Samuel Daniel has found few enthusiastic readers for his dramatic works. Sober minded, restrained, reflective, and frequently prosaic, Daniel stands outside the popular-stage tradition, yet as an innovator he is of considerable importance in the history of Renaissance drama. *Cleopatra* is one of the earliest and best attempts to trans-

plant French Senecan closet drama to the English stage; *The Vision of the Twelve Goddesses* inaugurated the vogue for the elaborate Jacobean court masque; and *The Queen's Arcadia* is the first English imitation of Italian pastoral drama.

Daniel was born in Somersetshire in 1562 or 1563, and little is known of his early life. His father is said to have been John Daniel, a musician. He matriculated at Magdalen Hall, Oxford, on 17 November 1581 and left three years later, apparently without taking a degree. During parts of 1585-1590 he traveled on the Continent, likely developing the knowledge of French and Italian literature which was to influence his dramatic work. His first published work, *The Worthy Tract of Paulus Jovius* (essentially a translation of Paolo Giovio's *Dialogo dell' imprese militari et amorose),* appeared in 1585, revealing an interest in emblems which was to surface later in *The Vision of the Twelve Goddesses.*

By 1592 Daniel had come under the patronage of Mary, Countess of Pembroke, to whom he dedicated *Delia. Containing Certain Sonnets: With the Complaint of Rosamond* (1592)–a volume which firmly established his reputation as a poet–and *Cleopatra.* It was under the influence of the literary circle at Wilton (his "best Schoole," as he refers to it in *Defense of Rhyme*) that Daniel wrote his first two plays.

Reflecting the political interests (in abuses of tyranny and limits of government) and literary ideals (derived from Sidney's *Defense of Poetry*) of the Countess of Pembroke's circle, Daniel sought in *Cleopatra* and *Philotas* "to reduce the stage from idlenes to those grave prsentments of antiquitie vsed by the wisest nations." More specifically, it was in the Wilton group's interest in the French Senecan drama of Robert Garnier and Etienne Jodelle that Daniel found a model for his early plays.

Encouraged by the Countess to compose a companion piece to her translation of Garnier's *Marc-Antoine* and heeding Spenser's advice to turn his pen to "tragic plaints and passionate mischance," Daniel wrote *The Tragedy of Cleopatra.* The play was first published in 1594, but Daniel, as he was to do for so many of his works, revised it: once in 1599 and more extensively in 1607.

In its emphasis on the destruction of the state through unrestrained ambition, on the doctrine of cyclical recurrence, and on the providential course of history, *Cleopatra* treats themes typical of much of Daniel's work. Tormented by her sins and aware of the disorder in Egypt brought about by her ambition, Cleopatra is determined to commit suicide, both to preserve her honor and to attest her love of the dead Antony. However, in an attempt to preserve her son Caesario so that he might restore Egypt's fallen glory, she pretends to submit to Octavius Caesar, who hypocritically promises her mercy. Caesar, however, plans to parade Cleopatra through Rome as his triumphant prize and, by bribing Caesario's tutor, arranges the murder of the prince. Apprised by Dolabella of Caesar's plans, Cleopatra has two asps smuggled to her and "Die[s] like a Queene," requesting to be buried in Antony's tomb. The play concludes with the Chorus emphasizing that Rome will be destroyed as was Egypt.

In the 1594 and 1599 versions, *Cleopatra* is closet drama: the lengthy monologues, dialogues on questions of political morality, and reported action render the play unsuitable for the popular stage. Yet, it is effective closet drama. As in *Rosamond* and *Letter from Octavia*, Daniel delineates the mind of an afflicted woman who bears herself with dignity and nobility. In her struggle over her divided role as Queen and mother, her awareness of the destruction she has caused in Egypt, the intensity of her love for Antony, and her resolution to die honorably, Cleopatra is an effective psychological portrait. Although all of the action is reported, Daniel handles this technique well, even dramatically (especially in Rodon's description of Caesario's betrayal and death, and the Nuntius's account of Cleopatra's suicide). Daniel addresses a variety of political issues, but the result is not the diffuseness we find in *Philotas.* Here Daniel makes effective use of the Chorus as a unifying device, for at the conclusion of each act the Chorus relates individual issues to the overriding emphases on the causes of civil disorder and its cyclical recurrence.

In 1607 Daniel so completely revised *Cleopatra* that it became in effect a new work. Apparently attempting to make the play more stage-worthy, he rearranged scenes and parts of scenes to break long monologues into dialogue or to turn reported into direct action, added passages to clarify action or theme, and deleted passages to reduce narration. Although the result is a more symmetrical action, Daniel's revisions–particularly of Cleopatra's opening monologue and Diomedes's report of Cleopatra's death–reduce the meditative, philosophical power of the verse, rendering the characterization of Cleopatra less powerful and the development of theme less full.

Of Daniel's plays, *Cleopatra* is the best known and most influential. Shakespeare drew upon the 1599 version in *Antony and Cleopatra,* which in turn probably influenced Daniel's 1607 version; Dryden was influenced in *All for Love* by Daniel's imagery. Among minor writers, Samuel Brandon, Fulke Greville, William Alexander, and Elizabeth Cary were indebted in various ways to *Cleopatra.*

As Joan Rees observes, *Cleopatra* marks an important stage in Daniel's development: "When he began *Cleopatra* he was 'Sweete hony-dropping Daniel'; by the time he finished it, he was

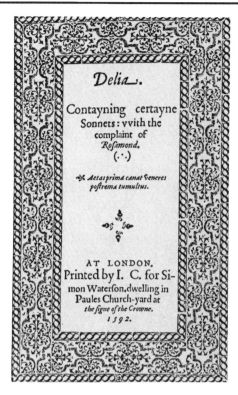

Title page for a 1592 quarto edition of the book that established Daniel's reputation as a poet (Anderson Galleries, sale number 2077, 20-21 May 1926)

Coleridge's 'sober-minded Daniel.' "

Until 1600, by which time he probably had begun *Philotas*, Daniel's attention was to his non-dramatic poetry. Some time during 1594 he came under the patronage of Lord Mountjoy, to whom *The First Four Books of the Civil Wars* (1595) and *The Poetical Essays* (1599) are dedicated. By 1600 he had possibly come under Elizabeth's favor, but the tradition that she appointed him poet laureate after the death of Spenser has no factual basis.

Daniel had written the first three acts of *Philotas* by 1600, intending the play to be acted by some gentlemen's sons as a Christmas entertainment. Revision of *The Civil Wars* interrupted work on the play, but, needing money, he completed the final two acts in 1604. The play was probably first performed on 3 January 1605 by the Children of the Queen's Revels. In 1607 Daniel extensively revised the work, principally to improve grammar, meter, or rhyme.

In *Philotas*, as he had in *Cleopatra*, Daniel treats themes common to much of his work: how unchecked ambition leads to civil disorder, how tyranny, through the unscrupulous use of the law, results in oppression, and how "To admire high hills, but liue within the plain" is the best

course of life. Philotas, a proud and ambitious soldier whom Alexander has raised above his rank, has entered into a conspiracy with his father to overthrow Alexander, whom they perceive as a vain and tyrannical ruler. Cloaking his ambition under protestations of honor, concern for the state, and a refusal to conform to the times by flattering the king, Philotas is esteemed by the people (represented by a Chorus). Partly motivated by self-interest and jealousy, Craterus (one of Alexander's "faithfull'st Counsellers") discerns Philotas's ambition and sets about to entrap him. Using Philotas's revelation of his ambition to his mistress Antigona and his failure to report a different plot by several nobles to murder Alexander—as well as masterful character assassination—Craterus, through rather Machiavellian maneuvering which subverts justice but providentially preserves the state, convinces the king of Philotas's guilt. At his trial Philotas is allowed to speak only after Alexander, presiding as judge, has pronounced him guilty and left. In protesting his innocence Philotas effectively underlines the trial's mockery of justice. Craterus, realizing the need for a confession to quell rumor and discontent, convinces Alexander to have Philotas tortured. At first Philotas, attempting to preserve his honor, resists, but eventually he reveals the conspiracy, even implicating an innocent bystander. As a result, Philotas loses all his supporters' respect, and the play concludes with the affirmation that the state has been spared from civil insurrection.

Philotas is justifiably acclaimed for elegance of diction and regularity of meter, qualities generally typical of Daniel's verse. However, his tendency to perceive an issue from more than one perspective—a trait which lends depth to many of his poems—works to disadvantage here. The examination of political morality and abuses of government at times is contradictory and structurally deficient. Although it is clear from the dedication to Prince Henry and the concluding apology that Daniel meant *Philotas* generally to condemn unchecked ambition which leads to civil disorder and to affirm the providential course of history, the equivocal nature of many of the issues and characters results in diffuseness and ambiguity rather than the complexity which Daniel sought.

Because of its political emphasis, many of Daniel's contemporaries read *Philotas* as a comment on the trial and execution of the Earl of Essex. Although Daniel was sympathetic to Essex and although the play, particularly in the trial

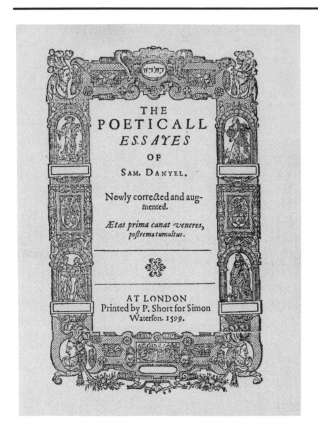

THE
POETICALL
ESSAYES
OF
SAM. DANYEL.

Newly corrected and aug-
mented.

Ætas prima canat veneres,
postrema tumultus.

AT LONDON
Printed by P. Short for Simon
Waterson. 1599.

Title page for the 1599 quarto edition of the book that includes the first revision of Cleopatra, *originally published in 1594 and revised again in 1607 (Anderson Galleries, sale number 2077, 20-21 May 1926)*

scene, bears several parallels to the Earl's trial, Daniel steadfastly denied before the Privy Council any connection between his play and the celebrated case. Whatever the relation to the Essex affair, Daniel turned away from history for subject matter in his later plays.

Although *A Panegyric Congratulatory to the King's Majesty* (1603) failed to gain the favor of the new king, James I, in 1604 Daniel came under the patronage of Queen Anne, for whom he wrote his last four dramatic works. The first of these was *The Vision of the Twelve Goddesses*, a masque performed by the Queen and her ladies at Hampton Court on 8 January 1604 and published later the same year. This was the first of several lavish and expensive masques which were so popular at the Jacobean court and included many of the finest specimens of this form of dramatic art.

As in his earlier plays, Daniel emphasizes order in the state: his intent is "to present the figure of those blessings, with the wish of their encrease and continuance, which this mightie Kingdome now enioyes by the benefit of his

most gracious Maiestie; by whom we haue this glory of peace, with the accession of so great state and power." To realize his theme, Daniel relies principally on an emblematic procession of the twelve goddesses, who represent "those blessings and beauties that preserue and adorne" the peaceful state. (For example, Pallas stands for "Wisedome and Defence"; Proserpina, riches; and Tethys, "power by Sea.") The goddesses, richly and symbolically dressed, descend from a hill at one end of the hall and march to the Temple of Peace, where they offer their respective gifts. For example, Pallas, played by the Queen, "was attyred in a blew mantle, with a siluer imbrodery of all weapons and engines of war, with a helmet-dressing on her head, and present[ed] a Launce and Target."

Although Daniel regarded *The Vision of the Twelve Goddesses* as entertainment and not one of his "grauer actions," he does unify text and spectacle, including dancing, singing, elaborate scenery, and emblematic costumes, to underscore his emphasis on the ordered state. From the opening speech of Night, who wields his white wand to "effect . . . significant dreames," to the closing speech of Iris, who justifies the representation of the goddesses in the forms of the Queen and her ladies, Daniel effectively manipulates levels of reality. Ultimately, however, *The Vision of the Twelve Goddesses* is not an accomplished example of the masque, a form with which Daniel was clearly uncomfortable.

In 1604 Daniel became Licenser to the Children of the Queen's Revels, a post he held until 28 April 1605. The appointment was not a fortunate one, for it involved Daniel in a lawsuit and monetary difficulties (which may have led him to complete *Philotas* for presentation by the company). And Daniel was not circumspect in his licensing of plays, for the Queen withdrew her patronage from the Children after *Philotas*, John Marston's *The Dutch Courtesan*, and George Chapman, Ben Jonson, and Marston's *Eastward Ho!* offended James I. Daniel did not, however, lose the favor of the Queen, and in 1607 he was appointed one of the Grooms of her Privy Chamber.

Daniel's next dramatic work, *The Queen's Arcadia*, is of considerable importance in the history of the drama, for it is the first attempt in English to imitate the Italian pastoral drama. Performed before the Queen at Christ Church, Oxford, on 30 August 1605, the play reflects Daniel's interest in Italian literature and attempt to appeal to the court's taste for extravagant dramatic entertain-

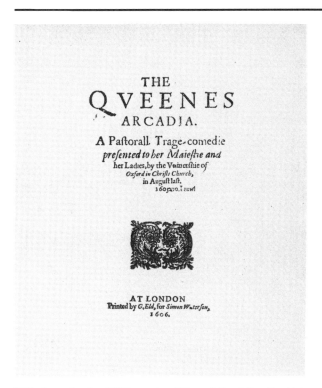

THE

QVEENES

ARCADIA.

A Paftorall Trage-comedie
prefented to her Maieftie and
her Ladies, by the Vniuerfitie of
Oxford in Chrifts Church,
in Auguft laft.

AT LONDON
Printed by G. Eld, for Simon Waterfon,
1606.

Title page for the 1606 quarto edition of Daniel's attempt to adapt the conventions of Italian pastoral drama to distinctly English concerns (Anderson Galleries, sale number 2077, 20-21 May 1926)

ment. Although heavily indebted to Guarini and Tasso, *The Queen's Arcadia* is distinctly English in its concerns. Like Daniel's earlier plays, it emphasizes order in the state, and, like much of his poetry, it glorifies the simple life.

Colax, "a corrupted traueller," and his accomplice Techne, "a subtle wench [that is, whore] of Corinth," are corrupting the natural harmony of Arcadia by introducing its virtuous lovers to lust, vanity, suspicion, and inconstancy. Three other foreigners also attempt to corrupt the Arcadians: Lincus, a pronotary's boy, passes himself off as a great lawyer and encourages needless litigation; Alcon, formerly a physician's servant, gains a reputation by distributing placebos and encouraging hypochondria; and Pistophoenax, a religious disputer who hides his ugly face behind a mask, works to subvert the natural religion of the country. The attempts of these outsiders to undermine "Rites, . . . Custome, Nature, Honesty"—"the maine pillors of . . . [the] state"—are frustrated by the revelations of Ergastus and Melibaeus, two elderly Arcadians who conveniently overhear all that takes place during the play.

Although commended by a member of the original audience as "being indeed very excellent, and some parts exactly acted," the play has not

been well received by modern readers. Daniel's treatment of the outsiders offers some effective comic satire on the hypocrisy and greediness of lawyers, on the quackery of physicians, and, generally, on a preference for foreign ideas and things. Most effective is a lengthy diatribe against tobacco, inserted perhaps because of King James's aversion to it. Yet, the satire is frequently blunted by Daniel's moralizing tendency and does not mesh with the conventional romantic treatment of pastoral love. The denouement is mechanical, and overall the play is rather dull.

During 1605-1610 Daniel published revisions of many of his earlier works (including *Cleopatra* and *Philotas*), completed the final version of *The Civil Wars,* and began his prose history, *The Collection of the History of England* (1618), which was to occupy him the remainder of his life.

Tethys' Festival, Daniel's second masque, was presented 5 June 1610 at Whitehall as part of the celebration of the creation of Prince Henry as Prince of Wales. This production, as befitted the occasion and Daniel's conception of masques as "Complements of State," was an elaborate, costly one (the charge for the costumes alone was nearly £1,000). In creating the entertainment, Daniel collaborated with Inigo Jones, the foremost stage architect of the period. As in *The Vision of the Twelve Goddesses,* the Queen (as Tethys) and her ladies (as the nymphs representing the rivers) assumed major roles.

Tethys' Festival consists of three scenes. The first represents "a Port or Hauen, with Bulworkes at the entrance, and the figure of a Castle commanding a fortified towne: within this Port were many Ships, small and great, seeming to be at Anchor, some neerer, and some further off, according to prospectiue: beyond all appeared the Horison, or termination of the Sea; which seemed to mooue with a gentle gale, and many Sayles, lying some to come into the Port, and others passing out." Zephyrus, accompanied by nyads and tritons, presents Tethys' gifts: a trident to the King and "a rich sword and skarfe," symbolizing respectively justice and "Loue and Amitie," to the Prince. The second scene is an elaborate architectural set compartmented into five niches, the middle one being Tethys' throne, the others representing the caverns of the river nymphs; from these the women issue forth to present "seuerall flowers in golden vrnes" at the Tree of Victory. In the final scene, the Queen and her ladies are revealed "in their owne forme" in an artificial grove.

Costume designs by Inigo Jones for Tethys' Festival, *the masque Daniel wrote for the celebration of the creation of Prince Henry as Prince of Wales: (above) Tethys or a nymph, (right) a naiad (Stephen Orgel and Roy Strong,* Inigo Jones, *1973)*

It is clear from Daniel's description of the sets and costumes and from Jones's extant drawings that the verse occupies a distinctly subordinate role in the entertainment. This is consistent with Daniel's conception of the masque as outlined in the preface to *Tethys' Festival:* "in these things . . . the onely life consists in shew; the arte and inuention of the Architect giues the greatest grace, and is of most importance: ours [the verse], the least part and of least note in the time of the performance thereof." Nevertheless, *Tethys' Festival* does display Daniel's fine lyric gift, particularly in the song beginning "Are they shadowes that we see?" Overall, as Rees points out, the work is a "feeble effort at a date when the masque form was in its full flower."

There is evidence of rivalry, even hostility, between Jonson and Daniel during the latter years of his life. This rivalry may have begun as early as 1604, when Daniel was chosen to write the first Queen's masque. William Drummond of Hawthornden records Jonson's assertion that "Daniel was at jealousies with him," and many references in the prefatory matter to Daniel's last four dramatic works seem directed at Jonson. Given their widely differing conceptions of the masque and pastoral drama, some kind of feud is not unlikely.

During the last years of his life, Daniel gave his attention to his prose history of England. His last major poetic work was also his final dramatic work, for which he again turned to pastoral drama. *Hymen's Triumph* was presented in February 1614 as part of the Queen's entertainment for the marriage of the Earl of Roxborough to Jean Drummond. A manuscript copy, with a dedicatory poem to Jean Drummond, is in Edinburgh University Library. The play was first published in 1615.

Appropriate to the occasion for which it was written, the play celebrates constancy in love. The theme is set in the prologue, an allegorical encounter of Hymen, who dons a pastoral disguise to effect a marriage between two of the most constant lovers, with Avarice, Envy, and Jealousy, "the disturbers of quiet marriage."

Thirsis, a young shepherd, remains constant in his love for Silvia, who, two years before, had been abducted by pirates and is apparently dead. Silvia, however, has escaped and returned to Arcadia, disguising herself as a boy and hiring out as a servant to Cloris. She maintains her disguise until after the marriage of Alexis, to whom her fa-

ther, out of avarice, had betrothed her. Before she can reveal herself to Thirsis, Silvia is stabbed by the jealous Montanus, who believes his beloved is in love with Silvia. Thirsis, having identified Silvia by a mole, vows to die with her, but they are miraculously saved and reunited.

Although *Hymen's Triumph* is less derivative than *The Queen's Arcadia*, Daniel's use of the conventional plot elements of pastoral drama–the female disguised as a male, the mistakes in love which ensue from the disguise, thwarted love, abduction by pirates, and an oracle–results in "sentimentality and bathos," as Cecil C. Seronsy points out. Although marred by some lengthy, incompletely assimilated passages on avarice and inconstancy, the masque has a "variety of mood and a rich lyricism," and many passages bear a striking resemblance to Shakespeare's romantic comedies, particularly *Twelfth Night* and *As You Like It.*

Five years after completing his final dramatic work, Daniel died. He was buried on 14 October 1619 at Beckington, Somersetshire, where in the church the Countess Dowager of Pembroke–who as Lady Anne Clifford had been his pupil–erected a monument to "that excellent poet and historian."

Although important for their innovations, Daniel's plays are little read and largely unappreciated today, especially by readers nurtured on the popular drama of this period. Daniel's seriousness, quietness, restraint, dignity, reflectiveness, sober-mindedness, preference for the abstract and general–qualities admirable in much of his nondramatic poetry–are not traits which serve him effectively in a dramatic medium. His fine lyric gift, which rightly earned him the epithet "well-languaged Daniel," surfaces too rarely in his plays. His pastoral dramas and masques–among the few works he did not revise–are serviceable occasional pieces, but it is the two tragedies on which Daniel would have wanted his reputation as a dramatist to rest.

Bibliographies:
Harry Sellers, "A Bibliography of the Works of Samuel Daniel, 1585-1623: With an Appendix of Daniel's Letters," *Proceedings and Papers of the Oxford Bibliographical Society,* 2, part 1 (1927): 29-54;

Sellers, "Supplementary Note to 'A Bibliography of the Works of Samuel Daniel,'" *Proceedings and Papers of the Oxford Bibliographical Society,* 2, part 4 (1930): 341-342;

James L. Harner, *Samuel Daniel and Michael*

Drayton: A Reference Guide (Boston: G. K. Hall, 1980).

References:

R. E. Brettle, "Samuel Daniel and the Children of the Queen's Revels, 1604-5," *Review of English Studies*, 3 (April 1927): 162-168;

Geoffrey Creigh, "Samuel Daniel's Masque *The Vision of the Twelve Goddesses*," *Essays and Studies by Members of the English Association*, new series 24 (1971): 22-35;

Thomas Gardner, " 'A Parodie! A Parodie!': Conjectures on the Jonson-Daniel Feud," in *Lebende Antike: Symposion für Rudolf Sühnel*, edited by Horst Meller and Hans-Joachim Zimmermann (Berlin: Schmidt, 1967), pp. 197-206;

W. W. Greg, *"Hymen's Triumph* and the Drummond MS.," *Modern Language Quarterly* (London), 6 (1903): 59-64;

Greg, *Pastoral Poetry & Pastoral Drama: A Literary Inquiry, with Special Reference to the Pre-Restoration Stage in England* (London: Bullen, 1906);

Russell E. Leavenworth, *Daniel's* Cleopatra: *A Critical Study*, Elizabethan & Renaissance Studies, no. 3 (Salzburg: Institut für Englische Sprache und Literatur, Universität Salzburg, 1974);

Kenneth Muir, "Elizabeth I, Jodelle, and Cleopatra," *Renaissance Drama*, new series 2 (1969): 197-206;

Arthur M. Z. Norman, "Daniel's *The Tragedie of Cleopatra* and *Antony and Cleopatra*," *Shakespeare Quarterly*, 9 (1958): 11-18;

Norman, *"The Tragedie of Cleopatra* and the Date of *Antony and Cleopatra*," *Modern Language Review*, 54 (January 1959): 1-9;

John Pitcher, *"In those figures which they seem": Samuel Daniel's* Tethys' Festival (Manchester: Manchester University Press, 1984);

Johanna Procter, *"The Queenes Arcadia* (1606) and *Hymens Triumph* (1615): Samuel Daniel's Court Pastoral Plays," in *The Renaissance in Ferrara and Its European Horizons/Il Rinascimento a Ferrara e i suoi orizzonti europei*, edited by J. Salmons and W. Moretti (Cardiff: University of Wales Press/Ravenna: Lapuccu, 1984), pp. 83-109;

Joan Rees, *Samuel Daniel: A Critical and Biographical Study*, Liverpool English Texts and Studies (Liverpool: Liverpool University Press, 1964);

Rees, "Samuel Daniel's *Cleopatra* and Two French Plays," *Modern Language Review*, 47 (January 1952): 1-10;

Ernest Schanzer, "Daniel's Revision of His *Cleopatra*," *Review of English Studies*, new series 8, no. 32 (1957): 375-381;

Cecil C. Seronsy, "The Doctrine of Cyclical Recurrence and Some Related Ideas in the Works of Samuel Daniel," *Studies in Philology*, 54 (July 1957): 387-407;

Seronsy, *Samuel Daniel* (New York: Twayne, 1967);

Seronsy, "Well-Languaged Daniel: A Reconsideration," *Modern Language Review*, 52 (October 1957): 481-497;

Pierre Spriet, *Samuel Daniel (1563-1619): Sa vie—son oeuvre*, Etudes Anglaises, no. 29 (Paris: Didier, 1968);

Brents Stirling, "Daniel's *Philotas* and the Essex Case," *Modern Language Quarterly*, 3 (December 1942): 583-594;

Ernest William Talbert, *The Problem of Order: Elizabethan Political Commonplaces and an Example of Shakespeare's Art* (Chapel Hill: University of North Carolina Press, 1962);

G. A. Wilkes, "Daniel's *Philotas* and the Essex Case: A Reconsideration," *Modern Language Quarterly*, 23 (1962): 233-242.

Papers:

The British Library holds manuscripts of the first two books of *The Civil Wars* and an early version of *A Panegyric Congratulatory to the King's Majesty*. A copy of *Hymen's Triumph* is at Edinburgh University Library, and an early version of *Letter from Octavia* is at Arundel Castle. Letters are at the Public Record Office, Hatfield House, and Longleat; Daniel's will is at Somerset House.

Recently, John Pitcher has convincingly ascribed to Daniel four verse epistles and a prose address in MS.Lt.q.36 in the Brotherton Collection, University of Leeds. Pitcher has also identified a manuscript in the Kerr Collection, National Library of Scotland, as Daniel's notebook of sources for *The Collection of the History of England*. See John Pitcher, *Samuel Daniel: The Brotherton Manuscript: A Study in Authorship*, Leeds Texts and Monographs, new series 7 (Leeds: University of Leeds, School of English, 1981).

John Day

(circa 1574-circa 1640)

Raymond S. Burns
Pace University

PLAY PRODUCTIONS: *The Conquest of Brute*, part 1, by Day, completed by Henry Chettle, London, Rose theater, summer 1598;

Cox of Collumpton, by Day and William Haughton, London, Rose theater, circa 1599-1600;

Thomas Merry (or *Beech's Tragedy*), by Day and Haughton, London, Rose theater, circa 1599-1600;

Lust's Dominion (possibly a revision of an earlier play, and presumably the same play as *The Spanish Moor's Tragedy*), by Day, Thomas Dekker, Haughton, and John Marston, London, Rose theater, spring 1600;

The Seven Wise Masters, by Day, Dekker, Haughton, and Chettle, London, Rose theater, March 1600;

The Golden Ass, or Cupid and Psyche, by Day, Dekker, and Chettle, London, Rose theater, May 1600;

The Blind Beggar of Bethnal Green, part 1, by Day and Chettle, London, Rose theater/part 2, by Day and Haughton, London, Rose or Fortune theater/part 3, by Day and Haughton, London, Fortune theater, between May 1600 and September 1601;

Six Yeomen of the West, by Day and Haughton, London, Fortune theater, summer 1601;

The Conquest of the West Indies, by Day, Haughton, and Wentworth Smith, London, Fortune theater, circa 1601-1602;

Friar Rush and The Proud Woman of Antwerp, by Day and Haughton, revised by Chettle, London, Fortune theater, circa 1601-1602;

The Bristol Tragedy, London, Fortune theater, summer 1602;

As Merry as May Be, by Day, Richard Hathway, and Smith, London, Fortune theater, autumn-winter 1602;

The Black Dog of Newgate, parts 1 and 2, by Day, Hathway, Smith, and another, London, Boar's Head theater, 24 November 1602-26 February 1603;

The Boss of Billingsgate, by Day, Hathway, and another, London, Fortune theater, spring 1603;

The Unfortunate General, by Day, Hathway, Smith, and another, London, Boar's Head theater, spring 1603;

Law Tricks, or Who Would Have Thought It, London, Blackfriars theater, circa 1604;

The Isle of Gulls, London, Blackfriars theater, February 1606;

The Travels of the Three English Brothers, by Day, William Rowley, and George Wilkins, London, Curtain theater, 1607;

Humor Out of Breath, London, Blackfriars theater, circa 1607-1608;

Guy of Warwick, by Day and Dekker, unknown theater (entered in the Stationers' Register, 15 January 1620);

The Bellman of London, by Day and Dekker, London, Curtain or Red Bull theater, licensed 30 July 1623;

Come See a Wonder (possibly the play revised by Dekker as *The Wonder of a Kingdom*), London, Red Bull theater, 18 September 1623.

BOOKS: *The Ile of Guls* (London: Printed for J. Trundle & sold by J. Hodgets, 1606);

The Travailes of the Three English Brothers, by Day, William Rowley, and George Wilkins (London: Printed by G. Eld for J. Wright, 1607);

Law-Trickes or, Who Woul'd Have Thought It (London: Printed by E. Allde for R. More, 1608);

Humour out of breath (London: Printed by R. Bradock for J. Helmes, 1608);

The Parliament of Bees (London: Printed for William Lee, 1641);

Lust's Dominion, or The Lascivious Queen (presumably the same play as *The Spanish Moor's Tragedy*), by Day, Thomas Dekker, William Haughton, and John Marston (London: Printed by F. K., sold by Robert Pollard, 1657);

The Blind-Beggar of Bednal Green, one of three plays by Day and Henry Chettle or Haughton (London: Printed for R. Pollard & Tho. Dring, 1659).

Editions: *The Works of John Day*, 2 volumes, edited

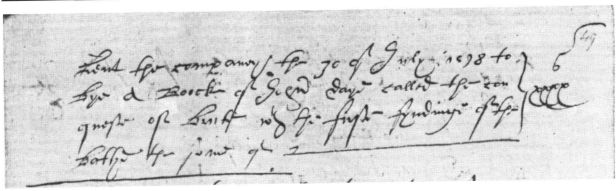

Entry in the diary of Philip Henslowe recording a payment on 30 July 1598 to buy Day's first known play, The Conquest of
Brute, *now lost (MSS VII, l. 49'; by permission of Dulwich College, London)*

by A. H. Bullen (London: Privately printed at the Chiswick Press, 1881)–comprises *Peregrinatio Scholastica, The Parliament of Bees, The Isle of Gulls, Humor Out of Breath, Law Tricks, The Travels of the Three English Brothers, The Blind Beggar of Bethnal Green;*

The Ile of Gulls, edited by Raymond S. Burns (New York: Garland, 1980);

The Parliament of Bees, edited by William T. Cocke (New York: Garland, 1981).

John Day, although not a playwright of perhaps even the second rank, is important historically. His was a career that illustrates the precarious fortunes of those young men who came to London to make their livings as playwrights, particularly of those who entered theater owner Philip Henslowe's stable of hacks. He seems, typically, to have been so busy following current interests and fashions that he never developed a dramatic interest or style of his own, though passages of lyrical loveliness in *Humor Out of Breath,* and the structural neatness and charm of the colloquies in *The Parliament of Bees,* suggest what, under more favorable conditions, he might have done. More important, however, his best-known work, *The Isle of Gulls,* illustrates the inbred character of the satiric comedies written for the private theaters of his time and can itself indicate what ultimately led to the closing of the theaters in 1642. On its own merits, finally, the induction to that play deserves to be better known as a shrewd and dramatically effective commentary upon the coterie plays and their jaded audiences at the private theaters.

Day is a shadowy figure whose name appears with some regularity in the pages of Philip Henslowe's diary from 1598 to 1603. The earliest record appears in the *Biographical History of Gonville and Caius College,* wherein he is described as "son of Walter Dey, husbandman. Born at Cawston, Norfolk. School, Ely. . . . Age 18. Admitted, Oct. 24, 1592, sizar. . . . He was expelled from the college for stealing a book, May 4, 1593." Some twenty-five years later William Drummond of Hawthornden recorded Ben Jonson's assertion "that Sharpham, Day, Dicker were all Rogues and that . . . Markham . . . was . . . a base fellow that such were Day and Midleton. . . ." In between those dates he appears in various records as the author or, more frequently, the collaborating author of more than a score of plays (most of them lost) before 1616. Most of these plays were written for Henslowe, many of them with Dekker. His nondramatic works, an allegorical prose treatise titled *Peregrinatio Scholastica* and a collection of twelve colloquies, *The Parliament of Bees,* came after he had written the bulk of his plays. He is known to have died by 1640 because an elegy by John Tatham, titled "On his loving friend M. John Day," appeared in a collection called *Fancies Theater* in 1640.

The few comments upon Day's life suggest a shadowy character that is consonant with what dramatist Robert Greene and some of the Puritan moralists said about the general run of Elizabethan and Jacobean playwrights and with the underlying cynical tone of his plays, especially *The Isle of Gulls.*

Although eight works wholly or partly by Day survive, he is finally known only for this play. Several editions or reprints of *The Isle of Gulls* are available. For the other plays one must resort mostly to facsimile reprints or the unreliable A. H. Bullen edition of the complete works (1881). Day has suffered a similar critical neglect; the little bit of scholarship there is usually ap-

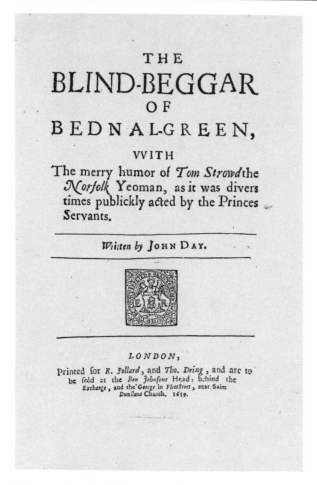

THE

BLIND-BEGGAR

OF

BEDNAL-GREEN,

WITH

The merry humor of *Tom Strowd* the *Norfolk* Yeoman, as it was divers times publickly acted by the Princes Servants.

Written by JOHN DAY.

LONDON,

Printed for *R. Pollard*, and *Tho. Dring*, and are to be sold at the *Ben Johnsons* Head, behind the *Exchange*, and the *George* in *Fleetstreet*, near Saint *Dunstans* Church. 1659.

Title page for the 1659 quarto edition of the only surviving part of a three-part play that Day wrote with Henry Chettle and William Haughton in 1600-1601 (Anderson Galleries, sale number 1375, 2-3 December 1918)

pears in unpublished dissertations. One must acknowledge, nevertheless, that though the Will Kemp scenes of *The Travels of the Three English Brothers* are of interest for the vivid impression they give of this colorful stage personality, though the pastoralism of *Humor Out of Breath* is often quite charming, and though T. S. Eliot paid *The Parliament of Bees* a great compliment by borrowing from it for *The Waste Land* (1922), the general neglect of all but one or two of Day's works by editors and critics is understandable. To speak of his reputation and importance is to speak of *The Isle of Gulls.*

This work was the first of his plays to appear in print and the only one to achieve a second edition within his lifetime. The date of performance has been established almost to the day, mid February 1606, by a letter that speaks of the men's parts being acted as of two nations, presumably the English and the Scots. The play

provoked royal indignation over lines that were interpreted as veiled references to the court of James I, and, as a result, several of those involved in its production were committed to Bridewell Prison. Publication followed soon after, very likely to capitalize upon the succès de scandale, and was itself the subject of difficulties, the insinuating titles "King" and "Queen" being replaced in the text by the "Duke" and "Duchess" of Day's source.

The play is prefaced by an Induction and then a Prologue, the former the most interesting part of the work. Three Gallants enter severally and ask the Prologue what kind of play it is to be. During the course of their questioning they comment upon other plays, alluding especially to the notorious lost play *The Isle of Dogs* by Ben Jonson and Thomas Nashe, which had led to Jonson's imprisonment and a brief closing of the theaters in 1597 and was now contributing a title to a new play. The First Gentleman asks whether it is critical (bitter), the Second if it is bawdy, and the Third if it is "high written." The first two features were the stock in trade of the private theaters, especially the children's companies, one of which—the Children of the Revels—was presenting the present play. To each the Prologue protests the playwright's inability to gratify the conflicting tastes of a "confused audience." He then addresses the audience and disingenuously pleads the author's innocence and good intentions.

The source of the play, acknowledged in the Induction, is Sir Philip Sidney's *Arcadia*, which Day used with a very free hand. Basilius has brought his Duchess, Gynetia, and their two daughters, Violetta and Hippolita, to a desert island in order to escape the unruly suitors whose impetuous concourse troubled the smooth stream of government in Arcadia. He has sent out a general challenge to all the youthful bloods of Africa to exercise their wit and policy to woo and win these daughters in a lovers' prize, and thus in turn to win his imperial crown. Against their easy success he has fenced in his island retreat and set up defense castles at each corner. In the royal entourage have come Dametas, counselor to Basilius; his wife and daughter; and Manasses, scribe-major to Dametas, and Manasses's wife.

The first to accept the Duke's challenge are Aminter and Julio, two princes disguised as a poor soldier and a scholar respectively, who have already enlisted the aid of the avaricious Dametas in their suits. Next come Prince Lysander, disguised as an Amazon, and Prince Demetrius, as a woodman. Because of the disguises employed by Lysander and Demetrius, they become the objects of unsought passion and the causes of a series of overlapping love rivalries, not least among these one involving the Duke and Duchess themselves. These intrigues, together with the impatience with which the sisters bear their virginity, the venality of Dametas, the hypocritical piety of Manasses, and the gaucherie of the three remaining women, form the plot and provide most of the comedy of the play. Just as Lysander and Demetrius are proclaiming their victory in the lovers' contest, the sisters announce that they have chosen Aminter and Julio.

Day's plot, for all the cleverness of its complication and resolution, is merely a line from which to hang his satire. His most obvious target— and the one that made for both the success and

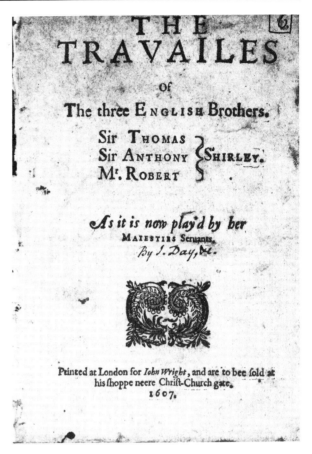

Title page for the 1607 quarto edition of a play that Day wrote with William Rowley and George Wilkins (Henry E. Huntington Library and Art Gallery)

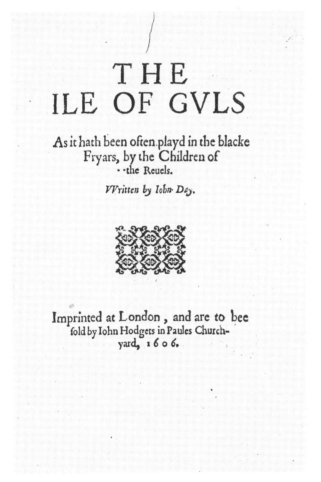

Variant title page for the 1606 quarto edition of the play that provoked the anger of James I when it was performed in February of that year. In the published version the titles of two characters have been changed from "King" and "Queen" to "Duke" and "Duchess" (Anderson Galleries, sale number 1375, 2-3 December, 1918).

the difficulties of the play—was King James I, the Scottish retainers who followed him to England in such numbers, and his favorites (in this case probably the Earl of Salisbury or the Earl of Dunbar). This satire was personal and political: it was aimed at James's prodigality, his neglect of his kingly responsibilities, his inordinate fondness for his favorites, his passion for hunting, and his strained relations with his wife. It was also aimed at his wasting of the treasury, the selling of patents, and the growing power of the Scots and Puritans. But Day's is such a broadly dispersed satire that it manages to cover a wide spectrum of presumed abuses and personalities: the "base upstarts" who were general targets for the playwrights of the private theaters, lawyers and usurers, Puritan divines, the Gunpowder conspirators, government spies, rival playwrights—Ben Jonson very likely chief among them. It might thus be more appropriate to describe his satire as unfocused.

The most remarkable difference between the play and its source is one of tone. The moral

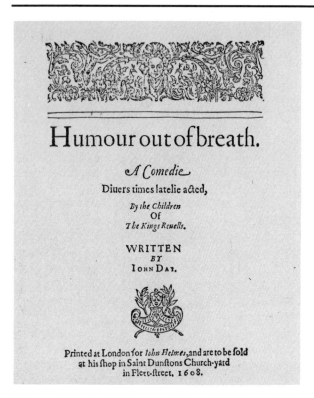

Title page for the 1608 quarto edition of the last surviving play written solely by Day (Anderson Galleries, sale number 2077, 20-21 May 1926)

earnestness of Sidney's romance has given way to a strange remoteness, as though, in viewing the singleminded pursuit of maidenheads, bedfellows, and gold, one were watching the scramblings of another species. Lacking the moral seriousness of a Jonson or the magnificent disdain of a Thomas Middleton, the comedy seems to be nothing so much as the reworking of a marketable formula. This is seen perhaps most notably in the final scene wherein, as promised in the Induction, "for fashion sake . . . all those which have to do in that desert are gulled in the reach of their hopes. . . ." Certainly Lysander and Demetrius have earned the princesses, and our sympathies have been directed to these young men from the beginning. The substance of the play has been their clever schemes to win the princesses according to the terms set by Basilius. Lysander and Demetrius alone attest lyrically to the ardor of their passions, are themselves loved in turn, actually win the sisters by "sweating in the field of invention," and engineer the dazzling coup of the last act—only to lose them to two plodding rivals. This capriciousness strikes the reader as a dramatic demonstration of the malaise often cited as an undercurrent in Jacobean comedy and tragedy, for it seems to be the mindless reduction of everything to the theme or trick of gulling. For all its vitality *The Isle of Gulls* provides as effective an illustration as any play contemporaneous with it of the artful portrayal of moral anarchy which so amused the audiences of the private theaters. Satire has begun running down a random pack of topical grievances; very fashionably, life has given way to theater. *The Isle of Gulls* unmistakably points the way to 1642.

References:

Gerald Eades Bentley, *The Jacobean and Caroline Stage,* 7 volumes (Oxford: Clarendon Press, 1941-1968), III: 238-240;

E. K. Chambers, *The Elizabethan Stage,* 4 volumes (Oxford: Clarendon Press, 1923), III: 284-289.

Papers:

The British Library has manuscripts for *The Parliament of Bees* (Lansdowne MS 725) and *Peregrinatio Scholastica* (Sloane MS 3150). An earlier manuscript for *Peregrinatio Scholastica* is at the Huntington Library.

Thomas Dekker
(circa 1572-August 1632)

Cyrus Hoy
University of Rochester

PLAY PRODUCTIONS: *Sir Thomas More,* probably by Anthony Munday, with revisions by Dekker, Henry Chettle, probably William Shakespeare, and perhaps Thomas Heywood, probably not produced, circa 1598;

Phaeton, London, Rose theater, January 1598;

The Triangle (or Triplicity) of Cuckholds, London, Rose theater, March 1598;

The Famous Wars of Henry I and the Prince of Wales (also known as *The Welshman's Prize*), by Dekker, Chettle, and Michael Drayton, London, Rose theater, March 1598;

Earl Godwin and his Three Sons, parts 1 and 2, by Dekker, Drayton, Chettle, and Robert Wilson, London, Rose theater, spring 1598;

Black Bateman of the North, part 1, by Dekker, Drayton, Chettle, and Wilson, London, Rose theater, May 1598;

The Mad Man's Morris, by Dekker, Drayton, and Wilson, London, Rose theater, July 1598;

Hannibal and Hermes, part 1 (also known as *Worse Afeard than Hurt*), by Dekker, Drayton, and Wilson, London, Rose theater, July 1598;

Pierce of Winchester, by Dekker, Drayton, and Wilson, London, Rose theater, July-August 1598;

Worse Afeard than Hurt (presumably part 2 of *Hannibal and Hermes*), by Dekker and Drayton, London, Rose theater, September 1598;

Conan, Prince of Cornwall, by Dekker and Drayton, London, Rose theater, October 1598;

The Civil Wars of France, parts 1, 2, and 3, by Dekker and Drayton, London, Rose theater, autumn 1598;

The First Introduction of the Civil Wars of France, London, Rose theater, January 1599;

Troilus and Cressida, by Dekker and Chettle, London, Rose theater, April 1599;

Agamemnon (apparently the same play as *Orestes' Furies*), by Dekker and Chettle, London, Rose theater, summer 1599;

The Shoemakers' Holiday, London, Rose theater, summer 1599;

Page of Plymouth, by Dekker and Ben Jonson, London, Rose theater, September 1599;

The Tragedy of Robert II, King of Scots, by Dekker, Chettle, Jonson, and perhaps John Marston, London, Rose theater, autumn 1599;

The Stepmother's Tragedy, by Dekker and Chettle, London, Rose theater, October 1599;

Old Fortunatus, London, Rose theater, autumn 1599;

Patient Grissell, by Dekker, Chettle, and William Haughton, London, Rose theater, January 1600;

Lust's Dominion (possibly a revision of an earlier play and presumably the same play as *The Spanish Moor's Tragedy*), by Dekker, John Day, Haughton, and Marston, London, Rose theater, spring 1600;

The Seven Wise Masters, by Dekker, Chettle, Haughton, and Day, London, Rose theater, March 1600;

The Golden Ass, or Cupid and Psyche, by Dekker, Chettle, and Day, London, Rose theater, May 1600;

Fair Constance of Rome, part 1, by Dekker, Drayton, Munday, Wilson, and Richard Hathway, London, Rose theater, June 1600;

Fortune's Tennis, London, Rose or Fortune theater, September 1600;

Sebastian, King of Portugal, by Dekker and Chettle, London, Fortune theater, May 1601;

Satiromastix, London, Globe theater and Paul's theater, autumn 1601;

Blurt, Master Constable, by Dekker and perhaps Thomas Middleton, London, Paul's theater, circa 1601-1602;

Pontius Pilate (anonymous play of circa 1597), prologue and epilogue added by Dekker, London, Fortune theater, January 1602;

Tasso's Melancholy (anonymous play of circa 1594), revised by Dekker, London, Fortune theater, January 1602;

Jephthah, by Dekker and Munday, London, Fortune theater, May 1602;

Caesar's Fall (also known as *Two Shapes*), by Dekker, Drayton, Munday, Middleton, and John Webster, London, Fortune theater, May 1602;

Sir John Oldcastle, part 2, by Drayton, Hathway, Munday, and Wilson (1600), revised by Dekker, London, Boar's Head or Rose theater, September 1602;

A Medicine for a Curst Wife, London, Boar's Head or Rose theater, September 1602;

Sir Thomas Wyatt (presumably the same play as *Lady Jane*), by Dekker, Webster, Chettle, Heywood, and Wentworth Smith, London, Boar's Head or Rose theater, autumn 1602;

Christmas Comes but Once a Year, by Dekker, Chettle, Heywood, and Webster, London, Boar's Head or Rose theater, November 1602;

The Magnificent Entertainment, by Dekker (with Zeal's speech by Middleton), streets of London, 15 March 1604;

The Honest Whore, part 1, by Dekker and Middleton, London, Fortune theater, spring 1604;

Westward Ho, by Dekker and Webster, London, Paul's theater, late 1604;

The Honest Whore, part 2, London, Fortune theater, circa 1604-1605;

Northward Ho, by Dekker and Webster, London, Paul's theater, 1605;

The Whore of Babylon, London, Fortune theater, winter 1605-1606;

The Roaring Girl, by Dekker and Middleton, London, Fortune theater, April-May 1611;

If This Be Not a Good Play, the Devil Is in It, London, Red Bull theater, May-June 1611;

Troia-Nova Triumphans, streets of London, 29 October 1612;

Guy of Warwick, by Dekker and Day (Stationers' Register, 15 January 1620), unknown theater;

The Virgin Martyr, by Dekker and Philip Massinger, London, Red Bull theater, October 1620;

Match Me in London, London, Red Bull theater, circa 1621;

The Witch of Edmonton, by Dekker, John Ford, and William Rowley, London, Cockpit theater, 1621;

The Noble Spanish Soldier (perhaps a revision of an earlier, circa 1600, collaboration with Day), unknown theater, circa 1622;

The Wonder of a Kingdom (apparently a revision and abridgment of a collaboration with Day), unknown theater, circa 1623;

The Bellman of Paris, by Dekker and Day, London, Curtain or Red Bull theater, licensed 30 July 1623;

The Welsh Ambassador (in part a revision of *The Noble Spanish Soldier* and perhaps a collaboration with Ford), unknown theater, circa 1623;

The Sun's Darling, by Dekker and Ford, London, Cockpit theater, licensed 3 March 1624;

The Fairy Knight, by Dekker and Ford, London, Red Bull theater, licensed 11 June 1624;

The Late Murder of the Son upon the Mother, by Dekker, Ford, Rowley, and Webster, London, Red Bull theater, September 1624;

The Bristow Merchant, by Dekker and Ford, London, Fortune theater, licensed 22 October 1624;

Lord Mayor's pageant, streets of London, 29 October 1627;

Britannia's Honor, streets of London, 29 October 1628;

London's Tempe, streets of London, 29 October 1629.

BOOKS: *The Pleasant Comedie of Old Fortunatus* (London: Printed by S. Stafford for W. Apley, 1600);

The Shoemakers Holiday. Or The Gentle Craft. With the Life of Simon Eyre, Shoomaker, and Lord Maior of London (London: Printed by V. Sims, 1600);

Blurt Master-Constable. Or The Spaniard's Night-Walke, by Dekker and perhaps Thomas Middleton (London: Printed by E. Allde for H. Rockytt, 1602);

Satiro-Mastix. Or The Untrussing of the Humorous Poet (London: Printed by E. Allde for E. White, 1602);

The Pleasant Comodie of Patient Grissell, by Dekker, Henry Chettle, and William Haughton (London: Printed by E. Allde for H. Rocket, 1603);

1603. The Wonderfull Yeare. Wherein Is Shewed the Picture of London, Lying Sicke of the Plague (London: Printed by T. Creede, sold by N. Ling, J. Smethwick & J. Browne, 1603);

Newes from Graves-End: Sent to Nobody (London: Printed by T. Creede for T. Archer, 1604);

The Meeting of Gallants at an Ordinarie: or The Walkes in Powles, by Dekker and perhaps Thomas Middleton (London: Printed by T. Creede, sold by M. Lawe, 1604);

The Honest Whore, with, the Humours of the Patient

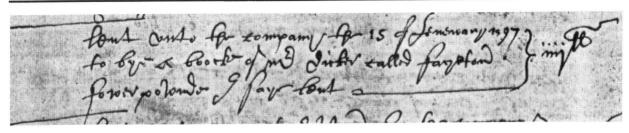

Entry in the diary of Philip Henslowe recording a payment on 15 January 1598 (1597 according to the calendar then in use) for Dekker's play Phaeton, *now lost (MS VII, l. 44'; by permission of Dulwich College, London)*

Man, and the Longing Wife [part 1], by Dekker and Middleton (London: Printed by V. Simmes & others for J. Hodgets, 1604); republished as *The Converted Curtezan* (London: Printed by V. Simmes, sold by J. Hodgets, 1604);

The Magnificent Entertainment: Given to King James upon His Passage through London (London: Printed by T. Creede, H. Lownes, E. Allde & others for T. Man the younger, 1604);

The Double PP. A Papist in Armes. Encountred by the Protestant. A Jesuite Marching before Them (London: Printed by T. Creede, sold by J. Hodgets, 1606);

Newes from Hell; Brought by the Divells Carrier (London: Printed by R. Blower, S. Stafford & V. Simmes for W. Ferebrand, 1606); enlarged as *A Knights Conjuring. Done in Earnest: Discovered in Jest* (London: Printed by T. Creede for W. Barley, 1607);

The Seven Deadly Sinnes of London: Drawne in Seven Severall Coaches, Through the Citie Bringing the Plague with Them (London: Printed by E. Allde & S. Stafford for N. Butter, 1606);

Jests to Make You Merie: With the Conjuring Up of Cock Watt, by Dekker and George Wilkins (London: Printed by N. Okes for N. Butter, 1607);

North-ward Hoe, by Dekker and John Webster (London: Printed by G. Eld, 1607);

The Famous History of Sir T. Wyat. With the Coronation of Queen Mary (presumably the same play as *Lady Jane*), by Dekker, Webster, Thomas Heywood, Chettle, and Wentworth Smith (London: Printed by E. Allde for T. Archer, 1607);

West-ward Hoe, by Dekker and Webster (London: Printed by W. Jaggard, sold by J. Hodgets, 1607);

The Whore of Babylon (London: Printed at Eliot's Court Press [?] for N. Butter, 1607);

The Dead Tearme. Or Westminsters Complaint for Long Vacations and Short Termes (London:

Printed by W. Jaggard, sold by J. Hodgets, 1608);

The Belman of London: Bringing to Light the Most Notorious Villanies Now Practised in the Kingdome (London: Printed by N. Okes for N. Butter, 1608);

Lanthorne and Candle-light. Or the Bell-mans Second Nights Walke (London: Printed by G. Eld for J. Busbie, 1608; corrected and amended edition, London: Printed by E. Allde for J. Busby, 1609); enlarged as *O per se o, or a new crier of Lanthorne and Candle-Light* (London: Printed by T. Snodham for J. Busbie, 1612); enlarged again as *Villanies Discovered by Lanthorne and Candle-Light* (London: Printed by W. Stansby for J. Busby, 1616; enlarged again, London: Printed by A. Mathewes, 1620); enlarged again as *English Villanies* (London: Printed by A. Mathewes, sold by J. Grismond, 1632);

Foure Birds of Noahs Arke (London: Printed by H. Ballard for N. Butter, 1609);

The Guls Horne-Booke (London: Printed by N. Okes for R. S., 1609);

The Ravens Almanacke Foretelling of a Plague, Famine, and Civill Warre (London: Printed by E. Allde for T. Archer, 1609);

Worke for Armorours: or, The Peace Is Broken (London: Printed by N. Okes for N. Butter, 1609);

The Roaring Girle. Or Moll Cut-purse, by Dekker and Middleton (London: Printed by N. Okes for T. Archer, 1611);

If It Be Not Good, The Divel Is in It. A New Play (London: Printed by T. Creede for J. Trundle, sold by E. Marchant, 1612);

Troia-Nova Triumphans. London Triumphing, or, The Solemne, Receiving of Sir J. Swinerton After Taking the Oath of Maioralty (London: Printed by N. Okes, sold by J. Wright, 1612);

A Strange Horse-Race, at the End of Which, Comes in the Catch-Pols Masque (London: Printed by N. Okes for J. Hunt, 1613);

Dekker's addition to Sir Thomas More, *in the manuscript preserved at the British Library (Harleian MS 7368, l. 13ᵛ; by permission of the British Library). These lines are the only preserved example of a dramatic composition in Dekker's hand.*

The Artillery Garden (London: Printed by G. Eld, 1616);

Dekker His Dreame. In Which, the Great Volumes of Heaven and Hell to Him Were Opened (London: Printed by N. Okes, 1620);

The Virgin Martir, A Tragedie, by Dekker and Philip Massinger (London: Printed by B. Alsop for T. Jones, 1622);

A Rod for Run-Awayes. Gods Tokens, of His Feareful Judgements, upon This City (London: Printed by G. Purslowe for J. Trundle, 1625);

Brittannia's Honor: Brightly Shining in Severall Magnificent Shewes or Pageants, to Celebrate R. Deane, at His Inauguration into the Majoralty of London, October the 29ᵗʰ. 1628 (London: Printed by N. Okes & J. Norton, 1628);

Warres, Warres, Warres (London: Printed by N. Okes for J. G., 1628);

Londons Tempe, or The Feild of Happines. To Celebrate J. Campebell, at His Inauguration into the Maioralty of London, the 29 of October, 1629 (London: Printed by N. Okes, 1629);

London Looke Backe, at That Yeare of Yeares 1625 (London: Printed by A. Mathewes, sold by E. Blackmoore, 1630);

The Blacke Rod: and the White Rod (London: Printed by B. Alsop & T. Fawcet for J. Cowper, 1630);

The Second Part of the Honest Whore (London: Printed by Eliz. Allde for N. Butter, 1630);

A Tragi-Comedy: Called, Match Mee in London (London: Printed by B. Alsop & T. Fawcet for H. Seile, 1631);

Penny-Wise Pound Foolish or, a Bristow Diamond, Set in Two Rings, and Both Crack'd (London: Printed by A. Mathewes for E. Blackmoore, 1631);

The Noble Souldier. Or, A Contract Broken, Justly Reveng'd. A Tragedy (London: Printed by J. Beale for N. Vavasour, 1634);

The Wonder of a Kingdome (London: Printed by R. Raworth for N. Vavasour, 1636);

The Sun's-Darling: A Moral Masque, by Dekker and John Ford (London: Printed by J. Bell for

Andrew Penneycuicke, 1656);

Lust's Dominion, or The Lascivious Queen (presumably the same play as *The Spanish Moor's Tragedy*), by Dekker, Haughton, John Day, and John Marston (London: Printed by F. K., sold by Robert Pollard, 1657);

The Witch of Edmonton, by Dekker, Ford, and William Rowley (London: Printed by J. Cottrel for Edward Blackmoore, 1658).

Editions: *The Non-Dramatic Works of Thomas Dekker*, edited by A. B. Grosart, 5 volumes (London, 1884-1886);

The Plague Pamphlets of Thomas Dekker, edited by F. P. Wilson (Oxford: Clarendon Press, 1925);

The Dramatic Works of Thomas Dekker, edited by Fredson Bowers, 4 volumes (Cambridge: Cambridge University Press, 1953-1961);

Thomas Dekker: Selected Prose Works, edited by E. D. Pendry (London, 1968);

Cyrus Hoy, *Introductions, Notes, and Commentaries to texts in 'The Dramatic Works of Thomas Dekker,'* 4 volumes (Cambridge: Cambridge University Press, 1980-1981).

Thomas Dekker was one of the most versatile of Renaissance English writers, and the plays and the nondramatic pamphlets (usually cast in

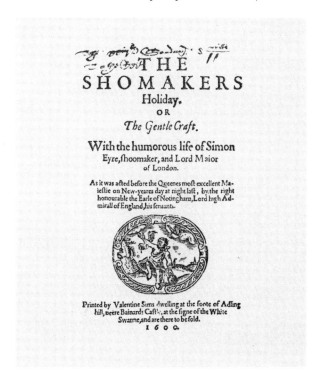

Title page for the 1600 quarto edition of the earliest surviving play solely written by Dekker (Anderson Galleries, sale number 2077, 20-21 May 1926)

the form of journalistic essays and narratives) that he produced during a career extending from the late 1590s to the early 1630s provide a record of popular taste during the last years of the reign of Queen Elizabeth I, through the reign of James I, and into the early years of Charles I. Dekker earned his living by his pen, and nearly everything he wrote shows signs of haste. Only rarely, as in such plays as *The Shoemakers' Holiday* or *The Honest Whore*, or such nondramatic pieces as *The Gull's Horn Book* or *Four Birds of Noah's Ark* does a single work of his seem entirely satisfactory, but nearly everything that he wrote bears witness to a sensitive and shrewd imagination and to a remarkable verbal range. His descriptive manner is by turns lyrical and boisterous. Where depiction of human feeling is concerned, he writes with a simplicity and a directness that carry great eloquence. At the other extreme of style, his accounts of human folly and error and vice and the lurid imbroglio these often make of worldly affairs exhibit a raucous delight in grotesquely personified detail. His work presents a striking blend of romantic sentiment and worldly awareness, a representation of the way things are combined with a vision of the way they ought to be. He is a compassionate but by no means uncritical commentator on the life of his times, and he mirrors it in language that, both in its quiet lyricism and its verbal exuberance, is typically Elizabethan.

The exact date of Dekker's birth is unknown. In the epistle to *English Villanies*, the 1632 edition of his *Lanthorn and Candlelight*, he speaks of his "three-score years," and this is the basis for the assumption that he was born in or around the year 1572. In his writings, he several times makes reference to London as the place of his birth and his upbringing, and his devotion to the city is manifest both in his plays and in his nondramatic works. Nothing is known of his life prior to January 1598, when his name begins to appear among the entries for payments to dramatists in the diary (that is the manuscript account book) of Philip Henslowe, theater owner and financier of two of the companies of players (the Lord Admiral's Men and the Earl of Worcester's Men) with whom Dekker was associated in the early years of his career.

The early 1590s witnessed the formation of a regular, theatergoing audience in London. The possibility of attending plays on anything like a regular, day-to-day basis had been available to the public only since 1576, when James Burbage

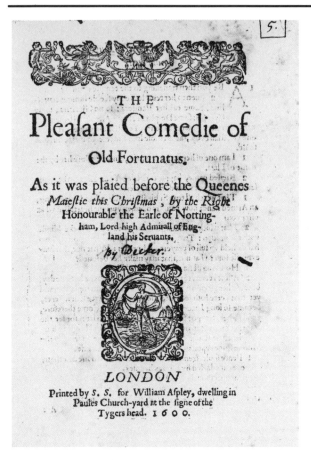

THE

Pleafant Comedie of

Old Fortunatus.

As it was plaied before the Queenes
Maieftie this Chriftmas, by the Right
Honourable the Earle of Nottingham, Lord high Admirall of England his Seruants.

by Dekker.

LONDON

Printed by S. S. for William Afpley, dwelling in
Paules Church-yard at the figne of the
Tygers head. 1 6 0 0.

*Title page for the 1600 quarto edition of Dekker's version of
an old play, which he wrote in autumn 1599 and revised for
a Court performance during the Christmas season of
1599-1600 (Henry E. Huntington Library and Art Gallery)*

built the first commercial theater in the vicinity
of London. More theaters were built in the years
that followed: the Curtain in 1577, the Rose in
1587, the Swan in 1595 or 1596, the Fortune in
1600. As their number increased, so the need increased for plays to be acted on their stages. Henslowe, who owned shares in the Rose and the
Fortune, kept in his employment a virtual crew of
playwrights, who turned out comedies, histories,
and tragedies, sometimes of an individual's own
devising but more often by collaborative teams
that might number anywhere from two to five or
six members. We first hear of Dekker when his
name appears in Henslowe's list of dramatists in
January 1598, but, since it was only in that year
that Henslowe began to include the names of
dramatists in his diary entries (prior to then he
had listed only the names of plays), one may assume that Dekker's career as a playwright had
begun several years before. By January 1598 he
was well launched as a professional dramatist.
Frances Meres, surveying the English literary

scene at just that time, cited Dekker (along with
such contemporary dramatists as William Shakespeare, Michael Drayton, George Chapman, and
Ben Jonson) as one of "our best for Tragedy" in
his *Palladis Tamia* (1598; the book was entered
for publication in the Stationers' Register on 7 September 1598).

During the four-and-a-half-year period
from January 1598 to June 1602, Henslowe's records show Dekker to have been associated in one
way or another with some forty plays for the Admiral's Men. Between July and December 1602
he was engaged on five more for Worcester's
Men. His services were variously employed, as
the dated entries in Henslowe's diary indicate. Occasionally, he is found writing a play unaided, as
in the case of *Phaeton* (January 1598), or *The Triangle* (or *Triplicity*) *of Cuckholds* (March 1598), or *The
Shoemakers' Holiday* (July 1599), or *A Medicine for
a Curst Wife* (July to September 1602). Sometimes he was employed to alter an old play by another dramatist or dramatists, as he did to *Tasso's
Melancholy* in January and again in November
and December 1602, or to *Sir John Oldcastle* (a
1600 play by Michael Drayton, Richard Hathway,
Anthony Munday, and Robert Wilson) in August
and September 1602. Or he might be hired to supply a prologue and an epilogue for someone
else's play, as he did for *Pontius Pilate* (January
1602). Sometimes he is found revising an old
play, but revising it so thoroughly as to make it virtually his own, as with *Old Fortunatus* (Novembo-
ber 1599). More often he is found working in collaboration with one or more other dramatists.

One of his more notable collaborators during this period was the poet Michael Drayton.
The two of them were coauthors of a three-part
play titled *The Civil Wars of France* (September to
December 1598), and of *Conan, Prince of Cornwall*
(October 1598). Dekker and Henry Chettle were
a frequent team (for example, *Troilus and Cressida*, April 1599; *Agamemnon*, also apparently
known as *Orestes' Furies*, May 1599; *The Stepmother's Tragedy*, August-October 1599; *Sebastian, King
of Portugal*, April-May 1601). Dekker collaborated
with Ben Jonson on *Page of Plymouth* in August-
September 1599; with Anthony Munday on *Jephthah* (May 1602). But in Henslowe's factory for
the assembling and production of plays, collaborative pairs could readily become trios. Thus
Dekker, Chettle, and Drayton wrote *The Famous
Wars of Henry I and the Prince of Wales*, also known
as *The Welshman's Prize* (March 1598). Dekker,
Drayton, and Robert Wilson put together *The*

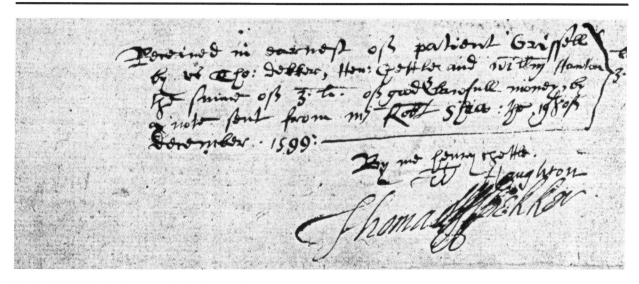

Receipt in the hand of Henry Chettle for an advance on the play Patient Grissell, *signed by Chettle, William Haughton, and Thomas Dekker (from the diary of Philip Henslowe; MS VII, l. 31'; by permission of Dulwich College, London)*

Mad Man's Morris (July 1598), *Hannibal and Hermes,* part one (July 1598; part two, also known as *Worse Afeard than Hurt,* was the work of Dekker and Drayton only, August-September 1598), and *Pierce of Winchester* (July-August 1598). Dekker, Chettle, and William Haughton wrote *Patient Grissell* (October to December 1599). Dekker, Chettle, and John Day wrote *The Golden Ass, or Cupid and Psyche* (April-May 1600). Dekker, Day, and Haughton collaborated on *The Spanish Moor's Tragedy* (February 1600). Trios grew into quartets: Dekker, Chettle, Jonson, and another (perhaps John Marston) wrote *The Tragedy of Robert II, King of Scots* (September 1599); Dekker, Drayton, Chettle, and Wilson put together a two-part play titled *Earl Godwin and his Three Sons* between March and June 1598. In April of the same year, the same foursome was at work on *Pierce of Exton,* though this play may not have been finished. In May of that year they produced part one of *Black Bateman of the North* (Chettle and Wilson wrote part two a month later). Dekker, Chettle, Haughton, and Day wrote *The Seven Wise Masters* (March 1600); Dekker, Chettle, Thomas Heywood, and John Webster assembled *Christmas Comes but Once a Year* (November 1602). Quartets could bloom into quintets: Dekker, Chettle, Heywood, Webster, plus Wentworth Smith wrote part one of what may have been a projected two-part play dealing with Lady Jane Grey (titled *Lady Jane,* but also known, it seems, as *The Overthrow of Rebels,* October 1602). Dekker, Drayton, Munday, Wilson, and Richard Hathway wrote *Fair Constance of Rome,* part one (June

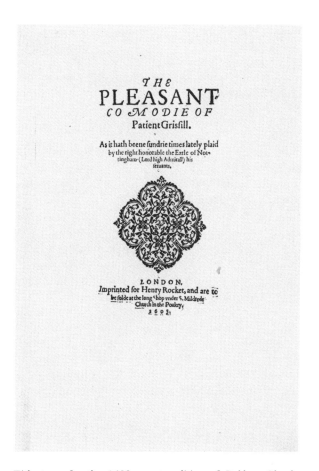

Title page for the 1603 quarto edition of Dekker, Chettle, and Haughton's dramatic version of the well-known story from Boccaccio's Decameron *that Chaucer's Clerk retells in* The Canterbury Tales *(Fredson Bowers, ed., The Dramatic Works of Thomas Dekker, volume 1, 1953)*

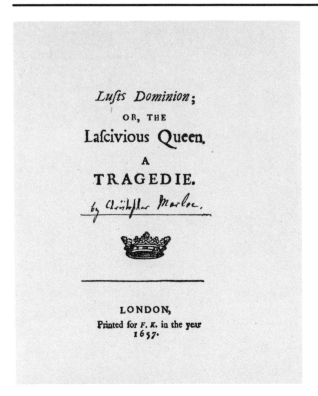

Title page for the unique copy of the first issue of the 1657 quarto edition of the play that is probably The Spanish Moor's Tragedy, *produced at the Rose theater in 1600 (Library of Congress). The play was first attributed to Christopher Marlowe, but that attribution is now generally rejected.*

1600; whether or not part two was ever completed is uncertain). Dekker, Drayton, Munday, Webster, and Thomas Middleton together wrote *Caesar's Fall,* also known as *Two Shapes* (May 1602).

All but five of these plays are lost. *The Shoemakers' Holiday or the Gentle Craft, Old Fortunatus,* and *Patient Grissell* survive under their own titles. *Lady Jane* is preserved in part at least in the play titled *Sir Thomas Wyatt. The Spanish Moor's Tragedy* is almost certainly the play now known as *Lust's Dominion.* It is possible that portions of one or another of Dekker's other plays for Henslowe are preserved in altered form in later work, either his own or another's. For example, two passages attributed to Dekker in Robert Allot's anthology of "the choicest flowers of our modern poets," *England's Parnassus* (1600), are reprinted in part in the 1636 text of Heywood's *Love's Mistress.* Two of Dekker's later plays, *The Noble Spanish Soldier* and *The Wonder of a Kingdom,* seem to derive in some way from earlier collaborations with Day. Certain anonymous plays that survive either in printed editions or in manuscript (such as *The Telltale, Look About You, The Weakest Goeth to the Wall, The London Prodigal, Captain Thomas Stukeley,*

The Merry Devil of Edmonton) have been claimed to be either wholly or partially Dekker's, but such claims, based as they are on stylistic evidence, are difficult to establish with any certainty.

Insofar as the titles of Dekker's lost plays yield any clues to their subjects, one gets the impression that he (like most of Henslowe's playwrights) could work in any dramatic genre. He wrote plays—or helped to write plays—on subjects drawn from English history (*The Famous Wars of Henry I, Earl Godwin, Lady Jane*), from recent European political events (*The Civil Wars of France* and *Sebastian, King of Portugal*), from classical legend (*Phaeton, Troilus and Cressida, Agamemnon,* and *The Golden Ass, or Cupid and Psyche*), from Biblical history (*Jephthah*), and he could produce tragedy of various kinds (*The Stepmother's Tragedy, The Tragedy of Robert II, King of Scots,* to say nothing of *Agamemnon*) as well as comedy (*The Shoemakers' Holiday* and *Old Fortunatus* among his extant plays bear witness to this fact, and so presumably would such lost plays as *The Triplicity of Cuckholds* and *A Medicine for a Curst Wife*). This sort of eclecticism is characteristic of the whole of his career as a dramatist.

What may be the earliest surviving example of Dekker's work is perhaps his contribution to a play not mentioned by Henslowe titled *Sir Thomas More,* a work commissioned, it would seem, by the joint companies of Lord Strange and the Lord Admiral during the period when they were acting together (circa 1590-1594). The play seems to have run into difficulties both with the company, which found it dramatically unsatisfactory, and with the Master of the Revels, who found it politically objectionable and declined to license it for production. The company attempted to salvage the play (the original version of which seems to have been the work of Munday) by hiring at least four different dramatists to revise or rewrite portions of it. The additions made to the play by way of revision have sometimes been dated as late as 1601, but a date circa 1593-1594 best fits the evidence. The manuscript of the play, together with the additions designed for it, is preserved in the British Library, London, and is one of the most important theatrical documents to survive from the Elizabethan period, not only for the notes by the censor that it contains concerning objectionable matter but for the handwriting of the various authors contained in the additions. One of the hands is almost certainly Shakespeare's, another may be Heywood's, a third is certainly Chettle's, and a fourth is certainly Dekker's (he seems to have revised one scene and added some thirty lines in his own hand).

The earliest surviving play of Dekker's sole authorship is *The Shoemakers' Holiday*. It is his most famous play, and it is one of his best. The setting is London, a place that Dekker found every bit as appropriate for the scene of a comedy as Shakespeare found the Forest of Arden in the exactly contemporary *As You Like It*. Here is a principal clue to the romantic quality of Dekker's literary imagination. Born and bred in London, he is as well acquainted with the city's capacity to breed vice and disease as he is with the daily toil required to make a living there; yet the city remained for him a place of wonders where honest industry combined with a shrewd business sense can raise a man from humble tradesman to of-

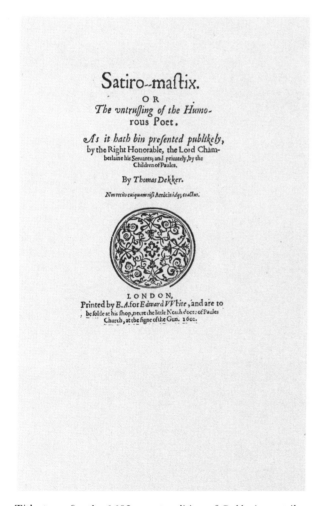

Title page for the 1602 quarto edition of Dekker's contribution to the "war of the theaters," written in response to Ben Jonson's Every Man out of His Humour, Cynthia's Revels, *and* Poetaster *(Fredson Bowers, ed.,* The Dramatic Works of Thomas Dekker, *volume 1, 1953)*

fices of civic dignity, where the turbulence and chicanery of city life can issue in the festivity of a communal feast, and where a sense of social harmony and order are seen to be the direct result of those forces of good government with which England's capital city, and England itself, are blessed. At the end of *The Shoemakers' Holiday*, the King of England himself comes to the feast that Simon Eyre makes for his apprentices after he has risen from shoemaker to Lord Mayor of London. Like any Shakespearean comedy, *The Shoemakers' Holiday* has two pairs of lovers, and part of the play's comic design is to eliminate the obstacles to their love. One pair, Rafe and Jane, are distinctly proletarian. He is one of Simon Eyre's journeymen, and she is his humble wife. He is drafted for service in the wars in France, and word comes back that he is dead; but he returns, a cripple, just in time to save Jane from being forced into marriage with another. Differences of social class separate the other pair, Lacy and Rose, for a time. He is of the nobility, nephew to the Earl of Lincoln; she is but a citizen's daughter though her father is a wealthy citizen, being in fact the Lord Mayor of London who precedes Simon Eyre in that office. Their families oppose their match, and Lacy plays truant from his colonelcy in the English armies in France and remains in London, disguised as a Dutch shoemaker in the employment of Simon Eyre, in order to pursue his love. The King pardons him in the final scene, affirms the union of the pair, and reconciles their elders to their match. But it is the madcap, merry-hearted but worldly wise Simon Eyre, with his lusty crew of singing and dancing apprentices swirling around him like so many attendant spirits of mischief, who is the center of the play, generating the air of festival and mirth and tolerant good cheer that is the life of the play. *The Shoemakers' Holiday* had the distinction of being acted at court before Queen Elizabeth I on New Year's Night 1600. Something of its contemporary popularity is suggested by the six printed editions of the play's text that were published between 1600 and 1657. The play continues to be staged from time to time, the most notable twentieth-century productions being the one performed at the Old Vic theater in London in 1926 and the one presented by Orson Welles and John Houseman at the Mercury theater in New York in 1938.

Old Fortunatus presents a similar blend of moral earnestness and quirky humor, but it is a sterner play than *The Shoemakers' Holiday*. The spirit of revelry may rule in it for a season, but by the end a series of punishments have been meted out against those who have abused life's gifts and have willfully strayed from the path of virtue. The play has its source in the German folk tale of Fortunatus, to whom the goddess of Fortune gives a purse that will never be empty of money. To this treasure Fortunatus adds another, a wonderful hat which will convey the wearer to any point in the world where he wishes to be (Fortunatus has stolen it from the Soldan of Babylon). When midway through the play, Fortunatus dies he leaves the purse and the hat to his two sons, and the last half of the play traces the manner in which the gifts reduce them to wretchedness and death. Like *The Shoemakers' Holiday, Old Fortunatus* was acted at court in the presence of the Queen during the Christmas season 1599-1600. Henslowe's records indicate that Dekker was paid to make alterations in the play for the court performance, and these are preserved in the printed edition that appeared in 1600. They include a prologue and an epilogue, each consisting of a dialogue in praise of the Queen and her court; and a specially designed

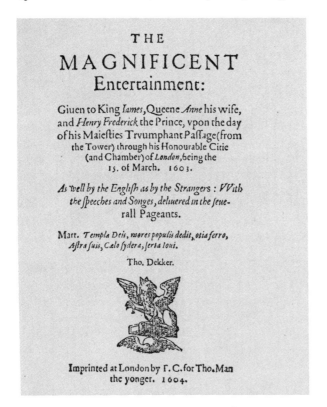

Title page for the first 1604 quarto edition of Dekker's contribution to the pageants and poetic speeches that the City of London had commissioned Dekker and his rival Ben Jonson to write for the celebration of the coronation of James I (Maggs Bros., catalogue 569, 1932)

ending to the play, wherein the Queen is complimented when the debate among Fortune, Vice, and Virtue as to which is most powerful is referred directly to her for a decision. In her presence, Vice flees, and Fortune admits herself overcome by the Queen's superior power, leaving Virtue, who represents what the Queen herself embodies, the victor.

Henslowe's records indicate that most of the work on *Patient Grissell* was done by all three collaborators (Dekker, Chettle, and Haughton) during the last weeks of December 1599. On 26 January 1600 Henslowe recorded payment of twenty shillings "to buy a grey gown for Grissell," so presumably the play was on the stage shortly thereafter. The story of patient Griselda was already famous in European literature. Boccaccio had told it in the closing tale of the *Decameron*, and Chaucer's Clerk had related it in English in *The Canterbury Tales*. The figure of Griselda–raised from the condition of her humble birth to high estate through marriage to a marquess who, though he loves her, persists in subjecting her to repeated trials in order to test her constancy–had become for Renaissance writers something of an exemplum for Christian humility and patience and for the rewards that attend on the successful pursuit of these virtues. Griselda never demurs at the trials to which she is put, and her devotion to her husband remains steadfast despite her distress at his repeated testings. By the time Dekker and his collaborators wrote their play, her story was well known in ballad and song and drama of a moralizing bent. Dekker's share in the play seems to have been chiefly confined to the treatment of Grissell's family: her simple, loving father, who stands staunchly by her through all her adversities; her brother, who strongly resents the marquess' treatment of her; and their devoted clown of a serving man.

The two other plays that survive from this period of Dekker's work for Henslowe are *Lady Jane* (in the play now known as *Sir Thomas Wyatt*) and *The Spanish Moor's Tragedy* (in the play now known as *Lust's Dominion*). *Sir Thomas Wyatt* treats of events from English history of half a century before: the plot to put Lady Jane Grey on the English throne upon the death of King Edward VI in 1553, together with the failure of this plan and the accession of Mary Tudor to the crown, and the subsequent rebellion of Sir Thomas Wyatt in protest against the Queen's alliance (specifically through her marriage to Philip of Spain) with foreign Roman Catholic powers. The text in

THE
Honeſt Whore,

With,

The Humours of the Patient Man,
and the Longing Wife.

Tho: Dekker.

LONDON
Printed by V. S. for Iohn Hodgets, and are to
be folde at his ſhop in Paules
church-yard 1604.

THE
SECOND
PART OF THE
HONEST VVHORE,

VVITH THE HVMORS
of the Patient Man, the Impatient
Wife: the Honeſt Whore, perſwaded by
ſtrong Arguments to turne Curtizan
againe: her braue refuting thoſe
Arguments.

And laſtly, the Comicall Paſſages of an Italian
Bridewell, where the Sцæne ends.

Written by THOMAS DEKKER.

LONDON,
Printed by *Elizabeth All-de*, for *Nathaniel Butter*.
An. Dom. 1630.

Title pages for the first 1604 quarto edition of part one and the only quarto edition of part two (1630) of Dekker's play about the reformation of a prostitute and her efforts to maintain her virtue (Fredson Bowers, ed., The Dramatic Works of Thomas Dekker, *volume 2, 1955). Both parts were written in 1604-1605, the first with the assistance of Thomas Middleton.*

which the play is preserved has been severely cut and may represent an abridgement of an original two-part play; further, the surviving text seems to have been put together from memory by a group of actors, and much of it is badly garbled. It is impossible to determine with any real precision Dekker's share in the play as it stands.

Lust's Dominion seems to be a revision of an older play. It is a revenge tragedy of the sort that came into vogue in the late 1580s with such plays as Thomas Kyd's *Spanish Tragedy*, Christopher Marlowe's *Jew of Malta*, and Shakespeare's *Titus Andronicus*. Eleazer the Moor of *Lust's Dominion* (presumably the titular figure of the play's original title, *The Spanish Moor's Tragedy*) is closely modeled on Aaron the Moor in Shakespeare's *Titus Andronicus*, and the Queen Mother of Spain, whose lust for him wrecks the kingdom, is a copy of Tamora, Queen of the Goths, whose erotic involvement with Aaron is the source of much of the violence that descends on Rome in Shakespeare's early tragedy. Henslowe's records suggest that the play was being worked on in the course of the fall and winter of 1599-1600, and that in addition to Dekker, Day, and Haughton, a fourth dramatist, Marston, may have had a hand

in it. There is some internal evidence from vocabulary and idiom for Marston's presence in the play. The point is of some importance for it provides our only basis for associating Dekker and Marston, and it is just at this time that the two playwrights come under attack from Ben Jonson, who parades them through three of his plays as a singularly ill-matched pair of would-be poet-dramatists.

Jonson's attack began with his *Every Man out of His Humour* (in existence by April 1600), continued in *Cynthia's Revels* (in existence by May 1601), and reached a virulent peak in *Poetaster* (in existence by December 1601). Marston seems to have been Jonson's original target: the language of his recent satiric poems (*Certain Satires* and *The Scourge of Villainy*, both published in 1598) had brought him a certain notoriety; Jonson parodies it in Clove's speeches in act three of *Every Man out of His Humour*. Marston had recently begun to write for the theater, urged in that direction perhaps by the ban on satire in June 1599, when his own books had been prominent among others of a scandalous or politically subversive nature that had been called in by the censor and burned. Two more disparate figures than Dekker

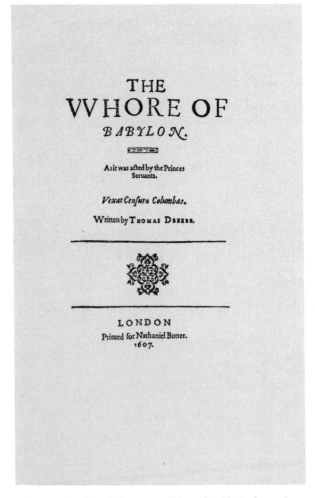

Title page for a 1604 quarto edition of the anti-Roman Catholic tract that Dekker wrote in response to the discovery of the Gunpowder Plot in November 1605 ("PP" alludes to the Pope) (Anderson Galleries, sale number 2077, 20-21 May 1926)

and Marston are hard to imagine: Dekker with his humble London background, toiling away for a living in Henslowe's factory; Marston, son of an old Shropshire family, educated at Oxford and now living in London, leading the privileged life of a member of the Middle Temple, where he was supposedly preparing himself for a legal career. The depiction of the pair in *Every Man out of His Humour* as the extravagantly verbal Clove, and Orange, his all-but silent companion who only speaks clichés, was but a preliminary sketch for what would follow. In *Cynthia's Revels*, Hedon (Marston) is presented as a frivolous fop, given over entirely to the pursuit of voluptuous pleasures. Anaides (Dekker), his constant companion, is a coarser type whose impudence and ignorance are stressed; he is much given to ridiculing what he does not understand. Both are notably envious of the honorable Crites, whom contemporary audiences regarded as Jonson's flattering portrait of himself. Hedon and Anaides try to detract from Crites' reputation for virtue, but to no avail, and they are increasingly frustrated by the high-minded manner in which he rises above their mean-spirited efforts to slander him. *Poetas-*

ter contains the most open attack on the pair. Again Marston is represented as a reveler who plays at being a poet when he is not gossiping or flirting; he is now called Crispinus. In need of money, he takes to writing for the players, and it is through them that he meets Demetrius (Dekker), a down-at-the-heels hack, described at one point as "a dresser of plays about the town," where "dresser" is an apt description of the alterations often performed by Dekker and his co-workers on old plays being refurbished as new ones to be acted in Henslowe's theaters. The envy and hatred directed by Hedon and Anaides against Crites in *Cynthia's Revels* is now directed by Crispinus and Demetrius against Horace (another piece of Jonsonian self-portraiture) in *Poetaster*. In the end both are accused of slander and found guilty: in a famous scene, pills are adminis-

Title page for the 1607 quarto edition of Dekker's dramatic response to the discovery of the Gunpowder Plot, an allegory in which Titania (Elizabeth I) triumphs over the Empress of Babylon (the Roman Catholic church) (Fredson Bowers, ed., The Dramatic Works of Thomas Dekker, volume 2, 1955)

tered to Crispinus, who shortly vomits up the more outrageous gobbets of his vocabulary; Demetrius is forgiven but made to wear a fool's coat and cap; both are made to take an oath never again to slander Horace.

Much is made in *Poetaster* of a play attacking Horace that a company of players has hired Demetrius to write; Crispinus is hired to help him with it. Such a play–Dekker's *Satiromastix*–in fact was written. Marston may (and probably did) help with the strategy of counterattack, but there is no evidence in the extant text of the play that he participated in the actual writing. He was busy throughout this period with his own responses to Jonson, in *Jack Drum's Entertainment* and *What You Will*. Dekker, in *Satiromastix*, replied to Jonson's satiric attacks by simply appropriating the two characters–Crispinus and Demetrius–who had been the vehicles of Jonson's satire, together with Jonson's admiring representation of himself in the figure of the high-minded Horace. Crispinus, Demetrius, and Horace all appear in *Satiromastix*, but their characters are completely changed. Here Crispinus and Demetrius are sober, responsible young men who look on in dismay as Horace (who is represented as a toady to the rich and powerful) demeans the genuine poetic talent which they acknowledge him to possess as he scrambles after wealthy patrons and vilifies anyone whom he suspects of standing in his way. *Satiromastix* makes the pretense that the bill of complaints drawn up against Jonson/Horace is lodged more in sorrow than in anger; but the complaints are pressed firmly, and in detail. His associates make it clear to the Horace of *Satiromastix* that they are tired of indulging him in his hypocrisy, tired of the high moral line he takes with all the world but never lives up to himself, tired of his efforts to pass himself off as a fearless champion of virtue when in fact he is as vicious as the next man and a sniveling coward into the bargain. As a piece of satiric retaliation, *Satiromastix* is an extremely clever play, and its effect seems to have been devastating: at any rate, Jonson made no attempt to answer it, and Dekker may be said to have had the last word in the famous war of the theaters.

This "stage quarrel" has been much discussed in histories of the Elizabethan theater. There was of course more to it than the quarrel between Jonson on the one hand, and Marston and Dekker on the other. On the basic level of box-office economics, it was a competition for London theater audiences. Essentially, the competition was between companies of adult actors, performing in large, open-air public theaters such as the Globe (where Shakespeare's plays were being acted at this time) or those owned by Henslowe, and companies of child actors performing in smaller, enclosed, private theaters where the price of admission was higher and the general tone of the audience more fashionable than at the public theaters. Companies of child actors (the children were choir boys) had performed in London before, but not for nearly a decade, when in 1599 the Children of Paul's began to perform plays in their song school near St. Paul's Cathedral; the following year, the Children of the Chapel Royal began to perform in Blackfriars. A novelty on the London theatrical scene, the children's companies enjoyed a vogue in the years around the turn of the century. Shakespeare, in *Hamlet* (II.ii.), alludes to the stiff competition the companies of boy actors were giving the adult companies in, presumably, the season of 1600-1601. The stage history of *Satiromastix* (performed it would seem in the fall of 1601) makes it clear, however, that the competition was not simply between child and adult acting troops performing respectively in private and public theaters. There also seems to have been rivalry between the two children's companies. Jonson's *Cynthia's Revels* and *Poetaster* were acted by the Chapel Children at Blackfriars. *Satiromastix* was performed both by child actors in a private theater (Paul's) and by adult actors (the Chamberlain's Men) in a public theater (the Globe). *Satiromastix*, with the prospect it held forth to audiences for satirizing Jonson the well-known satirist, must have seemed a sufficiently promising box-office success for Paul's Boys and the Chamberlain's Men, erstwhile rivals, to join forces in a common enterprise.

From the summer of 1600 to the end of 1601, Dekker's name appears less and less frequently in Henslowe's records, and the title page of *Satiromastix*, with its advertisement that the play had been acted by both Paul's and the Chamberlain's companies, suggests why: Dekker had begun to write for other companies besides Henslowe's. His only recorded play for Henslowe during the whole of 1601 is a collaboration with Chettle (*Sebastian, King of Portugal*) in May and June. But sometime during the late fall or winter of 1601-1602, presumably in the aftermath of his *Satiromastix* assignment, he wrote another play for Paul's, a comedy titled *Blurt, Master Constable or The Spaniard's Night-walk* (it was in existence by 7

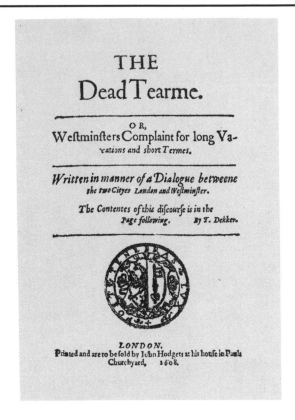

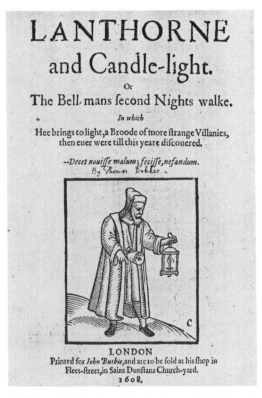

Title pages for four of the prose pamphlets Dekker wrote between 1605 and 1611 (top left: Anderson Galleries, sale number 2077, 20-21 May 1926; top right: Henry E. Huntington Library and Art Gallery; bottom left and right: Bodleian Library)

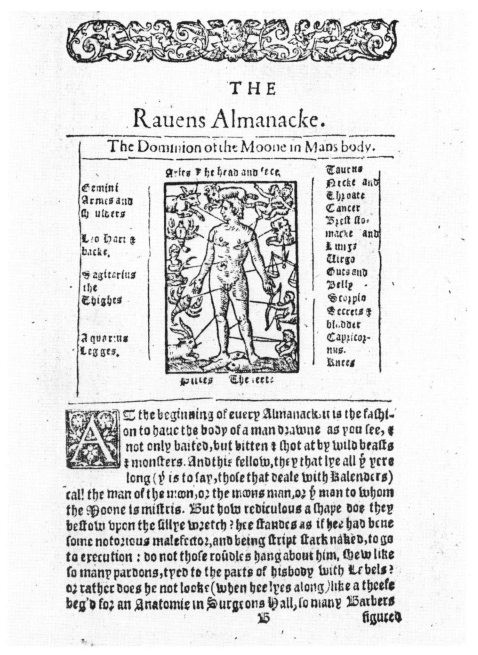

First page of text from Dekker's almanac "foretelling of a plague, famine, and civill warre" for 1609 (Bodleian Library)

June 1602 when it was licensed for printing). No author is named on the title page of the only edition of the play, and it was long attributed to Thomas Middleton. Only in recent years have scholars put forth an argument in support of Dekker's authorship of *Blurt, Master Constable*, and it is now generally acknowledged to be his (it may be a collaboration with Middleton, but if so, Middleton's share is a relatively small one). The play is unlike any of Dekker's extant work to this

time, but that is not surprising in view of the fact that it was written for a private theater and not a public one. It is a fashionable comedy, populated with witty ladies and the elegant gentlemen who are their lovers and the pert maids and cheeky pages who serve the ladies and the gentlemen. There is also a collection of low-comedy figures including the bumbling constable who gives the play its title and who is modeled on Shakespeare's Dogberry, and a fantastical Spaniard (referred to in the play's subtitle) whose efforts to make his way through the thickets of amorous intrigue which make up the play's plot are ridiculed.

Dekker resumed something like his former work load for Henslowe's companies in 1602. Henslowe records payments to him for one sort of assignment or another throughout that year: for providing a prologue and epilogue for *Pontius Pilate* in January, for altering *Tasso's Melancholy* in January (and for "mending" it in November and December), for collaborating with Munday on *Jephthah* in early May, for collaborating with Drayton, Middleton, Webster, and Munday on *Caesar's Fall or Two Shapes* later in the same month, for writing his own *A Medicine for a Curst Wife* from mid July to the beginning of September, for providing new additions to *Sir John Oldcastle* in August and September, for work on *Lady Jane* in October, for collaborating on *Christmas Comes but Once a Year* with Heywood, Webster, and Chettle in November.

Performances in all London theaters abruptly ceased on 19 March 1603, when Queen Elizabeth I became gravely ill; she died on 24 March. The theaters had hardly reopened following the period of official mourning before they were closed again on account of the plague, which had been raging since early April. They remained closed throughout the rest of the year and until the spring of 1604. Dekker, with his means of livelihood from the stage temporarily shut off, turned to writing nondramatic pamphlets. The first of these, *The Wonderful Year*, appeared near the end of 1603. It presents a vivid account of the changing climates of feeling during the events of the past momentous year: the anxiety of the opening months as the Queen's death approached; the relief felt throughout the land when James VI of Scotland succeeded peacefully to the English throne as James I; the sense of relief interrupted when the plague descended on the capital city like some heaven-sent reminder of the loss the land had suffered in the death of the great Queen. The latter half of *The Wonderful Year* presents (as the title page advertises) "the picture of London lying sick of the plague"; it is a grimly moving account of the appalling death tolls and the gallantry that the citizens of London displayed in enduring their ordeal. Early in 1604 Dekker published two further pamphlets dealing with London life during the plague: *News from Gravesend* and *The Meeting of Gallants at an Ordinary* (perhaps with Middleton).

The plague had caused the postponement of the coronation of King James, originally scheduled for the summer of 1603. It eventually took place on 15 March 1604, and the dramatists commissioned by the City of London to devise the pageants and compose the poetic speeches that would comprise the occasion were, ironically enough, Dekker and Ben Jonson. They had evidently not made their peace in the years since the stage quarrel, for Jonson published his share of the so-called *Magnificent Entertainment* separately, and when Dekker published the text of his own share together with a description of the whole affair, he merely summarized Jonson's contribution without naming him. He was careful, however, to acknowledge the share of Middleton, who contributed one speech to Dekker's part. Dekker's association with Middleton, which may have begun with *Blurt, Master Constable* in 1601, is a matter of record by the spring of 1604. At the same time Middleton was assisting Dekker with *The Magnificent Entertainment* he was also collaborating with him on a play that is now known as part one of the two-part play titled *The Honest Whore*. Henslowe's records for what had been the Admiral's Men but now, since the accession of

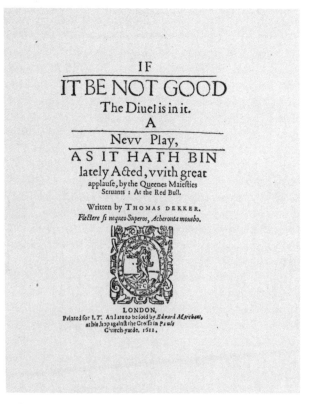

Title page for the 1612 quarto edition of the play that marked the end of Dekker's association with the Prince's Men (Fredson Bowers, ed., The Dramatic Works of Thomas Dekker, *volume 3, 1958)*

James I, was known as Prince Henry's Men, end with his entry for 14 March 1604; just before this final entry, he records payments to Dekker and Middleton for a play called "The Patient Man and the Honest Whore." It is one of Dekker's best (Middleton's share in it is comparatively small): a romantic, somewhat sentimental, but fiercely earnest account of the prostitute Bellafront's conversion to the ways of virtue, and her determined effort to persist in her reform despite all sensual and economic pressures to revert to her former life. The play's sequel, *The Honest Whore*, part two, is entirely the work of Dekker. It continues Bellafront's uphill battle to preserve her integrity, and it is chiefly notable for two of Dekker's finest pieces of characterization: that of Orlando Friscobaldo, Bellafront's father, who renounced her when she became a fallen woman and is skeptical when he hears of her conversion but is gradually brought to believe in the sincerity of her repentance and is reconciled with her; and that of Matheo, the lively but entirely unprincipled rogue who first led Bellafront astray and who, in her converted state, she feels constrained to marry.

During 1604-1605 Dekker was writing both for the Prince's Men (which produced the two parts of *The Honest Whore*) and for the Children of Paul's. For the latter company, near the end of 1604, he and John Webster (with whom he had worked on *Lady Jane/Sir Thomas Wyatt*) wrote *Westward Ho*, a satiric comedy set in contemporary London and dealing with the manner in which a group of citizens' wives outwit the amorous designs that a group of gallants have on them. It seems to have been popular enough to cause the rival comedy of boy actors, the Children of Her Majesty's Revels, performing at the Blackfriars, to produce a similar kind of comedy with a similar title, *Eastward Ho* (a three-part collaboration by Jonson, Chapman, and Marston, who was now reconciled with Jonson). The notoriety of this play (its unflattering remarks about the Scots brought down on the company the wrath of King James) must have encouraged Dekker and Webster to write another comedy of London life, this time titled *Northward Ho*, a lively account of how age outwits youth when a young gallant tries to seduce the virtuous wife of a London citizen. Dekker's remaining play for this period is *The Whore of Babylon*, acted by the Prince's Men and written either in late 1605 or early 1606. The play is a product of the anti-Roman Catholic passions that gripped England in the weeks follow-

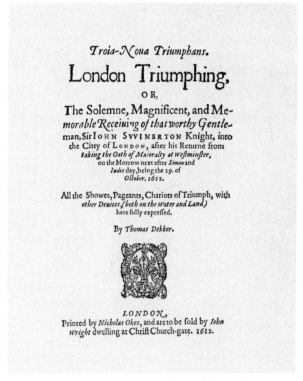

Title page for the 1612 quarto edition of Dekker's first Lord Mayor's pageant (Fredson Bowers, ed., The Dramatic Works of Thomas Dekker, *volume 3, 1958)*

ing the discovery of the Gunpowder Plot in November 1605. It bears a number of similarities with Dekker's anti-Roman tract, *The Double PP*, published in December 1605, in which the double *p* of the title alludes to the Pope. *The Whore of Babylon* is a religious and historical allegory. Its heroine is Titania (Queen Elizabeth I), and it dramatizes the many plots engineered by her enemy, the Empress of Babylon (the Roman church) to assassinate her and subvert her country and its religion.

The Whore of Babylon seems to have been Dekker's last play for some five years. Performances by the Paul's Boys gradually ceased after the summer of 1606 (the company came to an end in 1608), and this may have had something to do with Dekker's decision to give over (temporarily at least) writing for the stage. But it is also possible that he was discovering that writing his nondramatic pamphlets was more profitable than writing plays. In any case, it would seem (unless he wrote some plays that have vanished without a trace) that his pamphlets occupied him exclusively during the next five years. He turned out at least ten of them during this period: *News from Hell* (1606; revised in the following year as *A Knight's Conjuring*), *The Seven Deadly Sins of Lon-*

don (1606), *Jests to Make You Merry* (1607, with George Wilkins), *The Dead Term* (1608), *The Bellman of London* (1608), *Lanthorn and Candlelight* (1608), *Four Birds of Noah's Ark* (1609), *The Gull's Hornbook* (1609), *The Raven's Almanac* (1609), and *Work for Armorers* (1609). *Four Birds of Noah's Ark* is a collection of prayers and meditations. The rest are, in effect, journalistic essays and narratives on various aspects of the contemporary London scene, written in a vein that is by turns pleasantly humorous, satiric, didactic, and grotesquely jocular. The pamphlets are invaluable for the detailed evidence they provide concerning Jacobean London and its people. There are depictions of the city and its neighbor, Westminster, bustling with activity when the law courts are in session and all but deserted during the long summer vacation (*The Dead Term*); there are lively accounts of the latest fashions and fads and villanies (*News from Hell, The Raven's Almanac*); exposés of the confidence games–the so-called cony-catching schemes–practiced by rogues (*The Bellman of London, Lanthorn and Candlelight*); a shrewd appraisal of the social gulf that separates poverty and wealth (*Work for Armorers*); an account of an average day in the life of a would-be gentleman of fashion (*The Gull's Hornbook*). *The Bellman of London* and its sequel, *Lanthorn and Candlelight*, were immensely successful. *The Bellman of London* went through four separate editions in the year of its publication and appeared in subsequent editions in 1616 and 1640. *Lanthorn and Candlelight*, after its original edition in 1608, immediately went into a revised second edition in 1609; thereafter, Dekker periodically revised and expanded it in new editions with differing titles throughout the rest of his life: in 1612 (when it appeared as *O per se o, or a new crier of Lanthorn and Candlelight*); in 1616 (as *Villanies Discovered by Lanthorn and Candlelight*; reprinted with slight additions in 1620); in 1632 (as *English Villanies;* reprinted in 1638 and 1648). Dekker's indebtedness in *The Bellman of London* and *Lanthorn and Candlelight* to Robert Greene's cony-catching pamphlets of the early 1590s is considerable, but he manages to update Greene's material to a degree that stamps both works with his own distinctive style. The Elizabethan predecessor to whom that style owes most is Thomas Nashe. Dekker is not so aggressively witty as Nashe, and his satire is not so devastating; there is a gentleness, sometimes a sentimentality, in Dekker's nondramatic pamphlets that is quite foreign to the work of Nashe; but Nashe's verbal fecundity, the torrents of epithets and extravagantly developed metaphors that proceed from his pen by a sort of free association, clearly provided the rhetorical model that Dekker sought to emulate.

Dekker returned to writing for the stage in the spring of 1611 with *The Roaring Girl*, a collaboration with Middleton based on a contemporary figure, Mary Frith, known as Moll Cutpurse, who had achieved a certain notoriety for her exploits on the fringes of the London underworld. *The Roaring Girl* was acted by the Prince's Men, but a prefatory note to the published text of Dekker's next play, *If This Be Not a Good Play, the Devil Is in It*, written in the summer of 1611, indicates that a breach had occurred between the author and the company with which he had been associated for well over a decade. The Prince's Men seem to have rejected *If This Be Not a Good Play*, and it is in fact one of Dekker's weakest plays: an uneasy combination of raucous humor and moral didacticism concerning three devils sent to earth by Satan to corrupt mankind, and finding themselves outdone by mankind's superior deviltry. The play was performed by the Queen's Men at the Red Bull theater.

In October 1612 Dekker was commissioned to prepare the pageant celebrating the inauguration of London's new Lord Mayor (an annual event, occurring each October twenty-ninth). His pageant, *Troia-Nova Triumphans*, has for its motif the myth of London's founding by descendants of the ancient Trojans, who called their capital city Troynovant or New Troy: a myth that Dekker frequently alludes to in his nondramatic works. Not long after this, however, in Michaelmas Term 1612, Dekker's fortunes took a ruinous turn when he was arrested for debt and committed to the King's Bench Prison. There he remained for nearly seven years. Though his career as a playwright was brought to a halt, he did manage to do a certain amount of literary work during these years. In 1616 he wrote a poetical pamphlet, *The Artillery Garden*, praising the London militia, in the dedication to which he alludes to his present imprisonment. In the same year, he brought out a new edition of *Lanthorn and Candlelight* to which he added six new chapters dealing, appropriately enough, with prison life. In one of these he states that he has been in prison for more than three years. There is reason to believe that he contributed six new character descriptions (of "A Prison, A Prisoner, A Creditor, A Sargeant, His Yeoman, and A Jailor") to the ninth impression of Sir Thomas Overbury's collec-

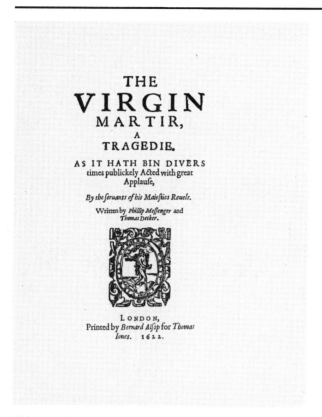

THE
VIRGIN
MARTIR,
A
TRAGEDIE.

AS IT HATH BIN DIVERS
times publickely Acted with great
Applause,

By the seruants of his Maiesties Reuels.

Written by *Philip Messenger* and
Thomas Dekker.

LONDON,
Printed by *Bernard Alsop* for *Thomas*
Iones. 1622.

Title page for the 1622 quarto edition of the play that Dekker
and Philip Massinger based on the life of Saint Dorothea
(Fredson Bowers, ed., The Dramatic Works of Thomas
Dekker, *volume 3, 1958)*

tion *Sir Thomas Overbury His Wife, with New Ele-*
gies, published in 1616. He may have contributed
as well to *Certain Characters and Essays of Prisons*
and Prisoners, compiled by Geoffray Mynshul, his
fellow prisoner in the King's Bench, and published in 1618. Dekker was apparently released
from prison sometime before 11 October 1619,
when another of his poetical pamphlets, *Dekker*
his Dream, was entered in the Stationers' Register
(it was published in 1620). In the preface to it he
refers to "the bed on which seven years [he] lay
dreaming," and to the "long sleep, which for almost seven years together, seized all [his] senses."

Dekker seems to have resumed his play-
writing activities by collaborating with Philip Massinger on a dramatization of the life of Saint
Dorothea in a play titled *The Virgin Martyr,* licensed for acting on 6 October 1620. The play is
a strange and often disconcerting mixture of
tender sentiment and raucous vulgarity. The mixture is in some degree inherent in the saint's life
on which the play is based; most of those among
whom Dorothea dwells in the still-pagan Roman
world that she inhabits would violate her if they
could. Most of the low-comedy scenes involving

Dorothea's two vicious servants (one described as
a drunkard and the other as a whoremaster) and
the evil spirit who savagely urges on her chief per-
secutor are Dekker's, but so too is the gently lyrical scene between Dorothea and the angelic spirit
who serves her: a passage that prompted Charles
Lamb's famous assertion that Dekker "had poetry
enough for anything." The play was acted by the
company at the Red Bull (where Dekker's last
play before his imprisonment, *If This Be Not a*
Good Play, had been performed) and was evidently successful. There were editions printed in
1622, 1631, 1651, and 1661. Though the Red
Bull company had broken up by the summer of
1623, *The Virgin Martyr* had evidently passed into
the repertory of another company; a new scene
was licensed for it in the summer of 1624, but
this was never printed. *The Virgin Martyr* is the
only play in the Dekker canon to have been revived on the Restoration stage.

What seems to have been Dekker's next
play, *The Witch of Edmonton,* is also a collaboration, this time with two others: the actor-
dramatist William Rowley and John Ford, whose
career as a dramatist may have begun with this
play and who would emerge in the course of the
next decade as the most significant figure in the
later Jacobean and Caroline theater. The central
plot of *The Witch of Edmonton* was based on a recent event: the trial and condemnation for witchcraft of one Elizabeth Sawyer in the spring of
1621, and her execution on 19 April of that year.
An account of her case was written by the Reverend Mr. Henry Goodcole, who had visited her in
Newgate during her imprisonment; his book, *The*
Wonderful Discovery of Elizabeth Sawyer, was entered in the Stationers' Register on 27 April and
provided the principal source for this one of the
play's two plots. The play was in existence by 29
December 1621, when it was acted at Court by
the Prince's Men. The figure of Mother Sawyer
in the play is the work of Dekker, and it is his greatest piece of dramatic portraiture. She is presented as a lonely and tormented old woman
whose neighbors have so long accused her of
being a witch that she begins to believe that in
fact she is one. The devil sends a familiar spirit
to her in the form of a black dog. It represents a
great rarity in her life, a creature that loves her
and will do her bidding; it indulges her crazed fantasies of vengeance on her enemies, and then having lured her to damnation, deserts her. The
play's other plot (chiefly the work of Ford) concerns Frank Thorney, a well-meaning but weak-

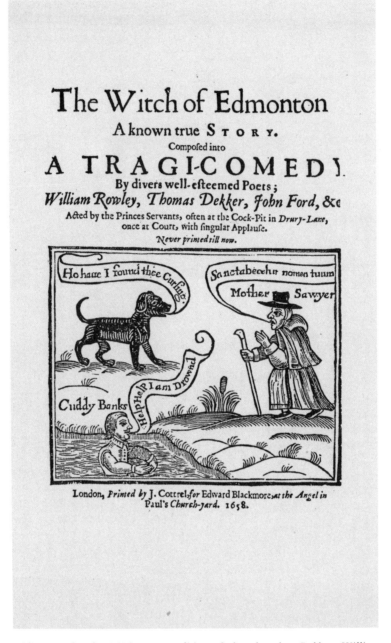

Title page for the 1658 quarto edition of the play that Dekker, William Rowley, and John Ford based on Henry Goodcole's 1621 account of Elizabeth Sawyer's trial and execution for witchcraft (Fredson Bowers, ed., The Dramatic Works of Thomas Dekker, *volume 3, 1958)*

willed young man who commits bigamy and, in an effort to extricate himself from this offense, murders his second wife. The demonic dog is put to extraordinarily effective use as it wanders from Mother Sawyer's scenes into the presence of Frank Thorney as his murderous intentions take shape. It makes another notable appearance in the scene where Thorney's guilt is discovered by the sister and father of his dead wife. The dog also strays across the path of a clownish yokel named Cuddy Banks, a part played on the stage by Rowley and written by him. The whiff of the diabolic that the dog's presence brings has the effect of turning scenes of conventional low-comic buffoonery into disquietingly bizarre and sinister episodes. *The Witch of Edmonton* is a remarkably unified play for a work of tripartite authorship, and much of the credit for its structural coherence must go to Dekker, for it is the scenes concerning Mother Sawyer and her dog, which he created, that provide the connective tissue linking all the play's principal strands of action, over which they cast that peculiarly combined glow of tenderness and grotesquerie which is a Dekker specialty. The play continues to be staged from time to time, at least in England. Sybil Thorndike acted the role of Mother Sawyer in a London production in 1921, and Edith Evans took the part in the Old Vic production of 1936 in a cast that also included Michael Redgrave and Alec Guinness. There was a production of the play at the Mermaid theater, London, in the fall of 1962, and in the fall of 1982 the Royal Shakespeare Company staged it with considerable success.

Dekker's first unaided play following his imprisonment seems to have been *Match Me in London*. The date of the play is uncertain. Sir Henry

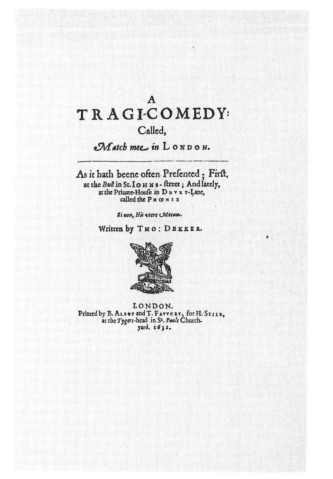

Title page for the 1631 quarto edition of Dekker's first play in the genre popularized by Beaumont and Fletcher (Fredson Bowers, ed., The Dramatic Works of Thomas Dekker, *volume 3, 1958)*

Herbert, Master of the Revels, whose office it was to license plays for performance, refers to it in August 1623 as an old play, but that could mean no more than that it had been previously licensed by one of his predecessors; Herbert had assumed his office only the month before. The text was not published until 1631, and the title page of that edition may tell us something when it prominently advertises the play as "A Tragicomedy." "Tragicomedy" is the most conspicuous word on the page; it appears at the top, and in far larger and bolder type than any other word. The vogue of romantic tragicomedy on the Jacobean stage may be said to have been launched in the years between 1608 or 1609 and 1611 (just prior to Dekker's imprisonment) with the great success achieved by such Beaumont and Fletcher tragicomedies as *Philaster* and *A King and No King*. During the years of Dekker's imprisonment the popularity of tragicomedy continued apace, and, when around 1619 or 1620 he resumed his career as a playwright, tragicomedy was the favorite dramatic form with London's theatergoers. *Match Me in London* is Dekker's attempt to produce a play in the new style. Its subject is the familiar tragicomic one: a lustful tyrant attempts to seduce a virtuous wife. Dekker seeks to develop his plot by means of the surprising disclosures and the sudden shiftings of a character's mood or motive which Beaumont and Fletcher handled with such easy virtuosity, but *Match Me in London* is an awkwardly contrived and derivative piece of work. It amply demonstrates how ill equipped Dekker was to master the new fashion in play making.

What survives from the work Dekker produced in his last decade is not distinguished. A number of his plays are lost, known to us only from licensing entries in Sir Henry Herbert's office book. These include *The Bellman of Paris*, a collaboration with John Day (licensed 30 July 1623) and two further collaborations with John Ford: *The Fairy Knight* (licensed 11 June 1624), and *The Bristow Merchant* (licensed 22 October 1624). In the summer of 1624 Dekker, Ford, and Rowley (the trio that had produced *The Witch of Edmonton*) joined forces again, together with Webster, to write a play that would combine two highly publicized recent events (a murder and a scandalous marriage). The play's title—*The Late Murder of the Son upon the Mother, or Keep the Widow Waking*—glanced at both news items, and it was performed at the Red Bull in September 1624, but the play is lost, and we know about it

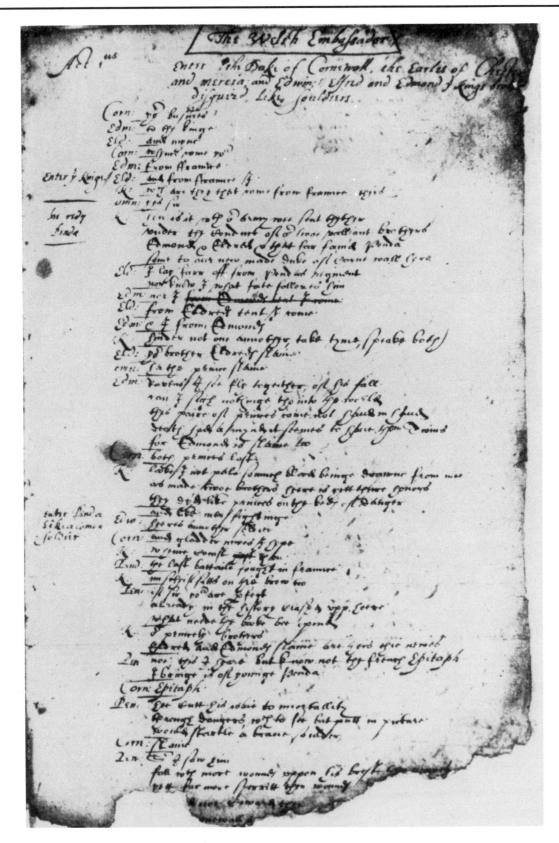

First page of the manuscript, written in the hand of a scribe, for The Welsh Ambassador *preserved in the Public Library of Cardiff, Wales (by permission of the Public Library of Cardiff)*

only from the lawsuits that followed in its wake. *The Sun's Darling* (licensed 3 March 1624) is the only certain Dekker-Ford collaboration that survives in addition to *The Witch of Edmonton*. It is a masque written for the public theater in emulation of the elaborate masques that by the 1620s had come to be such a notable feature of Stuart court entertainment. *The Sun's Darling* is a moral allegory of a prodigal's progress through the seasons of the year (and, by implication, through life), from spring to winter. It is full of songs and spectacle and might, in its original form, have been quite a pleasing show, but in the version in which it has come down to us (it was not printed until 1656) the ending has been altered so that the masque's original conclusion and thus its total design can no longer be discerned. Two plays connected with Dekker's last years—*The Wonder of a Kingdom* and *The Noble Spanish Soldier* (both entered together in the Stationers' Register on 16

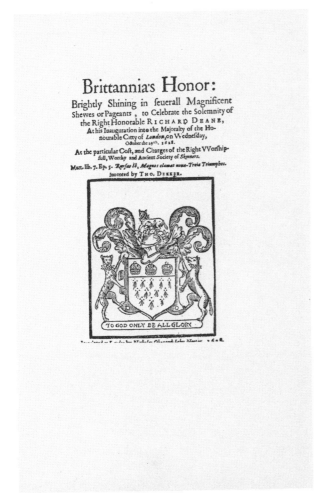

Title page for the unique copy of the 1628 quarto edition of Dekker's fourth Lord Mayor's pageant (British Library)

May 1631)—seem to be based in some degree on earlier collaborations with John Day. Passages from both plays appear in Day's *Parliament of Bees*. The central plot situation of *The Noble Spanish Soldier* (which seems in its extant version to date from circa 1622) was reworked by Dekker circa 1623 in *The Welsh Ambassador*. None of these three plays seems to have met with success. Two of them were published after Dekker's death (*The Noble Spanish Soldier* in 1634, *The Wonder of a Kingdom* in 1636). *The Welsh Ambassador* was never published until the twentieth century and is preserved in manuscript in the Public Library of Cardiff, Wales.

In 1627 Dekker was commissioned to provide the pageant for the Lord Mayor's inauguration. The show he provided is lost; we know that he wrote it from his statement in the dedication to his poetical pamphlet, *Wars, Wars, Wars* (published in 1628). He went on to provide Lord Mayor's shows for the next two years: *Britannia's Honor* in 1628, *London's Tempe* in 1629. Both are feeble performances, though it may be said in Dekker's defense that there is a general falling off in the quality of mayoral pageants in the 1620s. The form was becoming hackneyed. Dekker offered to prepare an inaugural pageant for Lord Mayor's Day in 1630, but no pageant—only a triumphal procession—was presented that year. The committee in charge of the occasion, however, paid him twenty shillings for his offer.

Just as in 1603 the death of Elizabeth I and the accession of James I had been accompanied by an outbreak of plague, so in 1625 the death of James and the accession of Charles I had been similarly attended. Dekker produced another plague pamphlet, *A Rod for Runaways*, for the occasion. When another epidemic of plague threatened in 1630, he put together two more: *The Black Rod and the White Rod*, and *London Look Back*. In 1631 he published *Penny Wise, Pound Foolish*, a piece of prose fiction retailing the amorous adventures of a Bristow (that is, Bristol) merchant. Scholars have wondered what, if any, relation the story may have had to Dekker and Ford's lost play of a Bristow merchant. In the same year, Dekker dedicated the published text of *Match Me in London* to Lodowick Carlell, the young courtier-dramatist and favorite of King Charles. He speaks poignantly of his advancing age: "I have been a priest in Apollo's temple many years, my voice is decaying with my age." In the following year, in the dedication to *English Villanies* (the 1632 edition of *Lanthorn and Candle-*

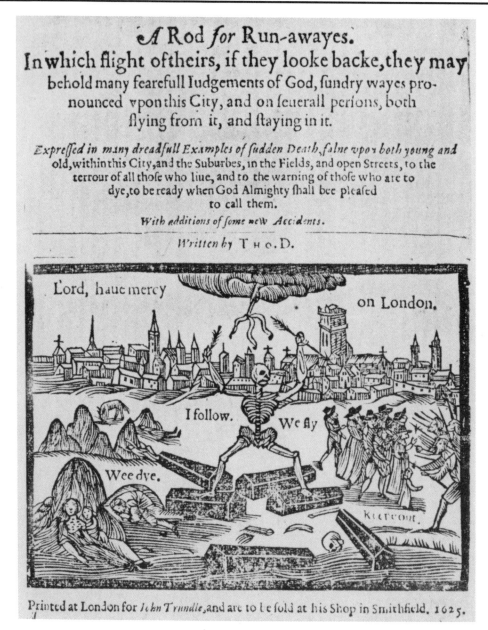

A Rod for Run-awayes.
In which flight of theirs, if they looke backe, they may behold many fearefull Iudgements of God, sundry wayes pronounced vpon this City, and on seuerall persons, both flying from it, and staying in it.

Expressed in many dreadfull Examples of sudden Death, falne vpon both young and old, within this City, and the Suburbes, in the Fields, and open Streets, to the terrour of all those who liue, and to the warning of those who are to dye, to be ready when God Almighty shall bee pleased to call them.

With additions of some new Accidents.

Written by T H O. D.

Lord, haue mercy ... on London.

I follow.   We fly

Wee dye.   ... kee out.

Printed at London for *Iohn Trundle*, and are to be sold at his Shop in Smithfield. 1625.

Title page for the 1625 revised quarto edition of the pamphlet Dekker wrote during the London plague that accompanied the death of James I and the accession of Charles I to the British throne (Bodleian Library, Oxford)

light) he speaks of his "three-score years."

It is in this year that Dekker is last heard of, and thus he was almost certainly the "Thomas Decker, householder," buried at St. James's, Clerkenwell, on 25 August 1632. The administration of his estate was renounced by his widow, Elisabeth, on 4 September 1632; this implies that Dekker died in debt. A few years before, in 1626 and 1628, he had been indicted for recusancy; fear of process for debt may explain why he had not been attending church. His widow Elisabeth was not his first wife. Years before, on 24 July 1616, while Dekker was in prison, "Mary wife of Thomas Deckers" had been buried in the same London parish (Clerkenwell) where sixteen years later Dekker died.

Dekker's work has elicited a varied range of critical response over the 350 years since he wrote. Lamb said he had poetry enough for anything. Swinburne admired his capacity to fuse humor with pathos, but he deplored the carelessness that mars so much of his work. The phrase "hack writer" has been hurled at him in one form or another since the days of Ben Jonson.

There is some truth in all these responses. Much of Dekker's work is hack writing. He is a prime example of a writer who made his living by his pen. This means that he was often working in haste and often writing about subjects that could not have interested him very much. This is especially true of some of the nondramatic pamphlets, especially those of the poetical kind, such as *Wars, Wars, Wars* or *The Artillery Garden* or *The Double PP*. Dekker's poetry on such occasions is mainly doggerel, and pieces such as these seem clearly to have been produced to capitalize on public excitement over some such special occasion as the Gunpowder Plot, or to secure some gift of patronage from the persons or groups to whom they are dedicated. The best of the nondramatic pieces, *The Gull's Hornbook* and *Four Birds of Noah's Ark*, demonstrate the dual strands of Dekker's literary personality with great clarity: *The Gull's Hornbook* is a lively, shrewd, and ironically amusing description of the swinging life-style to which sophisticated young men aspired in Jacobean London. The prayers and meditations of *Four Birds of Noah's Ark*, on the other hand, exhibit just how eloquent and affecting the simplicity of Dekker's style can be. Financial need evidently caused him to cease writing plays and to devote himself to writing nondramatic pamphlets for the five years or so from 1606 to 1611, but the interruption clearly did his career as a playwright no good. Just when he might have been expected to have consolidated all that he had gained from his early experience in the theater and to have built on such success as he had heretofore achieved to create more mature plays, his work for the stage ceased, and his career as a dramatist never regained the momentum that was driving it in the years from 1599-1605. When, in 1611, he resumed his activity as a playwright only to have it interrupted a year or so later by the half-dozen years of his imprisonment, his prospects for adding in any considerable way to the body of work he had already managed to produce for the stage were finished. Only *The Witch of Edmonton*, among the surviving plays with which he was associated after 1620, has any claim to real distinction. It is to this play, and to those earlier ones written in the period 1599-1605, that one must look to find the qualities that critics such as Lamb and Hazlitt and Swinburne so much admired.

They can be summarized under two heads: Dekker's compassion, and his humor. The compassion is most evident in the sympathy Dekker manages to generate for simple people who find themselves in the grip of very powerful feelings: feelings such as the guilt and shame aroused in Bellafront in *The Honest Whore*, part one; the fury and grief which her fall from virtue causes her father, Orlando Friscobaldo, and the renewed love and respect which he feels for his daughter when he is assured of her repentance in *The Honest Whore*, part two; the indignation that Grissell's brother, Laureo, feels in behalf of his sister's treatment by her royal husband, and by contrast the deep but uncomplaining sorrow felt by the father, Janicola, for his daughter, in *Patient Grissell;* the humiliation and outrage that drive Mother Sawyer to crazed visions of revenge on the neighbors who have persecuted her in *The Witch of Edmonton.*

As for Dekker's humor, it is of the genial kind that delights in eccentricities of personality and manner, and in his best work he has a fine gift for capturing his subject's typical quirks, fancies, and preoccupations in speech that is a compound of catch phrases and extravagant imaginative flights combined with the sort of nuances that particularize and characterize. The gift is most fully displayed in the character of Simon Eyre and his shop full of apprentices in *The Shoemakers' Holiday*, and in the titular character in *Old Fortunatus*. But nothing that Dekker wrote is ever entirely devoid of his energizing powers of language. They vitalize his nondramatic pamphlets, with their elaborate and often fantastic personifications (for example, *The Seven Deadly Sins*, the account of the armies of the poor in *Work for Armorers*, the grotesque description of the rout of thieves and rogues and the officers of the law who have them in chase in *A Strange Horse Race*). Side by side with the strain of eccentric fantasy in Dekker's art there is his clear-sighted vision of human strengths and weaknesses, and he gives voice to these in accents of the utmost simplicity. His powers of compassion and pathos exist in natural harmony with the genial humor of his comic manner, and together they give him a place in the tradition of English comic artists that includes such greater but nonetheless kindred spirits as Chaucer and Shakespeare, Fielding and Sterne and Dickens. Though his artistry is seldom equal to theirs, his poignant sense that human life contains much to be amused with and much to pity matches theirs.

Bibliographies:

Samuel A. Tannenbaum, *Dekker: A Concise Bibliography* (New York: Privately printed, 1939);

Samuel A. and Dorothy R. Tannenbaum, *Supplement to a Bibliography of Thomas Dekker* (New York: Privately printed, 1945);

Dennis Donovan, *Thomas Dekker, 1945-1965: Elizabethan Bibliographies Supplements, No. 2* (London: Nether Press, 1967);

A. F. Allison, *Thomas Dekker, c. 1572-1632. A Bibliographical Catalogue of the Early Editions to the end of the 17th Century* (Folkestone & London: Dawsons of Pall Mall, 1972);

Terence P. Logan and Denzell S. Smith, eds., *A Survey and Bibliography of Recent Studies in English Renaissance Drama: The Popular School* (Lincoln: University of Nebraska Press, 1975).

References:

Gerald Eades Bentley, *The Jacobean and Caroline Stage*, volume 3 (Oxford: Clarendon Press, 1956), pp. 241-275;

R. A. Foakes and R. T. Rickert, eds., *Henslowe's Diary* (Cambridge: Cambridge University Press, 1961);

M. T. Jones-Davies, *Un peintre de la vie londonienne: Thomas Dekker*, Collection des Etudes Anglaises, no. 6, 2 volumes (Paris, 1958).

Papers:

The manuscript for the play *Sir Thomas More*, containing Dekker's addition in his own hand, is preserved as Harleian MS 7368 in the British Library, London. The manuscript for *The Welsh Ambassador* is in the Public Library of Cardiff, Wales. The manuscript of Philip Henslowe's diary, with its many references to Dekker, is preserved among the papers of Edward Alleyn in the library of Dulwich College, London. Also preserved among the Alleyn papers are two letters in Dekker's hand, both written while he was a prisoner in the King's Bench prison; one is dated 12 September 1616, the other is undated. A commonplace book in the Folger Shakespeare Library, Washington, D.C. (MS V.a.160) contains two poems attributed to Dekker: "A New Ballad of the Dancing on the Ropes" and "Paul his Temple Triumphant." Both poems are reprinted by F. D. Hoeniger in "Thomas Dekker, the Restoration of St. Paul's, and J. P. Collier, the Forger," *Renaissance News*, 16 (1963): 181-200. Dekker's deposition (dated 3 February 1625) in the legal suit arising from the lost play titled *The Late Murder of the Son upon the Mother* is preserved in the Public Records Office, London. See C. J. Sisson, *Lost Plays of Shakespeare's Age* (Cambridge: Cambridge University Press, 1936), pp. 81ff.

Richard Edwards

(1524-31 October 1566)

D. Jerry White
Central Missouri State University

PLAY PRODUCTIONS: *Damon and Pithias,* Westminster, Whitehall Palace, Christmas season 1564-1565;
Palamon and Arcite, parts 1 and 2, Christ Church, Oxford, 2 and 4 September 1566.

BOOKS: *The Excellent Comedie of Two the Moste Faithfullest Freendes, Damon and Pithias* (London: Printed by W. Williamson for R. Johnes, 1571);
The Paradyse of Daynty Deuises, aptly furnished, with sundry pithie and learned inuentions: deuised and written for the most part, by M. Edwards, sometimes of her Maiesties Chappel: the rest, by sundry learned Gentlemen, both of honor, and woorshippe (London: Printed by R. Jones for [?] H. Disle, 1576).
Edition: *Richard Edwards' Damon and Pithias: A Critical Old-Spelling Edition,* edited by D. Jerry White (New York: Garland, 1980).

Though the literary merit of his one surviving play is itself sufficient, the stature of Richard Edwards as an important Tudor dramatist is assured by the sad historical fact that *Damon and Pithias* is the only extant example of a play unquestionably written by a Master of the Children of the Chapel Royal. Made up of thirty-two gentlemen singers and twelve children, the Chapel Royal was responsible for royal worship services outside Windsor and for providing the Court with other entertainment, including plays presented by the children.

Edwards's appointment to the post of master is evidence of his reputation as both a musician and dramatist. According to Leicester Bradner, it implies that he was "the chief ornament of polite literature in the eyes of his contemporaries." But Edwards's satiric wit in attacking less-polite abuses of the Court suggests also a humanist's awareness of the evils of power and of the dangers inherent in pointing out those evils. Though not a poet of the first order, Edwards is notable for his craft in developing characters, in organizing plot, and in presenting serious themes through devices such as comedy, romance, wordplay, and satire. His skill led to remarkable popularity in his own day and commends him to modern students of pre-Shakespearean drama.

Relatively little is known of the life of Richard Edwards; yet—perhaps in part because of the popularity he enjoyed among his contemporaries—some of the preserved details are surprisingly personal and provide an unusually intimate view of the life of an Elizabethan courtier. Edwards was born in Somersetshire in 1524. On 11 May 1540 he was admitted to Corpus Christi College, Oxford, and on 3 November 1544 he was awarded the Bachelor of Arts degree. Nearly three months earlier, on 11 August, he was elected a fellow at Corpus Christi, but it was at Christ Church College that he was named lecturer in logic in 1546 and advanced to the Master of Arts degree on 5 February 1547. Evidence suggests that Edwards was ordained between 1547 and 1550, and that he left Oxford shortly thereafter.

The next few years of Edwards's life are particularly vague, but he must have gained favor in the Court because a note written in early 1557 mentions a poet, "Edwards of the Chapel," who presented a New Year's gift of "certain verses" to Queen Mary and her husband, Philip of Spain. Court records show that Edwards was issued seven yards of black cloth for attire at Mary's funeral and four yards of scarlet for Elizabeth's coronation. After a brief assignment to the Queen's Chamber, Edwards was again appointed as a Gentleman of the Chapel in a patent dated 27 May 1560. Following the death of Richard Bower, who had served as Master of the Children of the Chapel Royal for sixteen years, Edwards became their master by a patent dated 27 October 1561.

When Edwards began writing plays is not certain, but by 1563 he had distinguished himself in the drama, as evidenced by twenty lines of doggerel praise for him that Barnabe Googe included in his *Eglogs, Epytaphes, and Sonettes.* The quality of Googe's verse aside, his "Of Edwards of the Chapel" praises Edwards's comedies as exceeding even those of Plautus and Terence. Further evidence of earlier dramatic activity is afforded by the prologue of Edwards's *Damon and Pithias,* which apologizes for earlier "toying Playes" that "did offende" because "to some he seemed too muche, in yonge desires to range." Unfortunately, nothing is known of these earlier works or of how serious the author was either in noting the offense or in offering the apology. Edwards's election as an honorary fellow of Lincoln's Inn in November 1564, however, is surely another indication of the popularity of his earlier plays. The lawyers probably selected him in part as a potential source of entertainment; at any rate that was one result of his admission, for records of Lincoln's Inn show at least two performances there by the children during the next two years.

Damon and Pithias, Edwards's only surviving play, was presented by the children at the Court during the Christmas season of 1564-1565, and apparently again at Lincoln's Inn the following February. Writing in a popular tradition that united the classical "friendship" theme with the morally instructive purpose of "courtesy" literature, Edwards borrowed most of his plot material from Thomas Elyot's *The Boke Named the Gouernour* (1531). His own invention was a series of structural parallels and plays on words that develop this simple drama into a powerful commentary on the evils of selfishness and duplicity in the court.

The play begins with the two friends arriving at the port of Syracuse despite a violent storm that has impeded their journey. In the company of Damon's servant, Stephano, the Greek students have come to visit the realm of Dionysius, a tyrant who is both feared and fearing. In fact, the king is so frightened of assassination that only his daughters are allowed to shave his beard, and even then not with a razor or knife but by singeing the hairs "with hote burning Nutshales."

Damon innocently examines the defenses of the city, a violation of Dionysius's law, and, through the testimony of a sycophantic courtier named Carisophus, he is subsequently sentenced to die. Even the advice of Eubulus, the good counselor, will not calm Dionysius's anger, and Aristippus, a philosopher-turned-courtier, selfishly refuses to defend Damon. The development of Aristippus's character seems especially poignant, for he probably reflects the fear of Edwards and other humanist courtiers that, put to the test, they might be tempted to bend their own values rather than sacrifice their positions in the Court.

Accepting his fate, Damon requests leave to return home and settle his affairs, promising to return for his execution. Incredulous, Dionysius jokingly grants the request, on the condition that someone will substitute for Damon and agree to accept the punishment should he fail to return within two months. Much to the King's surprise, Pithias volunteers as his friend's "pledge," and Damon must be allowed to depart.

The comic subplot of the play presents Jack and Will, lackeys of Aristippus and Carisophus. Dressed in huge pantaloons that apparently mocked a current fad in youthful clothing, these witty but immoral young men meet the greedy windbag Grim the Collier (probably portrayed by Edwards himself) as he is making his delivery of coals to the court. After engaging him in conversation, drink, and song, they give Grim a rough, slapstick shaving (reminding us of Dionysius's fearful barbering) and steal his purse.

The main plot returns with the executioner's axe about to fall on Pithias's neck when Damon comes running onto the stage, just back from Greece. The two argue over who should be executed; each pleads that he be allowed to die for his friend. Overwhelmed by the sincerity of their love, Dionysius repents, pardons them, and begs instruction in the ways of true friendship.

Thus the moral implications of Edwards's intricately parallel plots become clear. At the lowest and the highest levels–represented by Grim and Dionysius–the court is prey to false friends like the pairs of lackeys and courtiers. Only the trusting, selfless love of the two true friends can bring harmony to Dionysius's court and, Edwards seems to say, to Elizabeth's.

Perhaps such pointed allusions as these were responsible for the offense caused by his earlier drama, but quite clearly Edwards does little to disguise his moralizing purpose here. In fact the admonition of the prologue–"Wee talke of *Dionisius* courte, wee meane no Court but that"–intentionally hints that the play might be understood as topical. The closing song of the play only reiterates this purpose in the twice-repeated refrain: "The Lorde graunt her such friendes most noble Queene Elizabeth."

Later events in 1565 provide more glimpses of Edwards's life and some insight into the role

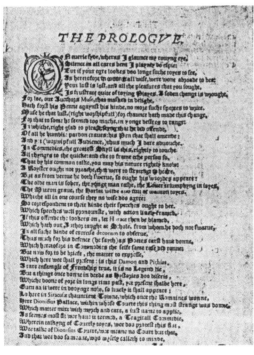

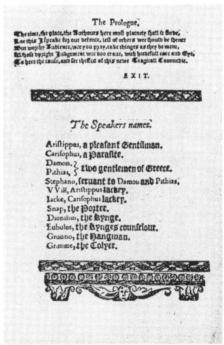

Title page, prologue, and dramatis personae from the 1571 quarto edition of Edwards's only surviving play (British Library)

of a courtier in Elizabeth's Court. No doubt applying his theatrical talent, Edwards served as a messenger to the Queen when, in August, he heralded the challenges of four knights who proposed to joust before the Court on the occasion of the marriage of the Earl of Bedford's daughter to the Earl of Warwick. In November, when the jousts were held, Edwards continued in this role, trumpet in hand, and asked the Queen's permission to begin the games.

As menial as this service sounds, it suggests a close relationship with the Queen, a relationship borne out in later records. In July of 1566 Elizabeth began a progression that would eventually take her to Oxford. Edwards not only accompanied her at Oxford, as he probably had throughout her progression in the summer of 1564 that included Cambridge, but he was also selected to present a play before the Queen. Since his own college of Christ Church was chosen as her residence and as site of the three plays to be performed, we may presume that Edwards played a major role in organizing the Oxford visit.

For the royal visit, Edwards wrote the now-lost play *Palamon and Arcite,* which was to be staged in two parts on consecutive evenings. Unfortunately, only one song (identified by Rollins) has survived, "An Elegy on the Death of a Sweetheart," to be sung by Emilia after Arcite's death. The failure of a copy of *Palamon and Arcite* to come down to us is even more frustrating because so much is known about the production. A Latin commentary written by John Bereblock describes the events in detail, and chronicles from several other contemporaries support and augment his reports.

That Edwards followed rather closely the plot of Chaucer's "Knight's Tale" seems to be evident from these accounts, and his choice of plots was certainly a calculated one in several ways. First, the romantic themes of a tragicomedy in which two friends battle for the love of the beautiful Athenian virgin Emilia provided an appropriate respite from the erudite, Latin dramas that preceded and followed Edwards's play. Second, through Emilia's marriage plans, Edwards may have joined other courtly voices in advising the Queen to marry and avoid the potential strife of a realm without an heir. Such a message had been expressed more pointedly in Norton and Sackville's 1562 play *Gorboduc,* and the Court was well aware of the Queen's usual displeasure at such advice. Nevertheless, Elizabeth's reaction to *Palamon and Arcite* suggests that she not only found herself allegorized in Emilia's character, but to Edwards's credit and probably his relief she regarded the reflection so complimentary that she awarded a prize of four pounds to the boy who played the part of Emilia.

Edwards also seems to have picked the play because of the potential it afforded for spectacle. The commentators noted the realism and splendor with which several scenes were staged: the howling of hounds in the courtyard to accompany Theseus's hunt; the prayers and intercessions that brought Diana, Mars, Venus, and Saturn to the stage; the lengthy battle between the two friends; the subterranean fire with which Saturn struck down Arcite after his victory; and the magnificent pyre constructed for Arcite's funeral.

Apparently *Palamon and Arcite* was an unqualified success for even a rehearsal drew great praise. According to Frederick S. Boas, Thomas Neale, a professor of Hebrew who witnessed the rehearsal, wrote that the play, "repeated before certayne courtiers . . . by ye players in their Schollers gownes before ye Queenes cōminge, was so well lyked that they saide it far surpassed Damon & Pythias, then ye whiche nothinge could be better."

On the first night of the performance, 2 September, so many spectators crowded onto a stairway that a stone wall collapsed, killing three people and injuring several others. Despite this unfortunate beginning, the first part continued and was well received. Because the Queen's schedule had left her indisposed to attend the next evening's performance, Edwards postponed the second half of his drama until 4 September. According to W. Y. Durand, Bereblock wrote that at its conclusion the play "was approved by the throng with a tremendous shout and clapping of hands"; furthermore, Boas quotes Neale's report that Elizabeth had Edwards brought to her and "gave him great thankes wth P[ro]mise of rewarde."

The Queen's affection for Edwards may be seen in the playful banter that occurred the following day when George Etherege, the musician and professor of Greek, presented her with a volume of Greek verses. Bradner quotes from Anthony à Wood's Oxford history in relating the exchange: "Edwards, who was standing near, said to the Queen: 'Madam, this man was my Master.' To which she merrily replied: 'Certainly he did not give thee whipping enough.' "

As Bradner notes, this final recorded incident in Edwards's life only shortly precedes "the brief statement in *The Old Cheque Book of the Chapel Royal*: '1566. Rich. Edwards died, Mr of the children, the last October.' " Neither a will nor a burial site has been located, but Bradner has identified a commission from the Prerogative Court of Canterbury that seems to give custody of Edwards's four children to their uncle, a Thomas Griffith. He speculates that Edwards was therefore married by 1562 and was a widower at the time of his death.

Even after his death, Edwards's reputation

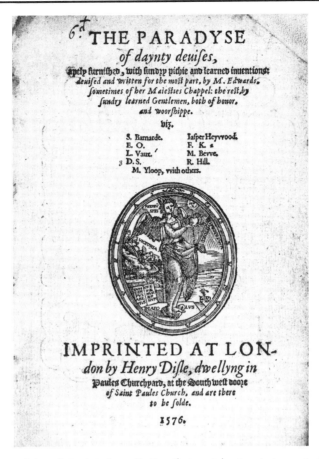

Title page for the 1576 quarto edition of the popular collection that contains twenty poems probably written by Edwards (Henry E. Huntington Library and Art Gallery)

seems to have been strong for some time. Indeed, literary hacks and notables alike found much to praise in his work; the list of Renaissance figures who offered plaudits includes Barnabe Googe, George Turberville, Thomas Twine, William Webbe, Richard Puttenham, and Francis Meres. In 1568 Merton College, Oxford, presented a revival of *Damon and Pithias*, probably in part recalling the popularity of the Oxford production of *Palamon and Arcite* two years earlier.

Another measure of Edwards's popularity among his contemporaries is the reception of his poetry. Including Emilia's song from *Palamon and Arcite*, twenty-seven poems have been identified as probably from his pen. Though these verses are generally too plodding in meter and too didactic in theme for modern tastes, they were popular in the sixteenth century. In fact ten years after Edwards's death, the poetic miscellany *The Paradyse of Daynty Deuises* was published with a subtitle purporting that it was his compilation: *aptly furnished, with sundry pithie and learned inuentions: deuised and written for the most part, by M. Edwards,*

sometimes of her Maiesties Chappel: the rest, by sundry learned Gentlemen, both of honor, and woorshippe.... The collection, containing twenty poems now identified as probably written by Edwards, went through eight editions between 1576 and 1606.

Though Edwards must remain a shadowy and relatively minor figure in comparison with Shakespeare or Jonson, several modern critics have pointed out that his influence extended even to these stellar figures of English Renaissance dramas. Peter's interrogation of the musicians in *Romeo and Juliet* (IV.v), for example, comically explicates one of Edwards's songs in *The Paradyse of Daynty Deuises*, and other possible borrowings have been suggested in *A Midsummer Night's Dream*, *The Merchant of Venice*, and *The Tempest*. To what extent *Palamon and Arcite* may have influenced *The Two Noble Kinsmen* by Shakespeare and John Fletcher remains uncertain. Even Jonson's parody of *Damon and Pithias* in the puppet show of *Bartholomew Fair* shows a keen awareness of Edwards's play and suggests other similarities in the two dramas.

It is indeed unfortunate that Edwards died at the early age of forty-two and that so much of his work has been lost. Certainly, as Master of the Children of the Chapel Royal, Edwards must have produced several plays and entertainments for the court during his five-year tenure, and we may safely assume that several were his own compositions. Given what has survived, though, students of pre-Shakespearean drama will continue to find Richard Edwards a significant figure whose career and works illuminate an important transitional period in the history of English drama and add to our understanding of the humanist-courtier's struggle to maintain his intellectual, artistic, and moral principles while serving effectively in the court.

Bibliography:

D. Jerry White, "Richard Edwards," in his *Early English Drama:* Everyman *to 1580* (Boston: G. K. Hall, 1986), pp. 116-120.

Biography:

Leicester Bradner, *The Life and Poems of Richard Edwards* (New Haven: Yale University Press, 1927).

References:

William A. Armstrong, "*Damon and Pithias* and Renaissance Theories of Tragedy," *English Studies*, 39 (October 1958): 200-207;

Frederick S. Boas, *University Drama in the Tudor Age* (Oxford: Clarendon Press, 1914);

W. Y. Durand, "*Palaemon and Arcyte, Progne, Marcus Geminus,* and the Theatre in Which They Were Acted, as Described by John Bereblock (1566)," *PMLA*, 20, no. 3 (1905): 502-528;

Allan Holaday, "Shakespeare, Richard Edwards, and the Virtues Reconciled," *Journal of English and Germanic Philology*, 66 (April 1967): 200-206;

J. E. Kramer, "*Damon and Pithias:* An Apology for Art," *ELH*, 35 (December 1968): 475-490;

Hyder E. Rollins, "A Note on Richard Edwards," *Review of English Studies*, 4 (April 1928): 204-206.

Robert Greene
(July 1558-3 September 1592)

Daniel Kinney
University of Virginia

PLAY PRODUCTIONS: *Alphonsus, King of Aragon,* London, unknown theater, circa 1588;

The History of Orlando Furioso, London, The Theatre, 1588-1591;

Friar Bacon and Friar Bungay, London, unknown theater, 1589-1591;

A Looking-Glass for London and England, by Greene and Thomas Lodge, London, The Theatre (?), circa 1590-1591;

Locrine, attributed to Greene, London, unknown theater, circa 1591;

Selimus, attributed to Greene, London, The Theatre, circa 1591;

The Scottish History of James IV, London, unknown theater, circa 1592;

George a Greene, The Pinner of Wakefield, attributed to Greene, London, Rose theater, by 1593;

John of Bordeaux, or The Second Part of Friar Bacon, attributed to Greene, London, Rose theater (?), by 1593.

BOOKS: *Mamillia. A Mirrour or Looking-Glasse for the Ladies of Englande* (London: Printed by T. Dawson for T. Woodcocke, 1583);

Mamillia [part 2]. *The Triumph of Pallas* (London: Printed by H. Middleton for W. Ponsonby, 1583?);

Arbasto. The Anatomie of Fortune (London: Printed by J. Windet & T. Judson for H. Jackson, 1584); republished with *Pyramus and Thisbe* (London: Printed by J. Beale for R. Jackson, 1617);

Gwydonius. The Carde of Fancie, translated by Greene (London: Printed by T. East for W. Ponsonby, 1584);

Morando the Tritameron of Loue (London: Printed by J. Charlewood & J. Kingston for E. White, 1584); enlarged as *Morando . . . The First and Second Part* (London: Printed by J. Wolfe for E. White, 1587);

The Myrrour of Modestie, Wherein Appeareth Howe the Lorde Deliuereth the Innocent (London: Printed by R. Warde, 1584);

Planetomachia: or The First Parte of the Generall Oppo-

Caricature of Robert Greene from the title page for the 1598 quarto edition of John Dickenson's Greene in Conceipt

sition of the Seuen Planets (London: Printed by T. Dawson & G. Robinson for T. Cadman, 1585);

Penelopes Web: Wherein a Christall Myrror of Faeminine Perfection Represents Vertues and Graces (London: Printed by T. Orwin [?] for T. Cadman & E. Aggas, 1587);

Euphues his Censure to Philautus (London: Printed by J. Wolfe for E. White, 1587);

Pandosto. The Triumph of Time (London: Printed by T. Orwin for T. Cadman, 1588); republished as *The Pleasant Historie of Dorastus and Fawnia* (London: Printed by T. Purfoot for F. Faulkner, circa 1635);

Perimedes the Blacke-Smith, A Golden Methode, How to Vse the Minde in Pleasant and Profitable Exercise (London: Printed by J. Wolfe for E. White, 1588);

Ciceronis Amor. Tullies Loue. Wherein is Discoursed the Prime of Ciceroes Youth (London: Printed by R. Robinson for T. Newman & J. Winnington, 1589);

Menaphon Camillas Alarum to Slumbering Euphues (London: Printed by T. Orwin for S. Clarke, 1589);

The Spanish Masquerado. Wherein . . . Is Discouered the Pride and Insolencie of the Spanish Estate (London: Printed by R. Ward for T. Cadman, 1589);

Greenes Mourning Garment, Giuen Him by Repentance (London: Printed by J. Wolfe for T. Newman, 1590);

Greenes Neuer Too Late. Or, A Powder of Experience [with *Francescos Fortunes: Or, The Second Part*] (London: Printed by T. Orwin for N. Ling & J. Busbie, 1590);

The Royal Exchange. Contayning Sundry Aphorismes of Phylosophie and of Morrall and Naturall Quadruplicities. Fyrst Written in Italian, translated, with commentary, by Greene (London: Printed by J. Charlewood for W. Wright, 1590);

Greenes Farewell to Folly. Sent to Courtiers and Schollers (London: Printed by T. Scarlet for T. Gubbin & T. Newman, 1591);

A Maidens Dreame. Vpon the Death of Sir Christopher Hatton (London: Printed by T. Scarlet for T. Nelson, 1591);

A Notable Discouery of Coosenage (London: Printed by J. Wolfe for T. Nelson, 1591);

The Second Part of Conny-Catching (London: Printed by J. Wolfe for W. Wright, 1591); enlarged as *The Second and Last Part of Conny-Catching* (London: Printed by J. Wolfe for W. Wright, 1592);

The Defence of Conny-Catching or a Confutation of Those Two Iniurious Pamphlets Published by R. G., possibly by Greene as Cuthbert Cony-Catcher (London: Printed by A. Jeffes for T. Gubbins, sold by J. Busbie, 1592);

The Thirde and Last Part of Conny-Catching (London: Printed by T. Scarlet for C. Burbie, 1592);

A Disputation, Betweene a Hee Conny-Catcher, and a Shee Conny-Catcher (London: Printed by A. Jeffes for T. Gubbin, 1592); republished as *Theeves Falling Out, True-Men Come by Their Goods* (London: Printed by W. White and another[?] for T. Gubbin, sold by R. [i.e. E.] Marchant, 1615);

The Blacke Bookes Messenger. Laying open the Life and Death of Ned Browne One of the Most Notable Cutpurses (London: Printed by J. Danter for T. Nelson, 1592);

Philomela. The Lady Fitzwaters Nightingale (London: Printed by R. Bourne & E. Allde for E. White, 1592);

A Quip for an Vpstart Courtier: or, A Quaint Dispute. Wherein is Plainely Set Downe the Disorders in All Estates and Trades (London: Printed by J. Wolfe, 1592);

Greenes Vision: Written at the Instant of His Death (London: Printed by E. Allde for T. Newman, 1592);

Greenes Groats-Worth of Witte . . . Written before His Death, doubtfully attributed to Greene, edited by H. Chettle (London: Printed by J. Wolfe & J. Danter for W. Wright, 1592);

The Repentance of Robert Greene, doubtfully attributed to Greene (London: Printed by J. Danter for C. Burbie, 1592);

The Historie of Orlando Furioso (London: Printed by J. Danter for C. Burbie, 1594);

A Looking Glasse for London and England, by Greene and Thomas Lodge (London: Printed by T. Creede, sold by W. Barley, 1594);

The Honorable Historie of Frier Bacon and Frier Bongay (London: Printed by A. Islip for E. White, 1594);

The First Part of the Tragicall Raigne of Selimus, doubtfully attributed to Greene (London: Printed by T. Creede, 1594);

The Lamentable Tragedie of Locrine, doubtfully attributed to Greene (London: Printed by T. Creede, 1595);

The Scottish Historie of James the Fourth (London: Printed by T. Creede, 1598);

A Pleasant Conceyted Comedie of George a Greene, the Pinner of Wakefield, attributed to Greene (London: Printed by S. Stafford for C. Burby, 1599);

The Comicall Historie of Alphonsus, King of Aragon (London: Printed by T. Creede, 1599);

Greenes Orpharion. Wherin is Discouered a Musicall Concorde of Pleasant Histories (London: Printed by J. Roberts for E. White, 1599);

Alcida Greenes Metamorphosis, Wherein is Discouered, a Pleasant Transformation of Bodies (London: Printed by G. Purslowe, 1617).

Editions: *The Life and Complete Works in Prose and Verse of Robert Greene. M. A. Cambridge and Oxford,* 15 volumes, edited by Alexander B. Grosart (London & Aylesbury: Privately printed, 1881-1886);

The Tragical Reign of Selimus, doubtfully attributed to Greene, edited by Grosart (London: Dent, 1898);

Title page for the 1606 quarto edition of the popular 1592 pamphlet that contains one of Greene's attacks on Gabriel and Richard Harvey (Maggs Bros., catalogue number 493, 1927)

The Plays and Poems of Robert Greene, 2 volumes, edited by J. Churton Collins (Oxford: Clarendon Press, 1905);

The History of Orlando Furioso, edited by W. W. Greg (Oxford: Oxford University Press, 1907);

Locrine, doubtfully attributed to Greene, in *The Shakespeare Apocrypha*, edited by C. F. Tucker Brooke (Oxford: Clarendon Press, 1908), pp. 37-65;

The Comedy of George a Green, edited by F. W. Clark (Oxford: Oxford University Press, 1911);

Alphonsus, King of Aragon, edited by Greg (London: Oxford University Press, 1926);

John of Bordeaux, or The Second Part of Friar Bacon, edited by William L. Renwick (Oxford: Oxford University Press, 1936);

Friar Bacon and Friar Bungay, edited by Daniel Seltzer (Lincoln: University of Nebraska Press, 1964);

Pandosto and *A Notable Discovery of Cozenage*, in *Elizabethan Prose Fiction*, edited by Merritt Lawlis (New York: Odyssey Press, 1967), pp. 226-277, 395-434;

The Scottish History of James IV, edited by J. A. Lavin (London: Benn, 1967);

Friar Bacon and Friar Bungay, edited by Lavin (London: Benn, 1969);

The Scottish History of James IV, edited by Norman Sanders (London: Methuen, 1970);

The History of Orlando Furioso, edited by

Tetsumaro Hayashi, in his *A Textual Study of Robert Greene's Orlando Furioso with an Elizabethan Text* (Muncie: Ball State University, 1973);

A Looking Glasse for London and England: A Critical Edition, edited by George A. Clugson (New York: Garland, 1980).

Few of Shakespeare's immediate precursors can be more notorious than Robert Greene, or more enigmatic. His purported excesses and his miserable end make a dubious substitute for accurate biography but an unequaled point of departure for lurid conjectures and simplistic moral critiques; only lately have scholars and critics begun to consider that Greene's image may well be as artful a fiction as any of his novels or plays, and at least as resistant to cursory survey.

What we know of Greene's life all derives from four sources: documentary evidence, including publication records; comments by Greene's contemporaries; personal statements in works which are definitely by Greene; personal statements in two well-known posthumous pamphlets, purportedly by Greene, which are more likely to be partly forgeries. Greene once signed himself "Norfolciensis" ("Of Norfolk"), and once elsewhere, "Nordouicensis" ("Of Norwich"); J. C. Collins discovered a baptismal record for one "Robert Greene, son of Robert Greene," baptized just outside Norwich on 11 July 1558, an appropriate year of birth for the playwright. His father was probably either a modest Norfolk saddler or a cordwainer-innkeeper boasting some prosperous connections in Yorkshire; the latter suggestion would explain the many Yorkshire names in Greene's early dedications and the sympathy with the values of the old landed gentry Greene displays in a number of his writings. He also signed himself "Graduate in Cambridge," "Maister of Arts, in Cambridge," "From my studie in Clarehall the vij of Iuli [1583]"; and he is probably the same Robert Greene who entered St. John's College as a sizar or poor working student in 1575, taking a middling B.A. in early 1580, and who moved to Clare Hall, where he took his M.A. three years later. As of 1588 Greene also held the courtesy title of "M.A. in both universities," his Cambridge M.A. being formally approved as the basis for an M.A. from Oxford. Greene undoubtedly relished his university status, and the stress that he gave it suggests that it helped to confirm his self-image as part of a clever and daring elite, the so-called University

Wits, including such figures as Thomas Nashe, George Peele, and Christopher Marlowe. One source, *The Repentance of Robert Greene* (1592), dates Greene's death 3 September 1592, and another, Gabriel Harvey's *Foure Letters* (1592), dates his burial the following day; though these sources may be unreliable in other respects, there would be little point in misrepresenting the actual date of Greene's death. Both agree that Greene sickened from a surfeit of pickled herring, spent his last days in pain and remorse, and died hopelessly poor. One of England's first professional writers, Greene finished his life like a character in an abusive depiction of Grub Street.

Part of this squalid picture is the work of Greene's enemy Gabriel Harvey, a self-righteous, frustrated Cambridge don who, along with his brother Richard, had personally provoked printed onslaughts from both Nashe and Greene. During this prolonged feud, described in more detail by Charles W. Crupi, Greene made his main attack on the Harveys in the first printing of his work *A Quip for an Upstart Courtier* (1592), where he assailed the Harveys' scholarly sense of self-worth from both bohemian and aristocratic standpoints; at the risk of anachronism, one could view the whole quarrel as a clash between bourgeois and bohemian notions of how intellectuals should live. This suggestion gains credence from Gabriel Harvey's triumphant review of Greene's vices and personal hardships and from Nashe's response in *Strange News* (1592). What Harvey presents as Greene's ruinous extravagance Nashe defends as courageous exuberance. At the same time Nashe tries to distance his own cause from Greene's and declines to supply a detailed firsthand justification of Greene against Harvey's attacks; thus, for reasons of his own, Nashe in large part accepted the tendentious character sketch promulgated by Harvey.

Nashe's reports about other details of Greene's flamboyant ways make it fairly clear that Greene did not dislike such notoriety. He wore a very long, pointed red beard, drank himself into debt and amusingly outfaced his creditors, and tossed off another popular pamphlet whenever his debts got oppressive. Further, Greene often wrote in the name of exposing the follies of youth and the evils of low life in London, and he even made a habit of recanting his own earlier "amorous" writings in his later works. Such activities, and Greene's premature death, would have made him a natural subject for lurid attacks and confessional pamphlets, even if he

Morando
The Tritameron of
Loue:

Wherein certaine pleasaunt conceites,
vttered by diuers woorthy personages, are perfectly
dyscoursed, and three doubtfull questyons of Loue,
most pithely and pleasauntly discussed : Shewing to the
wyse howe to vse Loue, and to the fonde, howe
to eschew Lust : and yeelding to all both
pleasure and profitt.
(***)

By Robert Greene , Maister of Artes
in Cambridge.

At London
Printed for Edwarde White, and are
to be solde at his shoppe, at the little North
doore of S Paules Church, at the
signe of the Gunne.
1584.

The Spanish Masquerado.

VVherein vnder a

pleasant deuise, is discouered

effectuallie, in certaine breefe sentences and
Mottos, the pride and insolencie of the
Spanish estate: with the disgrace
conceiued by their losse, and
the dismaied confusion
of their troubled
thoughtes.

Whereunto by the Author, for the better vnder-
standing of his deuice, is added a breefe glosse.

By Robert Greene, in Artibus Magister.

𝕿welue Articles of the state of Spaine.

The Cardinals sollicite all..
The King grauntes all.
The Nobles confirme all.
The Pope determines all.
The Cleargie disposeth all.
The Duke of Medina hopes for all.
Alonso *receiues all.*
The Indians minister all.
The Souldiours eat all.
The people paie all.
The Monkes and Friers consume all.
And the deuill at length wil cary away all.

❡ Printed at London by Roger Ward, for
Thomas Cadman. 1589.

CICERONIS AMOR.
Tullies Loue.

Wherein is discoursed the prime of Cice-
roes youth, setting out in luely portratures how young
Gentlemen that ayme at honour should leuell
the end of their affections, holding the loue of coun-
trie and friends in more esteeme then those
fading blossomes of beautie, that onely feede
the curious suruey of the eye.

A worke full of pleasure as following *Ciceroes* vaine,
who was as conceipted in his youth as graue in his age, profitable as conteining precepts worthie so famous an Orator.

Robert Greene in Artibus magister.

Omne tulit punctum qui miscuit vtile dulci.

AT LONDON,
Printed by *Robert Robinson,* for *Thomas Newman*
and *John Winington.* 1589.

---

*Title pages for quarto editions of three of the pamphlets that Greene wrote during the first decade of his career (top and bottom
left: Anderson Galleries, sale number 2077, 20-21 May 1926; bottom right: Henry E. Huntington Library and Art Gallery)*

himself had no hand in the pamphlets at all. Though computer analysis has been used to bolster longstanding suspicion that both *Greenes Groats-Worth of Witte* (1592) and *The Repentance of Robert Greene* are virtually pure forgeries, it is hard to rule out the conjecture that both works are editors' compilations largely based on known facts and Greene's notes; certainly both pamphlets support many of Harvey's assertions, though these pamphlets were published a few weeks before. As Richard Helgerson notes, the main interest of the subject may well be the way that Greene's life converged almost inevitably with a traditional prodigal-son narrative, a costly but neat way of "containing" Greene's heterodox conduct within orthodox categories. The ambivalence of the original parable ensured its appeal as a key to the writings and deeds of the new intellectuals: even solidly middle-class readers could season their smug disapproval of the way such men flouted convention with safely vicarious indulgence. From there, it is not such a great step to avowing such rebels as licensed aesthetes, modern martyrs to unmediated experience; in this one respect, Greene's flamboyant persona, despite his own scruples about "fancy" and "feigning" of all sorts, links him much more closely with modern aesthetes than with figures such as Ascham, for whom learning and literature were both pillars of the moral status quo. Relevant here is the fact that bohemian prodigals, even thinly disguised ones, play no part at all in Greene's dramas, though *Greenes Groats-Worth of Witte* decries playwrights as often the most unregenerate bohemians; the medium itself fairly clearly "selects for" persona, as well as vice versa.

After so many caveats, Greene's productive adult life as recorded in the extant sources may be summed up as follows: Greene took his B.A. in early 1580 and completed his first work, part one of *Mamillia* (1583), much later that year; meanwhile he may have traveled to Italy and Spain with some cronies from Cambridge (*The Repentance of Robert Greene*), and he probably married not much later if he was not married already. Harvey cites what may be a real letter from Greene to his wife giving her name as Dorothy or "Doll." The date of his marriage is important, though nowhere confirmed, because *Mamillia*, part one, is the first of Greene's numerous narratives about wayward husbands and because both the disputed confessional pamphlets and Harvey's *Foure Letters* imply that the principal model for these wayward husbands was Robert

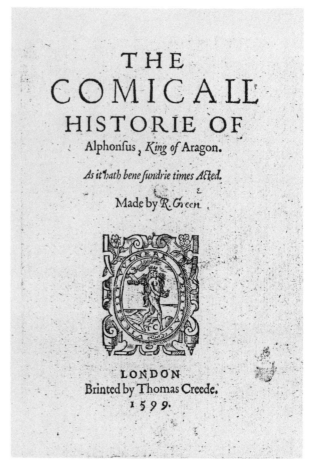

Title page for the 1599 quarto edition of Greene's first play (Victoria and Albert Museum). In this copy the printed credit "R. G." has been expanded.

Greene himself. *The Repentance of Robert Greene* indicates that Greene and his wife had been separated for six years as of 1592, so that the first wayward-husband adventures in Greene's works can scarcely be purely confessional if this marriage date is right. By his wife or by Em Ball, the prostitute sister of the noted London thug "Cutting Ball," Greene apparently had a son Fortunatus (branded "Infortunatus" by Harvey), who was buried in Shoreditch on 12 August 1593. Greene was working in Cambridge in 1583 when he finished his next pamphlet, *Mamillia*, part two (1583?); at some point in the next several years, relegating his wife and their child to Lincolnshire, Greene sought his fortune in London. Between 1583 and his death in September 1592, he produced on an average three or four lengthy pamphlets a year. Probably in 1587 he began writing dramas as well, his first play, the Marlovian *Alphonsus*, in no sense a brilliant debut. He is confidently assigned only three other plays and a part in composing another, but his progress in this mode was such that, according to Nashe, as a plotter of plays he was ultimately "his crafts master." One of Greene's wayward-husband alter egos, Francesco in *Never Too Late* (1590), is said to have had great success with a "Comedie," but the playwright's profession is treated as all of a piece with the rest of Francesco's base pastimes; it is mentioned at least as disdainfully in *The Repentance of Robert Greene* and *Greenes Groats-Worth of Witte.* Evidently the stage was perceived as beneath moral norms of the sort by which Greene at least claimed to be trying to reform his pamphlet-writing. One can argue for the presence of a real evolution in Greene's sense of his audience and aims as a writer of pamphlets; it is hard to detect any such thoroughgoing evolution in the theory or practice of the playwright.

Greene's self-presentation changed slightly along with the style and design of his pamphlets. He began (in parts one and two of *Mamillia*) with polite, verbose fictions contrasting abstractions such as "true love" and "fancy," reality and appearance, or reason and rhetoric in the general tradition of John Lyly's *Euphues* (1578); even in these first pamphlets, however, the proportion of real action to long-winded debate is much larger than in Lyly, and, as Jaroslav Hornat has noted, Greene counters Lyly's emphasis on feminine fickleness with a paragon of feminine longsuffering who overcomes a glib husband's inconstancy. Similar "suffering Griseldas" abound in Greene's works. But what is striking is not so much Greene's use of emblematic characters per se (see the classification in Crupi), but the unsettling way in which Greene half-resolves their not purely symbolic encounters. Characters such as Mamillia are not just abstractions and not just living everyday types; like the characters of *Measure for Measure*, Greene's characters challenge the simplest medieval conception of "pleasing instruction" based on totally lucid exemplars. On the other hand, as in *Mamillia,* the rejection of one emblematic position is often emphatic even when the supposed resolution is dubious. Such emphatic rejections were one way to lend at least some credibility to the Horatian formula "utile dulci" or "profit with pleasure," part of Greene's motto in many of these earliest pamphlets and the more complex romances and frame tales which followed. *Menaphon* (1589), perhaps Greene's most ambitious and daring romance, rings the changes on barely averted incest without ever ceasing to cel-

ebrate its chief characters' virtues; even more than *Pandosto* (1588), the chief source for *The Winter's Tale, Menaphon* "teaches" us, if at all, through the sort of symbolic self-mortification and communal self-affirmation constituting the ritual pattern behind most Shakespearean romance.

One important approach to Greene's pamphlets, developed by Walter R. Davis, indicates a progressive divorce between "idea" and "act" or ideal and reality. According to this view, the only way fiction can actually "teach" is by showing how beauty and beautiful ideals militate against truth, and vice versa. On this reading, Greene's implicit promise of "profit with pleasure" was bound to become more and more problematic, until Greene tried to segregate truth from illusion and profit from pleasure in the clear documentary bias and the instrusive moral directives of his later works. Certainly Greene's next body of works, heralded by the obscurely confessional *Never Too Late,* adjusted the promised proportions of profit and pleasure by adopting a new, chastened epigraph, "sero sed serio" ("late but in earnest"). Greene employed an even more austere-sounding epigraph, "nascimur pro patria" ("we are born for our country"), when he moved on to "cony-catching pamphlets," exposés of the shysters and swindlers of London, in 1591. But since Greene's nominal allegiance was always to truth and true love against "fancy," since the amorous elements of Greene's "farewells to love" have a great deal in common with those of his earlier fictions, and since fictional reworking of borrowed material is not lacking in Greene's cony-catching pamphlets, it would seem that the difference between the three modes may be largely a matter of making sensational content appeal more and more readily to a sensible middle-class readership. In his "farewells to love," Greene overtly abandoned the leisurely study of alternative systems of value that we find in more courtly romances such as *Menaphon*; the rejection of "fancy" in all forms is nominally a foregone conclusion. But even here, as in Greene's conycatching pamphlets, vicarious indulgence in formally censured behavior may be made all the easier for middle-class readers simply by amplifying the censures themselves (see Greene's own remarks to this effect in *Greenes Vision*); it may be less a question of dispensing with fancy or guile altogether than of finding a way to give each of them play safely distanced from working reality. Certainly, as both Merritt Lawlis and Crupi have pointed out, one of the voices dominating the

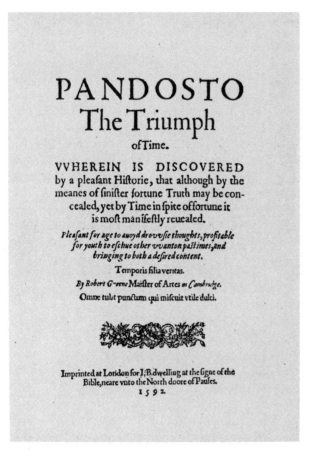

PANDOSTO
The Triumph
of Time.

VVHEREIN IS DISCOVERED
by a pleasant Historie, that although by the
meanes of sinister fortune Truth may be concealed, yet by Time in spite of fortune it
is most manifestly reuealed.

*Pleasant for age to auoyd drowsie thoughts, profitable
for youth to eschue other wanton pastimes, and
bringing to both a desired content.*

Temporis filia veritas.

By Robert Greene Maister of Artes in Cambridge.

Omne tulit punctum qui miscuit vtile dulci.

Imprinted at London for I; B. dwelling at the signe of the
Bible, neare vnto the North doore of Paules.
1592

*Title page for the unique copy of the 1592 quarto edition of
the 1588 prose romance that was the chief source for
Shakespeare's* The Winter's Tale *(Folger
Shakespeare Library)*

cony-catching pamphlets is a voice with a tone of
sly pleasure at the tricksters' success in defraud-
ing their middle-class victims. Whether by
Greene or not, the confessional pamphlets
Greenes Groats-Worth of Witte and *The Repentance of
Robert Greene* combine the two buffer devices deployed in the two earlier series of pamphlets, on
the one hand profuse deprecation of precisely
the sort of material Greene goes on to give us,
on the other, profuse exhortations to profit from
Greene's own risky firsthand experience, or in
other words, at his expense.

With no comparable role for an author-
persona to play in a drama, it is none too surprising that Greene's name appears on his dramas
with no motto at all or the Horatian motto of his
earlier pamphlets (which *The Scottish History of
James IV* shortens and *Friar Bacon and Friar
Bungay* gives in full: "omne tulit punctum qui
miscuit utile dulci"). Though the dramas stand
closest to his earlier pamphlets in substance, as
well, it would certainly be a mistake to take either

of these genre-linked features as a reason for dating all five dramas before 1590, as more than a
few scholars have done.

Like the other university wits, Greene took
little care to let the world know just which dramas he wrote; in fact, he generally speaks of vernacular drama per se with resounding contempt.
Greene's indifference to his own theatrical output helps account for the meagerness of the modern Greene canon; though as many as forty plays
have been claimed for the poet at one time or another, modern scholars agree on assigning him
only these few: *Alphonsus, King of Aragon; The History of Orlando Furioso; Friar Bacon and Friar
Bungay; The Scottish History of James IV*; and *A
Looking-Glass for London and England*, written with
Thomas Lodge. All these plays were first published after Greene's death, and just one, *The History of Orlando Furioso*, was linked with Greene's
name in his lifetime. The order in which they
were written is largely conjectural, and only the
last three were definitely ascribed to Greene in
the early editions. It is important to realize how
tenuous the basis for this canon is before we try
to study Greene's dramas alongside the rest of
his works or before we discount other plays with
some claim to be added to this list. Indeed, scholars might be better advised to consider such
plays in relation to a "period canon," a body of dramas all shaped in suggestively similar ways by the
tastes and capacities of their period, than in
terms of one ill-documented dramatic "career" or
conjectural stylistic development.

The chief reason for assigning *Alphonsus,
King of Aragon* to Greene is the title-page ascription to "R. G." Though these letters were probably chosen to suggest that the author was
Greene, such suggestions are often misleading
(compare the coy use of "W. S." to imply that William Shakespeare was the author of a play such
as *Locrine*). Once "R. G." was identified with
Greene, one could link the *Alphonsus* with a dis-
gruntled reference to Marlowe's theatrical bombast in Greene's *Perimedes* (1588); since *Alphonsus*
is clearly a crude imitation of *Tamburlaine* (produced circa 1587), one can take the unflattering
reference to Marlowe in Greene's *Perimedes* as an
oblique response to the failure of Greene's own attempts in an even more bombastic vein. If we assume that *Greenes Groats-Worth of Witte* is Greene's
work, we will find a clear parallel for Greene's
blustering dismissal of Marlowe in his famous, or
infamous, comments on Shakespeare or "Shake-
scene": perhaps Greene had a natural bent for dis-

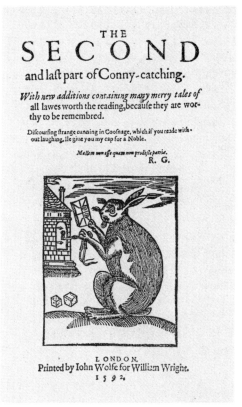

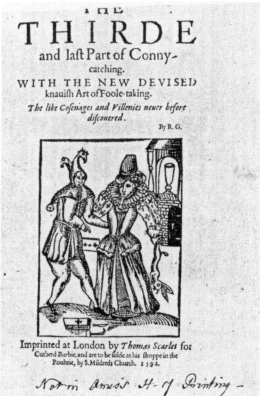

Title pages for 1591 and 1592 quarto editions of four of Greene's "cony-catching" pamphlets (top left [unique copy]: British Library; top right: Anderson Galleries, sale number 2077, 20-21 May 1926; bottom left [unique copy, Mal 575(3)] and bottom right: Bodleian Library, Oxford)

paraging talents that he could not emulate. Irving Ribner notes that already in *Alphonsus* Greene rejects Tamburlaine's mode of inexorable self-glorification for something much closer to faith in traditional noble prerogatives; it turns out that Alphonsus the lowly outsider is actually legitimate heir to one throne, and he ends his pursuit of another, his last, on being given the king's daughter in marriage. Certainly it would be hard to call *Tamburlaine* a "comicall historie," as the title page for the 1599 quarto describes *Alphonsus*, nor could even a bellicose Venus preside over Tamburlaine's exploits as she does over those of Alphonsus; but the very ineptness of the borrowings from Marlowe in this play makes it seem somewhat likelier that Greene simply bungled the job of adapting Marlowe's own "mighty line" to Alphonsus, as Una Ellis-Fermor has argued. The Alphonsus of this play has virtually no basis in fact, though the fairly renowned king Alphonsus of Naples did furnish a meager historical pretext by lending his name to Greene's hero. *Alphonsus* is Greene's first experiment in dramatic quasi-history, a mode that he never abandoned.

The ascription of *The History of Orlando Furioso* to Greene is a bit more secure: it is credited to Greene in his lifetime in a work which purportedly answers a pamphlet by Greene but which may actually be Greene's own sequel. In *The Defence of Conny-Catching* (1592), published under the pseudonym "Cuthbert Cony-Catcher," Greene is charged with selling the *Orlando Furioso* to two different theatrical companies and then challenged to distinguish his own double-dealing from "cony-catching"; Greene's response to this charge is not extant. Ellis-Fermor accounts for the play as Greene's effort to distance himself from Marlovian bombast through parody; this would "place" the *Orlando* just after the *Alphonsus* of 1588, as would what seems to be an allusion to the Spanish Armada, which sailed that same year. Unfortunately for this theory, the play survives only in a bad quarto and in a fragmentary actor's copy of Orlando's part, neither text offering any firm basis for judging how much of the bombast is Greene's and how much is pure muddle; it is thus hard to make a strong case for deliberate parody. Apart from the garbled Marlovian echoes, the play involves thorough recasting of Ariosto's *Orlando Furioso,* which it in fact cites in Italian: whereas Ariosto's Orlando goes mad after learning that his lady Angelica has actually eloped with another man, Greene's Orlando goes mad out of culpable jealousy after one of the lady's spurned suitors, the ambitious, unchivalrous Sacripant, slanders her to Orlando from sheer spite. Sacripant's language may or may not be a deliberate parody of Tamburlaine's. But as Crupi suggests, the surviving text offers far more cogent grounds for perceiving the politic Sacripant as an ironic foil to the amorous Orlando, or Orlando insane as a foil to Orlando triumphant. Something similar appears in chivalric accounts of the madness of Lancelot, where it constitutes not so much mockery of high-style romance as a test of its standards by means of inversion. It seems safest to stress that by making Angelica just another wronged heroine, Greene actually weakens the challenge to such standards which is posed by his source, Ariosto's *Orlando.*

Friar Bacon and Friar Bungay makes far more adroit use of the same subtle method of orientation by ironic doubling to be found in a play such as *Orlando Furioso. Friar Bacon and Friar Bungay* is generally assigned to the year 1589 on the strength of a casual reference in act one to "next Friday [. . .] St. James' [Day]," since St. James's Day actually fell on a Friday in 1589; in its fairly insistent patriotism it may also reflect English national sentiment not long after the defeat of the Spanish Armada in 1588. Though the language of *Friar Bacon and Friar Bungay* is a great deal more supple and fluent than that of *Orlando Furioso,* the difference may well be in large part a matter of textual transmission: the existing text of *Friar Bacon and Friar Bungay* is apparently based on a theatrical fair copy with generous stage directions, already a carefully "edited" text, but including a few casual notes about staging which may well go back to the author. The play's dating is also affected by its possible links with two other dramas. Critics often assume some connection between Greene's magicians and Marlowe's, though with Marlowe's *Doctor Faustus* now generally dated 1592 it seems likelier that Marlowe, if anyone, was the borrower for better or worse this time. Further, Greene blasts a play called *Fair Em* in the preface to *Greenes Farewell to Folly* (1591). Since that play's title-character bears a certain resemblance to Greene's Margaret in *Friar Bacon and Friar Bungay,* critics reason that Greene is attacking an unauthorized imitation, though of course he could also be trying to forestall any reference to his own indebtedness. According to Henslowe's diary, *Friar Bacon and Friar Bungay* was performed at least seven times by Lord Strange's Men between February 1592 and January 1593. The title page of the 1594 first edi-

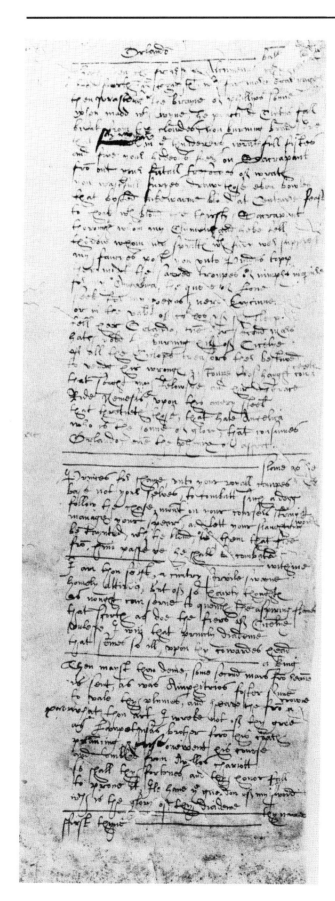

A portion of the actor's part for the title role in Orlando Furioso *that is preserved at Dulwich College. This manuscript is in the hand of a scribe with additions and corrections by Edward Alleyn, who may have used it when he acted in a 1591 performance of the play (MS I, item 138, fol. 267, strip 11; by permission of Dulwich College).*

tion alludes to additional performances by the Queen's Men, also mentioned as joint performances with Sussex's Men in Henslowe's diary entries for April 1594.

The play's principal source is a prose "famous history" of Friar Bacon, the oldest surviving edition of which dates from 1627. Roger Bacon and Thomas Bungay were renowned scholars and mathematicians who both worked in Oxford in the late thirteenth century; otherwise, both the "history" and the play are based almost entirely on popular legend. Once again, Greene's reworkings are striking: he condenses Friar Bacon's legendary career as a magician into one crucial sequence of incidents, elaborates one detachable incident from his source into virtually a parallel romantic plot, inverts Friar Bacon's role from the "history" as a friend of true love so that his magic works to oppose it, and in general gives Bacon's "science" so pervasive an air of unnatural black magic that only its outright rejection can possibly save him. William Empson applauded the way Greene connects his two plots by analogy: beauty is to the romantic plot as magic is to the rest of Bacon's exploits. Indeed, beauty thwarts Bacon's magic in one just as Bacon's own magic overreaches itself in the other. The link with Greene's favorite themes becomes clearer when we note that Bacon's magic promotes the young Prince Edward's lust for the "Fair Maid of Fressingfield," Margaret, while her beauty secures her not only Prince Edward's misguided attentions but also a noble and honorable suitor in the person of Edward's agent, Lacy. The two forces of magic and beauty are linked and opposed in the same way as "fancy" and "true love" in Greene's earlier works, with the difference that here the true love is a transfiguring power in its own right. This may help to explain the gratuitous "test" to which Lacy subjects Margaret's constancy by pretending to break their engagement: her show of Griselda-like patience helps to strengthen the link between her ideal love and transfiguring grace. Like Mamillia in Greene's earliest pamphlet, the "Fair Maid" is not just an abstraction and not just a living everyday type: though her speech is too lofty for a gamekeeper's daughter, it is also too lusty and matter-of-fact for a factitious saint. Though she plans to take vows as a nun after Lacy's pretended rejection, she can also protest, half in earnest, that her frailty condemns her to conjugal bliss, to a stock-comic fleshly reward, in almost the same way that the fleshly shortcomings of Bacon's assistant force his master into mortification and thus ultimate comic redemption. Although Margaret is no Isabella, this play does present us with problems of closure not unlike the ones which we encounter in *Measure for Measure* and the other Shakespearean "problem plays"; but to the extent that Margaret's marriage can be viewed as a token of genuine reintegration, as a triumph of amorous vision and not just as a pardonable lapse, *Friar Bacon and Friar Bungay* comprises a cautious apology for self-chastened poetic vision as well as a clear cautionary exemplum against its demonic abuses.

The Scottish History of James IV is in some ways the most carefully structured of Greene's plays but also his most irresponsible essay in pseudohistorical whimsy, assuming, of course, that the title it now bears is his. Since the extant allusions to the drama all postdate Greene's death, we may never be sure that the title is his, just as no one is sure when he actually wrote it (the ambitious structure suggests a late date, perhaps 1592). As the title page states, James IV, who was married to Henry VIII's sister, died in battle at Flodden in 1513, at the height of his quarrel with England. If purported to be about this Scottish king (whom the text never mentions by name), then the play in effect turns this famous result of the Scottish king's quarrel on its head, reassigning the marriage and quarrel to "the year 1520" in the process. It may be that the theme of the compromised marriage-alliance was all that the author—or editor—needed to justify linking the play to James IV. Otherwise, the play's intemperate hero may have more in common with hostile perceptions of James VI of Scotland, or of Richard II or III, or perhaps even Henry VIII of England. Greene's main source was in fact an Italian novella from Giraldi Cinthio's *Hecatommithi*, a source he probably read in a 1583 French translation; and once more, Greene's departures are telling. In its overall development, Greene's main plot has a definite affinity with such native morality dramas as John Skelton's *Magnificence*, though the wronged woman cast as redeemer in this tragicomedy has a quite different fictional lineage reaching back to the heroines of fairy tales and continuing through the novellas to dramas such as *All's Well that Ends Well*. Specific departures from Cinthio's version of the story are few but substantial: Greene's king, unlike Cinthio's, is already intent on enjoying another woman when he marries the neighboring king's daughter; Greene's wronged queen, Dorothea, displays a

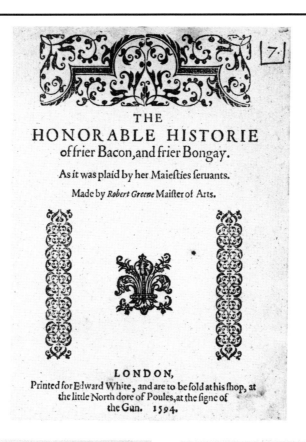

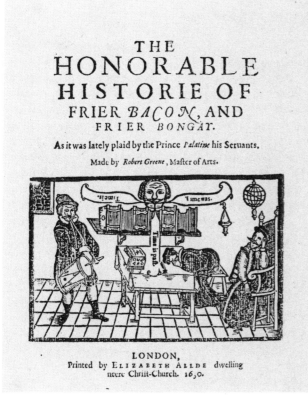

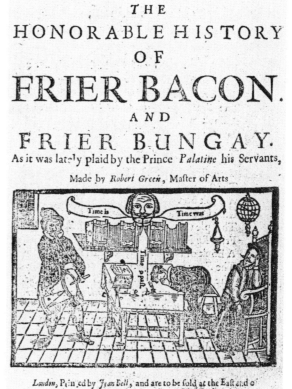

Title pages for the first three quarto editions of the popular play that Greene based on legends surrounding the careers of the renowned scholar-mathematicians Roger Bacon and Thomas Bungay (top: Henry E. Huntington Library and Art Gallery; bottom left: Bodleian Library, Oxford; bottom right: Victoria and Albert Museum)

more passive, Griselda-like fortitude than her model in Cinthio's narrative; Greene's disguised Dorothea, again unlike her model in Cinthio, actually rouses another woman's passion before she can drop her disguise; finally, Greene's king is exploited and egged on in his passion by a stock "evil counsellor," Ateukin, much more like a morality vice or the venal Chief Justice Tresilian in the anonymous drama *Woodstock* than like any of the characters in Cinthio (for further discussion of such points, see Sanders's edition of *The Scottish History of James IV*).

Greene's most radical departure from structural precedent will require a more detailed analysis. Tragicomedy of a more or less regular, normative sort here unfolds in a strange and ambiguous frame. We begin with a choric "induction" presenting the play as a scene from the past, an embittered recluse's exemplum (performed for the "King of the Fairies") against life at court; the recluse's sons start by enacting the scene from the past, then get thoroughly enmeshed in the same scene construed as a segment of present reality, to the point that the King of the Fairies himself must save one of the sons from a well-deserved hanging. The main action, the "history" proper, interwoven with choric exchanges and comic diversions, consists of the following incidents: a weak king decides to reject his state bride, Dorothea, and to woo the unspoiled maiden Ida, who spurns his advances and leaves court. The king then succumbs to the wicked advice of the schemer Ateukin and sends someone to kill Dorothea so that he will be free to wed Ida. Meanwhile, she weds her true love, Eustace, far from court. In the meantime Ateukin has hired the recluse's two sons as his servants and has casually given one of them ("Nano" or "Dwarf") to the queen; he stays with her through all her adversities, while his brother, named "Slipper," stays at court, collects bribes, and plays lackey and clown to Ateukin. The queen, finally convinced that her husband is trying to kill her, is wounded while fleeing disguised as a man and arouses the passion of her rescuer's wife, Lady Anderson, before laying aside her denaturing symbolic disguise. Meanwhile, Scotland is thrown into turmoil by England's invasion to punish its king. When Ateukin is told of the marriage of Eustace and Ida, he flees in disgrace. The repentant Scots king condemns him and his followers to death, and the queen intervenes to restore peace between the two kingdoms. The recluse and the

King of the Fairies appear to have quite different notions of how to respond to the play, the recluse melancholy, the King of the Fairies full of mirth, but they seem to agree that the play demonstrates the prevailing injustice of most worldly courts; yet precisely here, in the recluse's supposedly true-life exemplum of courtly injustice, a commonplace poetic justice quite clearly prevails. Greene appears to be experimenting cleverly but not very consistently with the various modes of comic containment or neutralization of potentially tragic material which Shakespeare was soon to exploit with much greater finesse in *A Midsummer Night's Dream*; if he did have Greene's games of containment in mind, this is one more example of how Shakespeare enhanced his own gifts by refining his precursors' virtues.

Greene's one known collaboration was with Thomas Lodge, on *A Looking-Glass for London and England*; though it cannot be dated precisely, Lodge's movements restrict the most probable date to not later than mid 1591. Attribution of various sections is highly conjectural, though most critics assign Greene the biblical action and Lodge the burlesque usurer subplot. The plot is a simple two-level development of the biblical story of Nineveh's sin and repentance. The usurer subplot helps to stress the pervasive analogy between Nineveh and present-day London. The play is worth noting, at least, for two reasons: it fuses historical drama, this time sacred historical drama, with the modified prodigal-son plot Greene found in the native morality (compare *The Scottish History of James IV*); and it once more incorporates a highly developed choric structure (the preachings of "Oseas") which seems rather redundant in the presence of an internal "chorus," namely Jonah. Both these characteristics connect the play closely with Greene, who may well have devised the whole plot by himself and assigned Lodge long segments of dialogue.

Greene's five dramas have more common features than mere summaries of each might suggest. All have something of the loosely processional structure found in earlier popular drama, though Greene seems to be trying for a tighter five-act structure in *The Scottish History of James IV*. All his dramas apart from *Alphonsus* owe much to the common morality structure in which some externalized evil genius or "vice" leads a not altogether degenerate protagonist astray, and the same plays amalgamate this simple morality pattern of sin and repentance with a crude "providential" recasting of what one might well label

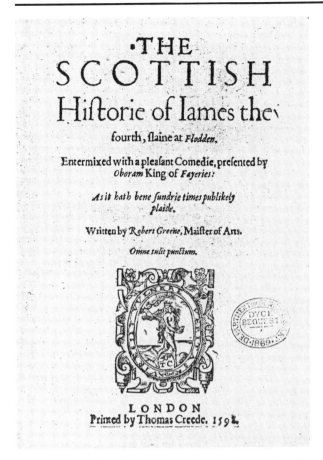

·THE·
SCOTTISH
Hiſtorie of Iames the
fourth, ſlaine at *Flodden*.

Entermixed with a pleaſant Comedie, preſented by
Oboram King of *Fayeries*:

As it hath bene ſundrie times publikely
plaide.

Written by *Robert Greene*, Maiſter of Arts.

Omne tulit punctum.

LONDON
Printed by Thomas Creede. 1598,

Title page for the 1598 quarto edition of the play that, despite its title, is not based on the life of James IV of Scotland (Victoria and Albert Museum)

"folk history." Corresponding to these outward representations of vice are the counterproductive assistants and clowns who externalize other, less grave, fleshly failings in plays like *Friar Bacon and Friar Bungay* and who people the subplots devoted to what some call the "comedy of evil." We have already spoken of Greene's many wronged heroines in connection with his prodigal heroes; suffice it to note that both character types invite quite different kinds of imaginative involvement, with the sufferer or with her triumphantly heedless oppressor, and that if these wronged heroines stand for undervalued *maternal* perfections, then Greene's heroes are bound to reject on one level what they are bound to regret rejecting on another. As a foil to these intricate Oedipal traceries Greene develops a number of strong, stable relationships between mother and daughter, even father and daughter, or father and son. The "bad father" of Oedipal fantasy seems to be more at home in Greene's pamphlets. Finally, Sanders notes the prevalence in Greene of disfiguring disguise, masks which hide the true self without offer-

ing any new scope for extending the self, as the state of disguise often does in the comedies of Shakespeare; this may be the most telling and crucial expression of Greene's own prevailing mistrust of all fancy and "feigning."

Several of the same features link Greene's plays just as closely to other plays written in the same period; since the canon of Greene's known plays is small while the corpus of plays from Greene's period is really quite large, it would probably be more worthwhile to begin by assembling a "period canon" of plays in the various modes than to go on attempting to sort out the disputed and unascribed dramas among the known dramatists on the basis of what may turn out to be quite commonplace modal links. Still, at least four such dubious plays have such promising links with Greene's name and known works that their status seems little more dubious than that of *Alphonsus*. The first of them, *Selimus* (published 1594), is in fact a good deal like *Alphonsus*, another bloody bombastic pastiche which, if his, would do Greene little credit; but six passages from *Selimus* are assigned to Greene in an anthology of 1600, perhaps no less reliably than *Alphonsus* is credited to "R. G." In its second issue (1638), *Selimus* was assigned to "T. G.," usually taken to mean "Thomas Goffe"; but it might be that Greene by that time was confused with another Greene, Thomas, who had handled a number of plays in almost the same period. Connected with *Selimus* is another quasi-history, this time British, not Turkish, *Locrine* (published in 1595, and ascribed to "W. S."): the two plays share a number of passages, enough that they may well be in large part the work of one author (see also the separate entry on *Locrine* and *Selimus*). Though *Locrine* is another bombastic pastiche, its low comedy is crude but ingenious; the whole play ranks at least with *Alphonsus*. Then we come to two plays which might even enhance Greene's achievement: *George a Greene, The Pinner of Wakefield* (published 1599), and *John of Bordeaux, or The Second Part of Friar Bacon*, surviving only in an imperfect manuscript. On one copy of *George a Greene*, a manuscript note probably written by some early drama enthusiast reads: "Ed. Juby saith that the play was made by R. Gree." This note seems to be meant as an answer to another note stating implausibly, on Shakespeare's authority, that the play was the work of a minister. Edward Juby, an actor and playwright who flourished around 1600, would make a good source if the note were undoubtedly authentic, but it actually may have been altered or forged by its finder, the shady Shakespearean J. Payne Collier. The play itself is a lusty processional quasi-history fairly close in most other respects to *Friar Bacon and Friar Bungay* and *The Scottish History of James IV* but distinctive for its generous use of creative disguise. *John of Bordeaux* is not only a competent sequel to *Friar Bacon;* it also includes an ingenious low-comic burlesque of the conjurer's exploits and perhaps the most moving wronged-heroine plot in Greene's works, one in which the wronged heroine's hardships gain meaning and substance as a practical lesson in empathy for all the oppressed. Whether by Greene or not, both these plays merit closer attention than unascribed plays generally get.

Not surprisingly, Greene's reputation has generally rested much more on his pamphlets than on his small canon of known plays; even this meager canon has yet to appear as a group in a scholarly modern edition. On the other hand, his fictional pamphlets prompted many imitations and sequels and continued to be read and reprinted well into the eighteenth century, while his possibly spurious confessional pamphlets fixed his character in the minds of most critics for centuries to come. He has suffered by being associated with the infamous "Shakescene" remark in *Greenes Groats-Worth of Witte*, as if no truly talented playwright could find fault with a talent like Shakespeare's; it took Norman Sanders to note that the genius of Greene's plays and Shakespearean comedy is in many ways one and the same. Greene's shortcomings as a dramatist may be less a reflection of any lack of talent, or even any lack of maturity, than a token of his basic lack of respect for the medium of drama itself; what Greene left incoherent, almost as a sign of contempt for his easily duped audience, his greater successor would tighten, or vary, or deliberately call into question as a way of enhancing the sort of communal awareness that drama uniquely promotes. Greene was probably more comfortable with the cooler, less sensuous, less provocative medium of print: in Greene's own view, perhaps only preachers could make demonstrations in public unless from the most dubious motives, the motives which dominate in Greene's own urban gallery of shysters. Even though all Greene's plays could be taken as dramas of comic redemption, in the firmly attributed plays make believe or role playing and genuine conversion remain mutually exclusive experiences, antithetical movements of error and anxious return, never

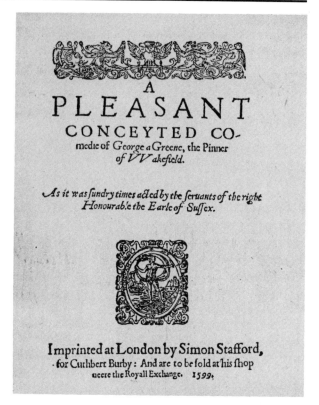

Title page for the 1599 quarto edition of one of the plays that has been conjecturally attributed to Greene (Anderson Galleries, sale number 1375, 2-3 December 1918)

part of the ritual continuum which informs the great comedies of Shakespeare.

Bibliographies:

A. F. Allison, *Robert Greene 1558-1592: A Bibliographical Catalogue of the Early Editions in English (to 1640)* (Folkestone, U.K.: Dawson, 1975);

James Seay Dean, *Robert Greene: A Reference Guide* (Boston: G. K. Hall, 1984).

References:

Eckhard Auberlen, *The Commonwealth of Wit: The Writer's Image and his Strategies of Self-Representation in Elizabethan Literature* (Tübingen: G. Narr, 1984), pp. 157-177;

Norbert Bolz, "Are Robert Greene's 'Autobiographies' Fakes?: The Forgery of *The Repentance of Robert Greene,*" *Shakespeare Newsletter,* 29 (December 1979): 43;

A. R. Braunmuller, "The Serious Comedy of Greene's *James IV,*" *English Literary Renaissance,* 3 (Autumn 1973): 335-350;

Michael D. Bristol, Discussion of *Locrine,* in his *Carnival and Theater* (London & New York: Methuen, 1985), pp. 143-150, 180-182;

Sandra Clark, *The Elizabethan Pamphleteers: Popular Moralistic Pamphlets 1580-1640* (Rutherford, Madison & Teaneck: Fairleigh Dickinson University Press, 1983);

Wolfgang Clemen, *English Tragedy before Shakespeare: The Development of Dramatic Speech,* translated by T. S. Dorsch (London: Methuen, 1961), pp. 178-191;

Charles W. Crupi, *Robert Greene* (Boston: Twayne, 1986);

Walter R. Davis, *Idea and Act in Elizabethan Fiction* (Princeton: Princeton University Press, 1969);

Paul Dean, "Shakespeare's Henry VI Trilogy and Elizabethan 'Romance' Histories: The Origins of a Genre," *Shakespeare Quarterly,* 33 (Spring 1982): 34-48;

Una Ellis-Fermor, "Marlowe and Greene: A Note on their Relation as Dramatic Artists," in *Studies in Honor of T. W. Baldwin,* edited by D. C. Allen (Urbana: University of Illinois, 1958), pp. 136-149;

William Empson, *Some Versions of Pastoral* (Norfolk, Conn.: New Directions, 1960), pp. 31-34;

Richard Helgerson, *The Elizabethan Prodigals* (Berkeley: University of California Press, 1976), pp. 79-104;

Jaroslav Hornat, "*Mamillia:* Robert Greene's Controversy with *Euphues,*" *Philologica Pragensia,* 5, no. 4 (1962): 210-218;

John C. Jordan, *Robert Greene* (New York: Columbia University Press, 1915);

Dean B. Lyman, "Apocryphal Plays of the University Wits," *English Studies in Honor of James Southall Wilson,* edited by F. Bowers (Charlottesville: University Press of Virginia, 1951), pp. 211-221;

David Margolies, *Novel and Society in Elizabethan England* (London & Sydney: Croom & Helm, 1985), pp. 105-143;

Kenneth Muir, "Robert Greene as Dramatist," in *Essays on Shakespeare and Elizabethan Drama in Honor of Hardin Craig,* edited by R. Hosley (Columbia: University of Missouri Press, 1962), pp. 45-54;

William Nestrick, "Robert Greene," in *The Predecessors of Shakespeare,* edited by T. P. Logan and D. S. Smith (Lincoln: University of Nebraska Press, 1973), pp. 56-92;

Rene Pruvost, *Robert Greene et ses romans (1558-1592)* (Paris: Société d'édition les belles lettres, 1938);

Irving Ribner, "Greene's Attack on Marlowe: Some Light on *Alphonsus* and *Selimus,*" *Studies in Philology,* 52 (April 1955): 162-171;

Brenda Richardson, "Robert Greene's Yorkshire Connexions: A New Hypothesis," *Yearbook of English Studies,* 10 (1980): 160-180;

Paul Salzman, *English Prose Fiction 1558-1700: A Critical History* (Oxford: Clarendon Press, 1985);

Norman Sanders, "The Comedy of Greene and Shakespeare," in *Early Shakespeare,* edited by J. R. Brown and B. Harris, Stratford-upon-Avon Studies, 3 (London: Arnold, 1961), pp. 35-53;

S. Schoenbaum, *Internal Evidence and Elizabethan Dramatic Authorship: An Essay in Literary History and Method* (Evanston: Northwestern University Press, 1966);

Werner Senn, "Robert Greene's Handling of Source Material in *Friar Bacon and Friar Bungay,*" *English Studies,* 54 (December 1973): 544-553;

Senn, *Studies in the Dramatic Construction of Robert Greene and George Peele,* Swiss Studies in English, volume 74 (Bern: Francke Verlag, 1973);

Barbara H. Traister, *Heavenly Necromancers: The Magician in English Renaissance Drama* (Columbia: University of Missouri Press, 1984), pp. 67-87.

Papers:

An incomplete copy of the speeches and cues for the title role in *Orlando Furioso* is at Dulwich College (MS I.138). This manuscript is in the hand of a scribe with additions and corrections by Edward Alleyn, who may have used it for a 1591 performance of the play.

Fulke Greville, First Lord Brooke

(3 October 1554-30 September 1628)

Charles Larson

University of Missouri at St. Louis

BOOKS: *The Tragedy of Mustapha* (London: Printed by J. Windet for N. Butter, 1609);

Certaine Learned and Elegant Workes (London: Printed by E. Purslowe for H. Seyle, 1633)–comprises *A Treatise of Humane Learning, An Inquisition upon Fame and Honour, A Treatise of Wars, Alaham, Mustapha, Cælica, Letter to an Honorable Lady, A Letter of Travel;*

The Life of the Renowned Sr Philip Sydney (London: Printed for Henry Seile, 1652);

The Remains of Sir Fvlk Grevill Lord Brooke: Being Poems of Monarchy and Religion: Never Before Printed (London: Printed by T. N. for H. Herringman, 1670)–comprises *A Treatise of Monarchy* and *A Treatise of Religion.*

Edition: *Poems and Dramas of Fulke Greville, First Lord Brooke*, 2 volumes, edited by Geoffrey Bullough (Edinburgh: Oliver & Boyd, 1939; New York: Oxford University Press, 1945)–comprises *Cælica, A Treatise of Humane Learning, An Inquisition upon Fame and Honour, A Treatise of Warres, Mustapha, Alaham.*

Although Fulke Greville's literary reputation rests principally upon the lyric poetry in his sonnet cycle *Cælica*, he was an unsettled experimenter in all of the genres available to a gentleman Renaissance author, including the drama. He is known to have written three plays–*Alaham, Mustapha,* and *Antony and Cleopatra*–none of which were produced and only the first two of which are extant, the manuscript of *Antony and Cleopatra* having been destroyed by Greville himself. The reasons for this act of artistic annihilation were pragmatic and political; for a courtier who was ambitious to rise through the ranks of his monarch's government, the sacrifice of a piece of writing that might retard that advance was a small price to pay.

Greville had been born with a sense of his own worth. The scion of a wealthy Warwickshire land-owning family (son of Sir Fulke Greville, *de jure* Lord Willoughby de Broke, and his wife Anne Neville), he had apparently determined at

an early age that his life would be spent in the service of his nation, rather than on his familial estate. A boyhood friend of Philip Sidney, he came to Elizabeth's court with Sidney in the mid 1570s, shortly after a three- or four-year stint at Jesus College, Cambridge, which he appears to have left without a degree. Both he and Sidney associated themselves with the radical Protestant faction of the court, and, although favorable recognition came slowly for anyone holding an extreme position (given Elizabeth's centrist penchant for compromise), he began making his way upward on the often-treacherous slopes of governmental power.

After the shock of Sidney's death in 1586, he hitched his wagon to the rising star of Robert Devereux, the Earl of Essex, Sidney's political heir and an increasing favorite of Elizabeth. It was as a friend of Essex that Greville at last achieved in 1598 a major office, that of the treasurer of the navy, and it was surely as a friend of Essex that Greville must have thought he had reached his political demise in 1601, when Essex revolted and was executed for treason. Oddly, however, Elizabeth continued to favor Greville, and his real political setback did not come until the first decade of the reign of James I. Then, because of the enmity of his old opponent Robert Cecil, a man close to the King, Greville was forced to relinquish office and retreat to Warwickshire.

When Cecil died in 1612, Greville moved with alacrity and evident skill to reestablish himself at court. Displaying as much adroitness as ever, he had arranged by 1614 to have himself named chancellor and under-treasurer of the Exchequer and privy councillor. He remained in power until his elevation to the peerage as Baron Brooke in 1621. This action seems to have been James's maneuver to ease an aging statesman out of a position of authority, although Greville stayed in London and in at least titular offices for seven more years, until he was fatally stabbed by a servant who felt himself to have been

Portrait by an unknown artist (by permission of Lord Willoughby de Broke)

slighted in Greville's recently drawn will. Never married and childless, Greville was buried in a tomb whose inscription he had written himself: "Fulke Greville, Servant to Queen Elizabeth, Councillor to King James, and Friend to Sir Philip Sidney, Trophaeum Peccati." That, after three distinctions of which he or any man could be deservedly proud, he should still choose to label himself a "trophy of sin" says much about his perception of the ultimate value of his life. It is with this astringent self-depreciation in mind that his highly political plays can most properly be read.

There is more of his Calvinistic contempt for the world reflected in his epitaph and in his literary production than there is in his career as a courtier and in his paradoxical concern for his own political fortunes. What *Antony and Cleopatra* had said about the difficulties and the follies of national leaders can only be speculated, but Greville seems to have decided shortly after Essex's failed rebellion of 1601 that it had to be destroyed. He must have felt that it was politically imprudent to preserve a play that presented a man's reckless passion for a female monarch, or so he suggested around 1610 in an autobiographical passage in the *Life of Sir Philip Sidney:* "many members in that creature [*Antony and Cleopatra*] (by the opinion of those few eyes, which saw it) having some childish wantonnesse in them, apt enough to be construed, or strained to a personating of vices in the present Governors, and government."

Having burned the play in 1601 or 1602, he never returned to the dramatic form, except to revise what he had already written. He was an habitual reviser of his work, a fact that makes the dating of any of his writings a problematic venture. Still, it is most likely that he wrote all three of his plays in the five-year period between 1595 and 1600. There is no certitude on the order of composition, although *Mustapha* (which exists in three somewhat different versions) may be first, followed by *Alaham* and then *Antony and Cleopatra*. Always the gentleman amateur, Greville never permitted any of his writings to be published while he was alive, and it was probably a considerable annoyance to him when an unauthorized printing of *Mustapha* appeared in 1609. His was not a drama written for the popular theater, and, indeed, he claimed in the *Life of Sidney* never to have had any intention of having his plays staged under any circumstances: "I have made these Tragedies, no Plaies for the Stage. . . . But he that will behold these Acts upon their true Stage, let him look on that Stage wherein himself is an Actor, even the state he lives in, and for every part he may perchance find a Player, and for every Line (it may be) an instance of life." This is one of the most explicit statements extant on the theory of Elizabethan closet drama, and it is important to put a positive face on it: Greville most certainly does approve of drama as a literary form. Staged plays might be merely entertainment and thus the fit recipients of the attacks that the Puritans were waging against the theater at that moment, but the drama as a literary text engages the mind seriously and leads to important discoveries about the nature of life.

Greville's interest in drama had come about as a result of his contact with a circle of closet-drama writers under the aegis of the Countess of Pembroke, Mary Sidney. The sister of his dead friend had translated a French play in 1592, and in the years that followed she was joined in translation or original composition by Samuel Daniel, Samuel Brandon, William Alexander, Thomas Kyd (the only one of the group to have an interest in the popular theater), and, of course, Grev-

ille. All of these playwrights were intent on bringing into English the spirit and the form of Senecan tragedy. Rome's greatest tragedian had already had a marked influence on Continental drama, and now the countess's circle was attempting to refine English drama according to his example. The attempt was probably futile from the start, for native English theater already was vigorously charting a different course for itself and was little inclined to pay much heed to a drama that insisted on the advancement of plot by means of long declamatory speeches and on obedience to conventions such as the use of a nuntius (messenger) to report undramatized violence.

Greville's fellow English Senecans had all taken material from Roman history and had made plays from it that emphasized political ideology rather than nonpolitical personal dramatic conflict. The motif of Roman politics may have predominated in *Antony and Cleopatra*, but *Alaham* and *Mustapha* set Greville apart from the others. The plots of both plays are non-Roman and are concerned with modern historical figures, although it must also be said that their Oriental exoticism probably serves to distance them from the reader to at least the degree that would a setting from the temporally remote but politically familiar Roman past.

Although *Alaham* was probably composed in about 1599, after the first version of *Mustapha* (which Greville wrote circa 1595), it definitely precedes the revised version of that play, and it manifests certain practices in organization, theme, and style that Greville was to bring to a higher state of perfection when he returned to rework *Mustapha* around 1608. Greville had found the story of Alaham, the sultan of the Arab kingdom of Ormus, in an early-sixteenth-century Italian travel narrative by Ludovico di Varthema. The story tells of Alaham's bloody climb to the throne, including the murder of his doddering father who was the rightful (if ineffectual) monarch. In this narrative of an ambitious and usurping son, Greville must have recognized that central Elizabethan theme of the overreacher. One can imagine Christopher Marlowe finding the story similarly attractive, and although *Tamburlaine* (produced circa 1587) was written in a different dramatic tradition, Marlowe's "Scourge of God" is a kindred spirit of Greville's protagonist. Both conquerors are frequently seized by fits of bombast, apparently believing that their capacity to impose their will on others is directly connected to their capacity to describe their desires in the most hyperbolic of ranting.

In the character of Alaham we are given what is potentially one of the most stirring dramatic spectacles: a man who, like Milton's Satan, deliberately chooses evil as his good and who is willing to deal with whatever consequences his choice might bring. The subject is probably too grandiose for the play, but if Greville fails to develop the concept with adequate dramatic plausibility, it may be because the emotions inherent in such a plot cannot be convincingly expressed by anyone but a superhuman epic creature.

Alaham is contrapuntally seconded in melodramatic treachery by his wife, Hala. No sooner has he explained his bloody ambitions to an aide in the first act but she begins act two with a soliloquy in which she reveals her greedy and lustful plan to feign agreement with her husband's strategems while actually advancing to power herself in the company of her lover, Caine, a royal counselor. Although she despises her husband, she is similar to him in her energy and her capacity to leap from introspective sessions of hate distilling to active spurts of conniving. Indeed, the second half of the play belongs mainly to her.

The turning point comes when Alaham, boasting to her about his successes, tells her that one fatality in his advance has been Caine. Infuriated, she privately vows revenge on her husband, and, in so doing, changes the nature of the play significantly. Unmentioned in the prose source for the play, she is Greville's addition to the story, and she turns the drama away from the direction of political tragedy and toward the equally classical example of passionate conflict between man and woman–in the direction, to cite a famous instance, of the story of Aegisthus and Clytemnestra. Hala thinks that she is in control of the play's final catastrophe, as she poisons her husband and adds to his death torment by slaying in front of him an infant whom she believes to be their child, screeching all the while that her only regret is that the baby is dying too quickly for her to feel fully revenged. Too late, she discovers that the child is in fact the one she has had by Caine. Nothing she can do now can reverse the error, and in a speech renouncing all hold on life, she condemns herself to hell, where her commitment to lust, fury, rage, and desire can be as permanent and excessive as she has always longed for it to be. Although not yet there physically, she has brought Hell to herself spiritually.

Overwritten in certain respects and implausible to a modern reader, this and other scenes in

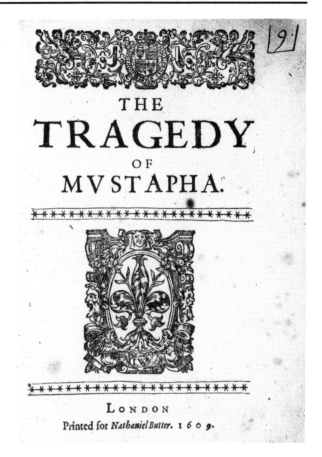

Title page for the unauthorized 1609 quarto edition of the only work by Greville published during his lifetime (Henry E. Huntington Library and Art Gallery)

the play nevertheless have the capacity for creating a type of terrifying horror that only Marlowe among Greville's English predecessors can equal. The playwright keeps sensationalism under control by the use of the classical chorus at the end of each of the first four acts in the play's five-act structure. The abstractions (such as, "Good Spirits," "Evil Spirits," "The People") who speak these choruses interrupt the flow of the action to offer ruminative generalizations on the meaning of the events. If the choruses afford Greville the opportunity to speak somewhat more directly on the themes of the play than he can through his characters, one can only conclude that he already was given to the same dark pessimism that he was to display in later years in verse treatises such as *An Inquisition upon Fame and Honour* (written circa 1613) and *A Treatise of Religion* (written circa 1625). Even the Good Spirits see man's middle position between animal and angel as nothing but a curse as long as he is alive, while the more severe speakers ridicule any belief in man's inherent goodness, a position that is certainly supported

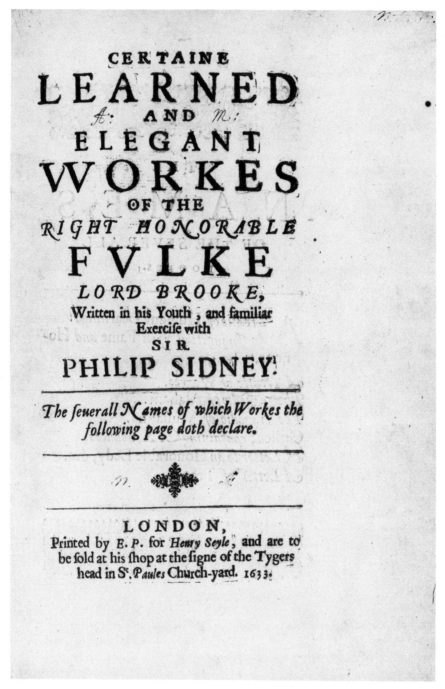

CERTAINE
LEARNED
AND
ELEGANT
WORKES
OF THE
RIGHT HONORABLE
FVLKE
LORD BROOKE,
Written in his Youth, and familiar
Exercise with
SIR
PHILIP SIDNEY.

The seuerall Names of which Workes the
following page doth declare.

LONDON,
Printed by E. P. for *Henry Seyle*, and are to
be sold at his shop at the signe of the Tygers
head in St. *Paules* Church-yard. 1633.

Title page for the 1633 folio edition of the posthumously published collection that includes
Alaham *and the revised version of* Mustapha *(Henry E. Huntington Library and*
Art Gallery)

by the evidence of the events in the play. Greville would seem to want to enforce the concept not only of the existence of evil in human affairs but also of its assured triumph on earth. He makes this point in a literary form that the reader understands to be essentially a fiction, but (as is almost always the case in Greville's "fictive" writing) it must be supposed that the fiction is reflective in some sense of the events that Greville had experienced in life.

There is a clearer biographical link to *Mustapha*, a play which, in its revised form, is a more polished work of art than is *Alaham*. Greville could have found information on the widely feared Turkish sultan Soliman the Magnificent in several histories and commentaries, all of which also speak of the title character Mustapha, Soliman's son, who was known to have been an innocent victim of his father's fears of rebellion, fears that had been fed by Soliman's wife Rossa, Mustapha's stepmother, who hoped to place her own son Zanger, Mustapha's younger half-brother, in the line of succession. Some, though by no means all, of the sources tell of Achmat, a counselor of the monarch, who recognizes the errors of the sultan's ways but who remains loyal to him to preserve the stability of the state. Greville's rendering of Achmat's dilemma gives the character a depth of personality that marks a clear advance over the flat characters of *Alaham*, and we may be fairly convinced that in this courtier with a complex, self-divided mind Greville is presenting a version of himself, a figure toward whom he can be both severely critical and benignly sympathetic. As an adviser to the sultan, Achmat holds a position of great responsibility to the national welfare, but with an imperfect monarch as ruler he is constantly uncertain as to how that welfare can best be maintained.

Achmat knows, for example, that Mustapha is innocent of Rossa's insinuations that he has committed treason, and he understands further how malleable Soliman is in his wife's hands. The counselor wants to pull the sultan out of his spell of benighted tyranny, but he does not know how to go about it without having his own credibility, and what he supposes to be his beneficial influence, damaged. He is able to win only a brief reprieve for Mustapha. Soliman continues to deteriorate as a monarch, and in act five he orders his son killed. This unnatural action provokes a popular revolt, and Achmat must decide whether he should aid this rebellion against a tyrant or continue to serve Soliman for the end of preserving the only government the nation knows. He opts for the latter, deciding to do what he can, at great personal risk, to prop up the unstable regime. Although it is not a pleasant thing to watch an essentially decent man make this kind of choice, Greville does what he can to right the moral balance of the play, foiling Rossa and Zanger's scheme and leaving Soliman in a humbled condition. Also, it may be helpful to note that whenever Greville speaks in his own voice in his other writings on issues such as this, he invariably comes down on the side of the preservation of stability and order, even if the price is tyranny. Since all men are hopelessly sinful and undependable, better the suffering caused by one tyrant than the anarchy caused by a mob who believe, mistakenly, that they understand truth and justice.

In revising the play, Greville expanded the choruses that conclude each act. The effect is, of course, to make the work less dramatic and more expository, intensifying and making explicit the philosophical and political themes that are otherwise more implicit in the drama. The topics of consideration are central to Greville's thought: political corruption, the necessity (and tragedy) of war, man's ineffectualness and sinfulness, the failure of the church to address human needs. The closing Chorus Sacerdotum is one of Greville's most anthologized passages, and its analysis of the human condition in terms of the difficulty of mortal man's living by immortal laws is extraordinarily striking: "Oh wearisome Condition of Humanity!/Borne under one law, to another bound."

That Greville should mix his presentation of his views on politics and religion is not surprising in an era when the two were inextricable for everyone. But Greville especially insists on inspecting them simultaneously. Although the action of both plays takes place in nominally non-Christian countries, Greville the Christian moralist presents his characters with political and personal dilemmas to which they are forced to respond in terms of Christian values. When, for example, a monarch has dealings with the "church" in these plays, it is always clear that the issue is the ability of the Christian church to avoid being seduced and destroyed morally by becoming as worldly as the society whose souls it purports to protect. Or, to come at the same issue from the perspective of the state, to what extent, the plays ask, can a temporal leader remain pure and take on some of the virtues of the cleric while at the same time performing his necessary duties? Such a question provides a way of analyzing Achmat's situation: all of his options are considered in terms of how they do or do not carry out God's will. To make a bad political choice is thus also to sin. Since there are no immediately apparent good political choices, there is similarly no escaping the taint of sin. Or is there? It would seem that the most sensible course of action would be to remove oneself completely from the political arena, but Greville never permits his characters this alternative, for to retreat would be to commit yet another sin, that of cowardice in leadership. It is a quandary that is as vexing for Greville's characters and choruses in his dramas as one may suppose it to have been for Greville himself in his life.

A portion of a page from the manuscript for A Treatise of Religion, *written entirely in Greville's hand (Alexander B. Grossart, ed.,* The Works in Verse and Prose Complete of the Right Honourable Fulke Greville, Lord Brooke, *volume 4, 1870)*

Greville's plays are thus works every bit as filled with ideas and theses as is the drama of Shaw. But Greville, unlike Shaw (or John Marston or George Chapman), had difficulty writing ideological drama that is credible as dramatic literature. Of course, one should recall that he did not intend these plays for the stage (a wish that, so far as is known, has always been respected). Still, it is often difficult for the reader who is in the middle of a 100-line speech to remember that he is reading a play at all. This fact is unfortunate, for the evidence of the texts shows Greville to be one of the most fascinating thinkers of his age, a man gloomily (but intelligently) obsessed with everything that might go wrong in his society. These two plays present this sobering corrective to late Elizabethan optimism in a form that is simultaneously too stylized and too personal. Greville's opinions on various matters that are at the core of human existence are recorded in the plays, but they are channeled into the stiff form of Senecan dialogue. Greville's aristocratic attitude toward the potential printing of these texts may have been correct: it is indeed possible that his original audience of fellow Senecans constituted the only group capable of giving them their full due.

Bibliography:

Paula Bennett, "Recent Studies in Greville," *English Literary Renaissance*, 2 (Autumn 1972): 376-382.

References:

Una Ellis-Fermor, "Fulke Greville," in her *The Jacobean Drama*, fourth edition, revised (London: Methuen, 1958), pp. 191-200;

Jean Jacquot, "Réligion et Raison d'Etat dans l'Oeuvre de Fulke Greville," *Etudes Anglaises*, 5 (August 1952): 211-222;

Charles Larson, *Fulke Greville* (Boston: Twayne, 1980);

Ivor Morris, "The Tragic Vision of Fulke Greville," *Shakespeare Survey*, 14 (1966): 66-75;

Ronald Rebholz, *The Life of Fulke Greville, First Lord Brooke* (Oxford: Clarendon Press, 1971);

Joan Rees, *Fulke Greville, Lord Brooke, 1554-1628* (Berkeley: University of California Press, 1971);

Peter Ure, "Fulke Greville's Dramatic Characters," *Review of English Studies*, new series 1 (October 1950): 308-323.

Papers:

There are three manuscript copies of two versions of *Mustapha*, none of them in Greville's own hand. The earlier version exists in two copies—one in the library of Trinity College, Cambridge, and the other in the Folger Shakespeare Library. The later is in the collected Warwick manuscript version of Greville's works, now in the British Library. The Warwick manuscripts provide the only manuscript version of *Alaham*; it is in the hand of the same scribe who had copied the later version of *Mustapha*, with a few corrections in Greville's hand.

Thomas Heywood

(1573 or 1574-August 1641)

Peter Davison
Westfield College, University of London

PLAY PRODUCTIONS: *Edward IV*, parts 1 and 2, London, Curtain theater(?), circa 1594-1599;

The Four Prentices of London, with The Conquest of Jerusalem (related to *Godfrey of Bologne*, part 2, circa 1594), London, Rose theater, circa 1594-1600;

The Fair Maid of the Exchange, doubtfully attributed to Heywood, London, unknown theater, 1594-1607;

The Fair Maid of the West, part 1, London, unknown theater, circa 1597-1610;

Sir Thomas More, probably by Anthony Munday, with revisions by Thomas Dekker, Henry Chettle, probably William Shakespeare, and perhaps Heywood, probably not produced until 1964, circa 1598;

War without Blows and Love without Suit (or *Strife*), London, Rose theater, early 1599;

Joan as Good as My Lady, London, Rose theater, 1599;

How a Man May Choose a Good Wife from a Bad, possibly by Heywood, Worcester's Men, circa 1601-1602;

Albere Galles (possibly the same play as *Nobody and Somebody*), by Heywood and Wentworth Smith, London, Rose theater, 1602;

The Royal King and the Loyal Subject, by Heywood and Smith (possibly the same play as *Marshal Osric*, London, Rose theater, autumn 1602);

Sir Thomas Wyatt (possibly incorporating *Lady Jane*, parts 1 and 2), by Heywood, Smith, Dekker, Chettle, and John Webster, London, Boar's Head or Rose theater, autumn 1602;

Christmas Comes But Once a Year, by Heywood, Dekker, Chettle, and Webster, London, Boar's Head or Rose theater, 1602;

The London Florentine, part 1, attributed to Heywood and Chettle, London, Rose theater(?), Christmas 1602;

The Blind Man Eats Many a Fly, London, Rose theater, early 1603;

A Woman Killed with Kindness, London, Rose theater, 1603;

If You Know Not Me You Know Nobody, parts 1 and 2, London, Boar's Head or Curtain theater, 1603-1605;

The Wise Woman of Hogsdon (possibly the same play as *How to Learn a Woman to Woo*, London, at Court, 30 December 1604);

The Bold Beauchamps, attributed to Heywood, London, unknown theater, circa 1606-1607;

The Rape of Lucrece, London, Red Bull theater, circa 1606-1608;

Fortune by Land and Sea, by Heywood and William Rowley, London, Red Bull theater, circa 1609;

The Golden Age, London, Red Bull theater, circa 1609-1611;

The Silver Age, London, Red Bull, Blackfriars, and Globe theaters(?), circa 1610-1612;

The Brazen Age, London, Red Bull theater (and possibly Blackfriars and Globe theaters?), circa 1610-1613;

The Iron Age, parts 1 and 2, London, Red Bull theater (and possibly Blackfriars and Globe theaters?), circa 1612-1613;

The Captives, London, Cockpit theater, autumn 1624;

The Escapes of Jupiter (or *Calisto*; scenes from *The Golden Age* and *The Silver Age*), London, unknown theater, circa 1625;

The English Traveller, London, Cockpit theater, circa 1625;

The Fair Maid of the West, part 2, London, Cockpit theater, circa 1630-1631;

London's Jus Honorarium, streets of London, 29 October 1631;

Londini Artium et Scientiarum Scaturigo, or London's Fountain of Arts and Sciences, streets of London, 29 October 1632;

A Maidenhead Well Lost, London, Cockpit theater, circa 1633;

Title page for the 1612 quarto edition of Heywood's defense of the stage against its Puritan attackers (Maggs Bros., catalogue number 517, 1929)

Londini Emporia, streets of London, 29 October 1633;

Love's Mistress, London, Cockpit theater, 1634;

The Late Lancashire Witches, by Heywood and Richard Brome, London, Globe theater, 1634;

The Apprentice's Prize, attributed to Heywood and Brome, London, Blackfriars theater(?), circa 1634(?);

The Life and Death of Sir Martin Skink, attributed to Heywood and Brome, London, Blackfriars theater(?), circa 1634(?);

A Challenge for Beauty, London, Blackfriars and Globe theaters, circa 1634-1636;

Londini Sinus Salutis, or London's Harbor of Health and Happiness, streets of London, 29 October 1635;

Londini Speculum, or London's Mirror, streets of London, 30 October 1637;

Porta Pietatis, or The Port of Piety, streets of London, 29 October 1638;

Londini Status Pacatus, or London's Peaceable Estate, streets of London, 29 October 1639;

Love's Masterpiece, London, unknown theater, 1640.

BOOKS: *Oenone and Paris,* attributed to Heywood (London: Printed by R. Jones, 1594);

The First and Second Partes of King Edward the Fourth (London: Printed by J. Windet for J. Oxenbridge, 1599);

A Pleasant Conceited Comedie, Wherein Is Shewed How a Man May Chose a Good Wife from a Bad, possibly by Heywood (London: Printed by T. Creede for M. Lawe, 1602);

If You Know Not Me, You Know No Bodie: or, The troubles of Queen Elizabeth (London: Printed by T. Purfoot for N. Butter, 1605);

The Second Part of, If You Know Not Me, You Know No Bodie (London: Printed by T. Purfoot for N. Butter, 1606);

The Fayre Maid of the Exchange, doubtfully attributed to Heywood (London: Printed by V. Simmes for H. Rockit, 1607);

A Woman Kilde With Kindnesse (London: Printed by W. Jaggard, sold by J. Hodgets, 1607);

The Famous History of Sir T. Wyat. With the Coronation of Queen Mary (possibly incorporating *Lady Jane,* parts 1 and 2), by Heywood, Thomas Dekker, John Webster, Henry Chettle, and Wentworth Smith (London: Printed by E. Allde for T. Archer, 1607);

The Rape of Lucrece. A True Roman Tragedie (London: Printed by E. Allde for J. Busby, sold by N. Butter, 1608);

Troia Britanica: or, Great Britaines Troy. A Poem, attributed to Heywood (London: Printed by W. Jaggard, 1609);

The Golden Age (London: Printed by N. Okes for W. Barrenger, 1611);

An Apology for Actors. Containing Three Briefe Treatises (London: Printed by N. Okes, 1612);

The Silver Age (London: Printed by N. Okes, sold by B. Lightfoote, 1613);

The Brazen Age (London: Printed by N. Okes for S. Rand, 1613);

A Funerall Elegie, Upon the Death of Henry, Prince of Wales, attributed to Heywood (London: Printed by N. Okes for W. Welbie, 1613);

A Marriage Triumphe. Solemnized in an Epithalamium, [for] *the Count Palatine. And the Lady Elizabeth,* attributed to Heywood (London: Printed by N. Okes for E. Marchant, 1613);

The Foure Prentises of London (London: Printed by N. Okes for J. Wright, 1615);

[Gunaikeion]: or, Nine Bookes of Various History. Concerninge Women (London: Printed by A. Islip, 1624); republished as *The Generall*

History of Women (London: Printed by
W. H. for W. H., 1657);

A Funeral Elegie, Upon the Death of King James (London: Printed by Eliot's Court Press for T. Harper, 1625);

Englands Elizabeth: Her Life and Troubles, During Her Minoritie, attributed to Heywood (London: Printed by J. Beale for P. Waterhouse, 1631);

The Fair Maid of the West, parts 1 and 2 (London: Printed by M. Flesher for R. Royston, 1631);

Londons Jus Honorarium. Exprest in Sundry Triumphs, at the Initiation of G. Whitmore, into the Maioralty (London: Printed by N. Okes, 1631);

The Iron Age, parts 1 and 2 (London: Printed by N. Okes, 1632);

Londini Artium & Scientiarum Scaturigo. Exprest in Sundry Triumphs, at the Initiation of N. Raynton into the Maior[al]*ty* (London: Printed by N. Okes, 1632);

The English Traveller (London: Printed by R. Raworth, 1633);

Londini Emporia, or Londons Mercatura. At the Inaugauration of R. Freeman into the Maior[al]*ty* (London: Printed by N. Okes, 1633);

A Pleasant Comedy, Called A Mayden-Head Well Lost (London: Printed by N. Okes for J. Jackson & F. Church, 1634);

The Late Lancashire Witches. A Comedy, by Heywood and Richard Brome (London: Printed by T. Harper for B. Fisher, 1634);

The Hierarchie of the Blessed Angells, attributed to Heywood (London: Printed by A. Islip, 1635);

Philocothonista, or, The Drunkard, attributed to Heywood (London: Printed by R. Raworth, 1635);

Londini Sinus Salutis, or, Londons Harbour of Health. At the Initiation of C. Cletherowe, into the Maioralty (London: Printed for R. Raworth, 1635);

A True Discourse of the Two Infamous Upstart Prophets, R. Farnham and J. Bull now Prisoners, with Their Examinations, attributed to Heywood (London: Printed by N. Okes for T. Lambert, 1636);

A Challenge for Beautie (London: Printed by R. Raworth, sold by J. Becket, 1636);

Loves Maistresse: or, The Queens Masque (London: Printed by R. Raworth for J. Crowch, sold by J. Emery, 1636);

The Royall King, and The Loyall Subject (London: Printed by N. & J. Okes for J. Becket, 1637);

Pleasant Dialogues and Dramma's, Selected Out of Lucian, Erasmus, Textor, Ovid, &c (London: Printed by R. Oulton for R. Hearne, sold by T. Slater, 1637);

A True Description of His Majesties Royall Ship (London: Printed by J. Okes for J. Aston, 1637);

Londini Speculum: or, Londons Mirror, at the Initiation of R. Fenn, into the Mairolty (London: Printed by J. Okes, 1637):

A Curtaine Lecture: As It Is Read by a Countrey Farmers Wife to Her Good Man (London: Printed by R. Young for J. Aston, 1637);

The Phœnix of These Late Times. Or The Life Of H. Welby (London: Printed by N. Okes, sold by R. Clotterbuck, 1637);

The Wise-Woman of Hogsdon. A Comedie (London: Printed by M. Parsons for H. Shephard, 1638);

Porta Pietatis, or, The Port or Harbour of Piety. At the Initiation of Sir M. Abbot into the Majoralty (London: Printed by J. Okes, 1638);

A True Relation, of the Lives and Deaths of the Two English Pyrats, Purser, and Clinton (London: Printed by J. Okes, 1639);

Londini Status Pacatus: or, Londons Peaceable Estate. At the Innitiation of H. Garway, into the Majoralty (London: Printed by J. Okes, 1639);

The Exemplary Lives and Memorable Acts of Nine of the Most Worthy Women of the World (London: Printed by T. Cotes for R. Royston, 1640);

Fortune by Land and Sea. A Tragi-Comedy, by Heywood and William Rowley (London: Printed for John Sweeting & Robert Pollard, 1655).

Editions: *The Dramatic Works of Thomas Heywood*, 6 volumes, edited by R. H. Shepherd (London: J. Pearson, 1874)—comprises *Edward IV*, parts 1 and 2; *If You Know Not Me You Know Nobody*, parts 1 and 2; *The Fair Maid of the Exchange; A Woman Killed With Kindness; The Four Prentices of London; The Fair Maid of the West; The Golden Age; The Silver Age; The Brazen Age; The Iron Age*, parts 1 and 2; *The English Traveller; A Maidenhead Well Lost; The Late Lancashire Witches; London's Jus Honorarium; Londini Sinus Salutis; Londini Speculum; A Challenge for Beauty; Love's Mistress; The Rape of Lucrece; Londini Porta Pietatis; The Wise Woman of Hogsdon; Londini Status Pacatus; The Royal King and the Loyal Subject; Pleasant Dialogues and Dramas; Fortune by Land and Sea;*

The Captives, in *A Collection of Old English Plays*, edited by A. H. Bullen, volume 4 (London: Privately printed, 1885);

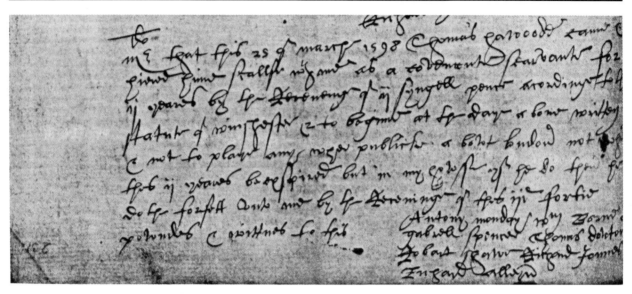

*Record in Philip Henslowe's diary of Heywood's agreement, on 25 March 1598, to write plays only for Henslowe for two years
(MSS VII, l. 231'; by permission of Dulwich College, London)*

If You Know Not Me You Know Nobody, parts 1 and 2, 2 volumes, edited by Madeleine Doran (London: Printed for the Malone Society at Oxford University Press, 1935);

The Rape of Lucrece, edited by Alan Holaday (Urbana: University of Illinois Press, 1950);

The Captives, edited by Arthur Brown (Oxford: Printed for the Malone Society at Oxford University, 1953);

A Woman Killed With Kindness, edited by R. W. Van Fossen (London: Methuen, 1961; Cambridge: Harvard University Press, 1961);

The Fair Maid of the Exchange, doubtfully attributed to Heywood (though not in this edition), edited by Peter H. Davison (Oxford: Printed for the Malone Society at Oxford University Press, 1963);

The Fair Maid of the West, parts 1 and 2, edited by Robert K. Turner, Jr. (Lincoln: University of Nebraska Press, 1967; London: Arnold, 1968);

The Escapes of Jupiter, edited by Henry D. Janzen (Oxford: Printed for the Malone Society at Oxford University Press, 1978);

The Late Lancashire Witches, by Heywood and Richard Brome, edited by Laird H. Barber (New York & London: Garland, 1979);

Thomas Heywood's The Four Prentices of London: A Critical, Old-Spelling Edition, edited by Mary Ann Weber Gasior (New York & London: Garland, 1980);

A Critical Edition of Fortune by Land and Sea *by*

Thomas Heywood and William Rowley, edited by Herman Doh (New York & London: Garland, 1980);

A Critical Edition of The Wise-Woman of Hogsdon, edited by Michael H. Leonard (New York & London: Garland, 1980).

Thomas Heywood's life and work were judiciously described about a quarter of a century ago by A. M. Clark. Born in Rothwell or Ashby, Lincolnshire, to the Reverend Robert and Elizabeth Heywood in 1573 or 1574, Heywood came from a Cheshire family that had some claim to gentility. Clark suggests that Heywood was "a man destined for the Church whom the accidents of the time rushed into dramatic journalism." There seems to be an association between Heywood's father's profession and the son's education and drama. Heywood was almost certainly one of the Heywoods who studied at Cambridge University, most likely at Emmanuel College, "the stronghold of Puritanism," circa 1591-1593. Though it has been suggested that he was a Fellow of Peterhouse, he is not recorded as being such, and his affiliation with the college is improbable.

Heywood seems to have started with "play-patching," as Clark aptly puts it, about 1594 or 1595. In Philip Henslowe's diary "hawodes bocke" is noted on 14 October 1596, and Heywood seems to have worked with Henslowe's company the Admiral's Men until the end of the century. By then he had "arrived," notably with the production of *Edward IV* (probably at the Curtain); thereafter he worked with many companies.

In addition to a large number of plays Heywood also wrote pseudohistory, poetry, translations, an apologia for the theater, pageants, accounts of the lives of women and pirates, and religious tracts. Much of this work is dull stuff, but he was clearly an exceptionally hardworking and versatile professional writer. Crediting Heywood with a greater concern for "religion and edification" than his fellow dramatists, Clark compares him to Thomas Dekker, calling both playwrights "essentially bourgeois, intensely loyal to King and Church, but with no love for courts and courtiers, and with an enthusiasm for London, its citizens and their standards, its wealth, splendour, and institutions." Clark goes on to call Heywood "a Puritan himself in all but name" and suggests that "it was his reputation among his persuasive fellows as a man of unblemished character" that caused Heywood to write *An Apology for Actors* (1612) as a defense of the stage against Puritan attacks.

On 13 June 1603 Heywood married Anne Buttler. There are baptismal records for a number of Heywood children–Isbell, Mary, Nicholas, Robert, Anne, Henry, Richard, and Thomas–but there cannot be complete certainty that all these children were the sons and daughters of the dramatist rather than another Heywood. After the death of his first wife, Heywood was married again, to Jane Span, on 18 January 1633. Heywood was buried on 16 August 1641 in St. James's, Clerkenwell, London, just before he would have had to make what Clark describes as "a decision for or against militant Puritanism."

The English Traveller (1633) has achieved a certain fame for Heywood's address to his readers, in which he claimed to have had "an entire hand, or at least a main finger" in the writing of 220 plays, many of which are now lost or unidentified. This prodigious output is indicative of the large-scale production of which an Elizabethan dramatist was capable. Also well known is Heywood's claim in his address that this play came "accidentally to the press," a fate which also befell part one of *If You Know Not Me You Know Nobody*, to which he added a prologue when the play "*was last revived at the* Cock-pit" circa 1630, describing the manner in which the text of the 1605 edition had been compiled for publication:

> some by Stenography drew
> The plot: put it in print: (scarce one word trew:)

And in that lamenesse it hath limp't so long,
The Author now to vindicate that wrong
Hath tooke the paines, upright upon its feete
To teach it walke, so please you sit, and see't.

Heywood's plays attracted sufficient interest to cause them to be printed surreptitiously and, as *If You Know Not Me You Know Nobody* demonstrates, to be revived nearly a quarter century later in an age, one would think, much out of tune with that for which it was composed.

The third point worth noting from the address to the reader of *The English Traveller* is Heywood's ironic statement that "*my Playes are not exposed vnto the world in Volumes, to beare the title of* Workes, *(as others).*" This rather deprecating attitude to his work occurs from time to time and may be partly conventional. The address to the reader of *The Rape of Lucrece* (1608) also maintains that it is not the author's custom to sell his labors "first on the Stage and after to the Presse." In part one of *The Fair Maid of the West* Heywood takes this even further: "*Cvrteous Reader, my Plaies have not beene exposed to the publike view of the world in numerous sheets, and a large volume; but singly (as thou seest) with great modesty, and small noise.*" By the time this play was published in 1631, the first folio of Shakespeare's plays had been published, and Ben Jonson had collected his plays as *The Workes of Ben Jonson*, to the derision of some contemporaries who considered plays insufficiently literary to be considered "works." Heywood seems to have shared their opinion, and he concluded his address with this description of his labors:

> Peruse it through, and thou maist finde in it,
> Some mirth, some matter, &, perhaps, some wit.

Although our conclusion so far as the *literary* value of his work may be little different, that it was theatrically effective in its own day is important. Further, there is much that is revealing of its own time, sociologically and morally, in Heywood's drama. Though Charles Lamb's description of Heywood as a "prose Shakespeare" may not be unjust, a fresh rereading of his oeuvre is remarkably rewarding. It might be claimed that though he wrote in his *Gunaikeion* (1624), "they that write to all, must strive to please all," he was by no means so narrowly inhibited.

There are some two dozen plays which may be attributed to Heywood with certainty or some confidence even without taking account of his seven City of London pageants and his *Pleasant Di-*

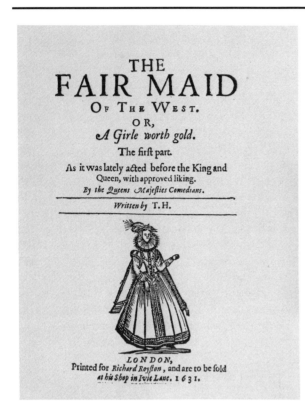

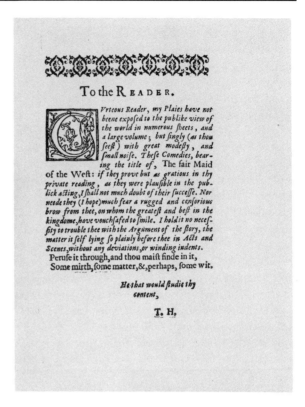

Title page and epistle to the reader for the first part of Heywood's comedy about a virtuous English barmaid (from the Bodleian Library copy of the 1631 quarto edition of parts 1 and 2)

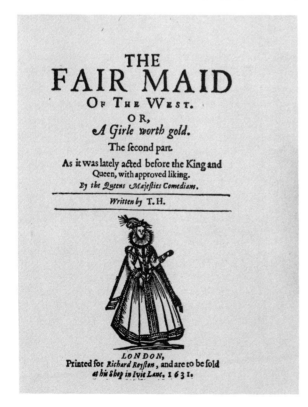

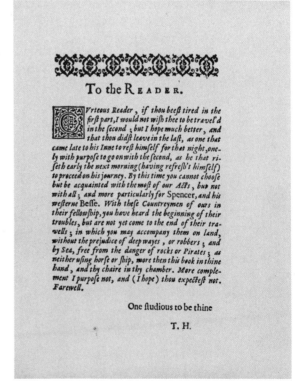

Interior title page and epistle to the reader for the second part of Heywood's comedy, written more than twenty-five years after part 1 (from the Bodleian Library copy of the 1631 quarto edition)

alogues and Dramas (1637). There is no adequate edition of Heywood's works, the most recent being R. H. Shepherd's edition of 1874, which omits two plays that existed only in manuscript form until A. H. Bullen published *The Captives* in *A Collection of Old English Plays* (1885) and Henry D. Janzen prepared a Malone Society edition (1978) of *The Escapes of Jupiter* (or *Calisto*).

No claim to greatness can be made for either of the two parts of *Edward IV* plays or the two parts of *If You Know Not Me You Know Nobody*, but to dismiss them out of hand would be mistaken. Their unevenness must debar successful revival today, but it is easy to see why they appealed in their own time in ways not restricted to oversimple patriotism, and they have elements that can still interest and entertain. They are, of course, the kind of chronicle plays that Heywood defended in his *An Apology for Actors* as instructing "such as cannot read in the discouery of all our *English* Chronicles."

Yet, part one of *Edward IV* opens in a way that would not shame the early Shakespeare:

> DUCHESS. Sonne I tell ye you haue done you
>   know not what;
> KING. I haue married a woman, else I am deceiued
>   mother.
> DUCHESS. Married a woman? married indeed,
>   Here is a marriage that befits a King:
>   It is no maruaile it was done in haste,
>   Here is a Bridall and with hell to boote,
>   You haue made worke.
> KING. Faith mother some we haue indeed, but
>   ere long you shall see vs make worke for an
>   heir apparant, I doubt not, nay, nay, nay, come
>   come, Gods will what chiding still?

The Duchess's spleen would immediately engage an audience's attention, and Edward's trivializing of the issue (his marriage to Lady Grey) is nicely hit off. In this opening section Heywood distinguishes the king by having him speak in prose even though he is royal: simple but effective.

The play proceeds with a certain sense of purpose until the attack on London by Falconbridge is repulsed. The common men of Kent and Essex are dramatized with a degree of individuality, and they are well answered by one of Heywood's favorite groups—the Apprentices. However, thereafter the play is a hodgepodge. A long section is made up of a series of exchanges between Hobs, the Tanner of Tamworth, and various characters, especially King Edward in disguise, and the play concludes with Edward's

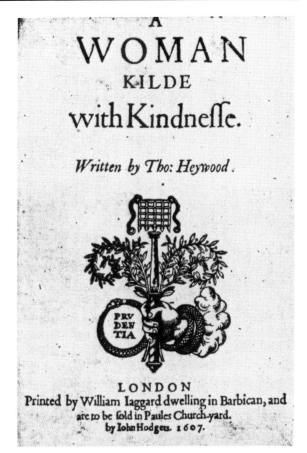

Title page for the unique copy of the 1607 quarto edition of Heywood's most popular play (British Library)

wooing and winning of Jane Shore—thus concupiscence first and last. Even these sections, though they cannot be integrated into the whole, are not without interest. Hobs, the ordinary workman, caught between the claims of Henry VI and Edward IV, responds vigorously to two nobles who warn him not to speak treasonably:

> for, by my troth, I know not when I speak treason, when I do not. There's such halting betwixt two kings, that a man cannot go vpright, but he shall offend t'one of them. I would God had them both, for me.

Jane Shore is depicted as genuinely perplexed and her husband as deeply troubled. It is easy to sense that, despite the genuflexions toward royalty in the shape of Edward IV, the commoners, whether rebels like Spicing, or, like Hobs the Tanner making his way as best he can, or Shore and his wife, loyal but suffering undeserved indignity and misfortune at the hands of a king they have defended, have more to be said for them than their rulers. At this early date, Heywood does not side unthinkingly with the powerful.

The play has one first-rate comic character in Josslin, one of the City Fathers. His repetitive "and so forth" anticipates by centuries, and much more comically, today's "you know," and it is beautifully taken out by Spicing:

> JOSSLIN. I, but you know what followed, and so forth.
> SPICING. Et cetera! are you there? methinks, the sight of the dun bull, the *Neuilles* honoured crest, should make you leaue your broken sentences, and quite forget euer to speake at all.

Edward IV, part two, is less mixed than the first part, but it is unartistically split down the middle. In the first part Edward pursues his claim to France, makes a compact with King Lewis, and—despite the machinations of Burgundy and the Constable of France, both seeking power at the expense of England, France, and each other—returns safe to England. A Chorus, the only one in the play, crudely announces a change of scene:

> King *Edward* is returned home to *England*,
> And *Lewis*, King of *France*, soon afterward
> Surprized both his subtil enemies,
> Rewarding them with traiterous recompence.
> Now do we draw the curtain of our Scene,
> To speake of *Shore* and his faire wife againe,
> With other matters thereupon depending.

The rest of the play is concerned with the death of Edward and the rise of Gloucester, culminating in his being crowned Richard III, and the fall of Jane Shore. The chief interest of the first of these strands of the story is the appearance of so many characters who appear in Shakespeare's *Richard III*, never with even the least touch of the same effect, except perhaps in the portrayal of Brackenbury. The stories must perforce overlap—even to the prophecy that "G" will murder Edward's heirs—but the relationship of Heywood's play to Shakespeare's, in content and style, is akin to that of the anonymous play *The Famous Victories of Henry the Fifth* to Shakespeare's Henry IV cycle.

The Jane Shore strand of the play is another matter, however. It is not great drama, but it is often touching, and once again Heywood shows his heart is with goodness and simplicity in whomsoever it might be found. Jane's tribulations—her walking *"in a white sheet barefooted with her hair*

about her eares, and in her hand a waxe taper," her desertion by those who batten on her, Richard's cruel proclamation that whoever gave her succour should die—contrast sharply with the relief she has shown to prisoners and the goodness of heart displayed by her husband and a young man, Mr. Aire, who aids her to repay her kindness to him. Heywood drives his lesson home: Aire speaks boldly for virtue, without priggishness, before he is executed onstage (*"Here he is executed"* is the stage direction). Jane and her husband beg his body, place it in a coffin onstage, and sit either side of it. Jane's husband addresses her: *"Jane, sit thou there! Here I my place will haue, / Giue me thy hand; thus we embrace our graue"*; he kisses her; and she dies. Shore then apostrophizes prior to his own death:

> Now, tyrant *Richard* do the worst thou canst.
> She doth defie thee. Oh, vnconstant world,
> Here lies a true anatomie of thee,
> A king had all my ioy, that her enioyed,
> And by a king again she was destroyed.

This powerful emblematic tableau, with its generous-hearted Magdalene and faithful husband, is immediately contrasted with the world of lust, cruelty, and power; as soon as the bodies are removed, Richard appears, crowned in place of Edward IV.

The Four Prentices of London, with The Conquest of Jerusalem is still remembered, if not known, because it served as the prime target for Francis Beaumont's satire, *The Knight of the Burning Pestle*, which was produced circa 1607. Not even Beaumont's most extravagant satire can, however, outmatch what Heywood does with such naive conviction. For that reason alone, Heywood's play must date from the beginning of his career, from earlier rather than later in the last decade of the sixteenth century. It should be noted, however, that, despite Beaumont, Heywood's play could be revived and republished after Beaumont's play was staged. That it could still, in the second decade of the seventeenth century, seemingly be the more popular of the two plays says something about the audiences of the time. Heywood dedicated the play to "the Honest and High-spirited Prentises." In the prologue (self-conscious enough in style to have been written later, perhaps, than the first production) the play's first title is given as "True and Strange" with "The Four Prentices" as the alternative, and it is also said to be a tale "euery one can tell by the fire in Winter." The time is avowedly

 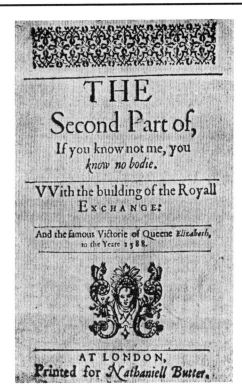

Title pages for the 1605 and 1606 quarto editions of the two-part play that Heywood probably began to write after the death of Elizabeth I in March 1603 (left: Anderson Galleries, sale number 2077, 20-21 May 1926; right: British Library)

that of William the Conqueror. The Earl of Boulogne has been dispossessed, and his sons have had to be apprenticed to London tradesmen. They prefer to fight, however, and go off to seek adventure, Guy to France, Godfrey to "Bulloigne," Charles to Italy, and Eustace to Ireland.

Despite being so dispersed it is no time at all before Eustace and his Irish kerns are confronting Charles and his Italian bandits. Charles and Eustace fight without recognizing each other; they both fall in love with their sister Bella Franca, who has surprisingly just appeared on the scene, without any of the three recognizing the others. There is much running between disputants to prevent their killing each other, and there are impossible and incongruous adventures aimed at the relief of Jerusalem, often described through hyperbolic language. Eventually the brothers win glory, which reflects upon the apprentices of London in general, as Eustace indicates in an aside—that is, in a direct address to such apprentices in the audience:

> oh that I had with mee
> As many good lads, honest Prentises,

From *Eastcheape*, *Canwicke-streete*, and *London-stone*,
To ende this Battle, as could with themselues
Vnder my conduct if they knew mee heere:
The doubtfull dayes successe wee neede not feare.

It is not difficult to see why Heywood's play was preferred to Beaumont's, in some theaters at least, in the middle of James I's reign.

The nadir of naiveté is to be found in the meeting and recognition of the brothers toward the end of the play:

> GODFREY. My brothers name was *Eustace*.
> EUSTACE. *Godfrey* mine.
> GUY. That Duke cal'd his sonne *Charles*
> CHARLES. Mine cal'd his *Guy*
> GODFREY. My brother *Eustace!*
> EUSTACE. *Godfrey!*
> CHARLES. *Guy!*
> GUY. And *Charles!*
> ALL. Brothers!

Robert might well be speaking on our behalf when he remarks, "This accident breeds wonders in my thoughts." It would still bring the house down today, as did Walter Reynolds's *Young England* in 1934, and for much the same reasons.

With Beaumont we may well laugh at *The Four Prentices*, but we should do so mindful that this century has seen unsophisticated good intent as simple and absurd–but that Heywood went on to better things than Reynolds.

The two parts of *The Fair Maid of the West* were written well over a quarter century apart, the later play being one of those written circa 1630-1631, after what seems to have been Heywood's ten-year break from writing for the theater. That he should have returned to this subject not only suggests that the first part had been very effective but that its extravagances could still be thought capable of winning an audience's favor at a time when the drama was seen by some critics as pandering to excess and as aesthetically and morally decadent. The story line of part one is absurd, toing and froing between Plymouth and Foy, and from England to the Azores and Morocco. It presents an exotic world but one in which good, honest, burgher values–*English* burgher values–triumph. The heroine, Bess Bridges, the "Fair Maid of the West," serves in a tavern (and Heywood's tavern scenes are always lively and convincing) but is virtuous, honest, and strong-hearted. Although Spencer, who loves her, is an honorable man, it is typical of Heywood that his "heroine of the people" stands out as the fount of native worth, a parallel being drawn between her name and that of Good Queen Bess. When Bess tells Mullisheg, King of Fez, her name is Elizabeth, he replies:

> MULLISHEG. There's vertue in that name.
> The Virgin Queene so famous through the world,
> The mighty Empresse of the maiden-Ile,
> Whose predecessors have ore-runne great France,
> Whose powerfull hand doth still support the Dutch,
> And keepes the potent King of Spaine in awe,
> Is not she titled so?
> BESS. She is.
> MULLISHEG. Hath she her selfe a face so faire as yours
> When she appears for wonder.
> BESS. Mighty *Fesse*,
> You cast a blush upon my maiden cheeke,
> To patterne me with her. Why Englands Queene
> She is the onely Phoenix of her age,
> The pride and glory of the Westerne Isles:
> Had I a thousand tongues they all would tyre
> And faile me in her true description.

There is no subtle undermining here: Bess says what she thinks, stating what audiences and probably Heywood himself believed. This naive patriotism is not the stuff of the committed drama of our century, yet it rings true in its context, and, as so often with Heywood, it gives modern readers a glimpse into many of the hearts that beat in England at that time. If not a contradiction in terms, this is "honest claptrap."

It should also be said that Heywood is not wholly uncritical of the world and people he so romanticizes. Early in the play, for example, Spencer reveals to his friend, Captain Goodlack, that he is attracted by Bess. (The 1631 edition, incidentally, lists Michael Bowyer, Richard Perkins, and Hugh Clark as playing these three roles respectively.) Goodlack's response is instructive:

> GOODLACK. Come, I must tell you, you forget your selfe,
> One of your birth and breeding, thus to dote
> Upon a Tanners daughter: why, her father
> Sold hydes in Somersetshire, and being trade-falne,
> Sent her to service.
> SPENCER. Prethee speake no more.
> Thou telst me that which I would faine forget,
> Or wish I had not knowne. If thou wilt humor me
> Tell me shee's faire and honest.
> GOODLACK. Yes, and loves you.
> SPENCER. To forget that, were to exclude the rest:
> All saving that, were nothing. . . .

Bess, of course, will prove faithful through thick and thin, and Spencer, a gentleman (at a time when the word had real meaning), will be united with her at the end of the play. It is the aptly named Goodlack who will prove false to his friend. As in Dekker's *The Shoemakers' Holiday* and much nineteenth-century melodrama, it is the ordinary folk who can be relied upon to be faithful and their "betters" who prove untrue, not only to their own codes of "honor" but to the norms of ordinary decent human dealing. Simply to depict such a contrast does not ensure convincing or aesthetically satisfying art, but Heywood's stance is consistent throughout his work with that described here–which makes one think that *The Fair Maid of the Exchange*, at least as we have it, is not Heywood's.

A more telling example of Heywood's stance, because critical of a kind of person or class who could be expected to be found in the public theater, is dramatized in act one. Carrol, a gentleman, has just been killed in a stupid tavern brawl. Two Drawers enter, and one immediately

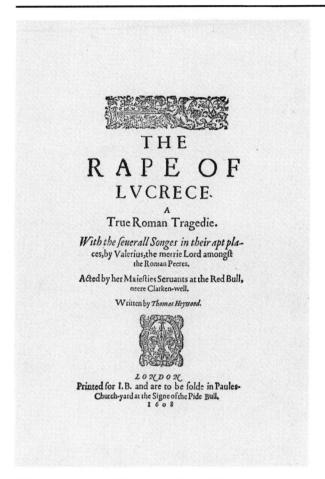

THE

RAPE OF

LVCRECE.

A

True Roman Tragedie.

With the feuerall Songes in their apt pla-
ces, by Valerius, the merrie Lord amongst
the Roman Peeres.

Acted by her Maiesties Seruants at the Red Bull,
neere Clarken-well.

Written by *Thomas Heywood.*

LONDON,
Printed for I. B. and are to be folde in Paules-
Church-yard at the Signe of the Pide Bull.
1 6 0 8

*Title page for the 1608 quarto edition of Heywood's dramatic
version of the story Shakespeare told in his long narrative
poem of 1594 (Anderson Galleries, sale number 2077, 20-21
May 1926)*

asks if the bill has been paid; for, " 'tis not so
much for the death of the man, but how shall we
come by our reckoning?" Later, Heywood inserts
a short scene of less than thirty lines, wholly unnec-
essary to the narrative line, to tell the audience
that the Drawers got their money. The act thus
ends with a splendid example of self-interest
from the Second Drawer: "Well, howsoever, I am
glad, though he kild the man wee have got our
money."

It is difficult to describe the second part of
The Fair Maid of the West as anything but a bad
play: a poor story, poorly constructed, poorly
written. Heywood was clearly capitalizing on his
earlier success. Of the original dramatis personae, Bess, Spencer, Goodlack, Mullisheg, the two
Bashaws, Clem the Clown, Ruffman, and Forset
appear. The significant characters added are
Mullisheg's Queen, Tota, and the Dukes of Florence, Mantua, and Ferrara, who help spin the action out into acts four and five. The play begins

on Bess and Spencer's wedding night. The King
of Fez, who was honorable in part one, now pines
and plots for Bess and his Queen for Spencer. Separately, and deceiving one another, they attempt
to suborn Ruffman and Goodlack (now a reformed character) to enable them to enjoy Bess
and Spencer. Ruffman and Goodlack perform a
double bed trick so that King and Queen find
themselves in each other's arms.

Some indication of Heywood's lack of
craftmanship and creative imagination in this
play may be gathered from one or two examples.
When Goodlack agrees to be shown how he
might win that which will make him "chronicled /
In thy own Countrey," Mullisheg responds:

> MULLISHEG. I am dull,
>   And drowsie on the sudden: whilst I sleep,
>   Captain, read there.
>
>   *He counterfets sleep, and gives him a letter.*
>
> GOODLACK. *To make Besse mine some secret means*
>   *devise,*
>   *To thy own height and heart Ile make thee rise.*
>   Is not this ink the blood of Basilisks,
>   That kills me in the eies, and blindes me so,
>   That I can read no further: 'twas compos'd
>   Of Dragons poyson, and the gall of Aspes,
>   Of Serpents venome, or of Vipers stings,
>   It could not read so harsh else. . . .

The last line reflects the author's work rather
than Mullisheg's. When Goodlack finishes his soliloquy, Mullisheg *"starts out of his chaire as from a
dream,"* and later, Spencer, seeking to escape, has
this aside:

> Sure this Moore hath been made private to
> the Kings intents, which if I finde, Ile
> make him the instrument for me to passe
> the Court gates. This man, whose office
> was to keep me, shall be the onely means
> to free me.

The Bashaw Alcade follows this speech with his
own aside: "On his marriage night, and up at
this hower?" Spencer gets away, but a mere
eleven lines later, without any change of scene,
he is brought back, a wounded captive, having
killed four of the guards. By the end of the
scene Bashaw Joffer has agreed to let him go on
his own to the escape ship (the totally black-
painted and rigged *Negro*) to bid Bess farewell
and prevent her committing suicide.

Of course, everyone escapes (though not be-

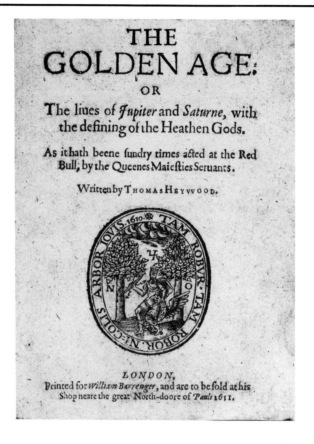

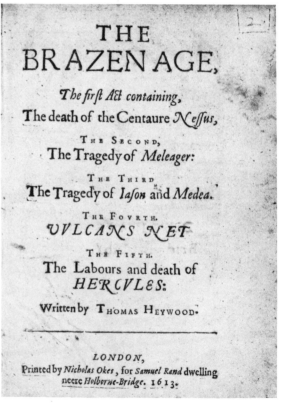

Title pages for quarto editions of the first three plays in Heywood's attempt to dramatize the entire body of classical mythology
(Henry E. Huntington Library and Art Gallery)

fore Clem the Clown has lost his "jewels"–the castration promised in act two of part one), but not for long. A banal Chorus between acts three and four tells how *"a French Pirate, who with two ships well rig'd / Way laies them in their voyage."* Goodlack and Spencer are separated from the rest and become champions of the Dukes of Ferrara and Mantua. They reconcile these warring lords, and all journey to Florence, where the Duke has arrived just in time to save Bess from rape by a Bandit Captain. Even Clem reappears, running a tavern in Florence, where all the friends meet and where Bashaw Joffer appears and is so impressed by honor of a quality not to be found in Barbary (despite what we have seen in part one) that "The vertue in these Christians hath converted me." We are back in the world of *The Four Prentices of London,* but this play lacks the natural naiveté of that early play. Not even Heywood's customarily fresh humor makes much appearance, and weaknesses in language, narrative, and structure coupled with coincidence and contrivance combine to ensure that this is hardly a play of which Heywood could be proud.

The lasting vitality of *The Fair Maid of the West*–especially part one–was delightfully demonstrated by the Royal Shakespeare Company in an adaptation produced by Trevor Nunn at the Swan Theater, Stratford-upon-Avon, 11 September 1986 (transferring to the Mermaid, London, 25 March 1987). The production was purportedly of both parts of the play, but the last two acts of part two were silently cut. Though fairly free, the adaptation was true of Heywood's spirit, and it was enjoyed by sophisticated scholars and little children–an audience range of Elizabethan proportions. Despite pruning and some first-rate business, the falling off between parts one and two was clearly apparent. This production did much to show why Heywood remained popular well into the seventeenth century, despite Beaumont's parody and changing tastes, and it cast doubts on the strictures of study-bound critics of early-seventeenth-century drama.

Although the three most significant full-length studies devoted to Heywood (by Otelia Cromwell, A. M. Clark, and Michel Grivelet) and the Malone Society edition of *The Fair Maid of the Exchange* decline to credit this play to Heywood, it is persistently attributed to him (especially by library cataloguers). The play was probably written some time between 1594 and 1602. It is likely to be the work of a tyro, and one new to London, for he gets the city's topography wrong. For example Phillis (the "fair Maid") and Ursula have to cross a bridge on their way from the Exchange to Mile End. The play is full of echoes of *Venus and Adonis* and a poem that could be by Heywood, T. H.'s *Oenone and Paris* (1594), and Shakespeare is frequently suggested (the "remuneration" scene in III.i of *Love's Labor's Lost,* for example).

It is possible that the play was revised. The business of the diamond that may be counterfeit (in scenes five and thirteen of the Malone Society edition) is singularly irrelevant; the Cripple is strangely silent and unaddressed by Phillis at a crucial moment at the end of the play; the speech heads at lines 2039-2041 in scene twelve give lines to the Cripple, who is offstage, and are embedded in a scene in which Frank is disguised as the Cripple, but he is correctly given the remaining six speeches. Finally, it is claimed that "Eleauen may easily acte this Comedie," which patently they cannot. This sentence could be an advertising puff, but it is at least as likely that it refers to an earlier version.

Despite the commercial milieu and Heywoodian comedy, especially via the family fool, Fiddle, as the play stands, with the repellent Frank Golding as the successful suitor of Phillis, Heywood seems an unlikely candidate for the authorship. Phillis plainly loves the Cripple and is prepared to marry him against her parents' wishes:

> Am not I a good childe thinke you,
> To play with both hands thus against my parents?
> Well, tis but a tricke of youth: say what they will,
> Ile loue the Cripple, and will hate them still.

Despite the plea to youth (as in *The English Traveller*), although Phillis's aim is worthy, its expression hardly idealizes her–especially in her reminiscence of the Vice, Ambidexter, in the second line.

Within 150 lines of the end of the play, she distinguishes so between Frank Golding and the Cripple:

> That golden *Golding* is but loathsome drosse,
> Nor is it golde that I so much esteeme;
> Dust is the richest treasure that we haue,
> Nor is the beauty of the fairest one,
> Of higher price or valew vnto me,
> Than is a lumpe of poore deformity.
> Father, you know my minde, and what I saide,
> Which if you graunt not, I will rest a maide.

The denouement which follows–provided by the appearance simultaneously of two "Cripples," one being Frank disguised–is totally unconvincing:

> PHILLIS. Hence foule deformitie.
>   Nor thou, nor he, shall my companion be,
>   If Cripples dead, the liuing seeme to haunt,
>   Ile neither of either, therefore I say auaunt[.]

She disposes of Frank's brothers, Ferdinand and Antonio (who also love her), much as Rosalynde will dispose of Phoebe in *As You Like It*, completely ignores the Cripple–who says nothing–and accepts Frank less than sixty lines later.

There is little good that can be said for Frank, and he wins Phillis by lies and deceit. Phillis is quite lively, but remarkably shrewish for such a heroine. There is a revealing shop scene–easily the best in the play (scene eight in the Malone Society edition)–which is worthy of Heywood and which does not idealize the heroine. (A similar scene in *The Wise Woman of Hogsdon*, I.ii, makes an interesting comparison.)

The most one might say so far as Heywood is concerned is that he might have had a finger in the play–main or otherwise, in association with others–when he was learning his trade. One would like to think that the story line once saw the union of Phillis and the Cripple–it would make the play imaginative and unusual in conception if not in execution–with Frank and his brothers sent packing. Perhaps that was too much for an audience of the time, but it would have accorded with the moral tone of the mature Heywood.

A final note on the play. There are two or three aspects that seem to anticipate–rather than reflect–Marston's *The Dutch Courtesan*. The business with the diamond and whether or not it is counterfeit appears (and just as peripherally) in Marston's play; Anthony, Frank's "second brother male-content" is a thinly sketched Malheureux; and the stage direction's references to Phillis's "sounds" when the man she is to marry appears disguised, are precisely what Beatrice does in *The Dutch Courtesan*.

The theme of *The Royal King and the Loyal Subject* is well expressed in act three by the leading figure in the subplot, Captain Bonville: " 'Tis generall thorow the world, each state esteemes / A man not what he is, but what he seemes." The play is well and simply constructed.

It comprises alternating actions centering on the King's testing of the Lord Marshal at the instigation of jealous courtiers and the exploits of a tatterdemalion Captain, his Corporal, and the Clown. The Lord Marshal is intensely loyal and generous. To ensure that these characteristics spring genuinely from the soul rather than as a means to rival the King as fount of honor, he is disgraced, sent from court, and first one daughter and then his second demanded by the King. The King is so taken by the first daughter that he marries her and makes her Queen, although that does not end the Lord Marshal's tribulations. He is himself married by the King to the Princess and, by a device, tried at a bar (a verbal tournament), awarded a laurel wreath–and the block. At the last moment, the King reveals that he trusts the Lord Marshal and not the Earl of Chester, whose envy has instigated the testing of the former.

Inevitably such a plot, well presented though it is, carries less conviction now than in Heywood's day. What still gives the play life, however, is the characterization and some of the language of the subplot. Here the theme of testing takes a different form. Instead of generosity being offered and its motives doubted, as in the main plot, charity is requested by those returned in tatters from the wars, but it is always denied. The best of the scenes is that between the Captain, Clown, and Bawd, and two Gentlemen in their finery with two prostitutes. The Bawd having first dismissed the Captain and Clown on grounds of their appearance, finds that the Gentlemen, though well dressed, have no money, while the Captain and Clown have chinking purses. We then get a new definition of Rascals and Gentlemen from the Bawd: "They be Rascalls that have no money; those be Gentlemen that have Crownes." To preserve Heywood's customary moral tone, whereas the Clown "goes learing away" after the prostitute ("shall I have no sport for my money, but even a snatch and away?"), Captain Bonville, having been accepted by the Bawd, flays her and her whores with his tongue, concluding with:

> Be he a *Lazar*, or a Leper, bring
> Coyne in his fist, he shall embrace your lust
> Before the purest flesh that sues of trust.

"Leper" implies ridden with venereal disease.

The play by which Heywood is best known to this day, and his one play that is quite frequently performed, is *A Woman Killed with Kindness.* It is a remarkable play, clear evidence–though it is apparent elsewhere–that Heywood, though by no stretch of the imagination the poet that was Shakespeare, had considerable dramatic inventiveness and originality. It is a tragedy of "ordinary people" and not, as *Arden of Faversham,* based on an historical incident; further, though there are deaths (and today we find Anne's "suffering penitent unto death" difficult to experience), none of the principals is killed. Indeed, the "staying of execution" is dramatically focused upon, most notably in scene eight when the Maid in her smock (compare Frankford's description of her as an angel in the ensuing speech) stays his hand as he follows the villain, Wendoll, who has seduced Frankford's wife, Anne, across the stage with his sword drawn:

> FRANKFORD. I thanke thee maide, thou like the
>   Angelles hand,
>   Hast stayd me from a bloody sacrifice.
>   Go, villen, and my wrongs sit on thy soule
>   As heauy as this greefe doth vpon mine.

These lines pick up something Wendoll has said in a soliloquy earlier in the play when, far more conscious-stricken than Richard III, he confesses, "I am a Villen if I apprehend / But such a thought" (of adultery) and concludes:

> And shall I wrong his bed? Thou God of Thunder
> Stay in thy thoughts of vengeance and of wrath,
> Thy great almighty, and all-iudging hand
> From speedy execution on a Villen,
> A villen and a Traitor to his friend.

The play is deeply moral. Its profound awareness of the sins of adultery and jealousy, of false friendship and revenge, are not only explored but carefully graded: jealousy and revenge are unforgiveable, but adultery and false friendship may be pardoned. Frankford, whom Heywood avoids making priggish, eschews jealousy and revenge, deeply though he is tormented; Anne is penitent to death; and Wendoll, the seducer, goes "free." The great, and surely telling, irony of the play (lost in those productions which crudely omit the subplot) is that it is the upright husband and the penitent wife who suffer most; the erring friend goes free; but in the subplot, the killing of two men in a fight and the attempt to prostitute a sister, together with double-dealing and revenge, can end "happily." The plots are only tenuously linked in narrative

terms. Their relationship is tonal and highly imaginative.

In the first quarto edition part one of *If You Know Not Me You Know Nobody* is alternatively titled *The troubles of Queene Elizabeth,* and the first quarto edition of the second part has two subtitles: *With the building of the Royall Exchange: And the famous Victorie of Queen Elizabethe in the Yeare 1588."* The first part is very short but was popular enough to be revived at the Cockpit theater many years after its first production.

Part one draws on John Foxe's *Acts and Monuments* and, as would be expected of its time and Heywood's own predilections, is written from a Protestant point of view. Queen Mary is peremptory and cruel toward her sister Elizabeth, and some of Mary's agents, notably the Constable of the Tower, where Elizabeth is imprisoned, are even worse. In response to Elizabeth's request that she might at least be allowed to walk in the Lieutenant Governor's garden, he replies:

> Ide lay her in a dungeon where her eyes
> Should not haue light to read her prayer-booke.
> So would I danger both her soul and body,
> Cause she an alien is to vs Catholikes:
> Her bed should be all snakes, her rest despaire;
> Torture should make her curse her faithlesse prayer.

Despite such attitudes and despite Heywood's often-noted chauvinism, King Phillip of Spain is presented sympathetically. He behaves honorably and mercifully obtains Elizabeth's release from detention. Again, the common people are shown as more capable of making humane decisions than are their masters. Elizabeth is guarded by Whitecoats from the north of England. The first soldier is incensed at Mary's treatment of Elizabeth and insists on giving vent to his feelings:

> Well, sirs, I haue two sisters, and the one loues the other, and would not send her to prison for a million. Is there any harm in this? Ile keepe myselfe within compasse, I warrant you; for I do not talke of the Queene; I talk of my sisters. Ile keepe myselfe within my compass, I warrant you.

Mary is too cruel and Elizabeth too idealized to make the contrast dramatically interesting, and the narrative is broken up by many short interposed dialogues, often by characters who appear only once–such as the Cook and Pantler followed then by three poor men. They are preceded by a Boy with a nosegay and he by the Clown beating

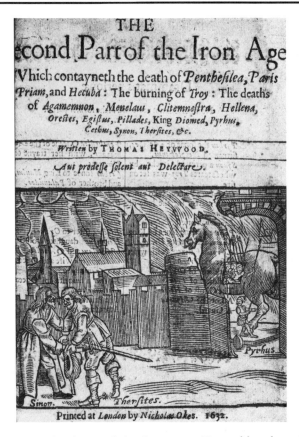

Title page and interior title page for a 1632 quarto edition of the two-part play that concludes the sequence Heywood hoped to collect in "an handsome Volumne . . . with an Explanation of all the difficulties, and an Historicall Comment of every hard name, which may appeare obscure or intricate to such as are not frequent in Poetry . . ." (Henry E. Huntington Library and Art Gallery)

a Soldier (neither of whom says anything and both immediately leaving the stage), and then by the Cook beating another Soldier, the Cook having four lines of dialogue and the Soldier none. Performance might have made this device pass muster, and certainly by the time Heywood wrote *A Maidenhead Well Lost* he was able to use this technique effectively (as at the beginning of act five). In *The Late Lancashire Witches* he achieves a fluidity, almost at times an impressionistic effect, that is a world apart from the crudity of this technique in his early work.

The religious cast of the play and its claim to be a belated Protestant morality—Heywood seems to have known the "Anti-Catholic Moral Interlude," *Lusty Juventus* of 1550—may be gauged not only from its dramatization of Elizabeth's "troubles" but in the climax to the play: the presentation to her by the Lord Mayor of London of a Bible—an *English* Bible as she notes:

This book, that hath so long conceald itself,
So long shut vp, so long hid, now, lords, see,
We here unclaspe: for euer it is free.

The milieu of *If You Know Not Me You Know Nobody*, part two, is commercial London. It opens with Gresham directing his multifarious merchant ventures and proceeds to dramatize—or rather, chronicle—the activities of merchants, factors, and tradesmen. Of these, Hobson has the best claim to our attention. As so often in Heywood, he has a catch phrase, "bones-a-me," and he incongruously follows Gresham to France dressed in nightgown, cap, and slippers. As well as depicting a thriving contemporary London, Heywood recalls the myths of London's past greatness, and this leads to the erection of the Royal Exchange, for which Gresham is knighted by Queen Elizabeth, who makes a belated entry into the play. Just as a Chorus crudely changes the course of events in part two of *Edward IV* so here a Chorus announces:

From fifty eight, the first yeare of her raigne,
We come to eighty-eight, and of her raigne
The thirtieth yeare.

Then is dramatized–chronicled–the defeat of the Armada, mainly through a succession of reports (though we see Elizabeth review her soldiers at Tilbury, and there is a scene on Medina Sidonia's ship). The defeat is attributed entirely to the bravery of the English seamen and the skill of their commanders: the storms that wreaked such havoc are not mentioned.

The play gives some sense of London's commercial life, idealized though it is, but for all these positive aspects it is rather heavy going, weighed down by its worthiness and lacking the sparkle of humor that Heywood so often can provide. One stage direction should, however, be picked out: the call for a comet to pass overhead. The direction reads, *"A blasing star,"* Hobson crying out, "Look how it streaks!"

The Wise Woman of Hogsdon (Hoxton, site of the nineteenth-century Britannia Theatre, in North London) can lay fair claim to being one of Heywood's best plays and, indeed, one of the best non-Shakespearean comedies of the period. It has something of the joie de vivre of the decades preceding 1600–Henry Porter's *The Two Angry Women of Abingdon* comes to mind, though Heywood's play is much the better. Like his own *The English Traveller*, and like *Lusty Juventus*, which Taber mentions in the play, it is a morality about wayward youth. Young Chartley, "a wild-headed Gentleman," tries to seduce Luce, a Goldsmith's daughter, by false marriage at the fortune-telling, baby-farming abode of the Wise Woman. But there are two Luces–a coincidence as acceptable and comic here as it is unfortunate in *The Fair Maid of the West*, part two. There is much deception and disguising, and in the end all comes out happily, *but* (and it is a very big but) not before Young Chartley has been thoroughly shamed, publicly exposed, and dramatized as truly repentant:

OLD CHARTLEY. Well art thou seru'd to bee a
    generall scorne,
To all thy bloud: and if not for our sakes,
For thy soules health and credit of the world,
Haue some regard to mee, to mee thy father.
CHARTLEY. Enough sir: if I should say I would become a new man; You would not take my word. If I should sweare, I would amend my life, you would not take mine oath, if I should bind my selfe, to become an honest man you would scarce take my bond.
OLD CHARTLEY. I should doe none of these.

CHARTLEY. Then see sir, when to all your judgements I see me past grace, doe I lay hold of *Grace*, and heere begin to retyre my selfe, this woman hath lent mee a glasse, in which I see all my imperfections, at which my conscience doth more blush inwardly, then my face outwardly, and now I dare confidently vndertake for my selfe I am honest.

Lies and deceptions are firmly put aside; the man who maintained in III.ii that "this 'Till death us do part' is tedious" has learned a different attitude, juxtaposed with that assertion:

LUCE'S FATHER. Son, Son, had I esteem'd my
    profit more
Then I have done my credit, I had now
Beene many thousands richer: but you see,
Truth and good dealing beare an humble saile;
That little I injoy, it is with quiet,
Got with good conscience, kept with good report:
And that I still shall labour to preserve.

Luce's father's speech has something of the measured propriety of Shakespeare's Corin in his defense of his livelihood against Touchstone's strictures. Once again Heywood shows ordinary humble folk as knowing and practicing *de vere nobilitate* whereas those to whom that phrase should be meaningful are the hollow men.

The play is firmly rooted in real speech, II.i being a good example. The comedy is often delightful, fresh, and vivid; yet it makes certain demands on the audience indicating that Heywood cannot have been relying solely on an appeal to "ordinary humble folk." Many jokes require a knowledge of Latin and, what is more, a quick ear to pick up what is obvious on the page but less so in the rapid interchange of dialogue onstage, as in these lines from act four:

SENCER. . . . Whats Latin for this Earth?
SIR BONIFACE. Facile and easy more fit
    for the pupill then the preceptor: whats
    Latin for this Earth? *Tellus.*
SENCER. Tell you; no syr, it belongs to
    you to tell mee.
SIR BONIFACE. I say *Tellus* is Latin for
    the Earth.
SENCER. And I say, I will not tell you
    what is Latin for the Earth; vnless you
    yeild mee victor.

The play has, like *The Fair Maid of the Exchange*, a shop scene in which gallants pester the tradesman's daughter: "I doe not love to sit thus publikely," says Luce, "And yet upon the traffique of our Wares, / Our provident Eyes and presence must still wayte"; Heywood's almost regulation tavern scene, familiar proverbs ("A Catt may looke at a King"); and some interesting directions, such as "&c" to indicate ad libbing is permissible and, near the end of act four, when Taber enters with *a bowle of Beere and a Napkine* and Sencer and Sir Boniface, an ignorant schoolmaster, *"dissemble one to another"*; shortly after, Chartley enters *"with his Napkin as from Dinner."*

As the Wise Woman says in III.i, "Here were even a Plot to make a play on," and this Heywood does excellently well. Of all his plays it is the one most worth reviving, given a production with style and panache.

Heywood's *The Rape of Lucrece* presents the twentieth-century reader with fascinating problems. Its mixture of the classical and comic, contemporary Europe, bawdy and song, has something superficially in common with *Cymbeline*, but the overall tone, despite the setting and frequent use of Latinate words, never suggests Rome as Shakespeare so wondrously does in his Roman plays. Its juxtaposition of the rape itself with a bawdy catch has struck most critics as being in the worst possible taste. Addington Symonds maintained, "This catch, which jokes in such a ribald fashion over Tarquin's crime, furnishes a pointed example of the way in which the dramatists of the period pandered to the tastes of the less refined among their audiences." But perhaps that is too superficial a view given Heywood's generally moral tone. Could he be attempting something more subtle?

The story is an extension back in time of that recounted in Shakespeare's poem and continued forward to include Horatio at the Bridge. It begins with Tarquin the Proud's usurpation of the throne of Rome from King Servius. Tarquin's consort, Tullia, has much in common with Lady Macbeth, and Shakespeare's influence is apparent very early in the play–in the third line:

TARQUIN. What would'st thou wife?
TULLIA. Be what I am not, make thee greater farre
  Then thou canst aime to be.
TARQUIN. Why I am *Tarquin.*
TULLIA. And I am *Tullia*, what of that?
....
  To be a queen I long, long, and am sicke.
  With ardency my hot appetite's a fire,
  Till my swolne fervor be delivered
  Of that great title Queene....

She is prepared to "lave our brows . . . in that crimson flood" for they "must be bold and dreadlesse."

King Servius is quickly disposed of, Heywood anticipating the "logic" of our times by having the usurper claim no fewer than four times in rapid succession that it is the usurped who usurps. Tullia completes the degradation of her father, the king, and of herself, by stepping on his body–"No matter," she says, "let his mangled body lie." Rebellious opposition is soon raised, and the usurping Tarquin's response is to make alliances and war abroad–again a common contemporary device. Heywood puts it succinctly when Tarquin says, "Kings that are proud, yet would secure their owne, / By love abroad, shall purchase feare at home."

These lines enable a transition to be made to the context of the rape. The town of Ardea is besieged; the Roman commanders boast of their wives' virtues and pay a surprise visit on them at home. Lucrece, of course, is not only the most virtuous but attracts the lustful eye of one of the king's sons, Sextus Tarquin. The scene is set for the sexual parallel to the rape of the throne by Tarquin son and father respectively. The entry of the Roman commanders into Lucrece's house is an excellent example of Heywood's craftsmanship. He provides a natural conversation which effectively summarizes the visits made to the other wives. Decorum requires that the rape is not carried out onstage (at least in Heywood's day), and, though Lucrece is discovered in bed, at the end of the scene, Sextus carries her off. The events thereafter are as told in Shakespeare's poem, coupled with Horatio at the Bridge, the eventual victory of the Romans, and the crowning of Collatinus, Lucrece's husband, as Consul, following the death of Brutus, who kills Sextus but is slain in the process.

So far, the play is, as Heywood called it, a tragedy. It is not particularly remarkable, having neither the virtues of Shakespeare's poem nor Lady Macbeth's dramatic power. What, paradoxically, distinguishes the play is its use of humor and song.

Brutus, though a heroic figure who behaves with rectitude and courage, is also clownish. Admittedly his humor is put on, rather as is Hamlet's antic disposition, but he nevertheless makes a good clown. There is also a genuine Clown, so named, who would have been more appropriate in one of Heywood's domestic dramas. But it is, perhaps, the songs that surprise one most. There

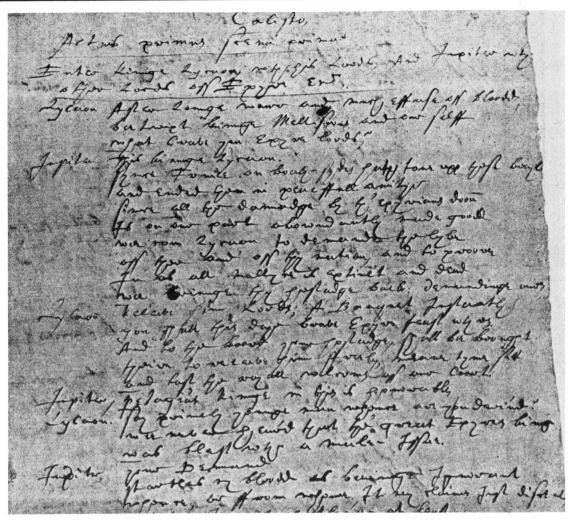

Upper portion of the first page from the manuscript for The Escapes of Jupiter. *Written in Heywood's hand, this manuscript is headed* Calisto, *a title that refers to the first act of the play, for which Heywood selected and revised scenes from* The Golden Age *and* The Silver Age *(MS Egerton 1994, f. 74'; by permission of the British Library).*

are no fewer than nineteen: none in the first and last acts but nine in act two, three in act three, and five in act four. Most of these are sung by one of the noble Romans, Valerius, though the Clown has a song, and Horatio and the Clown share in the bawdy catch. Simple arithmetic will show that two songs are unaccounted for. Heywood actually added two in an appendix, remarking that they "were added by the stranger that lately acted Valerius." One of these, "The Cries of Rome," is obviously a "Cries of London" song with Rome substituted for London. What is apparent is not only that Heywood did not object to the interjection of even more songs but that the use of songs must have appealed to the audiences. Neither of these additions is bawdy.

Many of the songs are inappropriate if only because out of topographical place–there are very "English" songs, a Scotch song, a Double-Dutch song, and a song devoted to the characteristics of all the nations of Europe and the Near East (to be repeated in *A Challenge for Beauty*). But it is the catch that attracts contumely, and it may offer a clue to what Heywood was up to. The catch occurs in the scene when Sextus returns to the camp after the rape. Its tone is well represented by its opening lines:

VALERIUS. *Did he take fair Lucrece by the toe man?*
HORATIO. *Toe man.*
VALERIUS. *I man.*
CLOWN. *Ha ha ha ha ha man.*
HORATIO. *And further did he strive to go man?*
CLOWN. *Goe man.*
HORATIO. *I man.*

There is no doubt that a Victorian critic such as Symonds would find this in poor taste, but are we not *meant* to be disgusted? It is noticeable that shortly after, as Lucrece is telling what happened to her and shortly before she stabs herself, Brutus demands they abjure such behavior:

> As you are Romans, and esteeme your fame
> More then your lives, all humorous toyes set off,
> Of madding, singing, smiling, and what else,
> Receive your native valours, be your selves,
> And joyne with *Brutus* in the just revenge
> Of this chaste ravisht Lady, sweare.

Valerius is among those who swear and who fight. There are no more songs, and the last act is dominated by Horatio's valor in defending the bridge leading to the downfall of the Tarquins.

Heywood may be guilty of combining titilation and morality, but he may also have been attempting a conflict of modes—of pathos and the comic, even the bawdily comic. Possibly it did not wholly succeed in his own day; perhaps the audiences enjoyed the songs too much; certainly we (though surely no more moral) would find the bawdy unacceptable today. *The Rape of Lucrece* may well have been intended to be a play rather like John Ford's *The Fancies Chaste and Noble*—also a much maligned play on similar grounds—which attempted from the juxtaposition of conflicting modes to test audiences anew, to make them "judge" just as Jonson had been prone to do earlier in the century.

Though seemingly written between 1607 and 1609, Heywood and William Rowley's *Fortune by Land and Sea* was not printed until 1655, after the theaters had been closed. It is a curiously mixed play, a characteristic which may be explained by joint authorship were it not typical of Heywood writing solo. What may characterize Rowley is a hard edge to some of the characters—Old Harding in particular. The play has some of Heywood's rapid, even absurd, turns of fate. Old Harding has married again, to the young, good-hearted Anne. His eldest son, Philip, against his father's wishes, marries Susan, from a family which has seen better times. As her father, Old Forrest, tells Old Harding:

> you called me then
> Your Landlord and young Master: then was then,
> But now the course of fortunes wheele is turned;
> You climbed, we fell, and that inconstant fate
> That hurled us down, hath lift you where we sate.

Old Harding disinherits his son and puts him and his bride into the family service, wearing clown's clothes, his brothers treating him with contempt.

Susan's family meets further setbacks. Her eldest brother is killed in a singularly unmotivated tavern quarrel (compare *The Fair Maid of the West*, part one); the younger brother, in revenge but in a fair duel, kills the murderer. Forced to flee, he is helped by Anne and a merchant (who turns out to be Old Harding's brother). He becomes a successful ship's master by raiding Spanish ships, rescues the Merchant (who had been captured by pirates), and returns home wealthy. The loss of the merchant's ship kills Old Harding, because he had wealth laid up therein, but before he can remake his will—so Philip inherits the estate. He shows his brothers the kindness they denied him, and Young Forrest marries Old Harding's widow, Anne. This turn of events led Barron Field (the self-claimed "first Australian Harmonist") in his 1846 edition to describe the play as "a very good drama, full of spirit and poetical justice." If such poetical justice, such spinning of the wheel of fortune, is less to our taste today, there are yet very interesting elements in the play.

Once again, it is a play which is indebted to the *Lusty Juventus*, youth-morality tradition. In I.i Old Forrest speaks against youthful rioting just prior to his eldest son's death in a tavern, and, when the wheel of fate has turned, Philip speaks similarly to his wastrel brothers in the play's penultimate speech. In IV.i there is a quite remarkable dramatization of a fight at sea between Philip's ship and that of the pirates, Purser and Clinton, who in the previous scene were the subject of an excellent parodic litany, not much to Barron Field's taste but in the tradition of those used elsewhere by Heywood (in *The Captives* and *The English Traveller*) and going back to the fifteenth century; act five opens with an interesting dialogue between two pirates on their way to execution. The pirates, Clinton and Purser, active in Elizabeth's time, were the subject of *A True Relation, of the Lives and Deaths of the Two English Pyrats, Purser, and Clinton*, written by Heywood and published in 1639. The use of travel imagery in Clinton and Purser's dialogue is similar to that in *The English Traveller*, and it anticipates the sea salt's language of the naval melodramas of the nineteenth century:

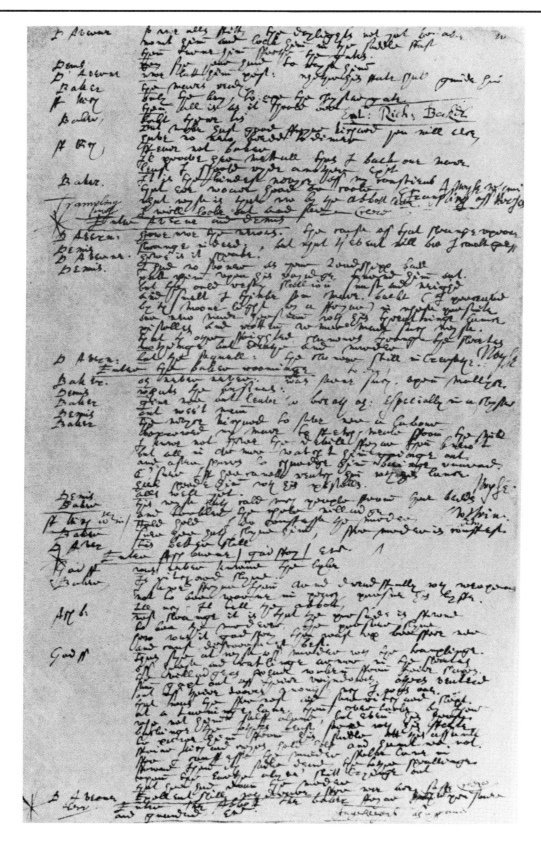

Page from the manuscript for The Captives. *This manuscript is written in Heywood's hand, with revisions by another (see lines 9, 17, and 78 of the portion of V.ii shown above) (MS Egerton 1994, f. 70*ʳ*; by permission of the British Library).*

CLINTON. What is our Ship wel tackled? we may
  lanch
  Upon this desperate voyage.
HANGMAN. Corded bravely.
PURSER. Call up the Boatswain, soundly lash the
  slave
  With a ropes end; have him unto the Chest,
  Or duck him at the Mainyard.
HANGMAN. Have me to the chest, I must first
  have you to the Gallows, and for Ducking, I'm
  afraid I shall see you duckt and drakt too.
....
CLINTON. Enough *Tom Watton,* with these sheets not
  sailes,
  A stiff gale blows to split us on yon rock.
PURSER. And set sail from the fatal Marshal seas,
  And *Wapping* is our harbour. . . .

Despite Heywood's diffidence about being
"exposed unto the world in volume," the five
plays on the Ages–*The Golden Age, The Silver Age,
The Brazen Age,* and *The Iron Age* (in two parts)–
were intended by him to be published in a single
"*handsome Volumne,*" and he proposed, "(Deo
Assistente,) *to illustrate the whole Worke, with an Explanation of all the difficulties, and an Historicall Comment of euery hard name, which may appear obscure or
intricate to such as are not frequent in Poetry.* . . . " Heywood never prepared this volume, and it was left
to R. H. Shepherd to say with justifiable pride
that in his 1874 edition of Heywood's works he
had accomplished what Heywood had wished, to
the extent at least of publishing the five plays in
a single volume. The plays were clearly a box-
office success in their own day–as they deserved
to be–for though Heywood begins in all modesty
when telling the reader in the first edition of *The
Golden Age* (1611), "As this is receiued, so you
shall find the rest: either fearefull further to
proceede, or encouraged boldly to follow," by
the time he came to address the reader of part
one of *The Iron Age* in 1632 he could claim:

> I desire thee to take notice, that these were the
> Playes often (and not with the least applause,)
> Publickely Acted by two Companies, vpon one
> Stage at once, and haue at sundry times
> thronged three seuerall Theaters, with numerous
> and mighty Auditories. . . .

The reason for Heywood's success is not
hard to find. Though these plays are not in the
same league as Shakespeare's "classical" dramas,
in his own way Heywood approaches the task he
has set for himself with a high sense of purpose.

As with his desire to instruct humble folk
through the medium of the chronicle history
plays, so here is he laying out, in detail and enter-
tainingly, the whole panoramic world of classical
myth. Most students of English literature in our
universities would benefit considerably from reading Heywood's account. He tells the story "*from*
Iupiter *and* Saturne, *to the vtter subuersion of*
Troy," and obviously this is an enormous under-
taking on a scale far larger even than a Shakespearean tetralogy. It is a precursor to the
television epic series of our own day, and, given
the limitations of the theater of his time, who
would deny that Heywood's single-handed
achievement is not considerably the more
impressive?

The title pages indicate the scope, though
not all the detail, of what Heywood covers and
are worth recapitulating:

THE GOLDEN AGE: OR The liues of *Jupiter* and
  Saturne, with the deifying of the Heathen
  Gods [some copies have *defining* rather than
  deifying];
THE SILVER AGE, INCLVDING. The loue of
  Iupiter to *Alcmena:* The birth of *Hercules.
  AND* The Rape of PROSERPINE. *CON-
  CLUDING,* With the Arraignement of the
  Moone;
THE BRAZEN AGE *The first Act containing,* The
  death of the Centaure *Nessus,* THE SEC-
  OND, The Tragedy of *Meleager:* THE
  THIRD, The Tragedy of *Iason* and *Medea.*
  THE FOVRTH, VVLCANS NET, THE
  FIFTH, The Labours and death of
  HERCVLES;
The Iron Age: Contayning the Rape of Helen:
  The siege of *Troy:* The Combate betwixt *Hec-
  tor* and *Aiax: Hector* and *Troilus* slayne by
  Achilles: Achilles slaine by *Paris: Aiax* and
  Vlisses contend for the Armour of *Achilles:*
  The Death of *Aiax, &c;*
The Second Part of the Iron Age Which
  contayneth the death of *Penthesilea, Paris,
  Priam,* and *Hecuba:* The burning of *Troy:*
  The deaths of *Agamemnon, Menelaus,
  Clitemnestra, Hellena, Orestes, Egistus, Pillades,
  King Diomed, Pyrrhus, Cethus, Synon, Thersites,
  &c.*

Another reason for the success of the series,
and a reason one can still appreciate, is the generally high level of Heywood's creative ability and
the ingenuity of his narrative structures. At times

THE
ENGLISH
TRAVELLER.
AS IT HATH BEENE
Publikely acted at the C O C K - P I T
in Drury-lane :
By Her Maiesties seruants.

Written by T H O M A S H E Y V V O O D.

Aut prodesse solent, aut delectare —————

L O N D O N,
Printed by *Robert Raworth :* dwelling in Old Fish-street,
neere Saint *Mary Maudlins* Church. 1 6 3 3.

Dramatis Personæ.

Geraldine. Dalauill.	Two yong Gentlemen.
Olde Wincott	The husband.
His Wife	A yong Gentlewoman.
Prudentilla	Sister to the wife.
Reignald	A parasiticall seruing-man.
Robin	A countrey seruing-man.
Lionell	A riotous Citizen.
Blanda	A Whore.
Scapha	A Bawde.
Rioter	A Spend-thrift
Two Gallants	His Companions.
Roger the Clowne	Seruant to Olde Wincott.
Two prostitutes	Companions with Blanda.
Olde Lionell	A Merchant father to yong Lionell.
A Seruant	To Olde Lionell.
Olde Mr. Geraldine	Father to yong Geraldine.
An Vsurer and his man.	
A Gentleman	Companion with Dalauill.
Besse	Chambermaid to Mistris Wincott.
A Tauerne Drawer.	
Master Ricott	A Merchant.
The Owner of the house, supposed to be possest.	

                                                                                   T O

To the Reader.

F Reader thou hast of this Play beene an audi-
tour ? there is lesse apology to be vsed by intrea-
ting thy patience. This Tragi-Comedy (being
one reserued amongst two hundred and twenty, in
which I haue had either an entire hand, or at
the least a maine finger, comming accidentally to the Presse,
and I hauing Intelligence thereof, thought it not fit that it
should passe as filius populi, a Bastard without a Father to acknowledge it : True it is, that my Playes are not exposed vnto
the world in Volumes, to beare the title of Workes, (as others)
one reason is, That many of them by shifting and change of Companies, haue beene negligently lost, Others of them are still
retained in the hands of some Actors, who thinke it against
their peculiar profit to haue them come in Print, and a third,
That it neuer was any great ambition in me, to bee in this
kind Volumniously read. All that I haue further to say at this
time is onely this : Censure I intreat as fauourably, as it is
exposed to thy view freely. euer

Studious of thy Pleasure and Profit,

                                             Thomas Heywood.

A 3   The

*Title page, dramatis personae, and epistle to the reader from the 1633 quarto edition of a play that Heywood is thought to have writ-
ten in 1625 (Bodleian Library)*

the language becomes incongruously colloquial–Juno as "you (gooddy witch)," in act three of *The Silver Age* for example–but in this Heywood's shortcomings are considerably fewer than many a twentieth-century writer who should have greater awareness of language perspective. The mass of material, as the "contents" show, is incredibly unwieldy, but not in Heywood's hands. If no Shakespeare or Marlowe, Heywood is never dull in his writing, at times moving (as in the fate of Semele, in act three of *The Silver Age),* nearly always interesting, often richly comic (the conversation between Socia and Ganymede in act two of *The Silver Age* is a good example), and on occasion he achieves a brilliantly judged seriocomic effect, as in these lines from act four of *The Golden Age:*

> Iupiter *puts out the light and makes vnready.*
> DANAE. Good my lord forbeare
> What do you meane? (oh heauen) is no man neere,
> If you will needs, for modesties chast law,
> Before you come to bed, the curtaines draw,
> But do not come, you shall not by this light,
> If you but offer't, I shall cry out right.
> Oh God, how hoarse am I, and cannot? fie
> *Danae* thus naked and a man so nye.
> Pray leaue me sir: he makes vnready still,
> Well I'le euen winke, and then do what you will.
> *The bed is drawne in, and enter the Clowne new wak't.*

The phrase "makes vnready" sums up the emotions perfectly.

The plays were also successful for a reason that Heywood himself gave–though he was not claiming such success. Homer, who acts as interlocutor in the first three plays, introduces act four of *The Brazen Age* by saying:

> Loath are we (curteous auditors) to cloy
> Your appetites with viands of one tast,
> The beauteous Venus we must next imploy[.]

The sheer variety of the plays is remarkable. It is not simply that many stories are told, but that they are so variously dramatized and so cunningly juxtaposed. Thus, there is no mention of Venus and Adonis in the title-page summaries but the story is dramatized in *The Brazen Age* in conjunction with that of Meleager's downfall, also set in a hunt. Further, each play has a different style. Thus, *The Silver Age* is less consciously elevated than *The Golden Age,* and it begins rather like an Italianate intrigue drama. It then shifts

gear smoothly into an excellent "Comedy of Errors," develops into a masque, elevates its tone for the rape of Proserpine, and concludes with something like a fireworks display:

> Hercules *sinkes himselfe: Flashes of fire; the Diuels appeare at euery corner of the stage with seuerall fire-workes. The Iudges of hell, and the three sisters run ouer the stage,* Hercules *after them: fire-workes all ouer the house. Enter* Hercules.

The fire continues in the next two stage directions. Are we really to believe the suggestion of "total theater" implied by *"fire-workes all ouer the house"*? Historical accounts of performances at outdoor theaters like the Red Bull suggest that we should.

Such pyrotechnics lead to another reason for these plays' attractiveness: spectacle. Literary scholars disdain spectacle, but it has a rightful place in the theater, and Heywood is masterful in his use of it. It does not take over (as it could in the late-nineteenth-century theater), and, after using it so exuberantly in *The Brazen Age* (with directions calling for fireworks, dragons, a sea monster, and fiery bulls, for example), he eschews it, relatively speaking, in the last two plays. This stage direction from the final scene of *The Brazen Age* suggests the sort of spectacle Heywood required:

> Iupiter *aboue strikes him with a thunder-bolt, his body sinkes, and from the heauens discends a hand in a cloud, that from the place where Hercules was burnt, brings vp a starre, and fixeth it in the firmament.*

The Silver Age also makes much use of gods descending in clouds and flying above. Earth rises up from the stage; there are fights, rainbows, many dumbshows, disguisings–everything that the combination of theatricality and masque could devise.

To cap all that, most members of the audience would feel that they were being richly and delightfully instructed. Justifiably, Heywood could feel proud of his achievement, not only as a popular success but in that curious genre of "learning entertainment" advocated by Horace and practiced so effectively in the United States through the museum and lyceum movements of the nineteenth century. Heywood, in these five plays, was perhaps the supreme artist of this genre.

Some measure of the popularity of the four

Ages is to be gathered from the fact that Heywood went on to complete *The Iron Age*–in two parts. The style of these parts, without rivaling Shakespeare, is much more in tune with that of *Troilus and Cressida* than that of the earlier *Ages,* and they include an interesting Thersites. Unlike the first three plays, these two have no Homer as interlocutor. Part one of *The Iron Age* dramatizes the Rape of Helen. This enables Heywood to mention her previously having been ravished by Theseus and that she was party to Paris's rape of her, suggesting the device of the feast aboard Paris's ship which enabled her to be brought away, something Agamemnon (or Heywood) overlooks in part two. Part one then covers much the same ground as *Troilus and Cressida* (touching on their story) and concludes with the funeral processions of Hector and Achilles.

Part two enables Heywood rightly to claim at its conclusion, glancing perhaps at Shakespeare, *"Here ends the whole History of the destruction of* Troy" (whereas Shakespeare treated only part of the story in *Troilus and Cressida*). Heywood includes the story of the Wooden Horse, evidently with a fabricated horse to appear on stage, from which the Greeks descend as described in a revealing stage direction: "Pyrrhus, Diomed, *and the rest, leape from out the Horse. And as if groping in the darke, meete with* Agamemnon *and the rest: who after knowledge imbrace."* In addition, Heywood involves the Amazons, the story of Laocoön, and, in acts four and five, the aftermath to Troy's destruction: the murder of Agamemnon, the revenge of Orestes, and, in an incredible fifth act, the slaughter of at least a dozen of the named characters–"at least" because Heywood himself adds "etc" when indicating those slain. Helen is the last to die, strangling herself, leaving Ulysses to found, among other places, "great Britaines *Troy-nouant"* (that is, London), at the behest of Hector's ghost. (In *A Challenge for Beauty* Heywood turns the Troy-Albion relationship on its head by having Bonavida assert that had "the *Trojan* Ravisher beheld" this English beauty, *"Troy* had still stood.")

Though too much ground is covered in these two plays–there is none of the artistic telescoping found in *Antony and Cleopatra*–Heywood does include much intriguing detail and often careful linkage of the material. Thus, in part two the shift to the story of the outcome of Clytemnestra's adultery is neatly related to that of Helen. If Menelaus pardoned Helen, may not Agamemnon pardon Clytemnestra? The answer (which actually precedes the question) is sharp:

> are not your adulteries
> Famous as *Hellens?* nay, more infamous,
> There was a rape to countenance what shee did,
> You nought saue corrupt lust and idlenesse:
> Tis blab'd in the Citty . . .
> To see what fearefull vengeance he will take
> For that your prostitution.

Heywood is not afraid to glance at Marlowe's Helen. The words "face," "grace," and "eternized" occur and reoccur in part one, and in part two she bemoans her fatal beauty, echoing the line in which Marlowe's Faustus asks, "Was this the face that Launcht a thousand ships":

> Where is that beauty? liues it in this face
> Which hath set two parts of the World at warre,
> ....
> . . . this the beauty,
> That launch'd a thousand ships from *Aulis* gulfe?

As with Hamlet and Gertrude, when Orestes sees the ghost of his father, Clytemnestra does not and thinks him mad. True to his interests in citizen drama, although these five plays are so dominated by gods and heroes, the destruction of Troy in part two of *The Iron Age* is first seen through a brief though sharply etched fifteen-line scene of a terrified citizen and his wife near the end of act two. Near the beginning of act one Thersites and Sinon are matched as "two meeting soules," and their comedy is often pointed:

> SINON: I am a pollitician, oathes with me
>   Are but the tooles I worke with, I may breake
>   An oath by my profession. . . .

Most interesting is the likening of Thersites to Richard III in part one:

> What if *Thersites* sprucely smug'd himselfe,
> And striu'd to hide his hutch-backe: No not I.
> Tis held a rule, whom Nature markes in show
> And most deformes, they are best arm'd below.

There is, it is true, something a little naive about this enterprise of the four *Ages*–as there is so often in Heywood–but that naiveté is not to be mistaken for simplemindedness. Without being a genius Heywood has "genius," and much of it is displayed in these five plays. Writing in his address to the reader in part two of *The Iron Age* (1632) he well summed up his work: *"I know not how they may bee receiued in this Age, where noth-*

ing but Satirica Dictaeria, *and* Comica Scommata *are now in request: For mine owne part, I neuer affected either, when they stretched to the abuse of any person publicke, or priuate."*

From the first two of these five plays, Heywood extracted a play that has survived in manuscript and is known as *The Escapes of Jupiter.* This play brings together Jupiter's escapades with Calisto, Danae, Semele, and Alcmena, reversing the order of the last two and devoting the two final acts to Alcmena. (Semele's misfortune would make a less dramatically satisfactory end to the play.) New links are written for Homer, and there is some revision, especially in the first three acts—such as the comic drag act given to Jupiter. Although it is probably correctly assumed that *The Escapes of Jupiter* is later, some of the revisions suggest weakening of the original, most notably Danae's seriocomic speech.

The Captives is a workmanlike drama of a kind that in a later age would doubtless have achieved a respectable run on Broadway or in the West End of London, but, partly because Heywood can so often surprise and partly because the text has come down to us in what is in all probability Heywood's foul papers (with some theatrical annotations), the play is of more than usual interest. The story is slight. It descends from the *Rudens* of Plautus (from which the names Palestra and Gripus in Heywood's play derive) and is not unakin to that which Mozart made into a far finer work of art, *Il Seraglio.* The play is set in Marseilles but features English merchants in the main plot. Two young women, Palestra and Scribonia, are held captive in a brothel by Mildew, "a trewe venereall broker." He agrees to sell Palestra to a young English merchant, Raphael, but, prompted by his unscrupulous ally, Sarleboys, attempts to make off with the money, both girls, and his material goods by ship. A sudden storm wrecks the boat and separates him from his treasures, and in due course the girls are united with their long-lost fathers, the brothers John and Thomas Ashburne, also merchants, to whom they were known as Mirabell and Winifred; in turn they are united with Raphael and his friend Treadway. The subplot is really quite extraordinary for a play that is, in the main, a typical "all's-well-that-ends-well" comedy. Lord and Lady de Averne have established a small monastery. Two of the monks, Friars John and Richard, are on anything but fraternal terms, and the former is accused of having "a leering eye." Believing his wife to be in love with

Friar Richard, Lord de Averne, with the help of his man, Dennis—a comic—kills the Friar. As the bookkeeper's annotation to the manuscript reads, "Fry: strangled"; and Dennis "comically" remarks, "I dare nwe / lodge him a whole night by my' systers syde / hees nwe past strmpetting."

The quality of the black humor is a feature of the subplot. Richard's body is hoisted over the monastery wall to lay the blame at its door (in a scene that is comic enough); Friar John sees his hated colleague, thinks he is ignoring him, and, to rouse his attention, is given one of the most famous stage directions in the Elizabethan theater: *"Eather strykes him with a staffe or Casts a stone."* Then, thinking he has killed Richard, he dumps the body at de Averne's door—creating more opportunity for grotesquerie. The dead Friar is then dressed in full armor, set upon a horse, and gives chase to Friar John who has—perchance—just borrowed the baker's horse. John admits to the murder and is on the way to be hanged when de Averne, in a fit of remorse, admits to the crime. Within fifty lines he is reprieved, after his widow, defying time and in a fair imitation of the Duchess of York in *Richard II,* refuses to rise from her knees until the king has signed a pardon. The absurdity of all this is obvious, but so is the *humour noir.* Also of moment is the fact that the subplot is not concluded until after the main plot, and the pattern of sudden resolution is precisely that of nineteenth-century melodrama. The casual killing of Friar Richard, who has not done anything reprehensible, goes unpunished and serves as no more than a source of cruel comedy. The fact that the subplot is rather funny leaves one uncertain as to whether to be amused or shocked.

A characteristic of the main plot is the considerable use of comic formulae from the popular dramatic tradition of the preceding two centuries. The family clown, John Ashburn, and his servant, Godfrey, engage in a highly alliterative comic turn in act three; there is a comic litany in act five and a rhyming litany in act five like those in *Jacob and Esau* (1554) and *As You Like It,* III.ii (there are also similar passages in *Fortune by Land and Sea* and *The English Traveller);* and soon after this litany Heywood includes a begging trick of the *Love's Labour's Lost* remuneration variety (III.i), like the one in *The Fair Maid of the Exchange.* The play reproduces a number of proverbs, such as "anythinge / for a quiet lyffe"; "nought venters nothinge gaynes"; and "I com to you wth the ould / proverbe, alls not ffishe that coms to nett." The grotesque is also to be found in such lines as Dennis's on the disposal of Richard's body: "shall wee poppe him in som privy," which is lively if not tasteful, and Heywood's chauvinism crops up in such lines as "I tell thee pesant, /Englands no broode ffor slaves." An echo of *An Apology for Actors,* which describes how a murderess confessed at a play performance in Lynn, Norfolk, as Hamlet plans with "The Mousetrap," may be found in V.ii: "Murders' a sinne / wch often is myraculously reveald" (compare Hamlet's "For murder, though it have no tongue, will speak / With most miraculous organ," II.ii). Lines from *As You Like It* III.v are quoted in II.ii: "who ever lovd that lov'd not att ffyrst sight / the poets exellent sayinge," and the Clown is called Jaques.

The English Traveller is a product of Heywood's maturity, its writing being attributed to the year 1625 when he would have been fifty-one. Furthermore, it is one of the first fruits of his return to theater writing after a seeming gap of nearly a decade between about 1616 and 1624. The play is, in one sense, remarkably old-fashioned. In theme and specifics it is strongly influenced by the morality plays of a century earlier. Perhaps Heywood was aware of this fact for he opens his prologue with:

> *A Strange Play you are like to haue, for know*
> *We vse no Drum, nor Trumpet, nor Dumbe show;*
> *No Combate, Marriage, not so much today*
> *As Song, Dance, Masque, to bumbaste out a Play.*

His tragicomedy (the genre to which he attributes it in his address to his readers) also looks back to *A Woman Killed with Kindness.* In the final act Young Geraldine adjures the errant wife of Old Wincott:

> bow to Heauen,
> Which thou hast most offended; . . .
> ....
> Die, and die soone, acquit me of my Oath,
> But prethee die repentant; Farewell euer,
> 'Tis thou, and onely thou hast Banisht mee,
> Both from my Friends and Countery.
> WIFE. Oh, I am lost.   *Sinkes downe.*

It is here that the influence of the morality is strong. When Delavil, who has seduced her and traduced his "friend" Young Geraldine, appears, he says, "See, I am Dalauill," and the wife replies:

> Th'art then a Deuille, that presents before mee
> My horrid sins; perswades me to dispaire;

> When hee like a good Angell sent from Heauen,
> Besought me of repentance. . . .

She is led off (though there is no stage direction), and shortly afterward comes news that she has expired. The Devil (note the deliberate, if strained, association with Delavil's name), sin, a good angel, and above all, despair take one back to the morality, perhaps, via Marlowe's *Dr. Faustus* (which is clearly suggested in act three of the play, when Old Geraldine proposes to "sift" his son's soul and when the Clown refers to a "Bottle of Hay").

Although the play's title suggests travel of a physical kind, and although it is true that Young Geraldine has just returned from a European journey when the play opens and that Old Lionel returns from his travels in act two, the "travel" of the play is really that through life and in particular in the development of social and spiritual maturity. Youth and age are strongly contrasted in the play, and the Clown early points out that his master, Old Wincott, "corresponds not with the youth of my Mistris, and you know cold Ianuary and lust May seldome meet in coniunction."

Young Geraldine has for his part an innocent relationship with Old Wincott's wife. Although he admits to loving her, he will not cuckold her husband and does no more than ask her to marry him when Old Wincott dies. In the meantime, he says, they will live as brother and sister. He confirms this with a kiss, and at his behest they then "diuide," "you to your priuate Chamber, / I to find out my friend." When Young Geraldine is traduced by Delavil, he abjures her company and Old Wincott's house completely. In the end it is the wife, as temptress, and Delavil, the false friend, who suffer, though, as in *A Woman Killed with Kindness,* the woman dies while the man merely leaves in disgrace. It is possible that Heywood, rather than thinking women should be more severely punished, believed them more sensitive to sin and shame. That he had an interest in a woman's point of view and sympathy for women can be seen not only in many of his female dramatic characters but in such works as *Gunaikeion: or Nine Books of Various History Concerning Women* (published in 1624, the year before *The English Traveller* was probably written).

Although Young Geraldine is mature enough to withstand temptation, the other young men are more clearly in accord with sixteenth-century moralities such as *Lusty Juventus.* Thus,

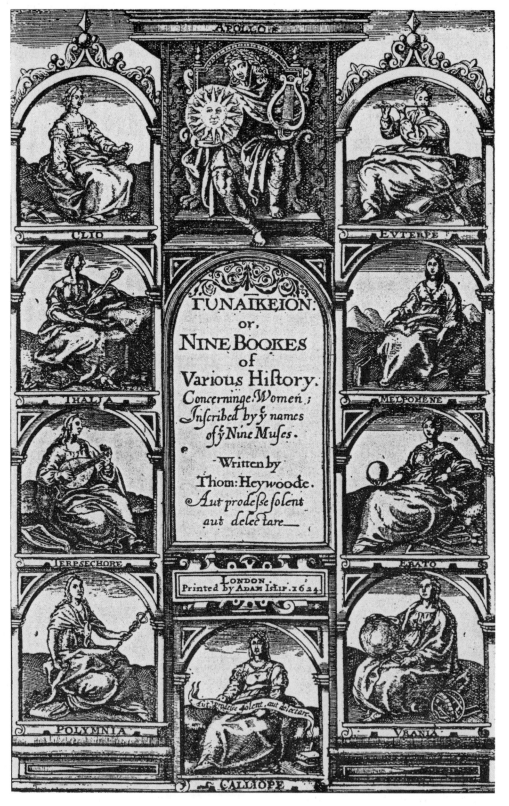

Title page, with engravings depicting the Muses, for the 1624 folio edition of a work that demonstrates the same sympathy for women displayed in many of Heywood's plays (from an undated Pickering & Chatto catalogue)

Young Lionel is described in the dramatis personae as "A riotous Citizen"; one character is called
a Rioter and is described as "A Spend-thrift,"
and Reignald is "A parasiticall seruing-man." In
I.ii, when Reignald is putting out of doors the
faithful serving man, Robin (he is restored at the
end of the play of course), he is told:

> Waste, Ryot, and Consume, Mispend your Howres
> In drunken Surfets, lose your dayes in sleepe,
> And burne the nights in Reuells, Drinke and Drab,
> ....
> . . . all that masse of wealth
> Got by me Masters sweat and thrifty care,
> Hauocke in prodigall vses.

Later in the same scene Young Lionel, at the end
of a long soliloquy, admits that "Lust, Disobedience, and profuse Excesse" drive out "The Thrift
with which our fathers tiled our Roofes" and
give place "to euery riotous sinne." Even the
Bawd, Scapha, can say, "heeres nothing but
Prodigallity and Pride, Wantoning, and Wasting,
Rioting, and Reuelling, Spoyling, and Spending, Gluttony, and Gormondising, all goes to
Hauocke . . ."—a virtual recall of the Seven
Deadly Sins.

Heywood makes considerable use of travel
imagery, and it is well related to his theme of the
journey through life. Thus Old Geraldine says to
his son in act three:

> You are growne perfect man, and now you float
> Like to a well built Vessell; 'Tweene two Currents,
> Vertue and Vice; Take this, you steere to harbour
> Take that, to eminent shipwracke.

William Hazlitt, as Symonds noted, regarded the
description of drunkenness in terms of a storm at
sea in act two as "the most splendid passage in
Heywood's comedies." The pervasive use of such
imagery, traditional though it is, is handled well
and, one imagines, very consciously by Heywood.
As ever, he is an excellent craftsman, and though
his theme is an old one he gives it life and interest. What is more, he solves that most difficult of
dramatic problems: he makes a morally good character interesting and avoids priggishness—a gift
he shares with George Bernard Shaw.

As would be expected of Heywood, the play
is not without a fair amount of comedy. In this
play it does not risk the charge of getting out of
hand as, perhaps, in *The Rape of Lucrece*. There is
a good Clown—a typical "family fool"—who has a
dramatic function in the play as well as being a

source of some respectable comedy; and the para-
sitical servant, Reignald, has one or two good
comic moments, particularly in act three, when
he is deceiving his master and holding off a Usurer simultaneously. Heywood makes considerable
use of forms of comedy from the sixteenth century. Reignald and Young Lionel have a comic litany in I.ii, and the Clown's monologue at the
end of the first scene would not have disgraced
Shakespeare. The Clown makes great use of
comic alliteration, and his account of the massacre at a dinner—of the food—is good fun. At the
end of act three, describing himself in a way that
antecedes Mrs. Malaprop as "something oblivious," he admits to being of Old Wincott's counsel: he is, he says, "His Priuy" (which the editor
of the Mermaid edition delicately glosses as
"Privy Council"). There is also comic reference
by Reignald to "a murdered Ghost," a line done
quite as comically as in Fielding.

A Maidenhead Well Lost shows Heywood writing in an alien mode: alien in that the play is set
in Italy, and alien in that its moral stance hardly accords with that underlying his London plays. For
Heywood, doubtless, as for many Englishmen
then and now, moral corruption starts once the
Channel is crossed. While showing his versatility,
it cannot be said to add stature to his reputation.
In his address to the reader Heywood makes two
interesting claims. There is nothing in the play,
he argues, that "*doth deuiate either from* Modesty,
or good Manners"—the kind of appeal to decorum
and "good taste" that would become so marked
at the end of the next century (and be pilloried
by Ludwig Tieck in his *Puss in Boots*, 1797). Nor,
says Heywood, can the play "*be drawne within the
Criticall censure of that most horrible* Histriomastix."
William Prynne's 1633 attack on the evils of the
theater may be monstrously large, but it is infinitely more learned than Heywood's *An Apology
for Actors*, and one might doubt that this play
would support the case against Prynne.

The play is an Italianate comedy of intrigue. Julia, the Duke of Milan's daughter, has become pregnant prior to her marriage to the
Prince of Parma. The machinations of Stroza, a
Machiavel ("More plot for mee; / My brain's in labour, and must be deliuered / Of some new
mischief," he says in act one), ensure the abandonment of Julia by Parma, the banishment of the virtuous Lauretta and her mother, and the putting
by of the newborn babe. All these complications
are resolved through the tired device of a bed
trick, no less, no more attractive than in *Measure*

A Pleaſant Comedy, called
A
MAYDEN-HEAD WELL LOST.
As it hath beene publickly Acted at the *Cocke-pit*
in *Drury-lane, with much Applauſe:*
By her Maieſties *Seruants.*

Written by THOMAS HEYVVOOD.

Aut prodeſſe ſolent, aut deleĉtare.

LONDON,
Printed by *Nicholas Okes* for *Iohn Iackſon* and *Francis Church,* and are
to be ſold at the *Kings Armes* in *Cheape-ſide,* 1634.

Title page for the 1634 quarto edition of the play that, according to Heywood, contains nothing that "doth deuiate either
from Modesty, *or good* Manners *(Maggs Bros., catalogue number 569, 1932)*

for *Measure* or *All's Well that Ends Well,* and rather less replete with black humor than in *The Changeling.* All is, in the end, "well"; virtue triumphs in the shape of the innocent Lauretta (despite her participation in the bed trick, as she says, not for the gold but for "that deere loue" she bears the Prince), the truly generous mother (who makes herself destitute to pay off her husband's soldiers), and the decently honourable Young Prince of Florence.

There are three dumb shows dramatizing the birth and concealment of Julia's illegitimate child (near the end of act two); the marriage of Julia (at the beginning of act four); and the bedding of the Prince of Florence on his wedding night, complete with stage direction *"others snatch his Pointes"*–the laces tying up his codpiece (at the end of act four). The dumb shows are effectively integrated into the play and genuinely serve to carry the story forward, and, of course, they counterpoint the normal course of wooing-marriage-procreation disturbed in Julia's relationship with the Prince. The snatching of points and the play's comedy (as well as the bed trick) would scarcely appeal to Prynne. Similarly, there is an expected play on "doing" at the beginning of act two. When Julia explains to Parma that she is pregnant by him and "it will ill become your Oathes and Vowes / To iest at my vndoeing," he responds, "You should say / Rather your doing." Parma follows up this speech with "why do you weepe? / You are not hungry, for your bellie's full." The Clown is probably the most sympathetic character. He has common sense–"I had rather beg a thousand times, then starue once"–and some modest humor, but here, far more than in *The Rape of Lucrece*, Heywood seems to be writing down to what he supposes is the audience's low taste. In *The Rape of Lucrece* Heywood may have been attempting something novel through the conflict of modes. Heywood does touch on the problem posed by the marriage of those of different classes (as he did in part one of *The Fair Maid of the West*) when the Prince says to Lauretta:

> would thou wert a Dutchesse,
> That I might court thee vpon equall tearmes;
> Or that I were of low deiected fortunes,
> To ranke with thee in Birth[;]

but he makes nothing of this problem; it is, indeed, forgotten.

Love's Mistress, or, The Queen's Masque is, as its second title indicates, more a masque than a drama–its settings were designed by Inigo Jones. It was presented at the Cockpit (or Phoenix) theater in Drury Lane as well as three times within eight days before the King and Queen and "sundry Forraigne Ambassadors," according to the 1636 title page. The play is founded on the story of Cupid's love for Psyche, the disapproval of Venus, Cupid's rejection of Psyche at one point, her being turned ugly and then recovering her beauty in a quest that takes her to the underworld. While this story is not particularly fascinating today, it is easy to see why the tale and the language in which Heywood told it pleased a court audience. What is, perhaps, of some interest today is the juxtaposition of the dance digressions, forming virtual antimasques at the ends of each of the first four acts, and the dialogues between the two presenters, Apuleius (who enters first carrying a pair of ass's ears) and Midas, which occur at the start of the play and at the conclusion of each act. Though they are not quite intermeans of the kind Ben Jonson devised for such plays as *Every Man out of His Humour* (produced in 1599) and *The Staple of News* (produced in 1626), Heywood learned from these examples and from Jonson's disposition of dances in his masques. The final dance, at the end of act five–instead of being performed by such characters as *"a Drunken Asse"* and "An Ignorant Asse" (as in act one); "Pan, Clowne, Swaines, *and Countrey-wenches*" (as in act two); *"a King and a Begger, a Young-man and an Old woman, a Leane man, a Fat woman"* (as in act three); and perhaps "Vulcan *and his* Ciclopps" (as in act four)–is evidently more refined–at least those involved are "Cupid, Psiche, *the gods and goddesses*," providing a formal shift in tone that marks the happy resolution of the work's issues.

The play includes a clown more Heywoodian than divine, who has an alliterative speech in act two where he lists Cupid's "stile in Folio":

> Hee is King of cares, cogitations, and cox-combes; vice-roy of vowes and vanities; Prince of passions, prate-apaces, and pickled livers; Duke of disaster, dissemblers, and drown'd eyes; Marquesse of molancholly, and mad-folkes, grand Signoir of griefes, and grones; Lord of Lamentations, Hero of hie-hoes, Admirall of aymes, and Mounsieur of mutton-lac'd.

This word play is part of a tradition that stretched back many decades and, in popular comedy, is still with us. The language at this level contrasts effectively and amusingly with the more decorous style of the gods and nobles. Thus, the conclusion of Cupid's address to Psyche near the end of act one–"Ile now crowne thy bed / With the sweet spoiles of thy lost Maiden-head"–is immediately followed by Midas's "Hand off, let goe my sheepe-hooke." In the speech by Apuleius that opens the play, there is a direct appeal to

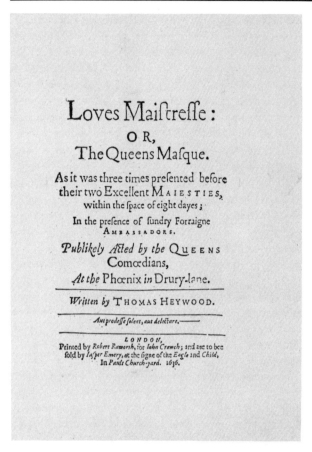

Title page for the 1636 quarto edition of the play whose "Argument" Heywood calls "a golden Truth, conteined in a leaden fable"

Psyche and Cupid—questions the morality of the play and is answered by Apuleius:

> Do they not teach the very feinds in hell
> Speake in blanke verse; doe wee not daily see
> Every dull-witted Asse spit Poetrie:
> And for thy Scene; thou bring'st heere on the stage
> A young greene-sicknesse baggage to run after
> A little ape-fac'd boy thou tearm'st a god
> Is not this most absurd?
> APULEIUS. Mis-understanding foole, thus much
>   conceive,
> *Psiche* is *Anima*, *Psiche* is the Soule,
> The Soule a Virgin, longs to be a bride,
> The soule's Immortall, whom then can shee wooe
> But Heaven? . . .

One wonders whose leg is being more violently pulled, the dull-witted reader's or the over-ingenious literary critic's. A speech by the Clown in act two anticipates the sort of epic burlesque associated with Paul Scarron, which was to find favor in its English version at the Restoration.

> by this *Troy* ranne a small Brooke, that one
> might stride over; on the other side dwelt
> *Menelaus* a Farmer, who had a light wench
> to his Wife call'd *Helen*, that kept his
> sheepe, whom *Paris*, one of *Priams* mad
> lads, seeing and liking, ticeth over the
> brooke, and lies with her in despight of
> her husbands teeth. . . .

Anyone who has seen or read *The Crucible* (1953), Arthur Miller's play about the Salem witch trials of 1692, before coming across Heywood and Richard Brome's *The Late Lancashire Witches* cannot but be astonished at the difference in attitudes about witches revealed by these plays: it is Miller, not Heywood and Brome, who takes witchcraft, ancient or modern, with deadly seriousness. Like *The Crucible*, Heywood and Brome's play is based on real events, having been written within months of a witchcraft trial in Lancashire. Those found guilty were not immediately executed but four—called Mal, Meg, Mawd, and Gillian in the play—were brought to London where further investigation took place. Although in time a witness at the trial confessed to having lied, so far as records show, the four women and others lingered on in prison but were not hanged. Whereas Miller's play is tragic, this play is described on its title page as "A well received Comedy, lately Acted at the *Globe* on the *Bankeside*, by the Kings Majesties Actors," and, most aptly, by Laird H. Barber in his edition as "a vari-

the audience which, evidently, Heywood did not expect to be answered:

> I faine would know the way to *Helicon*,
> Can none heere tell mee? Will none silence breake?
> It seems, these sit to heare then, not to speake[.]

After Venus mars Psyche's beauty because she has allowed herself to be deceived by the outward shape of things rather than divining inner beauty and truth, her disfigurement is described as "leprosie" (which is cleared by the labor Venus sets her—filling a vial with water from the source of the River Styx), and she is called "this Leoper." This leprosy is, of course, Venus's disease—venereal disease (to which Heywood had earlier alluded in *The Royal King and the Loyal Subject*). There is thus a slightly disturbing undercurrent to "the Queen's Masque."

Perhaps the most interesting aspect of *Love's Mistress* is its attacks on and defenses of the theater and poetry, which occur throughout. Near the end of act one Midas—referring specifically to

ety show." The play straddles a borderline between the world of farcical topsy-turvidom–with a range of "devilish" tricks far in excess of those in *Dr. Faustus* in kind and number–and that in which dark events and deep-seated fears dwell. It is the farcical world that is in the main dramatized, and one has, perhaps, to infer to a certain degree the extent to which an audience in the 1630s would contribute this dimension of fear. However, the upsetting of the Seely household so that the servants rule the son and daughter and they the father and mother, presents not only farce but, starkly and dramatically, an anarchic breakdown in the rules of order and natural hierarchy.

Acts two, three, and four are packed with strange and exciting incidents. The cats (witches) occupy a mill and drive out successive millers. Robin the servant embarks on a lightning ride to London to fill wine bottles at a favorite inn and returns to Lancashire in less time than it would take to fill the bottles locally. A man is ridden as a horse. The food at a wedding is bewitched, and the bride's cake crumbles to bran. There is wild dancing and a Skimmington (at that time a custom in England, Scotland, Scandinavia, and elsewhere of forcing a nagging wife or unfaithful husband to ride a horse in the company of a parade of derisive noise makers). Whetstone takes revenge by witchcraft, turning the tables on those who called him bastard. The play is crowded with incidents that might have pleased Vapid, the playwright in Frederic Reynolds's *The Dramatist* (1789), who continually demanded "incident," and was undoubtedly thoroughly entertaining to watch.

But it is not simple comedy–or farce. Early in the play, the aptly named Mr. Generous, whose wife stands accused, denies that there is any such thing as witchcraft:

> They that thinke so dreame,
> For my beliefe is, no such thing can be,
> A madnesse you may call it. . . .

At the end of the play, Mrs. Generous declines to be questioned as to her guilt: "I will say nothing, but what you know you know, / And as the law shall finde me let it take me." Doughty, her neighborly accuser, says, "we'l trifle w'yee no longer" (that is, with all those accused of witchcraft) and adds, "Now shall you all to the Iustices, and let them take order with you till the Sizes, and then let the Law take his course, and *Vivat Rex.* Mr. Gen-

erous I am sorry for your cause of sorrow, we shall not have your company?" There is something far removed from comedy, let alone farce, in Generous's reply:

> No sir, my Prayers for her soules recovery
> Shall not be wanting to her, but mine eyes
> Must never see her more.

In contrast, when Robin bids farewell to his sweetheart, Mal (one of the women accused of witchcraft) replies defiantly: "Well Rogue I may live to ride in a Coach before I come to the Gallowes yet." The shadow of the gallows tree is all too apparent, but the Seely house is now returned to its former hierarchical order, and in a dozen lines the play ends. The incursion of a Skimmington's Ride can be seen as no mere digression but, as it were, one piece of folklore exorcising another. Did the original audiences leave the Globe with a qualm of uneasiness, the more telling for their enjoyment of the farce? Was that how Heywood and Brome planned it? From the juxtaposition of modes in *The Rape of Lucrece* and the repudiation of triviality–"all humorous toyes set off," as Brutus demands in that play–perhaps that is precisely what Heywood did hope for.

A Challenge for Beauty, probably the last of Heywood's surviving plays, written when he was about sixty years old, is a remarkably lively piece of work. Its story is meretricious–a complex Italianate (or rather, Hispanic) intrigue–but it has a lively clown who would have graced Heywood's work in his youth and a variety of witty exchanges which, if rather conscious, yet can still engage the reader. But above all the play is of a kind that would have delighted Vapid, whose catch phrase applies so insistently to *A Challenge for Beauty:* "Here's incident!" It is almost as if Heywood were packing in every turn of event and all the old stock situations of the past forty years, in one last, glorious splurge. There is yet another bed trick–for a puritan writer, Heywood had a fondness for this device (see *A Maidenhead Well Lost* and the double trick in part two of *Fair Maid of the West*)–and he repeats a joke from Chapman, Jonson, and Marston's *Eastward Ho!* (produced in 1605) on a Nun/Noun Substantive (a prostitute), a pun that survived in English music halls as late as the 1930s.

The story, encrusted with incident though it is, is in essence very simple. Bonavida, a noble and honest Spanish lord, challenges the Spanish Queen's claim to incomparable beauty. The

Queen has more than her full share of that pride and arrogance conventionally given in the drama to Spanish nobility, and she is quite prepared that Bonavida should die for his presumption. He manages to stave off his execution while he goes in search of someone to outshine the Queen in beauty and—Heywood being the patriot he was—naturally finds her in England. The path to a happy resolution is tortuous but inevitable, and it is the events on the way that give the play its interest, even today. The reappearance, if rather more subtly, of the chauvinism of Heywood's earliest plays is also evident when the Queen of Spain, self-centered though she is, suggests that

> if any clyme
> Could yeeld rarietie to equall ours,
> It would be found in *England*.

For someone who knew something of drama's history, Heywood offers the surprising judgment in the opening of his prologue that "Roman *and* Athenian Drammaes" differ from those of England in being *"rather jiggs than Playes."* Yet some of the incidents in this play seem more like jigs themselves. The device by which a ring is wrested from the English beauty, Helena, involves her taking it off before she washes in a basin onstage and its being carried away by her maidservant. Heywood certainly strains the credulity of his audience, particularly in the resolution of the bed trick. Petrocella and an English lord, Ferrers, are in love. She is pursued by a Spanish lord, Valladaura, who hopes to win her by his valiant deeds. Valladaura has bought Ferrers out of Turkish slavery, and, though Ferrers loves Petrocella, he must, in honor and friendship, help Valladaura win Petrocella. Disguised as a priest, he "marries" her to Valladaura, who then requires Ferrers to spend the bridal night with his "bride," Ferrers being disguised as Valladaura. He must not, of course, act as a husband. Petrocella then enters with a *"bloody punyard,"* only to find that she has killed, not Valladaura, but the man she really loves disguised as her "husband." When this fact is revealed, she laughs, presumably hysterically; the man she has "killed" enters, and her expression of surprise is extraordinary:

> VALLADAURA. Dost laugh at sorrow?
> PETROCELLA. Would you have mee turne *Crocodile*, and weepe, *Ferrers*, Mont *Ferrers*, prithee come helpe me laugh to laugh a little.

> *Enter Ferrers.*
> VALLADAURA. *Ferrers!* my friend alive?
> PETROCELLA. By this blood of a Turtle, and that's a chaste oath, hee never died.

Petrocella's drawing attention to her oath is akin to the undercutting humor of the servant, Nicholas, as Anne Frankford lies dying in *A Woman Killed with Kindness:* "Ile wish to dye with thee," says her husband, and all around the deathbed save Nicholas chorus, "So do we all." The servant is more down to earth: "So will not I, / Ile sigh and sob, but by my faith not dye." Perhaps we have not given sufficient recognition to Heywood's use of such humor, a use once again common.

Another technique quite frequent in Heywood is the deliberate breaking of the illusion to remind an audience it is in a theater. Thus, Bonavida, on his way to execution, likens the staging for the execution to that of a theater (precisely as an engraving published in Amsterdam would soon depict the execution of Charles I in 1649):

> The Queene playes with my death,
> And bids me act a bold Tragedians part,
> To which, such moving action I will give,
> That it shall glaze this Theater round with teares,
> And all that shall behold me on this stage,
> Pitying my fate: shall taxe her cruelty[.]

Note not only "playes," "act," "Tragedians," and perhaps "moving action" but especially "this Theater round"—according to the title page of the 1636 edition *A Challenge for Beauty* was performed at the Blackfriars theater *"and at the* Globe *on / the* Banke-side" (the theater Shakespeare called "This wooden O"). Bonavida's speech forms an appropriate epitaph for the dramatist who so closely linked the theater and the world when he wrote in *An Apology for Actors,* "He that denyes these Theaters should be / He may as well deny a world to me."

Bibliographies:

Samuel A. Tannenbaum, *Thomas Heywood (A Concise Bibliography)* (New York: Privately printed, 1939);

Dennis Donovan, *Elizabethan Bibliographies Supplements,* volume 2 (London: Nether Press, 1967);

Otto Rauchbauer, "Thomas Heywood: An Annotated Bibliography, 1967- ," *Research Opportunities in Renaissance Drama,* 18 (1975): 45-50.

References:

Barbara J. Baines, *Thomas Heywood* (Boston: Twayne, 1984);

Frederick S. Boas, *Thomas Heywood* (London: Williams & Norgate, 1950);

Arthur Brown, "Heywood's Dramatic Art," in *Essays on Shakespeare and the Elizabethan Drama in Honor of Hardin Craig*, edited by Richard Hosley (Columbia: University of Missouri Press, 1962), pp. 327-339;

Arthur Melville Clark, *Thomas Heywood: Playwright and Miscellanist* (Oxford: Blackwell, 1931);

Otelia Cromwell, *Thomas Heywood: A Study in the Elizabethan Drama of Everyday Life* (New Haven: Yale University Press / London: Oxford University Press, 1928);

T. S. Eliot, "Thomas Heywood" (1931), in his *Selected Essays 1917-1932* (London: Faber & Faber, 1932), pp. 171-181;

W. W. Greg, "The Escapes of Jupiter: an autograph play of Thomas Heywood" (1925); republished in *Collected Papers*, edited by J. C. Maxwell (Oxford: Clarendon Press, 1966), pp. 156-183;

Michel Grivelet, *Thomas Heywood et le drame domestique élisabéthain* (Paris: Didier, 1957);

William Hazlitt, *Lectures Chiefly on the Dramatic Literature of the Age of Elizabeth* (London: Stodart & Steuart, 1820);

Marilyn L. Johnson, *Images of Women in the Works of Thomas Heywood* (Salzburg, 1974);

Norman Rabkin, "The Double Plot: Notes on the History of a Convention," *Renaissance Drama*, 7 (1964): 55-69;

Mowbray Velte, *The Bourgeois Elements in the Dramas of Thomas Heywood* (Mysore City, India: Wesleyan Mission Press, 1924);

Robert Wiemann, "Le déclin de la scène 'indivisible' élisabéthaine: Beaumont, Fletcher et Heywood," in *Dramaturgie et Société*, volume 2, edited by Jean Jacquot (Paris: Centre National de la Recherche Scientifique, 1968), pp. 815-827;

L. B. Wright, "Heywood and the Popularising of History," *Modern Language Notes*, 43 (May 1928): 287-293.

Papers:

The British Library has manuscripts for *The Captives* (MS Egerton 1994, ff. 52-73) and *The Escapes of Jupiter* (MS Egerton 1994, ff. 74-95).

Ben Jonson

(11 June 1572?-6 August 1637)

Kevin J. Donovan

University of New Hampshire

PLAY PRODUCTIONS: *The Isle of Dogs,* by Jonson, Thomas Nashe, and others, London, Swan theater, August 1597;

The Case Is Altered, London, unknown theater, 1597-1598;

Every Man in His Humour, London, Curtain theater, September (?) 1598;

Every Man out of His Humour, London, Globe theater, November or December, 1599;

Cynthia's Revels, London, Blackfriars theater, late 1600;

Poetaster, London, Blackfriars theater, early 1601;

The Entertainment at Althorp, Althorp, 25 June 1603;

Sejanus, London, Globe theater, late 1603 or early 1604;

The King's Coronation Entertainment, London, 15 March 1604;

A Panegyre, London, 19 March 1604;

The Entertainment at Highgate, Highgate, 1 May 1604;

Eastward Ho, by Jonson, George Chapman, and John Marston, London, Blackfriars theater, 1604-1605;

The Masque of Blackness, Westminster, Whitehall, 6 January 1605;

Hymenaei, Westminster, Whitehall, 5 and 6 January 1606;

Volpone, London, Globe theater, February-March 1606;

The Entertainment of the Two Kings at Theobalds, Theobalds, 24 July 1606;

An Entertainment of the King and Queen at Theobalds, Theobalds, 22 May 1607;

Entertainment for the Merchant Taylors' Company, London, 16 July 1607;

The Masque of Beauty, Westminster, Whitehall, 10 January 1608;

The Haddington Masque, Westminster, Whitehall, 9 February 1608;

Entertainment at Salisbury House, Westminster, Salisbury House, May 1608;

The Masque of Queens, Westminster, Whitehall, 2 February 1609;

Entertainment at Britain's Burse, London, 11 April 1609;

Epicoene, London, Whitefriars theater, December 1609 or January 1610;

The Speeches at Prince Henry's Barriers, Westminster, Whitehall, 6 January 1610;

The Alchemist, London, Globe theater, 1610;

Oberon, the Fairy Prince, Westminster, Whitehall, 1 January 1611;

Love Freed from Ignorance and Folly, Westminster, Whitehall, 3 February 1611;

Catiline, London, Globe theater, 1611;

Love Restored, Westminster, Whitehall, 6 January 1612;

The Irish Masque at Court, Westminster, at Court, 29 December 1613;

A Challenge at Tilt, Westminster, at Court, 1 January 1614;

Bartholomew Fair, London, Hope theater, 31 October 1614;

The Golden Age Restored, Westminster, Whitehall, 6 January 1615;

Mercury Vindicated from the Alchemists, Westminster, Whitehall, 1 January 1616;

Entertainment for the New Company of Merchant Adventurers, London, 14 June 1616;

The Devil Is an Ass, London, Blackfriars theater, November or December 1616;

Christmas, His Masque, Westminster, Whitehall, Christmas season 1616;

The Vision of Delight, Westminster, Whitehall, 6 January 1617;

Lovers Made Men, London, Essex House, 22 February 1617;

Pleasure Reconciled to Virtue, Westminster, Whitehall, 6 January 1618; revised as *For the Honor of Wales,* Westminster, Whitehall, 17 February 1618;

News from the New World Discovered in the Moon, Westminster, Whitehall, 7 January 1620;

Entertainment at the Blackfriars, London, May 1620(?);

Pan's Anniversary, Westminster, at Court, 19 June 1620(?);

Portrait by an unknown artist (by permission of the National Portrait Gallery, London)

The Gypsies Metamorphosed, Burley-on-the-Hill, 3 August 1621;

The Masque of Augurs, Westminster, Whitehall, 6 January 1622;

Time Vindicated to Himself and to His Honors, Westminster, Whitehall, 19 January 1623;

The Masque of Owls, Kenilworth, 19 August 1624;

The Fortunate Isles and Their Union, Westminster, Whitehall, 9 January 1625;

The Staple of News, London, Blackfriars theater, February 1626;

The New Inn, London, Blackfriars theater, early 1629;

Love's Triumph through Callipolis, Westminster, Whitehall, 9 January 1631;

Chloridia, Westminster, Whitehall, 22 February 1631;

The Magnetic Lady, London, Blackfriars theater, autumn 1632;

A Tale of a Tub, London, Cockpit theater, May 1633;

The King's Entertainment at Welbeck, Welbeck, 21 May 1633;

Love's Welcome at Bolsover, Bolsover, 30 July 1634.

BOOKS: *The Comicall Satyre of Every Man out of His Humor* (London: Printed by Adam Islip for William Holme, 1600);

Every Man in His Humor (London: Printed by Simon Stafford for Walter Burre, 1601);

The Fountaine of Selfe-Love. Or Cynthias Revells (London: Printed by Richard Read for Walter Burre, 1601);

Poetaster or the Arraignment (London: Printed by

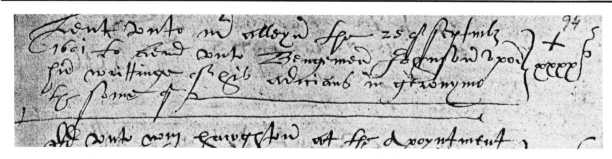

An entry in Philip Henslowe's diary recording a payment on 25 September 1601 for Jonson's additions to The Spanish Tragedy *(which Henslowe calls "geronymo") (MSS VII, l. 94'; by permission of Dulwich College, London)*

Richard Braddock for Matthew Lownes, 1602);

B. Jon: His Part of King James His Royall and Magnificent Entertainement through His Honorable Cittie of London, Thurseday the 15. of March. 1603 ... Also, A Briefe Panegyre of His Maiesties First and Well Auspicated Entrance to His High Court of Parliament, on Monday, the 19. of the Same Moneth. With Other Additions (London: Printed by Valentine Simmes and George Eld for Edward Blount, 1604);

Seianus His Fall (London: Printed by George Eld for Thomas Thorpe, 1605);

Eastward Hoe, by Jonson, George Chapman, and John Marston (London: Printed by George Eld for William Aspley, 1605);

Hymenaei: or The Solemnities of Masque, and Barriers (London: Printed by Valentine Simmes for Thomas Thorpe, 1606);

Ben: Jonson His Volpone or the Foxe (London: Printed by George Eld for Thomas Thorpe, 1607);

The Characters of Two Royall Masques. The One of Blacknesse, the Other of Beautie. . . . The Description of the Masque. With the Nuptial Songs. Celebrating the Happy Marriage of Iohn, Lord Ramsey, Vicount Hadington, with the Lady Elizabeth Ratcliffe (London: Printed by George Eld for Thomas Thorpe, 1608);

Ben: Jonson, His Case Is Altered (London: Printed by Nicholas Okes for Bartholomew Sutton, 1609);

The Masque of Queenes Celebrated from the House of Fame (London: Printed by Nicholas Okes for Richard Bonion & Henry Wally, 1609);

Catiline His Conspiracy (London: Printed by William Stansby? for Walter Burre, 1611);

The Alchemist (London: Printed by Thomas Snodham, for Walter Burre & sold by John Stepneth, 1612);

The Workes of Benjamin Jonson (London: Printed by William Stansby, 1616)—comprises *Every Man in His Humour, Every Man out of His Humour, Cynthia's Revels, Poetaster, Sejanus, Volpone, Epicoene, The Alchemist, Catiline, Epigrams, The Forrest, The King's Coronation Entertainment, A Panegyre, The Entertainment at Althorp, The Entertainment at Highgate, The Entertainment of the Two Kings at Theobalds, An Entertainment of the King and Queen at Theobalds,*

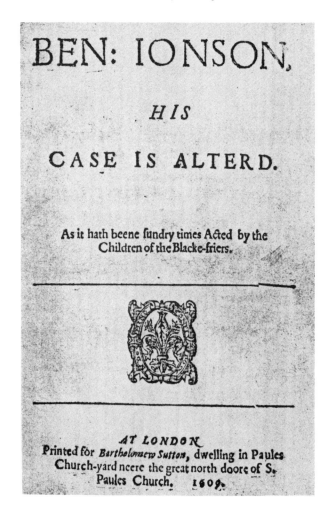

Title page for an unauthorized 1609 quarto edition of Jonson's first surviving play (British Library)

The Masque of Blackness, The Masque of Beauty, Hymenaei, The Haddington Masque, The Masque of Queens, Prince Henry's Barriers, Oberon the Fairy Prince, Love Freed From Ignorance and Folly, Love Restored, A Challenge at Tilt, The Irish Masque, Mercury Vindicated from the Alchemists, The Golden Age Restored;

Lovers Made Men. A Masque (London, 1617);

Epicoene, or The Silent Woman. A Comoedie (London: Printed by William Stansby & sold by John Browne, 1620);

The Masque of Augures. With Several Antimasques (London, 1621);

Time Vindicated to Himselfe and to His Honors (London, 1623);

Neptunes Triumph for the Returne of Albion, A Masque 1623 (London, 1624);

The Fortunate Isles and Their Union. A Masque 1624 (London, 1625);

Love's Triumph through Callipolis. A Masque, by Jonson and Inigo Jones (London: Printed by John Norton, Jr., for Thomas Walkley, 1630);

Chloridia, Rites to Chloris and Her Nymphs (London: Printed for Thomas Walkley, 1631);

Bartholmew Fayre. The Divell Is an Asse. The Staple of Newes (volume 2 of Jonson's works) (London: Printed by John Beale for Robert Allot, 1631);

The New Inne. Or, The Light Heart (London: Printed by Thomas Harper for Thomas Alchorne, 1631);

Ben: Jonson's Execration against Vulcan. With Divers Epigrams (London: Printed by John Okes for John Benson & Andrew Crooke, 1640);

Q. Horatius Flaccus: Horatius Flaccus: His Art of Poetry. Englished by Ben: Jonson. With Other Workes of the Author, Never Printed Before (London: Printed by John Okes for John Benson, 1640);

The Workes of Benjamin Jonson, volume 1 (London: Printed by Richard Bishop & sold by A. Crooke, 1640)–a reprint of *The Workes of Benjamin Jonson* (1616); volumes 2-3 (London: Printed for Richard Meighen & Thomas Walkley, 1640)–comprises the sheets of the 1631 works (volume 2) together with *The Magnetic Lady, A Tale of a Tub, The Sad Shepherd, The Fall of Mortimer, Christmas His Masque, Lovers Made Men, The Vision of Delight, Pleasure Reconciled to Virtue, For the Honor of Wales, News from the New World Discovered in the Moon, The Gypsies Metamorphosed, The Masque of Augurs, Time Vindicated,*

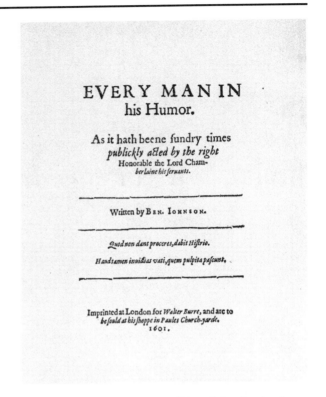

Title page for the 1601 quarto edition of the play that Jonson considered his first theatrical success (Anderson Galleries, sale number 2077, 20-21 May 1926)

Neptune's Triumph, Pan's Anniversary, The Masque of Owls, The Fortunate Isles, Love's Triumph through Callipolis, Chloridia, The Entertainment at Welbeck, Love's Welcome at Bolsover, The Underwood, Horace, His Art of Poetry, The English Grammar, Discoveries (volume 3) (London: Printed by John Dawson, Jr., for Thomas Walkley, 1640).

Editions: *Ben Jonson,* 11 volumes, edited by C. H. Herford and Percy and Evelyn Simpson (Oxford: Clarendon Press, 1925-1952)–comprises *A Tale of a Tub, The Case Is Altered, Every Man in His Humour* (original and revised texts), *Every Man out of His Humour, In Memoriam: Charles Harold Herford, Cynthia's Revels, Poetaster, Sejanus, Eastward Ho, Volpone, Epicoene, The Alchemist, Catiline, Bartholomew Fair, The Devil Is an Ass, The Staple of News, The New Inn, The Magnetic Lady, The Sad Shepherd, The Fall of Mortimer, Masques and Entertainments, The Poems, The Prose Works.*

By turns turbulent and weighty, scatalogical and refined, boisterous and delicate, Ben Jonson's works have always excited strong reactions among his readers and his playgoing audiences, just as his personality strongly impressed or offended his contemporaries. Jonson's life displays some of the same apparent contradictions as his work. He was a branded felon and for much of his life a recusant, whose career was punctuated by trouble with the officials of the church and state. Yet he rose to be a favored court poet, a companion of some of the most prominent men and women in the country, and a champion of royal authority. He was the greatest playwright of his age (with one notable exception) and one of the greatest English dramatists of all time; yet he seems to have distrusted the theater as a vehicle for the ethical program that informs his art.

Despite the contradictory impulses found in his life and work–or perhaps because of them–"honest Ben" is a more distinct personality than almost any of his contemporaries. Jonson was a man of strong convictions and equally strong prejudices. He was convinced of the necessity for rational control of the passions, especially for a poet; yet he often failed to manage his own notoriously unruly passions and appetites. In a censorious and aggressive age he was notably censorious and aggressive. However, he was also loyal and generous, and he had a special talent for making firm friendships.

Of Jonson's early life and family background relatively little is known. He told the Scottish poet William Drummond of Hawthornden, whose account of his conversations with Jonson is a valuable source of information about Jonson's life, that his grandfather was a gentleman who came from Carlisle and before that from Annandale. His father, a minister who lost his estate under Queen Mary, died in 1572, not long before the birth of his son Benjamin, near London, between 5 May 1572 and 19 January 1573 (probably on 11 June 1572). The character of his mother can be glimpsed in an anecdote about Jonson that is related in the *Conversations with Drummond*. In 1604 Jonson was arrested along with the playwrights John Marston and George Chapman for some satirical passages in their collaborative play *Eastward Ho*, and, after their release, Jonson feasted his friends in celebration: "at the midst of the Feast his old Mother Dranke to him & shew him a paper which she had (if the Sentence had taken execution) to have mixed jn ye Prisson among his drinke, which was full of Lūstie strong poison & that she was no chūrle she told she minded first to have Drunk of it herself." Such a mother does much to explain the tem-

perament of her famous son.

Within a few years of Jonson's birth, his mother remarried. Jonson's stepfather was a master bricklayer, a worker in one of the humbler crafts in the highly stratified society of Elizabethan England. According to tradition, the family lived in Westminster, in Hartshorn Lane, where Jonson attended St. Martin's parish school. Thus Jonson's stepfather may have been the bricklayer Robert Brett, who is found to have lived in Hartshorn Lane and whose name appears with Jonson's in the parish accounts of St. Martin's-in-the-Fields in 1597. In the normal course of affairs, Jonson would have followed his stepfather's trade immediately after finishing his studies at St. Martin's. However, as Jonson told Drummond, he was "putt to school by a friend" and attended Westminster School, where he studied under the great antiquarian William Camden. His affection and regard for Camden were expressed later in life in his dedication of the 1616 folio text of *Every Man in His Humour* to his former teacher, and in his Epigram 14, "To William Camden."

Although Jonson's experience at Westminster was brief, it profoundly affected him. Westminster School gave Jonson access to those Roman writers whose ethical and artistic ideals exerted so powerful an influence on his art. In addition he acquired there a love of classical literature and scholarship that would remain with him all his life. (One of Jonson's last surviving letters asks Sir Robert Cotton for the loan of a book that would tell "the true site, & distance betwixt *Bauli* or *portus Baiarum*, and *Villa Augusta*.") And Jonson was proud of his scholarship, as the marginal notes in the quarto editions of *Sejanus* and *The Masque of Queens* testify. We should also note that Westminster introduced Jonson to the drama; the Westminster scholars regularly performed three plays a year.

Jonson's formal education ended with Westminster, and he may not have even completed the course of studies there. He was taken out of school and set to work at his stepfather's trade. Drummond recorded Jonson's telling him that he was "taken from [school], and put to ane other Craft (I thinke was to be a Wright or Bricklayer) which he could not endure, then went he to ye low Countries, but returning soone he betook himself to his wonted studies." Jonson's apparent vagueness on the subject of his "other Craft" suggests a certain sensitivity; his early career as a bricklayer later provided a convenient source of

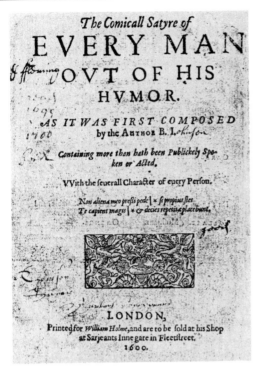

Title page for a 1600 quarto edition of the play that includes Jonson's opening salvo in the "war of the theaters," a satiric portrait of John Marston in the minor character Clove (British Library)

jibes for his enemies. Of his service in the Netherlands, Drummond recorded a famous anecdote: "he had jn the face of both the Campes Killed ane Enimie & taken opima spolia from him." Jonson probably refers to this exploit in Epigram 108, "To true Souldiers."

The lengths of Jonson's service in the Netherlands and of his career as a bricklayer as well as the nature of the "wonted studies" to which he returned are uncertain. Jonson left Westminster probably about 1589, was married in 1594, and appears as a playwright in Henslowe's diary in 1597. Besides these sketchy details, all that is known of him in these years is that he worked as an actor, at first probably in a touring provincial troupe and later at Paris Garden, a bear-baiting pit that doubled as a theater. The source of this information is not impartial; it appears in Thomas Dekker's *Satiromastix*, where Jonson is lampooned in the character of "Horace." Another character several times taunts "Horace" with references to his acting career: "I ha seene thy shoulders lapt in a Plaiers old cast Cloake, like a Slie knaue as thou art. . . . thou hast forgot how thou amblest (in a leather pilch) by a play-wagon, in the high way, and took'st mad Ieronimoes part, to get seruice among the Mimickes." Horace is also said

to have played the part of "Zulziman" at Paris Garden.

Jonson was married to Anne Lewis on 14 November 1594 in the London parish of St. Magnus Martyr. Relatively few facts are known about this marriage. Jonson told Drummond in 1618 or 1619 that his wife was "a shrew yet honest" and that he had lived apart from her for five years. Her "shrewishness" may well have been exacerbated by her marriage to a difficult man: Jonson narrated with evident glee a number of his episodes as a philanderer. As for her other epithet, Drummond also records that "of all stiles [Jonson] loved most to be named honest." At least two children were born of the marriage, Mary, "the daughter of [her parents'] youth," whose infant death is commemorated in Epigram 22, and Benjamin, the subject of Epigram 45, who died in 1603 at the age of seven. Other children were probably born of the marriage, including a Joseph Johnson, baptized on 9 December 1599, and another Benjamin, who was baptized on 20 February 1608 and died on 18 November 1611. "Elisib. daughter of Ben. Johnson," baptized on 25 March 1610, was probably an illegitimate daughter. Yet another Benjamin, described in the church records as "fil. Ben," was baptized on 6 April 1610; obviously this Benjamin and Elisabeth had different mothers if not different fathers. None of these children seems to have lived to adulthood.

By 1597 Jonson was earning a living as a playwright. In that same year he experienced the first of his many troubles with the authorities, this time over a lost play, *The Isle of Dogs*. The play was mainly written by Thomas Nashe, but Jonson seems to have supplied the play's conclusion. The Privy Council found that it contained "very seditious and sclandrous matter," and Jonson was arrested along with two fellow actors for his role as actor and part author. Nashe fled to Yarmouth and so escaped arrest. The incident caused a great stir; the Privy Council ordered the destruction of all the stages in London, an order which, fortunately, was rescinded; the theaters were closed for a time but soon reopened. The Privy Council also appointed a team of investigators, headed by the notorious recusant hunter Richard Topcliffe, to try to get the imprisoned actors to incriminate each other. Years later Jonson would still express contempt for the "two damn'd Villans" sent to trap him. He told Drummond that Epigram 59, "On Spies," was written in response to this incident.

141

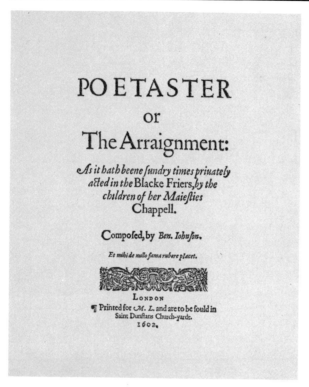

POETASTER
or
The Arraignment:

As it hath beene sundry times priuately acted in the Blacke Friers, *by the children of her Maiesties Chappell.*

Composed, by Ben. Iohnson.

Et mihi de nullo fama rubere placet.

LONDON
¶ Printed for *M. L.* and are to be sould in
Saint Dunstans Church-yarde.
1602.

Title page for the 1602 quarto edition of the play in which Jonson satirized Thomas Dekker as Demetrius, a writer of doggerel verse and "a dresser of plays about town," and John Marston as Crispinus, a vain fop who "pens high, loftie, in a new stalking strain" (Anderson Galleries, sale number 2077, 20-21 May 1926)

Jonson was imprisoned for more than two months. While still in prison he entered the employ of the theatrical entrepreneur Philip Henslowe. Henslowe, who owned the Rose and who eventually acquired other playhouses, financed the Lord Admiral's Men, a leading Elizabethan company whose foremost actor, Edward Alleyn, was Henslowe's son-in-law. From the evidence of Henslowe's diary, we know that Jonson wrote a number of plays for Henslowe. In July of 1597 he sold Henslowe his share of an unknown play, and in December of the same year he was working on an unnamed "boocke" for the Admiral's Men. In 1598 he cowrote with Henry Chettle and Henry Porter a comedy called *Hot Anger Soon Cold* and supplied the "plotte" for an unknown tragedy written by Chapman. In the following year he was working on a tragedy called *Robert II* and cowrote with his future enemy Thomas Dekker the tragedy *Page of Plimoth.* The year 1601 found him writing additions to Thomas Kyd's *The Spanish Tragedy* for Henslowe, and in 1602 he was writing a play called *Richard Crookback* and "new adicyons for Jeronymo."

Except for the additions to *The Spanish Tragedy*, which may or may not be those appearing in the play's 1602 edition, none of Jonson's work for Henslowe has survived. Jonson later told Drummond "that the half of his comedies were not jn Print," though at that date (1618-1619) the "half" would include *Bartholomew Fair, The Devil Is an Ass*, and also perhaps *The Case Is Altered*, which was published in 1609 without Jonson's approval. Jonson's lost tragedies were admired by the uncritical Francis Meres, who in *Palladis Tamia* (1598) groups Jonson among "our best for Tragedie." However, Jonson chose not to include any of the works written for Henslowe, or *The Case Is Altered*, written in 1597-1598 for the Children of the Chapel, in his 1616 collected works. Apparently these plays were not consistent with the image of his artistic development that Jonson wished to present to the world.

The entries in Henslowe's diary provide a valuable supplement to the image of Jonson's career which he consciously cultivated. Jonson always emphasized his departure from the practice of his contemporaries and immediate predecessors. Thus he would later refer to "those Comick Lawes/ Which I . . . first did teach the Age." However, the titles of the plays in Henslowe's diary suggest the standard fare of Elizabethan theater: popular comedy, chronicle history, domestic tragedy, and revenge tragedy. It is fascinating to observe that Jonson wrote *Richard Crookback* for Henslowe as late as 1602, by which time he had written both *Every Man* plays, *Cynthia's Revels*, and *Poetaster*, and was working on *Sejanus*.

The first play by Jonson to survive is *The Case Is Altered*. Jonson deliberately multiplied incidents and characters in the play, combining plots from two comedies by Plautus (*Captivi* and *Aulularia*) with a romantic love story and some clowning by Onion the servingman and Juniper the cobbler. Juniper seems to have been popular with Elizabethan audiences; Nashe refers in *Lenten Stuffe* to "the merry coblers cutte in that witty Play of *the Case is altered*." The text of the play as it has survived also includes a scene burlesquing playwright Anthony Munday, which was probably written at a later date than the play's original composition.

In its mingling of clowns and counts, its emphasis on love, its comic horseplay, and its reliance on such "romantic" plot elements from New Comedy as the finding of long-lost children—all of which are characteristic of Elizabethan popular comedy—*The Case Is Altered* is very different from the kind of comedy Jonson is most remembered for. As Jonson mastered a more classical dramatic idiom in his maturity, he came to prefer that this earlier work be forgotten. When in 1616 Jonson published his collected works, *The Case Is Altered* was omitted. However, in his later career Jonson would return to writing romantic comedy with *The New Inn,* a play which the Caroline public rejected.

In 1598 Jonson also wrote another play, *Every Man in His Humour,* this time for the Lord Chamberlain's Men at the Curtain. As the list of actors appended to the text of *Every Man in His Humour* in the 1616 folio edition of Jonson's collected works shows, Shakespeare acted in the original performance. Jonson regarded *Every Man in His Humour* as his first success. He chose it to head his collected works, although he first thoroughly revised it, changing the setting from Florence to London. At the end of his career while writing *The Magnetic Lady* and contemplating "the close, or shutting up of his Circle," he described himself as "beginning his studies of this kind, with *every man in his Humour.*"

The play's title exploits the popularity of the term "humour," which had become a fashionable catchword. Originally a medical term, "humours" were the fluids believed to regulate the body and by extension the temperament or "complexion" of man. An imbalance of one of them was supposed to cause a disturbance in man's body and his mind. However, the emphasis of Elizabethan psychology is always moral, rather than physiological. A person who allowed his passions to overwhelm his rational powers was considered morally guilty.

In popular speech the term had become less specific and was used to refer to any dominant trait or quirk of character. Chapman had already exploited the word's popularity with his comedy *A Humorous Day's Mirth.* However, in *Every Man in His Humour* and *Every Man out of His Humour,* which followed it, Jonson made the term forever his own.

The concept of "humour" was well suited to Jonson's comic vision. Typically Jonsonian comic characters are obsessed with a single idea or desire and pursue it to absurd lengths, spinning mon-

Variant title page for the 1605 quarto edition of the play Jonson wrote after deciding, "since the Comick MVSE/Hath prou'd so ominous to me, I will trie/If Tragoedie *haue a more kind aspect," and the first page of the text with scholarly notes that Jonson included to demonstrate the "truth of argument" he considered a criterion for tragedy (Bodleian Library)*

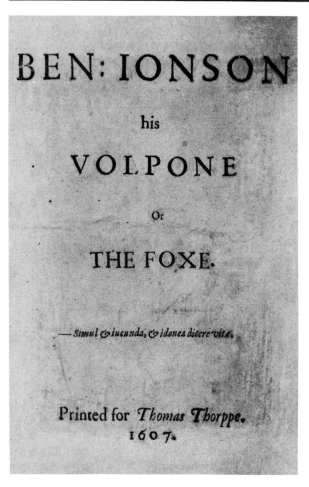 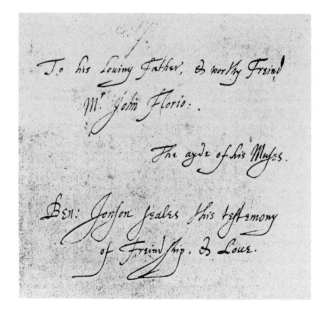

Title page for the 1607 quarto edition of the comedy that proved immensely popular with audiences at the Globe, where it was staged in early 1606, and at both Oxford and Cambridge, where it was performed later in the same year (Henry E. Huntington Library and Art Gallery); and Jonson's inscription to John Florio, groom of the privy chamber in the Court of James I and the first English translator of Montaigne's Essays, *in another copy of the same edition of the play (by permission of the British Library)*

strous fantasies out of their imaginations. The emphasis on a single trait or folly tends to reduce characters in one direction, but the exaggeration often attains a unique monstrous grandeur. "Humour" provided an explanation of sorts for such character types that was consistent with the classical principles espoused by Jonson. The imagery in Jonson's plays, poems, and masques shows that he had fully absorbed traditional Roman ethics, in which folly and vice are described as variable and liquid, and virtue as stable and solid. In the induction to *Every Man out of His Humour,* Jonson advocates the use of the term "humour" to describe the effect "when some one peculiar quality/Doth so possesse a man, that it doth draw/All his affects, his spirits, and his powers,/In their confluctions, all to runne one way."

The plot of *Every Man in His Humour* is original, but in its main outlines it owes a great debt to New Comedy. A young gallant (in this case a would-be poet) and his boon companion scheme with the aid of a tricky servant to outwit the young man's father and gain a pair of pretty brides. The play adheres to those infamous bugbears of neoclassical criticism, "the unities," and Jonson made much of the play's "correctness" in the prologue he wrote for the revised version of the play that appears in the 1616 folio. The fun of the play lies in its "humorous" characters, the braggart soldier Bobadill, the jealous husband Kitely, the country gull Stephen and the city gull Matthew, Downright the irascible country squire, and Justice Clement, "an old, merry Magistrate." In comparison to the comical satires that followed this play, *Every Man in His Humour* is genial and relaxed rather than satirical. The play "sport[s] with humane follies," as the prologue says. Fittingly it ends with the classic ritual affirmation of social harmony, the wedding feast.

Jonson had little time to celebrate the suc-

Costume designs by Inigo Jones for a Daughter of Niger (left) and a torchbearer, an Oceania (right), in The Masque of Blackness *(Stephen Orgel and Roy Strong,* Inigo Jones, *1973)*

cess of *Every Man in His Humour.* On 22 September 1598, probably within days of the first production of *Every Man in His Humour,* he killed a man in a duel and found himself on trial for murder. The victim, Gabriel Spencer, was an actor in Henslowe's company who had been arrested with Jonson over the *Isle of Dogs* affair the previous year. Jonson's Latinity saved his life; he escaped the gallows by pleading benefit of clergy (a privilege extended to all who could read enough Latin to construe a passage from the Bible). As it was, he suffered branding as a felon and the confiscation of all his property.

According to his statement to Drummond, Jonson was converted to Roman Catholicism while in prison for murder and continued in that faith for twelve years. The "priest who Visited him jn Prisson" and who converted him may have been Thomas Wright, the author of *The Passions of the Minde in Generall,* for which Jonson wrote a prefatory sonnet. Like Wright, Jonson maintained his loyalty to the Crown despite his religion. The authorities seem to have been aware of this fact, for in November 1605, within days of the discovery of the Gunpowder Plot, the Earl of Salisbury, then Secretary of State, employed Jonson to help find a priest willing to cooperate with the government's investigation.

Jonson spent only a few weeks in prison and was released in October 1598. In January 1599, however, Jonson was again committed to prison, this time to the Marshalsea in Southwark for a debt of ten pounds owed to a player named Robert Browne. Throughout his life Jonson had trouble making ends meet. At this time, having just suffered the loss of his goods to the Crown, he must have been in particularly dire straits. However, this debt must have been paid soon, because Jonson did not remain in prison for very long.

Part of 1599 was spent writing for Henslowe, but his most important work of that year was written for the Lord Chamberlain's Men. The title of *Every Man out of His Humour* capitalizes on the popularity of *Every Man in His Humour.* However, the play is in no sense a sequel; in fact, it is unlike anything previously presented on the Elizabethan stage. The character Cordatus, who is Jonson's mouthpiece in the play, describes it as "strange, and of a particular kind by it selfe, somewhat like *Vetus Comœdia.*"

The play is the first of three "comicall satires" written by Jonson. Satire was much in vogue in the 1590s. However, a decree by the Archbishop of Canterbury and the Bishop of London on 1 June 1599 had banned the printing of satires and epigrams because of the uproar raised by the works of Joseph Hall, John Marston, Thomas Nashe, and others. Jonson satisfied the public's hunger for satire by bringing it on the stage. However, he was not merely catering to the taste of his audience. The satirist's role of castigating vice strongly appealed to Jonson, who was convinced that responsible poetry, like philosophy, was supposed to educate its hearers, to teach them to love virtue and to shun vice. In addition he clearly enjoyed the linguistic license and exuberance characteristic of Elizabethan satire.

Elizabethan satire is a strange phenomenon. Because Renaissance critics had confused the classical terms *satura* and *satyra,* many spurious notions were attached to satire. The satirist was conceived of as a morally outraged satyr. Harshness was held to be "decorous" in terms of the genre, and satirists frequently took great liberties with language and with literary conventions. Some of this creative license is apparent in *Every Man out of His Humour.* The "scene" of the play is treated in a fluid way; at the outset of the play a satirist figure, Asper, appears, and we are told that the action which will follow is his own creation. A chorus frequently breaks in to comment on the main action of the play, shattering any dramatic illusion. Character, too, is fluid. Asper the censor plays a role, that of Macilente the envious man, in the drama that he supposedly creates.

Compared to *Every Man in His Humour* and *The Case Is Altered,* which are comedies of intrigue, *Every Man out of His Humour, Cynthia's Revels,* and *Poetaster* are relatively static. In the words of the prologue to *Cynthia's Revels,* these plays present "Words, aboue action: matter, aboue words." Another notable feature of the comical satires is their pronounced didacticism; the audience is invited to sit in judgment on the fools and knaves who are paraded out and systematically castigated. The didactic emphasis and static quality of these plays have not endeared them to later ages. The comical satires have virtually no stage history since the early seventeenth century. However, *Every Man out of His Humour* was a great success in its own day. Three editions of the play were published in 1600, and the many contemporary allusions to Jonson as the poet of "humours," where the context emphasizes satire, show how important the play was in establishing Jonson's literary reputation in London at the turn of the century.

In *Every Man out of His Humour,* Jonson's powers are most clearly shown in the frequent descriptions of the dramatis personae. Carlo Buffone, who is the embodiment of scurrility in the play, nearly steals the show with his "stabbing *simile's.*" Like the Theophrastan "characters" prefixed to the text of the play, Carlo's descriptions of his fellow "humorists" display the fertility of Jonson's imagination in their teeming mass of disparate images grotesquely yoked together. It is interesting to note that the same phrase used to characterize Carlo, "hee will sooner lose his soule then a iest," reappears only slightly modified in the *Conversations with Drummond* in reference to Jonson himself: "given rather to losse a friend, than a Jest." If the play's programmatic didacticism suggests the ordered, dispassionate ethos that Jonson adopts so often in his critical statements about poetry and true poets, Carlo's speeches show the more turbulent side of the mind of their maker, who told Drummond that "he heth consumed a whole night jn lying looking to his great toe, about which he hath seen tartars & turks Romans and Carthaginions feight in his jmagination."

The original ending of *Every Man out of His Humour* caused some unwelcome controversy for Jonson. The motive force in the play's slender plot is the envy of Macilente, who forces the other "humorists" into situations where their "humours" are purged. His own "humour," envy, was originally purged from him at the sight of the Queen, who was the embodiment of ideal virtue in Elizabethan literary convention. A boy actor dressed up as the Queen marched onto the stage of the Globe; at the sight of "the Queen" Macilente found himself completely dishumored. To many the impersonation of the Queen by a mere stage player was utterly distasteful, and Jonson revised the ending, cutting the offensive appearance of the Queen and having Macilente proclaim that his "humour" was gone now that his envy had no more objects to feed upon. However, in typical fashion Jonson included the original ending as an appendix when the quarto edition of the play was published in 1600, "that a right-ei'd and solide *Reader* may perceiue it was not so great a part of the Heauen awry, as [many] would make it."

Jonson's next play, *Cynthia's Revels,* which was performed in late 1600 by the Children of the Chapel at Blackfriars, is extraordinarily ambitious. While *Every Man out of His Humour* sought the acclaim of Elizabethan wits by castigating the follies and vices of various social classes, *Cynthia's Revels* bade directly for the Queen's recognition by the remarkable strategy of ridiculing the faults of the Court. Not surprisingly the attempt to win royal approbation was unsuccessful. If the two motives of the play—an appeal for royal favor and satire of courtiers—seem at odds, so do some of the play's formal elements. Jonson borrows elements of the Lylyan model of the courtly play, which had been so well suited both to complimenting the Queen and to performance by a company of boy actors. Thus *Cynthia's Revels* employs deliberately artificial groupings of allegorical and symbolic characters, passages of repartee between witty pages, and a number of very pretty lyrics that have often been anthologized. However, it is difficult to integrate this delicate mode of com-

HYMENAEI:

OR

The Solemnities of

Masque, and *Barriers,*

Magnificently performed on the eleventh, and twelfth Nights, from Christmas;

At Court:

To the auspicious celebrating of the Marriage-vnion, betweene *Robert,* Earle of *Essex,* and the Lady *Frances,* second Daughter to the most noble Earle of *Suffolke.*

By B **E** N: I **O** N S O **N** .

Iam veniet Virgo, iam dicetur Hymenæus.

A **T** L **ONDON**
Printed by *Valentine Sims* for *Thomas Thorp.*
1 6 0 6.

Title page for the 1606 quarto edition of the second masque Jonson wrote for performance at the Court of James I (Anderson Galleries, sale number 2077, 20-21 May 1926)

*Lucy Harington, Countess of Bedford, wearing a costume designed by
Inigo Jones for* Hymenaei *(by permission of the Marquess of Tavistock
and the Trustees of the Bedford Estate)*

edy with the demands of satire. Jonson's experiment is consciously daring; the play's prologue announces that,

> In this alone, his MVSE her sweetness hath,
> Shee shunnes the print of any beaten path,
> And proues new wayes to come to learned
>   eares.

However, Jonson's experiment is not entirely successful. At its best the play's blend of mythological allegory and dramatic satire provokes an intriguingly complicated aesthetic response. All too often, however, the mythology seems perfunctory and irrelevant, and the satire labored and tedious.

Also problematic is the role of Jonson's spokesman in the play, Crites (called Criticus in the quarto text). On the one hand he is a para-gon, "A creature of a most perfect, and diuine temper." On the other, his resemblance to the author is discomfiting: he is a poor and obscure scholar who earns the gratitude of the Queen by purging her court of its vanity by the efficacy of the revels over which he presides.

Certainly Jonson's enemies read the character of Crites as an idealized self-portrait. Some of Jonson's fellow playwrights were sufficiently annoyed by what they perceived as Jonson's arrogance that they were willing to satirize him personally. The grounds of Jonson's quarrels with John Marston and Thomas Dekker may go back farther than *Cynthia's Revels;* Jonson told Drummond that his quarrels with Marston had begun when Marston represented him on the stage. Apparently the character Chrisogonus in Marston's *Histriomastix* was meant to be a complimentary portrait of Jonson. However, Jonson resented the intended compliment and introduced into *Every Man out of His Humour* a minor character, Clove, intended to ridicule Marston. The attacks then went back and forth, with Marston lampooning Jonson in his *Jack Drum's Entertainment,* Jonson responding in *Cynthia's Revels* with the character Hedon, and Marston again retorting with the character Lampatho Doria in *What You Will.* The whole affair is rather murky up to this point. At any rate the Chamberlain's Men, angered at Jonson's having gone over to their new rivals, the Children of the Chapel, hired Dekker to write a play attacking him. Jonson learned of the coming attack, and in fifteen weeks he wrote *Poetaster,* which lampoons Dekker and Marston, and got it on the boards at the Blackfriars before the Chamberlain's Men could produce Dekker's *Satiromastix.* Thus was fought the famous "war of the theaters" obliquely alluded to in *Hamlet.*

In *Poetaster* Augustan Rome is the scene of Jonson's personal satire of Dekker and Marston. Jonson defends himself against his enemies by showing that the Roman poets whom he most admired, "VIRGIL, HORACE, and the rest/Of those great master-spirits," suffered from detraction just as he did. Jonson represents himself in the character of the Roman poet Horace, whom he greatly esteemed; Jonson later translated the *Ars Poetica,* and his nondramatic poetry is greatly indebted to Horatian precept and practice. Dekker and Marston are lampooned in the characters of Demetrius and Crispinus. Demetrius is a writer of witless doggerel verse and "a dresser of plays about the town" hired to abuse Horace. Crispinus is a vain fop who "pens high, loftie, in a new stalking strain"; a specimen of his verse is an obvious parody of Marston's style in his satires, characterized by such uncouth words as "lubrical," "glibberie," "snotteries," and "bespawles." The purgative function of comical satire is wittily translated into stage action in the play's final scene, when Crispinus is given an emetic and forced to vomit up his bizarre vocabulary onstage.

Poetaster is not merely an attack on Marston and Dekker. Most of the characters in the play do not refer to any of Jonson's contemporaries, and attempts by earlier scholars to identify Ovid and Virgil in the play with other Elizabethan poets have not met with acceptance. *Poetaster's* larger concerns are with the proper role of the poet in society. The ridicule of Crispinus and Demetrius occurs in the context of a general evaluation of poetry in which Ovid, Virgil, Horace, and Tibullus are also judged. However, the play's

stinging satire is the quality most remembered by posterity and by Jonson's contemporaries as well. *Poetaster* created yet more controversy for Jonson. Besides the attacks on Marston and Dekker, the play also satirizes lawyers, military braggarts, and professional actors. The satire of lawyers and the law seems to have riled certain government officials, and once again Jonson was threatened with prosecution. However, a friend, Richard Martin, intervened and defended Jonson. The author expressed his gratitude by dedicating the folio text of the play to Martin.

Jonson himself had sought to defend *Poetaster* in an "Apologeticall Dialogue" appended to the play. However, the dialogue was performed only once before being "suppressed by authority," and it was not included in the 1600 quarto edition of the play, although it was re-

Title page for the 1609 quarto edition of the masque whose production cost James I more than £3000 (Anderson Galleries, sale number 2077, 20-21 May 1926)

stored in the folio of 1616. In the "Apologeticall Dialogue" Jonson announces the end of his experimentation with comical satire:

> since the *Comick* MVSE
> Hath prou'd so ominous to me, I will trie
> If *Tragoedie* haue a more kind aspect.

The result would be *Sejanus*. Meanwhile Jonson needed some means of support. In 1602 his name appeared for the last time in Henslowe's accounts for work on the lost *Richard Crookback* and on additions to *The Spanish Tragedy*. In addition Jonson was seeking noble patronage. In February 1603 the law student John Manningham recorded in his diary that "Ben Johnson the poet nowe lives upon one Townesend and scornes the world."

The year 1603 ushered in a new reign. The ascension of James I to the throne of England would prove to be auspicious to Jonson, for under the new sovereign he would find royal favor and patronage. In addition, Jonson was now coming to know many noble men and women of the kingdom. Dekker had charged him in *Satiromastix* with trying to "skrue and wriggle himselfe into great Mens famyliarity," but the record of Jonson's friendship with a number of highly prominent people suggests an easy familiarity rather than servility on his part. Jonson's self-assurance among the great is seen not only in several anecdotes in the *Conversations with Drummond* but also in the tone in which he addresses such patrons as Lucy, Countess of Bedford (Epigrams 76 and 84), Sir Robert Wroth (*The Forrest* 3), Sir Robert Sidney (*The Forrest* 2), and the Earl of Pembroke (dedications to *Catiline* and *Epigrams*). Other nobles with whom Jonson was familiar included Lady Rutland, the daughter of Sir Philip Sidney; and Esmé Stuart, Lord D'Aubigny, a cousin of King James, with whom Jonson lived for five years. His relations with Salisbury, the Secretary of State, and Suffolk, Lord Chamberlain, were more ambiguous; epigrams of praise are addressed to both, but the *Conversations with Drummond* show that Jonson was not on the best of terms with either man.

Although the new reign was to bring Jonson fame and success, it began inauspiciously, with a personal loss, the death of his first son commemorated in Epigram 45. Drummond recorded a fascinating anecdote concerning the death. While the new King was journeying to London, the plague was raging in the city, and Jonson was staying in the country, at the house of the great antiquarian Sir Robert Cotton, with his old schoolmaster Camden. There one night he had a vision of his son Benjamin with the mark of a bloody cross on his forehead. The next morning he related the incident to Camden, who tried to reassure him that "it was but ane appreehension of his fantasie at which he sould not be disjected." Then a letter arrived from his wife telling of the boy's death of the plague. Jonson said that his son, who was seven years old at his death, appeared to him in "a Manlie shape & of yt Grouth that he thinks he shall be at the resurrection."

Another disappointment came with the first performance of *Sejanus* in late 1603 or early 1604. If Jonson had hoped to find "a more kind aspect" in tragedy than he had found in comedy, then he was greatly disappointed; *Sejanus* was hissed off the stage by the audience at the Globe. And once again Jonson found himself in trouble with the government, accused this time of popery and treason. Jonson believed that his troubles were due to the Earl of Northampton, with whose servant he had brawled. However, the Privy Council, who summoned Jonson to appear before them, tended to be wary on principle of plays dealing with conspiracy against monarchs. Fortunately no serious consequences ensued.

Sejanus is an unremittingly grim play. From beginning to end all power rests with the evil, crafty emperor Tiberius. Sejanus, his power-hungry underling, is as evil as his master and nearly his equal in intrigue, but his ambition proves fatal, and he is cruelly destroyed. The death of this villain at the close of the play, however, merely ushers in a worse, Macro. The play's good characters are wholly passive, "good, dull, noble lookers on," in the words of one of them.

The play as we have it differs from the version performed at the Globe, "wherein a second Pen had good share." Jonson replaced the work of the unnamed second poet (perhaps George Chapman) with passages of his own writing and published in 1605 a quarto edition of the play notable for its plethora of scholarly notes testifying to the "truth of argument" which he strongly emphasized as a criterion for tragedy. Having failed to please the populace in the theater, Jonson now appealed to the more literate sectors of society for their approbation. That this move was successful is shown by the many admiring references to the play by Jonson's contemporaries.

A new phase of Jonson's career, his employment as a writer of court masques and courtly en-

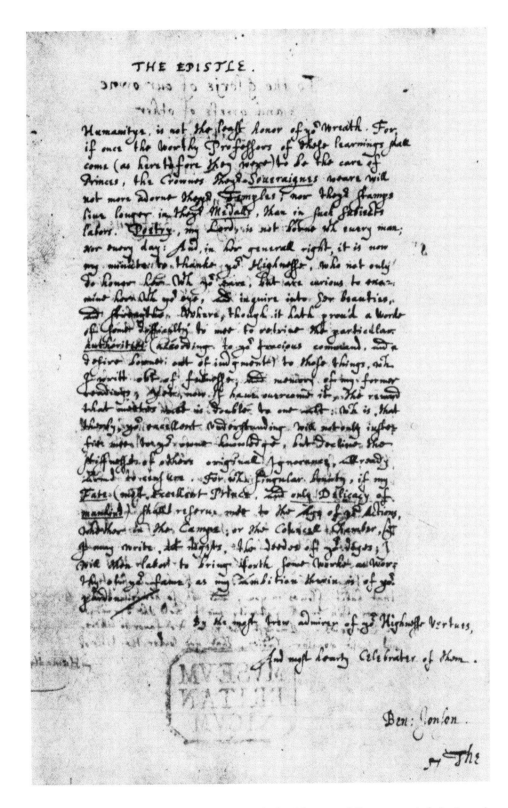

Letter of dedication from a presentation copy of The Masque of Queens, *entirely in Jonson's hand (Royal MS 18 A xlv, f.2ᵛ; by permission of the British Library)*

Costume designs by Inigo Jones for The Masque of Queens: *left (top) Penthesileia, (bottom) Camilla; right (bottom) Zenobia, (top) Atalanta (Stephen Orgel and Roy Strong,* Inigo Jones, *1973)*

tertainments, began in June 1603, when Jonson was commissioned to write an entertainment to greet the Queen and Prince at Althorp, the house of Sir Robert Spencer, on their way south from Scotland. In 1604, when the King arrived in London, the city hired Jonson to write speeches of greeting as part of its formal welcome of the new monarch; he also wrote a "Panegyre" for James's opening of Parliament a few days later. In the same year he wrote *The Entertainment at Highgate*, which welcomed the King and Queen to the house of Sir William Cornwallis. The King and Queen were sufficiently impressed by these performances that Jonson was commissioned to write the court masque for the next Christmas season's customary Twelfth Night revels.

Queen Anne requested a masque in which she and her chief ladies could appear disguised as "Black-mores." The result, *The Masque of Blackness*, performed on Twelfth Night 1605, launched Jonson's career as a deviser of court masques. Thereafter Jonson would produce a masque for the Court's Christmas festivities every year of the reign except for Christmas 1606-1607, when Thomas Campion's *Masque of Lord Hayes*, was written for that lord's wedding, which replaced the usual Christmas celebration; 1613, when he was absent in France; and Christmas 1620-1621.

Jonson is the most important writer of court masques, largely because he approached masque writing so seriously. Court masques were celebrations of royalty designed to impress foreign and domestic observers by their magnificence, and most people considered them to be primarily spectacles. Samuel Daniel, whose *Vision of the Twelve Goddesses* was performed at Court in January 1604, had ridiculed those who attempted "to shew most wit about these Puntillos of Dreames and shewes." However, Jonson insisted that masques be true poems, that they not only entertain but also move the spectators to virtue. The introduction to *Hymenaei* (produced on 5 and 6 January 1606) provides the clearest account of Jonson's lofty conception of the function of masques. There the spectacular elements of masques are compared to the body, and the intellectual elements to the soul. Jonson claims that the grounding of masques upon solid intellectual and moral ideas "hath made the most royall *Princes*, and greatest *persons* (who are commonly the *personaters* of these *actions*) not onely studious of riches, and magnificence in the outward celebration, or shew; (which rightly becomes them)

but curious after the most high, and heartie *inuentions*, to furnish the inward parts: (and those grounded vpon *antiquitie*, and solide *learnings*) which, though their *voyce* be taught to sound to present occasions, their *sense*, or doth, or should always lay hold on more remou'd *mysteries*."

Jonson recognized that poetry was only part of the masque; elaborate costumes and stage scenery, music, and dance were all integral parts of the form. However, he insisted that all spectacular elements should contribute to communicating a principle theme. And he believed that it was the poet's job to supply the theme around which the masque would be structured.

The opportunity to write court masques greatly attracted Jonson. For one thing, masque writing paid well. In 1620 Jonson was paid £100 for writing *News from the New World Discovered in the Moon;* in contrast he told Drummond in 1619 that "of all his Playes he never Gained 2 hundred pounds." However, Jonson was attracted by more than the financial rewards. The courtly masque satisfied both his desire for a more refined audience than was available in the public theater and his belief that poetry should serve the commonwealth. In the comical satires he had tried unsuccessfully to reform society from the stage. In the masques he could help to inform royalty with virtue, thus potentially reforming society from the top.

The royal entertainments and court masques of 1604-1605 were the beginning of a happy relationship between Jonson and King James. However, Jonson came very close to losing the foothold to royal favor that he had gained. In late 1604 or early 1605 he collaborated with Chapman and with his former adversary Marston on the play *Eastward Ho.* Imprudently the authors inserted some passages ridiculing the Scots, probably during an unlicensed production sometime between July and September 1605, while the King was on his Oxford progress. When James learned of the offense he was outraged. The three authors were imprisoned, and as Jonson told Drummond, "the report was that they should then had their ears cutt & noses." The three playwrights appealed to various powerful noblemen, Chapman even writing to the King himself, Jonson to the Earl of Salisbury. The intervention of Suffolk, the Lord Chamberlain, and of Lord D'Aubigny helped to bring about the release of the three authors.

A few months later Jonson found himself caught up in the government's response to a na-

THE ALCHEMIST.

VVritten
by
BEN. IONSON.

——*Neque, me vt miretur turba, laboro:*
Contentus paucis lectoribus.

LONDON,
Printed by *Thomas Snodham,* for *Walter Burre,*
and are to be sold by *Iohn Stepneth,* at the
West-end of Paules.
1612.

TO THE READER.

IF thou beeſt more, thou art an Vnderſtander, and then I truſt thee. If thou art one that tak'ſt vp, and but a Pretender, beware at what hands thou receiu'ſt thy commoditie; for thou wert neuer more fair in the way to be coſned (then in this Age, in Poetry, eſpecially in Playes: wherein, now, the Concupiſcence of Iigges, and Daunces ſo raigneth, as to runne away from Nature, and be afraid of her, is the onely point of art that tickles the Spectators. But how out of purpoſe, and place, doe I name Art? when the Profeſſors are growne ſo obſtinate contemners of it, and preſumers on their owne Naturalls, as they are deriders of all diligence that way, and, by ſimple mocking at the termes, when they vnderſtand not the things, thinke to get off wittily with their Ignorance. Nay, they are eſteem'd the more learned, and ſufficient for this, by the Multitude, through their excellent vice of iudgement. For they commend Writers, as they doe Fencers, or Wraſtlers; who if they come in robuſtuouſly, and put for it with a great deale of violence, are receiu'd for the brauer fellowes: when many times their owne rudeneſſe is the cauſe of their diſgrace, and a little touch of their Aduerſary giues all that boyſterous force the foyle. I deny not, but that theſe men, who alwaies ſeeke to doe more then inough, may ſome time happen on ſome thing that is good, and great; but very ſeldome: And when it comes it doth not recompence the reſt of their ill. It ſticks out perhaps, and is more eminent, becauſe all is ſordide, and vile about it: as lights are more diſcern'd in a thick darkneſſe, then a faint ſhadow. I ſpeake not this, out of a hope to doe good on any man, againſt his will; for I know, if it were put to the queſtion of theirs, and mine, the worſe would finde more ſuffrages: *becauſe*

---

becauſe the moſt fauour common errors. But I giue thee this warning, that there is a great difference betweene thoſe, that (to gain the opinion of Copie) vtter all they can, how euer vnfitly; and thoſe that vſe election, and a meane. For it is onely the diſeaſe of the vnskilfull, to thinke rude things greater then poliſh'd: or ſcatter'd more numerous then compos'd.

To my friend, Mr. Ben: Ionſon. vpon
his Alchemiſt.

A Maſter, read in flatteries great skill, (will,
Could not paſſe truth, though he would force his
By praiſing this too much, to get more praiſe
In his Art, then you out of yours doe raiſe.
Nor can full truth be vttered of your worth,
Vnleſſe you your owne praiſes doe ſet forth:
None elſe can write ſo skilfully, to ſhew
Your praiſe: Ages ſhall pay, yet ſtill muſt owe.
All I dare ſay, is, you haue written well,
In what exceeding height, I dare not tell.

George Lucy.

The Perſons of the Comœdie.

SVBTLE. The Alchemiſt.
FACE. The Houſe-keeper.
DOL: Common. Their Colleague.
DAPPER. A Clearke.
DRVGGER. A Tabacco-man.
LOVE-Wit. Maſter of the Houſe.

EPICVRE MAMMON. A Knight.
SVRLY. A Gamſter.
TRIBVLATION. A Paſtor of *Amſtredam.*
ANANIAS. A Deacon there.
KASTRIL. The Angry Boy.
Da: PLIANT. His ſiſter: A Widdow.
Neighbours.
Officers.
Mutes.

THE ARGVMENT.

T he Sickneſſe hot, A Maſter quit, for feare,
H is Houſe in Towne: and left one Seruant there.
E aſe him corrupted, and gaue meanes to know
A Cheater, and his Punque; who now brought low,
L eauing their narrow practiſe, were become
C os'ners at large: and, onely wanting ſome
H ouſe to ſet vp, with him they here contract,
E ach for a ſhare, and all begin to act.
M uch company they draw, and much abuſe
I n caſting Figures, telling Fortunes, Newes,
S elling of Flyes, flat Bawdry, with the *Stone:*
T ill It, and They, and All in *fume* are gone.

Title page, epistle to the reader, commendatory verse by George Lucy, dramatis personae, and the Argument from the 1612 quarto edition of one of Jonson's best-known plays (King's College Library, Cambridge)

tional crisis. The Gunpowder Plot to blow up Parliament on 5 November 1605 was thwarted just as the conspirators were about to put their plan into action. Jonson knew several of the conspirators; he had been at a supper party hosted by the conspirator Robert Catesby and attended by fellow Catholics some time around 9 October. However, Jonson was loyal to the crown. On 7 November Lord Salisbury commissioned Jonson to convey a promise of safe conduct to a priest "that offered to do good service to the State." Jonson sought him out unsuccessfully and was forced to write to Salisbury that "that Party will not be found, (for soe he returnes answere.)."

Jonson's cooperation did not keep him from trouble during the official reaction to the plot. In April of 1606 he and his wife were summoned before the Consistory Court for absenting themselves from Anglican communion; Jonson was also charged with being "a seducer of youthe to popishe religion." Jonson denied the latter charge on his own behalf and also denied all charges against his wife. With characteristic self-confidence, the poet told his examiners that his nonattendance at communion was due to "some scruple of conscience" and requested that learned men be appointed to resolve him in the matter.

In 1605 Jonson was living in a house in the district of the Blackfriars. There in five weeks he wrote *Volpone*, an undisputed masterpiece and his first unqualified success. The play was immensely popular at the Globe in early 1606; more gratifying still was the play's success at both universities later that year. The former bricklayer and itinerant actor who for years had demanded recognition of his scholarship and artistry had won the approval of the most prestigious centers of learning in the land. When Jonson published *Volpone* in 1607 he included a lengthy dedication to the universities expressing his gratitude.

Volpone marks a new phase in Jonson's struggle to develop a moral comedy. The comical satires had deliberately subordinated plot to characterization and to moral instruction. At the center of each stood an arbiter of morals–Asper, Crites, or Horace–surveying folly and vice from a position of lofty detachment while deftly managing the onstage action that exposes the fools and knaves. In the comedies from *Volpone* to *Bartholomew Fair*, there are no virtuous characters controlling the action. More often than not the rogues call all the shots; the virtuous Celia and Bonario seem relatively helpless in the world of *Volpone*.

After this play the depiction of ideal virtue disappears entirely from the comedies and is reserved for the masques and nondramatic poems of praise.

In *Volpone* and the comedies which follow it, the role of intrigue returns to the foreground as the plane of the ideal disappears. Plot becomes much more important in the middle and late comedies than in the comical satires. And the willingness to experiment with comic form seen in *Every Man out of His Humour* is replaced by an emphasis on critical orthodoxy: the prologue to *Volpone* promises "quick *comœdie*, refined,/As best Criticks haue designed."

Volpone has much in common with *Sejanus*. In both plays the action is wholly dominated by a crafty villain whose tricky henchman tries unsuccessfully to snatch power from him. Both Sejanus and Volpone are masters of theatricality. And in both plays virtue is helpless to deal with the machinations of the wicked.

The plot of *Volpone* is inspired by the Roman practice of *captatio*, whereby would-be legatees gave lavish gifts to old or sickly rich men in hopes of being named their heirs. The scene is not ancient Rome, however, but Renaissance Venice, which Jonson invests with all of the splendor and corruption that the Elizabethans associated with Italy. Elements from the genre of beast fable are woven into the plot, emphasizing the brutality of the world of the play. Thus most of the human characters have animal names, such as Volpone or fox, Mosca or fly, and Voltore, Corbaccio and Corvino–"vulture . . . Rauen, and gor-crow."

Brutality does not sufficiently qualify the description of the characters, however. Volpone and his assistant Mosca have intelligence and imagination as well. Volpone especially is not merely the crafty villain implied by the epithet "fox." He is a magnifico who combines the ruthless intelligence of Tiberius in *Sejanus* with the passionate will and daring imagination of a Marlovian overreacher, so that he attains a kind of perverse grandeur. Jonson gives him magnificent speeches packed with imagery that dazzles and glitters. Under the spell of his rhetoric we almost forget his villainy.

In the early part of the play Volpone also gains much of our sympathy because his victims are no better morally than he, while they lack his intelligence and imagination. They deceive themselves by their own greed and deserve to be cheated. However, Jonson forces his audience to condemn Volpone when "the fox" attempts to

Costume design by Inigo Jones for Oberon in the first of two Jonson masques performed at Court during the 1610-1611 Christmas season (Stephen Orgel and Roy Strong, Inigo Jones, *1973)*

rape an innocent woman and then tries to calumniate her equally innocent defender, Bonario. Volpone almost succeeds; but when he is betrayed by Mosca, who almost grabs all of his master's loot, he chooses to reveal his guilt in court and thus destroy himself along with Mosca, rather than allow himself to be cheated.

The play's catastrophe has excited a good deal of critical debate, for *Volpone* has one of the harshest endings of any comedy. Volpone is con-

demned "to lie in prison, crampt with irons" until he is truly lame and sick; Mosca is to be whipped and sentenced to life in the galleys; their dupes are also punished severely. Apparently Jonson still felt that in order to point the moral of the play retributive justice like that in the comical satires was necessary.

After *Volpone* Jonson remained absent from the stage for a period of four years. Meanwhile several masques appeared. January 1606 had seen the performance of *Hymenaei,* written for the wedding of Frances Howard to the Earl of Essex, which supplanted the usual Twelfth Night revels. The masque was performed on two consecutive nights, the first night's performance presenting the subjugation of the Humors and Affections to Reason at the behest of the god Hymen, and the second the victory of Truth over Opinion in a mock combat. That summer, on 24 July, *The Entertainment of the Two Kings at Theobalds* was performed to welcome James and his brother-in-law, King Christian of Denmark, to the Earl of Salisbury's house. On 22 May 1607 *An Entertainment of the King and Queen at Theobalds* was performed to mark the Earl of Salisbury's turning his house over to the King. That summer Jonson was also engaged by the Merchant Taylors' Company to provide an entertainment for the King, the Queen, and Prince Henry when

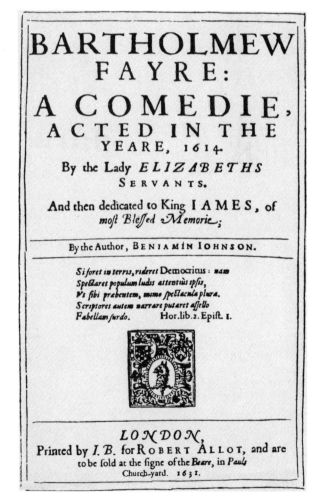

Title page for the first printing of Jonson's comedy, produced in 1614, from the 1631 folio edition of volume two of his works (C. H. Herford, Percy and Evelyn Simpson, eds., Ben Jonson, volume 6, 1938)

they came to attend the annual election of the company's Master and Warders.

On 10 January 1608 *The Masque of Beauty,* designed as a sequel to *The Masque of Blackness,* was performed in the newly completed Banqueting House at Whitehall, followed by *The Haddington Masque* on 9 February 1608, to celebrate the marriage of a favorite of the King's, Viscount Haddington. Both masques were very costly, but both were highly successful. A few months later Jonson was commissioned by the Earl of Salisbury to write a lesser piece, an entertainment welcoming King James to Salisbury House in the Strand. The text of this entertainment has not survived.

Jonson wrote *The Masque of Queens* for the next year's Twelfth Night festivities at the Court. However, because of diplomatic wrangling among the foreign ambassadors who were to attend the performance (a frequent problem during Jonson's tenure as a writer of court masques), the performance was postponed until 2 February 1609. When it was finally performed it made a great impression. However, it was also quite expensive, costing the King over £3000. Another entertainment, now lost, was performed before the Royal family on 11 April 1609, to celebrate the opening of "Britain's Burse," later known as the New Exchange. Jonson received over £13 for his share in devising the entertainment.

A prominent feature of Jonson's life during these years was his social activity. During the first half of the reign of King James, Jonson was one of a circle of literary men and wits who gathered in the famous Mermaid Tavern, whose "rich Canary wine" is mentioned in Epigram 101, "Inviting a Friend to Supper." A verse epistle from Francis Beaumont to Jonson has immortalized the gatherings at the tavern, and the tradition was embellished by Jonson's early biographers. Thomas Fuller (1608-1661) recorded that the tavern was the setting for "wit-combats" between Jonson and Shakespeare, "which two I behold like a *Spanish great Gallion,* and an *English man of War;* Master *Johnson* (like the former) was built far higher in Learning; *Solid,* but *Slow* in his performances. *Shake-spear,* with the *English man of War,* lesser in *bulk,* but lighter in *sailing,* could turn with all tides, tack about and take advantage of all winds, by the quickness of his Wit and Invention."

Jonson's relations with Shakespeare seem to have been friendly though not close. In the *Discoveries* Jonson wrote, "I lov'd the man, and doe honour his memory (on this side Idolatry) as much

THE DIUELL
IS
AN ASSE:

A COMEDIE
ACTED IN THE
YEARE, 1616.

BY HIS MAIESTIES
SERVANTS.

The Author BEN : IONSON.

HOR. *de* ART. POET.
Ficta voluptatis Causâ, sint proxima veris.

LONDON,
Printed by *J. B.* for ROBERT ALLOT, and are
to be sold at the signe of the *Beare*, in *Pauls*
Church-yard 1631.

Interior title page from the 1631 edition of volume two of Jonson's works for the first printing of the play whose 1616 production marked the beginning of Jonson's absence from the theater for nearly ten years (C. H. Herford, Percy and Evelyn Simpson, eds., Ben Jonson, *volume 6, 1938)*

as any." For the first folio collection of Shakespeare's plays (1623), Jonson composed a lengthy poem of praise. However, there was much in Shakespeare's writing that annoyed Jonson, and Jonson was never reluctant to criticize a perceived error. The famous remark in the *Conversations with Drummond*, "That Shaksperr wanted Arte," reappears in other guises elsewhere in Jonson's writing–in the induction to *Bartholomew Fair*, with its slighting references to "*Tales, Tempests*, and such like *Drolleries*"; in the prologue to *Every Man in His Humour*, which obliquely refers to Shakespeare's history plays as examples of "th'ill customes of the age"; in the reference to "some mouldy tale,/Like *Pericles*" in the "Ode to Himselfe" on the failure of *The New Inn;* and in

the observation in *Discoveries* that, "hee flow'd with that facility, that sometime it was necessary he should be stop'd: *Sufflaminandus erat.*"

Jonson's friends also included the poets John Donne, Francis Beaumont, and George Chapman. For Donne, Jonson held especially high regard. A letter has survived in which Jonson wrote to Donne, "You cannot but believe, how dear and reverend your friendship is to me." Jonson also respected greatly Donne's poetry. Although he criticized Donne's liberties with meter and his occasional obscurity, Jonson told Drummond that "he esteemeth John Done the first poet jn the World in some things." In an "Apologie" for *Bartholomew Fair*, which prefaced his translation of Horace's *Ars Poetica*, Jonson created a speaker named Criticus, who was intended to represent Donne. Unfortunately the preface was lost in the fire of 1623 that destroyed Jonson's library.

Jonson's friends were not all literary men. Among Jonson's closest friends were William Roe and his brother Sir John Roe. On one occasion, Sir John and Jonson were ejected from Whitehall by Lord Suffolk for boisterous behavior during the performance of a masque. In 1606 Sir John died of the plague in Jonson's arms, and Jonson paid the cost of his burial.

In late 1609 or early 1610 Jonson returned to the stage with the comedy *Epicoene*, performed by the Children of the Queen's Revels at Whitefriars. Ever since Dryden's discussion of the play in the *Essay of Dramatic Poesy, Epicoene* has been praised for the skill of its construction. But the play has also disturbed many readers by the heartlessness of the society it presents. None of the play's characters is ethically sound. Truewit and Dauphine, the comic heroes of the play, rise above their fellows in wit and breeding but are basically frivolous. And their treatment of Morose at the end of the play seems unnecessarily cruel.

The plot of the play, derived from two different classical sources, centers around the efforts of Dauphine, aided by his friend Truewit, to gain the inheritance of his uncle Morose, an old bachelor morbidly sensitive to noise of any kind. Morose is determined to disinherit his nephew, and thus decides to marry Epicoene, a woman remarkable for her silence. Truewit tries in a number of ways–each of which drives Morose to distraction–to dissuade him from marriage. However, Morose marries anyway, whereupon his bride immediately loses her silence. Dauphine then extracts from Morose a promise that he will make Dauphine his heir if Dauphine can find grounds to annul the marriage; when Dauphine reveals that Epicoene is not a woman but a boy in disguise, Morose is forced to keep his promise and is jeered off the stage.

In *Epicoene* Jonson's impulse to didacticism seems to have relaxed. This change is signaled in the play's prologue, which emphasizes entertainment rather than instruction. The poet is compared to a cook whose task is to please the palates of his guests—a striking contrast to the role of the poet in the comical satires, whose art is said to be "phisicke of the mind," good for the audience whether they like it or not.

However, not everyone was pleased by the feast which Jonson had prepared; in fact *Epicoene* involved Jonson in a new scandal, and by February the play was suppressed by the government. Some members of the audience detected a satirical reference to the King's cousin, Arabella Stuart, in a passage describing how Sir John Daw, a gull in the play, draws "maps of persons," including maps "of the Prince of *Moldauia*, and of his mistris, mistris EPICOENE." An imposter named Stephano Janiculo, who claimed to be the Prince of Moldavia, had come to England in 1601 and in 1607, on the latter occasion receiving a grant of £300 from King James. In 1608 Janiculo was in Venice bruiting it about that he was engaged to be married to Lady Arabella. By this time Lady Arabella had become engaged to Sir William Seymour; however, because she was a close relative of the King, her marriage plans were a matter of importance to the state and were watched closely by observers both foreign and domestic. On 8 February 1610 the Venetian ambassador made the following report: "Lady Arabella is seldom seen outside her rooms and lives in greater dejection than ever. She complains that in a certain comedy the play-wright introduced an allusion to her person and the part played by the Prince of Moldavia. The play was suppressed." We know of no further consequences for Jonson from the affair.

At about the same time as the performance of *Epicoene*, Jonson's *The Speeches at Prince Henry's Barriers* was performed, on Twelfth Night 1610. The festivities marked a special occasion, the investiture of Prince Henry as Prince of Wales. The Prince was portrayed as Meliadus, a knight destined to restore the lost glories of Chivalry. By all accounts the royal entertainment was a success.

Later that year the King's Men produced Jonson's next play, *The Alchemist*, which was en-

tirely successful in its own time and is regarded as one of his greatest works today. The tight construction seen in *Epicoene* is even more marked in this play; the action of the play takes place entirely within the two hours or so of the play's stage performance. The play centers around the desperate attempts of three rogues–Face the tricky butler, Subtle the alchemist, and Doll Common the whore–to swindle a variety of Londoners, all of whom are possessed by the dream of the philosophers' stone. Some of the dupes gulled by "the venter *tripartite*" are merely silly, like Dapper and Drugger. Sir Epicure Mammon, however, is a remarkable creation. For him the dream of infinite wealth is primarily a promise of infinite sensual variety; the dizzying speeches in which he describes his fantastic vision are among the most justly celebrated passages in Jonson's work.

Prominent among the victims of the alchemical conspiracy are the Puritans Ananias and Tribulation Wholesome. Jonson is unremittingly hostile toward the Puritans. They are depicted as entirely hypocritical, and their peculiar theological vocabulary as mere cant disguising their sordid greed. As early as *Every Man out of His Humour* Jonson had attacked those

> whose faces are all zeale,
> . . . that will not smell of sinne,
> But seeme as they were made of sanctitie!
> Religion in their garments, and their haire
> Cut shorter then their eye-browes!

In *Bartholomew Fair* he would continue his attack on the "Faction." It was not merely the Puritans' hostility toward the theater that earned Jonson's hostility, although that becomes a particular issue in *Bartholomew Fair*. Rather it is their rejection of the culture inherited from classical antiquity that earns Jonson's special contempt. "I hate *Traditions*," says Ananias; in the context of Jonson's work that is a damning statement.

Having proved so successful in comedy, Jonson decided to return to classical tragedy. In 1611 *Catiline* was performed by the King's Men. Unfortunately the play was even more of a failure with the public than *Sejanus*. Although *Sejanus* had been rejected by the multitude, the intellectuals had rallied to its defense. *Catiline*, however, seems to have been rejected even by the educated. Jonson's response to the play's failure on the stage was to rush it into print within the year, with a dedication to the Earl of Pembroke defending his "legitimate Poeme" from the

censure of "these Iig-giuen times," and a con-
temptuous address "TO THE READER IN
ORDINAIRIE." The Latin motto on the play's
title page was carefully chosen to attack the nobles as well as the commons for their lack of
judgment.

In the preface to *Sejanus*, Jonson had apologized for that play's failure to follow strictly the
classical model of tragedy. *Catiline*, with its chorus, and its adherence to "the strict laws of time"
was for Jonson a formal improvement, "a legitimate Poeme." And, as in *Sejanus*, Jonson again emphasized "truth of argument." Jonson followed
his main source, Sallust, in making Catiline and
his circle incarnations of evil. Thus the unmitigated malice, bloodlust, and delight in mischief expressed by the conspirators are melodramatic
rather than tragic. That in itself would not have offended Jonson's audience, however. More damag-
ing for the play's success was Jonson's treatment
of the play's hero, Cicero. Cicero was one of the authors for whom Jonson felt a special affinity.
Like Jonson he was a self-made man who had
risen to prominence on the strength of his eloquence. And like Jonson he placed a premium
on the moral function of eloquence. One of
Jonson's most firmly held principles was the relation between sound language and sound morals.
In the *Discoveries* he wrote, "Wheresoever, manners, and fashions are corrupted, Language is. It
imitates the publicke riot." In the comedies he
had repeatedly shown folly or vice expressed in degraded language–thus the uncouth style of
Crispinus, the hollow oratory of Voltore, the glib
prattle of Lady Would-be and the Collegiate ladies, and the cant of alchemy and Puritanism. In
the character of Cicero, Jonson could emphasize
the linguistic propriety of the well-settled soul.

Consequently *Catiline* places a good deal of
emphasis on Cicero's oratory; in fact the plot
hinges on the success of Cicero's famous oration
denouncing Catiline, which Jonson translates into

The Catalogue.

Euery Man in his Humor,	To Mr. CAMBDEN.
Euery Man out of his Humor,	To the INNES of COVRT.
Cynthias Reuells,	To the COVRT.
Poëtaster,	To Mr. RICH. MARTIN.
Seianus,	To ESME Lo. Aubigny.
The Foxe,	To the VNIVERSITIES.
The silent Woman,	To Sir FRAN. STVART.
The Alchemist,	To the Lady WROTH.
Catiline,	To the Earle of PEMBROK.
Epigrammes,	To the same.

The Forrest,
Entertaynments,
Panegyre,
Masques,
Barriers.

¶ 3

*Title page and table of contents from a 1616 folio edition of the volume that provoked criticism of Jonson for his classifying plays
as literary "works" (Bodleian Library, Oxford)*

Page from a manuscript for Christmas, His Masque, *possibly in Jonson's hand (Maggs Bros., catalogue number 569, 1932)*

nearly 300 lines of blank verse. As drama, however, the oration is tedious. The address "TO THE READER IN ORDINAIRIE" indicates that this long oration was the chief objection of the audience.

Meanwhile, for the court's celebration of Christmas 1610-1611, in which festivities the new Prince of Wales played a major role, Jonson had written two masques, *Oberon, the Fairy Prince*, performed on 1 January 1611, and *Love Freed from Ig-*

norance and Folly, scheduled for Twelfth Night but not performed until 3 February. For the next year's season he wrote *Love Restored*, performed on Twelfth Night 1612. Due to the King's severe financial difficulties at this time, little money could be spent on *Love Restored*, and the element of spectacle is drastically reduced in the masque, a circumstance to which Jonson refers wittily in the text.

By this time Jonson had returned to the Anglican church. Once again Drummond records an anecdote which vividly captures Jonson's personality: "after he was reconciled with the Church & left of to be a recusant at his first communion jn token of true Reconciliation, he drank out all the full cup of wyne."

In autumn 1612 Jonson traveled to France as the tutor of Sir Walter Raleigh's son. Raleigh had been imprisoned in the Tower of London since 1603; there he had written his *History of the World*, assisted, as Jonson told Drummond, by "the best wits of England. . . . Ben himselfe had written a peice to him of ye punick warre which he altered and set in his booke." Jonson may not have been the best choice for the position of tutor, however. His predilection to drink is well known; Drummond said it was "one of the Elements, jn which he liveth." One night in Paris the younger Raleigh got his tutor dead drunk and had him drawn through the streets stretched out on a cart, calling out at every corner that here was "a more Lively jmage of ye Crucifix then any they had." In seventeenth century Catholic Paris, such blasphemy could have caused serious trouble. Fortunately nothing came of the incident.

We also know of other more edifying episodes during Jonson's stay in France. Records have survived showing that Jonson was present at a theological debate between a Catholic and a Protestant on the subject of the Real Presence. The topic was of great interest to Jonson, who had twice converted; given his scholarly interests he must have been familiar with both sides of the issue. (Drummond rather snidely records his opinion that Jonson was "for any religion as being versed jn both.") Jonson's interest in theological matters is also shown in the reference to the "humble Gleanings in Divinitie" listed among the poet's writings lost in the fire that destroyed his library in 1623.

While in France Jonson also met the distinguished Cardinal Duperron, a powerful statesman who enjoyed a literary reputation in his own day. King James himself had expressed interest in Duperron's translations of Virgil. Jonson, however, was not impressed. When the cardinal showed his verses to Jonson, he was told that "they were naught."

Jonson was back in England by 29 June 1613; in the "Execration upon Vulcan" he mentions that he witnessed the burning of the Globe, which took place on that date. Jonson wrote two minor pieces, *The Irish Masque* and *A Challenge at Tilt*, for the next Christmas season at court, for which Campion wrote the principal masque. The annual festivities were dominated by another wedding–the notorious marriage of the Countess of Essex to the Earl of Somerset.

By the fall of 1614 Jonson had written for the Lady Elizabeth's Men the last of his comedies that ranks among his best works: *Bartholomew Fair*. The play was first performed at the Hope, a bear-baiting pit that doubled as a theater, on 31 October, and then at Whitehall the next day.

Bartholomew Fair is remarkable among Jonson's comedies for its relaxation of censoriousness. The tension between the comic spirit of delight in misrule and the satirist's passion for punishing disorder is here resolved in favor of the comic spirit to an extent unmatched in any of the earlier comedies. Although *Bartholomew Fair* abounds in unsavory characters–thieves, whores, cheats, fools, and even poetasters–the play's punishments are mainly reserved for its authority figures, who foolishly try to correct the "enormities" of the fair without first learning self-control. Parallel to the humbling of authority that occurs in the action of the play is the more accommodating stance that Jonson takes toward his audience. The inflexible elitism of the address "TO THE READER IN ORDINAIRIE" preceding the 1611 quarto of *Catiline* is replaced by a much more obliging attitude in the induction to *Bartholomew Fair*. There the author propounds "certaine Articles" of agreement between his audience and himself, a covenant whereby each side undertakes to fulfill certain conditions for the common good. For his part Jonson promises to try to please everyone in the audience, including the "grounded Iudgements" of the pit, as well as the more refined and educated hearers.

Yet Jonson does not abandon his critical principles in the play. The induction emphasizes his continued realistic emphasis: "Hee is loth to make Nature afraid in his *Playes*, like those that beget *Tales*, *Tempests*, and such like *Drolleries*." Jonson's impercipience to the glories of Shakespearean romance is sometimes embarrassing, but it derives from the same activity of ruthless critical judgment that is so essential to his artistic achievement. Jonson frequently invokes "truth to nature" as a criterion of his comedy, but Jonsonian "realism" is fundamentally satirical; the image reflected in the glass of Jonsonian comedy is never flattering. This is especially true in *Bartholomew Fair*, even though the would-be correctors of social mores, whose roles are analogous to those of the satirist figures in the comical satires,

Costume designs by Inigo Jones for Welsh dancers in For the Honor of Wales, *the revised version of* Pleasure Reconciled to Virtue, *for which Jonson wrote a new antimasque set in Wales (Stephen Orgel and Roy Strong,* Inigo Jones, *1973)*

are singled out for particular abuse. The activities of the fair which the authority figures try unsuccessfully to curb are never sentimentalized in the play. On the contrary, the play's imagery and action unsparingly indicate the animality of human activity at the fair: eating, drinking, copulating, fighting, urinating, sweating, and vomiting–all the indignities of the body dominate the language of *Bartholomew Fair*.

    The scene of the play is the annual fair held at Smithfield on St. Bartholomew's Day. Thither come people from every level of society, from the "Bartholomew-birds" hawking their shoddy wares and rotten gingerbread, selling roast pig and ale, stealing purses, and procuring whores, to the gentlefolks who come to eat, drink, and be amused. The plot involves a number of separate actions that interweave and crisscross; no one of them is dominant. The lack of focus on a single action might seem to be a relaxation of Jonson's critical standards; however, the management of the plot is exceptionally skillful. In fact the plot seems the least contrived of all Jonson's comedies.

    Into the world of the play come two notable opponents of saturnalia, Adam Overdo, a justice of the peace whose zeal in correcting "enormities" is exceeded only by his incompetence; and Zeal-of-the-Land Busy, a Puritan "rabbi." The

Costume designs by Inigo Jones for masquers in Time Vindicated. *The figure at top left, wearing a cat mask, is the Curious personified while the other figures represent the Eyes (bottom left), the Ears (bottom right), and the Nose (top right) (Stephen Orgel and Roy Strong,* Inigo Jones, *1973).*

character of Busy continues the attack on the Puritans that Jonson began in *The Alchemist*. As in the earlier play, the Puritans are depicted as utter hypocrites. *Bartholomew Fair*, however, presents a kind of defense of the theater by Jonson when Busy tries to overthrow the puppet show, which he attacks in the same terms that the Puritans used in attacking the stage. Jonson does nothing to defend the dignity of the theater; the puppet show is a witless farce in doggerel verse. Busy is confuted simply by being made ridiculous in confronting a puppet. The Puritan attack on the stage, although dangerous in its factiousness, is shown as merely silly.

The action of the fair may be mindless, greedy, and even vicious, but those who attempt to suppress it are made to look more foolish than those who come to enjoy it. The spirit of the play may be summed up in the rebuke addressed to Overdo at the close of the play: "remember you are but *Adam*, Flesh, and blood! you haue your frailty, forget your other name of Ouerdoo, and inuite vs all to supper." Yet Jonson does not encourage complacency in his audience. The frenetic animality that characterizes the fair is also associated with the larger world beyond the fair and beyond the playhouse in the last words of the play: "wee'll ha' the rest o' the *Play* at home."

The success of *Bartholomew Fair* was followed a few months later by the success of the masque *The Golden Age Restored*, which was performed at Court on Twelfth Night 1615 and again two days later. The next year Jonson produced another successful masque at Court, *Mercury Vindicated from the Alchemists*, first performed on 1 January and repeated on 6 January 1616 because of a quarrel over precedence among the foreign ambassadors in attendance.

Jonson's next play, *The Devil Is an Ass*, was followed by Jonson's absence from the stage for almost ten years. Yet *The Devil Is an Ass* is more often grouped with the plays that followed it than with those that preceded it. Dryden characterized Jonson's late plays as "dotages," and it is undeniable that they display less rigor in the management of the plot, difficulty in maintaining a consistency of tone, and, in the last plays especially, a weakening of the author's imaginative powers betrayed by a blunting of the wit of Jonson's language and a tendency to recycle old conceits. Yet the late plays are of interest in their experimentation.

A notable feature of all the late plays from *The Devil Is an Ass* to *A Tale of a Tub*, is their employ-

ment of older conventions of the Elizabethan stage. Thus *The Devil Is an Ass* is a reworking of the Elizabethan devil play; *The Staple of News* employs a number of morality-play elements; *The New Inn* is a thoroughly romantic comedy; *A Tale of a Tub*, whether or not it is a revision of an early original, is a lighthearted rustic comedy; and the two fragments *The Sad Shepherd* and *The Fall of Mortimer* are a pastoral involving Robin Hood and an English history play. The only one of the late plays which is not marked by a revival of "un-Jonsonian" popular Elizabethan conventions, is *The Magnetic Lady*, which so consciously reworks the formulas of Jonson's middle period that it is almost a caricature of Jonsonian comedy.

It is interesting to note that this experimentation with older dramatic forms is often accompanied by a greater emphasis on love as a dramatic motive than in the earlier plays, and that romantic love becomes a more prominent theme in the later nondramatic poetry, as well. In the *Epigrams* and *The Forrest*, love as a theme was conspicuously absent, and Jonson had addressed this fact in *The Forrest* 1, "Why I Write Not of Love." In *The Underwood*, however, erotic love is a much more prominent theme than in the earlier verse collections.

The Devil Is an Ass shows Jonson's new interest both in earlier dramatic forms and in romantic love. The play inverts the conventions of the older devil plays as Jonson understood them. In the *Conversations with Drummond* Jonson told his host that "according to Comedia Vetus, jn England the divell was brought jn either w' one Vice or other, the Play done the divel caried away the Vice." In Jonson's play, however, a minor devil named Pug is shown to be no match for the shrewder wickedness of contemporary London. Thus Pug is returned to hell on the back of the Vice Iniquity, who delivers the moral in doggerel rhyme:

> The *Diuell* was wont to carry away the euill;
> But, now, the Euill out-carries the *Diuell*.

The villain who most notably "out-carries the devil" is Meercraft, a "projector" whose brain teems with insubstantial money-making schemes. Meercraft's plans especially appeal to the gull Fitzdottrel who, like the gulls in *The Alchemist*, is utterly carried away by the prospect of infinite wealth. Fitzdottrel is especially attracted to a land-reclamation scheme which will make him the "Duke of Drownedland." Since there were actual

THE

FORTVNATE ISLES

and

THEIR VNION.

celebrated in a

M A S Q V E

defign'd for the Court, on the

Twelfth night.

1 6 2 4.

Hic chorea , cantúsque vigent.

Title page for the 1625 quarto edition of the Jonson masque that was performed at Court on 9 January 1625 (1624 according to the calendar then in use) (Anderson Galleries, sale number 2077, 20-21 May 1926)

land-reclamation projects in England at the time, and because Jonson's contemporaries were quick to identify characters satirized on the stage with actual men, he was accused of libel, and "the King desyred him to conceal" the offending passages. The discussion of this trouble in the *Conversations with Drummond* is vague, and there is no evidence that Jonson suppressed any part of the original play.

Besides being a gull like *The Alchemist*'s Sir Epicure Mammon, Fitzdottrel is also a jealous but sordid husband, like *Volpone*'s Corvino. Wittipol, a London gallant, becomes enamored of Mrs. Fitzdottrel and courts her with verses that also appear in *The Underwood* 2, "A Celebration of Charis." Although Wittipol's intentions are at first merely carnal, he comes to esteem Mrs. Fitzdottrel and at the end of the play places her honor ahead of his own desires.

Some scholars have speculated that the courtships dramatized in *The Devil Is an Ass* and "A Celebration of Charis" are based on an actual affair that Jonson engaged in at this time. The "Charis" lyrics especially seem to suggest a basis in fact, since the poet there describes himself, with comic detachment, as an aging lover:

> *Cupids* Statue with a Beard,
> Or else one that plaid his Ape,
> In a *Hercules*-his shape.

The year of *The Devil Is an Ass*, 1616, also saw two other important events in Jonson's career. The first was King James's grant to Jonson of a life pension of one hundred marks a year in recognition of his service to the King. Jonson thereby became the first Poet Laureate in English history. The second event was the publication of *The Workes of Benjamin Jonson*, a folio collection prepared for the press by the author himself. The collection contains nine plays (*Every Man in His Humour, Every Man out of His Humour, Cynthia's Revels, Poetaster, Sejanus, Volpone, Epicoene, The Alchemist,* and *Catiline*), the two verse collections *Epigrams* and *The Forrest*, and most of Jonson's masques and entertainments from 1604 to 1616. The absence of *Bartholomew Fair* is puzzling; otherwise it is clear that Jonson has selected his best works to date, those that most clearly present the image of himself and of his art that he wished to transmit to his contemporaries and to posterity.

Some of the works in the folio, such as the nondramatic poetry, were published for the first time in the collection. Others which had been previously printed were revised, revision being especially heavy in the earlier works. Thus *Every Man in His Humour* was wholly rewritten, with its scene transferred from Florence to London and the characters' Italianate names accordingly Anglicized. The references to the controversy surrounding the original ending to *Every Man out of His Humour* were tactfully suppressed. The "Apologeticall Dialogue" at the end of *Poetaster*, which had been suppressed by the government, was restored, as were several passages in *Cynthia's Revels* that were omitted from the quarto. Blasphemous oaths in the comedies were toned down, and the bad-tempered address "TO THE READER IN ORDINAIRIE" which had preceded *Catiline* was omitted from the folio.

The publication of plays from the professional stage in a folio collection with the haughty title "Works" was a bold move, and Jonson was ridiculed by some of his contemporaries for daring

Costume designs by Inigo Jones for masquers in The Fortunate Isles and Their Union: *(left to right) Johphiel, the Airy Spirit; Scogan, based on poet Henry Scogan (1361?-1407); Skelton, based on poet John Skelton (1460?-1529); and Merefool, the Rosicrucian (Stephen Orgel and Roy Strong,* Inigo Jones, *1973)*

to call his plays works. However, the publication of the folio was the logical culmination of Jonson's career up to this point. Ever since the 1600 publication of *Every Man out of His Humour* in a quarto "Containing more than hath been Publikely Spoken or Acted," Jonson had welcomed the opportunity to present his plays to the reading public. The measure of control thus effected over his texts, their freedom from the vagaries of dramatic performance, the recognition of literate men–all of these seem to have appealed greatly to Jonson. For Jonson insisted that his plays be regarded as literature, as true "poems," and he liked to emphasize his own distance from the practice of most of his contemporaries in the theater. Jonson may have coined the word "playwright"; it is certain that he only uses it disparagingly. His preferred term for himself is "poet" and for his plays, "poems."

Jonson seems always to have harbored some ambivalence toward the theater as an artistic medium. The famous "Ode to Himself" prompted by the failure of *The New Inn* in 1629, which begins "Come leaue the lothed stage," is only the most extreme manifestation of this ambivalence. In 1616 when he was at the height of his success, Jonson withdrew from writing plays for almost ten years. In the folio he had called the *Epigrams* "the ripest of my studies." Now that he had the leisure and the opportunity, thanks to his pension from the King, he chose to devote himself mainly to nondramatic poetry. There is one possible exception to this trend, however. There is some evidence that in 1617 or thereabouts Jonson contributed a scene or two to a play by John Fletcher called *The Bloody Brother*, which was later revised by Philip Massinger and known by the title of *Rollo, Duke of Normandy*. No performance before 1630 is known, and the evidence of Jonson's involvement is hardly conclusive.

His work as a writer of court masques continued, however. The Christmas season of 1616-1617 brought two masques to write. *Christmas, His Masque,* a burlesque mumming, was the slighter of the two. For the Twelfth Night revels Jonson wrote the more elaborate *The Vision of Delight.* Among the guests attending the performance of *The Vision of Delight* was Pocahontas, who was visiting London at that time. The very next month brought the performance of yet another masque, *Lovers Made Men,* presented at the home of Lord Hay for the entertainment of the French ambassador, and presided over by Jonson's longtime patron the Countess of Bedford.

The next year's Twelfth Night festivities marked an important occasion of state, the first appearance of Prince Charles, the new Prince of Wales, as a principal masquer. Jonson's offering for the occasion, *Pleasure Reconciled to Virtue,* is now recognized as one of his finest masques. However, the original performance was a disaster, so much so that King James lost his temper and shouted at the masquers. Illness had prevented Queen Anne from attending the Twelfth Night revels. For that reason and in order to try to make good the original failure of his debut, Prince Charles decided to repeat the masque on Shrovetide. Jonson revised the text, replacing the original antimasque with one set in the Welsh mountains, and giving the masque a new name, *For the Honor of Wales.* However, this performance, on 17 February, was hardly more pleasing than the first.

In the summer of 1618 Jonson set out on foot for Scotland, no small feat for the middle-aged and overweight poet. There he was received with great honor. John Taylor the "Water-Poet," who undertook a journey to Scotland on foot shortly after Jonson, met him in Leith in August and found him "amongst Noblemen and Gentlemen that knowes his true worth, and their owne honours, where with much respectiue loue he is worthily entertained." On 20 September Jonson was made a burgess and guildbrother of the city of Edinburgh, and in October the city spent more than £221 on a banquet in his honor.

For a few weeks in late December 1618 or early January 1619 Jonson was the guest of the Scottish poet William Drummond of Hawthornden, whose record of his guest's remarks during the visit and of his own impressions of the man—"Certain Informations and maners of Ben Johnsons," which have come to be known to posterity as the *Conversations with Drummond*—are an invaluable source of information. Particularly interesting are the accounts of the works that Jonson was engaged in at that time, most of which have not survived (perhaps lost in the fire of 1623 that destroyed his library). These works include a pastoral called "The May Lord" in which a number of noble ladies were to be represented allegorically, a description of his trip to Scotland, an apology for *Bartholomew Fair,* and a discourse written against Thomas Campion and Samuel Daniel defending couplets as "the bravest sort of Verses." We are also told "that he had ane jntention to perfect ane Epick Poeme jntitled Heroologia of the Worthies of [t]his Country, rowsed by fame, and was to dedicate it to his Country, it is all jn Couplets, for he detesteth all other Rimes."

Drummond described the character of his remarkable houseguest at the close of the *Conversations with Drummond,* revealing some annoyance with his proud and opinionated guest, whom he describes at times without any sympathy; yet the image of Jonson that emerges from the *Conversations with Drummond* is consistent with the view of him to be gained from his writing and the other known facts of his life: "he is passionately kynde and angry, carelesse either to gaine or keep, Vindicative, būt if he be well answered, at himself."

In July 1619 Jonson stayed at Christ Church College, Oxford, as the guest of his friend Richard Corbet, who became Dean of Christ Church in 1620. During this stay the university granted him the honorary degree of Master of Arts in recognition of his learning.

The next few years saw a renewal of Jonson's activity as a masque writer after the hiatus occasioned by the trip to Scotland. On 7 January 1620 *News From the New World,* which anticipates *The Staple of News* in its satire of the fledgling news industry of Jacobean London, was performed at Court. In May the *Entertainment at Blackfriars* was performed at the house of the Earl of Newcastle in celebration of the christening of Charles Cavendish, and in June *Pan's Anniversary* was performed at Court to celebrate the King's birthday.

In August and September 1621 *The Gypsies Metamorphosed* was produced. The original occasion of *The Gypsies Metamorphosed* was the entertainment of King James by his favorite, the Duke of Buckingham, and the masque is largely concerned with allusions to the Buckingham circle and the royal family, delivered through the dramatic device of a gypsy fortune-teller reading the palms of the distinguished members of the audience. The masque was a great success, and after its performance at the Duke of Buckingham's residence on 3 September and at the home of his mother on 5 September, it was performed at Windsor in September, with minor revisions for the changed circumstances of production.

In October 1621 Jonson was nominated by warrant of reversion to the office of Master of the Revels. Under the provisions of the warrant the office would revert to Jonson upon the deaths of Sir George Buc and Sir John Astley, but Astley outlived Jonson, and nothing came of the nomination.

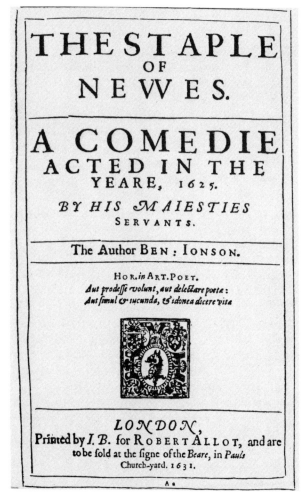

Interior title page from the 1631 folio edition of volume two of Jonson's works for the first printing of a play that was first produced by the King's Men in February 1626 (C. H. Herford, Percy and Evelyn Simpson, eds., Ben Jonson, volume 6, 1938)

On January 1622 occurred the first performance of *The Masque of Augurs*, which was revised for another performance on 6 May of the same year. One of the most interesting features of this masque is the character of Vangoose, a "projector" like Meercraft, but a projector of masques. Vangoose's remarks about the masque form provide an inverse reflection of Jonson's own opinions. Thus his remarks about the antimasque—"de more absurd it be, and vrom de purpose, it be ever all de better"—emphasize Jonson's care to make his own antimasques contribute to the masque's main theme.

Time Vindicated to Himself and to his Honors, performed on 19 January 1623, shows Jonson once again venturing into personal satire, this time of the poet George Wither, who is lampooned in the figure of Chronomastix. Not all of the audience were pleased with the attack on Wither, but Jonson did not suffer for his boldness.

In October 1623 Jonson testified in court in connection with a dispute between Sir Walter Raleigh's widow and a London jeweller. At that time he gave Gresham College as his residence, which may indicate that he was a lecturer in rhetoric at that institution.

In the same month or possibly November, a fire broke out in Jonson's lodgings and destroyed his personal library. *The Underwood* 43, "An Execration upon Vulcan," lists a number of the items lost in the fire and thus provides valuable information about Jonson's literary activity in the years immediately preceding the fire. Thus we know that in addition to "twice-twelve-yeares stor'd up humanitie,/With humble Gleanings in Divinitie," Jonson had already composed his translation of the *Ars Poetica*, including the apology for *Bartholomew Fair* mentioned in the *Conversations with Drummond*; a translation of John Barclay's *Argenis*, commissioned by the King; a verse account of his trip to Scotland; his English grammar; most of a history of the reign of Henry V, in which he was assisted by Richard Carew, Sir Robert Cotton, and Sir John Selden; and "parcels of a Play."

One of Jonson's best masques, *Neptune's Triumph for the Return of Albion*, was never performed due to a dispute between the French and Spanish ambassadors over precedence at the intended performance in January 1624. The masque celebrated the return of Prince Charles from his journey to Spain seeking the hand of the Infanta. By the next year Charles's return was old news and the Prince was already betrothed to Henrietta Maria. Jonson salvaged what

THE
NEVV INNE.
OR,
The light Heart.
A COMOEDY.
As it was neuer acted, but moſt
negligently play'd, by ſome, .
the Kings Seruants.
And more ſqueamiſhly beheld, and cēnſu-
red by others, the Kinge Subiects.
1629.
Now, at laſt, ſet at liberty to the Readers, his Maᵗⁱᵉ
Seruants, and Subiects, to be iudg'd.
1631.
By the Author, B. Ienſon.
Hor. . . . . *me lectori credere malim :*
Quàm ſpectatorii faſtidia ferre ſuperbi.

LONDON,
¶ Printed by *Thomas Harper,* for *Thomas Alcborne,* and
are to be ſold at his ſhop in Pauls Church-yeard,
at the ſigne of the greene Dragon.
MDCXXXI.

*The title page for the 1631 octavo edition of the Jonson com-
edy unsuccessfully performed by the King's Men in early
1629 expresses the playwright's anger at both the actors and
the audience (Anderson Galleries, sale number 2077, 20-21
May 1926)*

he could of the original composition and reworked it into *The Fortunate Isles and Their Union*,
which was performed on 9 January 1625. Meanwhile a slighter piece, the *Masque of Owls*, was performed at Kenilworth on 19 August 1624.

The accession of Charles I to the throne in
1625 caused a six-year hiatus in Jonson's career
as a masque writer. Jonson does not seem to
have been as well liked by Charles as he had
been by James. An undignified quarrel with
Inigo Jones, who was admired by Charles, can
only have worsened his situation at Court. Jonson
would only receive two masque commissions
from the new King. The loss of steady royal patronage may have contributed to Jonson's decision to return to the stage, although we know
that he had already composed "parcels of a Play"
in 1623. Whatever the motivating circumstances,
The Staple of News was acted by the King's Men at
the Blackfriars in February 1626.

The plot of *The Staple of News* centers
around the efforts of Pennyboy junior, a prodigal heir, to gain the hand of the Lady Pecunia,
the "*Infanta* of the *Mines*," who during much of
the play is a personification of wealth. Pennyboy

junior hearkens back to Quicksilver in *Eastward
Ho*, in that both characters are types of the
prodigal-son figure so common in Tudor drama.

A prominent rival of Pennyboy's for the
hand of Pecunia is Cymbal, the master of the Staple of News. The Staple is portrayed as "a weekly
cheat to draw mony," much like the intrigues of
Volpone and Mosca and of Subtle and Face. However, the satire of the Staple was highly topical;
the publication of news sheets was a recent development, and Jonson's satire touches specific individuals, most notably Nathaniel Butter, who
published a news sheet founded in 1622, and is alluded to in the figure of Nathaniel the stationer,
as well as in the frequent references to the "butter-
ing" of the news.

The play was not a great success with the public. In addition to the intended personal references, others were read into the play; for
instance, Lady Pecunia was wrongly interpreted
as a representation of the Infanta of Spain. Accordingly Jonson included a special address to
the readers prefixed to act three, in which he com-
plained of the "sinister" interpretation put upon
the play.

From this point on, the life of Jonson took
a decidedly downward turn. In 1628 the poet suffered a paralytic stroke which rendered him "A
Bed-rid Wit" for the rest of his life. Some solace
came in September of the same year with his appointment as "chronologer" or historian to the
city of London, with a pension of 100 nobles per
year. There is no evidence that Jonson ever performed any services for the city in his capacity as
chronologer, and in 1631 the city fathers ordered his wages frozen "vntill he shall have presented vnto this Court some fruits of his labours
in that his place." Jonson's attitude toward the
city's action is expressed in a letter to the Earl of
Newcastle: "Yesterday the barbarous Court of Aldermen haue withdrawne their Chander-ly Pension, for Veriuice, & Mustard." Eventually the
King intervened on Jonson's behalf, and the pension was restored in 1634.

Less than four weeks after his appointment
as chronologer, on 26 October 1628, Jonson was
examined by the attorney-general, Sir Robert
Heath, about his knowledge of some verses praising John Felton, who had assassinated the Duke
of Buckingham on 23 August. Jonson testified
that he had seen the verses lying on a table in Sir
Robert Cotton's house. He denied knowledge of
their authorship but said that he had heard them
attributed to Zouch Townly, a scholar and divine

Costume design by Inigo Jones for a "glorious boasting lover"
in Love's Triumph through Callipolis

"Cis," which the author changed to "Prue." But no such busy deciphering is needed to explain the play's failure. Jonson's experiment with romantic comedy pushes the conventions of the genre beyond their limits. The last scene's revelations of hidden identity occur too rapidly and too frequently; indeed the awkwardness of the last scene has been interpreted as evidence that the play should be read ironically, as a parody of romantic comedy, though the evidence for this interpretation is not strong. And the collection of "humorous" characters who frequent the Inn of the Light Heart are drawn without much vitality; their dialogue is utterly void of the rapid fire that had enlivened the earlier comedies.

A more interesting feature of the play is the portrait of Lovel, the melancholy "Platonic" lover. In the earlier works love is not treated as a serious topic, and Jonson had scoffed at the conventional poses of unrequited love. In *The New Inn*, however, Lovel is treated with great sympathy for his dignified perseverance in what seems to be a hopeless passion, and Jonson makes him quite eloquent in defining and defending the existence of love in a "court of love" at which he makes his address to his mistress. Lovel also gives an eloquent defense of true valor, a subject that Jonson had addressed in some of the early plays and in his nondramatic verse as well, but which seems to have especially interested him at this time of his life; it is also a major theme in his next play, *The Magnetic Lady*.

The public's rejection of *The New Inn* infuriated Jonson, who vented his wrath in the "Ode to Himself" beginning, "Come leaue the lothed stage," appended to the 1631 octavo edition of the play. After mercilessly attacking the public for what he perceived as its degraded taste, Jonson promised to sing the glories of King Charles. For his part, Charles granted Jonson a gift of £100, and upon Jonson's request increased his yearly pension from 100 marks to £100; in addition the King granted Jonson an annual tierce of canary wine.

Another welcome sign of royal favor was Jonson's commission to write a masque with the architect Inigo Jones for the 1630-1631 Christmas season. On 9 January 1631 *Love's Triumph through Callipolis* was performed, and on 22 February 1631 its companion piece, *Chloridia*. Collaboration between the two antipathetic artists was not easy. Although the two men had worked together harmoniously twenty-five years earlier, they had become estranged by the middle of James's

who later wrote two poems in praise of Jonson. Jonson was then asked about a dagger that he had given Townly. He explained that Townly had simply expressed a liking for it and that he had therefore made him a present of it. For Jonson the matter ended there. Townly, however, had to flee to Holland.

Another disappointment befell Jonson on the heels of his stroke when *The New Inn* was acted by the King's Men at the Blackfriars, early in 1629. The performance was a disaster. Jonson blamed the actors as well as the audience for the play's failure, and the title page of the octavo edition published in 1631 reads, "As it was neuer acted, but most negligently play'd, by some, the Kings Seruants. And more squeamishly beheld, and censured by others, the Kings Subiects." Apparently some kind of personal allusion was detected in the original name of the chambermaid,

reign. Thus in the *Conversations with Drummond* Jonson had several times expressed his dislike of Jones. Jones was now at the height of his career and of his powers, while Jonson was clearly on the decline, both artistically and in terms of his position at court. The texts of *Love's Triumph* and *Chloridia* suggest that Jonson was forced to relinquish much of the control over the masques that he had previously exercised. Spectacle clearly predominates over poetry in *Love's Triumph,* with its bare lists of names, and in *Chloridia,* with its elaborate antimasque containing eight separate "entries." The quarrel between Jones and Jonson came to a head in 1630 with the publication of *Love's Triumph.* Jonson included Jones's name on the title page but gave priority to his own, which angered Jones. Jonson's response was to attack Jones in verse with "An Expostulation with Inigo Jones," and two lesser pieces, "An Epigram of Inigo Jones" and "To Inigo Marquis Would-be." Jones's influence at court, however, worked against Jonson, and the poet was not commissioned to write a masque for the next Christmas season. In fact, Jonson would never write another court masque.

In 1631 Jonson decided to publish a second volume of his works. Three plays—*Bartholomew Fair, The Devil Is an Ass,* and *The Staple of News*—were printed before the project was abandoned. The printer, John Beale, treated the texts carelessly, and Jonson expressed his annoyance with "the lewd printer" in a letter to the Duke of Newcastle: "My Printer, and I, shall afford subiect enough for a Tragi-Comoedy. for wth his delayes and vexation, I am almost become blind...." The stock that was printed eventually was incorporated into the posthumous 1640 collected works.

By October 1632 Jonson had completed *The Magnetic Lady,* a play which consciously hearkens back to the triumphs of the early and middle comedies in its emphasis on "humours." The Boy who appears in the play's induction introduces the play with a speech emphasizing Jonson's consciousness that his career is almost at an end: "The *Author,* beginning his studies of this kind, with *everyman in his Humour,* and after, *every man out of his Humour:* and since, continuing in all his *Playes,* especially those of the *Comick* thred, whereof the *New-Inne* was the last, some recent humours still, or manners of men, that went along with the times, finding himselfe now neare the close, or shutting up of his Circle, hath phant'sied to himselfe, in *Idæa,* this *Magnetick Mistris.*" The play concerns the machinations of a

number of suitors for the hand of the well-dowried Placentia, the niece of Lady Loadstone. Also present at the house is Polish, Lady Loadstone's parasite, and her daughter Pleasance, Lady Loadstone's waiting woman. Complications arise first when Placentia goes into labor and gives birth to a baby boy, and second when it is revealed to the audience, though not to all of the characters, that Pleasance is actually Placentia and vice versa, the two having been switched in their cradles when infants. Meanwhile a valiant captain, Ironside, displays the meaning of true valor by refusing to quarrel over an empty cause with Sir Diaphanous Silkworm, and Compass, the friend of Lady Loadstone and in many respects the hero of the play, struggles to thwart the villain of the piece, the usurer Sir Moth Interest, and his accomplice Bias, in their efforts to obtain Placentia's inheritance. The play ends with Compass married to "Pleasance," the real Placentia; Ironside betrothed to Lady Loadstone; and Needle, the father of the illegitimate child, betrothed to "Placentia," that is, the real Pleasance.

The character of Compass is akin to Crites in *Cynthia's Revels* and Horace in *Poetaster,* in that he is Jonson's spokesman and seems in some respects to be an idealized portrait of the author. Of himself he says,

> You know I am a Scholler,
> And part a Souldier; I have beene imployed,
> By some the greates States-men o' the
>   kingdome,
> These many yeares: and in my time
>   convers'd
> With sundry humors....

His rule as spokesman is most clearly seen in his elaborate descriptions of the other characters in the play, which read like analogues in verse to the prose "characters" of *Every Man out of His Humour.*

Some trouble occurred during the play's first performance, when Sir Henry Herbert, the Master of the Revels, objected to a number of profane oaths delivered on the stage. When Herbert accused the players, they at first blamed the script but eventually admitted that they had added the offending matter themselves.

Perhaps this episode, following upon what Jonson perceived as a negligent treatment of *The New Inn,* caused a rift between Jonson and the King's Men. Whatever the cause Jonson's next play, *A Tale of a Tub,* was performed by their rivals, Queen Henrietta's Men, at the Cockpit in

Costume design by Inigo Jones for Chloris in Chloridia *(Stephen Orgel and Roy Strong,*
Inigo Jones, *1973)*

May of 1633. On 14 January 1634 the play was presented at court, where it was "not likte," according to Sir Henry Herbert.

A Tale of a Tub presents unusual textual difficulties. Scholars are divided over the question of whether the play is Jonson's reworking of an original version composed in the 1590s or a composition of 1633 incorporating deliberate archaisms and possibly incorporating some passages composed earlier. The text of the play reveals striking stylistic differences, which seem to suggest different strata of composition. In addition the play is set in the reign of Queen Mary, and there are a number of references to figures from the early Tudor period. This may indicate a certain nostalgia for a much earlier period; much depends upon whether the allusions would be intelligible to an audience of 1633.

Whether the play is early or late, Jonson was conscious of its unusual position in the context of his work. The play is mainly a lighthearted rural comedy based on the crisscrossing intrigues of a number of homely suitors for the hand of a country maid, Audrey. The self-deprecating tone of the prologue and of the Latin motto printed on the title page are unusual for Jonson and suggest that he did not regard his experiment in the play with a great deal of confidence.

Into this rural comedy Jonson introduced some personal satire of Inigo Jones. Sir Henry Herbert's records show that originally the play had included "Vitruvius Hoop," a character clearly intended to represent Jones; his part and an earlier version of "the motion of the tubb," which must have been a more scathing attack on Jones's work than that which survives in the play, were struck out at the instigation of the Lord Chamberlain, to whom Jones had appealed for redress. However, Jonson continued his attack on Inigo Jones in the character of In-and-in Medlay, a cooper who is called upon to prepare a masque for a rustic wedding. The other characters sometimes call him a joiner, with pointed emphasis; Jones had begun his career as a joiner. Medlay's main device in the masque, the motion of the tub, is a parody of the *machina versatilis* that Jones had designed for the *Masque of Queens*.

In May 1633, the month in which *A Tale of a Tub* was originally performed, *The King's Entertainment at Welbeck* was performed at the house of Jonson's friend and patron the Duke of Newcastle. The King was pleased with the performance, and Jonson was commissioned to write another en-

tertainment, *Love's Welcome at Bolsover*, to celebrate the King's visit to another Newcastle estate in July 1634. Once again Jonson introduced satire of Inigo Jones into a work, this time in the figure of the surveyor Coronell Vitruvius. Although Jonson's satire of Jones in *A Tale of a Tub* had not pleased the court the previous January, no offense seems to have been taken by the King and Queen on this occasion. Shortly afterward Charles intervened on Jonson's behalf with the City of London authorities to see that Jonson was paid his pension as city chronologer.

Thereafter little is heard of Jonson before his death. No new plays or masques appeared, though Jonson left incomplete a pastoral play, *The Sad Shepherd*, and a mere fragment of another play, *Mortimer his Fall*. We do know that to the end of his life Jonson remained a sociable man. Although the paralytic stroke had put an end to Jonson's reign at the Apollo room of the Devil Tavern, which had replaced the Mermaid as the chief gathering place for the poet's circle of friends and admirers, who now styled themselves "the Tribe of Ben" in his honor, his chamber in Westminster continued to draw admiring visitors. Among the friends of Jonson's later years were the Duke and Dutchess of Newcastle; Sir Kenelm Digby, who served as Jonson's literary executor, and his wife, Lady Venetia Digby; Lord Falkland; and the writers Thomas Carew, James Howell, and Richard Brome.

Ben Jonson died in Westminster on 6 August 1637. Although he had earned a considerable pension, the poet died intestate; the total value of his property was estimated at eight pounds, eight shillings, and ten pence. Jonson was buried on 9 August in Westminster Abbey, accompanied to his grave by a great crowd of mourners. In 1638 a volume of undistinguished commemorative verse, *Jonsonus Virbius*, was published. In addition, a subscription was organized to raise money for a monument, but the outbreak of the Civil War caused the project to be abandoned. Jonson's grave was marked only by a square flagstone on which was later carved "O rare Ben Jonson." In 1640 the second folio edition of his works, containing a number of works published for the first time, was published posthumously.

Today, as in the seventeenth century, Ben Jonson's status as a major dramatist and poet seems well established and unlikely to be shaken, but appreciation of his work has varied with the vicissitudes of critical fashion. Since the eighteenth

Engraved portrait of Jonson by Robert Vaughan with verses by Abraham Holland, circa 1625 (Hope Collection, Oxford). This engraving was later used as the frontispiece for the 1640 quarto edition of Ben: Jonson's Execration against Vulcan *and the first volume of the 1640 folio edition of Jonson's works.*

century it has been Jonson's misfortune inevitably to be compared to his great contemporary, Shakespeare, and, because Jonson's artistic commitments are so frequently at odds with Shakespeare's, the comparison has often been an odious one for Jonson, whose (in-)famous strictures against the romantic drama of his contemporaries, which include a few shots at specific plays of Shakespeare, brought the wrath of bardolatry upon his head in the nineteenth century. The twentieth century has seen a renewal of critical ap-

preciation of Jonson. The publication of the monumental Oxford *Ben Jonson* has been a great stimulus to Jonson scholarship, and there have also been excellent considerations of Jonson's use of language, his social and ethical ideals, and his use of classical and native English literary traditions. The nondramatic poetry and the masques as well as the plays have received critical attention. No longer is Jonson seen as the author of a handful of good comedies and a few pretty lyrics. We are now able to appreciate the diversity of

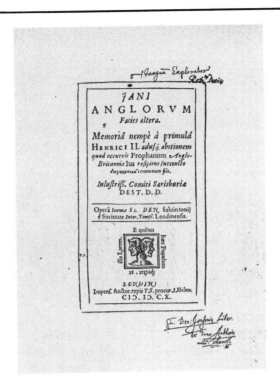

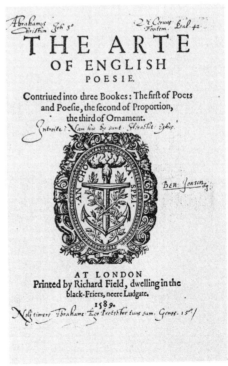

Title pages for three books from Jonson's library: (top) John Selden's Jani Anglorum Facies altera *(1610), later owned by Robert Davies, in which Jonson wrote his motto at top right ("as an explorer," from a line in Seneca's* Epistles *that may be translated as "I am accustomed as it were to go into the foreign camp not as a deserter to the enemy but as an explorer") and at bottom right Latin phrases that read "I am Ben Jonson's book. A gift from the author dear to me" (Anderson Galleries, sale number 1394, 29-30 January 1919); (bottom left) Giovanni Baptista Pigna's* Carminvm *(1553), with similar annotations by Jonson and note by a later owner (by permission of the British Library); and George Puttenham's* The Arte of English Poesie *(1589), in which Jonson wrote quotations from John 8, Psalm 42, and Genesis 15 in the Latin Bible and from Hereclites of Ephesus*
(by permission of the British Library)

Jonson's achievement and his continued willingness to experiment with new literary forms.

Bibliographies:

Samuel A. Tannenbaum, *Ben Jonson: A Concise Bibliography* (New York: Privately printed, 1938) and Samuel A. Tannenbaum and Dorothy R. Tannenbaum, *Supplement to a Concise Bibliography of Ben Jonson* (New York: Privately printed, 1947); both republished as volume 4 of *Elizabethan Bibliographies* (Port Washington, N.Y.: Kennikat Press, 1967);

D. Heyward Brock and James M. Welsh, *Ben Jonson: A Quadricentennial Bibliography, 1947-1972* (Metuchen, N.J.: Scarecrow, 1974);

James Hogg, *Recent Research on Ben Jonson* (Salzburg, Austria: Institut für Englische Sprache und Literatur, 1978);

Walter D. Lehrman, Dolores J. Sarafinski, and Elizabeth Savage, *The Plays of Ben Jonson: A Reference Guide* (Boston: G. K. Hall, 1980);

David C. Judkins, *The Nondramatic Works of Ben Jonson: A Reference Guide* (Boston: G. K. Hall, 1982).

Biographies:

Marchette Chute, *Ben Jonson of Westminster* (New York: Dutton, 1953);

Rosalind Miles, *Ben Jonson: His Life and Work* (London & New York: Routledge & Kegan Paul, 1986).

References:

Judd Arnold, *A Grace Peculiar: Ben Jonson's Cavalier Heroes*, Penn State University Studies, no. 35 (University Park: Pennsylvania State University, 1972);

J. B. Bamborough, *Ben Jonson* (London: Hutchinson, 1970);

Bamborough, "The Early Life of Ben Jonson," *Times Literary Supplement*, 8 April 1960, p. 225;

Jonas A. Barish, "*Bartholomew Fair* and Its Puppets," *Modern Language Quarterly*, 20 (March 1959): 3-17;

Barish, *Ben Jonson and the Language of Prose Comedy* (Cambridge: Harvard University Press, 1960);

Barish, "The Double Plot in *Volpone*," *Modern Philology*, 51 (November 1953): 83-92;

Barish, "*Volpone*": *A Casebook* (London: Macmillan, 1972);

Barish, ed., *Ben Jonson: A Collection of Critical Essays* (Englewood Cliffs, N.J.: Prentice-Hall, 1963);

Anne Barton, *Ben Jonson, Dramatist* (Cambridge & New York: Cambridge University Press, 1984);

C. R. Baskervill, *English Elements in Jonson's Early Comedy*, Bulletin of the University of Texas, no. 178, Humanistic Series, no. 12; Studies in English, no. 1 (Austin: University of Texas, 1911);

Helena Watts Baum, *The Satiric and the Didactic in Ben Jonson's Comedy* (Chapel Hill: University of North Carolina Press, 1947);

L. A. Beaurline, *Jonson and Elizabethan Comedy: Essays in Dramatic Rhetoric* (San Marino, Cal.: Huntington Library, 1978);

Beaurline, "Volpone and the Power of Gorgeous Speech," *Studies in the Literary Imagination*, 6 (April 1973): 61-76;

Gerald Eades Bentley, *Shakespeare and Jonson. Their Reputations in the Seventeenth Century Compared*, 2 volumes (Chicago: University of Chicago Press, 1945);

David Bergeron, "Harrison, Jonson and Dekker: The Magnificent Entertainment for King James (1604)," *Journal of the Warburg and Courtauld Institutes*, 31 (1968): 445-448;

Normand Berlin, "Ben Jonson," in his *The Base String: The Underworld in Elizabethan Drama* (Rutherford, N.J.: Fairleigh Dickinson University Press, 1968), pp. 130-171;

Ralph W. Berringer, "Jonson's *Cynthia's Revels* and the War of the Theatres," *Philological Quarterly*, 22 (January 1943): 1-22;

David Bevington, "Shakespeare vs. Jonson on Satire," in *Shakespeare 1971: Proceedings of the World Shakespeare Congress, Vancouver, August 1971*, edited by Clifford Leech and J. M. R. Margeson (Toronto: University of Toronto Press, 1972), pp. 107-122;

William A. Blissett, Julian Patrick, R. W. Van Fossen, eds., *A Celebration of Ben Jonson* (Toronto: University of Toronto Press, 1973);

Daniel C. Boughner, *The Devil's Disciple: Ben Jonson's Debt to Machiavelli* (New York: Philosophical Library, 1968);

Fredson T. Bowers, "Ben Jonson the Actor," *Studies in Philology*, 34 (July 1937): 392-406;

J. F. Bradley and J. Q. Adams, *The Jonson Allusion-Book, 1597-1700* (New Haven: Yale University Press, 1922);

D. Heyward Brock, *A Ben Jonson Companion* (Bloomington: Indiana University Press, 1983);

Joseph A. Bryant, Jr., "*Catiline* and the Nature of Jonson's Tragic Fable," *PMLA,* 69 (March 1954): 265-277;

Bryant, *The Compassionate Satirist: Ben Jonson and His Imperfect World* (Athens: University of Georgia Press, 1972);

Bryant, "Jonson's Revision of *Every Man in His Humour,*" *Studies in Philology,* 59 (October 1962): 641-650;

O. J. Campbell, *Comicall Satyre and Shakespeare's Troilus and Cressida* (San Marino, Cal.: Huntington Library, 1938);

M. Castelain, *Ben Jonson: l'Homme et l'Oeuvre* (Paris: Librairie Hachette, 1907);

Fran D. Chalfant, *Ben Jonson's London: A Jacobean Placename Dictionary* (Athens: University of Georgia Press, 1978);

Larry S. Champion, *Ben Jonson's "Dotages": A Reconsideration of the Late Plays* (Lexington: University of Kentucky Press, 1967);

Mary Chan, *Music in the Theatre of Ben Jonson* (Oxford: Clarendon Press, 1980);

John Creaser, "*Volpone:* The Mortifying of the Fox," *Essays in Criticism,* 25 (July 1975): 329-356; 329-356;

Joe Lee Davis, *The Sons of Ben: Jonsonian Comedy in Caroline England* (Detroit: Wayne State University Press, 1967);

Barbara Nielson De Luna, *Jonson's Romish Plot: A Study of "Catiline" and Its Historical Context* (Oxford: Clarendon Press, 1967);

Alan C. Dessen, *Jonson's Moral Comedy* (Evanston: Northwestern University Press, 1971);

Aliki L. Dick, *Paedeia Through Laughter: Jonson's Aristophanic Appeal to Human Intelligence* (The Hague: Mouton, 1974);

Ian Donaldson, "Jonson and the Moralists," in *Two Renaissance Mythmakers,* edited by Alvin Kernan (Baltimore: Johns Hopkins University Press, 1977), pp. 146-164;

Donaldson, "Language, Noise and Nonsense: *The Alchemist,*" in *Seventeenth-Century Imagery: Essays on Uses of Figurative Language from Donne to Farquhar,* edited by Earl Miner (Berkeley: University of California Press, 1971), pp. 69-82;

Donaldson, *The World Upside Down: Comedy from Jonson to Fielding* (London: Oxford University Press, 1970);

Kevin J. Donovan, "The Final Quires of the Jonson 1616 *Workes*: Headline Evidence," *Studies in Bibliography,* 40 (1987): 106-120;

Douglas J. M. Duncan, *Ben Jonson and the Lucianic Tradition* (Cambridge: Cambridge University Press, 1979);

Richard Dutton, *Ben Jonson: To the First Folio* (Cambridge & New York: Cambridge University Press, 1983);

Mark Eccles, "Jonson and the Spies," *Review of English Studies,* 13 (October 1937): 385-397;

Eccles, "Jonson's Marriage," *Review of English Studies,* 12 (July 1936): 257-272;

T. S. Eliot, "Ben Jonson," in his *The Sacred Wood: Essay on Poetry and Criticism* (London: Methuen, 1920), pp. 95-111;

John J. Enck, *Jonson and the Comic Truth* (Madison: University of Wisconsin Press, 1957);

Willa McClung Evans, *Ben Jonson and Elizabethan Music* (Lancaster, Pa.: Lancaster Press, 1929);

R. A. Foakes and R. T. Rickert, eds., *Henslowe's Diary. Edited with Supplementary Material, Introduction and Notes* (Cambridge: Cambridge University Press, 1961);

Franz Fricker, *Ben Jonson's Plays in Performance and the Jacobean Theatre* (Bern: A. Francke, 1972);

W. Todd Furniss, "Ben Jonson's Masques," in *Three Studies in the Renaissance: Sidney, Jonson, Milton,* edited by B. C. Nangle (New Haven: Yale University Press, 1958), pp. 89-179;

Judith K. Gardiner, *Craftsmanship in Context: The Development of Ben Jonson's Poetry* (The Hague: Mouton, 1975);

Johann Gerritsen, "Stansby and Jonson Produce a Folio: A Preliminary Account," *English Studies,* 40 (1959): 52-55;

Brian Gibbons, *Jacobean City Comedy: A Study of Satiric Plays by Jonson, Marston, and Middleton* (Cambridge: Harvard University Press, 1968);

Allan H. Gilbert, *The Symbolic Persons in the Masques of Ben Jonson* (Durham: Duke University Press, 1948);

D. J. Gordon, "Poet and Architect: The Intellectual Setting of the Quarrel Between Ben Jonson and Inigo Jones" and "*Hymenaei:* Ben Jonson's Masque of Union," in *The Renaissance Imagination,* edited by Stephen Orgel (Berkeley: University of California Press, 1975), pp. 77-101, 157-184;

Stephen J. Greenblatt, "The False Ending in *Volpone,*" *Journal of English and Germanic Philology,* 75 (January-April 1976): 90-104;

Thomas Greene, "Ben Jonson and the Centered Self," *Studies in English Literature,* 10 (Spring 1970): 325-348;

Sir W. W. Greg, "The Riddle of Jonson's Chronology," *Library,* 6 (March 1926): 340-347;

Greg, ed., *Jonson's "Masque of Gipsies" in the Burley, Belvoir and Windsor Versions: An Attempt at Reconstruction* (London: Oxford University Press, 1952);

Nicholas Grene, *Shakespeare, Jonson, Molière: The Comic Contract* (London: Macmillan, 1980);

Colburn Gum, *The Aristophanic Comedies of Ben Jonson: A Comparative Study of Jonson and Aristophanes* (The Hague: Mouton, 1969);

William Hazlitt, "On Shakespeare and Ben Jonson," in his *Lectures on the English Comic Writers* (London: Taylor & Hessey, 1819);

Ray L. Heffner, Jr., "Unifying Symbols in the Comedy of Ben Jonson," in *English Stage Comedy*, edited by W. K. Wimsatt, Jr., English Institute Essays, 1954 (New York: Columbia University Press, 1955), pp. 74-97;

G. R. Hibbard, ed., *The Elizabethan Theatre IV* (London & Basingstoke: Macmillan, 1974);

Peter Hyland, *Disguise and Role-Playing in Ben Jonson's Drama* (Salzburg, Austria: Institut für Englische Sprache und Literatur, 1977);

Gabriele B. Jackson, *Vision and Judgment in Ben Jonson's Drama* (New Haven: Yale University Press, 1968);

Bertil Johansson, *Religion and Superstition in the Plays of Ben Jonson and Thomas Middleton* (Cambridge: Harvard University Press, 1950);

George Burke Johnston, *Ben Jonson: Poet.*, Columbia University Studies in English and Comparative Literature, no. 162 (New York: Columbia University Press, 1945);

Robert C. Jones, "The Satirist's Retirement in Jonson's 'Apologetical Dialogue,'" *ELH*, 34 (December 1967): 447-467;

Marie Thérèse Jones-Davies, *Inigo Jones, Ben Jonson et le Masque* (Paris: Didier, 1967);

R. J. Kaufman, ed., *Elizabethan Drama: Modern Essays in Criticism* (New York: Oxford University Press, 1961);

W. David Kay, "The Shaping of Ben Jonson's Career: A Re-examination of Facts and Problems," *Modern Philology*, 67 (February 1970): 224-237;

William R. Keast, ed., *Seventeenth-Century English Poetry: Modern Essays in Criticism*, revised edition (New York: Oxford University Press, 1971);

Alvin B. Kernan, *The Cankered Muse: Satire of the English Renaissance* (New Haven: Yale University Press, 1959);

Kernan, ed., *Two Renaissance Mythmakers: Christopher Marlowe and Ben Jonson*, Selected Papers from the English Institute, 1975-1976, new series 1 (Baltimore & London: Johns Hopkins University Press, 1977);

Arthur C. Kirsch, "Guarini and Jonson," in his *Jacobean Dramatic Perspectives* (Charlottesville: University Press of Virginia, 1972), pp. 7-24;

George Lyman Kittredge, "King James I and *The Devil Is an Ass*," *Modern Philology*, 9 (October 1911): 195-209;

David Klein, *The Elizabethan Dramatists as Critics* (New York: Philosophical Library, 1963);

L. C. Knights, *Drama and Society in the Age of Jonson* (London: Chatto & Windus, 1937);

Robert E. Knoll, *Ben Jonson's Plays: An Introduction* (Lincoln: University of Nebraska Press, 1964);

Louis Kronenberger, *The Thread of Laughter: Chapters on English Stage Comedy from Jonson to Maugham* (New York: Knopf, 1952);

Alexander Leggatt, *Ben Jonson: His Vision and His Art* (London: Methuen, 1981);

J. W. Lever, "Roman Tragedy: *Sejanus, Caesar and Pompey*," in his *The Tragedy of State* (London: Methuen, 1971), pp. 59-77;

Harry Levin, "Jonson's Metempsychosis," *Philological Quarterly*, 22 (July 1943): 231-239;

Eric Linklater, *Ben Jonson and King James: Biography and Portrait* (London: Cape, 1931);

Hugh Maclean, "Ben Jonson's Poems: Notes on the Ordered Society," in *Essays in English Literature from the Renaissance to the Victorian Age, Presented to A. S. P. Woodhouse*, edited by Millar MacLure and F. W. Watt (Toronto: University of Toronto Press, 1964), pp. 43-68;

Leah Marcus, "Present Occasions and the Shaping of Ben Jonson's Masques," *ELH*, 45 (June 1978): 201-225;

Arthur Marotti, "All About Jonson's Poetry," *ELH*, 39 (June 1972): 208-237;

Katherine Eisaman Maus, *Ben Jonson and the Roman Frame of Mind* (Princeton: Princeton University Press, 1984);

Scott McMillin, "Jonson's Early Entertainments: New Information from Hatfield House," *Renaissance Drama*, new series 1 (1968): 153-166;

John C. Meagher, *Method and Meaning in Jonson's Masques* (Notre Dame: University of Notre Dame Press, 1966);

Earl Miner, *The Cavalier Mode from Jonson to Cotton* (Princeton: Princeton University Press, 1971);

J. G. Nichols, *The Poetry of Ben Jonson* (New York: Barnes & Noble, 1969);

Allardyce Nicoll, *English Drama: A Modern Viewpoint* (New York: Barnes & Noble, 1968), pp. 56-74;

Robert Gale Noyes, *Ben Jonson on the English Stage, 1660-1776* (Cambridge: Harvard University Press, 1935);

Stephen Orgel, *The Illusion of Power: Political Theater in the English Renaissance* (Berkeley: University of California Press, 1975);

Orgel, *The Jonsonian Masque* (Cambridge: Harvard University Press, 1965);

Robert Ornstein, *The Moral Vision of Jacobean Tragedy* (Madison: University of Wisconsin Press, 1960);

John Palmer, *Ben Jonson* (New York: Viking, 1934);

George Parfitt, *Ben Jonson: Public Poet and Private Man* (New York: Barnes & Noble, 1977);

R. B. Parker, Introduction to *Volpone, or The Fox,* edited by Parker, The Revels Plays (Dover, N.H.: Manchester University Press, 1983);

Parker, "The Problem of Tone in Jonson's 'Comicall Satyrs,' " *Humanities Association Review,* 28 (Winter 1977): 43-64;

Edward B. Partridge, *The Broken Compass: A Study of the Major Comedies of Ben Jonson* (London: Chatto & Windus, 1958; New York: Columbia University Press, 1958);

Partridge, "The Symbolism of Clothes in Jonson's Last Plays," *Journal of English and Germanic Philology,* 56 (July 1957): 396-409;

Richard S. Peterson, *Imitation and Praise in the Poems of Ben Jonson* (New Haven & London: Yale University Press, 1981);

Norbert H. Platz, *Ethik und Rhetorik in Ben Jonsons Dramen* (Heidelberg: Winter, 1976);

Elke Platz-Waury, *Jonsons Komische Charaktere: Untersuchungen zum Verhältnis von Dichtungstheorie und Bühnenpraxis* (Nürnberg: Hans Carl, 1976);

Mario Praz, "Ben Jonson's Italy," in his *The Flaming Heart: Essays on Crashaw, Machiavelli, and Other Studies in the Relations Between Italian and English Literature from Chaucer to T. S. Eliot* (Garden City: Doubleday, 1958), pp. 168-185;

Dale B. Randall, *Jonson's Gypsies Unmasked: Background and Theme of "The Gypsies Metamorphos'd"* (Durham: Duke University Press, 1975);

James D. Redwine, Jr., "Beyond Psychology: The Moral Basis of Jonson's Theory of Humour Characterization," *ELH,* 28 (December 1961): 316-334;

James A. Riddell, "Variant Title-Pages of the 1616 Jonson Folio," *Library* series 6, 8 (June 1986): 152-156;

Andrew J. Sabol, ed., *A Score for "Lovers Made Men"* (Providence, R.I.: Brown University Press, 1963);

A. H. Sackton, *Rhetoric as a Dramatic Language in Ben Jonson* (New York: Columbia University Press, 1948);

Leo Salingar, "Comic Form in Ben Jonson: Volpone and the Philosopher's Stone," in *English Drama: Forms and Development: Essays in Honour of Muriel Clara Bradbrook,* edited by Marie Axton and Raymond Williams (Cambridge: Cambridge University Press, 1977), pp. 48-69;

James E. Savage, *Ben Jonson's Basic Comic Characters, and Other Essays* (Hattiesburg: University & College Press of Mississippi, 1973);

Evelyn Mary Simpson, "Jonson and Dickens: A Study in the Comic Genius of London," *Essays and Studies by Members of the English Association,* 22 (1944): 82-92;

C. J. Sisson, "Ben Jonson of Gresham College," *Times Literary Supplement,* 21 September 1951, p. 604;

R. A. Small, *The Stage-Quarrel between Jonson and the So-Called Poetasters* (Breslau: M. & H. Marcus, 1899);

Frederick W. Sternfeld, "Song in Jonson's Comedy: A Gloss on *Volpone,*" in *Studies in the English Renaissance Drama,* edited by Josephine W. Bennett, Oscar Cargill, and Vernon Hall, Jr. (New York: New York University Press, 1959), pp. 310-321;

Theodore A. Stroud, "Ben Jonson and Father Thomas Wright," *Journal of English Literary History,* 14 (December 1947): 274-282;

Claude J. Summers and Ted-Larry Pebworth, *Ben Jonson* (Boston: Twayne, 1979);

Summers and Pebworth, eds., *Classic and Cavalier: Essays on Jonson and the Sons of Ben* (Pittsburgh: University of Pittsburgh Press, 1982);

John Gordon Sweeney III, *Jonson and the Psychology of Public theater: "To Coin the Spirit, Spend the Soul"* (Princeton: Princeton University Press, 1985);

A. C. Swinburne, *A Study of Ben Jonson* (London: Chatto & Windus, 1889);

C. G. Thayer, *Ben Jonson: Studies in the Plays* (Norman: University of Oklahoma Press, 1963);

Mary Olive Thomas, ed., "Ben Jonson: Quadricentennial Essays," special issue of *Studies in the Literary Imagination,* 6 (April 1973);

Freda L. Townsend, *Apologie for Bartholomew Fayre: The Art of Jonson's Comedies* (New York: Modern Language Association of America, 1947);

Wesley Trimpi, *Ben Jonson's Poems: A Study of the Plain Style* (Palo Alto: Stanford University Press, 1962);

Eugene M. Waith, "The Staging of *Bartholomew Fair*," *Studies in English Literature*, 2 (Spring 1962): 181-195;

Geoffrey Walton, "The Tone of Ben Jonson's Poetry," in *Seventeenth-Century Poetry: Modern Essays in Criticism*, edited by William R. Keast (New York: Oxford University Press, 1962), pp. 193-214;

C. F. Wheeler, *Classical Mythology in the Plays, Masques, and Poems of Ben Jonson* (Princeton: Princeton University Press, 1938);

Glynne Wickham, "The Privy Council Order of 1597 for the Destruction of all London's Theatres," in *The Elizabethan Theatre I*, edited by David Galloway (Toronto: Macmillan of Canada, 1969), pp. 21-44.

Papers:
Several autograph manuscripts of Jonson have survived, including letters, inscriptions on books, a few poems, and the entire text of *The Masque of Queens*. These are located at the British Library; the Public Record Office, Kew; Dulwich College and Christ Church, Oxford; Hatfield (among the Cecil papers); the Folger Shakespeare Library; Harvard; Princeton; and in private hands. They are listed in the Herford and Simpson edition of Jonson.

Thomas Kyd

(November 1558-August 1594)

Gordon Braden
University of Virginia

PLAY PRODUCTIONS: *Hamlet* (the lost play now known as the *Ur-Hamlet*), attributed to Kyd, London, unknown theater, no later than 1589;

The Spanish Tragedy, London, unknown theater, 1585-1590(?); London, Rose theater, 1592;

Soliman and Perseda, attributed to Kyd, London, unknown theater, no later than 1592.

BOOKS: *The Housholders Philosophie*, a translation of Tasso's *Il Padre di Famiglia*, attributed to Kyd (London: Printed by J. Charlewood for T. Hacket, 1588);

The Spanish Tragedie (London: Printed by E. Allde for E. White, 1592);

The Tragedye of Solyman and Perseda, attributed to Kyd (London: Printed by E. Allde for E. White, 1592?);

Cornelia, Kyd's translation of Robert Garnier's *Cornélie* (London: Printed by J. Roberts for N. Ling & J. Busbie, 1594).

Editions: *The Works of Thomas Kyd*, edited by Frederick S. Boas, enlarged edition (Oxford: Clarendon Press, 1955);

The Spanish Tragedy, edited by Philip Edwards (London: Methuen, 1959; Cambridge: Harvard University Press, 1959).

OTHER: *Verses of Prayse and Ioye, Written vpon Her Maiesties Preseruation*, includes a poem attributed to Kyd (London: Printed by J. Wolfe, 1586);

Robert Allott, ed., *Englands Parnassus: or The Choysest Flowers of Our Moderne Poets*, includes selections attributed to Kyd (London: Printed for N. Ling, C. Burby & T. Hayes, 1600).

Thomas Kyd's place in the history of English Renaissance drama is secured by one surviving play, *The Spanish Tragedy*. Impressive in itself, it is also momentous in its influence as one of the first mature plays on the Elizabethan stage and as the great original for all subsequent revenge tragedies. Oblique evidence also points to Kyd as the author of the so-called *Ur-Hamlet*, the lost play of which Shakespeare's *Hamlet* is evidently an adaptation and critique. Yet for this indisputable achievement we have very little in the way of context. Except for one spectacular event, the biographical record is sketchy and uncertain; and what there is of Kyd's oeuvre beyond *The Spanish Tragedy* comes nowhere near that play in interest. Of the major English dramatists of the time, only Cyril Tourneur is more shadowy.

It is highly probable, if not altogether certain, that the playwright is the Thomas Kyd baptized in St. Mary Woolnoth on 6 November 1558; he would then be the son of Francis Kyd, a London scrivener of some standing, and his wife Anna. Both parents survived this child, who was buried at St. Mary Colchurch on 15 August 1594; for unspecified reasons, they refused to administer his estate. We have records of a brother, William, of uncertain age, and a younger sister, Ann. Thomas was enrolled in 1565 at Merchant Taylors' School (where Edmund Spenser had come four years earlier); there is no evidence of university affiliation. There is also little trace of his name in the theatrical annals of the age. Inference from a passage in Thomas Dekker's *A Knight's Conjuring* (1607) associates him with the actor John Bentley and hence the Queen's Company during the period 1583-1585. *The Spanish Tragedy* was first published in 1592, anonymously. We are sure of its authorship only because of three lines quoted and attributed by Thomas Heywood in his *Apology for Actors* (1612); for all its popularity, the play was never printed under Kyd's name until the eighteenth century. A fairly mechanical reply to Chidiock Tichborne's famous elegy is assigned to "T. K." in *Verses of Praise and Joy Written upon Her Majesty's Preservation* (1586); the only other contemporary literary figure with those initials is the unlikely Timothy Kendall, and the poem may well be Kyd's. The same initials appear on the title page of *The Householder's Philosophy*, a translation of Tasso's *Il Padre*

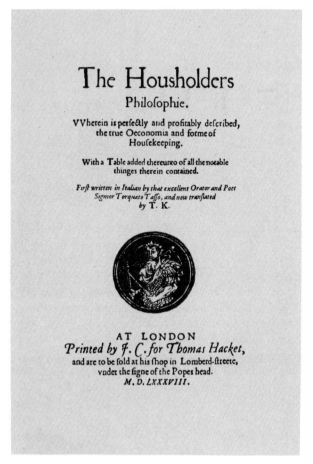

The Housholders
Philofophie.

VVherein is perfeßly and profitably defcribed,
the true Oeconomia and forme of
Houfekeeping.

With a Table added thereunto of all the notable
thinges therein contained.

Firft written in Italian by that excellent Orator and Poet
Signior Torquato Taffo, and now tranflated
by T. K.

AT LONDON
Printed by F. C. for Thomas Hacket,
and are to be fold at his fhop in Lomberd-ftreete,
vnder the figne of the Popes head.
M. D. LXXXVIII.

Title page for the unique copy of the 1588 quarto edition of a translation of Tasso's Il Padre di Famiglia *that has been attributed to Kyd (Mal 233[3]; Bodleian Library, Oxford)*

di Famiglia published in 1588; internal evidence makes its ascription to Kyd fairly convincing. When in 1594, though, a translation of Robert Garnier's *Cornélie* appears with "Tho. Kyd" printed under the last line, it is the first and only publication so signed during the Renaissance.

This almost invisible life suddenly flares in May 1593, with Kyd's arrest on order of the Privy Council. Their action was apparently prompted by the publication of some anonymous xenophobic "libels," but attention quickly shifted to "vile hereticall Conceiptes denyinge the deity of Jhesus" found among Kyd's papers. There survive two letters written by Kyd in his own defense to Sir John Puckering, Keeper of the Great Seal (reprinted in Arthur Freeman's *Thomas Kyd: Facts and Problems*, 1967, pp. 181-183). Kyd denies the charge of atheism—"a deadlie thing wch I was vndeserved chargd wthall"—and attributes the offending manuscript to Christopher Marlowe: "shufled wth some of myne (vnknown to me) by some occasion of o^r wrytinge in one chamber

twoe yeares synce." The letters are important both for their assertion of a special intimacy between Kyd and Marlowe and for their claims about Marlowe's character. The two were associated, according to Kyd, in service to an unnamed patron, "although his L^p never knewe his service, but in writing for his plaie^{r}s, ffor never cold my L. endure his name, or sight, when he had heard of his conditions, nor wold indeed the forme of devyne praiers vsed duelie in his L^{ps} house, haue quadred [squared] wth such reprobates." Marlowe was "intemp[er]ate & of a cruel hart"; the second letter further details his "monstruous opinions": "He wold report S^t. John to be o^r savio^r Christes Alexis . . . that is that Christ did loue him wth an extraordinary loue." These accusations are substantially corroborated by an extant memorandum by Richard Baines, a spy in the service of Sir Francis Walsingham, Elizabeth's secretary of state. Marlowe was summoned before the Privy Council soon after Kyd's arrest, then released on the condition that he report back daily; on 30 May he was killed in an apparent dispute over a tavern bill in Deptford.

The situation is rich with suggestions of treachery: that Marlowe set Kyd up, that Kyd returned the favor, that Marlowe's death was covertly arranged as a result. Countervailing evidence, however, suggests that Marlowe was himself an *agent provocateur* employed by the Privy Council in its anti-Catholic activities; and Kyd's letters were written some indeterminate time after Marlowe's death, their aim not revenge but Kyd's own rehabilitation in what, despite his release, was evidently a desperate situation. Kyd was especially concerned for Puckering's intercession with his patron, "whom I haue servd almost theis vj yeres nowe, in credit vntill nowe, & nowe am vtterlie vndon wthout herein be somewhat donn for my recoverie." Reference is also made to "my paines and–vndeserved tortures," presumably suffered during interrogation; Kyd's death a year later at the age of thirty-five may have been that of a man ruined physically as well as professionally.

The publication of the Garnier translation in 1594 looks like a last attempt on Kyd's part to restore his reputation and fortune. It is dedicated, with dark mention of "those so bitter times and priuie broken passions that I endured in the writing it," to the Countess of Suffolk. Her father-in-law, the ninth earl, who had died in December 1593, maintained a small theatrical company and may possibly have been Kyd's unidentified pa-

will say throughly w'h me & the same perpetuall tenor
& consent.

188

what the Scriptures do witnes of God it is clere &
manifest inough for first Paul to the Romains declareth
that he is euerlasting. And to Timothi mortall & inuisible
to the Thessalonians liuing & true. James teacheth also
that he is incommutable which things in the old law &
prophets likwise ar thought in incu inculcate so often
that they cannot escape the Reader. And yf we think
thes epithetons not vainly put but truly & proffitably
adiect. And that they agree to God. And that they we
must not beleue him to be God to whom the same agree not
we therfor call God which onlie is worthie this name &
appellation Euerlasting, Inuisible, Incommutable Incom=
prehensible Immortall &c.

what the Scriptures do witnes of God it is clere &
manifest inough &c so forth as is aboue rehearced.

And yf Jhesus Christ euen he which was borne of Marie
was God so shull he be a visible God comprehensible &
mortall which is not compted God w'h me quoth great
Athanasius of Alexandria &c.

For yf we be not able to comprehend nor the Angels
nor owr own Sowles which ar things creat so wrongfully
then & absurdly we mak the Creator of them comprehen
sible especiallie contrary to so manifest testimonies of
the Scriptures &c

A page from the manuscript containing "vile heretical Conceiptes denyinge the deity of Jhesus" that was found among Kyd's papers in May 1593 (Harleian MSS 6848, f. 188; by permission of the British Library)

Letter to Sir John Puckering in which Kyd asserted that the heretical manuscript was Christopher Marlowe's "and shufled wth some of myne (vnknown to me) by some occasion of or wrytinge in one chamber twoe yeares synce" (Harleian MSS 6849, f. 218; by permission of the British Library)

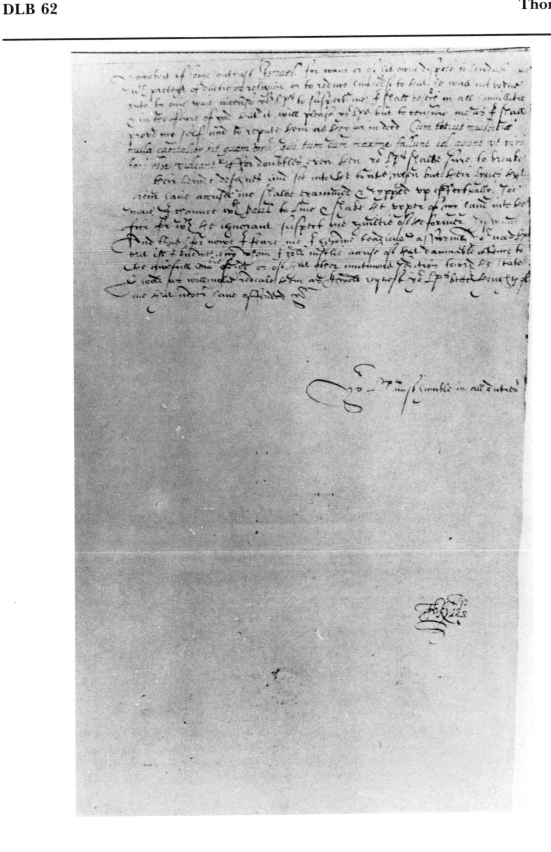

tron. Whatever Kyd's relations with this particular family, the translation is clearly a bid for aristocratic literary dignity, inspired by the appearance in 1592 of the Countess of Pembroke's translation of Garnier's *Marc Antoine*. Garnier's plays are among the best examples of the neoclassical dramaturgy that was a recurring ambition for Continental humanism. Philip Sidney spoke for many intellectuals when in his *Apology for Poetry* he stated his forceful preference for this austere tradition, as exemplified by Thomas Sackville and Thomas Norton's *Gorboduc*, over the mongrel disreputability of the popular stage; his sister's translation was part of a deliberate program—which included original works by Samuel Daniel, Fulke Greville, and others—to nurture such a tradition in England. Traces of *Cornélie* in the battle descriptions of *The Spanish Tragedy* suggest that Kyd had been familiar with Garnier for some time, but the translation itself is a popular playwright's late effort to enter a new kind of literary circle. Kyd's dedication ends with an unfulfilled promise to continue the effort with a translation of Garnier's *Porcie*.

As a translator, Kyd makes his share of sometimes colorful mistakes: "ou les trespassez vont" in act two, for instance, is metamorphosed into "where sinnes doe maske vnseene." Even when not actually misconstruing the text, he is often casually paraphrastic and expansive. Later in the same act, "Apres l'Hyuer glacé le beau Printemps fleuronne,/L'Esté chaud vient apres, apres l'Esté Autonne" becomes:

> When Isie Winter's past, then comes the spring,
> Whom Sommers pride (with sultrie heate) pursues,
> To whom mylde Autumne doth earths treasure bring,
> The sweetest season that the wise can chuse.

There are also abridgments and omissions, and some wholly original passages without warrant in the French—such as the lengthy opening of III.i:

> The cheerefull Cock (the sad nights comforter),
> Wayting vpon the rysing of the Sunne,
> Doth sing to see how *Cynthia* shrinks her horne,
> While *Clitie* takes her progresse to the East [.]

Yet if these practices contrast with the rigorous, line-for-line meticulousness of Lady Pembroke's rendering of the same author, they are only the common trade of a distinguished line of Elizabethan translators, and Kyd's is on the whole a respectable and spirited piece of work. His efforts gave England a new Roman play unusually eloquent about the suicidal deadliness of empire; in act one Garnier's Cicero sees the victory of Julius Caesar both as evil in itself and as the logical culmination of Rome's much-envied success:

> Carthage and Sicily we haue subdude,
> And almost yoked all the world beside:
> And, soly through desire of publique rule,
> Rome and the earth are waxen all as one:
> Yet now we liue despoild and robd by one
> Of th' ancient freedom wherein we were borne.
> And euen that yoke, that wont to tame all others,
> Is heauily return'd vpon our selues—
> A note of Chaunce that may the proude controle,
> And shew Gods wrath against a cruell soule.

To the Elizabethan mythology of Rome Kyd imports a particularly lucid disillusion.

The achievement nevertheless now seems of little import. Whatever thematic interest the play has is almost fatally compromised by the static dramaturgy. The only scene in which anything notable happens is a dialogue between Cassius and Decimus Brutus in which the conspiracy against Caesar is organized. But the assassination comes after the play's end; the other major event, Pompey's death, has already occurred when the play begins. Cassius and Brutus never share the stage with Caesar and Antony; nor do any of them ever encounter the play's main character, Pompey's widow, Cornelia. The bulk of the play is given over to her operatic *Klagereden;* the sole change in her condition during the play is that news of her father's death is added to that of her husband's. The avoidance of action to enhance the declamatory set speech is of course deliberate on the part of both Garnier and his English avatars, and in France it does lay some of the ground for the classically spare theater of Corneille and Racine. Yet in itself it is theatrical deadweight, and Lady Pembroke's movement came, unsurprisingly, to nothing of consequence. A handful of favorable comments suggests that Kyd's attempt to attach himself to that movement achieved a minor *succès d'estime;* the translation was republished in 1595, with Kyd's name brought forward to the title page, and widely quoted (with what may be some fragments from lost works) in *England's Parnassus* (1600). But in the long view the whole enterprise seems Kyd's almost perverse turning away from the authentic genius of the Elizabethan stage for the pointless refinement of closet drama.

Further mapping of Kyd's career is more speculative. On some readings of the evidence, his abandonment of the public theater may have come even earlier. Thomas Nashe's preface to Robert Greene's *Menaphon* (1589) includes a screed against "a sort of shifting companions, that runne through euery art and thriue by none to leaue the trade of *Nouerint*, whereto they were borne, and busie themselues with the indeuors of art," and eventually "to imitate the Kidde in *Aesop*, who enamored with the Foxes newfangles, forsooke all hopes of life to leape into a new occupation; and these men renowncing all possibilities of credit or estimation, to intermeddle with Italian translations." The trade of "Noverint" is that of the scrivener; and there being no suitable fable of "the Kid" in Aesop, scholars have long suspected a specific reference to the playwright. The date of the reference tallies with the reported beginning of Kyd's service to his patron and with the appearance of *The Householder's Philosophy*. The work Kyd chose to translate is one of several Renaissance descendants of Xenophon's *Oeconomicus*, of which Alberti's *Della Famiglia* is the most thorough and famous. Tasso reports the inherited wisdom sustaining a modest but impressively autonomous rural household near Vercelli: "It lightlie happeneth not . . . that I send to the Cittie for any thing necessarie or fit for the life of a poore Gentlema[n], for (God be praised) I haue aboundaunce of euery thing ministred vnto me vpon myne owne ground." The strategies for such a goal concern the choosing of a wife, the education of children, the husbanding of resources, and, perhaps most interestingly, a wary involvement in commerce in which the profit motive is kept under strict control: "When mony . . . is changed with mony, not directed and imployed to some other vse, it is vsed beyond the proper vse, and so abused. In which exchange Nature is not imitated, for as well may exchaunge that doth multiply or accumulat infinite and excessiue profits be said to haue no end or absolute determination as Vsurie." Such prescriptions put mercantile savvy at the service of aristocratic gentility; Kyd's interest in them, and in their marketability, may well be related to his own move from the turmoil of the public theater to the more dignified world of the great house.

What evidence we have for dating Kyd's genuine theatrical activity neither points to 1588 as an effective terminus nor decisively precludes the possibility. Nashe's preface is the principal reason for assigning Kyd authorship of the *Ur-Hamlet;* between the references to "the trade of *Nouerint*" and "the Kidde in *Aesop*" come sarcastic com-

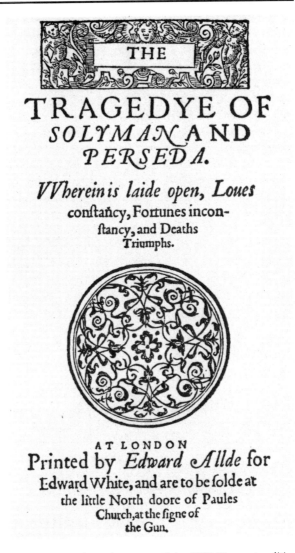

Title page for the unique copy of the 1592(?) quarto edition of the play that has been attributed to Kyd on the basis of its similarities to The Spanish Tragedy (British Library)

ments on the target's dramatic productions: "English Seneca read by candle-light yeeldes manie good sentences as '*bloud is a begger*' and so forth: and if you intreate him faire in a frostie morning, he will affoord you whole *Hamlets*, I should say handfulls of tragical speeches." The play in question must be no later than 1589; and if Kyd is indeed being attacked as the author, he would already have to be sufficiently well established to be worth the trouble. There is, however, no firm necessity for dating *The Spanish Tragedy* much earlier than its first publication. A certain amount of scholarly consensus favors 1585-1587 (Frederick S. Boas, Arthur Freeman), though it relies on such unavoidably subjective favors as a sense that the play's image of Spain must be "pre-Armada"; serious arguments have been made (by scholars such as Philip Edwards) for a later date, closer to 1590. A comparatively brief *First Part of Jeronimo* published in 1605 and dramatizing the story of Don Andrea's murder has numerous inconsistencies with *The Spanish Tragedy* and contains what seem to be allusions to Shakespeare's *Hamlet* and *Julius Caesar* and Chapman's *The Gentleman Usher;* it seems datable circa 1602 and is now acknowledged not to be Kyd's. It may, however, draw on the "spanes comodye" mentioned in Henslowe's records for 1591-1592, which could have been an authoritative prologue to the more famous play. There are also reasons for attributing to Kyd the *Soliman and Perseda* published anonymously in, probably, 1592; it treats, in fuller and slightly different form, the story of the play-within-the-play of *The Spanish Tragedy,* and contains some striking verbal conjunctions with that work. It also contains some strong parallels with Marlowe's *Edward II,* which is itself usually dated, also indecisively, 1592; the best we can say is that Kyd's career in the public theater may or may not have continued that long.

Within this oeuvre, *Soliman and Perseda* has attracted the least attention, though it has its interest among the early Elizabethan dramas of murderous despotism, for which *Tamburlaine* is the great exemplar and inspiration. Based on a story in Henry Wotton's *Courtly Controversy of Cupid's Cautels* (1578), *Soliman and Perseda* concerns a Turkish emperor of Marlovian arbitrariness and savagery who finds himself trapped by his own simultaneous attraction to two young Christian lovers who come under his power. Soliman admires Erastus's martial reputation and prowess, and desires Perseda's beauty, both almost to distraction; in IV.i, after some turmoil, he rises to an act of Cornelian generosity:

> I loue them both, I know not which the better:
> They loue each other best: what then should follow,
> But that I conquer both by my deserts,
> And ioyne their hands, whose hearts are knit already?

He not only marries them but also makes Erastus governor of Rhodes. His nobility, however, almost immediately snaps into bloodthirsty frenzy. Soliman has Erastus strangled on a fictitious charge of treason, and then has the executioners and all those involved in the trial killed as well. Perseda tricks Soliman into killing her, and then into poisoning himself by kissing her venomed lips. In V.iv he dies partly repentant but also tranced by the pattern of it all:

> My last request, for I commaund no more,
> Is that my body with *Persedas* be
> Interd, where my *Erastus* lyes intombd,
> And let one Epitaph containe vs all.

In V.v this end settles the allegorical argument among Fortune, Love, and Death with which the action is framed:

> DEATH: Hence foolish *Fortune,* and thou wanton Loue:
>   Your deedes are trifles, mine of consequence.
> FORTUNE: I giue worlds happines and woes increase.
> LOVE: By ioyning persons I increase the world.
> DEATH: By wasting all I conquer all the world.

The complicated plot is handled with efficiency and skill, though the play does illustrate the vices of its genre; the almost universal slaughter that underscores its theme–including, almost as an afterthought on Soliman's part, the last-minute depopulation of Rhodes–which threatens to be unintentionally comic as things pile up. But the play also exemplifies some of Elizabethan tragedy's unpredictable strengths, most notably in a running counterpoint that is quite deliberately comic, and not just by way of relief. One of Perseda's other lovers, Basilisco, is a *miles gloriosus* of Falstaffian resonance. He explains himself handsomely in V.iii:

> Let me see: where is that *Alcides,* surnamed *Hercules,*
> The onely Club man of his time? dead.
> Where is the eldest sonne of *Pryam,*
> The abraham-coloured Troian? dead.
> Where is the leader of the Mirmidons,
> That well knit *Accill[es]*? dead.
> ....
> To conclude in a word: to be captious, vertuous, ingenious,
> Are to be nothing when it pleaseth death to be enuious.
> ....
> I loue *Perseda,* as one worthie;
> But I loue *Basilisco,* as one I hould more worthy,
> My fathers sonne, my mothers solace, my proper selfe.
> Faith, he can doe little that cannot speake,
> And he can doe lesse that cannot runne away:
> Then sith mans life is as a glasse, and a phillip may cracke it,
> Mine is no more, and a bullet may pearce it:
> Therefore I will play least in sight.

Moved nevertheless to kiss the dying Perseda, he

is swiftly killed by Soliman. His unavailing practicality sets off the play's tragic passions in a way that both mocks and intensifies them; Lear's fool is among his memorable descendants.

Soliman and Perseda, however, pales in influence and significance beside the *Ur-Hamlet* and *The Spanish Tragedy*. There is no sign that the former was ever printed; nothing specific survives of it aside from the widely quoted "Hamlet, revenge" and (on Nashe's oblique testimony) "Blood is a beggar." Reconstructions of the play rely heavily on the strong similarities between Shakespeare's *Hamlet* and *The Spanish Tragedy*—similarities in which both contrast with the source material for the Hamlet story in Saxo Grammaticus and Belleforest. The popular and resonant device of the play-within-the-play—a literalized metaphor which now seems the definitive emblem for Elizabethan theater itself—very probably began its life with these two plays. It seems reasonable as well to credit the *Ur-Hamlet* with introducing the father's ghost, and with giving dramatic prominence to Hamlet's delay under the hectoring of that ghost; the addition of Hamlet's own death to those of his eventual victims also probably was Kyd's innovation. These changes give new meaning to the avenger's feigned madness, and raise revenge beyond mere satisfaction to a tragic and indeed suicidal action. Revenge so conflicted is a rich and compelling theme, one capable not merely of inspiring a few good plays, but of sustaining a major theatrical tradition. Even if Kyd is not in fact responsible for whatever achievement the *Ur-Hamlet* may have represented, he indubitably clinched matters with *The Spanish Tragedy*, a play whose power established revenge tragedy as the central genre of English tragedy for the next three generations.

In one form or another, revenge is indeed one of the dominant themes throughout Renaissance tragedy, in Spain and France as well as in England. The concern was not merely artistic; personal satisfaction through violence, especially as the formalized cult of dueling spread, was a sufficiently common and visible occurrence to constitute a civic threat which the regimes of Western Europe all had to address. The literature of official admonishment on the subject is considerable; Kyd's Hieronimo himself cites the pertinent biblical text (Romans 12.19) in act three of *The Spanish Tragedy*. What made things touchy was that the violence in question was not primarily a lower-class affair but rather something practiced by the conspicuously privileged. Vengeance carried an air of aristocratic dignity, a cultural memory of the baronial right of private justice which the monarchies of the fifteenth and sixteenth centuries had struggled so hard to extinguish; even under the successfully centralized authority of the new state, the *lex talionis* attached itself tenaciously to an ideal of personal honor as, in effect, the most dramatic form in which such honor could assert its force as a motivation. The honor plays of the Continental theater are occasionally quite explicit about the taking of vengeance as a way of claiming through one's own demeanor the sort of personal prestige that is traditionally associated with aristocratic birth: defending his honor, even the poor man becomes noble. The outcome can be tragic, but is not invariably so. In England, however—in great part, it would seem, under Kyd's influence—the revenge play is expected to end in a holocaust that consumes the avenger as well as his prey; playwrights who break that rule—John Marston in *Antonio's Revenge*, Cyril Tourneur in *The Atheist's Tragedy*—know that they must have their reasons for doing so. Coming to his end, the English stage avenger characteristically takes on the style of a Machiavellian villain—deceitful, treacherous, cold—even as his goal, more often than not, remains just and necessary. This torsion is only hinted at in *Tamburlaine* and its progeny; the generic rules established by Kyd nurture a wider and subtler exploration of combative self-respect and its paradoxes.

The popularity of *The Spanish Tragedy* was swift and durable—unparalleled, in fact—even as English tragedy evolved and changed. Copies of the play from ten printings between 1592 and 1633 have survived, and there is evidence of an earlier edition in the former year. Stage allusions to the play are numerous; their tone can be ironic and superior, but, as in these lines from Thomas May's *The Heir* (produced in 1620), they also customarily involve an admission that Kyd had crafted a virtual synecdoche for effective theater:

ROSCIO: Has not your lordship seen
  A player personate *Hieronimo*?
POLYMETES. By th' mass 'tis true. I have seen the
    knave paint grief
  In such a lively colour that for false
  And acted passion he has drawn true tears
  From the spectators. Ladies in the boxes
  Kept time with sighs and tears to his sad accents
  As he had truly been the man he seemed.

Ben Jonson dealt slightingly with the play and its

devotees on several occasions–"He that will swear *Ieronimo* or *Andronicus* are the best plays yet, shall pass unexcepted at here as a man whose judgment shows it is constant, and hath stood still these five and twenty or thirty years" (*Bartholomew Fair*, Induction)–but we also have record of two rather large payments by Henslowe to him for "adicions in Geronymo" in 1601-1602; these may be the supplements that become part of the standard text with the 1602 printing. The play's staying power appears to have extended to the closing of the theaters; indeed, antitheatrical polemicists in the 1630s eagerly retailed the story of a woman "of good rank" who put by all spiritual attention on her deathbed and cried instead, "Hieronimo, Hieronimo, O let me see Hieronimo acted." As late as 1675, Charles Cotton could write, nostalgically, "of all plays *Hieronimo*'s the best." The play also accompanied Shakespeare's *Hamlet* to the Continent, to become one of English literature's rare international hits; two German and two Dutch adaptations were published in the seventeenth century, and there are records of several lost versions. One of the Dutch editions was republished as late as 1729–a ninth printing.

Aside from the play-within-the-play, Kyd seems, unusually for an Elizabethan dramatist, to have worked from no particular source. Neither the main plot nor a somewhat tangential Portuguese subplot is based on any specific event in recent Iberian history; some details attest a fairly casual acquaintance with that history (as in a fanciful catalogue in the first scene of English military successes there), and even with Spanish geography (in III.xiv the Portuguese viceroy is said to have "crost the seas" to reach Spain). A few incidents, such as Lorenzo's treachery toward his own henchman Pedringano, may be drawn from recent English politics. Senecan tragedy supplied a few significant *sententiae*–some of them quoted in slightly altered Latin–and probably helped authorize a tone of hyperbolic outrage: "What age hath euer heard such monstrous deeds?" (IV.iv). The framing device of Don Andrea's colloquy with Revenge has some formal affinity with the scene between Tantalus and Furia that opens Seneca's *Thyestes,* and the numerous and lengthy set speeches of Kyd's first act and a half suggest that he might have begun with the intention of writing in a loosened form of the Senecan neoclassicism to which he eventually returned in *Cornelia.*

If so, he made his mark when he abandoned his original intentions. The complicated, rather stately plotting of the play's early part, rife with vengeful motives, shifts gears sharply with the killing of Horatio: an act that in effect decides whose revenge play this is to be. And Hieronimo's instant arrival on stage in II.v brings the first of the play's great speeches:

> What out-cries pluck me from my naked bed,
> And chill my throbbing hart with trembling feare,
> Which neuer danger yet could daunt before?
> Who cals *Hieronimo*? speak, heere I am.

There is no answer; he finds instead the body of his murdered son. With it comes a stark sense of purpose:

> Seest thou this handkercher besmerd with blood?
> It shall not from me, till I take reuenge.
> Seest thou those wounds that yet are bleeding fresh?
> Ile not intombe them, till I haue reueng'd.
> Then will I ioy amidst my discontent.

Yet the purpose also brings an urgent need for its concealment, in which he instructs his distraught wife:

> Meane while, good *Isabella,* cease thy plaints,
> Or, at the least, dissemble them awhile:
> So shall we sooner finde the practise out,
> And learne by whom all this was brought about.

It is the dramatic spectacle of consuming rage made desperately private that gives the succeeding action its famous power: "Thus therefore will I rest me in vnrest, / Dissembling quiet in vnquietnes" (III.xiii).

One component of this spectacle is a Machiavellian detective story. Hieronimo in fact learns the identity of the murderers early on, but understandably he distrusts the information. As he says in III.ii,

> This is deuised to endanger thee,
> That thou by this *Lorenzo* shouldst accuse,
> And he, for thy dishonour done, should draw
> Thy life in question and thy name in hate.

The needed corroboration is ironically provided by Lorenzo himself, when his attempt to cover his tracks by disposing of an accomplice delivers the latter's confession to Hieronimo. Lorenzo's efforts to head off Hieronimo's direct access to the king further play into Hieronimo's hands when the highminded Duke of Castile, suspecting only

The Spanish Tragedie:

OR,

Hieronimo is mad againe.

Containing the lamentable end of *Don Horatio*, and
Belimperia; with the pittifull death of *Hieronimo*.

Newly corrected, amended, and enlarged with new
Additions of the *Painters* part, and others, as
it hath of late been diuers times acted.

LONDON,

Printed by W. White, for I. White and T. Langley,
and are to be fold at their Shop ouer againft the
Sarazens head without New-gate. 1615.

*Title page for the unique copy of the seventh surviving quarto edition of the popular play that served as
a model for later English revenge tragedies (Trinity College, Cambridge). The earliest extant edition, published in 1592, is thought to have been preceded by an edition printed the previous year.*

the usual court infighting, takes it upon himself
to arrange a reconciliation, to which Hieronimo
disarmingly agrees (in III.xiv):

> see, Ile be freends with you all:
> Specially with you, my louely Lord;
> For diuers causes it is fit for vs

That we be freends: the world is suspitious,
And men may think what we imagine not.

Requested to provide an entertainment for the visiting Portuguese, Hieronimo calls on this new
friendship to secure the participation of Lorenzo
and Balthazar in his production of *Soliman and*

Perseda. In IV.i, at Balthazar's demurral—"would you haue us plaie a Tragedie?"—Hieronimo cites imperial precedent:

> Why, Nero thought it no disparagement,
> And Kings and Emperours haue tane delight
> To make experience of their wits in plaies.

These are the lines to which we owe our certainty about the play's authorship; with them, Heywood cites the stories that are evidently on Hieronimo's mind, of how condemned Roman prisoners were made to act roles in which they were literally killed on stage. Accepting their parts, Lorenzo and Balthazar go to their doom.

Against this cool calculation presses Hieronimo's tumultuous fury:

> The blustring winds, conspiring with my words,
> At my lament haue moued the leaueles trees,
> Disroabde the medowes of their flowred greene,
> Made mountains marsh with spring tides of my
>   teares,
> And broken through the brazen gates of hell.

In such speeches—this one from III.vii—the least ruly part of the Senecan heritage wings free of neoclassical decorum to merge with a native tradition of theatrical rant, out-Heroding Herod. This is the language for which Kyd's play was most famous in its own time, the note most amplified in the 1602 additions. It is similar to the violent extravagance of Tamburlaine's comparably famous speeches, but Marlowe's emphasis is time and again on Tamburlaine's ability to translate that violence into immediate public action. Hieronimo's rage is for most of the play impotent, blocked. The speech just quoted continues:

> still tormented is my tortured soule
> With broken sighes and restles passions,
> That winged mount, and, houering in the aire,
> Beat at the windowes of the brightest heauens,
> Solliciting for iustice and reuenge:
> But they are plac't in those empyreal heights,
> Where, countermurde with walles of diamond,
> I finde the place impregnable; and they
> Resist my woes, and giue my words no way.

Hieronimo deliberately confines much of this rhetoric to his soliloquies, in response to the practical danger of his situation: "*Hieronimo* beware; goe by, goe by," he tells himself in III.xii. But even when it slips out, as it does before the king later in the same scene, it baffles far more than it terrorizes: "What accident hath hapt *Hieronimo*? / I

haue not seene him to demeane him so." He acquires a reputation for madness that if anything further screens his intentions, though that is not itself part of the plan; rather, he is in the grip of an emotion whose sheer intensity is unintelligible to most of those around him.

At moments of special dramatic force, this passion seems nevertheless shareable. In III.xiii an encounter with an old man whose own son has been murdered brings unexpected pause:

> Thou art the liuely image of my griefe;
> Within thy face my sorrowes I may see.
> ....
> Come in, old man, thou shalt to *Izabell;*
> Leane on my arme: I thee, thou me shalt stay,
> And thou, and I, and she will sing a song [.]

And at the beginning of the fourth act, Hieronimo finally makes contact with Bel-imperia, the lover of both Don Andrea and Horatio, who has been secretly intent on vengeance since the play's start. Discovery of her passion gives Hieronimo the conviction that God is now securely on his side:

> Why then I see that heauen applies our drift,
> And all the Saintes doe sit soliciting
> For vengeance on those cursed murtherers.

Their teamwork brings off the lethal play-within-the-play, and clears the way at last for Hieronimo's triumphant public statement in IV.iv:

> know I am *Hieronimo,*
> The hopeles father of a hapless Sonne,
> Whose tongue is tun'd to tell his latest tale.

And he tells the stunned court the full story of what has been done to him and what he has just done.

Yet Kyd also cancels Hieronimo's triumph even as he achieves it. Isabella and Bel-imperia are already dead by their own hands, and Hieronimo ends his speech announcing the same intent:

> Princes, now beholde *Hieronimo,*
> Author and actor in this Tragedie,
> Bearing his latest fortune in his fist;
> And will as resolute conclude his parte
> As any of the Actors gone before.

An attempt to prevent him fails, but it lasts long enough to produce the play's most notorious piece of stage business:

Indeed thou maiest torment me, as his wretched
  Sonne
Hath done in murdring my *Horatio:*
But neuer shalt thou force me to reueale
The thing which I haue vowd inuiolate.
And therefore in despight of all thy threats,
Pleasde with their deaths, and easde with their
  reuenge,
First take my tung, and afterwards my hart.

He bites out his tongue.

It is not at all clear what Hieronimo means by the "thing which I haue vowd inuiolate," since he seems to have just told all. Textual corruption has been suggested–possibly two alternative endings inadvertently printed in sequence–though Kyd may also have simply skimped verisimilitude in pursuit of an overriding goal to end his avenger's story not in victory and justification but in death and silence.

That closure, in any case, gives the play its final resonance. It embodies a stern and enduring moral judgment on revenge, but it is more than just that. Hieronimo's end is mirrored in characters as diverse as Iago and Hamlet: "O I could tell you– / But let it be. . . ." The tragic fate of which Kyd writes is in a sense the mortal isolation of humanity itself, of the individual life as a secret taken to the grave.

Bibliography:

Dickie Spurgeon, "Thomas Kyd," in *The Predecessors of Shakespeare: A Survey and Bibliography of Recent Studies in English Renaissance Drama,* edited by Terence P. Logan and Denzell S. Smith (Lincoln: University of Nebraska Press, 1973), pp. 93-106.

References:

Fredson T. Bowers, *Elizabethan Revenge Tragedy 1587-1642* (Princeton: Princeton University Press, 1940);

Gordon Braden, *Renaissance Tragedy and the Senecan Tradition: Anger's Privilege* (New Haven: Yale University Press, 1985);

Félix Carrère, *Le Théâtre de Thomas Kyd* (Toulouse: Edouard Privat, 1951);

Wolfgang Clemen, *English Tragedy before Shakespeare: The Development of Dramatic Speech,* translated by T. S. Dorsch (London: Methuen, 1961);

Arthur Freeman, *Thomas Kyd: Facts and Problems* (Oxford: Clarendon Press, 1967);

Charles A. Hallett and Elaine S. Hallett, *The Revenger's Madness: A Study of Revenge Tragedy Motifs* (Lincoln: University of Nebraska Press, 1980);

Peter B. Murray, *Thomas Kyd* (New York: Twayne, 1969);

Alexander Maclaren Witherspoon, *The Influence of Robert Garnier on Elizabethan Drama* (New Haven: Yale University Press, 1924).

Papers:

Kyd's two autograph letters to Sir John Puckering are in the Harleian manuscripts in the British Library.

John Lyly

(circa 1554-November 1606)

Leah Scragg
University of Manchester

PLAY PRODUCTIONS: *Campaspe,* London, Blackfriars theater, 1583-1584;

Sapho and Phao, London, Blackfriars theater,
1583-1584;

Gallathea, London, Paul's theater(?), 1585-1588(?);

Endimion, Greenwich, at Court, 2 February 1588;

Love's Metamorphosis, London, Paul's theater, circa
1588-1590;

Mother Bombie, London, Paul's theater, 1588-
1590(?);

Midas, London, Paul's theater, 1589-1590;

The Woman in the Moon, London, unknown theater, 1591-1594(?).

BOOKS: *Euphues. The Anatomy of Wyt* (London:
Printed by T. East for G. Cawood, 1578);

*Euphues and His England. Containing His Voyage
and Aduentures* (London: Printed by T. East
for G. Cawood, 1580);

*A Moste Excellent Comedie of Alexander, Campaspe,
and Diogenes* (London: Printed by T. Dawson for T. Cadman, 1584); republished as
Campaspe (London: Printed by T. Dawson
for T. Cadman, 1584);

Sapho and Phao (London: Printed by T. Dawson
for T. Cadman, 1584);

*Pappe with an Hatchet. Alias, A Figge for My God
Sonne* (London: Printed by J. Anoke & J.
Astile for the Bayliue of Withernam [T.
Orwin], 1589);

Endimion, The Man in the Moone (London: Printed
by J. Charlewood for the Widdow Broome,
1591);

Gallathea (London: Printed by J. Charlwoode for
the Widdow Broome, 1592);

Midas (London: Printed by T. Scarlet for J.
Broome, 1592);

Mother Bombie (London: Printed by T. Scarlet for
C. Burby, 1594);

The Woman in the Moone (London: Printed by J.
Roberts for W. Jones, 1597);

Loves Metamorphosis. A Wittie and Courtly Pastorall
(London: Printed by S. Stafford for W.
Wood, 1601);

Sixe Court Comedies, edited by Edward Blount (London: Printed by W. Stansby for E. Blount,
1632)–comprises *Endimion, Campaspe, Sapho
and Phao, Gallatea, Midas,* and *Mother Bombie.*

Editions: *The Complete Works of John Lyly,* 3 volumes, edited by R. Warwick Bond (Oxford:
Clarenden Press, 1902);

Euphues, The Anatomy of Wit; Euphues His England,
edited by Morris W. Croll and Harry
Clemons (London: Routledge, 1916);

Alexander and Campaspe, edited by W. W. Greg
(London: Printed for the Malone Society at
Oxford University Press, 1934);

Mother Bombie, edited by Kathleen M. Lea, with
the assistance of D. Nichol Smith (London:
Printed for the Malone Society at Oxford
University Press, 1948);

Gallathea and Midas, edited by Anne B. Lancashire (Lincoln: University of Nebraska
Press, 1969; London: Arnold, 1970).

Until the early 1960s John Lyly's reputation
as playwright and prose writer rested largely
upon the influence his plays were thought to
have exerted upon the work of later dramatists
(notably Shakespeare) and upon his creation of a
unique prose style (euphuism) that enjoyed a
brief period of popularity and rapidly fell into dis-
repute. Only in the last twenty years has it been
recognized that Lyly's dramatic works are significant in their own right, and that the style their creator evolved is inseparable from his vision of life.

Lyly was born into a family with close connections with the humanist movement. His grandfather was William Lily, the famous grammarian
and High Master of St. Paul's School, while his
uncle, George Lily, was secretary to the learned
Reginald Pole, kinsman of Henry VIII. His father, Peter, a minor ecclesiastical official in the
Archbishopric of York, had married Jane Burgh
(possibly a distant relative of Lord Burghley)
some time before 1559. The date of Lyly's birth
is uncertain. The statement of Anthony à Wood
that he matriculated at Oxford in 1569 and

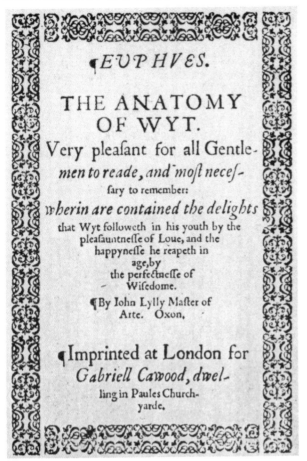
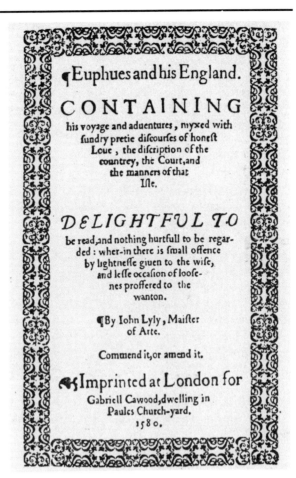

Title pages for the 1578 quarto edition of the book that established Lyly as one of the foremost prose writers of his time (British Library) and for a 1580 quarto edition of its equally popular sequel (Hampstead Public Library)

Lyly's supplication for the degree of B.A. in 1573 point to the year 1552, while the appearance of his name on the 1571 matriculation list at Magdalen College, Oxford, suggests 1554. Since his brothers attended the King's School at Canterbury (where Christopher Marlowe was also a pupil) it is likely that Lyly received his early education there before entering the college formerly attended by his uncle and grandfather. At Oxford he appears to have gained a reputation as a wit and possibly as a profligate, but the ultimate seriousness of his academic ambitions is indicated by a letter to Lord Burghley, written in May 1574, in which he asks Burghley to use his good offices to obtain him a university fellowship. Like the majority of Lyly's subsequent appeals for patronage, his plea went unregarded, and he left Oxford, after obtaining his M.A. in 1575, to take lodgings in the Savoy in London. (In 1579 Cambridge awarded him an M.A. by incorporation.)

At what point Lyly decided to advance his position by literary means is uncertain, but in 1578

he published the work which was to establish him as one of the foremost prose writers of his day–*Euphues: The Anatomy of Wit. Euphues* (the name means well-endowed) traces the career of an intelligent, but inexperienced, young man who leaves Athens (Oxford) to sojourn in Naples (London), "a place of more pleasure than profit and yet of more profit than piety." In Naples Euphues is offered good counsel by Eubulus and pledges his friendship to Philautus, only to fall in love with the object of his friend's affections–Lucilla, daughter of Don Ferardo. Euphues wins Lucilla's love and quarrels with Philautus, but he is ultimately forsaken by Lucilla and reconciled with his friend, to whom he addresses a series of increasingly grave and pious letters which bring the work to a close.

Though *Euphues* is set in a highly sophisticated society remote from day-to-day reality, it nevertheless deals with issues highly relevant to Lyly's contemporaries. The romance is an "anatomy" of "wit" in that it lays bare, or explores in full, the limitations of intellectual capacity divorced from wisdom or experience, dealing with a range of moral issues through the opposing positions the characters take up. Approached via the prose fiction of a later period, it appears structurally weak and lacking in psychological realism, but the conventions of the modern novel are, in fact, entirely alien to the genre to which *Euphues* belongs. The tale follows a traditional "prodigalson" pattern and is commended to its readers as a "simple pamphlet" in which the folly and wisdom of Euphues are equally displayed. To the sixteenth-century reader it offered a delightful compendium of literary motifs, combined with elegance of expression and moral edification. The uniqueness of Lyly's achievement, however, lies in his fusion of seemingly contradictory impulses within a single composition. In some respects *Euphues* might be said to resemble a Renaissance "perspective" painting, in that it yields contrasting interpretations depending upon the angle from which it is viewed. According to G. K. Hunter, "looked at one way it is sophisticated and flippant; looked at from another angle it is seriously concerned with conduct." It is this ambivalence which was to be the hallmark of Lyly's subsequent work, his plays evolving ever more complex ways of projecting the "doubleness" characteristic of his vision of reality.

One of the principal vehicles through which Lyly's distinctive vision is conveyed is his prose style, the "euphuistic" mode which took its name from his earliest work. The characteristic features of euphuism did not originate with Lyly, but he used them more systematically, and subtly, than any of his predecessors or imitators. The style is rooted in antithetical balance, a sentence characteristically falling into a series of paired clauses, the second matching the first syntactically but contrasting with it in meaning, and the opposition between the two being pointed by alliteration and assonance. For example, Euphues asks Eubulus, "Doe you measure the hotte assaultes of youth by the colde skirmishes of age? whose yeares are subiect to more infirmities then our youth, we merry, you melancholy, wee zealous in affection, you ielous in all your dooinges, you testie without cause, wee hastie for no quarrel." Equally characteristic of the style is the use of illustrative analogies drawn from the natural world (both real and imaginary), which constantly emphasize the presence of contrasting properties within a single phenomenon. For example, we are told that "the Birde *Taurus* hath a

Title page for the 1584 quarto edition of the first play Lyly wrote for the joint company of the Children of the Chapel Royal and the Children of St. Paul's (Anderson Galleries, sale number 2077, 20-21 May 1926)

great voyce, but a small body, the thunder a greate clappe, yet but a lyttle stone" and that "yᵉ *Camelion* thoughe hee haue most guttes, draweth least breath . . . the Elder tree thoughe hee bee fullest of pith, is farthest from strength." In Lyly's work, particularly in his plays, the emphasis upon the fusion of opposites in the phenomenological world is so great, and the use of antithetical balance so insistent, that the style ceases to be merely ornamental and becomes a major vehicle for the projection of a universe conceived in terms of paradox and duality.

Though the success of *Euphues* was instantaneous, the sequel promised by the author in his closing lines, *Euphues and His England*, did not appear until 1580–Lyly's intentions in relation to it having apparently changed in the intervening period. Whereas the closing lines of *Euphues* suggested that the second part would concern itself with the Court, and the postscript to the second edition (1579) implied the forthcoming work would include a survey of the universities, *Euphues and His England* focuses upon love rather than upon the education of the young or the nature of power and patronage and is explicitly directed toward a female audience. In the words of the letter to "The Ladies and Gentlewoemen of England" with which the second part opens, "*Euphues* had rather lye shut in a Ladyes casket, then open in a Schollers studie." The method by which the narrative proceeds has also undergone a change, with the use of exemplary tales or incidents replacing the moral reflections characteristic of the earlier work. Nevertheless, it would be a mistake to overestimate the difference between the two parts. In the address to the ladies and gentlewomen of England, and in the letter to the gentlemen readers which immediately follows it, Lyly stresses the multifaceted nature of the composition, the variousness of its appeal, and the active participation it requires from the reader for its full enjoyment. Its limitation of subject matter is more apparent than real, numerous topics of contemporary interest being woven into the narrative. In short, *Euphues and His England* shares both the inclusiveness of its predecessor and its concern with contrasting attitudes or perspectives.

Euphues and *Euphues and His England* were the most successful literary works of their period. Five editions of *Euphues* were published by the end of 1581, and thirty-three editions of *Euphues* and *Euphues and His England* had appeared by the end of 1636, including four combined editions of the two works. To write like Lyly became instantly fashionable, a spate of imitations and parodies testifying to the popularity of these works and the literary prestige of their creator.

The success of the two parts of *Euphues* coincided with Lyly's entry into the household of the Earl of Oxford, to whom *Euphues and His England* is dedicated. Securing Oxford's patronage represented a major advance in Lyly's career in that Oxford was both Lord Great Chamberlain and a royal favorite (and hence a channel to courtly preferment), while being a highly cultured individual in his own right, with strong artistic inclinations and his own company of actors. During his association with Oxford, Lyly's personal and professional life prospered. In 1583 he made an advantageous marriage to a member of an affluent and well-connected Yorkshire family, Beatrice Browne (their many offspring include

John, baptized 1600; Frances, baptized 1603; and Elizabeth, died 1605); while through Oxford, Lyly became a partner in the Blackfriars theater, writing a succession of plays for a joint company of boy actors performing both at the Blackfriars itself and at Court.

The first Blackfriars theater was a private, indoor playhouse that had been created, at considerable expense, by Richard Farrant, Master of the Children of Windsor Chapel and Deputy Master of the Children of the Chapel Royal, from what had been the upper frater of the former Dominican Priory that constituted one of the "liberties" within the city of London (that is, one of the areas not subject to the jurisdiction of the civic authorities). Farrant had initially used the building as a rehearsal room for his troupe of boy actors, but the concept of rehearsal had rapidly become a fiction, and by 1580, when Farrant died, the Blackfriars was firmly established as an indoor theater. After Farrant's death, the management of the playhouse had passed first to William Hunnis and then to Henry Evans, who formed a joint company from the Children of St. Paul's and the Chapel Children with himself as manager and his fellow leaseholders, Lyly and Oxford, as principal dramatist and patron.

Though there is no evidence that Lyly had any dramatic ambitions prior to his association with the Blackfriars, the kind of production in which the boy companies specialized proved the ideal medium for the projection of his distinctive vision. Though the boy actors were not capable of their seniors' range and depth of emotion, they performed highly efficiently as a troupe, excelling in debate, witty repartee, and the graceful execution of stylized scenes. Where the public theaters drew upon emotion, the private theaters depended upon pattern, seeking to engage the spectator's intellect in the unfolding of an idea. The success of *Campaspe* (produced in 1583-1584), the first fruit of his entry into this theatrical milieu, demonstrates how congenial Lyly found this new medium. In common with many plays written for boy actors, the plot of *Campaspe* is relatively slight. Alexander, on his return from his conquest of Thebes, falls in love with one of his prisoners, the relatively lowly Campaspe, who is also loved by the painter Apelles. Alexander hesitates between love and duty until the closing scene, when he asserts his superiority to love and relinquishes Campaspe to her lover. Interlaced with the main action is a subplot concerning a group of philosophers and their young servants,

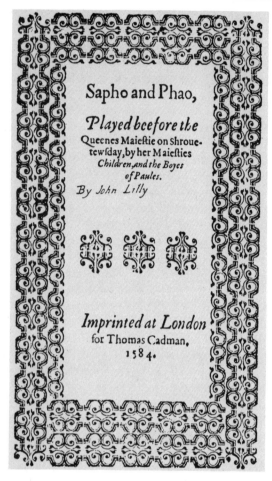

*Title page for the unique copy of the 1584 quarto edition of
the play that Lyly called a "Labyrinth of conceites"
(British Library)*

which serves to widen the implications of the main plot through an examination of the role of individuals within the state. Clearly, the interest of such a play does not lie in what happens or in the experience the individuals undergo. Instead the attention of the audience is directed toward a host of issues that are raised by the central situation. Thus the starting point of the action, the overthrow of Thebes, becomes the occasion for a debate upon the limitations of human conquest, which is then extended, through Alexander's love for Campaspe, into a consideration of the proper uses of power and the relationship between king and subject. The choice Alexander is forced to make leads to a consideration of the public and private selves of the king, while Campaspe's situation raises the question of the extent to which the individual is bound to obey his superior. This list could be extended almost indefinitely. As in *Euphues*, the slow evolution of a central situation allows for a range of issues relevant to contemporary society in general, and, in the case of *Campaspe*, a courtly society in particular, to be explored.

It would be wrong, however, to suggest that the play is no more than a series of minor debates set within the context of a larger discussion of the relative value of love and duty. The Prologue at Court comments, not upon the firm dialectical structure of the drama, but upon the fluidity of the performance that is to ensue, emphasizing the active role played by the spectator in determining the meaning of the action:

> Whatsoeuer we present, we wish it may be
> thought the daunsing of *Agrippa* his
> shadowes, who in the moment they were
> seene, were of any shape one woulde
> conceiue,

while the epilogue at the Blackfriars maintains that

> Our exercises must be as your iudgment is,
> resembling water, which is alwaies of the
> same colour into what it runneth.

The action which these declarations frame, while taking conventional debate topoi as its starting point, evolves from debate into a more complex demonstration of the inherent instability of both the physical and intellectual worlds. From the single word, which is discovered in III.ii and IV.i to be capable of "diuerse significations," an expanding circle of ambivalence is developed which moves outward from the ambiguous word to the antithetical sentence, from the antithetical sentence to juxtaposed speeches, and from juxtaposed speeches to contrasting scenes. Thus at one extreme it is revealed that the word *fly* may mean different things to different people, while, on a larger scale, the theoretical assertion toward which I.i builds—that "needes must that common wealth be fortunate, whose captaine is a Philosopher, and whose Philosopher is a Captaine"—is counterpointed by the observations of the servants in I.ii, which demonstrate in practical terms the inability of the philosopher to rule the petty commonwealth of his household. The concluding gesture of magnanimity with which Alexander relinquishes Campaspe and asserts his superiority to love is undercut by his decision to return to war (the value of which has already been called into question), while the renunciation itself is undermined by the terms in which it is made:

Go *Apelles*, take with you your *Campaspe,*
Alexander is cloied with looking on that
which thou wondrest at.

What the audience is offered is not a conventional debate leading to the demonstration of the superiority of one viewpoint to another but an image of a universe conceived in terms of antithetical elements, susceptible of a variety of different interpretations according to the perspective from which it is viewed, and hence dependent for its ultimate "meaning" upon the judgment of the individual spectator.

As noted above, the euphuistic style is of prime importance in the projection of Lyly's vision. Not only does the insistent use of antithetical balance imply that any given proposition is capable of being answered or matched, but Lyly's idiosyncratic imagery constantly reiterates the coexistence of contrasting properties within a single phenomenon, thus widening the ambiguities of the intellectual arena to the universe of the play as a whole. For example, the Prologue at the Blackfriars points out that "Basill softly touched, yeeldeth a sweete sent but chafed in the hand, a ranke sauour"; Hephaestion reminds Alexander that "Hermyns haue faire skinnes, but fowle liuers; Sepulchres fresh colours, but rotten bones; women faire faces, but false heartes"; while in the prologue that preceded the play's court performance Lyly remarks upon the transformation which the drama has undergone in being transposed from one theatrical milieu to another: "Wee are ashamed that our birde which fluttered by twilight seeming a swan, should bee proued a Batte set against the sunne."

The use of debate as a starting point for the exploration of a universe conceived in terms of the paradoxical union of opposites remained central to Lyly's dramatic technique, his use of antithetical balance becoming more complex in succeeding plays. The setting of the drama, too, is typical of the plays which follow. The classical location distances the audience from the statuesque dramatis personae, the union of a remote time with topical issues giving the play a timelessness characteristic of all Lyly's dramatic work. The division of the cast between self-controlled, cultured men and women, whose predicaments are explored through elegant yet emotionally sensitive set speech, and quick-witted servants delighting in wordplay and song similarly remains basic to succeeding compositions, while the sense of pattern underlying the evolution of the action (as in

the counterpointing of I.i and I.ii noted above) becomes increasingly pronounced as Lyly's career progresses. In short, *Campaspe* inaugurates a drama of a highly stylized kind, appealing to a cultivated (rather than a popular) audience, capable of appreciating the subtlety both of a supremely nonnaturalistic dramatic idiom and of an elegantly articulated dramatic design which exploits to the full the capabilities of its boy performers.

Sapho and Phao, the second play produced by Lyly at the Blackfriars, and subsequently at Court, followed quickly upon *Campaspe* and has much in common with it. Once again the plot is relatively slight and turns upon the love between a person of noble rank and a social inferior. Venus, resentful of the chaste Queen Sapho's resistance to the assaults of love, endows the humble ferryman, Phao, with irresistible beauty, to which the Queen inevitably falls subject. Phao,

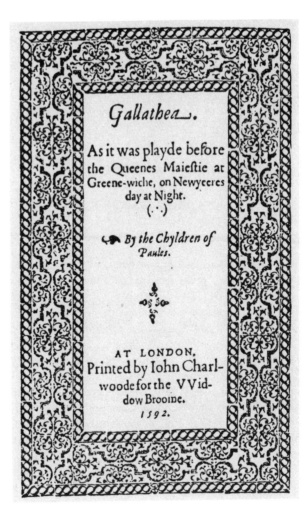

Title page for the 1592 quarto edition of the play that is often considered Lyly's finest dramatic achievement (British Library)

ENDIMION,

The Man in the
Moone.

Playd before the Queenes Maieftie at Greenewich on Candlemas day
at night, by the Chyldren of
Paules.

AT LONDON,
Printed by I. Charlewood, for
the widdowe Broome.
1591.

*Title page for the 1591 quarto edition of a play that was first
produced before Elizabeth I on 2 February 1588
(British Library)*

dramatis personae generate. The central opposition between chastity and amorousness (embod-
ied in the conflict between Sapho and Venus)
frames a series of related debates upon the advantages and disadvantages of contrasting ways of
life. The play opens, for example, with a medita-
tion by Phao upon the benefits of a humble lot,
and the disadvantages of greatness, while in the
following scene Trachinus and Pandion debate
the relative worth of the scholar's life and that of
the courtier. Nevertheless the play does not simply repeat the formula established in *Campaspe*.
Where the plot of the earlier play is minimally progressive, in that Alexander surrenders Campaspe
to Apelles at the close and elects to return to
war, the plot of *Sapho and Phao* is essentially circu-
lar, with Phao withdrawing once again to his se-
cluded life and Sapho reinstated as superior to
Venus. Moreover, the epilogue is at pains to
point out the circularity of the composition, likening the experience of those watching it to that of
people entering a maze, who "walke oftentimes
in one path, and at the last come out where they
entred in," while comparing the play itself to a
"daunce of a Farie in a circle." The lack of progression suggested by these images is counterpointed
by the implication of complexity that the concepts of a maze and a fairy dance carry, and it is
this union of simplicity with complexity which is
the hallmark of this composition. While the basic
pattern of the "dance" is clear-cut, the individual
"steps" are of a highly intricate nature, the overall meaning of the design that is unfolded being
characteristically elusive and dependent, once
again, upon the perspective from which it is
viewed. On a primary level the play may be seen
as a conventional love versus chastity debate, but
the significance of the action is deepened by the
equation that is clearly set up between the figure
of Sapho and that of Elizabeth. On this level, the
play may be seen as an elaborate compliment to a
sovereign whose passions are controlled by wisdom. The play, however, is not merely a tribute
to the decorum of the Tudor Court. The
speeches of the scholar, Pandion, afford us an
image of the potentiality for corruption which underlies all courtly societies, while incipient frivol-
ity is manifest in Sapho's ladies. Thus while on
one level the Queen's victory over Venus appears
clear-cut, the potentiality for that situation to be
reversed is clearly indicated, the circularity of the
composition implying that the entire pattern of
the play, which includes Venus's temporary triumph over Sapho, may be repeated. The mean-

overcome by Sapho's appearance, conceives an un-
dying love for her, but Venus, having fallen in
love with Phao herself, causes Vulcan to forge
fresh arrows to make Phao inconstant and Sapho
indifferent to him. Cupid, however, is seduced
from Venus's service to Sapho's, and having
struck Sapho with the arrow of disdain, causes
Phao to loathe rather than love Venus. Venus
vows revenge upon both Cupid and Sapho; but
the Queen is established as the new sovereign of
love, while Phao, unable to free himself of his passion for her, returns desolate to his native land.
As in the previous play, the main action is inter-
mingled with a series of scenes contrasting the intellectual life with that of the Court, while both
are commented upon by a group of quick-witted
pages. Moreover, as in *Campaspe*, the interest of
the play lies not in what happens, which is predict-
able, but in the ideas which the situations of the

ing of the play is further complicated by an additional structure of allegory erected through the use of dream and the prophetic utterances of the Sybil. The whole of IV.iii, for example, is taken up with a series of highly enigmatic dreams related by Sapho and her ladies, the emblematic nature of which serves to widen the implications of the action in a variety of ways. For example, Sapho's dream of a stock dove seeking to build its nest in a tall cedar crawling with parasites has obvious reference to her relationship with Phao, but the dream restates the situation in more erotic terms than hitherto while simultaneously, through the equation that is set up between Sapho and Elizabeth, inviting a political interpretation. Similarly, utterances of the Sybil, which are also couched in emblematic terms, have a range of implications outside the immediate situations of the protagonists. In short, *Sapho and Phao*, as its author proclaims, is a "Labyrinth of conceites," yielding layer upon layer of possible meanings the more carefully its structure is scrutinized.

In two further respects *Sapho and Phao* represents a development of Lyly's dramatic art from the point achieved in *Campaspe*. In the earlier play it was Alexander who stood at the center of the action and the choice he was called upon to make which framed the other issues raised by the play. In *Sapho and Phao*, though Phao's predicament is explored, it is the response of a sensitive, intelligent, female character to the love experience which is now the center of dramatic interest. Moreover, for all the heart searchings involved for *Campaspe*'s triangle of lovers, the play ends on a positive note. Alexander relinquishes Campaspe and returns to a life of conquest, while Campaspe and Apelles are united. In *Sapho and Phao*, by contrast, the play's central amatory relationship is incapable of a happy outcome, the social gulf between the lovers precluding a direct courtship and generating an atmosphere of wistfulness and bitterness.

In 1584 the landlord of the building housing the Blackfriars theater retook possession of the property, and the grouping for which Lyly's first two plays had been written broke up. There is evidence to suggest, however, that a third play, *Gallathea*, was also composed for performance by this company, the play being entered in the Stationers' Register in 1585, though there is no record of a performance before 1588.

Gallathea represents the culmination of this period of Lyly's career and is probably his outstanding dramatic achievement. Once again the plot involves a conflict between love and chastity, but the structure as a whole is more complex than those of previous plays in that it combines three areas of dramatic interest. The first strand of action to be introduced involves the attempt by two fathers, Tyterus and Melebeus, each of whom believes his daughter to be the fairest maiden in the community, to avoid the sacrifice of his child to Neptune, who has ordained that the loveliest virgin available must be surrendered to his instrument, the Agar. Tyterus and Melebeus disguise their daughters, Gallathea and Phillida, as boys, but the maidens meet, fall in love, and are freed from the dilemma this creates

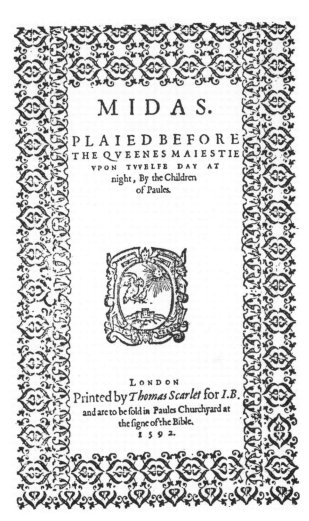

Title page for the 1592 quarto edition of the play whose prologue states, "what heretofore hath beene serued in seuerall dishes for a feaste is now minced in a charger for a Gallimaufrey. If wee present a mingle-mangle, our fault is to be excused, because the whole world is become a Hodge-podge" (Anderson Galleries, sale number 2077, 20-21 May 1926).

only by the intervention of Venus, who turns one of them into a youth. Interwoven with this thread of the plot is a second strand involving Venus and Diana. Cupid, having been slighted by one of Diana's nymphs, exacts vengeance by making the followers of the virgin huntress fall in love, only to be captured himself by Diana and forced to obey her behests, until restored to Venus by the intervention of Neptune. These two major interests are punctuated by the activities of three boys, Robin, Rafe, and Dick, who are seeking to make their fortunes by apprenticing themselves to a series of masters, but whose aspirations are repeatedly dashed. The three lines of action are linked in a variety of ways. In terms of plot Neptune remits the virgin sacrifice in order to secure harmony between Venus and Diana, while the boys are employed to sing at the marriage between the girls. More important, a number of themes are common to all three. All involve an exploration of destiny, of the relationship between mankind and the gods, and the presentation of deceptive appearance. The principal unifying factor, however, is the concept of metamorphosis, and it is in the utilization of every aspect of the composition to project a universe conceived in terms of flux and compounded of antithetical properties that the achievement of the play lies.

From the very outset the audience is presented with an image of transmutation. The setting of the action is a place that was once land, then sea, is now land, and may well be covered by the sea again if the wrath of Neptune, the play's principal deity, is aroused. The character upon whom attention is focused is a girl transformed to a boy, while the opening dialogue emphasizes the concept of change. And the ensuing scenes reiterate the transformation motif. I.ii introduces the conflict between Cupid and Diana's nymphs which is to lead in II.ii to Cupid's disguise as a maiden and to the transformation of the followers of Diana into devotees of love. In I.iii we learn that Phillida, too, is to play the part of a youth, while in II.ii Neptune himself assumes the role of a shepherd. The conceptual universe in which the characters function is also characterized by a paradoxical fluidity. Fortune, we are told, is "constant in nothing but inconstancie," Neptune's immutable will proves to be mutable, while the experience of love is seen as making "constancie ficklenes, courage cowardice, modestie lightnesse; working things impossible . . . and tempering hardest harts like softest

wooll." However, the play does not merely project an image of a universe incessantly oscillating between contrary states. As the drama progresses it is the oneness of seeming opposites, or the synthesis of contraries in a single entity of which the audience becomes aware, rather than alternation and polarity. Thus Gallathea and Phillida are ultimately perceived not as maidens disguised as youths but as epicoene beings with both masculine and feminine potentialities; Cupid is seen as at once powerful and powerless, both a "great" and a "little" god; while the ultimate union of Gallathea and Phillida signifies, not the victory of one of the striving goddesses over the other but the reconciliation of the polarized impulses they embody.

The dazzling complexity of *Gallathea* is not solely the product of action and imagery–the design of the composition is itself a major achievement. Individual scenes are elegantly crafted to project a series of contrasting perspectives on the play's central issues, while the relationship between dramatic sequences itself contributes to the elaboration of meaning. For example, the alternation between contrasting states which is the basic condition of the play world is also a facet of the structure, with successive scenes presenting mirror images of one another. The vision of a maiden disguised as a youth, for instance, which is projected in act one, is counterpointed by the vision of a youth disguised as a maiden in act two, while the decision of a god to disguise himself as a humble man (II.ii) is juxtaposed against a humble man's presentation of himself as a god (II.iii).

The treatment of the central human figures, Gallathea and Phillida, also represents a significant advance both in the development of Lyly's art and in the evolution of Renaissance drama. Not only are both central figures now women but their masculine disguises allow them a freedom not normally available to their sex, while their mutual passion places them in an amusing but highly pathetic situation. The result is a kind of comedy that depends not upon the conventional rituals of heterosexual courtship but upon the conflicting impulses within a sensitive individual caught between the pressure to advance imposed by disguise and the instinct to withdraw dictated by sex, and between an intellectual awareness of the futility of the situation and an emotional commitment to its maintenance. The wooing scenes produced by these conflicting impulses are characterized by delicate wordplay, obliquity, wistfulness, and regret, and they were to exercise a considerable influence upon the work of Shakespeare.

The closure of the first Blackfriars theater did not bring to an end Lyly's relationship with the boy actors. During the second half of the decade he appears to have been the principal dramatist for the Children of St. Paul's, his plays being performed both at the troupe's own theater in the cathedral precincts and at court. Though he seems to have lost Oxford's patronage around 1588, his hopes of courtly preferment were high, in that there is evidence to suggest that during this period the Queen herself proposed that he should consider himself as a candidate for the Reversion of the Revels (the position of putative successor to the Master of the Revels).

Four plays belong to this period of Lyly's career: *Endimion*, *Love's Metamorphosis*, *Midas*, and *Mother Bombie*. The first of these, *Endimion*, is very closely related in terms of both structure and theme to Lyly's earlier compositions. Once again, the plot turns upon a poignant amatory relationship involving an insuperable barrier between lovers and sets up an opposition between love and chastity. Endimion, caught up in a hopeless passion for Cynthia (the moon goddess), is cast into a forty-year sleep by his former love, Tellus (an earth goddess), from which he is awakened only by the devotion of his friend Eumenides, who discovers that he can be roused by a kiss from Cynthia and persuades the goddess to waken him. Into this main action is woven the love of Eumenides for the disdainful Semele (whom he also wins by his devotion), that of the jailor, Corsites, for Tellus (who is in love with Endimion), and the ludicrous passion of the braggart Sir Tophas for the enchantress, Dipsas, the whole tissue of frustrated relationships being interleaved with the comments of philosophers on the one hand and, more prominently, of witty pages on the other. The play's emphasis upon flux also forges a link with previous compositions. The presiding goddess is Cynthia, embodiment of chastity but also of change (and hence a synthesis of the deities of *Gallathea*), while all the principal dramatis personae undergo an alteration of person or affections. The play itself, like its predecessors, insists upon its elusiveness (for example, "for there liueth none vnder the Sunne, that knowes what to make of the Man in the Moone"), while, as in *Sapho and Phao*, the implied equation between the central female character and the Queen, together with a tissue of dreams and visions, invites a range of topical interpretations.

However, *Endimion* is more than an amalgam of modes and themes of earlier comedies. Its organization is more complex than that of any of its predecessors in that it involves more lines of action, while a greater number of debate issues (such as love versus friendship, art versus nature) are elicited from its design, frustrating any simple statement with regard to its meaning. More important, unlike the plays up to and including *Gallathea*, the significance of the action does not arise solely from an assemblage of situations and perspectives. The characters are more fully differentiated than in previous plays, and one level of meaning arises from the contrasts that are set up between the responses of individuals placed in comparable situations. Thus, while from one angle *Endimion* might be regarded as among the more remote and abstract of Lyly's works, with its overt allegorical structure, nonnaturalistic action, and emphasis on ideas, from another it appears a more popular composition, with a greater degree of narrative interest and a wider spectrum of characters–Sir Tophas, in particular, affording amusement, not as the embodiment of an untenable intellectual position, but through his absurdity as a human being. It is probably this greater degree of engagement with character and event and the possible application of both to Elizabethan court life, that accounts for the inclusion of the play in so many nineteenth- and twentieth-century anthologies of Renaissance drama.

Love's Metamorphosis, by contrast, is an uncompromisingly stylized composition. Whereas *Endimion* is by far the longest of Lyly's plays and combines a number of areas of dramatic interest, *Love's Metamorphosis* is much the shortest of his extant works, with only two strands of action (there is no subplot of witty pages), few scenes, and a comparatively small cast. Nevertheless, the play is very closely related to the comedies which precede it, being heavily dependent upon *Gallathea* in terms of structure and theme. As in the earlier drama, the action opens in a pastoral setting and adjacent to a grove of trees and a seacoast, the stage being dominated by a tree associated with one of the play's principal deities. The plot involves the mollification of a divine being whose place of devotion has been violated, together with the punishment by Cupid of a group of nymphs who have slighted his power–the resolution of both elements being achieved by a compromise between the offended gods. Once again, the concept of mutability is inherent from the outset, with a variety of metamorphoses having taken place before the start of the play or occurring in the course of it, while the theme of transformation is universalized through imagery and by such general observations as "in my affections shall there be no staiednesse but in vnstaiednes." The dramatic technique of the two plays is also similar. Both expositions evolve through patterned repetition, while the serial entries of III.i echo those of the corresponding scene of the earlier play. However, *Love's Metamorphosis* is not simply an exercise in repetition. A rigorous process of selection has transformed the prismlike structure of *Gallathea* into a design remarkable for its simplicity, clarity of outline, and sense of completeness. Whereas, in the earlier play, a variety of incidents, from the misadventures of apprentices to the mutual passion of maidens, projected a complex image of a world in process of transmutation and capable of being perceived in more than one way at any given moment, in *Love's Metamorphosis* all the elements of the composition concern some aspect of love and contribute to an inclusive definition of that concept. Similarly, the dramatis personae, rather than being placed in situations that call forth divergent and conflicting responses, exhibit one unambiguous facet of amatory experience, from lust to spiritual love, their schematic opposition producing an anatomy of an emotional condition. In short, where *Gallathea* presents its audience with a series of potentialities upon which the mind of the spectator imposes a final meaning, *Love's Metamorphosis* projects a sharply defined image of a multifaceted state.

Not unnaturally, of all Lyly's plays *Love's Metamorphosis* relies most heavily on emblem. For example, the three scornful maidens, Nisa, Celia, and Niobe, are all transformed into objects representative of their natures, while the setting itself is highly emblematic. Cupid's temple stands at the center of the stage, with properties suggesting chastity on the one hand and lust on the other positioned on either side of it; Protea's transformations take place on the seashore; and Erisichthon's lovelessness is symbolized by his destruction of Ceres' tree. The use of emblem forms a link with a third play in this group, *Midas*, in which the ass's ears that appear on the hero's head are a visual representation of the folly he exhibits throughout. In other respects, however, *Midas* stands aside from the main body of Lyly's work. The prologue suggests that it was written to conform with a shift in public taste

Title page for the 1594 quarto edition of the only play by Lyly that has its roots in Roman New Comedy (R. Warwick Bond, ed., The Complete Works of John Lyly, volume 3, 1902)

that ran counter to the artistic principles of the dramatist himself, and the play lacks much of the richness of previous compositions. Though the subject of love is not wholly excluded, the plot does not turn, like those of earlier plays, upon man's amatory nature, and hence there is no place for the evasive exchanges in which Lyly's lovers excel. The structure lacks the complexity of previous creations, the action falling into two halves corresponding to two tales by Ovid (of Midas's golden touch and preference for the music of Pan to that of Apollo) which constitute the source. Debate, which forms the starting point of virtually all Lyly's work but which is subsumed into a more intricate exploration of ideas in the majority of plays, is here the basic structural principle, with Midas making a series of improper choices among the various options proposed. Above all, the play lacks the multifacetedness of the major works. The moral implications of Midas's choices are clear-cut, with his daughter Sophronia functioning as a mouthpiece for right action unambiguously perceived. Overt references to contemporary events set up a clear equation between Midas and Philip II of Spain, limiting the implications of the action and leaving no room for the ambivalent responses elicited by earlier plays. Nevertheless, in some ways *Midas* is still closer to the court comedies as a group than to the fourth play of this period, *Mother Bombie*. It draws heavily upon classical mythology, with the gods playing a major part in events. The action revolves around a monarch and his court, and the principal characters display their refinement through their dramatic idiom. A strong sense of pattern underlies the evolution of the action, with attention focused, not upon individualized experience but the significance of the choices that are made. Metamorphosis remains a central concern, Midas initially being endowed with the ability to change all things to gold and then undergoing a transformation himself. Opportunities for spectacle and set piece abound, while the nonnaturalistic mode is emphasized by the use of music and song.

Mother Bombie, by contrast, represents a radical departure from this formula. The gods play no part in the dramatic action; the concerns of the play are domestic rather than courtly; and the dramatic interest lies in intrigue, rather than in an unfolding pattern of ideas. Two rich old men, each having a mentally defective child but ignorant of the deficiencies of the other's offspring, plot to bring about a marriage between their children, while two other old men, who oppose a love match between their issue, plan to marry their children to the fools, of whose intellectual limitations they know nothing. The plans of all the fathers are circumvented by their servants who succeed in marrying the lovers to one another. The foolish offspring, Maestius and Serena, are then revealed to be supposititious, while a further pair of lovers, who had believed themselves to be siblings of low birth, are revealed to be the true Maestius and Serena, and are thus at liberty to marry.

The plot of the play clearly relies heavily upon Roman New Comedy, rather than being rooted, like those of Lyly's earlier compositions, in debate, and it is upon the outcome of the action, rather than in a structure of ideas, that the interest of the play lies. Thus, whereas in the earlier plays, the intellectual dexterity of the dramatis personae was an index to their sensitivity and an instrument for the exploration of antithetical concepts, in *Mother Bombie* it becomes a means of achieving a desired goal, with the characters with the greatest play of mind winning the approbation of the audience, not for the delicacy of their perceptions but for their ability to manipulate others. The lovers, who had formerly occupied the center of Lyly's stage, have consequently given way to the witty servants, who, like their classical predecessors, out-maneuver their masters for the benefit of the younger generation. The descent from deities to domestics as the controlling agency within the play, together with the familiarity of the setting (the action takes place, for all the classical nomenclature, in Rochester), strip the play of the abstract, ethereal quality characteristic of earlier works, while opportunities for spectacle are much more limited than in the changing worlds of the more courtly comedies.

Nevertheless, *Mother Bombie* cannot be dismissed simply as a changeling in the Lylian canon. The exposition is conducted in the highly stylized manner characteristic of earlier works, with act one introducing a succession of fathers, each concerned with the matrimonial prospects of a child. The love of complexity, expressed through a "maze of conceits" in preceding comedies, is here manifested through a labyrinthine plot which more than doubles the convolutions of its Terentian counterparts, while the capabilities of the boy actors are, as always, exploited through the use of song and witty repartee. Above all, the geometric outline of the composition is softened by the curious title figure whom the dramatist has grafted onto the classical structure. Mother Bombie is a fortune-teller who plays no essential part in the action but who knows the outcome of events in advance, so that, in one sense, the play takes place within her mind. The presence of this character, and the ambiguous relationship of the action to her, give the play a strangeness quite alien to the inherited form on which it is based.

Two nondramatic ventures brought Lyly's most productive decade to a close. In 1589 he appears to have been asked by the bishops to contribute to the Martin Marprelate controversy—a pamphlet war occasioned by a decree of 1586 seeking to stem the rising tide of Presbyterian tracts. Though the Marprelate pamphlets themselves are among the finest prose satires of the period, the replies by the professional men of letters who

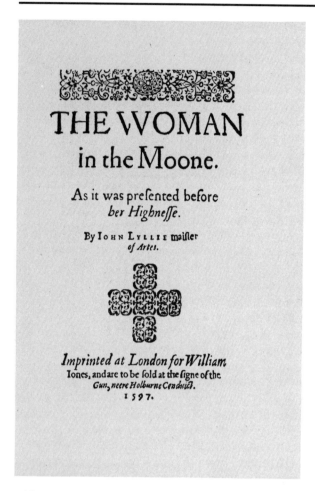

Title page for the 1597 quarto edition of Lyly's last play (R. Warwick Bond, ed., The Complete Works of John Lyly, *volume 3, 1902)*

were employed to rebut them are less distinguished, and Lyly's *Pap with a Hatchet* is no exception. As the title indicates, the work aspires to the raciness of the Martinist publications, but it lacks their satirical thrust, descending to pointless ribaldry and abuse. In the same year, possibly through the patronage of the bishops on whose behalf *Pap with a Hatchet* was composed, Lyly was elected M.P. for the borough of Hindon in Wiltshire. The Parliament sat for less than two months, and there is no record of any contribution by Lyly to its debates, but his election is indicative both of his social standing and of the patronage he enjoyed.

Promising as his future must have seemed at this point, in fact, the beginning of the last decade of the century marks a downturn in Lyly's fortunes. In 1590 Paul's Boys, the company for which, either singly or as a combined troupe, all his plays were composed, came into conflict with the authorities and was suppressed, leaving him

with no outlet for his work. He appears to have left London not long afterward to take up residence in his wife's hometown of Mexborough, though he must have returned to the capital in February 1593 when he was again elected to Parliament, this time as the member for Aylesbury. It was probably during this period, 1591-circa 1594, that his last play, *The Woman in the Moon*, was composed, though for which company it was intended is not certain.

The Woman in the Moon is unique among Lyly's works in that in it he exchanges the euphuistic prose upon which his reputation had been founded for the medium current upon the public stage–blank verse. The prologue makes clear that the play is an experiment in an unfamiliar vein:

> Remember all is but a Poets dreame,
> The first he had in *Phoebus* holy bowre,
> But not the last, vnlesse the first displease,

while the multilevel staging and absence of witty pages also point to an attempt to adapt to the demands of a new kind of theatrical milieu. Nevertheless, the play has much in common with earlier compositions. The action is set in the most remote of all locations–Utopia–while the dramatis personae are deities, planets, and shepherds. The plot is designed to explain the presence of a woman in the moon, together with the man in the moon and his thorn bush, and thus moves toward the creation of myth rather than the definition of actuality. The meaning unfolds through set-piece scenes rather than realistic action, while the structure is interwoven with music and song. Lyly's preoccupation with change is also apparent. The plot turns upon Nature's creation of the beautiful Pandora "for a solace vnto men" and the ensuing resentment of the planets, who determine to subject her, in turn, to their influence. Pandora runs through a gamut of personalities, tormenting the shepherds who love her, until placed by Nature in the moon as the epitome of inconstancy. Pandora is not the only character to undergo a transformation, however. Stesias, a Utopian shepherd, assumes the guise of a woman, while the clown Gunophilus is changed to a thorn bush. Lyly's concern with the dual nature of the universe is also implicit throughout. For example, in the opening scene Nature tells Discord and Concord:

> your worke must prooue but one;
> And in your selues though you be different,
> Yet in my seruice must you well agree.

However, *The Woman in the Moon* cannot be defined simply in terms of an attempt to pour old wine into a new bottle. In some respects it represents two divergent developments from earlier structures that might have borne fruit in later plays had *The Woman in the Moon* met with success. On the one hand, from act three onward, the relationships between Pandora and the shepherds are presented in terms of a skilfully plotted intrigue (as in *Mother Bombie*) that demonstrates the dramatist's facility in handling a kind of comedy very different from that upon which his reputation as a playwright principally rests, while, on the other hand, the career of Pandora constitutes an anatomy of the female mind, assembled, like a jigsaw puzzle, before the eyes of the audience, and thus represents an entirely novel application of his "mosaic" technique. Both developments point to a kind of dramaturgy at a considerable remove from the conventional "debate" with which Lyly's name is so often associated.

The Woman in the Moon was presented at Court and clearly lends itself to courtly performance. It is hard to see, however, how it could have succeeded on the public stage, and with no other avenue open to him as a dramatist, it is not surprising that Lyly's association with the stage came to an end at this point. Nevertheless, his hopes of employment in London seem not to have deserted him. Early in 1595 he gave up his home in Mexborough to take up residence in the capital and the following year was reelected to Parliament for the constituency of Appleby. But the remaining years of his life brought only disillusion. His hoped-for preferment to the Reversion of the Revels never materialized, while his numerous powerful friends and acquaintances seemed unable to provide him with any employment. Though *Euphues* and the plays continued to appear on the bookstalls, his literary talents seem to have found no outlet during this period beyond the famous petitions which he addressed to the Queen asking for some recognition of his services. Even in these disillusioned epistles, however, the singular character of Lyly's genius is apparent. Though the writer is clearly embittered and his situation desperate, he presents his case with such elegance he leaves his reader poised between pity and respect. A single sentence will serve to sum up Lyly's view of his own career: "Thirteen years your Highness' servant, and yet nothing; twenty friends that though they say they will be sure, I find them sure to be slow; a thousand hopes, but all nothing; a hundred promises, but yet nothing." In 1601, while still pleading with the Queen for reward of any kind, "lands, goods, fines or forfeitures," he was once more reelected to Parliament, this time for his old constituency of Aylesbury, but his financial situation apparently continued to deteriorate. A year later his wife also petitioned the Queen for help, but it seems likely that Elizabeth's death in 1603 forestalled any projected favor. The steady expansion of Lyly's family during these years must have aggravated his problems, and he appears to have been in considerable financial difficulties when he died in 1606.

Lyly's career as a creative artist is among the most remarkable of the period. His very first work established him as one of the leading prose writers of the day, and it inaugurated a literary vogue, while his seemingly chance association with the Blackfriars precipitated him into the role of leading dramatist to Elizabeth's Court. Yet his star was eclipsed almost as rapidly as it rose. The reaction against euphuism was quick to set in, while the suppression of the boy actors and the emergence of Shakespeare shifted the focus of histrionic activity away from coterie drama to the public stage. Only ten years after Lyly's appearance on the literary scene his preeminence as a dramatist was wholly at an end, while his style was soon to be ridiculed as absurd and old-fashioned.

Nevertheless, Lyly's achievement during his brief period of ascendancy was considerable. He inaugurated a new kind of drama, one directed toward a highly sophisticated audience and designed, in his own words, "to moue 'inward delight, not outward lightnesse . . . soft smiling, not loude laughing" through the presentation of sensitive individuals poised between amatory commitment and reserve. His structures achieved a degree of polish unprecedented during the period, while his dialogue was without parallel for its elegance and wit. He transformed debate into an instrument for the projection of a vision of a universe founded upon the harmonious conjunction of opposites, creating a series of dramas that evade analysis through the variety of meanings they yield up. Above all, through the exquisite nature of his structures, settings, and dramatic language, together with his use of song and delicacy of sentiment, he succeeded in generating an aura of fragile loveliness in his plays that endows their central female characters with a charm unsurpassed on the Renaissance stage outside the work of Shakespeare.

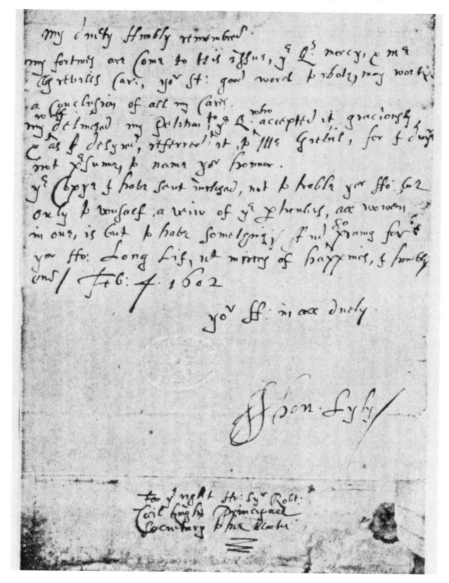

Letter to Secretary of State Sir Robert Cecil, 4 February 1603 (1602 according to the calendar then in use), in which Lyly asks Cecil to speak to Elizabeth I and Fulke Greville on behalf of a petition for help that Lyly's wife had given to the Queen, who had subsequently passed it to Greville (Cecil Papers 91/103, Hatfield House Library; by permission of the Marquess of Salisbury)

While being an important literary figure in his own right, Lyly is also of significance for the influence which he exerted. Not only did his two prose works produce a flood of imitations but the "dancing shadows" which he created on the stage clearly captured the imagination of his fellow dramatists. Robert Greene reworked *Campaspe* for the popular stage, while Shakespeare drew freely on the court comedies (particularly *Endimion* and *Gallathea*) for the structure of specific scenes (as in *Love's Labour's Lost*, IV.iii),

for the use of comic servants (as in *Love's Labour's Lost*), sexual disguise (as in *As You Like It* and *Twelfth Night*), and the handling of his female characters (as in *As You Like It* and *Twelfth Night*). As late as 1623, when the first folio of Shakespeare's works was published, Lyly is one of the four Renaissance dramatists mentioned by Ben Jonson in his commendatory verses, and it is interesting to note that he refers to him, not simply by his name, but as "our Lyly."

Lyly's influence did not extend far into the

seventeenth century, however. After the publication of a collected edition of his plays in 1632, his work fell into total neglect, and the recrudescence of interest in it in the nineteenth and early-twentieth centuries has owed more to its relationship with Shakespearian comedy than to its intrinsic merit. It was not until the publication of G. K. Hunter's *John Lyly: The Humanist as Courtier* in 1962 that the extent of Lyly's achievement began to be recognized, his reputation as a dramatist now being higher than it has been for nearly four hundred years. Modern scholars, in short, are at last coming to perceive that Lyly is a writer who can "court it with the best and scholar it with the most, in whom [one knows not whether one should] more commend his manners or his learning, the one so exquisite, the other so general" (Barnaby Rich).

Bibliography:

S. A. Tannenbaum, *John Lyly: A Concise Bibliography* (New York: S. A. Tannenbaum, 1940).

References:

J. A. Barish, "The Prose Style of John Lyly," *English Literary History*, 23 (March 1956): 14-35;

M. R. Best, "Lyly's Static Drama," *Renaissance Drama*, new series 1 (1968): 75-86;

A. Feuillerat, *John Lyly: Contribution à l'Histoire de la Renaissance en Angleterre* (Cambridge: Cambridge University Press, 1910);

Reavley Gair, *The Children of Paul's: The Story of a Theatre Company, 1553-1608* (Cambridge: Cambridge University Press, 1982);

Joseph W. Houppert, *John Lyly* (Boston: Twayne, 1975);

G. K. Hunter, *John Lyly: The Humanist as Courtier* (London: Routledge & Kegan Paul, 1962);

Hunter, *Lyly and Peele*, Writers and their Work, no. 206 (London: Longmans, Green, 1968);

G. Wilson Knight, "Lyly," *Review of English Studies*, 15 (April 1939): 146-163;

M. Mincoff, "Shakespeare and Lyly," *Shakespeare Survey*, 14 (1961): 15-24;

Harald Mitterman and Herbert Schendl, *A Complete Concordance to the Novels of John Lyly* (Hildesheim: Olms, 1984);

W. Ringler, "Immediate Source of Euphuism," *PMLA*, 53 (September 1938): 678-686;

Peter Saccio, *The Court Comedies of John Lyly* (Princeton: Princeton University Press, 1969);

Leah Scragg, *The Metamorphosis of "Gallathea": A Study in Creative Adaptation* (Washington, D.C.: University Press of America, 1982);

Michael Shapiro, *Children of the Revels* (New York: Columbia University Press, 1977);

J. Dover Wilson, *John Lyly* (Cambridge: Macmillan & Bowes, 1905).

Papers:

A number of Lyly's autograph letters are extant, including a group of four addressed to Sir Robert Cecil, discovered at Hatfield, and a fifth addressed to Sir Robert Cotton among the Cotton manuscripts in the British Library.

Christopher Marlowe

(February 1564-30 May 1593)

Roma Gill

PLAY PRODUCTIONS: *Dido Queen of Carthage*, Children of Her Majesty's Chapel, circa 1586;

Tamburlaine the Great, parts 1 and 2, London, Rose theater, 1587-1588;

The Jew of Malta, London, Rose theater, circa 1590;

The Massacre at Paris, London, Rose theater, circa 1590;

Edward II, Pembroke's Men, winter 1592-1593;

Dr. Faustus, London, Rose theater, 30 September 1594.

BOOKS: *Tamburlaine the Great . . . . Deuided into Two Tragicall Discourses* (London: Printed by R. Jhones, 1590);

The Tragedie of Dido Queene of Carthage (London: Printed by the Widdowe Orwin for T. Woodcocke, 1594);

The troublesome raigne and lamentable death of Edward the second, King of England (London: Printed by R. Robinson for W. Jones, 1594);

The Massacre at Paris: With the Death of the Duke of Guise (London: Printed by E. Allde for E. White, 1594?);

Certaine of Ouides Elegies, in *Epigrammes and Elegies*, by Marlowe and John Davies (Middleborugh [i.e. London], 1595?); enlarged as *All Ouids Elegies* (Middlebourgh [i.e. London], after 1602);

Hero and Leander (London: Printed by A. Islip for E. Blunt, 1598);

Lucans First Booke Translated Line for Line (London: Printed by P. Short, sold by W. Burre, 1600);

The Tragicall History of D. Faustus (London: Printed by V. Simmes for T. Bushell, 1604);

The Famous Tragedy of the Rich Jew of Malta, edited by Thomas Heywood (London: Printed by J. Beale for N. Vavasour, 1633).

Editions: *Christopher Marlowe: The Poems*, edited by Millar Maclure (London: Methuen/ Manchester: Manchester University Press, 1968);

The Plays of Christopher Marlowe, edited by Roma Gill (Oxford: Oxford University Press, 1971);

Complete Plays and Poems, edited by E. D. Pendry and J. C. Maxwell (London: Dent, 1976);

The Complete Works of Christopher Marlowe, revised edition, 2 volumes, edited by Fredson Bowers (Cambridge: Cambridge University Press, 1981);

The Complete Works of Christopher Marlowe, 1 volume to date, edited by Roma Gill (Oxford: Oxford University Press, 1987).

The achievement of Christopher Marlowe, poet and dramatist, was enormous–surpassed only by that of his exact contemporary, Shakespeare. A few months the elder, Marlowe was usually the leader, although Shakespeare was able to bring his art to a higher perfection. Most dramatic poets of the sixteenth century followed where Marlowe had led, especially in their use of language and the blank-verse line. The prologue to Marlowe's *Tamburlaine* proclaims its author's contempt for the stage verse of the period, in which the "jygging vaines of riming mother wits" presented the "conceits [which] clownage keepes in pay"; instead the new play promised a barbaric foreign hero, the "Scythian Tamburlaine, Threatning the world with high astounding terms." English drama was never the same again.

The son of John and Catherine Marlowe, Christopher Marlowe was born in Canterbury, where his father was shoemaker, in 1564. He received some of his early education at The King's School, Canterbury, and an Archbishop Parker scholarship took him from this school to Corpus Christi College in the University of Cambridge. In 1584 he graduated as Bachelor of Arts. The terms of his scholarship allowed for a further three years' study if the holder intended to take holy orders, and Marlowe appears to have fulfilled this condition. But in 1587 the University at first refused to grant the appropriate degree of Master of Arts. The college records show that Marlowe was away from Cambridge for considerable periods during his second three years, and

Portrait of a young man found in 1953 when workmen were repairing the Master's Lodge at Corpus Christi College, Cambridge. Authenticated as a genuine painting from the Elizabethan period, it is possibly a portrait of Christopher Marlowe, who—like the young man in the painting—was twenty-one and enrolled at Corpus Christi in 1585 (by permission of the Master, Fellows, and Scholars of Corpus Christi College).

the university apparently had good reason to be suspicious of his whereabouts. Marlowe, however, was not without some influence by this time: Archbishop Whitgift, Lord Burghley, and Sir Christopher Hatton were among members of Queen Elizabeth's Privy Council who signed a letter explaining, "Whereas it was reported that Christopher Morley was determined to have gone beyond the seas to Reames and there to remaine, Their Lordships thought good to certefie that he had no such intent, but that in all his accions he had behaved him selfe orderlie and discreetlie wherebie he had done her Majestie good service, & deserved to be rewarded for his faithfull dealinge . . . . " The reference to "Reames" makes everything clear. The Jesuit seminary at Rheims was the refuge of many expatriate Roman Catholics, who were thought to be scheming to over-

throw the English monarch: the Babington Conspiracy was plotted here—and its frustration in 1586 was achieved through the efforts of secret agents placed by Sir Francis Walsingham.

In 1587 Christopher Marlowe, M.A., went from Cambridge to London; and for the next six years he wrote plays and associated with other writers, among them the poet Thomas Watson and the dramatist Thomas Kyd. His friendship with Watson brought trouble: the two friends were arrested in 1589, charged with the homicide of William Bradley, and committed to Newgate Prison. Marlowe was released after a fortnight, and Watson (whose sword had killed Bradley) pleaded that he had acted "in self-defence" and "not by felony"; he was set free after five months in prison. The association with Kyd was also the cause of trouble some years later. In the spring of 1593

Kyd was arrested on a charge of inciting mob violence in riots against Flemish Protestants. His home was searched, and papers were found there containing "vile hereticall Conceiptes Denyinge the Deity of Jhesus Christ our Savior." Kyd denied that the document was his, asserting that the papers belonged to Marlowe and had been "shuffled with some of myne (unknown to me) by some occasion of our wrytinge in one chamber twoe yeares synce." Perhaps Kyd, a professional scrivener, had been transcribing the manuscript for Marlowe–who was not, however, the author (the ideas had been published in 1549 by John Proctor under the title *The Fal of the Late Arrian*). Riots combined with the plague made the spring of 1593 an unusually tense period; and the Privy Council (Archbishop Whitgift and Lord Burghley were still members, as they had been in 1587) acted quickly on Kyd's information and instructed a court messenger "to repaire to the house of Mr. Tho: Walsingham in Kent, or to anie other place where he shall understand Christofer Marlow to be remayning, and . . . to apprehend, and bring him to the Court in his Companie. And in case of need to require ayd." Marlowe–who had perhaps retreated to Kent in order to avoid the plague which had closed the London theaters–was commanded to report daily to the council. The treatment was proper for a gentlemen: a lesser person would have been imprisoned.

Attempting to exculpate himself from the charges of heresy and blasphemy, and to deny any continuing friendship with his former chamber mate, Kyd sent two letters to the Lord Chancellor, Sir John Puckering. In the first he affirmed Marlowe's ownership of the papers that had been "shuffled" with his own, declaring "That I shold love or be familiar frend, with one so irreligious, were very rare . . . besides he was intemperate & of a cruel hart." In the second he enlarged upon the subject of "marlowes monstruous opinions," offering examples of how Marlowe would "gybe at praiers, & stryve in argument to frustrate & confute what hath byn spoke or wrytt by prophets & such holie men."

Kyd was not alone in making such accusations at this time. Puckering also received a note from a certain Richard Baines, who may have been a government informer and had previously been arrested with Marlowe at Flushing in 1592. On this occasion the Governor of Flushing commented in a letter which he sent to Lord Burghley along with the prisoners, that "Bains and he

[Marlowe] do also accuse one another of intent to goe to the Ennemy or to Rome, both as they say of malice one to another." In 1593 Baines denounced Marlowe for his "Damnable Judgement of Religion, and scorn of gods word." Marlowe, he said, had stated

> That the first beginning of Religioun was only to keep men in awe. . . .
> That Christ was a bastard and his mother dishonest . . . .
> That if there by any god or any good Religion, then it is in the papistes because the service of god is performed with more Cerimonies, as Elevation of the mass, organs, singing men, Shaven Crownes & cta. that all protestantes are Hypocriticall asses. . . .

It is perhaps understandable that the Elizabethans, fearful for their Church and their State, should have given some credence to these wild statements, but it is astonishing to find that some readers of Marlowe's works–to the present day–are prepared to accept the slanders of Kyd and Baines and believe in Marlowe's "atheism."

Although such slanders have affected the dramatist's reputation, they did no harm to the man. By the time Puckering received Kyd's second letter and the note from Baines, Marlowe was probably already dead.

Marlowe's death and the events which immediately preceded it are fully documented in the report of the inquest (which was discovered by Leslie Hotson and published in *The Death of Christopher Marlowe*). The report tells of a meeting at the house of Mrs. Eleanor Bull in Deptford–not a tavern, but a house where meetings could be held and food supplied. On 30 May 1593 Marlowe spent the whole day there, talking and walking in the garden with three "gentlemen." In the evening there was a quarrel, ostensibly about who should pay the bill, "*le recknynge*"; in the ensuing scuffle Marlowe is said to have drawn his dagger and wounded one of his companions. The man, Ingram Frizer, snatched the weapon and "in defence of his life, with the dagger aforesaid of the value of 12d. gave the said Christopher then & there a mortal wound over his right eye of the depth of two inches & of the width of one inch; of which mortal wound the aforesaid Christopher Morley then & there instantly died." Ingram Frizer was granted a free pardon within one month, and returned to the service of the Walsinghams. One of his accomplices was Robert

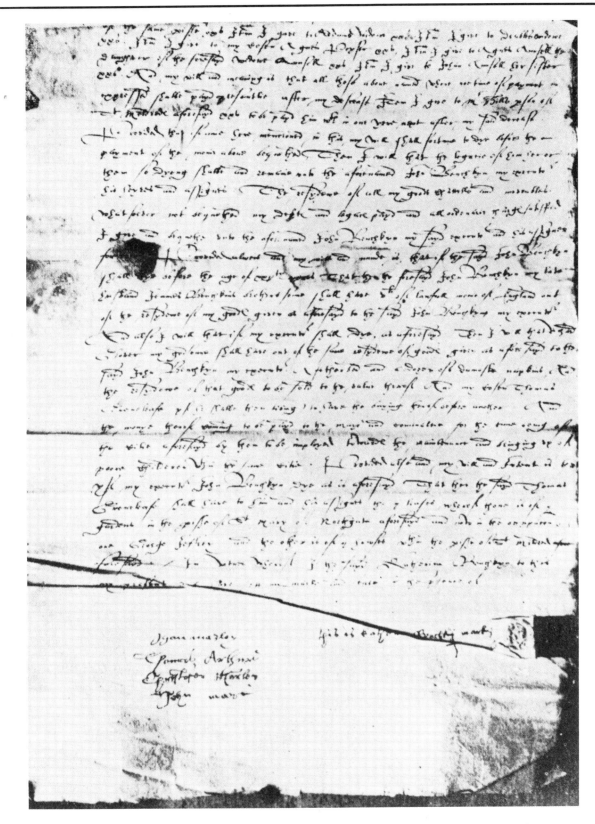

Last page of the will of Katherine Benchkyn, witnessed November 1585 by Christopher Marlowe (third signature, lower left) (by permission of the Kent Record Office, Maidstone). The other witnesses were John Morley, Marlowe's father; Thomas Arthur, probably Marlowe's uncle; and John Moore, Marlowe's brother-in-law.

Poley, the man largely responsible for the discovery of the Babington Conspiracy in 1586. The third man was Nicholas Skeres, who may have been the "Skyrres" who was with Poley and some of the conspirators shortly before the discovery. Such a combination of events and personalities makes it unlikely that this was a mere tavern brawl.

Some contemporary moralists seized on the story with an unholy glee; in 1597, for example, Thomas Beard recognized in it "a manifest signe of Gods judgement ... in that hee compelled his owne hand which had written those blasphemies to be the instrument to punish him, and that in his braine, which had devised the same." The poets were more generous: Thomas Nashe described Marlowe as "a diviner Muse" than Musaeus; George Peele called him "the Muses' darling"; and Michael Drayton observed in him "those brave translunary things That the first poets had." This early appreciation has extended over the years, so that now most critics–sharing the benefits of hindsight–would agree with A. C. Swinburne that Marlowe was "the father of English tragedy and the creator of English blank verse." According to Havelock Ellis, "Marlowe's place is at the heart of English poetry"; and T. S. Elliot even predicted "the direction in which Marlowe's verse might have moved ... [which was toward] ... intense and serious and indubitably great poetry."

In his 1592 letter to Lord Burghley, the Governor of Flushing described his prisoners and said that Marlowe was "by his profession a scholar." Marlowe's earliest writings are certainly those one would expect from a learned man–at the beginning of his career. Marlowe began writing verse by translating the Roman poets Ovid and Lucan. He could well have encountered Lucan while he was at grammar school; and at school too he would have read some of Ovid's verse–but not the *Amores,* which he chose to translate.

The Latin poems are written in the elegiac meter: a hexameter line followed by a pentameter. They show Ovid at his most sophisticated, writing of love in many different aspects with complete confidence in his linguistic brilliance. Marlowe's translations of these elegies are not uniformly successful; but they nevertheless form an impressive achievement. For the Latin elegiac couplet, Marlowe substituted the rhymed pentameter couplet–which John Donne later followed, imitating Marlowe with his own elegies. Instead of the polished artifice with which Ovid manipulated

his inflective language, Marlowe wrote with the directness of the spoken voice, using the range and variety of speech tones to approach the "masculine perswasive force" for which Donne is so highly esteemed. The couplet and the speaking voice often combine to give a dramatic immediacy and wit to lines such as these from elegy 18 of book two, where the poet makes his excuses for writing of love when he should be contemplating epic matters:

> Often at length, my wench depart, I bid,
> Shee in my lap sits still as earst she did.
> I sayd it irkes me: halfe to weping framed,
> Aye me she cries, to love, why art a shamed?
> Then wreathes about my necke her winding armes,
> And thousand kisses gives, that worke my harmes:
> I yeeld, and back my wit from battells bring,
> Domesticke acts, and mine owne warres to sing.

Here the closing of the couplet enacts the speaker's resignation as well as bringing to a close the first section of the poem.

There are forty-eight poems in the collection *All Ovids Elegies,* and many are less satisfying than this one. Sometimes Marlowe seems to be bored with his work and snatching at the most obvious English word without reflecting on its aptness ("admonisht" for *admonitus);* at other times the exigencies of rhyme force the English language new strange shapes to take ("forbod" to rhyme with "god"); and often the attractive circumlocutions of the Latin are rendered with a pedantry which assumes an ignorant readership (the worst example is the translation of Ovid's pretty reference to the birth of Bacchus in III.iii *"non pater in Baccho matris haberet opus"* becomes "The fathers thigh should unborne *Bacchus* lacke"). More often, however, we see the praiseworthy attempts of a young poet to master the foreign language *and* his native tongue–and on occasion we see the genesis of a notion which is developed later in his career.

The translating of book one of Lucan's epic poem the *Pharsalia* was in many ways less demanding than the translating of the *Amores:* the poem's narrative line and the medium (blank verse) were better guides to Marlowe–and when his comprehension of the Latin was inadequate, he had a copiously annotated commentary to help him. Neither this translation nor that of the *Amores* can be dated with any accuracy, but it seems likely that such academic–and apprentice– work would be undertaken at a time of (comparative) leisure such as the Cambridge years. For the

Beginning of Richard Baines's 1593 letter denouncing Marlowe for his "Damnable Judgement of Religion, and scorn of gods word" (Harleian MS 6648, f. 185; by permission of the British Library)

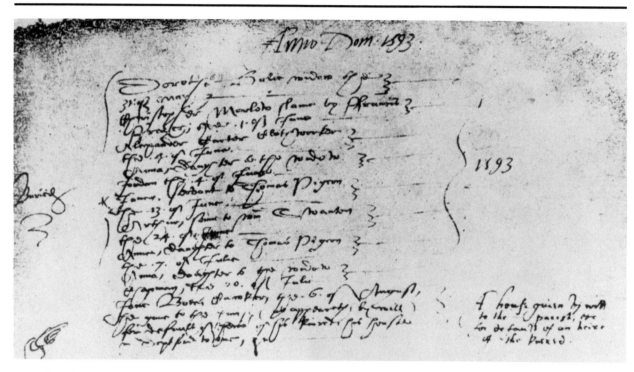

A portion of a page from the register of the Church of St. Nicholas, Deptford, listing the burial on 1 June 1593 of "Christopher Marlow slaine by ffrancis ffrezer" (by permission of the Church of St. Nicholas, Deptford)

nation, these were times of political tension, with events such as the unmasking of the Babington Conspiracy, the execution of Mary, Queen of Scots, and the threat of the Spanish Armada. In literature the national unease manifested itself in works such as Lodge's play *The Wounds of Civil War* and Shakespeare's *Henry VI* trilogy. In this context book one of *Pharsalia* takes on a new dimension: it is not merely an academic and personal exercise but a warning of grim topicality against the horrors and dangers of civil butchery. Lucan's Centurion promises to wage war against his city at Caesar's command, even if he should "Intombe my sword within my brothers bowels;/ Or fathers throate. . . [.]" The lines may be compared with the stage direction which, for Shakespeare, indicated the greatest of civil (and natural) disorders: *"Enter a Sonne that hath kill'd his Father . . . and a Father that hath kill'd his Sone"* (*Henry VI*, part three, II.v).

In the preface to his translations of *Ovid's Epistles* (1680) John Dryden distinguished three kinds of translation, of which the first was "that of Metaphrase, or turning an Author word by word, and line by line, from one language into another." Marlowe's translations of Ovid and Lucan are of this kind—which is good reason to suppose that they are early works, where Marlowe might be reluctant to allow himself too much freedom

because he lacked the confidence to use it. Dryden's second method offers greater scope: "Paraphrase, or Translation with Latitude," which is a useful term to describe Marlowe's handling of Virgil's *Aeneid* for what was probably his first play, *Dido Queen of Carthage.*

Dryden explained "Paraphrase" by saying that in this kind of translation "the Author is kept in view by the Translator, so as never to be lost, but his Words are not so strictly followed as his Sense, and that too is admitted to be amplified, but not altered." Marlowe took the plot of his play from book six of Virgil's poem, but he moved easily around the epic, taking details from books one and two for his dramatic purposes. His translation changes the Latin into English, transforms epic narrative into stage action, and takes the part for the whole—the story of Dido occupies only one twelfth of the *Aeneid*, so that the episode can be viewed *sub specie aeternitatis.*

Another difference—which is of great importance for the appreciation of the play—is that whereas Virgil's characters are superhuman, of proper epic proportions, Marlowe's are slightly less than human in size: they were meant to be acted by children. The title page of the first quarto edition advertises that the play was "Played by the Children of her Majesties Chappell." The plays written for these highly professional children obeyed conventions different from those obtaining in plays written for adult performers: *Dido* is more appropriately compared—in respect of its technique—with the plays of Peele than with *Antony and Cleopatra* (whose subject matter is comparable).

Marlowe took from Virgil the account of Dido's passion for Aeneas, the Trojan hero shipwrecked on the Carthaginian coast after the destruction of Troy, and he added a subplot of the unrequited love of Anna, Dido's sister, for one of Dido's suitors, whose name—Iarbus—is mentioned only infrequently in the *Aeneid*. Virgil's hero is a man of destiny, ordained by the gods to sail to Italy and there establish the Roman race, the true descendants of the Trojans. The interlude with Dido is only a part of the divine plan, and Aeneas must not allow himself to be detained in Carthage, even though his departure is a tragic catastrophe for the Queen. Virgil's gods are always in control of the action.

Marlowe introduces the gods at the beginning of his play, daringly presenting them as a bunch of rather shabby immortals subject to very human emotions: Venus is anxious for the welfare of her shipwrecked son, Aeneas; Juno is jealous of Venus and irritated by her husband's infidelities; and Jupiter is besotted with a homosexual passion for Ganymede. This is a grotesquely "domestic" comedy, which might seem to endanger the tragic stature of the play's heroine and the epic status of its hero, since both Dido and Aeneas are at the mercy of such deities. The character of Aeneas has provoked varying reactions in critics of the play (one sees him as "an Elizabethan adventurer"; another adopts the medieval view in which he is the betrayer of Troy; and for yet another he is the unheroic "man-in-the-street" who has no desire for great actions). Dido, however, is unambiguously sympathetic. At first a majestic queen, she becomes almost inarticulate as she struggles with a passion that she does not understand; her grief at Aeneas's departure brings back her eloquence, and then, preparing for death, she achieves the isolated dignity of a tragic heroine. The inarticulateness was described by Virgil (*incipit effari, mediaque in voce resistit*), and Marlowe adds the immediacy of speech when in III.iv Dido is overcome with love:

> AENEAS. What ailes my Queene, is she falne sicke of late?
> DIDO. Not sicke my love, but sicke:—I must conceal

> The torment, that it bootes me not reveale,
> And yet Ile speake, and yet Ile hold my peace,
> Doe shame her worst, I will disclose my griefe:—
> *Aeneas*, thou art he, what did I say?
> Something it was that now I have forgot.

At the end of the play Marlowe does not translate the Latin, and this has been called by Harry Levin "an evasion that smells of the university." Rather, it shows Marlowe's respect, both for his author and for his audience. The lines that he takes from Virgil are beautiful—and well known: he could not hope to equal them. When the stage Aeneas is adamant to Dido's entreaties, he utters the words of the epic hero (which include one of the best-known half lines in all poetry): *"Desine meque tuis incendere teque querelis,/Italiam non sponte sequor."* ("Cease to inflame both me and yourself

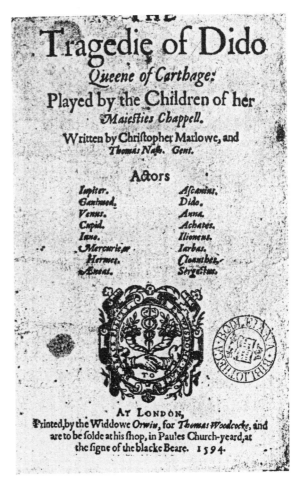

Title page for the 1594 quarto edition of the play Marlowe based on the story of Dido in book six of Virgil's Aeneid (Bodleian Library, Oxford). Thomas Nashe may have prepared the manuscript for publication, but he is not believed to have had a hand in the play's composition.

with your lamentations. It is not of my own free will that I seek Italy.") And Dido's last words, as she curses Aeneas before her self-immolation, are the words of Virgil–but the dramatic moment is intensified by the interpolation of an English line:

> *Littora littoribus contraria, fluctibus undas*
> *Imprecor: arma armis: pugnent ipsíque nepotes:*
> Live false *Aeneas*, truest *Dido* dyes,
> *Sic sic juvat ire sub umbras.*

("I pray that coasts may be opposed to coasts, waves to waves, and arms to arms; may they and their descendants ever fight . . . . Thus, thus I rejoice to enter into the shades.")

Implicit tribute is paid in these lines not only to the verse of Virgil and the understanding of the audiences but also to the skills of the child actors, who were chosen from the (already highly selected) boys of the royal choirs and given special coaching for their theatrical roles. Writers in the sixteenth century such as Peele and Lyly (and in the seventeenth century, Jonson and Middleton) were proud to write for such companies, recognizing that special demands were made on them to exploit the assets and minimize the limitations of the child actors.

Immaturity was the most obvious limiting factor: verisimilitude was not to be looked for, and the presentation of "character" (in the modern sense of the word) was clearly impossible. Instead the productions compensated by offering spectacle, where the emphasis was always on artifice and where imitation was always ready to draw attention to itself qua imitation–expecting applause for the excellence of its craftsmanship in equalling (and, if possible, surpassing) nature. For example, an Oxford boys' production of an entertainment in 1583 was reported with wonder, for there was "a goodllie sight of hunters with full crie of a kennel of hounds . . . the tempest wherein it hailed small confects, rained rose water, and snew an artificial kind of snew, all strange, marvellous, and abundant" (in John Nichols, *The Progresses, and Public Processions, of Queen Elizabeth,* 1788-1807). The dramatists' choice of subject matter also emphasized the artificiality of the performances: boys with unbroken voices took the parts of the great figures from classical mythology–"Hercules and his load too," as Rosencrantz tells Hamlet.

The great strength of the children was their *elocution,* taught as part of the discipline of rhetoric in every Elizabethan grammar school. It included not only the training of the voice but practice in the appropriate accompanying gestures and facial expressions. And the child actors were, of course, far more accomplished than the average schoolboy. Marlowe's play calls for such talent–especially in Aeneas's account of the Fall of Troy, where more than sixty lines are punctuated only occasionally by comments from the other character, orchestrating pity and terror in fine narrative verse.

The play was published in 1594, and the title page claims Thomas Nashe as part author–but there is no trace of his hand in the composition. Perhaps Nashe secured, or even transcribed, the manuscript for publishers eager to take advantage of the notoriety of Marlowe's death and unable to obtain possession of the other plays since these were all the valued property of adult theatrical companies.

The earliest of these plays had, however, already been published: the two parts of *Tamburlaine the Great,* subtitled *Two Tragicall Discourses,* appeared in print in 1590, two or three years after the plays were performed by the Admiral's Men. The first of these "Discourses" appears to be complete in itself, leaving the eponymous hero triumphantly alive at the end of act five, where he announces that now *"Tamburlaine* takes truce with al the world." The second "Discourse" opens with a prologue which testifies to the popularity of the first, explaining its own raison d'être:

> *The generall welcomes* Tamburlain *receiv'd,*
> *When he arrived last upon our stage,*
> *Hath made our Poet pen his second part[.]*

At the end of this play's act five, "earth hath spent the pride of all her fruit": Tamburlaine is dead.

In outline, the action of *Tamburlaine* is simple. The hero of part one, a Scythian shepherd of boundless aspiration, encounters no serious opposition in his rise to power and majesty. By force, either of rhetoric or of arms, he overcomes all resistance–winning allies, conquering kings and kingdoms, and captivating the beautiful Zenocrate. The play ends with amatory as well as martial triumph, anticipating the "celebrated rites of mariage." In part two the opposition grows and is not merely human in origin: Tamburlaine is disappointed in his sons; Zenocrate falls sick and dies; lastly Tamburlaine himself is

The verse sweeps to its climax at the end of the paragraph, verbally enacting the speaker's breathless impetuousness and captivating audiences just as Tamburlaine's person vanquishes all resistance.

But the play does not ask for *uncritical* applause, either for the character or for the "high astounding tearms" of his utterances. Marlowe is well aware that both ambition and hyperbole are potentially ludicrous, and in the first scene he encourages laughter, thereby establishing criteria for the appreciation of his protagonist.

The very first lines of the play, spoken by Mycetes, King of Persia, make the proper association between personality and linguistic command:

> Brother *Cosroe*, I find my selfe agreev'd,
> Yet insufficient to expresse the same:
> For it requires a great and thundring speech [.]

Marlowe demonstrates the comic range of such "thundring speech" as soon as Mycetes attempts to speak as befits his dignity. His comedy includes the grimly incongruous–in the description of "milk-white steeds"

> All loden with the heads of killed men.
> And from their knees, even to their hoofes below,
> Besmer'd with blood, that makes a dainty show.

There is even one of the crude "conceits [which] clownage keeps in pay" which are scorned in the prologue:

> MYCETES. Well here I sweare by this my royal seate–
> COSROE. You may doe well to kisse it then.
> MYCETES. Embost with silke as best beseemes my
>   state [.]

The folly and weakness of Mycetes justify Cosroe in his determination to overthrow his brother and wear the crown himself; and this act of usurpation serves to justify Tamburlaine in his subsequent decision.

Tamburlaine first appears in the company of Zenocrate, to whom he offers comfort and protection. Although he is dressed as a shepherd, his behavior is more like that of a knight in some medieval romance. Before our eyes, he seems to increase in stature as he sheds his humble garments ("weedes that I disdaine to weare") and exchanges them for "adjuncts more beseeming"–a "compleat armour" and a "curtle-axe." So accoutred, he is compared by his companions to a lion (the emblem of kingship), and he himself refers

---

Title page for the 1590 octavo edition of the two-part tragedy whose "high astounding tearms" were both imitated and parodied by Marlowe's contemporaries (C. F. Tucker Brooke, ed., The Works of Christopher Marlowe, 1910)

forced to confess that "sicknesse proove[s] me now to be a man."

The play's style suits the character. In verses prefixed to the first folio edition of Shakespeare's plays (1623), Ben Jonson referred to "Marlowe's mighty line," and it is in part one of *Tamburlaine* that this line is evolved, especially when in II.vii the hero enunciates his credo:

> Nature that fram'd us of foure Elements,
> Warring within our breasts for regiment,
> Doth teach us all to have aspyring minds:
> Our soules, whose faculties can comprehend
> The wondrous Architecture of the world:
> And measure every wandring plannets course:
> Still climing after knowledge infinite,
> And alwaies mooving as the restles Spheares,
> Wils us to weare our selves and never rest,
> Untill we reach the ripest fruit of all,
> That perfect blisse and sole felicitie,
> The sweet fruition of an earthly crowne.

to "Empires"; but the first impassioned speech is made to Zenocrate–and Tamburlaine is thereby associated with beauty, jewels, love, and richness, rather than bloodthirsty conquests. The advance of the Persian horsemen also places Tamburlaine in a favorable position for winning the sympathy of the audience–he asks the Soldier to confirm the enemy numbers: "A thousand horsemen? We five hundred foote?" Undeterred he outlines a stratagem and declares his willingness to combat against far greater odds–"Weele fight five hundred men at armes to one"–and to face the foe himself–"My selfe will bide the danger of the brunt."

By the end of act two, Tamburlaine is secure in his position of "super-man," because he has been seen to deserve it and to be morally as well as physically superior to those he has defeated. He reaches a pinnacle of success in act three, when he fights against the Turkish Emperor Bajazeth.

The Turk's proud boasts overtop Tamburlaine's own claims, and Bajazeth is accompanied by apparently powerful allies–so that once again Tamburlaine's army seems to be heavily outnumbered. Furthermore, Tamburlaine is now presented as a defender of the faith, opposed to the infidel Turks and promising to

> inlarge
> Those Christian Captives, which you keep as slaves,
> Burdening their bodies with your heavie chaines,
> And feeding them with thin and slender fare,
> That naked rowe about the Terrene sea.

The battle is splendidly managed. Fought offstage, its progress is commented on by Zabina and Zenocrate, who also wage a verbal battle which parallels the conflict of the warriors. But although Tamburlaine once again deserves victory, his treatment of the conquered Bajazeth gives rise to audience suspicion that he is beginning to overreach himself.

For the rest of part one, and throughout most of part two, Marlowe balances scenes of great brutality, performed with a ritual solemnity, against speeches of amazing beauty in praise of Zenocrate and in lament for her death. Themes of ambition, love, power, and justice are introduced in part one and developed further in part two, so that the two parts form a symphonic unity.

Increasingly in part one and throughout the whole of part two, Tamburlaine images himself as "the Scourge and Wrath of God," the instru-

ment of some divine retribution; this must be accepted by the audience–who must also recognize (as an Elizabethan audience certainly would acknowledge) that the scourge itself must be scourged and destroyed. Even Tamburlaine seems sporadically aware of this fact–as when, at the death of Zenocrate, he inveighs in II.iv against the

> Proud furie and intollorable fit,
> That dares torment the body of my Love,
> And scourge the Scourge of the immortall God [.]

Thus admiration (for the valor) and horror (at the cruelty) are tempered with respectful anticipation of the inevitable catastrophe.

The style of *Tamburlaine* was immediately infectious: but imitation soon turned to parody and then to scorn. In *Timber* Ben Jonson warns his "true Artificer" that the language of his play should not "fly from all humanity, with the *Tamerlanes,* and *Tamer-Chams* of the late Age, which had nothing in them but the *scenicall* strutting, and furious vociferation, warrant them to the ignorant gapers." The actor responsible for the *"scenicall* strutting" was Edward Alleyn, the star performer of the Admiral's Men, for whom Marlowe wrote this play. For Alleyn, also, he created the role of Barabas in his next play, *The Jew of Malta.*

Internal evidence (mainly stylistic) suggests that *The Jew of Malta* was written circa 1589; it was frequently performed by The Admiral's Men in the years immediately following Marlowe's death, and the recorded "box-office receipts" testify to its popularity. There was no printed text until 1633 when a quarto edition was published carrying new prologues and epilogues written by Thomas Heywood; it seems likely that Heywood was also responsible for a complete revision of the play–but the full extent of his revising cannot be ascertained. In both of his new prologues Heywood alludes to the play's antiquity: addressing the "Gracious and Great" in the "Prologue spoken at Court," he explains that *The Jew of Malta* was "writ many years agone," and he adds that it was "in that Age, thought second unto none."

The play has always been "second unto none" in the sense that nothing else in English drama is quite like it: it has no place in any recognizable dramatic tradition. The theme of *radix malorum cupiditas* is not unknown in English drama. Shakespeare's Shylock is a distant relation of Marlowe's Barabas, and Jonson's Volpone

*Portrait of Edward Alleyn, who played the roles of Tamerlaine
and Barabas in* The Jew of Malta *(by permission of the
Dulwich College Picture Gallery, London)*

shares his interest: but these similarities only emphasize the differences between *The Jew of Malta*
on the one hand, and *The Merchant of Venice* or
Volpone on the other.

Marlowe's play has no obvious source. The
action is set on the tiny Mediterranean island of
Malta, which at the end of the sixteenth century
was a Spanish possession occupied by the
Knights of St. John Hospitaller after their expul-
sion from Rhodes in 1522. Marlowe's Knights
(and audience) are reminded of this fact in II.ii:

> Remember that to *Europ's* shame,
> The Christian Ile of *Rhodes*, from whence you came,
> Was lately lost, and you were stated here
> To be at deadly enmity with Turkes.

The Knights of the play, however, have a truce
with the Turks, to whom they owe a tribute. In
order to pay this tribute Ferneze, the Governor
of Malta, determines to levy tax on the island's
Jews, who must either pay one half of their estates, or else be converted to Christianity. The

wealthiest Jew, Barabas, rejects both alternatives. To punish him, Ferneze confiscates his entire property; the rest of the play shows Barabas's efforts to reinstate himself—he in fact becomes Governor of Malta—and to take revenge on those who have injured him. There follows a rapid succession of murders: Ferneze's son, who is in love with the Jew's daughter, fights a duel—in which both he and his rival are killed; Abigail, the object of their affections, is poisoned—and an entire convent of nuns dies with her; two suspicious friars quarrel—one is strangled and the other hanged; Ithamore, a villainous Turkish slave who has been Barabas's instrument, is poisoned before he can betray his master—a prostitute and her pimp die with him; a monastery housing the Turkish forces is blown up while their leader is preparing to banquet with Barabas—but the leader (the son of the Turkish emperor) is saved when Ferneze operates the mechanism which should have precipitated him into a cauldron of boiling water. It is Barabas who is boiled to death, caught in his own trap; and he dies with a fine, melodramatic defiance: "Dye life, flye soule, tongue curse thy fill and dye."

The speed with which these crimes are dispatched encourages in the spectator the detachment appropriate to comedy, precluding any sympathy with the victims. And only Abigail is presented as an attractive character—"The hopelesse daughter of a haplesse Jew." Her death is pathetic: in III.vi she expires in the arms of the friar who converted her, with the laudable sentiment

> ah gentle Fryar,
> Convert my father that he may be sav'd,
> And witnesse that I dye a Christian.

But pathos is immediately dissolved in laughter with the friar's response: "I [Aye], and a Virgin too, that grieves me most." None of the other murder victims emerges as more than a comic stereotype—the romantic lover, the avaricious friar (an anti-Catholic caricature), a slave whose curriculm vitae includes "setting Christian villages on fire, Chaining of Eunuches, binding gally-slaves," and a prostitute lamenting the decline of trade in Malta ("my gaine growes cold ... now against my will I must be chast").

In contrast to all these Barabas is presented as a richly unique character. A "bottle-nos'd knave," he opens the play as a mercantile adventurer, discovered "*in his Counting-house, with*

heapes of gold before him." Absorbed in his enterprises, he is a businessman who keeps his accounts straight. In I.i he says,

> So that of thus much that returne was made:
> And of the third part of the Persian ships,
> There was the venture summ'd and satisfied.

But he soon shows frustration and envy:

> Fye; what a trouble tis to count this trash.
> Well fare the Arabians who so richly pay
> The things they traffique for with wedge of gold [.]

Ambition turns him into a dreamer—a visionary lost in the admiration of

> Bags of fiery *Opals, Saphires, Amatists,*
> *Jacints,* hard *Topas,* grasse-greene *Emeraulds,*

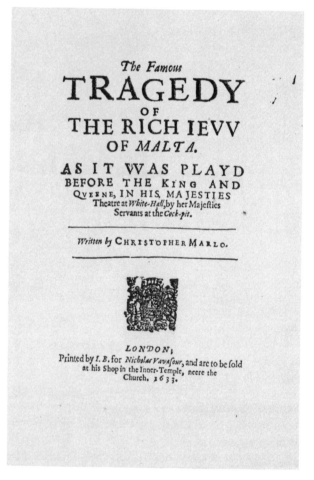

Title page for the 1633 quarto edition of the play that—according to Thomas Heywood, who added new prologues and epilogues to this first printing of Marlowe's popular tragedy—was "writ many years agone" and was "in that Age, thought second unto none" (Anderson Galleries, sale number 2032, 15-16 February 1926)

Beauteous *Rubyes*, sparkling *Diamonds*,
And seildsene costly stones. . . [.]

The speech builds to a crescendo, rising to one of Marlowe's best-known lines when Barabas longs to "inclose/Infinite riches in a little roome." There are further revelations to come, but already we (as audience or readers) have begun to understand Barabas; we are more inward with him than any of the other dramatis personae. This sense of intimacy is developed in the ensuing action through the use of asides which allow us to feel superior to the other characters–to the Jews, for instance, when later in I.i Barabas seems to be promising his support:

> 2. JEW. But there's a meeting in the Senate-house,
>   And all the Jewes in *Malta* must be there.
> BARABAS. Umh; All the Jewes in *Malta* must be
>   there?
>   I [Aye], like enough, why then let every man
>   Provide him, and be there for fashion-sake.
>   If any thing shall there concerne our state
>   Assure your selves I'le looke——*unto my*
>   *selfe.*   *Aside.*

Barabas is also a sympathetic character in that, at the beginning of the play, he is a man more sinned against than sinning: the victim of prejudice, his fault lies in his Jewishness–and the Knights of Malta are prepared to use religion as a cloak for theft when they take the Jews' property to pay the Turks. Barabas discloses their hypocrisy–"Preach me not out of my possessions."

In this confrontation of Jew and Roman Catholic, Marlowe is presenting two objects of fear, hatred, and suspicion to the Elizabethan Protestants who formed the play's contemporary audience. As Christians, the Elizabethans believed the Jews to be the race that betrayed and crucified their God; but as Englishmen they recognized in Roman Catholicism a threat to their church and their monarch. From the very beginning of the play there is a complexity of emotional response which is by no means reconciled at the end of act five.

By overreaching himself in his villainy Barabas, like Tamburlaine in the earlier play, has alienated the audience; his ignominious death in the cauldron–standard Elizabethan punishment for the poisoner–is seen to be most appropriate. At the same time, it is impossible to share in the unctuous piety of Ferneze's closing couplet: "let due praise be given/Neither to Fate nor Fortune, but to Heaven." It is, perhaps, the last joke of this early "black comedy."

THE
MASSACRE
AT PARIS:

With the Death of the Duke
of Guife.

As it was plaide by the right honourable the
Lord high *Admirall* his Seruants.

Written by *Chriftopher Marlow.*

AT LONDON
Printed by *E. A.* for *Edward White,* dwelling neere
the little North doore of S. Paules
Church at the figne of
the Gun.

Title page for the 1594(?) octavo edition of the play that Marlowe must have written after the death of Henry III of France in August 1589 (Bodleian Library, Oxford)

Marlowe seems to be well acquainted with the history of Malta–whence Jews were expelled in 1422 unless they cared to purchase Christian baptism at the price of forty-five percent of their individual estates. In the 1580s the island seems to have had a particular interest for the English. There were suspicions–still imperfectly understood–of conspiracies and espionage which might have been known to Marlowe, whose interest in politics and current events did not cease with his Cambridge career.

This interest is clearly evidenced by *The Massacre at Paris*, a play linked stylistically with *The Jew of Malta* by its grim humor. The date of *The Massacre at Paris* is unknown: it was performed in 1593, and must have been written after the death, in August 1589, of Henry III of France. The first scenes of the play present the bloody violence of the French riots in 1572, when more than thirty thousand French Protestants were murdered at the hands of Roman Catholics led by the Duke of Guise (drawing support from Catherine de Medici). The play ends after Guise has been murdered (December 1588) at the instigation of Henry III, and when Henry himself is dying, passing the French crown to Henry of Navarre (Henry IV of France). Among the accusations made against Guise is the rhetorical reminder

> Did he not draw a sorte of English priestes
> From Doway to the Seminary at Remes,
> To hatch forth treason gainst their naturall Queene?
> Did he not cause the King of *Spaines* huge fleete,
> To threaten *England* . . . ?

Marlowe could, of course, have gained this information from the printed sources that he was using; but it must not be forgotten that he may well have been at Rheims in the service of Walsingham and the Privy Council. Just before his death Henry III addresses the "Agent for *England*," instructing him to "send thy mistres word, What this detested Jacobin [the Duke of Guise] hath done"; swearing to "ruinate that wicked Church of *Rome*," he vows his loyalty to the Protestant cause, "And to the Queene of *England* specially,/ Whom God hath blest for hating Papestry." The "Agent for *England*" at the time of Henry III of France was Walsingham himself.

Unfortunately, *The Massacre at Paris* survives only in a pitifully mangled form, and the undated octavo edition cannot offer adequate material for an assessment of Marlowe's work. There are the traces of a fine theatricality in the very first scene, where the religious tensions are shown at the wedding of the Protestant Navarre to the Catholic Margaret–a union which Catherine de Medici threatens to "desolve with bloud and crueltie." The character of Guise is presented with typical Marlovian ambivalence: unquestionably a brutal, ruthless murderer, he nevertheless is possessed of aspiration and a high disdain which in themselves are praiseworthy:

> That like I best that flyes beyond my reach.
> Set me to scale the high Peramides,
> And thereon set the Diadem of *Fraunce,*
> Ile either rend it with my nayles to naught,
> Or mount the top with my aspiring winges,
> Although my downfall be the deepest hell.

And although Henry III's deeds are sanctioned by his Protestant sympathies, the character is not given uncritical approval: his hypocrisy is blatant, and we are clearly shown the weakness to which

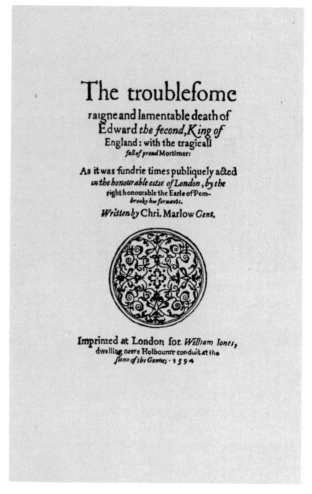

Title page for the 1594 quarto edition of the play that Marlowe may have written for a provincial touring company (C. F. Tucker Brooke, ed., The Works of Christopher Marlowe, *1910)*

Queen Catherine draws attention: "His minde you see runnes on his minions." In this last respect, the character seems to adumbrate the protagonist of *Edward II.*

The eponymous hero of this play on the subject of English history is the only one of Marlowe's protagonists who is totally lacking in the charismatic energy with which the rest are driven, and which is voiced in the "high astounding tearmes" of *Tamburlaine.* This was not a part designed for Edward Alleyn.

According to the title page of the first (1594) edition, *Edward II* was "sundrie times publiquely acted in the honourable citie of London, by the right honourable the Earle of Pembrooke his servants." Pembroke's Men seem to have been a scratch troupe of actors who toured the provinces in time of plague; in September 1593 they were penniless and forced to disband, pawning their costumes and selling their playbooks. Marlowe might have written his play especially for this company: it demands few elaborate costumes and asks for no multilevel staging, and in such respects it would suit a touring company. But it offers no roles comparable with those of Tamburlaine, Barabas, or Dr. Faustus—the parts played by Alleyn for the Admiral's Men.

Most of the events of *Edward II* were taken from Holinshed's *Chronicles of England* (1597). The five acts of Marlowe's play span twenty-three years of English history, from the accession of Edward II in 1307 until the events of 1330 when Mortimer's treachery was discovered. Edward was a weak king, besotted by love for his "minion," Piers Gaveston. Neglecting—and even abusing—both his queen and the realm, he was imprisoned and cruelly murdered.

The play also shows the rise to power and "the tragicall fall of proud Mortimer." At first Mortimer is an impetuous patriot, resenting the honors which the King bestows on Gaveston because the country is thereby impoverished. But ambition leads him to rebel. He becomes the Queen's lover; forces Edward to resign the crown to his son; and takes upon himself the position of Protector to the young King. For a short time he can gloat over his power, saying in V.iv:

> Now all is sure, the Queene and *Mortimer*
> Shall rule the realme, the king, and none rule us,
> Mine enemies will I plague, my friends advance,
> And what I list commaund, who dare controwle?
> *Major sum quam cui possit fortuna nocere.*
> ("I am great beyond Fortune's harm.")

He has arranged the murder of Edward, who dies in agony; but the crime is discovered, and the new King condemns Mortimer to a traitor's death.

Sympathies in this play are never fixed, and the characters are unusually complex. From a passionate patriot Mortimer becomes a Machiavellian usurper and a sadistic regicide. Isabella, the Queen, is at first (in II.iv) a cruelly wronged wife, "Whose pining heart, her inward sighes have blasted,/And body with continuall moorning wasted." Love and obedience are eventually destroyed, and she finds comfort in Mortimer's gentle courtesy. Soon she is quite dominated by her lover: in IV.vi we are told by the Earl of Kent (always a useful guide to the direction our sympathies should take) that "*Mortimer* And *Isabell* doe kisse while they conspire," and in V.ii the Queen herself acknowledges her new love:

> Sweet *Mortimer*, the life of *Isabell*,
> Be thou perswaded, that I love thee well,
> And therefore so the prince my sonne be safe,
> Whome I esteeme as deare as these mine eyes,
> Conclude against his father what thou wilt,
> And I my selfe will willinglie subscribe.

Isabella's rival for her husband's attentions is the young Frenchman, Piers Gaveston. He too is a character who develops—or at least changes—during the course of the play's action. He opens the play with a soliloquy, outlining schemes he has devised to "draw the pliant king which way I please"; although he speaks of Edward with affection, it is certain that self-interest is a powerful motivating force. As the play progresses, however, it becomes equally certain that his self-interest gives way to an unselfish love that overcomes the bitterness of captivity and the imminence of an ignoble death—in II.iv, for example, Gaveston looks forward to a final meeting with his lover: "Sweete soveraigne, yet I come To see thee ere I die."

Toward Edward II Marlowe's attitude (and consequently *our* attitude) seems to be ambivalent. Edward is a danger to the country's stability in his free dispensation of offices and wealth to a commoner. Wailing over Gaveston's departure, or on tiptoe with excitement at his return, the King is ludicrous. And the husband who flaunts a lover before his wife, making her acceptance of Gaveston the condition for the continuance of their marriage, is utterly despicable. Against such charges Marlowe sets the solitary redeeming fact that Edward loves Gaveston:

> MORTIMER. Why should you love him, whome the world hates so?
> EDWARD. Because he loves me more then all the world.

Edward is a man of extremes, swerving violently from the blackest depression to carefree exuberance with no intervening stage of reasonable moderation. In his death he is the object of intense pity—and admiration.

Edward's death is a parody of the homosexual act. The details were supplied by history, and Marlowe accumulated them from various chronicle sources. The King is arrested at the Abbey of Neath, where he has tried to find sanctuary among friends and sympathizers; in IV.vii Marlowe, the poet of striving and aspiration, becomes the poet of weariness and despondency:

good father on thy lap
Lay I this head, laden with mickle care,
O might I never open these eyes againe,
Never againe lift up this drooping head,
O never more lift up this dying hart!

It is the last comfort he will find. After his capture he is bundled "from place to place by night," shaved in puddle water, and finally imprisoned in a stinking cell–"the sincke/Wherein the filthe of all the castell falles" and where "One plaies continually upon a Drum." Edward recounts his pitiful story to Lightborn, a character of Marlowe's own imagination, who is in fact the murderer. Lightborn is subhuman, a machine for murder. He is the only character in the play who has no emotional response to Edward, and his heartless efficiency seems to intensify the King's muddled, suffering humanity. For one moment Edward becomes a king again as in V.v, with an almost habitual grace, he bestows his last jewel–"Know that I am a king . . . ."

Not until he lost his throne did Edward rise to kingship, and the sad eloquence of his final speeches is in contrast to the empty rhetoric that precedes them. The "mighty line" is subdued in this play, whose characteristic modes are irony and deflation: when in IV.iv Isabella begins a peroration to justify the rebellion against Edward, she is abruptly silenced by Mortimer:

QUEENE. ....
   Misgoverned kings are cause of all this wrack,
   And *Edward* thou art one among them all,
   Whose loosnes hath betrayed thy land to spoyle,
   And made the channels overflow with blood,
   Of thine own people patron shouldst hou be
   But thou——
MORTIMER. Nay madam, if you be a warriar,
   Ye must not grow so passionate in speeches [.]

Only Mortimer is allowed to hold up the play's action with a heroic parting speech, but the words of stoical courage are preceded and followed by references to Mortimer as "traitor" and "murderer" which effectively reduce the speech's impact.

Frustration and weakness are Marlowe's themes in *Edward II*. There is no superman hero–and the soaring splendor of *Tamburlaine*'s verse would be inappropiate here. In his next play, *Dr. Faustus*, Marlowe sets the mighty lines of the hero's aspirations in a critical balance against the

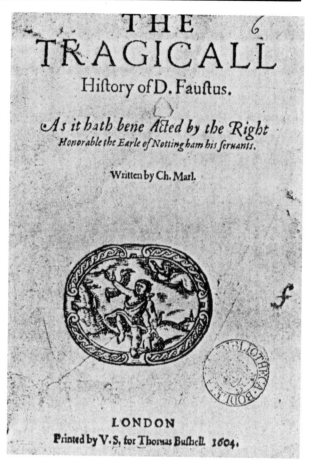

Title page for the unique copy of the 1604 quarto edition of the play that may have been left unfinished at Marlowe's death in May 1593 (Antiq.e E 1588[3]; Bodleian Library, Oxford)

cool tones of experience, achieving thereby a tragedy which is still–in the twentieth century–able to startle and terrify with its thoughtful intensity.

At the beginning of the play Faustus, having excelled in all branches of human knowledge, finds his intellectual ambitions still unsatisfied: although as a physician, for instance, he has achieved renown in the treatment of "thousand desperate maladies," he longs for greater power:

Couldst thou make men to live eternally,
Or being dead, raise them to life againe,
Then this profession were to be esteem'd.

At last he turns to Divinity, but upon opening the Bible he is confronted with an apparently insoluble dilemma when he juxtaposes two sentences: "The reward of sin is death"; and "If we say that we have no sinne we deceive our selves, and there is no truth in us." From these two premises he proceeds to the syllogism's logical conclusion:

> Why then belike
> We must sinne, and so consequently die,
> I [Aye], we must die, an everlasting death.

Throwing his books aside, he opts for the study of magic, resolving be this means "to get a Deity."

In I.iii, with his first invocation, he conjures up the devil, Mephostophilis, and makes a bargain with him: in exchange for twenty-four years of power and knowledge, when Mephostophilis will be his servant, Faustus will hazard his immortal soul. Mephostophilis, a surprisingly honest devil, tries to dissuade the eager conjurer by painting a bleak picture of the torments of the damned

> Think'st thou that I who saw the face of God,
> And tasted the eternall Joyes of heaven,
> Am not tormented with ten thousand hels,
> In being depriv'd of everlasting blisse?
> O *Faustus* leave these frivolous demandes,
> Which strike a terror to my fainting soule.

Faustus is undeterred, refusing to believe "that after this life there is any paine." At the devil's request he writes a formal legal document in his own blood, which is "A Deed of Gift, of body and of soule."

For the next twenty-four years he pursues knowledge and pleasure, but finds only disappointment. All the time he is accompanied by two Angels, Good and Evil; the former urges him to turn to God in repentance and hope for mercy, while the Evil Angel persuades him that he cannot repent, that he can never be forgiven, and that "devils will teare [him] in peeces" if he attempts to break the promise he has made to the devil. In the last act of the play he twice conjures up the spirit of Helen of Troy—the first time for the benefit of his scholar friends, who have requested to see "the admirablest Lady that ever lived." The second conjuration is for his own delight and comfort; he asks for Helen as his "paramour,"

> Whose sweet embraces may extinguish cleare,
> Those thoughts that do disswade me from my vow,
> And keepe mine oath I made to *Lucifer*.

The second appearance of Helen calls forth from Faustus the most famous lines that Marlowe ever wrote:

> Was this the face that Launcht a thousand ships,
> And burnt the toplesse Towers of *Ilium*?
> Sweet *Hellen* make me immortall with a kisse:
> Her lips sucke forth my soule, see where it flies.

Such hyperbole is by no means uncommon in the love poetry of the sixteenth century, but here there is a cruel irony. In Helen's embraces Faustus "from [his] soule exclud[es] the grace of heaven" (V.i) and indeed assures himself of immortality—"in hell for ever" (V.ii).

The final soliloquy enacts his last hour on earth and reverses the movement of the first soliloquy. The proud scholar, who had fretted at the restrictions imposed by the human condition and longed for the immortality of a god, now seeks to escape from an eternity of damnation. To be physically absorbed by the elements, to be "a creature wanting soule," "some brutish beast," even—at the last—to be "chang'd into little water drops": this is the final ambition of the man who had once tried "to get a Deity." Time is the dominant. in this speech. The measured regularity of the opening gives way to a frantic tugging in two directions as Faustus is torn between Christ and the devil: "O I'le leape up to my God: who puls me downe?" The pace and passion increase as the clock strikes relentlessly, and the second half hour passes more quickly than the first. We are agonizingly aware of the last minutes of Faustus's life, trickling away like sand through the hourglass with what seems like ever-increasing speed. But as each grain falls, bringing Faustus closer to his terrible end, we become more and more conscious of the deserts of vast eternity and damnation that open up beyond death.

The critic Leo Kirschaum said in 1943 that "there is no more obvious Christian document in all Elizabethan drama than *Doctor Faustus*" (*Review of English Studies*). But its ideology is not simple. The form is, in some respects, that of the old morality plays—with two significant differences. Firstly, the central figure is not the generic Everyman: Dr. Faustus is an individual, with a history (born in Germany, "within a Towne cal'd *Rhode*," to parents "base of stocke") and an impressive curriculum vitae. And, in the second place, the fate of this individual is not that of the type character, whose fall into sin is condemned and then—before the end of the play—redeemed.

It is important to remember that Marlowe spent some time as a student of theology; and a close reading of *Dr. Faustus* reveals the dramatist's recollections of his study. Dr. Faustus sins willfully: he has full knowledge of the consequences of his deed (even though he does not believe in the reality of the threatened hell), and in II.i he takes complete responsibility:

> MEPHOSTOPHILIS. Speake *Faustus,* do you deliver this as your Deed?
> FAUSTUS. I [Aye], take it, and the devill give the good of it.

Throughout the play there is a conflict in Faustus's mind, encouraged and expressed by the two Angels, as in these lines from II.ii:

> GOOD ANGEL. *Faustus* repent, yet God will pitty thee.
> BAD ANGEL. Thou art a spirit, God cannot pity thee.

Orthodox theology taught that the devils–in this context "spirit" is a synonym–were by their very nature incapable of repentance and therefore of receiving divine forgiveness; and Faustus acknowledges this doctrine when he hears the two promptings and responds:

> FAUSTUS. Who buzzeth in mine eares I am a spirit?
> Be I a devill yet God may pitty me,
> Yea, God will pitty me if I repent.
> BAD ANGEL. I [Aye], but *Faustus* never shall repent.
> FAUSTUS. My heart is hardned, I cannot repent [.]

He confesses to despair–a "deepe despaire" which even prompts him to suicide, but which is overcome by "sweete pleasure."

The triviality in the central scenes of the play has often drawn attention away from its profound seriousness. Acts three and four, where Faustus explores his magic powers, show scenes of slapstick farce and simple conjuring. Some suggestions for these scenes could have come from the prose narrative which was the main source of Marlowe's plot–*Das Faust-Buch* (1587) translated into English by 1592 as *The Historie of the Damnable Life and Deserved Death of Doctor John Faustus.* This prose work was a mixture of jestbook and moral fable, which offered also a guidebook to Europe and a tour of hell. But the storyteller's license was not available to the playwright, and the middle part of the dramatic *Dr. Faustus* is a disappointment.

But it is unlikely that Marlowe himself was responsible for this flaw. Perhaps the manuscript of the play, unfinished when Marlowe died in 1593,

came into the hands of the impresario Philip Henslowe, who found other writers to complete the piece for performance in 1594. Eight years later Henslowe recorded in his diary a payment to two hack dramatists, Samuel Rowley and William Birde, for their "adicyones" to *Dr. Faustus.* The play in its earlier form was not published until 1604 (the A Text); the later edition, published in 1616 (the B Text), incorporates the 1602 "adicyones." These complications of writing and printing make *Dr. Faustus* one of the major bibliographical problems of English literature.

Before his death, Marlowe had returned to the writing of nondramatic verse and was again working on a form of translation–the kind that Dryden describes as "imitation." In Dryden's sense, "imitation" does not seek to translate the words, or even the sense, of an author but "to set him as a pattern and to write as [the translator] supposes that author would have done, had he lived in our age and in our country." The "pattern" for Marlowe was Musaeus, a Greek poet of the fourth or fifth century A.D., whose narrative poem *Hero and Leander* earned him the title of "grammatikos"–which distinguished him as a scholarly writer, learned in the poetry, rhetoric, and philosophy of his own time and expert in the interpretation of the great authors of the past. Marlowe's poem is a worthy imitation; and to the necessary qualities of a "grammatikos" the English writer adds one more: wit.

The Greek poem briefly describes the first encounters of the two lovers and then narrates Leander's final attempt to swim the Hellespont on a winter's night; the youth was drowned, and his Hero died by his side. Marlowe's poem, however, is a comedy, lavishing care on the meeting of Hero, "*Venus* Nun," with the stranger from Abydos. The two lovers are described in great detail. Hero is a masterpiece of art–her footwear, for example, is a technological tour de force:

> Buskins of shels all silvered, used she,
> And brancht with blushing corall to the knee;
> Where sparrowes pearcht, of hollow pearle and gold,
> Such as the world would woonder to behold:
> Those with sweet water oft her handmaid fils,
> Which as shee went would cherupe through the bils.

The verse admires the elaborate luxury, while at the same time revealing its absurdity. In complete contrast to the description of Hero is Marlowe's portrait of Leander, which lingers erotically over the boy's naked body:

Even as delicious meat is to the tast,
So was his necke in touching, and surpast
The white of *Pelops* shoulder. I could tell ye,
How smooth his brest was, and how white his bellie,
And whose immortal fingers did imprint,
That heavenly path, with many a curious dint,
That runs along his backe. . . [.]

The admixture of comedy (especially through the rhymes) prevents the sensual and mythological richness from becoming self-indulgent.

Using persuasions taken from Ovid's *Amores*, Leander starts his seduction of Hero; he is at first a "bold sharpe Sophister," but quickly shows himself to be a "novice . . . rude in love, and raw." Hero responds by protecting herself, initially, with her status as priestess, but instinctive attraction soon leads to unconscious encouragement as "unawares *(Come thither)* from her slipt." She shows her true innocence when she opens the door to Leander, who has just swum across the Hellespont, and "seeing a naked man, she schriecht for feare,/Such sights as this, to tender maids are rare." Marlowe's poem moves toward a climax as the poet slowly describes the encounter of the two lovers which leads to the consummation of their love. The passage is splendidly orchestrated. It begins with the human comedy of Leander's appeal to Hero's pity ("This head was beat with manie a churlish billow,/And therefore let it rest upon thy pillow"); a second movement is the sympathetic presentation of Hero's conflicting emotions as she halfheartedly tries to ward off Leander's assaulting hands; then, after a brief and "metaphysical" comparison of Hero's breasts to "a globe," we reach the moment of Leander's triumph, when he achieves the status of a superman and, "like Theban *Hercules*," accomplishes his mission.

Hero and Leander reveals qualities in its author which the plays seem to suppress or deny: tenderness, sympathy, and generous humor which can laugh without cruelty. The poem is not without flaws, of course; but the achievement is great in itself and suggests enormous potential for the future, which can only be lamented in the words of the epilogue to *Dr. Faustus:*

Cut is the branch that might have growne full
straight,
And burned is *Apollo's* Lawrell bough,
That sometime grew within this learned man [.]

But Marlowe's actual achievement (rather than his unfulfilled potential) is best summed up in the words of a contemporary: Shakespeare's reference to Marlowe's death (in *As You Like It*) serves as an epitaph on the writer's work–it was "A great reckoning in a little room."

References:

John E. Bakeless, *The Tragicall History of Christopher Marlowe* (Cambridge: Harvard University Press, 1942);

J. Leslie Hotson, *The Death of Christopher Marlowe* (London: Nonesuch Press, 1925);

Paul H. Kocher, *Christopher Marlowe: A Study of his Thought, Learning, and Character* (Chapel Hill: University of North Carolina, 1946);

Constance Brown Kuriyama, *Hammer or Anvil: Psychological Patterns in Christopher Marlowe's Plays* (New Brunswick: Rutgers University Press, 1980);

Clifford Leech, *Christopher Marlowe: Poet for the Stage* (New York: AMS Press, 1986);

Leech, ed., *Marlowe: A Collection of Critical Essays* (Englewood Cliffs, N.J.: Prentice-Hall, 1964);

Harry Levin, *The Overreacher: A Study of Christopher Marlowe* (Cambridge: Harvard University Press, 1952);

J. B. Steane, *Marlowe: A Critical Study* (Cambridge: Cambridge University Press, 1964);

Judith Weil, *Christopher Marlowe: Merlin's Prophet* (Cambridge: Cambridge University Press, 1977).

Anthony Munday

(October 1560-August 1633)

Philip J. Ayres
Monash University

PLAY PRODUCTIONS: *Fedele and Fortunio,* translation and adaptation, attributed to Munday, of an Italian play by Luigi Pasqualigo, London, at Court, circa 1584;

John a Kent and John a Cumber, London, Rose theater, December 1594(?);

Mother Redcap, by Munday and Michael Drayton, London, Rose theater, 1597-1598;

The Downfall of Robert, Earl of Huntingdon, London, Rose theater, licensed 28 March 1598;

The Death of Robert, Earl of Huntingdon, by Munday and Henry Chettle, London, Rose theater, licensed 28 March 1598;

Richard Coeur de Lion's Funeral, by Munday, Chettle, Drayton, and Robert Wilson, London, Rose theater, June 1598;

Valentine and Orson, by Munday and Richard Hathway, London, Rose theater, July 1598;

Sir Thomas More, by Munday, with revisions by Thomas Dekker, Chettle, probably William Shakespeare, and perhaps Thomas Heywood, probably not produced, circa 1598;

The True and Honorable History of Sir John Oldcastle, parts 1 and 2, by Munday, Drayton, Hathway, and Wilson, London, Rose theater, October-December 1599;

Fair Constance of Rome, part 1, by Munday, Dekker, Drayton, Hathway, and Wilson, London, Rose theater, June 1600;

Fair Constance of Rome, part 2, by Munday, Hathway, and others, London, Rose theater, summer 1600;

The Rising of Cardinal Wolsey, by Munday, Chettle, Drayton, and Wentworth Smith, London, Fortune theater, August-November 1601;

Jephthah, by Munday and Dekker, London, Fortune theater, 1602;

Caesar's Fall, or The Two Shapes, by Munday, Dekker, Drayton, Thomas Middleton, and John Webster, London, Fortune theater, May 1602;

The Set at Tennis, London, Fortune theater, December 1602;

The Triumphs of Reunited Britannia, streets of London, 29 October 1605;

Camp-Bell, or The Ironmongers Fair Field, streets of London, 29 October 1609;

London's Love to Prince Henry, streets of London, 31 May 1610;

Chruso-Thriambos, streets of London, 29 October 1611;

Himatia Poleos, streets of London, 29 October 1614;

Metropolis Coronata, streets of London, 30 October 1615;

Chrysanaleia, streets of London, 29 October 1616;

Siderothriambos, streets of London, 29 October 1618;

The Triumphs of the Golden Fleece, streets of London, 29 October 1623.

BOOKS: *The Mirrour of Mutabilitie, or Principall Part of the Mirrour for Magistrates* (London: Printed by J. Allde, sold by R. Ballard, 1579);

The Paine of Pleasure (London: Printed by J. Charlewood for H. Car, 1580);

A View of Sundry Examples. Reporting Many Straunge Murthers (London: Printed by J. Charlewood for W. Wright, sold by J. Allde, 1580);

Zelauto. The Fountaine of Fame (London: Printed by J. Charlewood, 1580);

A Courtly Controuersie betweene Looue and Learning (London: Printed by J. Charlewood for H. Carre, 1581);

The Araignement and Execution of a Wilfull and Obstinate Traitor, named E. Ducket, alias Hauns (London: Printed by J. Charlewood for E. White, 1581);

A Breefe Discourse of the Taking of Edmund Campion (London: Printed by J. Charlewood for W. Wright, 1581);

A Discouerie of Edmund Campion and His Confederates (London: Printed by J. Charlewood for E. White, 1582);

A Breefe Aunswer Made vnto Two Seditious Pamphlets (London: Printed by J. Charlewood, 1582);

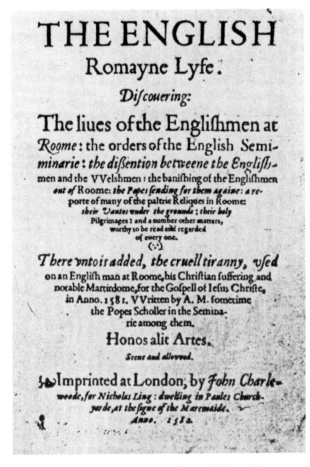

THE ENGLISH
Romayne Lyfe.

Dilcouering:

The liues of the Englifhmen at
Roome: the orders of the English Semi-
narie: the diſſention betweene the Engliſh-
men and the VVelshmen: the baniſhing of the Englifhmen
out of Roome: the Popes ſending for them againe: a reporte of many of the paltrie Reliques in Roome:
their Vauntes vnder the grounde: their holy
Pilgrimages: and a number other matters,
worthy to be read and regarded
of every one.

(∴)

There vnto is added, the cruell tiranny, vſed
on an Engliſh man at Roome, his Chriſtian ſuffering and
notable Martirdome, for the Goſpell of Ieſus Chriſte,
in Anno. 1581. VVritten by A. M. ſometime
the Popes Scholler in the Semina-
rie among them.

Honos alit Artes.

Seene and allowed.

Imprinted at London, by John Charle-
woode, for Nicholas Ling: dwelling in Paules Church-
yarde, at the ſigne of the Mermaide.

Anno. 1582.

Title page for the 1582 quarto edition of Munday's account of his stay at the English College in Rome (Bodleian Library, Oxford)

A Breefe and True Reporte, of the Execution of Certaine Traytours at Tiborne (London: Printed by J. Charlewood for W. Wright, 1582);

The English Romayne Lyfe (London: Printed by J. Charlewoode for N. Ling, 1582);

A Watch-Woord to Englande to Beware of Traytours (London: Printed by J. Charlewood for T. Hacket, 1584);

Fedele and Fortunio. The Deceites in Loue, translation and adaptation, attributed to Munday, of an Italian play by Luigi Pasqualigo (London: Printed by J. Charlewood [?] for T. Hacket, 1585);

A Banquet of Daintie Conceits (London: Printed by J. Charlewood for E. White, 1588);

The First Part of the True and Honorable Historie, of the Life of Sir J. Oldcastle, by Munday, Michael Drayton, Richard Hathway, and Robert Wilson (London: Printed by V. Simmes for T. Pavier, 1600);

The Downfall of Robert, Earle of Huntington, After-

ward called Robin Hood of merrie Sherwoode, by Munday, revised by Henry Chettle (London: Printed by R. Bradock for W. Leake, 1601);

The Death of Robert, Earle of Huntington, by Munday and Chettle (London: Printed by R. Bradock for W. Leake, 1601);

The Triumphes of Re-United Britania. Performed in Honor of Sir L. Holliday Lorde Mayor. 1605 (London: Printed by W. Jaggard, 1605);

Camp-Bell, or The Ironmongers Faire Field (London: Printed by E. Allde, 1609);

Londons Love, to the Royal Prince Henrie, Meeting Him at His Returne from Richmonde (London: Printed by E. Allde for N. Fosbrooke, 1610);

A Briefe Chronicle of the Successe of Times, from the Creation (London: Printed by W. Jaggard, 1611);

Chruso-Thriambos. The Triumphes of Golde. At the Inauguration of Sir J. Pemberton, in the Dignity of Lord Maior (London: Printed by W. Jaggard, 1611);

Himatia-Poleos. The Triumphes of Old Draperie. At the Enstalment of S'. T. Hayes in the High Office of Lord Maior (London: Printed by E. Allde, 1614);

Metropolis Coronata, The Triumphes of Ancient Drapery. In Honour of the Advancement of Sir J. Jolles, to the High Office of Lord Maior (London: Printed by G. Purslowe, 1615);

Chrysanaleia: The Golden Fishing: Or, Honour of Fishmongers. Applauding the Advancement of J. Leman, to Lord Maior (London: Printed by G. Purslowe, 1616);

Sidero-Thriambos. Or Steele and Iron Triumphing. Applauding the Advancement of Sir S. Harvey, to the Dignitie of Lord Maior (London: Printed by N. Okes, 1618);

A Suruay of London, by John Stow, continued and enlarged by Munday (London: Printed by G. Purslowe, 1618); completed by Munday, Humphrey Dyson, and others (London: Printed by E. Purslow, sold by N. Bourne, 1633);

The Triumphs of the Golden Fleece. For the Enstaulment of M. Lumley in the Maioraltie (London: Printed by T. Snodham, 1623).

Editions: *The Life of Sir John Oldcastle*, by Munday, Michael Drayton, Richard Hathway, and Robert Wilson; edited by Percy Simpson (London: Printed for the Malone Society, 1908);

Fidele and Fortunio, translation and adaptation, attributed to Munday, of an Italian play by Luigi Pasqualigo; edited by Simpson (London: Printed for the Malone Society, 1909);

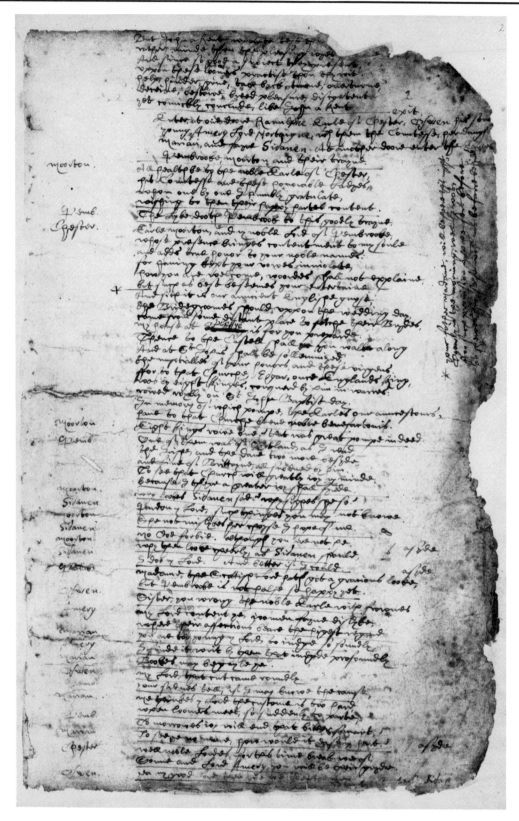

Page from the manuscript for John a Kent and John a Cumber. *This manuscript, in Munday's hand with notations by others, may have been used as a promptbook (HM 500, fol. 2'; by permission of the Henry E. Huntington Library and Art Gallery).*

supplement, edited by W. W. Greg (London: Printed for the Malone Society at Oxford University Press, 1933?);

The Book of Sir Thomas More, by Munday, with revisions by Thomas Dekker and Henry Chettle, probably William Shakespeare, and perhaps Thomas Heywood; edited by W. W. Gregg (London: Printed for the Malone Society at Oxford University Press, 1911);

The Downfall of Robert, Earl of Huntingdon, by Munday, revised by Chettle; edited by John C. Meagher (Oxford: Printed for the Malone Society at Oxford University Press, 1965);

The Death of Robert, Earl of Huntingdon, by Munday and Chettle; edited by Meagher (Oxford: Printed for the Malone Society at Oxford University Press, 1967);

The English Roman Life, edited by Philip J. Ayres (Oxford: Clarendon Press, 1980);

An Edition of Anthony Munday's John a Kent and John a Cumber, edited by Arthur E. Pennell (New York: Garland, 1980).

TRANSLATIONS: Anonymous, *The Famous, Pleasant, and Variable Historie, of Palladine of England*, translated by Munday from Claude Colet's French translation of part 1 of the romance *Florando de Inglaterra* (London: Printed by E. Allde for J. Perrin, 1588);

Palmerin de Oliva, *The Mirrour of Nobilitie*, part 1 (London: Printed by J. Charlewoode for W. Wright, 1588); parts 1 and 2 (London: Printed by T. Creede, 1597);

François de la Noue, *The Declaration of Lord de la Noue, vpon His Taking Armes* (London: Printed by J. Woolfe, 1589);

Francisco de Moraes, *The Honorable, Pleasant and Rare Conceited Historie of Palmendos* (London: Printed by J. Charlewood for S. Watersonne, 1589);

Anonymous, revised by Garci Ordóñez or Rodríguez Montalvo, *The First Book of Amadis of Gaule*, translated by Munday from Nicholas de Herberay's French translation of the original Spanish (London: Printed by E. Allde, 1590?); books 3 and 4 (London: Printed by N. Okes, 1618);

L.T.A., *The Masque of the League and the Spanyard Discovered* (London: Printed by J. Charlewoode for Richard Smyth, 1592);

Etienne de Maisonneuve, *Gerileon of England. The Second Part* (London: Printed by T.

Scarlet [?] for C. Burbie, 1592);

Guillaume Telin, *Archaioplutos. Or the Riches of Elder Ages. Proouing that the Ancient Emperors Were More Rich than Such Liue in These Daies* (London: Printed by J. Charlewood for R. Smith, 1592);

Ortensio Landi, *The Defence of Contraries. Paradoxes against Common Opinion, Debated in Forme of Declamations to Exercise Yong Wittes*, translated by Munday from the French translation, usually attributed to Charles Estienne, of *Paradossi* (London: Printed by J. Windet for S. Waterson, 1593);

Primaleon of Greece, *The First Booke of Primaleon of Greece* (London: Printed by J. Danter for C. Burby, 1595); *The Second Booke of Primaleon of Greece* (London: Printed by J. Danter for C. Burby, 1596); books 1-3 published as *The Famous and Renowned Historie of Primaleon of Greece* (London: Printed by T. Snodham, 1619);

de Moraes, *The First and Seconde Parts, of the No Lesse Rare, Historie of Palmerin of England* (London: Printed by T. Creede, 1596); *The Third and Last Part of Palmerin of England* (London: Printed by J. Roberts for W. Leake, 1602);

Anonymous, *A Breefe Treatise of the Vertue of the Crosse* (London: E. Allde for E. White, 1599);

José Teixeira, *The Strangest Adventure that Ever Happened. Containing a Discourse of the King of Portugall Dom Sebastian, from 1578. unto 1601. First Done in Spanish, then in French, and now into English* (London: Printed by R. Field for F. Henson, 1601);

Philippe de Mornay, *The True Knowledge of a Mans Owne Selfe* (London: Printed by J. Roberts for W. Leake, 1602);

François Citois, *A True and Admirable Historie, of a Mayden of Confolens, that for Three Yeeres Hath Lived, without Receiving either Meate or Drinke*, translated by Munday from Marc Lescarboux's French translation (London: Printed by J. Roberts, 1603);

Jacopo Affinati d'Acuto, *The Dumbe Divine Speaker ... A Treatise, in Praise of Silence* (London: Printed by R. Bradock for W. Leake, 1605);

Charlotte Brabantine of Nassau, *The Conversion of a Most Noble Lady of Fraunce. Madame Gratiana, Wife to Claudius, Duke of Thouars. Written by Her, to the Ladyes of Fraunce* (London: Printed by T. Purfoot for N. Butter, 1608).

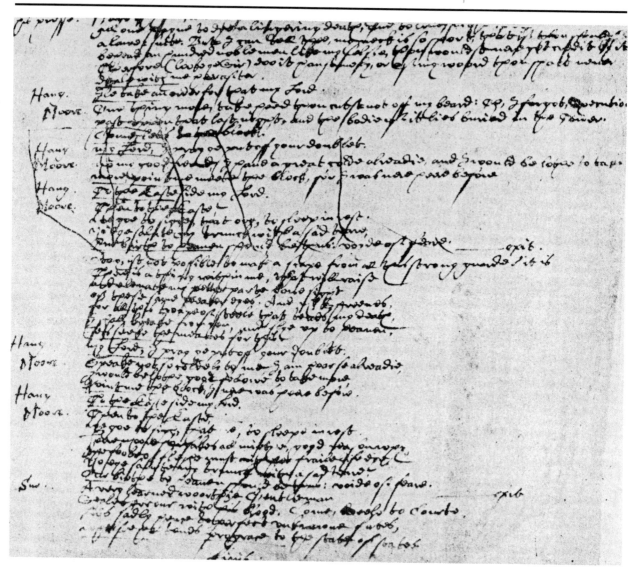

A portion of a page, in Munday's hand, from the manuscript for Sir Thomas More, *written by Munday and revised by Thomas Dekker, Henry Chettle, probably William Shakespeare, and possibly Thomas Heywood (Harleian MSS 7368, f. 22ʳ; by permission of the British Library)*

Few Elizabethan and Jacobean authors produced as varied a canon as did Anthony Munday. He wrote plays, translated Continental prose romances, produced original prose fiction, apparently wrote ballads in his earlier years, was, in the early 1580s, by far the most controversial "news reporter" in London, and in his later years devised pageants for the City of London, as well as expanding and bringing up to date Stow's chronicle of the city. As is frequently the case with people who throw themselves into a host of literary fields, he excelled in none. However, much of his work is interesting, some of it still eminently readable.

As he was baptised on 13 October 1560, it is probable that he was born in that month, although the precise date of his birth is unknown. He was buried on 9 August 1633 after a long life, but not quite as long as the eighty years that his tombstone, quoted in the 1633 edition of John Stow's *Survey of London*, which Munday had enlarged, reported him to have lived. His father, Christopher Munday (a stationer trained as a draper), and mother, Jane, died early, and in 1576 the orphaned Anthony was apprenticed to the stationer John Allde, working for him until the autumn of 1578 when his indentures were canceled on his own request to allow him to travel abroad.

His destination was Rome, but his motive is unlikely to have been religious. While there he

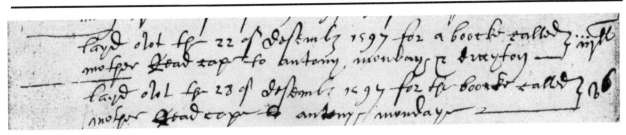

Entries in Philip Henslowe's diary listing payments on 22 and 28 December 1597 for Mother Redcap, *by Munday and Michael Drayton (MSS VII, l. 38'; by permission of Dulwich College, London)*

stayed from February to May 1579 at the English College, which had recently been converted to a seminary. It was an interesting time to visit the city. He was able to see the carnival, the catacombs had just been rediscovered, and the English College was about to suffer dramatic changes, with Munday a participator. He published an account of all these events in 1582 in his *English Roman Life,* the most readable of his books.

After his return to England he busied himself with the moralistic *The Mirror of Mutability* (1579), which contains much undistinguished rhyme and blank verse, wrote prose fiction in the shape of the not particularly outstanding *Zelauto* (1580), produced a ballad and perhaps a pamphlet against the stage, and in 1581 turned to anti-Catholic propaganda, putting his knowledge of Catholic circles in Europe to maximum use. He was among those who, on 20 November 1581, testified against certain priests, some of whom Munday had met in Lyons and Rome, and others, including Edmund Campion, whom he had never before seen. His *A Discovery of Edmund Campion and His Confederates* (1582) reports these courtroom revelations and the "treasons" of the accused and describes in great detail their executions. *The English Roman Life* was produced shortly afterward to prove his credentials and refute those who doubted he had ever been to Rome. As a historical document this work has a double claim to importance. It offers a unique and highly detailed record of daily life in the English College in Rome at that time and a participant's account of the successful rebellion early in 1579 of the English students against the rector. At the request of the students, the Jesuits were given control of the institution. It also has value as a vivid document on contemporary Roman social history. Of all his books, it is probably this one that most deserves to be read today. While working on a variety of projects, but particularly translations of Continental prose fiction (for exam-

ple, the Palmerin romances) through the 1580s, Munday is believed to have found time to translate the play *Fedele and Fortunio,* if indeed it is his, from the Italian. Munday's translation (published in 1585), however, is a rather free adaptation of the play for the English stage of the day, with much of the prose turned to verse and the comic elements enhanced, and it should be regarded as a substantially original work. It seems to have been particularly successful and was performed at Court.

His second play was probably *John a Kent and John a Cumber,* written in the late 1580s or early 1590s. This romantic pastoral comedy capitalizes on the contemporary popularity of plays such as Robert Greene's *Friar Bacon and Friar Bungay* by embodying magic and disguises. Two magicians compete, pit their skills against one another, and John a Kent, assisted by Shrimp, proves superior to John a Cumber. The action is developed through Kent's promotion of the love between Sidanen and Marian. Like the later Robin Hood plays, *John a Kent and John a Cumber* mines English folklore successfully and has a good deal of genuine charm, particularly in the clowning scenes.

Sir Thomas More is a collaborative play surviving in a manuscript largely in Munday's hand. It was revised by four other playwrights, one of whom has been identified as Shakespeare (hand D). The play attempted to make capital out of anti-alien sentiment in London in the 1590s, was censored by the Master of the Revels on that account, and was never acted, despite substantial rewriting. It is based on Hall's Chronicle, and shows More's successful handling of an insurrection, his subsequent favor with the King, his close friendship with Erasmus, and his principled opposition to the King's policy, which leads to his execution, before which he is allowed some exercise of wit.

Philip Henslowe's diary reveals that Munday worked on *Mother Redcap* (in collaboration with Mi-

Designs for Chrysanaleia: The Golden Fishing, *Munday's 1616 Lord Mayor's pageant: (top left) the bower and tomb of William Walworth, who was Lord Mayor twice in the fourteenth century; (bottom left) fishing-boat device honoring the new Lord Mayor, John Leman of the Fishmongers Company; (top right) lemon-tree and pelican device suggesting an analogy between the new Lord Mayor (the lemon tree a pun on his name) and the pelican as the tender parent to her family; (bottom right) pageant chariot of Richard II and the Royal Virtues, an allusion to Walworth, who was Lord Mayor during Richard's reign (John Gough Nichols, ed.,* Chrysanaleia, *1844)*

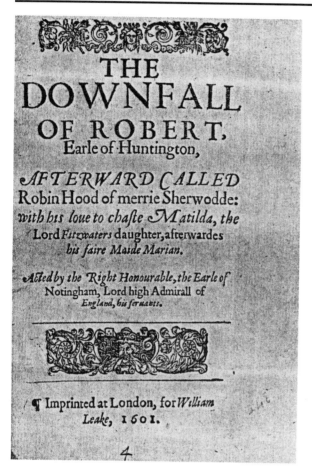
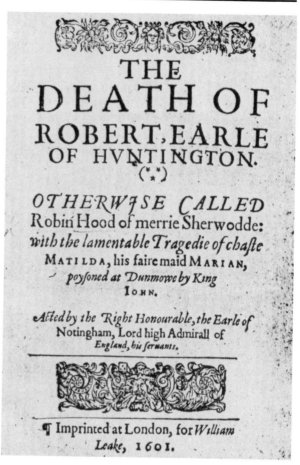

Title pages for the 1601 quarto editions of Munday and Chettle's popular plays about the English folk hero Robin Hood (left: Bodleian Library, Oxford; right: British Library)

chael Drayton in late 1597), now lost. Its heroine was a well-known witch of English folklore, but how Munday and Drayton chose to handle her is, unfortunately, a mystery. Munday continued to write for Philip Henslowe, following *Mother Redcap* with *The Downfall of Robert, Earl of Huntingdon* (later revised by Henry Chettle), which was quickly followed by *The Death of Robert, Earl of Huntingdon* (in collaboration with Chettle). Like Munday's earlier plays, these draw on English folklore, in this case the legend of Robin Hood, and they proved highly popular. Munday used a wide variety of sources for *The Downfall of Robert, Earl of Huntingdon* and combined them in an original and successful amalgam that embodies some of the best elements of pastoral comedy. (Quite possibly, Munday's play had an influence on Shakespeare's *As You Like It.*) *The Death of Robert, Earl of Huntingdon* transforms the story into bloody melodrama. Robin Hood dies, but Maid Marian (called Matilda in these plays) fights on. Both plays show Munday's ability to maintain an

audience's interest in the excitement of the rapidly moving action, and, indeed, the development of an exciting plot is Munday's chief strength in these plays. Theme, development of character, the moral dimensions of the action, were obviously of much less interest to him.

Success for these two plays led to a lost sequel, *Richard Coeur de Lion's Funeral* (also written in 1598), by Munday, Chettle, Drayton, and Robert Wilson. Other lost plays written for Henslowe in about 1598 were *Valentine and Orson* (with Richard Hathway) and *Worse Afeard than Hurt* (with Drayton and Thomas Dekker). In this same year Francis Meres in his *Palladis Tamia* praised Munday as "our best plotter" in a list of writers Meres judged "The best for Comedy amongst us." In view of the fact that Meres is occasionally tongue-in-cheek, however, this praise may be intentionally ironic, a reference more to Munday's activities as government spy and discoverer (some would say fabricator) of "plots," than as a dramatist.

In the following year, 1599, Munday, with Drayton, Hathway, and Wilson, wrote an answer to Shakespeare's presentation of Sir John Oldcastle in the character of Falstaff. Their play was titled *The True and Honourable History of the Life of Sir John Oldcastle* (revised by Dekker in 1602), which turned out to be quite as unhistorical as Shakespeare's portrait of the same man. The prologue informs the audience that

> It is no pamperd glutton we present,
> Nor aged Councellor to youthfull sinne,
> But one, whose vertue shone aboue the rest,
> A valiant Martyr, and a vertuous peere.

Oldcastle is said to have shown "true faith and loyaltie . . . Unto his soueraigne, and his countries weale." Shakespeare's character was a "forg'de inuention" which "defac'te" historical truth. In fact, the play transforms a historical heretic pictured in the chronicle histories as boastful, dishonest, and a drunken reveller into a good Protestant born before his proper time, a loyal and courageous friend to his king, and a victim of unjust Romish persecution. It was successful enough to cause Henslowe to commission a second (lost) part.

Early in 1600 Munday was again at work, with these same collaborators, on *Owen Tudor*, another historical play, which seems never to have been completed; and in June of that year he was writing, with others, parts one and two of *Fair Constance of Rome*, presumably based on Chaucer's Man of Law's Tale–both lost.

In the following year Munday wrote, with Chettle, Drayton, and Wentworth Smith, *The Rising of Cardinal Wolsey* (lost), and in 1602 another three lost plays–*Jephthah* (with Dekker), *Caesar's Fall, or The Two Shapes* (with Dekker, Drayton, Middleton, and Webster), and *The Set at Tennis* (alone).

After 1602 Munday wrote no more for the stage. His pageants, however, written for the City of London, were dramatic in quality, and a natural enough field for talents trained in Henslowe's employ. The Lord Mayor's annual pageant was a spectacular affair, and Munday was a regular contributor. After 1616, to Munday's disappointment, Thomas Middleton, his one-time collaborator in play writing, replaced him as the favored author of the pageants, and Munday returned to reediting romances and to completing his expanded edition of John Stow's *Survey of London* (1618), which he then proceeded to enlarge further, making this project the work of his remaining years. This greatly expanded edition of Stow finally appeared in 1633, some little time after Munday's death in August of that year.

Anthony Munday was not a dramatist of the first or even of the second rank. He was what is rather disparagingly referred to as a "hack-writer." He did, however, write plays that were well constructed, entertaining, and highly original in their treatment of popular and traditional material and which reflected and satisfied the tastes of their audiences more successfully than did some of the august offerings of his contemporary Ben Jonson. Indeed, Jonson's low opinion of Munday, whom he ridiculed as Antonio Balladino in *The Case is Altered*, was perhaps partly conditioned by the very favor Munday seems to have found with his audiences.

References:

David M. Bergeron, "Anthony Munday: Pageant Poet to the City of London," *Huntington Library Quarterly*, 30 (August 1967): 345-368;

Bergeron, *English Civic Pageantry, 1558-1642* (London: Arnold, 1971);

Mark Eccles, "Anthony Munday," in *Studies in the English Renaissance Drama*, edited by J. W. Bennett, Oscar Cargill, and Vernon Hall (London: Peter Owen/Vision Press, 1959), pp. 95-106;

Frank L. Huntley, "Ben Jonson and Anthony Munday or, *The Case is Altered* Altered Again," *Philological Quarterly*, 41 (January 1962): 205-214;

MacDonald P. Jackson, "Anthony Munday and 'Sir Thomas More,'" *Notes and Queries*, new series 208 (March 1963): 96;

J. M. R. Margeson, "Dramatic Form: the Huntingdon Plays," *Studies in English Literature*, 14 (Spring 1974): 223-238;

J. C. Meagher, "Hack-writing and the Huntingdon Plays," in *Elizabethan Theatre*, edited by J. R. Brown and B. Harris (London: Arnold, 1966), pp. 196-219;

Mary Patchell, *The Palmerin Romances in Elizabethan Prose Fiction* (New York: Columbia University Press, 1947);

Celeste Turner, *Anthony Munday: An Elizabethan Man of Letters* (Berkeley: University of California, 1928).

Papers:

The manuscript for *John a Kent and John a Cumber* is at the Huntington Library. The British Library has the manuscript for *Sir Thomas More*.

George Peele

(circa 25 July 1556-9 November 1596)

Stanley J. Kozikowski
Bryant College

PLAY PRODUCTIONS: *Iphigenia*, Peele's translation of Euripides' play, Christ Church, Oxford, circa 1579;

Entertainment for Count Palatine, Christ Church, Oxford, May 1583;

The Arraignment of Paris, London, at Court, 1584;

The Pageant before Woolstone Dixie, streets of London, 29 October 1585;

The Pageant for Martin Calthrop, streets of London, 29 October 1588;

The Battle of Alcazar, London, the Theatre, circa 1590;

Edward I, London, the Theatre or Curtain theater, circa 1590-1592;

Descensus Astraeae, streets of London, 29 October 1591;

The Old Wives Tale, London, the Theatre, Curtain, or Rose theater, circa 1591-1594;

David and Bethsabe, London, unknown theater, by 1594.

BOOKS: *The Araynement of Paris: A Pastorall* (London: Printed by H. Marsh, 1584);

The Device of the Pageant Borne before Wolstan Dixi Lord Maior of London (London: Printed by E. Allde, 1585);

A Farewell. Entituled To the Famous and Fortunate Generalls of Our English Forces: Sir J. Norris & Syr F. Drake. Whereunto Is Annexed A Tale of Troy (London: Printed by J. Charlewood, sold by W. Wright, 1589);

Polyhymnia: Describing the Honourable Triumph at Tylt (London: Printed by R. Jhones, 1590);

Descensus Astrææ. The Device of a Pageant Borne before M. William Web, Lord Maior of London, 1591 (London: Printed by T. Scarlet for W. Wright, 1591);

The Honour of the Garter. Displaied in a Poeme Gratulatorie: Entitled, To the Earle of Northumberland. Created Knight of That Order, and Installd Anno Regni Elizabethæ. 35. die Iunij 26 (London: Printed by the Widdowe Charlewood for F. Busbie, 1593);

The Famous Chronicle of King Edward the First (London: Printed by A. Jeffes, sold by W. Barley, 1593);

The Battell of Alcazar (London: Printed by E. Allde for R. Bankworth, 1594);

The Old Wiues Tale. A Pleasant Conceited Comedie (London: Printed by J. Danter, sold by R. Hancocke & J. Hardie, 1595);

The Love of King Dauid and Fair Bethsabe (London: Printed by A. Islip, 1599).

Edition: *The Life and Works of George Peele*, 3 volumes, general editor Charles Tyler Prouty (New Haven: Yale University Press, 1952-1970).

OTHER: R. S., ed., *The Phoenix Nest*, includes poems by Peele (London: Printed by J. Jackson, 1593);

Robert Allott, ed., *Englands Parnassus*, includes poems by Peele (London: Printed for N. Ling, C. Burby & T. Hayes, 1600);

Englands Helicon, includes poems by Peele (London: Printed by J. Roberts for J. Flasket, 1600).

George Peele has long been regarded as one of the playwrights who gave significant direction to the rapidly evolving theater which Shakespeare, Jonson, and others inherited. Within the group known as the University Wits—which also includes Thomas Nashe, Robert Greene, John Lyly, and Thomas Lodge—Peele stands alone as a writer of extraordinary variety. Although he is known primarily as the author of the courtly *The Arraignment of Paris* and the folksy *The Old Wives Tale*, a number of Peele's other writings deserve attention. He wrote a fair number of university pieces, court entertainments, and occasional verses, as well as biblical and historical drama, which in addition to comedy, pastoral drama, and tragedy identify him as a writer of astonishing range and scope. The works of such writers as Sidney, Lyly, and Marlowe have been given greater attention; but in George Peele we find a writer closer to his times, who worked within certain literary conventions but explored, in some instances boldly, literary innovations. Also perhaps the most hybrid literary figure of his day, Peele wrote for the court with an eye to the public, and he wrote for the general public without betraying his university upbringing and concomitant sense of aesthetic obligation. His life reflects that tendency which always characterized his art–to seek fame in both the court and the general marketplace. Peele's reputation has perhaps never been more secure than it is today. He is well regarded as an imaginative, responsive, and even intriguing literary craftsman, who left works of unusual variety and meaning.

Born in London on or about 25 July 1556, George Peele was the son of a reasonably successful Elizabethan tradesman, James Peele, and his first wife, Anne. James Peele was a man of some learning in his own right who, among other things, wrote some material which was presented during the annual Lord Mayor's pageants. An accountant by profession, he became an official at a London charity home and school, teaching in that school and later at a private school of his own. Evidently ambitious in his own right, James Peele sought out every advantage on behalf of his son. In 1565 George Peele was sent to the primary school of Christ's Hospital, an excellent preparatory school for boys intent upon attaining a good education. Peele matriculated in April of 1571 at Oxford, and he established himself as a student at Christ Church, Oxford, in 1574, earning a B.A. in 1577 and an M.A. in 1579. Peele was hardly unique in his aspirations: by then both Cambridge and Oxford universities were attracting good numbers of young men from England's rapidly growing middle class. As a consequence, opportunities for advancement in the professions and in the service of the state were becoming limited.

Whether confident of his own special talents or apprehensive about following opportunities in other directions, Peele began preparing for a career as a professional writer while in college. Well regarded by fellow students and by his college, Peele certainly received encouragement. William Gager, a fellow student who became a renowned Latin dramatist, praised Peele's English translation of Euripides' *Iphigenia*. Although the play is lost, it represents the first manifestation of Peele's always-keen interest in classical antiquity. In May of 1583 the college paid Peele the

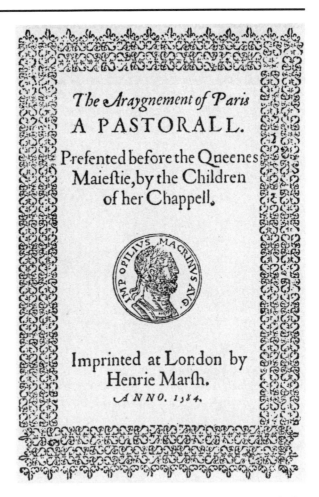

Title page for the 1584 quarto edition of the pastoral play Peele wrote for presentation before Elizabeth I (Anderson Galleries, sale number 2078, 24-25 May 1926)

extraordinary sum of twenty pounds "in respect of the playes & intertaynemt of the palatine laskie." What Peele did to earn the sum is unclear; but the occasion involved some sort of collegiate entertainment for Count Palatine of Siradia (Poland), Albert Alasco, who was traveling that year in England. Peele no doubt had a significant hand in some sort of entertainment, much like that playlet held at Oxford twenty years later to England's newly enthroned King James, who was praised by students dressed as three sybils in much the same way that Shakespeare's three witches flatter Macbeth. Such entertainments were elaborate, often proceeding for several days, attracting writers and aspiring writers of talent and ambition. This fact is especially significant because by 1583 Peele had already earned his M.A., had married a local woman, Anne Cooke, in 1580, and had apparently launched his career in London, where he had settled in 1581. It is clear that he maintained close ties at Oxford and that he had established a reputation as a worthy man of letters whose work did merit royal attention.

It is likely that Peele had a highly influential advocate for his art, someone with extraordinary influence at court. For within a year after the Oxford entertainment, Peele wrote a play which was performed before Queen Elizabeth and her court, a play unmistakably written for the occasion of its presentation to the Queen–*The Arraignment of Paris*. Peele's pastoral play not only reveals his confident artistry as a writer of court entertainment, but it also looks ahead to his excellence as a writer of civic pageants. The play, based upon the origin of the Trojan War, presents a subject of special interest to the Elizabethans and a subject which Peele had written about during his college days (Peele would refer to *A Tale of Troy*, published in 1589, as "an olde Poeme"). Peele's play refers to England as "a seconde Troie" because according to legend King Priam's descendants established Rome and later founded Britain. Although *The Arraignment of Paris* does echo Peele's poem in part, the play brings a variety of materials together in a unique, compelling fashion. Drawing upon classical mythology, legend, and the English pastoral tradition, Peele's play culminates with an extraordinary compliment to the Queen.

Critical opinion concerning Peele's play has been divided. Some scholars view Peele's work as disunified and chaotic; others have praised its ingenious skill in synthesizing diverse elements. Certain facts, however, are beyond dispute: Peele's work represents the earliest surviving English pastoral play, and on that score alone it warrants special attention. Also, the play is regarded as the product of the first known playwright in England who sought to vary metrical patterns artfully with changes in subject and characterization. Such aesthetic sensitivity in prosody suggests the presence of equivalent deliberation with respect to the play's structure. *The Arraignment of Paris*, accordingly, contains a carefully presented succession of events, each of which represents a special type of conflict or discord. As the play alternates between divine and human conflict, disorder in one seemingly perfect realm (the heavens) mirrors disorder in another such realm on earth (the pastoral). Of course, at Diana's insistence, contention among the gods and goddesses is resolved by the human agency of Paris. This shift in perspective from heaven to earth becomes the perfect vehicle to draw attention and tribute to

Queen Elizabeth. The goddess Diana praises England as a kingdom comparable to her own, and she maintains that all of the best qualities that may be found in Juno, Pallas, Venus, and herself exist within England's Regent. As the goddesses sing praises to the Queen, so too do the three Fates–Clotho, Lachesis, and Atropos–who yield the symbols of their offices (the distaff, reel, and knife) just before the goddesses agree to present the golden apple, which Paris was to have given to the one whom he judged fairest among them, in dramatic, most sublime judgment–to Queen Elizabeth, who is praised in conclusion for her chastity, purity, and learning.

Peele's play is not unique within his canon as a work which defies classification. With its reiterative song, dance, and music it evokes some of the quality but not the predominant character of an Elizabethan masque. In its display of colorful spectacle, didactic catalogue, and highly representative personages, it evokes but does not replicate the court revels which traditionally honored the Queen when she went on a progress. Even as conventional drama *The Arraignment of Paris* contains notable departures, the most significant of which lies with its obvious break from its genre as it addresses directly and gathers itself around the personage of the Queen, becoming itself an audience instead of a play, reversing convention extraordinarily, in the fashion of contemporary neorealistic literature. Peele's play reminds us of how intimate the Elizabethan and Jacobean theater was with the throne–a fact not always appreciated by readers of many plays from *Gorboduc* to *Macbeth*.

Peele's work as a dramatist cannot be separated from his efforts as a writer of occasional poetry designed for both public and private audiences. In fact, after presenting *The Arraignment of Paris*, Peele tried his hand at some literary enterprises aimed at keeping favor at court and at securing lasting influence with the officialdom of London. To appreciate Peele's efforts, we must remember that virtually all forms of ceremony and entertainment, whether directed to the court or to the city, were equally cherished by their divergent audiences, who celebrated annually and with relish the anniversary of Elizabeth's accession to the throne and the installation of the Lord Mayor of London. The seventeenth of November, the holiday honoring Elizabeth's accession, grew with every year into an increasingly spectacular event. James I, decades later, would keep the tradition intact as he made his accession

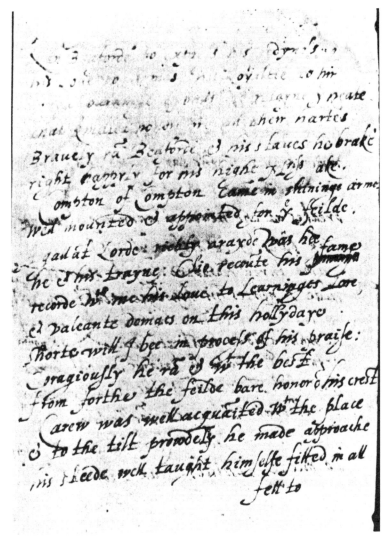

Page from the manuscript, in Peele's hand, for Anglorum Feriae, *a poem he wrote for the Accession Day tilts of 1595 (MS Add. 21432, f. 9ʳ; by permission of the British Library)*

day a day of thanksgiving, recalling to mind how he was delivered from death at the hands of the Scottish Earl of Gowrie and other Protestant nobles, while a guest in Gowrie's castle–a fact evoked in Shakespeare's *Macbeth*. Accession Day, from the 1570s onward, was celebrated as England's greatest secular holiday of the year. One mode of celebration took the form of tilts or jousts in which a nobleman might communicate with the Queen through a clever use of armor, supporting riders, uniforms, and symbolic decoration. Through these means of expression the nobleman might request, beseech, flatter, protest, or caution against some royal prerogative or initiative. Other tilters might negatively or unfavorably modulate that communication to the Queen. And the Queen, always, responded as she chose

in whatever tone that she might choose. In two works–*Polyhymnia* (1590) and *Anglorum Feriae* (possibly the ballad entered in the Stationers' Register on 18 November 1595)–Peele depicts two Accession Day tilts, capturing the exact flavor of communication between petitioner and sovereign. He describes how each tilter presents himself, how he is challenged, and how the Queen responds. Peele's poems, like his plays, represent a large "cast" of characters, contain some fine dramatic moments, and focus thematically upon the purposes of state. The highlight of *Polyhymnia* is a description of the "show" presented by the Earl of Essex in mourning for the death of Sir Philip Sidney. In sable livery, a distinct contrast to the various colors worn by the other noblemen, the train of Essex provides by its unique sartorial splendor the spectacular sense of pageantry which Peele, in varying contexts, always found attractive. Five years later, in his *Anglorum Feriae*, Essex's cavalcade is again primary among the spectacles. On this occasion, dressed in the red and white so appealing to the Tudors, Essex is greeted by personages who symbolize courses of life available to him: a hermit representing the contemplative extreme, a political figure evoking the life of thought and action, and a soldier suggesting the purely active state. Essex responds with uncertainty; and this episode, which was added to the text by Francis Bacon, anticipates, again, the heralding of King James by the three sybils during his progress to Oxford. Underlying the *Anglorum Feriae* is a special celebratory note which was to remain customary for the remainder of Elizabeth's reign and which was always to characterize the reign of King James I—a thanksgiving for the sovereign's having successfully escaped assassination. Peele's poem commends Elizabeth's good fate in having been saved from two groups of plotters, one of which, a Portuguese group, was supposedly instigated by the Queen's personal physician, Dr. Lopez. Peele's commendation of Queen Elizabeth's blessed rule in *Anglorum Feriae* should be understood as distinguished among many such tributes paid by the great poets of the age to their sovereigns. Since these literary endeavors were tied to national holidays for the most part, they very likely attracted widespread attention. (In 1603 Shakespeare's company, the King's Men, greeted the accession of King James with a play about his near assassination by the Earl of Gowrie.) The Elizabethans were indeed artfully mindful of the fates of their Regent.

At the time that Peele was writing his Accession Day poems, he also seems to have gotten involved in writing some scripts for pageants honoring the annual installations of London's Lord Mayors. Peele's civic pageants bear unmistakable similarity to his tilting poems honoring Elizabeth. His pageant for the installation of Wolstone Dixie in 1585 enjoys the distinction of "being the earliest extant complete Lord Mayor's pageant," according to David H. Horne, the editor of Peele's minor works. It represents the first of three such pageants which Peele wrote, the others being a pageant for the installation of Martin Calthrop in 1588, which has not survived, and *Descensus Astraeae*, published in 1591 with the subtitle *The Device of a Pageant Borne Before M. William Web*. Both extant pageants use symbolic and classi-

cal mythology figures to sing the praises of Queen Elizabeth, and both remind their audiences of the great prosperity of England and London under the rule of Queen Elizabeth. In the more sophisticated *Descensus Astraeae* Elizabeth is equated with "Astraea daughter of the immortall Jove," and she is celebrated as the "Celestiall sacred Nymph, that tendes her flocke." It also bears noting that Astraea, the goddess of justice, was the last immortal to depart from earth and that she became the constellation Virgo. The incongruity of Peele's lofty pastoral theme invoked in celebration of a city pageant creates a somewhat dramatic sense of expectancy because the City of London is not mentioned in the entire "device" until its very end. Instead, repeatedly, the fair Astraea-Elizabeth is heralded as preserver of the flock against a range of threats and dangers. Elizabeth's role as protector far surpasses any special meritorious role which the Lord Mayor might possess. It may therefore be concluded that the last, and most elaborate, of Peele's city pageants evokes more the spirit of an Accession Day poem than the quality of a celebration for the Lord Mayor.

Peele's occasional poems are some of the finest accounts of the important celebratory events of the day. Peele takes care, in his poetical flights of fancy (which include a special proclivity for unusual and sustained puns), to record precisely the events of the important day. On one occasion Peele was commissioned to write a poem celebrating the Earl of Northumberland's installation as a Knight of the Garter—the only recorded instance of Peele's having been requested to compose a work to order. This work—in addition to presenting a history of the order revived by Elizabeth—along with a stirring account of the inductees and the heroic pageantry honoring them, may be described justly as the most self-referential of Peele's occasional verses. Northumberland, his patron, receives Peele's mild complaint, which becomes a hope, that poetry finds protection and sustenance among those such as Elizabeth and Northumberland, who have proven to be worthy protectors of the art of poets. Peele is sincere, direct, and unabashedly defensive in this work, written in curious tones of self-consciousness. Peele saw his role as purposive, in that he might be allowed to deploy his special and recognized talents in the service of his country as well as those most mighty in the affairs of state—the very Order of the Knights of the Garter themselves—whose patronage Peele no

THE BATTELL,

OF ALCAZAR, FOVGHT

in Barbarie, betweene Sebaſtian king
of Portugall, and Abdelmelec king
of Marocco. With the
death of Captaine
Stukeley.

Aſit was ſundrie times plaid by the Lord high Admirall his ſeruants.

Imprinted at London by Edward Allde for Richard
Bankworth, and are to be ſolde at his ſhopp e in
Pouls Churchyard at the ſigne of the
Sunne. 1 5 9 4.

Title page for the 1594 quarto edition of the play Peele probably started soon after the defeat of the Spanish Armada in 1588 (Anderson Galleries, sale number 2078, 24-25 May 1926)

doubt devoutly sought. But unfortunately Peele's aspirations were not to be fulfilled. In the few years left in his brief life Peele appeared to confine his energies to writing several remarkably different plays.

Probably written second to *The Arraignment of Paris* though published later, *The Battle of Alcazar* appeared in a quarto edition in 1594. Peele is generally thought to have started the play shortly after the defeat of the Spanish Armada in 1588. It concerns itself with an actual historical event which took place on 4 August 1578, the Battle of Alcazar, in which the young King of Portugal, Sebastian, was defeated and killed in his efforts to as-

sist Mohammed el-Mesloukh (the villain of the play, known as "Muly Mahamet" or more commonly "the Moor") against his uncles, whom Mohammed's father had viciously, and partially, succeeded in wiping out in order to preserve for his son the kingdoms of Fez and Morocco. Peele's treatment of this background story, which is at variance with history (he has the Moor doing most of the killing), is presented in the prologue to *The Battle of Alcazar*. The chief line of action in Peele's play consists of the efforts of the Moor's surviving uncles–Abdelmelec and Muly Mahamet Seth–to remove and punish the usurping Moor. Abdelmelec immediately moves successfully

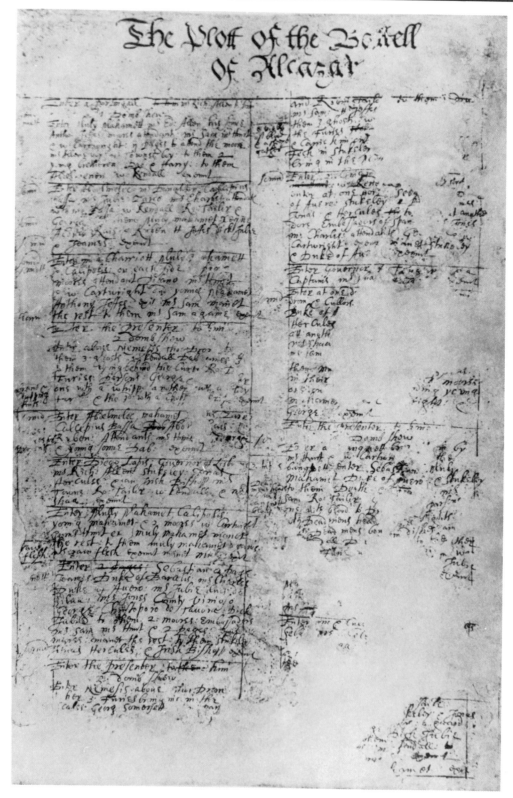

First page from a theatrical plot for The Battle of Alcazar, *prepared by a scribe for a revival of the play by the Admiral's Men probably during the months of December 1598-February 1599. The prompter and actors used such outlines to keep track of role assignments, actors' entrances and exits, props, sound effects, and other staging information (MS Add. 10449, f. 3; by permission of the British Library).*

against the Moor, who enlists the support of King Sebastian and an English soldier of fortune by the name of Thomas Stukeley, who was something of a national English hero and who served Queen Elizabeth, King Philip of Spain, and finally King Sebastian in his checkered career. The party supporting the Moor, in a succession of sensational dramatic scenes, is defeated and killed. Stukeley is put to death by the army of Italian mercenaries which he had led.

Peele's play is generally regarded as having been of exceptional interest to the Elizabethans, and it should be studied as a primary instance of the sort of play in which the theatergoing public and the professional acting companies delighted. The role of the Moor attracted the attention of the great Elizabethan actor Edward Alleyn. Alleyn had achieved notoriety in having acted the role of the hero in Christopher Marlowe's two-part *Tamburlaine*, which was one of the most successful plays of the Elizabethan stage. *The Battle of Alcazar* is very much a succession piece to Marlowe's play. In its ringing blank-verse speeches, its unusual subject and location, its depictions of overweening ambition, and its scenes of spectacular violence and triumph, it evokes *Tamburlaine* convincingly. The artistically ambitious Peele was not merely intent upon presenting another Marlovian play. Aside from Anglicizing a portion of the play's characterization by featuring Thomas Stukeley as a major fixture, Peele appropriated a few structural devices from earlier, well-known Elizabethan tragedies—particularly *Gorboduc* and *The Spanish Tragedy*. Peele reintroduced the dumb show, which was used in both previous plays, but he extended it imaginatively and admirably by having a Presenter preside over the dumb show that introduced each act and functioned effectively in the dual role of popular interpreter and Senecan chorus. By employing this device Peele created yet another "first": he is generally regarded as having been the first English dramatist to make use of a presenter. The use of this presenter gives his historically dense play an expository concision which allows him to concentrate dramatic attention upon key events and to shape his audience's sense of heightened expectancy. Also, the play compares favorably with Kyd's popular *The Spanish Tragedy*. Peele deftly involves Senecan furies, ghosts, and figures of Death and Nemesis in the psychological pattern of his dumb shows. In this regard Peele's dumb shows are solidly transitional, implicated in the mood, pace, and action of the play. While Peele's play illustrates, in this respect and others, a dependence upon the distinctive art forms of Marlowe and Kyd, it also demonstrates an admirable native talent, expressive and compelling in its own right. Peele's distinctiveness is evident in the processional aspects of the dumb show as well as in those moments in the play when characters enter leading a train or when, for example, the Moor enters upon a chariot. The visual excitement generated by Peele's extraordinary skill as a crafter of civic pageants must have added a very special dimension for its Elizabethan audience.

Edward I was entered on 8 October 1593 in the Register of the Stationers' Company, but it was probably written between 1590 and 1592, certainly after *The Battle of Alcazar*. It is very likely a candidate for being Peele's least distinguished effort; even as a "failure" it commands and repays special attention. The play traces the intractable events of some twenty-two years in the reign of Edward I of England, beginning with his return to England from the Holy Land and ending with the settlement of the throne of Scotland. Peele, with an extraordinary amount of telescoping and melding of his historical sources, creates the dramatic impression of Edward as a powerful ruler and uniter of England, Wales, and Scotland—an interpretation that is not historically documented. Along with the main plot, which focuses upon King Edward, his play has two subplots—the account of "Lluellen, alias Prince of Wales" and an account of the disappointed ambitions of Edward's Queen—Elinor of Castile. Peele uses both subplots, which are heightened by legendary materials and historical inaccuracies, to counterpoint Edward's triumphant rule over Wales and Scotland. The text of the play contains numerous loose ends which have been puzzling to critics and scholars alike—but Peele's glorifying focus upon Edward remains clear from start to finish. Edward's triumphs in the Holy Land are celebrated at the outset of the play. Meanwhile, the rebellious Prince Lluellen is encouraged and entertained by a comic band which includes a ribald friar, his novice, his wench, and a prophetic Welshman. At the same time Queen Elinor is seen tempering her love for her husband with a haughty disdain for the subjects of England, the brunt of which is borne by the Lord Mayor of London's wife. As the Welsh rebellion continues to foment beyond necessary complication, Edward sends his wife, to her chagrin, to Wales in the hope of, since she is with child, establishing succession rights there. Edward's efforts earn

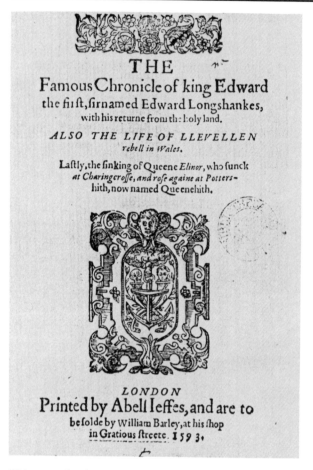

THE
Famous Chronicle of king Edward
the first, firnamed Edward Longshankes,
with his returne from the holy land.

ALSO THE LIFE OF LLEVELLEN
rebell in Wales.

Laftly, the finking of Queene *Elinor*, who funck
at *Charingcroffe*, and rofe againe at *Potters-*
hith, now named Que enchith.

LONDON
Printed by Abell Ieffes, and are to
befolde by William Barley, at his fhop
in Gratious ftreete. 1 5 9 3.

Title page for the 1593 quarto edition of the play in which Peele traces the events of twenty-two years in the reign of Edward I of England (Bodleian Library, Oxford)

him a physical thrashing from his Queen when he meets her in Wales; and to carry things to an even greater height of madness, Lluellen inexplicably retreats to the forests of Wales with his merry crew to rove about in imitation of Robin Hood. Peele's plots, counterplots, and numerous arbitrarily interwoven sidelights resemble, in their grand discontinuity and complexity, a contemporary American novel by Thomas Pynchon. What seems in the play to be perfectly bizarre verges upon becoming profoundly incredible: in an assertion of vicious and sadistic power, just as things appear to have somewhat stabilized, the irrepressible Queen Elinor demands that her husband order all male subjects to shave their beards and all Englishwomen to have their right breasts severed. Edward debunks Elinor by advising that they, as royal couple, set the precedent. The plot of *Edward I* thickens like cement as a profusion of plots and counterplots become mixed by a rapid hardening of wills on all sides. The King, in league with Mortimer, Earl of March, de-

feats and beheads Lluellen. Meanwhile, more spectacularly, Queen Elinor, forswearing her involvement in the merciless torturing of the Lady Mayoress, is condemned to Hell only to be, for whatever reason, released–in a wonderfully comic scene–before some unimpressed countryfolk. In this high historical farce of a play Peele was clearly teasing his audience just as he had teased a wildly improbable story out of his historical sources. The ending of *Edward I* is admirably consistent in its adhesion to its mad plot. The King and his brother Edmund, Duke of Lancaster, disguise themselves as priests upon their return from Wales to England, where a repentant Elinor confesses to them that she had been unfaithful to Edward, having had sexual liaison with Edmund. The play ends, true to its letter and spirit, with a succession of fantastic spectacles, which defy normal as well as historical truth.

Critics have tended to either dismiss *Edward I* as a crude, poorly wrought effort, or they have quietly defended the play as having some structural integrity despite its eccentricities of plot and theme. In his excellent study of Peele, A. R. Braunmuller has shown how the play frames both public and private demands upon King Edward, pointing to how the threat that Lluellen presents on the field of battle is paralleled on the personal front by the siege to the King's heart caused by Elinor's crimes and sins. Elinor, it should be noted, by the example of her monstrous villainy, may stand unique in the canon of Elizabethan literature as perhaps the only naturalized image, in the form of a woman, of the Vice figure. Her speech is as rhetorically distinct from that of the other characters in the play as her behavior. In its repeated assertion of malign intent it distinguishes her from the remaining humanity of Peele's play. She is clearly more than an example of a fallen queen. She represents a radical image of morally formulated reality, as comically absurd as evil is irrational, and so understood, by its Elizabethan audience.

The highly innovative artistry of Peele's genre-splitting drama was to strain definition further in what for many readers is his most interesting play–*The Old Wives Tale*, published in 1595. The date of its authorship is uncertain. Peele in this play extends and sophisticates the device of the presenter, which he had deployed so successfully in *The Battle of Alcazar*. The frame of the play begins with two characters, Frolicke and Fantasticke, who hear a third character, Madge, narrate "an old wives winters tale." As Madge begins haltingly to tell her tale, attention is shifted to the main action. The original characters remain off to the side on the stage, occasionally making observations about the very complicated series of actions in Peele's brief play. In typical folktale fashion Madge's story concerns a Princess who was abducted by a sorcerer from her father ("a King or a Lord or a Duke"). The Princess's two brothers set out to rescue her from her imprisonment in a castle. On the way they meet an old holy man, whom, we discover, has been transformed by the sorcerer from a handsome young man whose love the sorcerer has kidnapped. These two misfortunes constitute the main thrust of the action, but their consequences form but a small part of an exceedingly complicated plot construction, which proves to be nothing less than amazing given the brevity of the play (only 928 lines). Again, we have to go to the twentieth century for an analogue—a "young wive's tale," Pynchon's *The Crying of Lot 49* (1966). Peele's play is astonishingly modern in its penchant for fabulation, its neat ordering of constantly supervening plot, its artful narrative self-consciousness, its concentration upon the idea that plot is less a comfortable mode of action than a constant form of antagonism, its cavalcade of wildly surnamed characters, its extraordinary linguistic sophistication, its fascination with scientifically indeterminate phenomena, and its ever-constant focus upon song, magic, and protean shifts or disguises of character. Peele's wonderful and intelligent eclecticism should commend him to a large and faithful modern readership, if not for the entire canon of his dramatic work, certainly for *The Old Wives Tale.* Needless to say, Peele's play has attracted diverse responses from its critics. It has been read as a blending of romance with realism, a burlesque with an unfocused sense of purpose, a fascinating reflection of Madge's disheveled mind, a satire on medieval romance, and a highly allusive private play with many muted references to people whom Peele knew. Others have proclaimed the play, in different fashions, a total artistic failure. There is no denying that Peele's play, whatever its exact orientation, was unprecedented both in its technical and in its linguistic sophistication. Clearly, it presents one of the most interesting interpretative challenges in all of Elizabethan drama.

Published three years after Peele's death, *David and Bethsabe* is considered to be the best example of a Bible-inspired Elizabethan play. In the figure of David, Peele created the ideal image

of man—king, lover, father, military leader, victim, hero, poet, and visionary. Among these roles are numerous juxtapositions between the personal and the public life; and the central tension of the play draws upon the public consequences of King David's private life. The issue of succession looms large in this play, as it would to an Elizabethan audience, whose ruler had by then served, without issue, for nearly a half century. To the degree that Peele's David is weak, vacillating, and self-indulgent, we are reminded that any sovereign, no matter how powerful or how revered, is a human being subject to the frailties, whims, and bemusements that all share. The larger, grander side of David, which some critics believe is notably downplayed in Peele's play, is to some degree apparent in the verse uttered by David. Some of the most stirring and haunting poetry in all of Peele's writings, many of David's lines are sonorous, figuratively rich, and dignified. As the central figure in the play, David as a kind of poet surrogate shapes events by the influence of his personal presence, his language, his royal policy.

Peele's reputation, although not his fortune, was fairly well established by the 1590s. In addi-

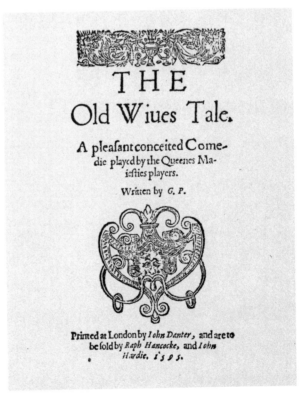

Title page for the 1595 quarto edition of Peele's "old wives winters tale" (Anderson Galleries, sale number 2078, 24-25 May 1926)

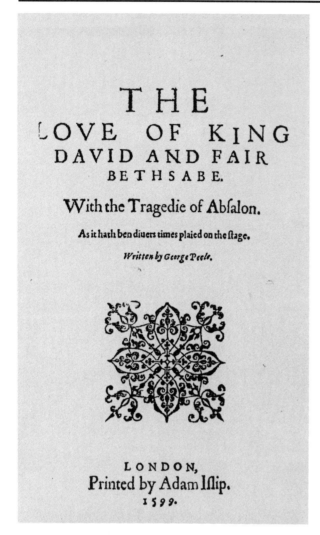

THE
LOVE OF KING
DAVID AND FAIR
BETHSABE.

With the Tragedie of Abſalon.

As it hath ben diuers times plaied on the ſtage.

Written by George Peele.

LONDON,
Printed by Adam Iſlip.
1599.

Title page for the 1599 quarto edition of the play in which Peele dealt with the topic of royal succession, an issue of great concern in Elizabethan England (Anderson Galleries, sale number 2078, 24-25 May 1926)

tion to his involvements in various types of occasional celebrations, entertainments, and plays, Peele saw his work included in the popular anthologies of the day–*The Phoenix Nest* (1593), *Englands Parnassus* (1600), and *Englands Helicon* (1600). In fact, a number of his colleagues writing late in Peele's life or just after his death praise him highly. Thomas Nashe, known more for his dim view of then-prevailing poets, singled out Peele for special praise. In *Greenes Groats-Worth of Wit* (1592), Robert Greene placed Peele in the company of Marlowe and Nashe. There is some evidence that all four poets were part of a literary circle referred to by Thomas Dekker in his *A Knights Conjuring* (1607).

It should also be noted that although Peele was a member of the Elizabethan literary establishment, he appears to have suffered financial problems and ill health. Only a year before his death, Peele wrote a pitiable letter to the powerful Lord Burleigh begging for support for a promised work and explaining "Longe sickness hauinge so enfeebled me maketh bashfullnes allmost become impudency." Within a year Peele died. The register of his parish at Saint James Clerkenwell recorded the death of "George Peele, householder" on 9 November 1596, a reference which suggests that he was the head of a family that had settled within that London parish. Peele's letter to Burleigh, state records show, was filed with correspondence from people regarded as eccentrics and crackpots.

Bibliography:
Thorleif Larsen, "A Bibliography of the Writings of George Peele," *Modern Philology*, 32 (November 1934): 143-156.

References:
Leonard R. N. Ashley, *George Peele* (New York: Twayne, 1970);

David M. Bergeron, *English Civic Pageantry 1558-1642* (London: Arnold, 1971);

Muriel C. Bradbrook, "Peele's *Old Wives' Tale:* A Play of Enchantment," *English Studies*, 43 (1962): 323-330;

A. R. Braunmuller, *George Peele* (Boston: Twayne, 1983);

P. H. Cheffaud, *George Peele (1558-1596?)* (Paris: Felix Alcan, 1913);

Sarah Lewis Carol Clapp, "Peele's Use of Folk-Lore in *The Old Wives' Tale*," *Studies in English* (University of Texas), 6 (1926): 146-156;

John D. Cox, "Homely Matter and Multiple Plots in Peele's *Old Wives Tale*," *Texas Studies in Literature and Language*, 20 (1978): 330-346;

John Crow, "Folklore in Elizabethan Drama," *Folk-Lore*, 58 (September 1947): 297-311;

John P. Cutts, "Peele's *Hunting of Cupid*," *Studies in the Renaissance*, 5 (1958): 121-132;

John Doebler, "The Tone of George Peele's *The Old Wives' Tale*," *English Studies*, 53 (October 1972): 412-421;

Inga-Stina Ewbank, "The House of David in Renaissance Drama: A Comparative Study," *Renaissance Drama*, 8 (1965): 3-40;

Ewbank, "On the Background of Peele's 'Arraygnment of Paris,'" *Notes and Queries*, new series 3 (June 1956): 246-249;

Thelma N. Greenfield, *The Induction in Elizabethan Drama* (Eugene: University of Oregon, 1969);

Walter W. Greg, *Pastoral Poetry and Pastoral Drama* (London: Bullen, 1906);

Greg, *Two Elizabethan Stage Abridgements* (Oxford: Clarendon Press, 1923);

George K. Hunter, *John Lyly: The Humanist as Courtier* (London: Routledge, 1962);

Harold Jenkins, "Peele's 'Old Wive's Tale,'" *Modern Language Review,* 34 (April 1939): 177-185;

Henry G. Lesnick, "The Structural Significance of Myth and Flattery in Peele's *The Arraignment of Paris,*" *Studies in Philology,* 65 (April 1968): 163-170;

Joan C. Marx, " 'Soft, Who Have We Here?': the Dramatic Technique of *The Old Wives Tale,*" *Renaissance Drama,* new series 12 (1981): 117-143;

Louis Adrian Montrose, "Gifts and Reasons: The Contexts of Peele's *Araygnement of Paris,*" *ELH: Journal of English Literary History,* 47 (Fall 1980): 433-461;

S. Musgrove, "Peele's 'Old Wives Tale': An Afterpiece?," *AUMLA,* 23 (1965): 86-95;

Irving Ribner, *The English History Play in the Age of Shakespeare,* revised edition (London: Methuen, 1965);

Murray Roston, *Biblical Drama in England: From the Middle Ages to the Present Day* (Evanston: Northwestern University Press, 1968);

Arthur M. Sampley, "Plot Structure in Peele's Plays as a Test of Authorship," *PMLA,* 51 (September 1936): 689-701;

Werner Senn, *Studies in the Dramatic Construction of Robert Green and George Peele,* Swiss Studies in English, no. 74 (Bern: Francke, 1973);

Emily B. Stanley, "The Use of Classical Mythology by the University Wits," *Renaissance Papers* (1956): 25-33;

Susan T. Viguers, "The Hearth and the Cell: Art in *The Old Wives Tale,*" *Studies in English Literature,* 21 (Spring 1981): 209-221;

Andrew Von Handy, "The Triumph of Chastity: Form and Meaning in *The Arraignment of Paris,*" *Renaissance Drama,* new series 1 (1968): 87-101;

Robert H. Wilson, "Reed and Warton on *The Old Wives Tale,*" *PMLA,* 55 (June 1940): 605-608.

Papers:

A manuscript for *Anglorum Feriae* (MS Add. 21437), in Peele's hand, is at the British Library, which also has a scribe's copy of a plot summary for *The Battle of Alcazar* (MS Add. 10449, f. 3), which probably dates from the late-sixteenth century. A scribal copy of *Polyhymnia* (MS 216) is in the library of St. John Baptist College, Oxford.

Henry Porter

(birth date and death date unknown)

Karen Wood

University of California, Berkeley

PLAY PRODUCTIONS: *The Two Angry Women of Abington,* Admiral's Men, by 1590;

Love Prevented, possibly by Porter, London, Rose theater, circa 1598;

Black Bateman of the North, part 2, by Robert Wilson, Henry Chettle, and possibly Porter, London, Rose theater, circa 1598;

Hot Anger Soon Cold, by Porter, Chettle, and Ben Jonson, London, Rose theater, circa 1598;

The Two Angry Women of Abington, part 2, London, Rose theater, circa 1599;

Two Merry Women of Abington, London, Rose theater, circa 1599;

The Spencers, by Porter and Chettle, London, Rose theater, circa 1599.

BOOK: *The Pleasant Historie of the Two Angrie Women of Abington* (London: Printed by E. Allde for J. Hunt & W. Ferbrand, 1599).

Editions: *The Two Angry Women of Abington: A Critical Edition,* edited by Karen Wood (Ann Arbor: University Microfilms, 1979);

The Two Angry Women of Abington: A Critical Edition, edited by Marianne B. Evett (New York: Garland, 1980).

Henry Porter is the author of *The Two Angry Women of Abington,* a remarkably innovative comedy of the late sixteenth century. He is listed in Philip Henslowe's diary as the author and coauthor of plays for the Admiral's Men in 1598 and 1599, and the diary also notes that he borrowed money from Henslowe in 1596-1599. The plays attributed to him in the diary are *Love Prevented* (part of this entry may be forged), *Black Bateman of the North,* part 2 (with Henry Chettle and Robert Wilson), *Hot Anger Soon Cold* (with Ben Jonson and Chettle), part 2 of *The Two Angry Women of Abington, Two Merry Women of Abington,* and *The Spencers* (with Chettle). All of these works are lost. That Porter enjoyed a moderate success as a dramatist may be inferred from the two sequels to *The Two Angry Women of Abington* (which the

diary does not mention), from Henslowe's having placed him under exclusive contract in February of 1599, and from Francis Meres's description of him in *Palladis Tamia* (1598) as one of the "best Poets from Comedy . . . amongst us."

Little is known about Porter's life. The name Henry Porter appears in various records of the late sixteenth century, but these records clearly refer to more than one person. A 1599 epigram by John Weever is addressed "Ad Henricus Porter," who seems, though the poem is not explicit on this point, to be a poet-clergyman. The *Calendar of State Papers* shows that a pardon *"de se defendendo"* was granted to a Henry Porter on 1 December 1591 "for the death of Cotterell." Another calendar entry, for August 1584, mentions a Henry Porter who was captain of the pirate ship *Charles Jones.* Leslie Hotson claimed that Porter died 7 June 1599 of a wound inflicted the previous day by the playwright John Day. He quotes the 1599 file for the Southwark assizes for that year to show that Day was found guilty of having "with malice aforethought . . . killed and murdered . . . Henry Porter." Hotson's conclusion is poorly documented, but it is not contradicted by Henslowe's diary, whose final entry concerning Porter is dated 26 May 1599.

The *Alumni Cantabrigienses* records two Henry Porters as matriculants in the time of Elizabeth—one as sizar at Christ's College in 1586, the other as pensioner at Corpus Christi in 1590. The *Brasenose College Register* shows a Henry Porter of London, son of a gentleman and sixteen years of age, as a matriculant in 1589. The *Register of the University of Oxford* lists a Henry Porter of Christ's Church College as applicant for the bachelor's degree in 1600, and Anthony à Wood's *Athenae Oxonienses* indicates that the degree was awarded:

1600: Bach of Musick

Jul . . . Henry Porter of Ch.Ch.—Some of his compositions I have seen. . . . He was fa-

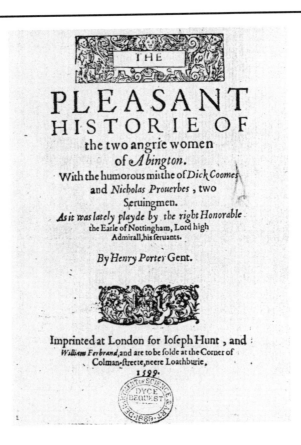

THE

PLEASANT
HISTORIE OF

the two angrie women
of *Abington*.
With the humorous miithe of *Dick Coomes*
and *Nicholas Prouerbes*, two
Seruingmen.
As it was lately playde by the right Honorable
the Earle of Nottingham, Lord high
Admirall, his seruants.

By Henry Porter Gent.

Imprinted at London for Ioseph Hunt, and
William Ferbrand, and are to be solde at the Corner of
Colman-streete, neere Loathburie,
1599.

The Prologue.

entlemen, I come to yee like one
that lackes and would borrow, but
was loth to aske leaft he should be
denyed: I would aske, but I would
aske to obteine: O vvould I knew that manner
of asking: to beg vvere bafe, and to cooche low
and to carrie an humble shew of entreatie, were
too Dog-like that favynes on his maifter to get
a bone from his Trencher: out Curre I cannot
abide it, to put on the shape and habit of this
nevv vvorlds nevv found beggars, miftermed
Souldiers, as thus: fvveet Gentlemen, let a poore
Scholler implore and exerate, that you would
make him riche in the poffeffion of a mite of
your fauours, to keepe him a true man in vvit,
and to pay for his lodging among the Mufes:
fo God him helpe he is driuen to a moft lovve
eftate, tis not vnknowne what feruice of words

A 2   he

A pleafant Comedie of the tvvo
But kindly take the fauour of good will.
If any thing be in the pen to blame,
Then here ftand I to blufh the writers fhame,
If this be bad, he promifes a better,
Truft him, and he will prooue a right true debter.

FINIS.

Title page and prologue from a 1599 quarto edition of Porter's only surviving play (Victoria and Albert Museum)

255

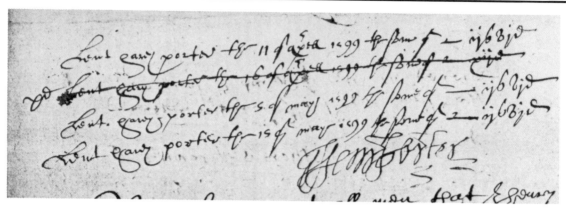

Records of Philip Henslowe's loans to Henry Porter, 11 April-15 May 1599, written and signed by Porter in Henslowe's diary (MSS VII, l. 30ʳ; by permission of Dulwich College, London)

ther to Walt. Porter sometimes Gentleman of the royal Chappel of King Ch. I and Master of the Choristers at Westminster. . . .

Whether any of the Henry Porters who attended the universities was the dramatist–who claims in the prologue to *The Two Angry Women of Abington* to be a scholar–cannot now be determined, partly because the records contain so few facts, partly because they were often inaccurately kept, and partly because, at Cambridge from 1590 to 1601, they were not kept at all. Perhaps the most probable candidate is the Porter of Christ's Church, who had undergone twelve years of study when he applied for his degree. The leniency with which university residency requirements were enforced would have allowed him, during this time, to write plays and to pay occasional visits to London. The application for the degree in 1600 and the disappearance of his name from Henslowe's diary after 1599 could indicate a decision to devote his energies entirely to music. It might also suggest that he no longer needed the income provided by the plays. The appointment in 1603 of a Henry Porter to the office of royal sackbut supports this conjecture. Then also, Porter's use of the Spencer family as the subject of his last play, along with the fact reported by Anthony à Wood that Walter Porter, Henry's son, had received the patronage of the Spencers, indicates a family connection between them and the Christ's Church Porter that could identify him as the dramatist. Finally, though, no definite conclusions are possible.

The Two Angry Women of Abington, Porter's only extant play, teaches an old and misogynistic lesson: women are innately irascible and ruled by will, not, as men are, by reason. Mistress Barnes and Mistress Goursey quarrel because one sus-

pects the other, groundlessly, of adultery with her husband. To reconcile the two women the husbands plan a marriage between their children, Mall Barnes and Frank Goursey, but the wives' violent opposition to that union results in everyone's getting lost outside at night.

The play was published in 1599, but its date of composition is unknown; external evidence indicates that the play was written before 1590. For its period *The Two Angry Women of Abington* is an unusually original play. During and preceding the 1580s, dramatic subjects were typically mythological or biblical. Porter's play is the first extant example of sustained realistic treatment of country life. It is also, in its use of idiosyncratic styles of language to render aberrances of character, an early humors play.

Finally, it is the earliest extant comedy with a fully formed night scene, a nocturnal world governed by its own special laws and principles and charged with metaphoric implications of moral error and psychic disequilibrium. In other words, Porter's play is a possible source for the humors comedies that were to follow, as well as for later plays with night scenes–such as *The Merry Wives of Windsor, The Merry Devil of Edmonton, A Midsummer Night's Dream*–and it contains raw materials which Shakespeare, Jonson, and others were to refine and perfect.

References:

R. H. Bowers, "Notes on *The Two Angry Women of Abington,*" *Notes & Queries,* 193 (24 July 1948): 311-314;

E. K. Chambers, *The Elizabethan Stage* (Oxford: Clarendon Press, 1923), III: 466-467;

Leslie Hotson, "The Adventures of the Single Rapier," *Atlantic Monthly,* 148 (July 1931): 26-31;

William J. Lawrence, "The Elizabethan Nocturnal," in his *Pre-Restoration Stage Studies* (Cambridge: Harvard University Press, 1927), pp. 122-144;

Baldwin Maxwell, "*The Two Angry Women of Abington* and *Wily Beguiled,*" *Philological Quarterly,* 20 (1941): 334-339;

J. M. Nosworthy, "Henry Porter," *English,* 6 (1946): 65-69;

Nosworthy, "Notes on Henry Porter," *Modern Language Review,* 35 (1940): 517-521;

Nosworthy, *Shakespeare's Occasional Plays, Their Origin and Transmission* (New York: Barnes & Noble, 1965);

E. H. C. Oliphant, "Who Was Henry Porter?," *PMLA,* 43 (June 1928): 572-575;

Felix E. Schelling, *Elizabethan Drama, 1588-1642* (Boston: Houghton Mifflin, 1908), I: 321-323;

Rosetta E. Shear, "New Facts About Henry Porter," *PMLA,* 42 (September 1927): 641-655;

Karen Wood, Introduction to *The Two Angry Women of Abington* (Ann Arbor: University Microfilms, 1979).

Thomas Preston
(1537-1598)

Irby B. Cauthen, Jr.
University of Virginia

PLAY PRODUCTIONS: *Cambises, King of Persia* (possibly the same play as *Huff, S[n]uff, and Ruff,* London, at Court, Christmas season 1560-1561);

Sir Clyomon and Clamydes, doubtfully attributed to Preston, London, unknown theater, circa 1570.

BOOKS: *A Lamentable Tragedy Mixed ful of Pleasant Mirth, Conteyning the Life of Cambises King of Percia* (London: Printed by J. Allde, 1570?);

The Historie of the Two Valiant Knights, Syr Clyomon and Clamydes, doubtfully attributed to Preston (London: Printed by T. Creede, 1599).

Editions: *Cambises,* in *Tudor Plays,* edited by Edmund Creeth (Garden City: Doubleday, 1966), pp. 443-503;

Cambises, in *Minor Elizabethan Tragedies,* edited by T. W. Craik (London: Dent, 1974), pp. 59-104;

A Critical Edition of Thomas Preston's Cambises, edited by Robert Carl Johnson (Salzburg: Institut für Englische Sprache und Literatur, 1975);

Cambises, in *Drama of the English Renaissance: The Tudor Period,* edited by Russell A. Fraser and Norman Rabkin (New York: Macmillan, 1976), pp. 59-80.

The Thomas Preston whose name appears on the title page and in the colophon of the first quarto edition of *Cambises* has been traditionally identified as the distinguished academic of the University of Cambridge who, after study at Eton, entered King's College in 1553 and became a fellow there in 1556, earning a B.A. in 1557 and an M.A. in 1561. When Queen Elizabeth visited Cambridge in 1564, he acted in a performance of *Dido* which she attended, disputed before her with a redoubtable Puritan, Thomas Cartwright, and addressed her in a Latin oration on her departure. She invited him to kiss her hand and gave him a pension of £20 a year with the title of "her scholar." He became proctor of the university in 1565, began the study of civil law in 1572, and proceeded to the degree of LL.D. four years later. He left in 1581 and seems to have joined the College of Advocates, a group of judges and lawyers housed in Doctors' Commons near St. Paul's in London, who heard and pled cases involving civil and canon law, but not criminal law. Returning to Cambridge in 1584 as master of Trinity Hall, he eventually, in his last year (1598), was appointed vice-chancellor of the university. Interestingly, in 1592 he had signed, along with others, a petition asking for the banning of plays in Cambridge.

That such a learned, even cloistered man could have written the bombastic *Cambises* was questioned first by John M. Manly in 1910; E. K. Chambers in 1923 thought it "incredible" that he should be taken as the author of a play that contains "nothing academic," and thus Chambers attributed *Cambises* to "a popular writer of the same name." In his 1924 edition of the play John Q. Adams seconded their doubts, and the play's most recent editor, R. C. Johnson, suggested in 1975 that the play is the work of an itinerant actor-playwright. But other critics, among them Felix E. Schelling in 1908 and W. A. Armstrong in 1955, support Preston's authorship.

If only from the title, one can understand why authorship by the distinguished scholar Pres-

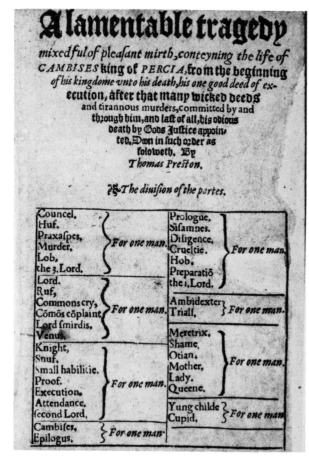

Title page for the 1570(?) quarto edition of the play whose well-known rhetorical excesses Falstaff refers to in Henry IV, *part 1, when he declares, "I must speak in passion, and I will do it in King Cambises' vein" (Henry E. Huntington Library and Art Gallery)*

ton can be questioned: "A lamentable tragedy *mixed ful of pleasant mirth, conteyning the life of CAMBISES king of PERCIA, from the beginning of his kingdome vnto his death, his one good deed of ex*ecution, after that many wicked deeds and tirannous murders, committed by and through him, and last of all, his odious death by Gods Justice appointed." The play closely follows its source, Richard Taverner's *The Garden of Wisdom* (1539), a collection of moralizing anecdotes about great men of antiquity. Both accounts of Cambises relate his one good deed, the flaying of a corrupt judge, Sisamnes, whose skin was then placed over the judgment seat of his son who succeeded him as a constant reminder of his father's guilt and punishment. Then follow three crimes: first, when urged by his counselor Praxaspes to cease his drunkenness, Cambises shoots an arrow through the center of his counselor's son's heart to prove his steady hand is not that of a drunkard. Second, Cambises murders his brother so he will not become king. Finally, he marries his cousin, his "own sister germain," whom he puts to death when she reminds him of his fratricide. God's vengeance, Taverner and Preston agree, waits to plague the sinner: when Cambises is mounting his horse, his sword falls out of its scabbard and so sorely wounds him in his side that he dies. Preston, following the moralizing Taverner, declares that such a death is "a just reward for his misdeeds that God above hath wrought."

From this naive story comes a play that is difficult to fit into a genre. At its simplest level it is a Renaissance story of the fall of the mighty that goes back to Boccaccio's *De Casibus Virorum Illustrium* (1363-1364) and was brought into English with Chaucer's *Monk's Tale*, John Lygate's *The Fall of Princes*, and *A Mirror for Magistrates*. But it is not a simple play. It harks back as well to early religious drama; J. M. R. Margeson points out that in Preston's play pathos is aroused by the killing of Praxaspes's son in the same way that it is aroused by the murder, or imminent murder, of children in the medieval miracle plays *The Slaughter of the Innocents* and *Abraham and Isaac*. Also Cambises is like the tyrant Herod of *The Slaughter of the Innocents*, arrogant and irreligious, the ranting embodiment of the world's enmity against God. It recalls also the later morality plays, particularly in its most vivid character, Ambidexter, "the double dealer," who descends from the traditional Vice. Other characters are given moralitylike names—"Preparation," "Proof," "Execution"—when they could as well have been called "First Servant" and the like. The comic scenes, particularly those with Huff, Snuff, and Ruff, remind us of English folk plays; they speak like English rustics who could just as well have been called Diccon or Hodge. By their doggerel they relieve the monotonous "fourteeners," the alexandrine lines given to the king and his courtiers. Because *Cambises* combines so many of its dramatic antecedents it has been classified as a "mixed" type–history, morality, comedy, and folk play.

But like its near contemporary *Gorboduc*, it does more than draw from its predecessors: it, too, is an expression of the *speculus principis*, a "mirror" play about the relationship of the ruler and the governed. As William A. Armstrong points out, the necessity for obedience to a lawful monarch, even if he is a tyrant, is insistently emphasized. Only God can remove an evil ruler; the evil deeds a king commits will not be tolerated long. Cambises reigns less than two years. The accidental, self-inflicted wound is a sign of God's retribution: "A just reward for my misdeeds my death doth plain declare" are his last words.

In the comic scenes when the commoners, urged on by Ambidexter, speak of sedition, the message again is clear: susceptible to demagoguery as the commoners are, they must defer to the nobles, who must maintain the unity of the realm. But passive obedience by both noble and commoner is not enough; God will uphold those who support the ordained hierarchical order and will deliver them in good time from the tyrant.

Yet *Cambises*, one must admit, was not famous for its historical precedents or its orthodox political philosophy. It was popular for its sensationalism and its rhetoric. Violence occurs on the stage; it is not reported by a messenger–a judge is flayed (according to stage directions, by use of "a false skin"); a child's heart is cut out after his pathetic cry, "Good master king, do not shoot me; my mother loves me best of all!"; the king's brother is struck "in divers places" with his blood spurting out (an effect created by *"A little bladder of vinegar pricked"*); and finally, when Cambises dies, the stage direction–which must have pleased the actor–reads *"Here let him quake and stir."* The onstage violence anticipates that in Thomas Kyd's *The Spanish Tragedy*.

The rhetoric of *Cambises* was well known and sometimes affectionately parodied. Falstaff, in assuming the mock throne and role of Hal's father in part one of *Henry IV* (II.iv), declares that "I must speak in passion, and I will do it in King

THE
HISTORIE OF
the two valiant Knights,
Syr *Clyomon* Knight of the Golden
Sheeld, fonne to the King of
Denmarke:

And Clamydes *the white Knight, fonne to the*
King of Suauia.

As it hath bene fundry times Acted by her
Maiesties Players.

LONDON
Printed by Thomas Creede.
1599.

Title page for the 1599 quarto edition of a play that has sometimes been attributed to Preston (Anderson Galleries, sale number 2077, 20-21 May 1926)

Cambises' vein." Shakespeare also seems to be remembering *Cambises* in the Pyramus and Thisbe interlude in *A Midsummer Night's Dream*, "very tragical mirth"; and one wonders if there are not echoes of the *Cambises* vein in the scene where Nurse and the Capulets discover Juliet presumed dead (IV.v). In the prologue to *Tamburlaine*, which presents a king not unlike his dramatic predecessor Cambises, Marlowe, too, alludes to the style and matter of *Cambises*: "From jigging veins of rhyming mother wits/And such conceits as clownage keeps in pay. . . ."

What the play makes up in action and words, it lacks in staging. Though it may have been performed at Court during the 1560-1561 Christmas season, it seems to have been designed for a touring company, as it is played on a stage nearly bare; but stage props are named, including a board for the banquet and staves for a mock fight. Eight men, two of them probably boys, take thirty-eight parts. The actors playing Cambises and Ambidexter each take only one other part; others take either six or seven. Adams suggests that Shakespeare possibly acted one of the roles in a later production.

Sir Philip Sidney, in his *Defense of Poesie*, may have been the first to condemn *Cambises* when he deplores the play's mixing of kings and clowns, particularly where the clowns "play a part in majestical matters, with neither decency or discretion." Succeeding critics have found the play "barbaric," "wretched," lacking in "any real tragic intent," and too filled with grandiloquence and bombast. But others, such as J. P. Myers, have found it, despite its lack of genius and style, "the most interesting and successful of hybrid morality-history plays." The highest praise perhaps comes from Emile Legouis, who wrote that the playwright "has rendered [Cambises] lifelike and complex enough, has shown his double physical and moral nature, and given him a temperament. There is here a character which ought already to be called Shakespearean."

Another play, *Sir Clyomon and Clamydes* (produced circa 1570), has been attributed to Preston by G. L. Kittredge, who noted that it is written in the vein of *Cambises* and that the Vice is similar to Ambidexter; he also found parallels to *Cambises* in one speech. More recently, David Bevington has found the attribution plausible. *Sir Clyomon and Clamydes* is a romance–much unlike *Cambises* in its lack of seriousness–that suggests *The Faerie Queene* with enchanters such as Archimago keeping knights and ladies under their spells. There is a lady in the plot, Neronis, who–disguised as a page–attends her beloved, not the last of such patient heroines.

But it is *Cambises* that is important for dramatic history. It was written most likely by a learned man; for, despite Chambers's claims to the contrary, there are things academic in it (such as the classical allusions in the prologue, for example). It sets forth a political philosophy that would be appropriate for Preston the scholar; and it shows a familiarity with a simple stage, as in a banqueting house, that a youthful, although university, actor might know. Even a man established in an academic profession could have written such a play, perhaps as an escape from

scholarship. The perceptive mind that lies behind the naive story explores, both through comedy and tragedy, a seriousness in man's destiny. And, as William D. Wolf properly asserts, "for all its crudity and rant, the play is a considerable *tour de force* when compared to the popular drama preceding it."

Bibliography:

Philip Dust and William D. Wolf, "Recent Studies in Early Tudor Drama: *Gorboduc, Ralph Roister Doister, Gammer Gurton's Needle,* and *Cambises,*" *English Literary Renaissance,* 8 (Winter 1978): 107-119.

References:

William A. Armstrong, "The Authorship and Political Meaning of *Cambises,*" *English Studies,* 36, no. 6 (1955): 289-299;

David Bevington, *From* Mankind *to* Marlowe (Cambridge: Harvard University Press, 1962), pp. 183-188;

Bevington, *Tudor Drama and Politics* (Cambridge: Harvard University Press, 1968), pp. 156-160;

E. K. Chambers, *The Elizabethan Stage* (Oxford: Clarendon Press, 1923), III: 469-470;

George Lyman Kittredge, "Notes on Elizabethan Drama," *Journal of English and Germanic Philosophy,* 2, no. 1 (1898): 8-9;

Emile Legouis, *A History of English Literature* (New York: Macmillan, 1957), pp. 243-245;

John M. Manly, "The Children of the Chapel Royal and Their Masters," in *The Cambridge History of English Literature,* edited by A. W. Ward and A. R. Waller, volume 6, part 2 (Cambridge: Cambridge University Press, 1910), pp. 320-321;

J. M. R. Margeson, *The Origins of English Tragedy* (Oxford: Clarendon Press, 1967);

James P. Myers, Jr., "The Heart of King Cambises," *Studies in Philology,* 70 (October 1973): 367-376;

Irving Ribner, *The English History Play in the Age of Shakespeare* (London: Methuen, 1957), pp. 49-56;

Felix E. Schelling, *Elizabethan Drama 1558-1642,* 2 volumes (Boston: Houghton Mifflin, 1908), I: 72, 120-121, 199; II: 16.

Thomas Sackville
(1536-19 April 1608)

Thomas Norton
(1532-10 March 1584)

Irby B. Cauthen, Jr.
University of Virginia

PLAY PRODUCTION: *Gorboduc, or Ferrex and Porrex*, acts 1-3 by Norton, acts 4-5 by Sackville, London, Inner Temple, 6 January 1562.

WORKS BY SACKVILLE: *Induction* and *Complaint of Henry, Duke of Buckingham*, in *A Myrroure for Magistrates*, edited by William Baldwin (London: Printed by T. Marshe, 1559);

Commendatory verse in *The Courtyer of Baldessar Castilio*, translated by Thomas Hoby (London: Printed by W. Seres, 1561).

WORKS BY NORTON: *An Epistle vnto the Right Honorable . . . the Duke of Somerset*, by Peter Martyr, translated by Norton (London: Printed by N. Hill for G. Lynne, 1550);

Epitaph of Henry Williams, in *Songs and Sonnettes [Tottel's Miscellany]* (London: Printed by R. Tottel, 1557);

Orations, of Arsanes agaynst Philip of Macedone, edited and translated by Norton (London: Printed by J. Daye, 1560?);

The Institution of Christian Religion, by John Calvin, translated by Norton (London: Printed by R. Woolfe & R. Harison, 1561);

To the Queenes Maiesties Poore Deceyued Subiectes of the Northe Contreye (London: Printed by H. Bynneman for L. Harrison, 1569);

A Warning agaynst the Dangerous Practises of Papistes (London: Printed by J. Day, 1569?);

A Catechisme, or First Instruction of Christian Religion, translated by Norton from the Latin catechism by Alexander Nowell (London: Printed by J. Day, 1570);

A Bull Graunted by the Pope to Doctor Harding and Other. . . . With a True Declaration of the Intention and Frutes Thereof (London: Printed by J. Day, 1570);

A Disclosing of the Great Bull (London: Printed by J. Daye, 1570);

An Addition Declaratorie to the Bulles (London: Printed by J. Daye, 1570);

A Message, Termed Marke the Truth of the Worde of God, in These .xiii. Bloes, at the Popes Bull, attributed to Norton (London: Printed by W. How for J. Arenolde, 1570);

The Seueral Confessions of T. Norton and C. Norton, by Thomas Norton and Christopher Norton (London: Printed by W. How for R. Johnes, 1570);

A Catechisme, or Institution of Christian Religion, to Bee Learned of All Youth Next After the Little Catechisme: Appointed in the Booke of Common Prayer, translated by Norton from the Latin catechism by Alexander Nowell (London: Printed by J. Daye, 1572).

WORK BY SACKVILLE AND NORTON: *The Tragedie of Gorboduc*, acts 1-3 by Norton, acts 4-5 by Sackville (London: Printed by W. Griffith, 1565); republished as *The Tragidie of Ferrex and Porrex* (London: Printed by J. Daye, 1570).

Editions: *Gorboduc*, in *Tudor Plays*, edited by Edmund Creeth (Garden City: Doubleday, 1966), pp. 383-442;

Gorboduc, or Ferrex and Porrex, edited by Irby B. Cauthen, Jr. (Lincoln: University of Nebraska Press, 1970);

Gorboduc, in *Minor Elizabethan Tragedies*, edited by T. W. Craik (London: Dent, 1974), pp. 1-58;

Gorboduc, in *Drama of the English Renaissance: The Tudor Period*, edited by Russell A. Fraser and Norman Rabkin (New York: Macmillan, 1976), pp. 81-100.

Thomas Sackville and Thomas Norton, joined by little else in their lives, collaborated in the writing of *Gorboduc*, the first important play in the history of English literature. Not only is it the first "regular" English tragedy (one that follows classical rules), but it is marked by innovations that were to become traditional. Both authors were members of the Inner Temple—one of the four Inns of Court in London—when they prepared the play for the 1562 Twelfth Night celebrations there. Both men were to serve the crown later in different ways; the play they wrote together may present, almost improbably, the only political philosophy they shared, and even on that they may not have agreed.

Born in Buckhurst, Sussex, into a wealthy family that had served the crown through many distinguished generations, Thomas Sackville was the only son of Sir Richard Sackville, cousin of Anne Boleyn. The son most likely studied briefly at Oxford, but later in life received honorary M.A.'s from both Oxford and Cambridge. Although there are problems about assigning an exact date for their composition, it is in this early period of his life—most likely between 1554 and 1557—that he wrote his *Induction* and the *Complaint of Henry, Duke of Buckingham*, which were eventually included in *A Mirror for Magistrates* (1559), edited by William Baldwin. In this admonitory volume—a continuation of John Lydgate's *The Fall of Princes*—figures of English history tell their stories so that present and future rulers ("magistrates") may see how vice has been punished and thus be moved to "the sooner amendment." Sackville's poems were praised by Jasper Heywood, but he is known to have written only one more, a commendatory sonnet for Sir Thomas Hoby's 1561 translation of Baldassare Castiglione's *The Courtier*. After the composition of these pieces and *Gorboduc*, he devoted himself to his duties in Parliament and at Court.

In preparation for those duties, not for the practice of law, he was admitted to the Inner Temple in 1555. The previous year he had married Cecily, daughter of Sir John Baker of Sissinghurst in Kent. He was elected to Parliament in 1558. During his long tenure there he undertook various services, including diplomatic missions to the Continent. He was knighted and made a peer, created Baron Buckhurst, on the same day in 1567 that the Queen called him her "beloved kinsman."

In 1586 Sackville was one of the forty chosen to bring the news of her impending execution to Mary Queen of Scots, who, by Sackville family tradition, was so impressed with his demeanor that she gave him a piece of the "furni-ture of her private chapel," a carving of the procession to Calvary. Two years after his election to the Order of the Garter in 1589, he was chosen Chancellor of the University of Oxford upon the Queen's recommendation. He became Lord High Treasurer in 1599, and in that office he conducted the trial of the Earl of Essex for treason in 1601; in pronouncing the death sentence "with gravity and solemnity," as Lord Bacon said, he compassionately suggested that the Earl call upon the Queen's mercy. Sackville's service to the crown continued under James I, who in the second year of his reign created him Earl of Dorset.

In poor health for many years, Sackville wrote that he was "always subject to rheums and colds in the winter." Characteristically, he died, on 19 April 1608, while working at the Council Table. At that meeting, one of his contemporaries reported, "He spake as well and temperately as ever he did, and as free he seemed from all pain and distemperature as any of the rest, and suddenly in the midst of the Lords went away in a manner unperceived as though he had slumbered."

His collaborator in the writing of *Gorboduc* presents a contrast to this gentle and gracious man. The eldest son of Thomas Norton and his first wife, Elizabeth Merry, the younger Thomas Norton was born into a family closely associated with the Grocers' Company in London, at whose expense he was sent to Cambridge. Nothing further is known of his academic career but he received an M.A. from Cambridge in 1570. Admitted to the Inner Temple in 1555—the same year in which he married Margery, the third daughter of Archbishop Thomas Cranmer—he had published before his collaboration with Sackville various verses, one of them appearing in *Tottel's Miscellany*, and some translations, such as John Calvin's *Institutes of the Christian Religion*.

He too had been elected to Parliament in 1558 and was a member of the 1563 commission that considered the limitation of the succession to the throne, a matter central to *Gorboduc*; he read the report that recommended the Queen's marriage. In 1571 he was appointed "remembrancer" to the City of London, an office established to remind the mayor of his official engagements and to report the doings of Parliament to him. But despite his ability for "wise, bold, and eloquent" orations, he became more and more involved in the persecutions of the Catholics. In 1581 he was ap-

Title page for the 1559 quarto edition of the volume that contains Sackville's Induction *and* Complaint of Henry, Duke of Buckingham *(Anderson Galleries, sale number 2078, 24-25 May 1926)*

pointed the official censor of the Queen's Catholic subjects and licenser of the press, and on 28 April of that year he directed the torture of a seminary priest, Alexander Briant. He boasted (lamely excusing it later) that he had stretched Briant on the rack to a foot longer than God had made him—a deed and a boast that earned him the nickname of "Rackmaster-General." Others, among them Edmund Campion the martyr, suffered from his zeal.

His treatment of Catholics and his growing (even violent) dissatisfaction with the episcopal establishment became so intense that early in

1584 he was placed under house arrest and later sent to the Tower. His health broken, he was released to return home, where he died on 10 March 1584.

Sackville, wealthy, aristocratic, the perfect courtier, and Norton, intolerant, cruel, and morally repugnant—so they are now remembered. But when they wrote *Gorboduc*, they were still young and maturing men who could agree—in general if not in detail—on what was for them and the realm a matter of great concern—the succession to the crown. Of the five acts of the play, Norton wrote the first three, Sackville the last two,

¶ Orations, of Arſanes agaynſt Philip the trecherous kyng of Macedone: of the Embaſſadors of Venice againſt the Prince that vnder crafty league with Scanderbeg, layed ſnares for Chriſtendome : and of Scanderbeg prayeng ayde of Chriſtian Princes agaynſt periurous murderyng Mahumet and agaynſt the old falſe Chriſtian Duke Mahumetes confederate. With a notable example of Gods vengeance vppon a faithleſſe Kyng, Quene, and her children.

¶ Imprinted at London, by Iohn Daye.

Title page for the 1560(?) octavo edition of one of Norton's translations (Bodleian Library, Oxford)

but the design of the whole may have been Sackville's. And the consistency of the play may be evidence that Sackville, the more skilled poet, saw it into finished form.

The play is based on the story of Gorbodugo as told by Geoffrey of Monmouth in his *History of the Kings of Britain;* it is the prototype of the King Lear story, and Shakespeare may have known Sackville and Norton's dramatic retelling of it. In their play, Gorboduc, growing old, divides his kingdom, with the best of intentions and after much advice, between his two sons, Ferrex and Porrex. Both sons, envying and suspecting each other, plunge the realm into civil war. Porrex kills Ferrex, and their mother, Queen Videna, kills the murderer. The people rise up against Gorboduc and Videna, and the kingdom is thrown into chaos: "Thus shall the wasted soil yield forth no fruit, / But dearth and famine shall possess the land. / The towns shall be consumed and burnt with fire, / The peopled cities shall wax desolate."

The tragedy had an implied political message for contemporary audiences: a childless queen, then nearing thirty and seemingly reluctant to marry, could leave the realm rulerless. The play does not overtly advise the Queen: such directness would not only be impolite but possibly fatally impolitic, particularly since she commanded and attended a second performance on 18 January 1562, less than two weeks after the first. Instead, it advises more obliquely that to insure a peaceful succession there be "certain heirs appointed to the crown, / To stay the title of established right, / And in the people plant obedience." It thus advocates a line of succession that would eliminate, or at least reduce, the danger of civil war.

It is not for its political import that *Gorboduc* is remembered but for other more important literary matters. It is the first "regular" English tragedy, one that follows classical rules. It modifies a Senecan tradition to English matters, employing the classical five-act structure, a chorus and a messenger, and Senecan themes, particularly revenge; but it has no Senecan ghost, and the unities are almost ignored. The Senecan influence should not be overstated, for the play descends as well from a native English tradition of the morality play, in which allegorical forces battle over a human soul; it also reminds us of Sackville's early work that appeared in *A Mirror for Magistrates* and its insistence upon retributive justice. The play is a conscious joining of classical and native traditions.

Gorboduc is also the first English drama written in blank verse. Although the claims are not clear, it is usually accepted that Henry Howard, Earl of Surrey, first used this verse form for parts of his translation of the *Aeneid* (completed before 1547). The verse of *Gorboduc* is ponderous, sometimes highly rhetorical, sometimes bombastic. For the first audiences it may have been exciting to hear such a metrical form in the dialogue, a far cry from the more usual rhyming fourteen-syllable line, as in Thomas Preston's *Cambises*. Certainly in a somber play such as *Gorboduc*, the language is appropriate and even becomes part of the action of the play by its gravity.

Further, *Gorboduc* is the first English drama to use dumb shows, perhaps adapted from the Italian dramatic tradition but more likely derived from court masques and civic pageants. Appear-

¶ The Tragidie of Ferrex and Porrex, set forth without addition or alteration but altogether as the same was shewed on stage before the Queenes Maiestie, about nine yeares past, *vz.* the xviij. day of Ianuarie. 1561. by the gentlemen of the Inner Temple.

Seen and allowed. &c.

Imprinted at London by Iohn Daye, dwelling ouer Aldersgate.

¶ The argument of the Tragedie.

Gorboduc king of Brittaine, diuided his realme in his life time to his sonnes, Ferrex and Porrex. The sonnes fell to discention. The yonger killed the elder. The mother that more dearely loued the elder, for reuenge killed the yonger. The people moued with the crueltie of the fact, rose in rebellion and slew both father and mother. The nobilitie assembled and most terribly destroyed the rebels. And afterwardes for want of issue of the prince whereby the succession of the crowne became vncertaine, they fell to ciuill warre, in which both they and many of of their issues were slaine, and the land for a long time almost desolate and miserably wasted.

¶ The P. to the Reader.

Where this Tragedie was for furniture of part of the grand Christmasse in the Inner Temple first written about nine yeares agoe by the right honourable Thomas now Lorde Buckhurst, and by T. Norton, and after shewed before her Maiestie, and neuer intended by the authors therof to be published: yet one W. G. getting a copie therof at some yongmans hand that lacked a litle money and much discretion, in the last great plage. an. 1565. about v. yeares past, while the said Lord was out of England, and T. Norton farre out of London, and neither of them both made priuie, put it forth exceedingly corrupted: euen as if by meanes of a broker for hire, he should haue entised into his house a faire maide and done her villanie, and after all to bescratched her face, torne her apparell, berayed and disfigured her, and then thrust her out of dores dishonested. In such plight after long wandring she came at length home to the sight of her frendes who scant knew her but by a few tokens and markes remayning. They, the authors I meane, though they were very much displeased that she so ranne abroad without leaue, whereby she caught her shame, as many wantons do, yet seing the case as it is remedilesse, haue for common honestie and shamefastnesse new apparelled, trimmed, and attired her in such forme as she was before. In which better forme since she hath come to me, I haue harbored her for her frendes sake and her owne, and I do not dout her parentes the authors will not now be discontent that she goe abroad among you good readers, so it be in honest companie. For she is by my encouragement and others somewhat lesse ashamed of the dishonestie done to her because it was by fraude and force. If she be welcome among you and gently entertained, in fauor of the house from whence she is descended, and of her owne nature courteously disposed to offend no man, her frendes will thanke you for it. If not, but that she shall be still reproched with her former mishap, or quarelled at by enuious persons, she poore gentlewoman wil surely play Lucreces part, & of her self die for shame, and I shall wishe that she had taried still at home with me, where she was welcome: for she did neuer put me to more charge, but this one poore blacke gowne lined with white that I haue now geuen her to goe abroad among you withall.

A.ij.   ¶The

¶ The names of the Speakers.

Gorboduc, King of great Brittaine.
Videna, Queene and wife to king Gorboduc.
Ferrex, elder sonne to king Gorboduc.
Porrex, yonger sonne to king Gorboduc.
Clotyon, Duke of Cornewall.
Fergus, Duke of Albanye.
Mandud, Duke of Loegris.
Gwenard, Duke of Cumberland.
Eubulus, Secretarie to the king.
Arostus, a counsellor to the king.
Dordan, a counsellor assigned by the king to his eldest sonne Ferrex.
Philander, a counsellor assigned by the king to his yongest sonne Porrex.
     { Both being of the olde
     { kinges counsell before.
Hermon, a parasite remaining with Ferrex.
Tyndar, a parasite remaining with Porrex.
Nuntius, a messenger of the elder brothers death.
Nuntius, a messenger of Duke Fergus rising in armes.
Marcella, a lady of the Queenes priuie chamber.
Chorus, foure auncient and sage men of Brittaine.

¶The

Title page, argument, the printer's note to the reader, and dramatis personae from the 1570 authorized, octavo edition of Gorboduc, or Ferrex and Porrex, *published as a corrective to the "exceedingly corrupted" unauthorized edition of 1565 (British Library)*

ing before each act and suggesting the action that is to come, they, like the drama itself, are moral as well as dramatic.

Gorboduc is the first English drama to receive serious literary criticism. Sir Philip Sidney in his *Defence of Poesie* praised its "stately speeches and well-sounding phrases, climbing to the height of Seneca's style, and full of notable morality." However, deploring its lack of unities of place and time, he declared it could not be "an exact model" for all tragedies.

Rarely performed after its two initial productions, *Gorboduc* is the prototype of the English history plays that have an almost obsessive concern with the destiny of the realm, its monarch, and its people. It announced clearly the dangers of a divided country, an unwise ruler, and civil war; those dangers are made more dramatic in Marlowe and in Shakespeare's "thinly veiled sermons on government," in Glynn Wickham's phrase. It is indeed a landmark in the history of English drama.

The play was first printed in 1565 from a copy secured by a young man who "lacked a little money and much discretion"; this pirated edition was followed by a corrected version in 1570, one that modern editors follow.

Bibliography:

Philip Dust and William D. Wolf, "Recent Studies in Early Tudor Drama: *Gorboduc, Ralph Roister Doister, Gammer Gurton's Needle,* and *Cambises,*" *English Literary Renaissance,* 8 (Winter 1978): 107-119.

References:

Paul Bacquet, *Un contemporain d'Elizabeth I: Thomas Sackville l'homme et l'oeuvre* (Geneva: Droz, 1966);

Howard Baker, *Induction to Tragedy, A Study in the Development of Form in Gorboduc, The Spanish Tragedy, and Titus Andronicus* (Baton Rouge: Louisiana State University Press, 1939);

Normand Berlin, *Thomas Sackville* (New York: Twayne, 1974);

Wolfgang Clemen, *English Tragedy before Shakespeare* (London: Methuen, 1961);

Madeleine Doran, *Endeavors of Art: A Study of Form in Elizabethan Drama* (Madison: University of Wisconsin Press, 1954);

M. T. Herrick, "Senecan Influence in *Gorboduc,*" in *Studies in Speech and Drama in Honor of Alexander M. Drummond,* edited by Herbert A. Wilchelns, Donald C. Bryant, Barnard Hewitt, and Karl R. Wallace (Ithaca: Cornell University Press, 1944), pp. 78-104;

Irving Ribner, *The English History Play in the age of Shakespeare* (London: Methuen, 1965);

Jacob Swart, *Thomas Sackville: A Study in Sixteenth-Century Poetry* (Groningen: Wolters, 1948);

Ernest W. Talbert, "The Political Import and First Two Audiences of *Gorboduc,*" *Studies in Honor of Dewitt T. Starnes,* edited by Thomas P. Harrison, Archibald A. Hill, Ernest C. Mossner, and James Sledd (Austin: Humanities Research Center, University of Texas, 1967), pp. 89-115;

H. A. Watt, *Gorboduc; or, Ferrex and Porrex* (Madison: University of Wisconsin Press, 1910).

Papers:

Some of Norton's papers on affairs of state are at the British Library (Lansdale MS 155, folios 84 seq.). Letters and other manuscripts by and relating to Sackville are in various collections at the Bodleian Library.

William Shakespeare

(on or about 23 April 1564-23 April 1616)

John F. Andrews
National Endowment for the Humanities

PLAY PRODUCTIONS: *Henry VI*, part 1, London, unknown theater (perhaps by a branch of the Queen's Men), circa 1589-1592;

Henry VI, part 2, London, unknown theater (perhaps by a branch of the Queen's Men), circa 1590-1592;

Henry VI, part 3, London, unknown theater (perhaps by a branch of the Queen's Men), circa 1590-1592;

Richard III, London, unknown theater (perhaps by a branch of the Queen's Men), circa 1591-1592;

The Comedy of Errors, London, unknown theater (probably by Lord Strange's Men), circa 1592-1594; London, Gray's Inn, 28 December 1594;

Titus Andronicus, London, Rose or Newington Butts theater, 24 January 1594;

The Taming of the Shrew, London, Newington Butts theater, 11 June 1594;

The Two Gentlemen of Verona, London, Newington Butts theater or the Theatre, 1594;

Love's Labor's Lost, perhaps at the country house of a great lord, such as the Earl of Southampton, circa 1594-1595; London, at Court, Christmas 1597;

Sir Thomas More, probably by Anthony Munday, revised by Thomas Dekker, Henry Chettle, Shakespeare, and possibly Thomas Heywood, evidently never produced, circa 1594-1595;

King John, London, the Theatre, circa 1594-1596;

Richard II, London, the Theatre, circa 1595;

Romeo and Juliet, London, the Theatre, circa 1595-1596;

A Midsummer Night's Dream, London, the Theatre, circa 1595-1596;

The Merchant of Venice, London, the Theatre, circa 1596-1597;

Henry IV, part 1, London, the Theatre, circa 1596-1597;

Henry IV, part 2, London, the Theatre, circa 1597;

The Merry Wives of Windsor, Windsor, Windsor Castle, 23 April 1597;

The Flower Portrait of Shakespeare, which came into the possession of Mrs. Charles Flower in 1895 (Royal Shakespeare Theatre, Stratford-upon-Avon, Picture Gallery; by permission of the Governors). When the previous owner, H. C. Clements, acquired the portrait in 1840, he said he had seen it exhibited seventy years earlier, but his claim is unsubstantiated. Once thought to have been the original from which the engraving on the title page of the 1623 First Folio of Shakespeare's plays was copied, this portrait is now generally believed to have been based on that engraving.

Much Ado About Nothing, London, the Theatre, circa 1598-1599;

Henry V, London, Globe theater(?), between March and September 1599(?);

Julius Caesar, London, Globe theater, 21 September 1599;

As You Like It, London, Globe theater, circa 1599-1600;

Hamlet, London, Globe theater, circa 1600-1601;

Twelfth Night, London, at Court(?), no earlier than 6 January 1601(?); London, Globe theater(?), circa 1601-1602(?); London, Middle Temple, 2 February 1602;

Troilus and Cressida, London, Globe theater(?), circa 1601-1602(?);

All's Well That Ends Well, London, Globe theater, circa 1602-1603;

Measure for Measure, London, Globe theater(?), 1604(?); London, at Court, 26 December 1604;

Othello, London, Globe theater(?), 1604(?); Westminster, Whitehall, 1 November 1604;

King Lear, London, Globe theater(?), by late 1605 or early 1606; London, at Court, 26 December 1606;

Timon of Athens (possibly unperformed during Shakespeare's lifetime); possibly London, Globe theater, circa 1605-1608;

Macbeth, London, Globe theater(?), 1606(?); London, at Court, probably 7 August 1606;

Antony and Cleopatra, London, Globe theater, circa 1606-1607;

Pericles, possibly by Shakespeare and George Wilkins, London, at Court, between January 1606 and November 1608; London, Globe theater, probably circa 1607-1608;

Coriolanus, London, Globe theater, circa 1607-1608;

Cymbeline, London, Blackfriars theater or Globe theater, 1609;

The Winter's Tale, London, Globe theater, 15 May 1611;

The Tempest, London, at Court, 1 November 1611;

Cardenio, probably by Shakespeare and Fletcher, London, Globe theater(?), circa 1612-1613;

Henry VIII, possibly by Shakespeare and John Fletcher, London, Globe theater, 29 June 1613;

The Two Noble Kinsmen, by Shakespeare and Fletcher, London, probably Blackfriars theater (possibly Globe theater), 1613.

BOOKS: *Venus and Adonis* (London: Printed by Richard Field, sold by J. Harrison I, 1593);

The First Part of the Contention betwixt the two famous Houses of Yorke and Lancaster [abridged and corrupt text of *Henry VI,* part 2] (London: Printed by Thomas Creede for Thomas Millington, 1594);

Lucrece (London: Printed by Richard Field for John Harrison, 1594); republished as *The Rape of Lucrece. Newly Revised* (London: Printed by T. Snodham for R. Jackson, 1616);

The Most Lamentable Romaine Tragedie of Titus Andronicus (London: Printed by John Danter, sold by Edward White & Thomas Middleton, 1594);

A Pleasant Conceited Historie, Called The Taming of a Shrew [corrupt text] (London: Printed by Peter Short, sold by Cuthbert Burbie, 1594);

The True Tragedie of Richard Duke of Yorke, and the death of good King Henrie the Sixt [abridged and corrupt text of *Henry VI,* part 3] (London: Printed by Peter Short for Thomas Millington, 1595);

The Tragedy of King Richard the Third (London: Printed by Valentine Simmes & Peter Short for Andrew Wise, 1597);

The Tragedie of King Richard the second (London: Printed by Valentine Simmes for Andrew Wise, 1597);

An Excellent conceited Tragedie of Romeo and Juliet [corrupt text] (London: Printed by John Danter [& E. Allde?], 1597); *The Most Excellent and lamentable Tragedie of Romeo and Juliet. Newly Corrected, Augmented, and Amended* (London: Printed by Thomas Creede for Cuthbert Burby, 1599);

A Pleasant Conceited Comedie Called, Loues Labors Lost (London: Printed by William White for Cuthbert Burby, 1598);

The History of Henrie the Fourth [part 1] (London: Printed by Peter Short for Andrew Wise, 1598);

A midsommer nights dreame (London: Printed by R. Bradock for Thomas Fisher, 1600);

The most excellent Historie of the Merchant of Venice (London: Printed by James Roberts for Thomas Heyes, 1600);

The Second part of Henrie the fourth, continuing to his death, and coronation of Henrie the fift (London: Printed by Valentine Simmes for Andrew Wise & William Aspley, 1600);

Much adoe about Nothing (London: Printed by Valentine Simmes for Andrew Wise & William Aspley, 1600);

The Cronicle History of Henry the fift [corrupt text] (London: Printed by Thomas Creede for Thomas Mullington & John Busby, 1600);

The Phoenix and Turtle, appended to *Loves Martyr:*

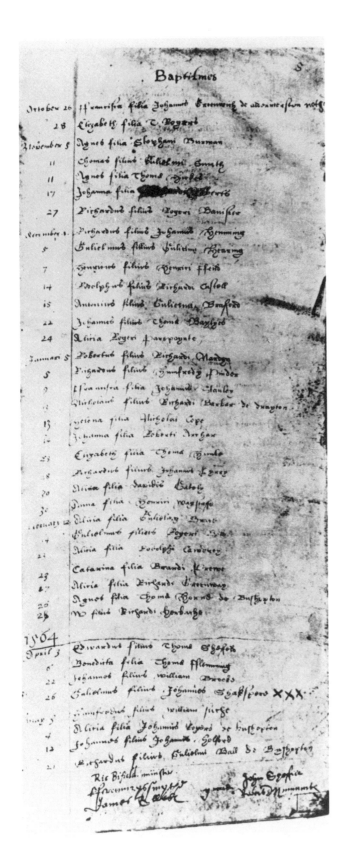

Page from the baptismal register of Holy Trinity Church, Stratford-upon-Avon, recording Shakespeare's christening on 26 April 1564 (Shakespeare's Birthplace Trust Records Office, Stratford-upon-Avon; by permission of the Trustees and Guardians of Shakespeare's Birthplace)

or, Rosalins Complaint, by Robert Chester (London: Printed by Richard Field for E. Blount, 1601);

A Most pleasaunt and excellent conceited Comedie, of Syr John Falstaffe, and the merrie Wives of Windsor [corrupt text] (London: Printed by Thomas Creede for Arthur Johnson, 1602);

The Tragicall Historie of Hamlet Prince of Denmark [abridged and corrupt text] (London: Printed by Valentine Simmes for Nicholas Ling & John Trundell, 1603); *The Tragicall Historie of Hamlet, Prince of Denmarke. Newly Imprinted and Enlarged to Almost as Much Againe as It Was, According to the True and Perfect Coppie* (London: Printed by James Roberts for Nicholas Ling, 1604);

M. William Shak-speare: His True Chronicle Historie of the life and death of King Lear and his three daughters (London: Printed by N. Okes for Nathaniel Butter, 1608);

The Historie of Troylus and Cresseida (London: Printed by G. Eld for R. Bonian & H. Walley, 1609);

Shake-speares Sonnets (London: Printed by G. Eld for Thomas Thorpe, sold by W. Aspley, 1609);

The Late, and Much Admired Play, Called Pericles, Prince of Tyre (London: Printed by W. White for Henry Gosson, 1609);

The Tragædy of Othello, The Moore of Venice (London: Printed by Nicholas Okes for Thomas Walkley, 1622);

Mr. William Shakespeares Comedies, Histories, & Tragedies. Published according to the True Originall Copies (London: Printed by Isaac Jaggard & Edward Blount, 1623)–comprises *The Tempest; The Two Gentlemen of Verona; The Merry Wives of Windsor; Measure for Measure; The Comedy of Errors; Much Ado About Nothing; Love's Labor's Lost; A Midsummer Night's Dream; The Merchant of Venice; As You Like It; The Taming of the Shrew; All's Well That Ends Well; Twelfth Night; The Winter's Tale; King John; Richard II; Henry IV,* parts 1 and 2; *Henry V; Henry VI,* parts 1-3; *Richard III; Henry VIII; Troilus and Cressida; Coriolanus; Titus Andronicus; Romeo and Juliet; Timon of Athens; Julius Caesar; Macbeth; Hamlet; King Lear; Othello; Antony and Cleopatra; Cymbeline;*

The Two Noble Kinsmen, by Shakespeare and John Fletcher (London: Printed by Thomas Cotes for John Waterson, 1634).

Editions: *A New Variorum Edition of Shakespeare,* 29 volumes to date, volumes 1-15, 18, edited by Horace Howard Furness; volumes 16-17, 19-20, edited by Horace Howard Furness, Jr. (Philadelphia & London: Lippincott, 1871-1928); volumes 1-25, general

The earliest depiction of the house where Shakespeare spent his childhood, a watercolor painted by Richard Greene circa 1762 (by permission of the Folger Shakespeare Library; Art Vol. d 75, no. 27c)

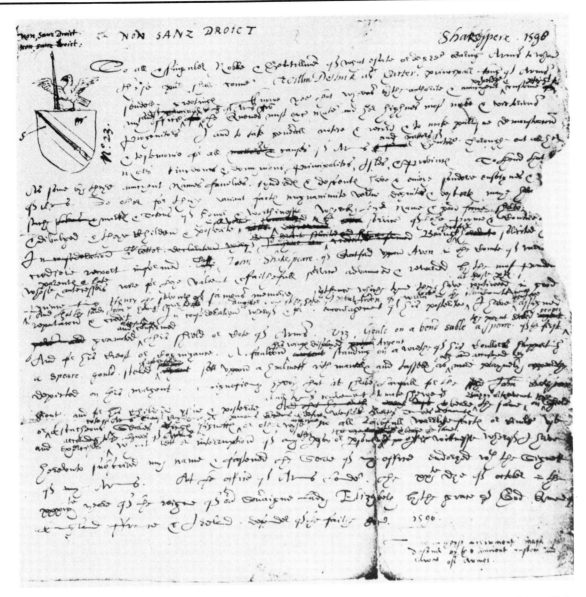

Grant of Arms to John Shakespeare, the first of two rough drafts prepared by William Dethick, Garter King-of-Arms (College of Arms, MS Vincent. 157, art. 23; by permission of the Chapter)

editor Joseph Quincey Adams; volumes 26-27, general editor Hyder Edward Rollins (Philadelphia & London: Lippincott for the Modern Language Association of America, 1936-1955); volumes 28-   , general editors Robert K. Turner, Jr., and Richard Knowles (New York: Modern Language Association of America, 1977-   );

The Works of Shakespeare, The New Cambridge Shakespeare, edited by J. Dover Wilson, Arthur Quiller-Couch, and others, 39 volumes (Cambridge: Cambridge University Press, 1921-1967);

The Complete Works of Shakespeare, edited by

George Lyman Kittredge (Boston: Ginn, 1936); revised by Irving Ribner (Waltham, Mass.: Ginn, 1971);

Shakespeare Quarto Facsimiles, edited by W. W. Greg and Charlton Hinman, 14 volumes (Oxford: Clarendon Press, 1939-1966);

William Shakespeare: The Complete Works, edited by Peter Alexander (London & Glasgow: Collins, 1951; New York: Random House, 1952);

The Arden Shakespeare, general editors Harold F. Brooks and Harold Jenkins, 38 volumes to date (London: Methuen, 1951-   );

The Complete Works of Shakespeare, edited by

Hardin Craig (Chicago: Scott Foresman, 1961); revised by Craig and David Bevington (Glenview, Ill.: Scott Foresman, 1973); revised again by Bevington (Glenview, Ill.: Scott Foresman, 1980);

The New Penguin Shakespeare, general editor T. J. B. Spencer, 33 volumes to date (Harmondsworth: Penguin, 1967-);

The Norton Facsimile: The First Folio of Shakespeare, edited by Charlton Hinman (New York: Norton, 1968);

William Shakespeare: The Complete Works, The Complete Pelican Shakespeare, general editor Alfred Harbage (Baltimore: Penguin, 1969);

The Complete Signet Classic Shakespeare, general editor Sylvan Barnet (New York: Harcourt Brace Jovanovich, 1972);

The Riverside Shakespeare, general editor G. Blakemore Evans (Boston: Houghton Mifflin, 1974);

Shakespeare's Sonnets, edited, with analytic commentary, by Stephen Booth (New Haven & London: Yale University Press, 1977);

Shakespeare's Plays in Quarto: A Facsimile Edition of Copies Primarily from the Henry E. Huntington Library, edited by Michael J. B. Allen and Kenneth Muir (Berkeley: University of California Press, 1982);

The Complete Works, general editors Stanley Wells and Gary Taylor (Oxford: Clarendon Press, 1986);

The Complete Works: Original-Spelling Edition, general editors Wells and Taylor (Oxford: Clarendon Press, 1986).

"He was not of an age, but for all time." So wrote Ben Jonson in his dedicatory verses to the memory of William Shakespeare in 1623, and so we continue to affirm today. No other writer, in English or in any other language, can rival the appeal that Shakespeare has enjoyed. And no one else in any artistic endeavor has projected a cultural influence as broad or as deep.

Shakespeare's words and phrases have become so familiar to us that it is sometimes with a start that we realize we have been speaking Shakespeare when we utter a cliché such as "one fell swoop" or "not a mouse stirring." Never mind that many of the expressions we hear most often– "to the manner born," or (from the same speech in *Hamlet*) "more honored in the breach than the observance"–are misapplied at least as frequently as they are employed with any awareness of their original context and implication. The fact remains that Shakespeare's vocabulary and Shakespeare's cadences are even more pervasive in our ordinary discourse today than the idiom of the King James Bible, which Bartlett lists as only the second most plentiful source of *Familiar Quotations*.

And much the same could be said of those mirrors of our nature, Shakespeare's characters. From small delights like Juliet's Nurse, or Bottom the Weaver, or the Gravedigger, to such incomparable creations as Falstaff, King Lear, and Lady Macbeth, Shakespeare has enlarged our world by imitating it. It should not surprise us, therefore, that personalities as vivid as these have gone on, as it were, to lives of their own outside the dramatic settings in which they first thought and spoke and moved. In opera alone there are enough different renderings of characters and scenes from Shakespeare's plays to assure that the devotee of Charles-François Gounod or Giuseppe Verdi, Richard Wagner or Benjamin Britten, could attend a different performance every evening for six months and never see the same work twice. Which is not to suggest, of course, that the composers of other musical forms have been remiss: Franz Schubert, Felix Mendelssohn, Robert Schumann, Franz Liszt, Hector Berlioz, Pyotr Tchaikovsky, Claude Debussy, Jean Sibelius, Sergey Prokofiev, and Aaron Copland are but a few of the major figures who have given us songs, tone poems, ballets, symphonic scores, or other compositions based on Shakespeare. Cole Porter might well have been addressing his fellow composers when he punctuated *Kiss Me Kate* with the advice to "Brush Up Your Shakespeare."

Certainly the painters have never needed such reminders. Artists of the stature of George Romney, William Blake, Henry Fuseli, Eugene Delacroix, John Constable, J. M. W. Turner, and Dante Gabriel Rossetti have drawn inspiration from Shakespeare's dramatis personae; and, thanks to such impresarios as the eighteenth-century dealer John Boydell, the rendering of scenes from Shakespeare has long been a significant subgenre of pictorial art. Illustrators of Shakespeare editions have often been notable figures in their own right: George Cruikshank, Arthur Rackham, Rockwell Kent, and Salvador Dali. Meanwhile, the decorative arts have had their Wedgwood platters with pictures from the plays, their Shakespeare portraits carved on scrimshaw, their Anne Hathaway's Cottage tea cozies, their mulberry-wood jewelry boxes, and their Superbard T-shirts.

The Guild Chapel and the Guild Hall with the schoolroom of the King's New School on the second floor (top) and the interior of the schoolroom (bottom). Though no school records for the period survive, Shakespeare may have attended this grammar school.

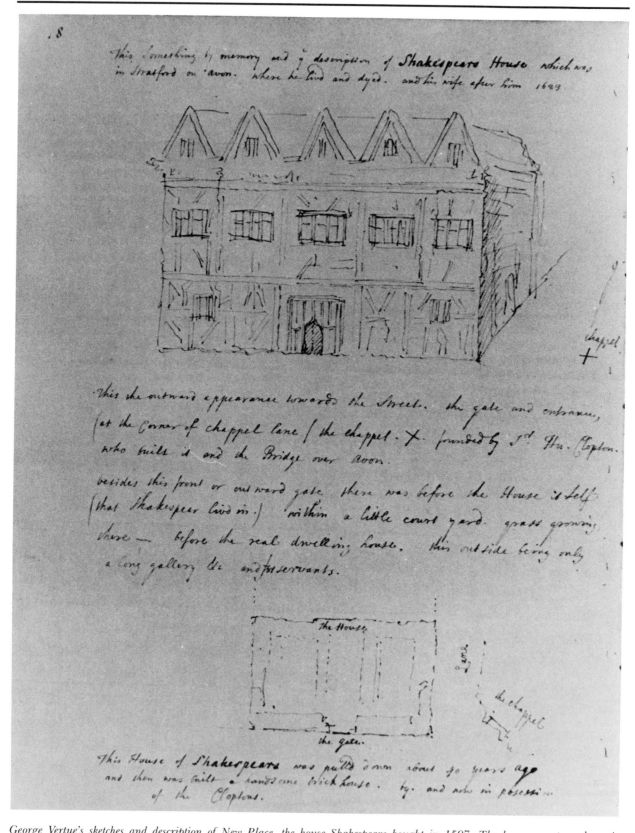

George Vertue's sketches and description of New Place, the house Shakespeare bought in 1597. The house was torn down in 1702, and Vertue, who visited Stratford-upon-Avon in autumn 1737, based his notes and drawings on the reminiscences of a local inhabitant, perhaps a descendant of Shakespeare's sister Joan Hart (British Library, MS Portland Loan 29/246, p. 18; by permission of the British Library Board).

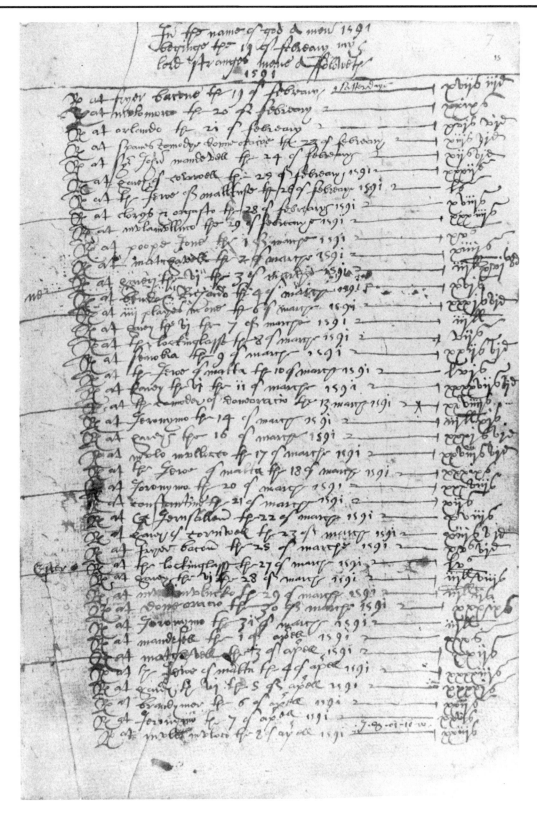

The first mention of a Shakespeare play in the diary of Philip Henslowe came on 3 March 1592 (1591 according to the calendar then in use) when the receipts for a performance of Henry VI *("harey the vj") by the Lord Strange's Men were recorded. Now considered a forgery, the page shown above also records performances of the play on 7, 11, 16, and 28 March and 5 April. It was staged fourteen times between 3 March and 20 June of that year earning large receipts (MSS VII, l. 7ᵛ; by permission of Dulwich College, London).*

Every nation that has a theatrical tradition is indebted to Shakespeare, and in language after language Shakespeare remains the greatest living playwright. Not merely in terms of the hundreds of productions of Shakespeare's own plays to be blazoned on the marquees in any given year, either: no, one must also bear in mind the dozens of film and television versions of the plays, and the countless adaptations, parodies, and spinoffs that accent the repertory—from musicals such as *The Boys from Syracuse* (based on *The Comedy of Errors*) and *West Side Story* (Leonard Bernstein's New York ghetto version of the gang wars in *Romeo and Juliet*), to political lampoons like *Macbird* (contra LBJ) and *Dick Deterred* (the doubly punning anti-Nixon polemic), not to mention more reflective dramatic treatments such as Edward Bond's *Bingo* (a "biographical drama" about Shakespeare the man) and Tom Stoppard's *Rosencrantz and Guildenstern Are Dead* (an absurdist re-enactment of *Hamlet* from the perspective of two innocents as bewildered by the court of Renaissance Elsinore as their twentieth-century counterparts would be in a play such as Samuel Beckett's *Waiting for Godot*).

When we broaden our survey to include the hundreds of novels, short stories, poems, critical appreciations, and other works of serious literature that derive in one way or another from Shakespeare, we partake of an even grander view of the playwright's literary and cultural primacy. Here in America, for example, we can recall Ralph Waldo Emerson's awestruck response to the Stratford seer, his exclamation that Shakespeare was "inconcievably wise," all other great writers only "conceivably." On the other side of the coin, we can indulge in the speculation that Shakespeare may have constituted an aspect of the behemoth that obsessed Herman Melville's imagination, thus accounting for some of the echoes of Shakespearean tragedy in the form and rhetoric of *Moby-Dick*. In a lighter vein, we can chuckle at the frontier Bardolatry so hilariously exploited by the Duke and the King in Mark Twain's *Huckleberry Finn*. Or, moving to our own century, we can contemplate William Faulkner's *The Sound and the Fury* as an extended allusion to Macbeth's "tomorrow and tomorrow and tomorrow" soliloquy. Should we be disposed to look elsewhere, we can puzzle over "the riddle of Shakespeare" in the meditations of the Argentine novelist and essayist Jorge Luis Borges. Or smile (with perhaps but an incomplete suspension of disbelief) as the Nobel Prize-winning African poet

and dramatist Wole Soyinka quips that "Sheikh Zpeir" must have had some Arabic blood in him, so faithfully did he capture the local color of Egypt in *Antony and Cleopatra*.

Implicit in all of these manifestations of Shakespeare worship is a perception best summed up, perhaps, in James Joyce's rendering of the charismatic name: "Shapesphere." For in showing "the very age and body of the time his form and pressure" (as Hamlet would put it), Shakespeare proved himself to be both the "soul of the age" his works reflected and adorned and the consummate symbol of the artist whose poetic visions transcend their local habitation and become, in some mysterious way, contemporaneous with "all time" (to return once more to Jonson's eulogy). If Jan Kott, a twentieth-century existentialist from eastern Europe, can marvel that Shakespeare is "our contemporary," then, his testimony is but one more instance of the tendency of every age to claim Shakespeare as its own. Whatever else we say about Shakespeare, in other words, we are impelled to acknowledge the incontrovertible fact that, preeminent above all others, he has long stood and will no doubt long remain atop a pedestal (to recall a recent *New Yorker* cartoon) as "a very very very very very very very important writer."

So important, indeed, that some of his most zealous admirers have paid him the backhand compliment of doubting that works of such surpassing genius could have been written by the same William Shakespeare who lies buried and memorialized in Stratford-upon-Avon. Plays such as the English histories would suggest in the writer an easy familiarity with the ways of kings, queens, and courtiers; hence their author must have been a member of the nobility, someone like Edward de Vere, the seventeenth Earl of Oxford. Plays such as *Julius Caesar,* with their impressive display of classical learning, would indicate an author with more than the "small Latin and less Greek" that Ben Jonson attributes to Shakespeare; hence the need to seek for their true begetter in the form of a university-trained scholar such as Francis Bacon. Or so would urge those skeptics (whose numbers have included such redoubtable personages as Henry James and Sigmund Freud) who find themselves in sympathy with the "anti-Stratfordians." Their ranks have never been particularly numerous or disciplined, since they have often quarreled among themselves about which of the various "claimants"—the Earl of Derby, Christopher Marlowe, even Queen

Robert Greene's attack on "Shake-scene" in Greene's Groatsworth of Wit *(1592; British Library). In saying that Shakespeare is "as Tygers hart wrapt in a Players hyde," Greene was alluding to a line in* Henry VI, *part 3, where the Duke of York calls Queen Margaret "tiger's heart wrapped in a woman's hide."*

Elizabeth herself—should be upheld as the "true Shakespeare." And because many of their arguments are methodologically unsophisticated, they have never attracted adherents from scholars with academic credentials in the study of English Renaissance history and dramatic literature. But, whatever their limitations, the anti-Stratfordians have at least helped keep us mindful of how

frustratingly little we can say for certain about the life of the man whose works have so enriched the lives of succeeding generations.

One thing we do know is that if Shakespeare was a man for all time, he was also very much a man of his own age. Christened at Holy Trinity Church in Stratford-upon-Avon on 26 April 1564, he grew up as the eldest of five chil-

Anthony van Wyndgaerde's 1594 drawing of Greenwich Palace (top), where the Lord Chamberlain's Men performed during the Christmas season of 1594 (by permission of the Ashmolean Museum, Oxford); and a portion of a page from the Accounts of the Treasurer of the Queen's Chamber (bottom) recording payment to Shakespeare, William Kempe, and Richard Burbage—all members of the Lord Chamberlain's company—for their part in those festivities. This entry is the earliest documentation of Shakespeare's membership in an acting company (Public Record Office, Exchequer, Pipe Office, Declared Accounts, E. 351/542, f. 107ᵛ; by permission of the Controller of Her Majesty's Stationery Office).

dren reared by John Shakespeare, a tradesman who played an increasingly active role in the town's civic affairs as his business prospered, and Mary Arden Shakespeare, the daughter of a gentleman farmer from nearby Wilmcote. Whether Shakespeare was born on 23 April, as tradition holds, is not known; but a birth date only a few days prior to the recorded baptism seems eminently probable, particularly in view of the fear his parents must have had that William, like two sisters who had preceded him and one who followed, might die in infancy. By the time young William was old enough to begin attending school, he had a younger brother (Gilbert, born in 1566) and a baby sister (Joan, born in 1569). As he attained his youth, he found himself with two more brothers to help look after (Richard, born in 1574, and Edmund, born in 1580), the younger of whom eventually followed his by-then-prominent eldest brother to London and the theater, where he had a brief career as an actor before his untimely death at twenty-seven.

The house where Shakespeare spent his childhood stood adjacent to the wool shop in which his father plied a successful trade as a glover and dealer in leather goods and other commodities. Before moving to Stratford sometime prior to 1552 (when the records show that he was fined for failing to remove a dunghill from outside his house to the location where refuse was normally to be deposited), John Shakespeare had been a farmer in the neighboring village of Snitterfield. Whether he was able to read and write is uncertain. He executed official documents, not with his name, but with a cross signifying his glover's compasses. Some scholars interpret this as a "signature" that might have been considered more "authentic" than a full autograph; others have taken it to be an indication of illiteracy. But even if John Shakespeare was not one of the "learned," he was certainly a man of what a later age would call upward mobility. By marrying Mary Arden, the daughter of his father's landlord, he acquired the benefits of a better social standing and a lucrative inheritance, much of which he invested in property (he bought several houses). And by involving himself in public service, he rose by sure degrees to the highest municipal positions Stratford had to offer: chamberlain (1561), alderman (1565), and bailiff (or mayor) and justice of the peace (1568). A few years after his elevation to the office of bailiff, probably around 1576, John Shakespeare approached the College of Heralds for armorial

bearings and the right to call himself a gentleman. Before his application was acted upon, however, his fortunes took a sudden turn for the worse, and it was not until 1596, when his eldest son had attained some status and renewed the petition, that a Shakespeare coat of arms was finally granted. This must have been a comfort to John Shakespeare in his declining years (he died in 1601), because by then he had borrowed money, disposed of property out of necessity, ceased to attend meetings of the town council, become involved in litigation and been assessed fines, and even stopped attending church services, for fear, it was said, "of process for debt." Just what happened to alter John Shakespeare's financial and social position after the mid 1570s is not clear. Some have seen his nonattendance at church as a sign that he had become a recusant, unwilling to conform to the practices of the newly established Church of England (his wife's family had remained loyal to Roman Catholicism despite the fact that the old faith was under vigorous attack in Warwickshire after 1577), but the scant surviving evidence is anything but definitive.

The records we do have suggest that during young William's formative years he enjoyed the advantages that would have accrued to him as the son of one of the most influential citizens of a bustling market town in the fertile Midlands. When he was taken to services at Holy Trinity Church, he would have sat with his family in the front pew, in accordance with his father's civic rank. There he would have heard and felt the words and rhythms of the Bible, the sonorous phrases of the 1559 Book of Common Prayer, the exhortations of the Homilies. In all likelihood, after spending a year or two at a "petty school" to learn the rudiments of reading and writing, he would have proceeded, at the age of seven, to "grammar school." Given his father's social position, young William would have been eligible to attend the King's New School, located above the Guild Hall and adjacent to the Guild Chapel (institutions that would both have been quite familiar to a man with the elder Shakespeare's municipal duties), no more than a five-minute walk from the Shakespeare house on Henley Street. Though no records survive to tell us who attended the Stratford grammar school during this period, we do know that it had well-qualified and comparatively well-paid masters; and, through the painstaking research of such scholars as T. W. Baldwin, we now recognize that a curriculum such as the one offered at the

The Workes of William Shakespeare,

containing all his Comedies, Histories, and
Tragedies : Truely set forth, according to their first
ORJGJNALL.

The Names of the Principall Actors
in all these Playes.

Illiam Shakespeare.	Samuel Gilburne.
Richard Burbadge.	Robert Armin.
John Hemmings.	William Ostler.
Augustine Phillips.	Nathan Field.
William Kempt.	John Underwood.
Thomas Poope.	Nicholas Tooley.
George Bryan.	William Ecclestone.
Henry Condell.	Joseph Taylor.
William Slye.	Robert Benfield.
Richard Cowly.	Robert Goughe.
John Lowine.	Richard Robinson.
Samuell Crosse.	Iohn Shancke.
Alexander Cooke.	Iohn Rice.

List, from the First Folio edition of Shakespeare's works (1623; Folger Shakespeare Library), of the members of the company that Cuthbert and Richard Burbage formed as the Lord Chamberlain's Men in 1594. In 1603 the company came under the patronage of James I and was renamed the King's Men.

King's New School would have equipped its pupils with what by modern standards would be a rather formidable classical education.

During his many long school days there, young Shakespeare would have become thoroughly grounded in Latin, acquired some background in Greek, and developed enough linguistic facility to pick up whatever he may have wanted later from such modern languages as Italian and French. Along the way he would have become familiar with such authors as Aesop, Caesar, Cicero, Sallust, Livy, Virgil, Horace, Ovid, and Seneca. He would have studied logic and rhetoric as well as grammar, and he would have been taught the principles of composition and oratory from the writings of such masters as Quintilian and Erasmus. In all probability, he would even have received some training in speech and drama through the performance of plays by Plautus and Terence. If Shakespeare's references to schooling and schoolmasters in the plays are a reliable index of how he viewed his own years as a student, we must conclude that the experience was more tedious than pleasurable. But it is difficult to imagine a more suitable mode of instruction for the formation of a Renaissance poet's intellectual and artistic sensibility.

Meanwhile, of course, young Shakespeare would have learned a great deal from merely being alert to all that went on around him. He would have paid attention to the plant and animal life in the local woods that he would later immortalize, in *As You Like It*, as the Forest of Arden. He may have hunted from time to time; one legend, almost certainly apocryphal, has it that he eventually left Stratford because he had been caught poaching deer from the estate of a powerful squire, Sir Thomas Lucy, four miles upstream. He probably learned to swim as a youth, skinny-dipping in the river Avon. He may have participated in some of the athletic pursuits that were the basis of competition in the Elizabethan equivalent of the Olympics, the nearby Cotswold Games. He would undoubtedly have been adept at indoor recreations such as hazard (a popular dice game), or chess, or any of a number of card games. As he grew older, he would have become accustomed to such vocations as farming, sheepherding, tailoring, and shopkeeping. He would have acquired skills such as fishing, gardening, and cooking. And he would have gathered information about the various professions: law, medicine, religion, and teaching. Judging from the astonishing range of daily life and human endeavor reflected in his poems and plays, we can only infer that Shakespeare was both a voracious reader and a keen observer, the sort of polymath Henry James might have been describing when he referred to a character in one of his novels as "a man on whom nothing was lost."

Once his school years ended, Shakespeare married, at eighteen, a woman who was eight years his senior. We know that Anne Hathaway was pregnant when the marriage license was issued by the Bishop of Worcester on 27 November 1582, because a daughter, Susanna, was baptized in Holy Trinity six months later on 26 May 1583. We have good reason to believe that the marriage was hastily arranged: there was only one reading of the banns (a church announcement preceding a wedding that allowed time for any legal impediments against it to be brought forward before the ceremony took place), an indication of unusual haste. But whether the marriage was in any way "forced" is impossible to determine. Some biographers (most notably Anthony Burgess) have made much of an apparent clerical error whereby the bride's name was entered as Anne Whateley of Temple Grafton in the Worcester court records; these writers speculate that Shakespeare was originally planning to marry another Anne until Anne Hathaway of Shottery (a village a mile or so from Shakespeare's home in Stratford) produced her embarrassing evidence of a prior claim. To most scholars, including our foremost authority on Shakespeare's life, S. Schoenbaum, this explanation of the Anne Whateley court entry seems farfetched. Such hypotheses are inevitable, however, in the absence of fuller information about the married life of William and Anne Hathaway Shakespeare.

What we do have to go on is certainly compatible with the suspicion that William and Anne were somewhat less than ardent lovers. They had only two more children–the twins, Hamnet and Judith, baptized on 2 February 1585–and they lived more than a hundred miles apart, so far as we can tell, for the better part of the twenty-year period during which Shakespeare was employed in the London theater. If we can give any credence to an amusing anecdote recorded in the 1602-1603 diary of a law student named John Manningham, there was at least one occasion during those years when Shakespeare, overhearing the actor Richard Burbage make an assignation, "went before, was entertained, and at his game before Burbage came; then, message being brought that Richard the Third was at the door, Shakespeare caused return to be made that William the Conqueror was before Richard the Third." If we read the sonnets as in any way autobiographical, moreover, we are shown a poet with at least one other significant liaison: a "Dark Lady" to whom Will's lust impels him despite the self-disgust the affair arouses in him (and despite her infidelity with the fair "Young Man" to whom many of the poems are addressed and for whom the poet reserves his deepest feelings).

But even if there is reason to speculate that Shakespeare may not have always been faithful to the marriage bed, there is much to suggest that he remained attached to Anne as a husband. In 1597 he purchased one of the most imposing houses in Stratford—New Place, across the street from the Guild Chapel—presumably settling his wife and children there as soon as the title to the property was clear. He himself retired to that Stratford home, so far as we can determine, sometime between 1611 and 1613. And of course he remembered Anne in his will, bequeathing her the notorious "second-best bed"—which most modern biographers regard as a generous afterthought (since a third of his estate would have gone to

the wife by law even if her name never occurred in the document) rather than the slight that earlier interpreters had read into the phrasing.

Naturally we would like to know more about what Shakespeare was like as a husband and family man. But most of us would give just as much to know what took place in his life between 1585 (when the parish register shows him to have become the father of twins) and 1592 (when we find the earliest surviving reference to him as a rising star in the London theater). What did he do during these so-called "dark years"? Did he study law, as some have suspected? Did he travel on the Continent? Did he become an apprentice to a butcher, as one late-seventeenth-century account had it? Or—most plausibly, in the view of many modern biographers—did he teach school for a while? All we can say for certain is that by the time his children were making their own way to school in rural Stratford, William Shakespeare had become an actor and writer in what was already the largest city in Europe.

Shakespeare probably traveled the hundred miles to London by way of the spires of Oxford, as do most visitors returning from Stratford to

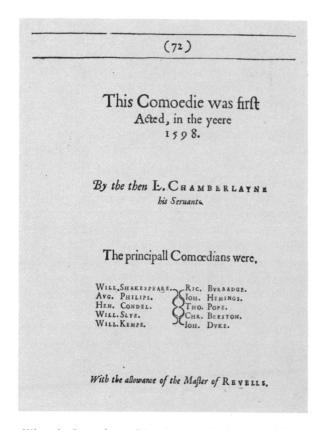

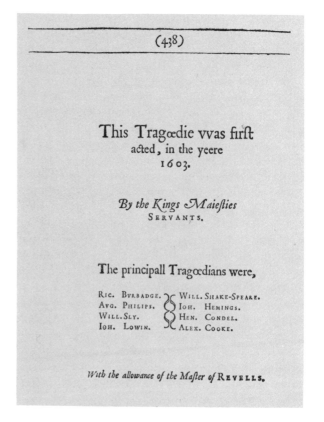

When the first volume of Ben Jonson's Works *was published in 1616, Shakespeare was listed as a cast member for the first performances of* Every Man in His Humour *(left) and* Sejanus *(right) (Bodleian Library)*

Self-portrait of Richard Burbage, who played roles such as Richard III, Othello, and King Lear (by permission of Dulwich College Picture Gallery, London)

London today. But why he went, or when, history does not tell us. It has been plausibly suggested that he joined an acting troupe (the Queen's Men) that was one player short when it toured Stratford in 1587. If so, he may have migrated by way of one or two intermediary companies to a position with the troupe that became the Lord Chamberlain's Men in 1594. The only thing we can assert with any assurance is that by 1592 Shakespeare had established himself as an actor and had written at least three plays. One of these–the third part of *Henry VI*–was alluded to in that year in a posthumously published testament by a once-prominent poet and playwright named Robert Greene, one of the "University Wits" who had dominated the London theater in the late 1580s. Dissipated and on his deathbed, Greene warned his fellow playwrights to beware of an "upstart crow" who, not content with being a mere player, was aspiring to a share of the livelihood that had previously been the exclusive province of professional writers such as himself. Whether *Greene's Groatsworth of Wit* accuses Shakespeare of plagiarism when it describes him as "beautified with our feathers" is not clear; some scholars have interpreted the phrase as a complaint that Shakespeare has borrowed freely from the scripts of others (or has merely revised existing plays, a practice quite common in the Elizabethan theater). But there can be no doubt that Greene's anxieties signal the end of one era and the beginning of another: a golden age, spanning two full decades, during which the dominant force on the London stage would be, not Greene or Kyd or Marlowe or even (in the later years of that period) Jonson, but Shakespeare.

If we look at what Shakespeare had written by the early 1590s, we see that he had already become thoroughly familiar with the daily round of one of the great capitals of Europe. Shakespeare knew St. Paul's Cathedral, famous not only as a house of worship but also as the marketplace where books were bought and sold. He knew the Inns of Court, where aspiring young lawyers studied for the bar. He knew the river Thames, spanned by the ever-busy, ever-fascinating London Bridge. He knew the Tower, where so many of the characters he would depict in his history plays had met their deaths, and where in his own lifetime such prominent noblemen as the Earl of Essex and Sir Walter Raleigh would be imprisoned prior to their executions. He knew Westminster, where Parliament met when summoned by the Queen, and where the Queen herself held court at Whitehall Palace. He knew the harbor, where English ships, having won control of the seas by defeating the "invincible" Spanish Armada in 1588, had begun in earnest to explore the New World.

In Shakespeare's day London was a vigorous city of somewhere between 150,000 and 200,000 inhabitants. If in its more majestic aspects it was dominated by the court of Queen Elizabeth, in its everyday affairs it was accented by the hustle and bustle of getting and spending. Its Royal Exchange was one of the forerunners of today's stock exchanges. Its many marketplaces offered a variety of goods for a variety of tastes. Its crowded streets presented a colorful pageant of Elizabethan modes of transport and dress, ranging from countrywomen in homespun to elegant ladies in apparel as decorative as their husbands' wealth—and the Queen's edicts on clothing—would allow. Its inns and taverns afforded a rich diversity of vivid personalities—eating, tippling, chatting, and enjoying games and pleasures of all kinds. It was, in short, an immensely stimulating social and cultural environment, and we can be sure that Shakespeare took full advantage of the opportunity it gave him to observe humanity in all its facets. Like Prince Hal, he must have learned "to drink with any tinker in his own language," and it was this as much as anything he was taught at school (or might have acquired by attendance at university) that equipped him to create such vibrant characters as Mistress Quickly, proud Hotspur, and the imperturbable Bottom.

Not that all was always well. Like any major city, London also had its problems. Preachers and moralists were constantly denouncing the excessive use of cosmetics. Thus, when Hamlet speaks out against "your paintings," telling Ophelia that "God hath given you one face, and you make yourselves another," he would have been sounding a note familiar to everyone in Shake-

Robert Armin, who specialized in "wise fool" parts such as Touchstone in As You Like It, *Feste in* Twelfth Night, *and the Fool in* King Lear *(woodcut from the title page of the 1609 quarto edition of Armin's* The Two Maids of Moreclacke; *Anderson Galleries, sale number 2077, 20-21 May 1926)*

speare's audience. So also with the "furred gowns" so roundly cursed by Lear: courtiers and their ladies were accustomed to lavishing as much "pride" on a single article of bejeweled finery as a modern man or woman might pay for a very expensive automobile. But luxury was only one of the evils of the age. London's Puritan authorities, regarding the theaters as dens of iniquity, closed them down on any available pretext, particularly when the plague was rampant. Meanwhile, even without the plague or the theaters to concern them (and one gathers that some of the authorities were anything but sure about which was the greater peril), the city fathers had to contend with gambling, drunkenness, prostitution, and other vices, especially in the Bankside district south of the Thames and in the other "liberties" outside the city walls to the west, east, and north (such as Shoreditch, where James Burbage had erected the first permanent commercial playhouse, the Theatre, when Shakespeare was only twelve, and where many of Shakespeare's plays prior to 1599 were first performed). Here most blatantly, but elsewhere as well, pickpockets, vagabonds, and other members of the fraternity of urban lowlife lay in wait for "conies," as they called their unsuspecting victims. Given so many "notorious villainies" for spokesmen like Thomas Dekker's "Belman of London" to bring to light, it is hardly surprising that among the most prolific literary genres of the period were the scores of books and tracts that spewed forth from reformers incensed by the decadence of the Renaissance metropolis.

In such a setting did Shakespeare write and help perform the greatest theatrical works the world has ever experienced. And he did so in suburbs known primarily for entertainments that we would regard as totally alien from the sweet Swan of Avon's poetic grace. For if Shoreditch and, later, Bankside were to blossom into the finest theatrical centers of that or any other age, they were also, for better or worse, the seedbeds for such brutal spectator sports as bearbaiting, bullbaiting, and cockfighting. This may help account for the blood and violence so frequently displayed on the Elizabethan stage, most notably in such early Shakespearean experiments as the *Henry VI* trilogy and *Titus Andronicus*, but also in mature works such as *Julius Caesar* and *King Lear*. But of course there was a good deal more than murder and mayhem in the "wooden O" that served as amphitheatre for most of Shakespeare's dramatic productions.

On a stage largely devoid of scenery but by no means lacking in spectacle, the playwright and his actors made efficient use of language, properties, and gesture to establish time, locale, situation, and atmosphere. In the process, through all the resources of rhetoric, symbolism, and what Hamlet in his advice to the players calls "action," the "artificial persons" of the drama (its dramatis personae) imitated humanity in such a way as to convey whatever "matter" an author and his company envisaged for a scene, an act, or a full dramatic sequence. By twentieth-century standards, the means they used were relatively primitive–no spotlights, too few furnishings to achieve verisimilitude through setting and dress, only the crudest of "special effects," no curtains to raise and lower as a way of signaling the beginning and end of a scene or act–but by any standards, the results they achieved were brilliant. It has taken us nearly four centuries to rediscover what they

seem to have understood intuitively: that in some things theatrical, less is more.

Our best estimate is that approximately 3,000 spectators could be crammed into a ninety-nine-foot-wide, polygonal structure such as the Theatre (which opened in 1576 and was dismantled in 1598, after the owner of the land on which it stood refused to negotiate a lease acceptable to Shakespeare's acting company) or its successor the Globe (which opened in 1599, after the company transported the lumber from the Theatre across the Thames and used it as the scaffolding for an even more handsome playhouse on the Bankside). More than half of the audience stood in the yard (which measured about fifty-five feet in diameter); the remainder sat in the three galleries that encircled the yard and rose to a thatched roof some thirty-six feet above the ground.

The stage was probably about forty-three feet wide, and it thrust some twenty-seven feet into the yard from the "tiring house" at the rear of the building. It was covered by a pillar-supported superstructure–the "heavens"–that protected the actors and their costumes from the elements and housed the equipment Elizabethan companies used for ascents, descents, and other "flying" effects. In the floor of the stage platform (about five feet above the surrounding yard) was a trapdoor that could be opened for visitations from below or for access into what, depending on the context, might represent a grave or a pit or even hell itself. At the back of the stage in all likelihood, concealing the tiring house where the actors effected their costume changes and awaited their cues to enter, were three doors. The two at the corners were probably used for most of the entrances and exits of the actors; the large middle one was capable of being employed as a shallow, draped "discovery space" that might be drawn open for tableaux (as when Ferdinand and Miranda are disclosed playing chess in *The Tempest*) or adapted to represent small enclosures such as closets, studies, bedrooms, or shops like the Apothecary's cell in *Romeo and Juliet*. On the level above the tiring house, probably divided into five bays, was a balcony that accommodated a select number of the theater's highest-paying customers and functioned in many of the plays as the "upper stage" where brief scenes requiring a higher vantage point could be enacted. Sentinels on watch, lovers at a second-story bedroom window, seamen crying out from a ship's crow's nest: these and other situations called for the use of

A portion of the inset John Norden prepared for the panorama of London he published in 1600 as
Civitas Londini *(Royal Library, Kungliga Biblioteket, Stockholm). The first Globe theater, built from
the timbers of the Theatre in 1598, is shown just south of the Rose theater (here mislabeled "The Stare").*

one or more of the upper-level bays (probably the central one in most instances) for characters to speak their lines and render the movements called for in the script.

Because the main playing area was surrounded on all four sides by spectators, the poet and the performer benefited from a more intimate relationship with the audience than is customary in present-day theaters fitted with a curtain and a proscenium arch. For Shakespeare, this meant that he could allow a character to confide in a nearby playgoer through asides, as does Iago in *Othello,* or to be overheard while he meditates in solitude, as does Brutus in the soliloquy in which he talks himself into joining the plot to assassinate Caesar. Such devices may strike a modern viewer as less sophisticated than, say, the cinematic voice-over, but they proved eminently acceptable to an audience that was willing to "piece out" a performance's "imperfections with [its] thoughts." And it says a great deal about the intelligence and sensitivity of Elizabethan theatergoers that they attended and were capable of appreciating dramatic works which, in many respects, were both responses to and sublimations of the coarser activities that competed for at-

tention (and people's entertainment budgets) only a short distance away from the magic circle defined by the walls of a Theatre or a Globe.

Just who composed the audiences of these public playhouses is still a matter of debate, but recent research by Ann Jennalie Cook and Andrew Gurr suggest that they were a more affluent cross-section of Elizabethan society than earlier writings by such scholars as Alfred Harbage would have led us to believe. An examination of wages and prices during the period indicates, for example, that those who attended performances on weekday afternoons would have had to have more leisure, and more disposable income, than seems compatible with the view that even the groundlings (who paid the lowest admission, a penny to stand in the yard and risk getting soaked in the event of rain) were predominantly working-class people and illiterate apprentices. Because their position in the yard put their eyes on a level with the feet of the players, the groundlings were sometimes derided as "understanders"; it now begins to appear that a substantial percentage of these theatergoers were "understanders" in a more favorable sense. To be sure, some of them may at times have been a bit ob-

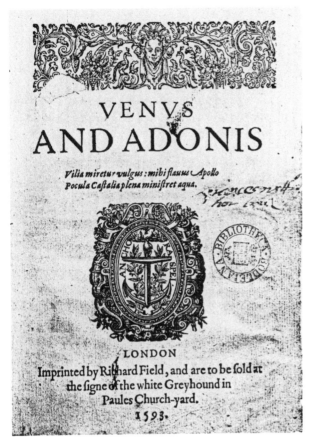

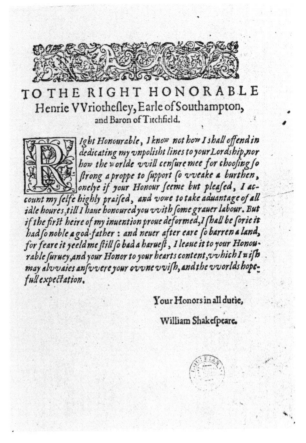

Title page and dedication page from the 1593 quarto edition of Shakespeare's first book, an erotic mythological poem based on Ovid's Metamorphoses *(Bodleian Library, Oxford)*

streperous, and their number may well have included an assortment of men and women (including prostitutes) preoccupied with extra-theatrical pursuits. It may be, too, that the groundlings were more susceptible than other members of the audience (if merely because of their greater proximity to the stage) to manipulation by what we now call "naughty" actors, the overweening "clowns" whom Hamlet rebukes for their tendency to ply the crowd for inappropriate laughter, interrupting the flow of the action and causing spectators to miss "some necessary question of the play." But even if the groundlings were not quite as cultivated, on the average, as those members of the audience who could afford to sit while they watched a play, it is difficult to reconcile the subtlety and indirection of Shakespeare's plotting and characterization, not to mention the complexity of his language and the incomparable music of his verse, with the assumption that the majority of an average house at the public theaters was unable to respond to anything more elevated than the broad humor of a

Launce or a Dogberry. Even if we still find it valuable, then, to preserve something of the traditional distinction between the groundlings and the more "privileged" spectators who sat in the three-tiered galleries encircling the yard, we should now open our minds to the possibility that there were more of what Hamlet would call "judicious" viewers in every segment of the Elizabethan audience, including those who stood in the yard, than we have tended to assume until very recently in our analyses of Shakespearean drama.

Which is not to say, of course, that Shakespeare and his fellow dramatists were *completely* satisfied with *any* of their audiences (but then what writer ever is?). Hamlet bestows high praise on a play that he says "was never acted, or if it was, not above once," for "it pleased not the million, 'twas caviary to the general." He then exhorts the players to disregard "a whole theatre of others," if necessary, in order to please "those with judgments in such matters." Whether Hamlet's creator would himself have endorsed such extreme elitism is difficult to determine, but such a view is certainly consonant with the epistle to the reader that prefaced the revised 1609 first quarto edition of *Troilus and Cressida*. Here we are assured that we have "a new play, never staled with the stage, never clapper-clawed with the palms of the vulgar, and yet passing full of the palm comical"; and we are given to believe that it is to the credit rather than the discredit of the work that it has never been "sullied with the smoky breath of the multitude." Inasmuch as this preface and the title page preceding it replaced an earlier title page advertising *Troilus and Cressida* "as it was acted by the King's Majesty's servants at the Globe," we are probably correct to assume that whoever wrote it had in mind the kind of vulgar "multitude" who would have seen the play at one of the outdoor public theaters.

All of which is to acknowledge that even if the audiences that attended the public theaters were sophisticated enough to support the vast majority of Shakespeare's dramatic efforts, they may nevertheless have proven deficient in their response to some of the extraordinary challenges he placed before them after he arrived at his artistic maturity. This should not surprise us, given Shakespeare's continual experimentation with inherited generic forms and his ever-more-complex approaches to traditional material. Nor should we assume that by terms such as "the million" and "the general" he and his fellow playwrights referred only to the groundlings. Writers of the period were equally acidulous in their criticism of the gallants who attended the theater to be "the observed of all observers"–the ostentatiously attired young men who sat not only in the galleries near the stage (where the admission price was thrice as much as for the places in the yard) and in the balconies above and behind the stage (which cost six times as much as the places in the yard), but even on the stage itself at some performances in the indoor "private" theaters (where the least expensive seat cost six times the price of general admission to the Theatre or the Globe, and where

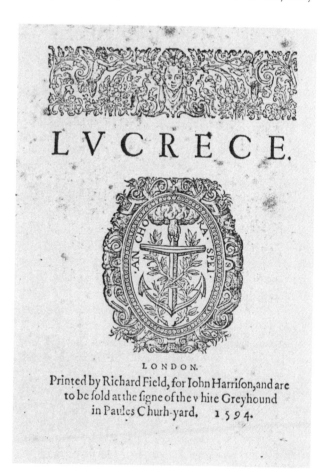

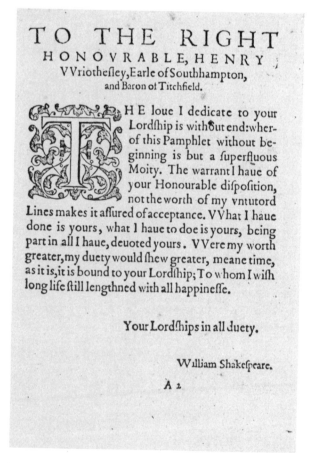

Title page and dedication page from the 1594 quarto edition of the long narrative poem that was later republished as The Rape of Lucrece *(Elizabethan Club, Yale University)*

some of the seats cost a full thirty times as much). It is difficult to believe that Shakespeare any more than Dekker (who satirized such gallants in *The Gull's Hornbook*) would have considered these foppish Osrics even slightly more "judicious" than their fellow spectators at the lower end of the economic scale. And one can easily imagine that after 1609, when his company began using the Blackfriars theater as its primary venue during the colder months (the London authorities having finally dropped the restrictions that had prevented James Burbage from operating a commercial adult theater in the old monastery he had purchased and adapted in 1596), Shakespeare felt that he had simply exchanged one kind of less-than-perfect audience for another.

One gathers, nevertheless, that, like other playwrights of the period, Shakespeare was careful not to refer too overtly to deficiencies in the well-to-do members of his audiences, especially when such members might include the nobility or persons close to them. After all, an acting company's livelihood depended upon its securing and retaining favor at Court—not only because of the extra income and prestige that accrued from periodic Court performances commissioned by the Master of the Revels, but even more fundamentally because a company could perform in or near London only if it were licensed to do so by the Crown and enjoyed the protection of a noble or royal patron. A prudent playwright would not wish to jeopardize his company's standing with the monarch. And Shakespeare and his colleagues—the other "sharers" who owned stock in the company that was known as the Lord Chamberlain's Men from 1594 until 1603 (when Queen Elizabeth died and was succeeded by King James I) and the King's Men thereafter (having received a patent as the new monarch's own players) —must have been prudent, because theirs was by far the most prosperous and the most frequently "preferred" theatrical organization in the land, from its inception in the early 1590s until the triumph of Puritanism finally brought about the closing of the theaters half a century later in 1642.

Shakespeare's position with the Lord Chamberlain's Men was a source of professional stability that probably had a great deal to do with his growth and maturation as a writer. For one thing, it freed him from some of the uncertainties and frustrations that must have been the lot of other playwrights, virtually all of whom operated as free-lancers selling their wares to impresa-

Henry Wriothesley, Earl of Southampton, to whom Shakespeare dedicated his first two books (miniature by Nicholas Hilliard, 1593 or 1594; Fitzwilliam Museum, Cambridge, by permission of the Syndics)

rios such as Philip Henslowe (often for as little as five pounds), and most of whom thus forfeited any real say about how their plays were to be produced and, in time (if a given acting company so wished or if chance provided), published. From at least 1594 on Shakespeare was a stockholder of the theatrical organization for which he wrote his plays. After 1598 (when the sons of the recently deceased James Burbage, Cuthbert and Richard, invited four of the principal actors in the Lord Chamberlain's Men to become their partners and put up half the capital needed to rebuild the Theatre across the Thames as the Globe), Shakespeare was also a co-owner of the playhouse in which that company performed the plays. As such, he shared in all the profits the Lord Chamberlain's Men took in at the gate, and he was undoubtedly a participant in most, if not all, of the major decisions affecting the company's welfare. We know from the surviving legal records of the playwright's various business transactions that he prospered financially by this arrangement: like his father, Shakespeare invested wisely in real estate, purchasing properties in both Stratford and London. And we can infer from the evidence of his rapidly developing sophistication as a dramatist that Shakespeare's membership in a close-knit group of theatrical entrepreneurs also helped him flourish artistically.

It meant, for example, that he could envisage and write his plays with particular performers in mind: Richard Burbage for leading roles such as Richard III, Othello, and King Lear; Will Kempe for clowning parts such as Launce or Dogberry in the early years of the company, and thereafter (following Kempe's departure from the Lord Chamberlain's Men around 1599) Robert Armin, who seems to have specialized in "wise fools" such as Touchstone, Feste, and Lear's Fool; Shakespeare himself, perhaps, for "old men" such as Adam in *As You Like It;* "hired men" (adult actors who, not being shareholders in the company, were simply paid a sum of money for each job of work) for most of the lesser roles; and apprentice boy-actors for the youthful parts and many, if not all, of the female roles (there being no actresses on the English stage until the theaters reopened after the Restoration). Working as the resident playwright for a company in

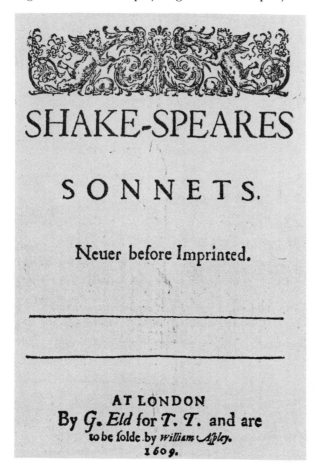

SHAKE-SPEARES

SONNETS.

Neuer before Imprinted.

AT LONDON
By *G. Eld* for *T. T.* and are
to be folde by *William Apley.*
1609.

Title page for the 1609 quarto edition of the volume publisher Thomas Thorpe dedicated to "Mr. W. H.," fueling speculation about the identity of the young man in the sonnets (Anderson Galleries, sale number 1405, 4-5 March 1919)

which he was both an actor and a business partner meant that Shakespeare could revise and rewrite his scripts in rehearsal prior to a given play's first performance, and that he could adapt and further revise them later as differing circumstances required: such as performances commissioned at Court during holiday seasons or on ceremonial occasions, or performances solicited by the great houses of the nobility, or (during sieges of plague when the London theaters were closed) performances on tour in the provinces, during which, in all likelihood, the troupe was reduced to entertaining with fewer actors and was required to make do with provisional playing areas in guild halls, inn yards, and other less-than-ideal theatrical spaces.

Because the conditions under which Shakespeare worked required him, above all, to be pragmatic and flexible, we would probably be correct to infer that as he composed his plays he thought of his scripts, not as fixed "literary" texts, but as provisional production notes—susceptible of lengthening or shortening or other modes of alteration as determined by the constraints of particular venues and performance situations. He would have had to prepare each script with an eye to the number of actors available for speaking parts (one recent scholar has concluded that most of Shakespeare's plays were composed with a cast of thirteen performers in mind), and he probably planned each scene with a view to the possibilities for "doubling" (a principle of theatrical economy whereby a given actor would alternate among two or more roles in the same play). It may well be that, in the absence of anyone else in the organization designated to function in that capacity, Shakespeare was the first "director" his plays had. If so, we can be sure that he approached the task with an awareness that the devising of a production was a collaborative process and that the playscript, though normative, was never to be revered as a monument carved in stone. Shakespeare was, after all, a play*wright* (that is, a "maker" rather than merely a writer of plays), and he would have been the first to recognize that the final purpose of a dramatic text was a fully realized performance rather than a piece of literature to be read in the privacy of a patron's parlor or pondered in the lamplight of a scholar's study.

If in his capacity as theater professional Shakespeare conceived of himself, then, as a maker of "plays" (by definition ephemeral and "insubstantial" pageants, as Prospero observes in

The Tempest) rather than as an author of literary "works" (the term that earned Ben Jonson the derision of his fellow playwrights when he came out with a pretentiously titled folio volume of his collected plays in 1616), it is hardly surprising that he appears to have had little or nothing to do with the publication of any of his own dramatic scripts. Nor is it surprising that several of the texts that were published in Shakespeare's lifetime or shortly thereafter have come down to us in forms that vary from one printing to another.

Some of these variations probably result from authorial revisions or from theatrical adaptations of one kind or another. Others undoubtedly derive from the vicissitudes of textual transmission, with the extant state of a given text or passage dependent on whether it was printed from the author's own manuscript (either in draft form or in a more finished version) or from a manuscript prepared by someone else (a scribe's "fair copy" of a manuscript owned by the author or the company, for example, or a rough compilation by one or more actors relying on faulty memories to pull together an abridged script for a reduced cast touring the provinces)— quite apart from any further complications that may have occurred in the printing house itself (where one copy editor, one compositor, or one proofreader differed from another in the accuracy with which he reproduced the manuscript before him). Whatever their origins, these variations are eloquent testimony to the difficulty–if not indeed the impossibility–of our ever arriving at an absolutely "final" version of a Shakespearean play. For if the conditions under which plays were written, performed, and preserved make it clear that a "definitive" playtext was rare, if not unknown, in Shakespeare's own time, we must recognize that any effort to produce an authoritative edition for our own time can aspire, at best, to reconstitute as accurately as possible the closest surviving approximation to a given script at some point in its compositional or theatrical history.

And even this kind of edition will remain stubbornly "incomplete," for the simple reason that a Shakespearean script was originally intended for the use, not of a reading audience, but of a small company of theater professionals who would employ it as a "score" from which to orchestrate a complex, multidimensional performance. The texts that do survive are mostly dialogue, and a sensitive analysis of them can tell us a great deal about how the words were meant

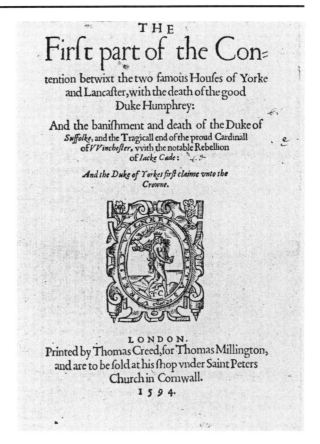

Title page for the 1594 quarto edition of an abridged and corrupt text of Henry VI, *part 2 (Folger Shakespeare Library)*

to be spoken, where the emphases were to be placed, and what character motivations were to be indicated at specific points in the action. But because we can no longer recover the context in which these scripts were first realized–a context that would have included a good deal of oral communication about gesture, movement, blocking, and other stage business–we must content ourselves with editions that will always be to some degree indeterminate. Perhaps this is just as well: it teases the critic and the director with enough interpretive liberty to ensure that we will never be faced with a dearth of innovation in Shakespearean commentary and production.

We should bear in mind, of course, that a considerable investment of additional work would have been required to transform a production script into a reading text for the public–not altogether unlike what is required nowadays to turn a screenplay into a coherent piece of narrative fiction–and that Shakespeare may never have had the time (even if we assume that he ever had the inclination) to effect such a generic adaptation. Still, those of us who would not object to a little more detail about some of the "matter" of Shakespeare's plays may perhaps be pardoned for wishing that the playwright had been able to spare more thought for the morrow–for the after-life that most (though who is to say all?) of his plays were eventually to have as a consequence of publication. Our sentiments are echoed in the 1623 address "To the Great Variety of Readers" at the beginning of that posthumous edition of Shakespeare's works known as the First Folio: "It had been a thing, we confess, worthy to have been wished, that the author himself had lived to have set forth and overseen his own writings."

He did set forth and oversee some of his own writings, of course. But, significantly, these were not dramatic scripts.

In 1593 Shakespeare published an 1194-line narrative poem that appears to have been intended as his opening bid for serious attention as an author of "literary works." Based on Ovid's *Metamorphoses* and capitalizing on a fashion for elegant romances that was being catered to by such writers as Thomas Lodge (whose *Scilla's Metamorphoses* had been published in 1589) and Christopher Marlowe (whose *Hero and Leander* may well have circulated in manuscript prior to his death in 1593 and certainly before it appeared in print in 1598), Shakespeare's *Venus and Adonis* was an erotic mythological poem printed by fellow Stratfordian Richard Field and bearing a florid dedication to "the Right Honorable Henry Wriothesley, Earl of Southampton." Its six-line stanzas employed an *ababcc* rhyming scheme whose authority had been established by such contemporary Renaissance poets as Edmund Spenser, and its ornamented, "artificial" style solicited a favorable reception from the "wiser sort" of readers to be found in the Inns of Courts, at the universities, and at Court. Although Shakespeare decorously apologized for the poem as "the first heir of my invention," he must have done so in full confidence that *Venus and Adonis* was an achievement worthy of his talent. And it proved to be an immediate and sustained success, with nine reprints by 1616 and six more by 1640. The large number of references to it during the late 1590s and early 1600s suggest that it was the work for which Shakespeare was most widely recognized during his own lifetime.

Within a year of the publication of *Venus and Adonis*, Shakespeare was back to press with another long narrative poem. This time he chose a seven-line stanza rhyming *ababbcc* (rhyme royal, a verse form whose tradition in English poetry ex-

tended all the way back to Chaucer), and once again he drew on Ovid for a work dedicated (this time even more warmly) to the Earl of Southampton. If *Venus and Adonis* is most aptly approached as a quasi-comic treatment of love (depicting the frustrations of an insatiate goddess who falls all over herself as she fumbles to seduce an unresponsive youth), despite the fact that it ends with the death of the innocent young mortal, *Lucrece* is more properly described as a tragic "complaint," a moving exploration of the personal and social consequences of a noble Roman's surrender to lust, against his better nature and at the cost, ultimately, of both his victim's life and his own. In his foreword to *Venus and Adonis*, Shakespeare had promised the dedicatee "a graver labor" if his first offering pleased its would-be patron; in all likelihood, then, *Lucrece* was under way as a companion piece to *Venus and Adonis* at least a year before its eventual publication in 1594. It may be, as some have suggested, that Shakespeare's narrative of Tarquin's rape of Lucrece and her suicide was motivated by a desire to persuade anyone who might have considered the earlier work frivolous that the poet's muse was equally capable of a more serious subject. In any case it is clear that once again he struck a responsive chord: *Lucrece* went through eight editions prior to 1640, and it seems to have been exceeded in popularity only by *Venus and Adonis*.

Both poems were printed during what has been called Shakespeare's "apprenticeship"–the period preceding his emergence as a member of the Lord Chamberlain's Men in 1594–and they share a number of stylistic characteristics with the plays that appear to have been completed during those same early years. As with such youthful dramatic efforts as the three parts of *Henry VI*, *Titus Andronicus*, *The Two Gentlemen of Verona*, *The Comedy of Errors*, and *The Taming of the Shrew*, the writing in *Venus and Adonis* and *Lucrece* is generically imitative (closely adhering to received poetic and dramatic forms), structurally and verbally derivative (echoing the poet's sources almost slavishly at times), and rhetorically formal (with a rigidly patterned verse containing far more rhymes, end-stopped lines, syntactic balances, and allusions to the classics than are to be observed in Shakespeare's writing after the mid 1590s). One feels immediately that *Venus and Adonis* and *Lucrece* are artistically of a piece with Shakespeare's first tentative experiments as a dramatist.

The two poems were probably written dur-

Quee. Welcome to *England*, my louing friends of *Frāce*,
And welcome *Summerset*, and *Oxford* too.
Once more haue we spread our sailes abroad,
And though our tackling be almost consumde,
And *Warwike* as our maine mast ouerthrowne,
Yet warlike Lords raise you that sturdie post,
That beares the sailes to bring vs vnto rest,
And *Ned* and *I* as willing Pilots should
For once with carefull mindes guide on the sterne,
To beare vs through that dangerous gulfe
That heretofore hath swallowed vp our friends.
Prince. And if there be, as God forbid there should,
Amongst vs a timorous or fearefull man,
Let him depart before the battels ioine,
Least he in time of need intise another,
And so withdraw the souldiers harts from vs,
I will not stand aloofe and bid you fight,
But with my sword presse in the thickest thronges,
And single *Edward* from his strongest guard,
And hand to hand enforce him for to yeeld,
Or leaue my bodie as witnesse of my thoughts.
Oxf. Women and children of so high resolue,

And Warriors faint, why twere perpetuall
Shame? Oh braue yong Prince, thy
Noble grandfather doth liue againe in thee,
Long maiest thou liue to beare his image,
And to renew his glories.

Qu. Great Lords, wise men ne'r sit and waile their losse,
But chearely seeke how to redresse their harmes.
What though the Mast be now blowne ouer-boord,
The Cable broke, the holding-Anchor lost,
And halfe our Saylors swallow'd in the flood?
Yet liues our Pilot still. Is't meet, that hee
Should leaue the Helme, and like a fearefull Lad,
With tearefull Eyes adde Water to the Sea,
And giue more strength to that which hath too much,
Whiles in his moane, the Ship splits on the Rock,
Which Industrie and Courage might haue sau'd?
Ah what a shame, ah what a fault were this.
Say *Warwicke* was our Anchor: what of that?

And *Mountague* our Top-Mast: what of him?
Our slaught'red friends, the Tackles: what of these?
Why is not *Oxford* here, another Anchor?
And *Somerset*, another goodly Mast?
The friends of France our Shrowds and Tacklings?
And though vnskilfull, why not *Ned* and I,
For once allow'd the skilfull Pilots Charge?
We will not from the Helme, to sit and weepe,
But keepe our Course (though the rough Winde say no)
From Shelues and Rocks, that threaten vs with Wrack.
As good to chide the Waues, as speake them faire.
And what is *Edward*, but a ruthlesse Sea?
What *Clarence*, but a Quick-sand of Deceit?
And *Richard*, but a raged fatall Rocke?
All these, the Enemies to our poore Barke.
Say you can swim, alas 'tis but a while:
Tread on the Sand, why there you quickly sinke,
Bestride the Rock, the Tyde will wash you off,
Or else you famish, that's a three-fold Death,
This speake I (Lords) to let you vnderstand,
If case some one of you would flye from vs,
That there's no hop'd-for Mercy with the Brothers,
More then with ruthlesse Waues, with Sands and Rocks.
Why courage then, what cannot be auoided,
'Twere childish weakenesse to lament, or feare.

Queen Margaret's speech at the beginning of V.iv of Henry VI, *part 3, as it appears in the* True Tragedie of Richard Duke of Yorke *(from the unique copy in the Bodleian Library, Oxford; Arch G f1)–the 1595 octavo edition of an abridged and corrupt text of the play—and in the 1623 First Folio edition of Shakespeare's plays (Folger Shakespeare Library), which drew its text from the 1602 and 1622 quarto editions, evidently with some reference to the promptbook*

ing the two-year period from June 1592 to June 1594 when the London theaters were closed owing to the plague. But whether they indicate an inclination to leave the theater altogether and essay a career as a traditional poet (as Shakespeare's quest for the patronage of the young Earl of Southampton would seem to imply), or merely demonstrate that Shakespeare was resourceful enough to turn his pen to other uses while he waited for the theaters to reopen, is more than we can say. The only thing that seems beyond doubt is that Shakespeare regarded what he was doing when he wrote *Venus and Adonis* and *Lucrece* as something fundamentally different from what he was doing, prior to that and subsequent to it, in his capacity as a playwright and theater professional.

Like his fellow playwrights when they donned personae as men of letters, Shakespeare was addressing his efforts, first of all, to a noble patron and, second, to a cultivated readership. He was therefore concerned that his compositions be published as he had written them, and he took pains to assure that they were accompanied by a graceful appeal for the approval of an audience presumed to embody the highest standards of literary taste and judgment. It may be that during the same period when he was seeing *Venus and Adonis* and *Lucrece* through the press in carefully proofed editions he was also writing other nondramatic poetry. Many scholars believe that this was when he composed most if not all of the 154 sonnets that bear his name. And if he was in fact the author of *A Lover's Complaint* (a narrative poem in rhyme royal that was attributed to Shakespeare when it was published, along with the *Sonnets*, in an unauthorized edition in 1609), he probably wrote that labored lyric during his years "in the workshop" too. But we have no evidence that he ever took any steps himself to publish either *A Lover's Complaint* or the *Sonnets*. Apart from *Venus and Adonis* and *Lucrece*, the only other literary work that Shakespeare may have had anything to do with publishing on his own behalf was a curious poem called *The Phoenix and Turtle*, which appeared in 1601 as part of a collection "Shadowing the Truth of Love" and appended to Robert Chester's *Love's Martyr*. The Phoenix and Turtle is a sixty-seven-line lyric, probably allegorical, about one bird (the phoenix) legendary for its rarity and beauty and another (the turtledove) proverbial for its constancy. Its scholastic imagery—reminiscent in some ways of the highly technical language to be found in writing of the same liter-

ary climate by such "metaphysical" poets as John Donne—suggests that, if indeed it is by Shakespeare (which many have questioned), it was probably written expressly for the Chester volume at about the time that Shakespeare was at work on such "philosophical" plays as *Hamlet* and *Troilus and Cressida*.

If we except *The Phoenix and Turtle*, then, and assume that the *Sonnets* and *A Lover's Complaint* were published without Shakespeare's active participation, we are left with the conclusion that Shakespeare's "literary career," narrowly defined, was more or less limited to the two-year interruption in his activities as a theater professional when the London playhouses were closed because of the plague. This does not require us to presume, of course, that he ceased to have literary aspirations after 1594. He may have allowed his "sugared sonnets" to circulate in manuscript "among his private friends" (as Francis Meres asserted in *Palladis Tamia* in 1598, a year prior to William Jaggard's surreptitious printing of two of the sonnets in a volume called *The Passionate Pilgrim*) while he continued to revise and augment them in the expectation that he would publish an anthology at a later time. And it is not inconceivable that he would have published a collected edition of his plays had he lived (Jonson having braved the critical tempest that such audacity was bound to generate when he came out with his works in 1616, the year of Shakespeare's death). But the fact is that Shakespeare did not himself publish any of the compositions we now value the most, and we can only infer that doing so was of less importance to him than what he did choose to devote his professional life to: the "wrighting" of plays.

If so, he must at times have had his doubts about the choice he made. In Sonnet 110 (if we may be permitted to assume that the poet was either speaking in his own voice or echoing sentiments that he himself had felt), he allows that he has made himself "a motley to the view" and "sold cheap what is most dear." He then goes on in Sonnet 111 to lament that he "did not better for [his] life provide/Than public means which public manners breeds."

> Thence comes it that my name receives a brand,
> And almost thence my nature is subdu'd
> To what it works in, like the dyer's hand.

Wordsworth believed the *Sonnets* to be the key whereby Shakespeare "unlocked his heart," and it

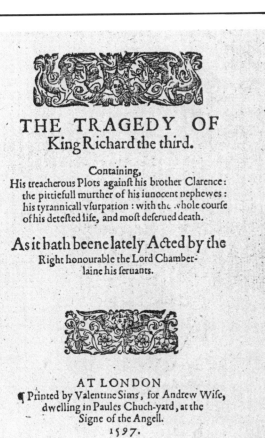

THE TRAGEDY OF
King Richard the third.

Containing,
His treacherous Plots againft his brother Clarence:
the pittiefull murther of his innocent nephewes:
his tyrannicall vfurpation: with the whole courfe
of his deteſted life, and moſt deferued death.

As it hath beene lately Acted by the
Right honourable the Lord Chamberlaine his feruants.

AT LONDON
¶ Printed by Valentine Sims, for Andrew Wife,
dwelling in Paules Chuch-yard, at the
Signe of the Angell.
1597.

Enter Richard Duke of Gloiceſter ſolus.

Ow is the winter of our difcontent,
Made glorious fummer by this fonne of Yorke:
And all the cloudes that lowrd vpon our houfe,
In the deepe bofome of the Ocean buried.
Now are our browes bound with victorious wreathes,
Our bruifed armes hung vp for monuments,
Our fterne alarmes changd to merry meetings,
Our dreadfull marches to delightfull meafures.
Grim-vifagde warre, hath fmoothde his wrinkled front,
And now in fteed of mounting barbed fteedes,
To fright the foules of fearefull aduerfaries,
He capers nimbly in a Ladies chamber,
To the lafciuious pleafing of a loue.
But I that am not fhapte for fportiue trickes,
Nor made to court an amorous looking glaffe,
I that am rudely ftampt and want loues maiefty,
To ftrut before a wanton ambling Nymph:
I that am curtaild of this faire proportion,
Cheated of feature by diffembling nature,
Deformd, vnfinifht, fent before my time
Into this breathing world fcarce halfe made vp,
And that fo lamely and vnfafhionable,
That dogs barke at me as I halt by them:
Why I in this weake piping time of peace
Haue no delight to paffe away the time,
Vnleffe to fpie my fhadow in the funne,
And defcant on mine owne deformity:
And therefore fince I cannot prooue a louer
To entertaine thefe faire well fpoken daies,

A 2   I am

Title page and first page of text from the 1597 quarto edition of the fourth part of Shakespeare's "first tetralogy" of history plays
(British Library)

may be that these intriguing poems are to some degree a spiritual testament—imitating, as was traditional with lyric verse, the thought processes and shifts in sensibility of a person responding to the vicissitudes of private life. That granted, we may be correct to interpret Sonnets 110 and 111 as expressions of Shakespeare's own dissatisfaction with the lot of an actor and playwright.

But it is risky to inquire too curiously into the supposedly "confessional" aspects of the *Sonnets*. Like Shakespeare's other writings, they employ the artifice of "fictions," and they may have been but another form of story telling—different in kind from the plays and narrative poems, to be sure, but similar to them in being "about" something quite other than (or in addition to) the poet's own experience. If we examine them in the context of earlier sonnet sequences—Petrarch's lyrics to Laura in fifteenth-century Italy, for instance, or such late-sixteenth-century English sequences as those by Philip Sidney, Edmund Spenser, Samuel Daniel, and Michael Drayton—we discover that they are quite "conven-tional" in many respects. They display the speaker's wit and attest to his originality; they imply a deeply felt personal situation and hint at a coherent narrative, but they usually stop short of connecting their emotional peaks and valleys into a fully textured autobiographical landscape; they assert the immortality of verse and claim its sovereignty over the ravages of time and change; and usually they deal with themes of truth and beauty in the context of love and friendship and all the circumstances that life arrays in opposition to such values.

To a far greater degree than with most sonnet sequences, Shakespeare's *Sonnets* have "the ring of truth." This is partly because, like all his works (from his earliest plays onward), they portray humanity so convincingly. But it is also a consequence of the extent to which they seem to go beyond, or even to disregard, convention. Thus, instead of praising a lady by cataloging all the attributes that make her lovely, Shakespeare turns Petrarchan tradition on its head by denying his "dark lady" any of the expected beauties and virtues. "My mistress' eyes are nothing like the sun," he says in Sonnet 130; and far from being ethereal and inaccessible in her idealized spirituality, the woman described in Shakespeare's *Sonnets* is sensual, coarse, and promiscuous. Petrarch's Laura may have inspired that earlier poet to Platonic transcendence, but Shakespeare's mistress leaves only the bitter aftertaste of "Th' expense of spirit in a waste of shame," "A bliss in proof, and prov'd, a very woe" (Sonnet 129). And what is more, she alienates the affection of the fair young man to whom most of the first 127 sonnets in the sequence are addressed: the friend who occasions some of the deepest verses in English on such themes as fidelity, stewardship (Shakespeare seems to have been preoccupied with the Parable of the Talents, as rendered in Matthew 25: 14-30), and man's struggle against "never-resting time."

As one reads the sonnets directed to the young man, one detects a descent from unquestioned devotion ("This thou perceiv'st, which makes thy love more strong,/To love that well, which thou must leave ere long"–Sonnet 73) to a fear that the older man's love may be unrequited or at least taken for granted by the young friend to whom he has given so much of himself ("For sweetest things turn sourest by their deeds;/Lilies that fester smell far worse than weeds"–Sonnet 94) to a courageous but probably quixotic determination to remain true to his convictions despite his doubts about the young man's worthiness of such absolute faith ("love is not love/Which alters when it alteration finds/Or bends with the remover to remove"–Sonnet 116). The intensity of feeling expressed in these sonnets has led many interpreters to infer that they must have been based on a homoerotic passion. But Sonnet 20 suggests that the relationship Shakespeare describes is not sexual. Nature, he says, has given the young man "one thing to my purpose nothing." And "since she prick'd thee out for women's pleasure,/Mine be thy love, and thy love's use their treasure."

Several of the sonnets addressed to the friend refer to a "rival poet" who is also bidding for his favors and affection (Sonnets 79, 80, 83, and 86, for example), and others (Sonnets 78, 82, 84, and 85) imply that the young aristocrat is the subject of praise by a great many poetic suitors. As he reflects upon his own position vis-à-vis his many competitors for the friend's love, the speaker in Shakespeare's sonnets is subject to a depth of insecurity that sometimes borders on de-

spair: "Wishing me like to one more rich in hope,/Featur'd like him, like him with friends possess'd,/Desiring this man's art, and that man's scope" (Sonnet 29). And many of the greatest sonnets in the sequence derive their peculiar power from what Robert Frost has termed a "sense of difficulty overcome"–the poet working through the tensions and conflicts described in the first three quatrains (linked by an *abab cdcd efef* rhyme scheme) to some kind of hard-won (though perhaps not completely convincing) resolution in the concluding couplet (rhymed *gg*): "For thy sweet love remem'bred such wealth brings,/That then I scorn to change my state with kings" (again Sonnet 29).

Because the other personalities who figure in the psychodrama of the *Sonnets* seem so vivid, at least as they impinge upon the personality of the speaker, interpreters of the sequence have been inexorably drawn toward speculation about real-life identities for the Dark Lady, the Young Man, and the Rival Poet. Some commentators (such as Oxford historian A. L. Rowse) have persuaded themselves, if not everyone else, that these characters can be positively linked with such contemporaries of Shakespeare as Emilia Lanier, the Earl of Southampton (or, alternatively, the Earl of Pembroke), and Christopher Marlowe (or possibly George Chapman). Unless further information should come to light, however, we are probably best advised to content ourselves with a position of agnosticism on such questions. Until we can be sure about how the *Sonnets* came to be published, and just what kind of debt the publisher Thomas Thorpe refers to when he dedicates the 1609 quarto to the "only begetter" of these poems "Never before Imprinted"–the mysterious "Mr. W. H."–we are unlikely to be able to pin down the "real names" of any of the persons who inhabit the world of the *Sonnets*. Until then, indeed, we cannot even be certain that the *Sonnets* have any autobiographical basis in the first place.

Turning from Shakespeare's nondramatic poetry to the fruits of his two decades as a playwright, we should probably begin where scholars now think he himself began: as the principal practitioner, if not in many ways the originator, of a new kind of drama that sprang from native patriotism. The most immediate "source" of the English history play appears to have been the heightened sense of national destiny that came in the wake of the royal navy's seemingly providential victory over the Spanish Armada in 1588. Proud of the new eminence their nation had

Richard III as portrayed by David Garrick in the eighteenth century (top; engraving by Thomas Cook from a painting by William Hogarth), Edmund Kean in the nineteenth century (bottom left; mezzotint by Charles Turner), and Laurence Olivier in 1949 (bottom right)

The hall in Gray's Inn, where The Comedy of Errors *was performed on 28 December 1594*

achieved, and immensely relieved that the threat of invasion by a Catholic power had been averted, many of Shakespeare's contemporaries were disposed to view England's deliverance as a sign of heaven's favor. As such, it seemed to be a vindication of the reign of Queen Elizabeth and a substantiation of the Tudor order's claim to divine sanction–a claim that had been asserted by a succession of Renaissance chroniclers from Polydore Vergil (circa 1470-1555) through Edward Hall (circa 1498-1547) to Raphael Holinshed (circa 1529-1580), and a claim that was implicit in such government documents as the "Exhortation concerning Good Order and Obedience to Rulers and Magistrates," a 1547 homily read in churches throughout England.

Given this context, it must have seemed entirely fitting that sometime in the late 1580s or early 1590s an enterprising young playwright began dramatizing a sequence of historical developments that were almost universally regarded as

the "roots" of England's current greatness. Most of the material for the four history plays with which Shakespeare began his career as playwright he drew from Edward Hall's *Union of the Two Noble and Illustre Families of Lancaster and York* (1548) and Raphael Holinshed's *Chronicles of England, Scotland, and Ireland* (1587 edition). Here he found narratives of late-medieval English history that began with the reign of King Richard II (1377-1399), focused on Richard's deposition and execution by Henry Bolingbroke (Henry IV), described the Wars of the Roses (1455-1485) that were the eventual consequence of Bolingbroke's usurpation, and concluded with the restoration of right rule when Henry Richmond defeated the tyrannical Richard III (1483-1485) and acceded to the crown as Henry VII, inaugurating a Tudor dynasty that was to last until the death of Queen Elizabeth in 1603. Here he also found a theological reading of political history that treated England as a collective Everyman–falling into sin, undergoing a terrifyingly bloody punishment for its disobedience, and eventually finding its way back to redemption through the emergence of Henry VII.

The chances are that as Shakespeare matured in his craft he came to view the "Tudor myth" (as E. M. W. Tillyard has termed this official dogma) with a degree of skeptical detachment; but even so, he seems to have found in its clear, broad sweep a pattern that served quite well as a way of organizing the disparate materials he chose to dramatize. It gave him a theme of epic proportions, not altogether unlike the "matter" of Greece and Rome that had inspired such classical authors as Homer and Virgil in narrative genres and Aeschylus, Sophocles, Euripides, and Seneca in dramatic genres. It accorded with the biblical treatment of human destiny that Shakespeare's age had inherited from earlier generations, an approach to historical interpretation that had been embedded in such didactic entertainments as the Morality Play (allegorizing the sin, suffering, repentance, and salvation of a typical member of mankind) and the Mystery Play (broadening the cycle to a dramatization of the whole of human history, from man's fall in the Garden of Eden to man's redemption in the Garden of Gethsemane to man's bliss in the Paradise of the New Jerusalem). And it provided a rationale for Shakespeare's use of such powerful dramatic devices as the riddling prophecy and the curse—projecting retribution for present crimes, as the Old Testament would put it, to the third and fourth generations.

When we approach the four plays known as Shakespeare's "first tetralogy" (the three parts of *Henry VI* and *Richard III,* all written, so far as we can tell, by 1592) from the perspective of his "second tetralogy" (*Richard II, Henry IV,* parts 1 and 2, and *Henry V,* all of which appear to have been written between 1595 and 1597), the earlier plays seem comparatively crude. Like their sources, they place more emphasis on providential design and less on human agency. Their verse is more declamatory and less supple. And they provide less individuation of character. Still, they have their virtues, and successful recent productions by the Royal Shakespeare Company and the British Broadcasting Corporation have proven that they can be surprisingly effective in performance.

Henry VI, part 1 did not achieve print until the 1623 First Folio, but it is now generally thought to have been written prior to parts 2 and 3, which first appeared in bad texts, respectively,

in a 1594 quarto edition titled *The First Part of the Contention betwixt the two famous Houses of Yorke and Lancaster* and in a 1595 octavo entitled *The True Tragedie of Richard Duke of Yorke. Henry VI,* part 1, begins with the funeral of King Henry V (which occurred in 1422), details the dissension at home and the loss of life and territory abroad that result from the accession of a new monarch too young and weak to rule, and concludes with King Henry VI's foolish decision to marry Margaret of Anjou—a step that places the saintly King in the very unsaintly hands of an ambitious woman and a lustful nobleman (the Earl of Suffolk, who plans to enjoy Margaret as his own mistress and thereby "rule both her, the King, and realm") and virtually assures the further degradation of a kingdom that has been in decline since the death of Henry VI's famous warrior-king father. *Henry VI,* part 2, covers a ten-year span from Margaret of Anjou's arrival in England (1445) to the Duke of York's victory over his Lancastrian enemies at St. Albans in the first major battle of the Wars of

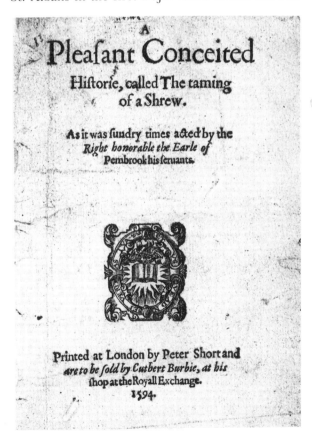

Title page for the 1594 quarto edition of what is generally believed to be a corrupt text of The Taming of the Shrew *(Henry E. Huntington Library and Art Gallery). The authoritative version of the play, first published in the 1623 First Folio, is significantly different from the text of this quarto.*

the Roses (1455). The same kind of internecine strife that has left the noble Talbot exposed to the forces of the strumpet-witch Joan of Arc in *Henry VI*, part 1, works here to undo Henry VI's protector, Duke Humphrey of Gloucester, topple two of the good Duke's enemies (Cardinal Beaufort and Suffolk), unleash the anarchic rebellion of the peasant Jack Cade, and further divide the warring factions (the Yorkists, who have chosen the red rose as their symbol in the famous Temple Garden scene, II.iv, of part 1, and the Lancastrians, who have rallied behind the white rose) that seem hell-bent to tear the kingdom asunder. In *Henry VI*, part 3, the war is at full pitch. As the feeble Henry VI withdraws into a private realm of pastoral longing, his brutal Queen and her allies exchange outrages with one Yorkist enemy after another, father killing son and son killing father in a nightmarish world that has degenerated into a spectacle of unmitigated cruelty. By the time the dust settles, Henry VI and a number of other would-be claimants to the throne are dead or on their way to the grave, and the ominously crookbacked figure of Richard, Duke of Gloucester is slouching his rough way to the crown he will don in the blood-drenched final movement of this hitherto unprecedented cycle of historical tragedies.

Richard III was first published in a 1597 quarto edition that many scholars believe to have been reconstructed from memory by actors plagued out of London theaters between July and October of that year. The play was evidently quite popular, because it went through at least five more printings before it appeared in the 1623 First Folio edition based largely on the third and sixth quartos. And it has remained popular ever since, with a stage tradition highlighted by Richard Burbage in Shakespeare's own theater, David Garrick in the eighteenth century, Edmund Kean in the nineteenth, and Laurence Olivier in the twentieth. Nor is the reason hard to find. For despite the bold strokes with which he is portrayed, Richard III is a character of sufficient complexity to sustain a great deal of dramatic interest. However much we find ourselves repelled by his ruthless treachery, we cannot help admiring the eloquence, resourcefulness, and virtuosity with which he confides and then proceeds to execute his wicked intentions. His wooing of the grieving Lady Anne in the first act is a case in point: having set himself the seemingly impossible task of seducing a woman whose husband and father-in-law he has recently mur-

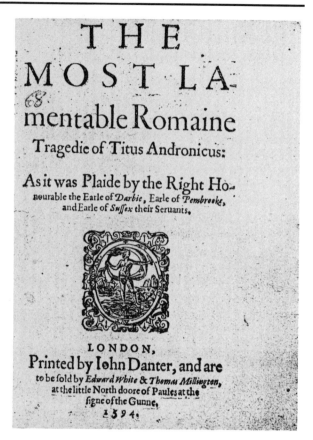

Title page for the only surviving copy of the 1594 quarto edition of Shakespeare's first experiment with revenge tragedy (Folger Shakespeare Library)

dered, Richard is just as astonished as we are by the ease with which he accomplishes it.

In many ways Richard seems, and would have seemed to Shakespeare's first audiences, a conventional, even old-fashioned stage villain: the quick-witted, clever, self-disclosing Vice of the late-medieval Morality Play, the dissimulating Devil familiar from the scriptures. In other, more important, ways he seems, and would have seemed, disturbingly modern: the Machiavellian politician who acknowledges no law, human or divine, in restraint of his foxlike cunning and leonine rapacity; the totalitarian dictator who subverts every social and religious institution in pursuit of his psychopathic grand designs; the existentialist cosmic rebel whose radical alienation is a challenge to every form of order. But if Richard seems in many ways a relentlessly twentieth-century figure, we learn by the end of the play that his "vaulting ambition" (so proleptic of Macbeth's) is ultimately but an instrument of the same providential scheme that he scorns and seeks to circumvent. Richard may be a "dreadful minister of hell," as Lady Anne calls him, but members of Shakespeare's audience (familiar with the story through such earlier renderings of it as the portrait painted by Thomas More) would have seen him simultaneously as a "scourge of God," unleashed to punish England for her sins of the past. Prophetic Margaret reminds us over and over that had there not been strife in the kingdom prior to the advent of Richard, there would have been no ripe occasion for "this poisonous bunch-backed toad" to ascend the throne in the first instance. And as the play ends, an action that has drawn our attention again and again to the past looks optimistically to the future. "By God's fair ordinance," the "bloody dog is dead," and Richmond and Elizabeth (the forebears of Shakespeare's sovereign Elizabeth) are ushering in "smooth-faced peace,/With smiling plenty, and fair prosperous days."

One other English history play is now commonly believed to have been written during Shakespeare's apprenticeship, though scholars differ about whether to date it in the early 1590s or (more probably, in the opinion of most) in the transition years 1594-1595. The earliest surviving text of *King John* is the version printed in the 1623 First Folio, and it offers a drama about a king of doubtful title whose reign (1199-1216) had been viewed in widely divergent ways. Medieval Catholics, focusing on King John's presumed complicity in the death of his nephew Arthur (whose claim to the throne was stronger than John's) and on his feud with Pope Innocent III (which had resulted in the King's excommunication before he finally capitulated five years later and "returned" his kingdom to the Church), had seen him as a usurper, a murderer, and a heretic. Sixteenth-century Protestants, on the other hand, had rehabilitated him as a proto-Tudor martyr and champion of English nationalism. In many respects, Shakespeare's own portrayal is closer to the medieval view of King John: he does away with any ambiguity about John's role in the removal of Arthur, for example, presents the saintlike Arthur and his impassioned mother, Constance, as thoroughly engaging characters, and endows John with few if any sympathetic traits. At the same time, however, Shakespeare's King John continues to receive the loyalty of characters who are portrayed sympathetically—most notably the bastard son of Richard the Lionhearted, Philip Faulconbridge—and by the end of the play it seems evident that a higher cause, the good of England, is to take precedence over such lesser concerns as John's weak title, his execution

of a potential rival, and his inadequacies as a leader. The Bastard, a political realist who seems quite Machiavellian at first—particularly in his analysis of the all-pervasiveness of "commodity" (self-interest) in human affairs—eventually becomes a virtual emblem of patriotism. To him is given the concluding speech of *King John,* and it is frequently cited as Shakespeare's most eloquent summary of the moral implicit in all his early history plays:

> This England never did, nor never shall,
> Lie at the proud foot of a conqueror
> But when it first did help to wound itself.
> ....
> . . . Naught shall make us rue
> If England to itself do rest but true.

If Shakespeare's earliest efforts in the dramatization of history derived from his response to the political climate of his day, his first experiments in comedy seem to have evolved from his reading in school and from his familiarity with the plays of such predecessors on the English stage as John Lyly, George Peele, Robert Greene, and Thomas Nashe. Shakespeare's apprentice comedies are quite "inventive" in many respects, particularly in the degree to which they "overgo" the conventions and devices the young playwright drew upon. But because they have more precedent behind them than the English history plays, they strike us now as less stunningly "original"—though arguably more successfully executed—than the tetralogy on the Wars of the Roses.

Which of them came first we do not know, but most scholars incline toward *The Comedy of Errors,* a play so openly scaffolded upon Plautus's *Menaechmi* and *Amphitruo* (two farces that Shakespeare probably knew in Latin from his days in grammar school) that one modern critic has summed it up as "a kind of diploma piece." Set, ostensibly, in the Mediterranean city familiar from St. Paul's Epistle to the Ephesians, the play begins with a sentence on the life of a luckless Syracusan merchant, Aegeon, who has stumbled into Ephesus in search of his son Antipholus. After narrating a tale of woe that wins the sympathy of the Duke of Ephesus, Aegeon is given till five in the afternoon to come up with a seemingly impossible ransom for his breach of an arbitrary law against Syracusans. Meanwhile, unknown to Aegeon, the object of his search is in Ephesus too, having arrived only hours before him; Antipholus had set out some two years earlier to find a twin brother

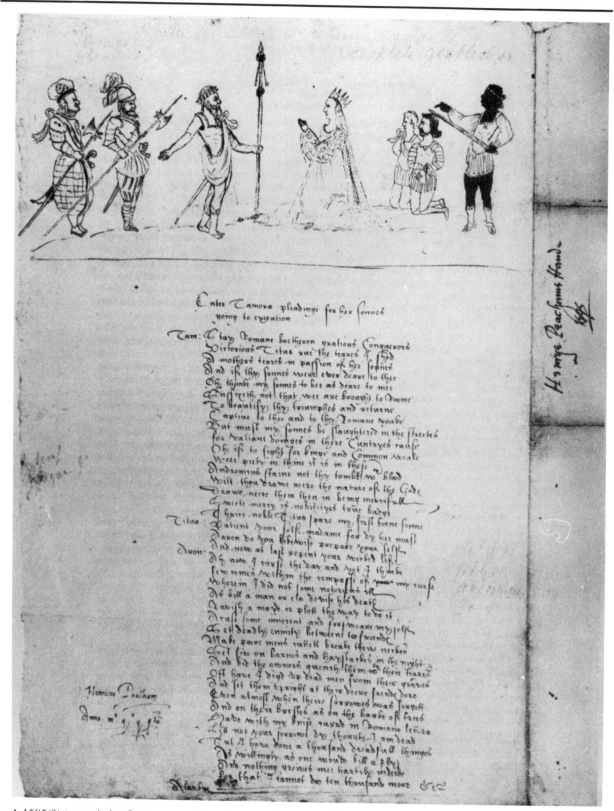

A 1595(?) transcription from memory of lines from a performance of Titus Andronicus, *with sketches of some of the charac-*
ters. At center Tamora is shown begging Titus to spare her two sons, kneeling behind her. Aaron the Moor is at far right.
Henry Peacham, whose name is at lower left, may have made the transcription and perhaps the drawing (Harley Papers,
vol. i, f. 159ᵛ, Longleat; by permission of the Marquess of Bath).

by the same name who was separated from the rest of the family in a stormy shipwreck more than twenty years in the past. By happy coincidence, the other Antipholus has long since settled in Ephesus, and so (without either's knowledge) has their mother, Aegeon's long-lost wife, Aemilia, who is now an abbess. To complicate matters further, both Antipholuses have slaves named Dromio, also twins long separated, and of course both sets of twins are indistinguishably appareled. Into this mix Shakespeare throws a goldsmith, a set of merchants, a courtesan, a wife and a sister-in-law for the Ephesian Antipholus, and a conjuring schoolmaster. The result is a swirling brew of misunderstandings, accusations, and identity crises–all leading, finally, to a series of revelations that reunite a family, save Aegeon's life, and bring order to a city that had begun to seem bewitched by sorcerers.

The Comedy of Errors reached print for the first time in the 1623 First Folio. We know that it was written prior to 28 December 1594, however, because there is record of a performance on that date at one of the four Inns of Court. Some scholars believe that the play was written for that holiday Gray's Inn presentation, but most tend to the view that it had been performed previously, possibly as early as 1589 but more likely in the years 1592-1594. Most critics now seem agreed, moreover, that for all its farcical elements, the play is a comedy of some sophistication and depth, with a sensitivity to love that anticipates Shakespeare's great comedies later in the decade: when Luciana advises her sister Adriana about how she should treat her husband Antipholus, for example, she echoes Paul's exhortations on Christian marriage in Ephesians. And with its use of the devices of literary romance (the frame story of Aegeon comes from Apollonius of Tyre), *The Comedy of Errors* also looks forward to the wanderings, confusions of identity, and miraculous reunions so fundamental to the structure of "late plays" such as *Pericles* and *The Tempest*.

What may have been Shakespeare's next comedy has also been deprecated as farce, and it is frequently produced today with staging techniques that link it with the commedia del l'arte popular in Renaissance Italy. But for all its knockabout slapstick, *The Taming of the Shrew* is too penetrating in its psychology and too subtle in its handling of the nuances of courtship to be dismissed as a play deficient in feeling. Its main event is a battle of the sexes in which Petruchio, who has "come to wive it wealthily in Padua," takes on a

dare no other potential suitor would even consider: to win both dowry and docility from a sharp-tongued shrew avoided as "Katherine the curst." Apparently recognizing that Katherine's willfulness is a product of the favoritism her father has long bestowed upon her younger sister, and having the further good sense to realize that the fiery Kate is capable of becoming a much more attractive wife than the much-sought-after but rather devious Bianca, Petruchio mounts a brilliant campaign to gain Kate's love and make her his. First, he insists that Kate is fair and gentle, notwithstanding all her efforts to disabuse him of that notion. Second, he "kills her in her own humour," with a display of arbitrary behavior–tantrums, scoldings, peremptory refusals–that both wears her down and shows her how unpleasant shrewishness can be. At the end of the play Petruchio shocks his skeptical fellow husbands by wagering that his bride will prove more obedient than theirs. When Kate not only heeds his commands but reproaches her sister and the other wives for "sullen, sour" rebellion against their husbands, it becomes manifest that Petruchio has succeeded in his quest: Kate freely and joyfully acknowledges him to be her "loving lord." If we have doubts about whether Kate's transformation can be accepted as a "happy ending" today–and alterations of the final scene in many recent productions would suggest that it may be too offensive to current sensibilities to be played straight–we should perhaps ask ourselves whether the Kate who seems to wink conspiratorially at Petruchio as she puts her hands beneath his foot to win a marital wager is any less spirited or fulfilled a woman than the Kate who drives all her would-be wooers away in the play's opening scene.

Whether or not *The Taming of the Shrew* is the mysterious *Love's Labor's Won* referred to by Francis Meres in 1598, it seems to have been written in the early 1590s, because what is now generally believed to be a bad quarto of it appeared in 1594. *The Taming of a Shrew* differs significantly from the version of Shakespeare's play that was first published in the 1623 Folio–most notably in the fact that the drunken tinker Christopher Sly, who appears only in the induction to the later printing of the play, remains on stage throughout *The Taming of a Shrew*, repeatedly interrupting the action of what is presented as a play for his entertainment and resolving at the end to go off and try Petruchio's wife-taming techniques on his own recalcitrant woman. Some directors retain the later Sly scenes, but no one seriously questions that the Folio text is in general the more authoritative of the two versions of the play.

The Folio provides the only surviving text of *The Two Gentlemen of Verona*, a comedy so tentative in its dramaturgy (for example, its ineptitude in the few scenes where the playwright attempts to manage more than two characters on the stage at once), and so awkward in its efforts to pit the claims of love and friendship against each other, that many scholars now think it to be the first play Shakespeare ever wrote. Based largely on a 1542 chivalric romance (*Diana Enamorada*) by Portuguese writer Jorge de Montemayor, *The Two Gentlemen of Verona* depicts a potential rivalry between two friends–Valentine and Proteus–who fall in love with the same Milanese woman (Silvia) despite the fact that Proteus has vowed his devotion to a woman (Julia) back home in Verona. Proteus engineers Valentine's banishment from Milan so that he can woo Silvia away from him. But Silvia remains faithful to Valentine, just as Julia (who has followed her loved one disguised as his page) holds true to Proteus, notwithstanding the character he discloses as a man who lives up to his name. In the concluding forest scene Valentine intervenes to save Silvia from being raped by Proteus; but, when Proteus exhibits remorse, Valentine offers him Silvia anyway, as a token of friendship restored. Fortunately, circumstances conspire to forestall such an unhappy consummation, and the play ends with the two couples properly reunited.

Unlike *The Comedy of Errors* and *The Taming of the Shrew*, *The Two Gentlemen of Verona* has never been popular in the theater, even though it offers two resourceful women (whose promise will be fulfilled more amply in such later heroines as Rosalind and Viola), a pair of amusing clowns (Launce and Speed), and one of the most engaging dogs (Crab) who ever stole a stage. In its mixture of prose and verse, nevertheless, and in its suggestion that the "green world"

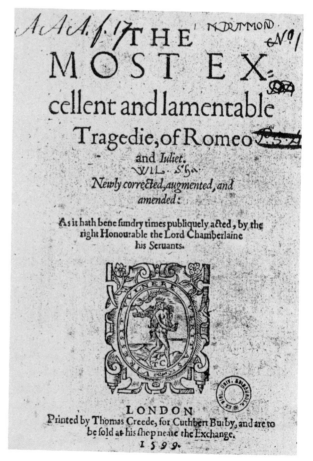

Title pages for the 1597 corrupt quarto edition (Henry E. Huntington Library and Art Gallery) and the 1599 "corrected, augmented, and amended" quarto edition (Edinburgh University) of the play for which Shakespeare drew on a didactic narrative poem of the same title by Arthur Brooke, first published in 1562. The copy of the second quarto shown here once belonged to William Drummond of Hawthornden, who wrote his name on the title page.

A
PLEASANT
Conceited Comedie
CALLED,
Loues labors loft.

As it vvas prefented before her Highnes
this laft Chriftmas.

Newly correƈted and augmented
By W. Shakeſpere.

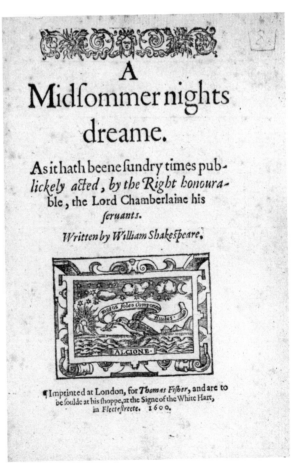

Imprinted at London by W.W.
for Cutbert Burby.
1598.

Title page for the 1598 quarto edition of a play that was performed before Elizabeth I during the 1597 Christmas season (British Library)

of the woods is where pretensions fall and would-be evildoers find their truer selves, *The Two Gentlemen of Verona* looks forward to the first fruits of Shakespeare's maturity: the "romantic comedies" of which it proves to be a prototype.

The one remaining play that most critics now locate in the period known as Shakespeare's apprenticeship is a Grand Guignol melodrama that seems to have been the young playwright's attempt to outdo Thomas Kyd's *Spanish Tragedy* (produced circa 1589) in its exploitation of the horrors of madness and revenge. The composition of *Titus Andronicus* is usually dated 1590-1592, and it seems to have been drawn from a ballad and *History of Titus Andronicus* that only survives today in an eighteenth-century reprint now deposited in the Folger Shakespeare Library. (The Folger also holds the sole extant copy of the 1594 first quarto of Shakespeare's play, the authoritative text for all but the one scene, III.ii, that first appeared in the 1623 Folio.) If Shakespeare did take most of his plot from the *History of Titus*

Andronicus, it is clear that he also went to Ovid's *Metamorphoses* (for the account of Tereus's rape of Philomena, to which the tongueless Lavinia points to explain what has been done to her) and to Seneca's *Thyestes* (for Titus's fiendish revenge on Tamora and her sons at the end of the play).

Although *Titus Andronicus* is not a "history play," it does make an effort to evoke the social and political climate of fourth-century Rome; and in its depiction of a stern general who has just sacrificed more than twenty of his own sons to conquer the Goths, it anticipates certain characteristics of Shakespeare's later "Roman plays": *Julius Caesar*, *Antony and Cleopatra*, and *Coriolanus*. But it is primarily as an antecedent of *Hamlet* (influenced, perhaps, by the so-called lost *Ur-Hamlet*) that *Titus* holds interest for us today. Because whatever else it is, *Titus Andronicus* is Shakespeare's first experiment with revenge tragedy. Its primary focus is the title character, whose political misjudgments and fiery temper

A
Midſommer nights
dreame.

As it hath beene fundry times publickely aƈted, by the Right honourable, the Lord Chamberlaine his
feruants.

Written by William Shakeſpeare.

¶ Imprinted at London, for Thomas Fiſher, and are to
be ſoulde at his ſhoppe, at the Signe of the White Hart,
in Fleeteſtreete. 1600.

Title page for the 1600 quarto edition of the Shakespeare comedy that probably dates from 1595-1596, the same period as the tragedy Romeo and Juliet *(Henry E. Huntington Library and Art Gallery)*

put him at the mercy of the Queen of the Goths, Tamora, and her two sons (Demetrius and Chiron). They ravish and mutilate Titus's daughter Lavinia, manipulate the Emperor into executing two of Titus's sons (Martius and Quintus) as perpetrators of the crime, and get Titus's third son (Lucius) banished for trying to rescue his brothers. Along the way, Tamora's Moorish lover Aaron tricks Titus into having his right hand chopped off in a futile gesture to save Martius and Lucius. After Lavinia writes the names of her assailants in the sand with her grotesque stumps, Titus works out a plan for revenge: he slits the throats of Demetrius and Chiron, invites Tamora to a banquet, and serves her the flesh of her sons baked in a pie. He then kills Tamora and dies at the hands of Emperor Saturninus. At this point Lucius returns heading a Gothic army and takes over as the new Emperor, condemning Aaron to be half-buried and left to starve and throwing Tamora's corpse to the scavenging birds and beasts.

As Fredson Bowers has pointed out, *Titus Andronicus* incorporates a number of devices characteristic of other revenge tragedies: the protagonist's feigned madness, his delay in the execution of his purpose, his awareness that in seeking vengeance he is taking on a judicial function that properly rests in God's hands, and his death at the end in a bloody holocaust that leaves the throne open for seizure by the first opportunist to arrive upon the scene.

Revenge is also a significant motif in Shakespeare's other early tragedy, *Romeo and Juliet,* usually dated around 1595-1596. It is a blood feud between their two Veronan families that forces the lovers to woo and wed in secret, thereby creating the misunderstanding that leads Mercutio to defend Romeo's "honor" in act three when the just-married protagonist declines his new kinsman Tybalt's challenge to duel. And it is both to avenge Mercutio's death and to restore his own now-sullied name that Romeo then slays Tybalt and becomes "fortune's fool"–initiating a falling action that leads eventually to a pair of suicides and a belated recognition by the Capulets and the Montagues that their children have become "poor sacrifices of our enmity."

But it is not for its revenge elements that most of us remember *Romeo and Juliet.* No, it is for the lyricism with which Shakespeare portrays the beauty and idealism of love at first sight–all the more transcendent for the ways in which the playwright sets it off from the calculations of

Juliet's parents (intent on arranging their daughter's marriage to advance their own status) or contrasts it with the earthy bawdiness of Juliet's Nurse or the worldly-wise cynicism of Romeo's friend Mercutio. The spontaneous sonnet of Romeo and Juliet's initial meeting at Capulet's ball, their betrothal vows in the balcony scene later that evening, the ominous parting that concludes their one night together and foreshadows their final meeting in the Capulet tomb–these are the moments we carry with us from a performance or a reading of what may well be history's most famous love story.

Romeo and Juliet may strike us as an "early" tragedy in its formal versification and in its patterned structure. It has been faulted for its dependence on coincidence and on causes external to the protagonists for the conditions that bring about the tragic outcome–an emphasis implicit in the play's repeated references to Fortune and the stars. And critics have encountered difficulty in their attempts to reconcile the purity of Romeo and Juliet's devotion to each other ("for earth too dear") with the play's equal insistence that their relationship is a form of idolatry–ultimately leading both lovers to acts of desperation that audiences in Shakespeare's time would have considered far more consequential than do most modern audiences. But whatever its supposed limitations and interpretive problems, *Romeo and Juliet* seems likely to hold its position as one of the classics of the dramatic repertory.

Romeo and Juliet first appeared in a 1597 quarto edition that most scholars believe to be a memorial reconstruction, though one with isolated passages (such as Mercutio's celebrated Queen Mab speech) printed in a form that some scholars believe superior to their rendering in the text today's editors accept as the best authority: the 1599 second quarto, "newly corrected, augmented, and amended," and apparently derived primarily from Shakespeare's own "foul papers." Two more printings appeared before the 1623 Folio, whose text–essentially a reprint of the third quarto edition (1609)–has no independent authority. The principal source for the play was a 1562 narrative, *The Tragical History of Romeus and Juliet,* by Arthur Brooke, a didactic poem urging children to be obedient to their parents. By telescoping three months into four days and by dramatizing the story in a manner more sympathetic to the young lovers, Shakespeare transformed a sermon into a tragedy whose urgency must have been just as moving in the Elizabethan theater as

A Midsummer Night's Dream: *(top)* Titania and Bottom, *painting by Henri Fuseli, 1780-1790; and (bottom), William Blake's watercolor,* Oberon, Titania and Puck with Fairies Dancing, *circa 1785-1787 (Tate Gallery, London)*

we know it to be in our own.

If *Romeo and Juliet* is a play that has lost none of its freshness in the four centuries since its first appearance, *Love's Labor's Lost* now strikes us as so thoroughly "Elizabethan" in its rhetoric and topicality as to be nearly inaccessible to modern audiences. Evidently another product of the "transition years" when Shakespeare was working his way back into the theater after a two-year hiatus due to the plague, *Love's Labor's Lost* appears to have been written in 1594-1595 for private performance and may well have been revised in 1597 for a performance before the Queen during the Christmas revels. Its earliest known printing was a 1598 quarto announcing itself as "newly corrected and augmented" and probably set from Shakespeare's "foul papers." The Folio text was essentially a reprint of this first quarto, which has the distinction of being the first play to bear Shakespeare's name on its title page. Until recently no literary source had been found for the plot of *Love's Labor's Lost,* but Glynne Wickham has now turned up a 1581 analogue, *The Four Foster Children of Desire,* that helps account for much of the play's structure and several of its themes.

What emerges for a theatergoer or reader of the play today is a highly "artificial" comedy about a company of men whose well-intended but ill-conceived attempt to outwit nature makes them all look foolish and lands them in a pickle. No sooner have King Ferdinand of Navarre and his friends Longaville, Dumaine, and Berowne–hoping to conquer the frailties of the flesh and find an antidote to "cormorant devouring time"–forsworn the company of women and withdrawn to their quasi-monastic Academe than they find their fortress besieged by four beautiful ladies–the Princess of France and her attendants Maria, Katherine, and Rosaline–who camp in the park outside and watch with amusement as each of the "scholars" falls in love, forsakes his vows, and gets caught by the others. Eventually the men surrender and propose marriage, but by this time it has become clear that they are so far gone in artifice that they need at least a year of penance–and time in real-world settings such as the hospital to which Berowne is consigned–before their protestations of devotion can be given any credit. Love's labor is "lost," then, in the sense that this is a comedy without the traditional happy consummation in wedding, feasting, and dancing. Its concluding lyrics move from spring ("When daisies pied") to winter ("When icicles hang"), and the year of penance to come is one

that requires all of the men to reevaluate their aspirations with a renewed awareness of the omnipresence of disease and the inevitability of death.

Love's Labor's Lost is one of Shakespeare's most self-conscious plays generically, and it is also one of his most demanding plays linguistically. Much is made of the "literary" artifice of the four men's rhetoric, and it is shown to be detrimental to normal human feeling. It is also shown to be an infection that touches such lesser characters as the bombastic braggart soldier Don Adriano de Armado, the pedant schoolmaster Holofernes, and the clown Costard, all of whom, like the poor curate Nathaniel in the Pageant of the Nine Worthies, prove "a little o'erparted." It is one of the ironies of the play that the four major male characters, who laugh so cruelly at the participants in the pageant, also prove "o'erparted" in the end. Such are the wages of affectation.

Affectation of another kind is depicted in a delightful scene from what many regard as Shakespeare's most charming comedy, *A Midsummer Night's Dream.* As the Athenian courtiers are quick to observe in their critiques of the "tragical mirth" of Pyramus and Thisby in V.i, the "mechanicals" who display their dramatic wares at the nuptial feast of Theseus and Hippolyta are even more fundamentally "o'erparted" than the hapless supernumeraries of *Love's Labor's Lost.* But there is something deeply affectionate about Shakespeare's portrayal of the affectations of Bottom and his earnest company of "hempen homespuns," and the "simpleness and duty" with which they tender their devotion is the playwright's way of reminding us that out of the mouths of babes and fools can sometimes issue a loving wisdom that "hath no bottom." Like "Bottom's Dream," the playlet brings a refreshingly naive perspective to issues addressed more seriously elsewhere. And, by burlesquing the struggles and conflicts through which the lovers in the woods circumvent the arbitrariness of their elders, "Pyramus and Thisby" comments not only upon the fortunes of Demetrius and Helena, Lysander and Hermia, but also upon the misfortunes of Romeo and Juliet. After all, both stories derive ultimately from the same source in Ovid's *Metamorphoses,* and Shakespeare's parallel renderings of the "course of true love" in *Romeo and Juliet* and *A Midsummer Night's Dream* are so closely linked in time and treatment that it is tempting to regard the two plays as companion pieces–tragic and comic masks, as it were, for the same

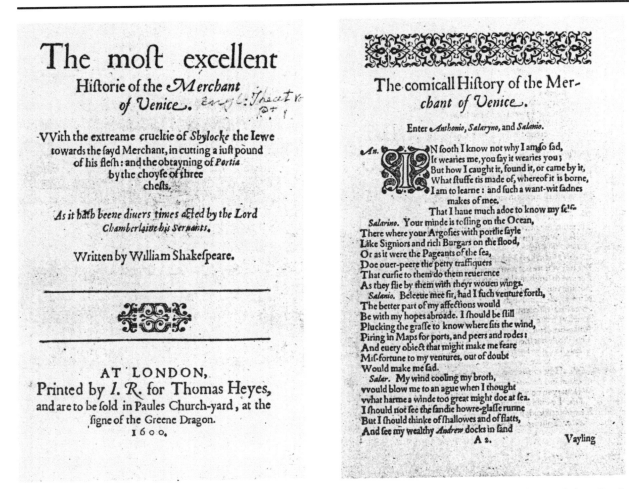

Title page and first page of text from the 1600 quarto edition of the play that serves as a prototype for Shakespeare's later "problem comedies" (British Library)

phase (1595-1596) of Shakespearean dramaturgy.

Whether or not *A Midsummer Night's Dream* was commissioned for a wedding ceremony at Whitehall, as some scholars have speculated, the play is in fact a remarkable welding of disparate materials: the fairy lore of Oberon and Titania and their impish minister Puck, the classical narrative of Theseus's conquest of the Amazons and their queen Hippolyta, the confused comings and goings of the young Athenian lovers who must flee to the woods to evade their tyrannical parents, and the rehearsals for a crude craft play by a band of well-meaning peasants. It is in some ways the most original work in the entire Shakespearean canon, and one is anything but surprised that its "something of great constancy" has inspired the best efforts of such later artists as composer Felix Mendelssohn, painters Henry Fuseli and William Blake, director Peter Brook, and filmmakers Max Reinhardt and Woody Allen.

A Midsummer Night's Dream is in many re-

spects the epitome of "festive comedy," an evocation of the folk rituals associated with such occasions as May Day and Midsummer Eve, and its final mood is one of unalloyed romantic fulfillment. Romance is also a key ingredient in the concluding arias of Shakespeare's next comedy, *The Merchant of Venice*, where Bassanio and Portia, Lorenzo and Jessica, and Gratiano and Nerissa celebrate the happy consummation of three love quests and contemplate the music of the spheres from a magical estate known symbolically as Belmont. But the "sweet harmony" the lovers have achieved by the end of *The Merchant of Venice* has been purchased very dearly, and it is hard for a modern audience to accept the serenity of Belmont without at least a twinge of guilt over what has happened in far-off Venice to bring it about.

Whether *The Merchant of Venice* is best categorized as an anti-Semitic play (capitalizing on prejudices that contemporaries such as Marlowe had catered to in plays like *The Jew of Malta*) or

King Richard the Second.

Peace shall go sleepe with turkes and infidels,
And in this seate of peace, tumultuous warres,
Shall kin with kin, and kinde with kind confound:
Disorder, horror, feare, and mutiny,
Shall heere inhabit, and this land be cald,
The field of Golgotha and dead mens sculs.
Oh if yon raise this house against this house,
It will the wofullest diuision proue,
That euer fell vpon this cursed earth:
Preuent it, resist it, let it not be so,
Lest child, childs children, crie against you wo.
  North. Well haue you argued sir, and for your paines,
Of Capitall treason, we arrest you heere:
My Lord of Westminster, be it your charge,
To keepe him safely till his day of triall.
  Bull. Let it be so, and loe on wednesday next,
We solemnly proclaime our Coronation,
Lords be ready all.   *Exeunt.*
       Manent West. Caleil, Aumerle.
  Abbot. A wofull Pageant haue we heere beheld.
  Car. The woe's to come, the children yet vnborne,
Shall feele this day as sharpe to them as thorne.
  Aum. You holy Clergy men, is there no plot,
To ridde the realme of this pernitious blot?
  Abbot. My Lo. before I freely speake my mind heerein,
You shall not onely take the Sacrament,
To burie mine intents, but also to effect,
What euer I shall happen to deuise:
I see your browes are full of discontent,
Your harts of sorrow, and your eies of teares:
Come home with me to supper, Ile lay a plot,
Shall shew vs all a merrie daie.   *Exeunt.*
       Enter the Queene with her attendants.
  Quee. This way the King will come, this is the way,
To Iulius Cæsars ill erected Tower,
To wohse flint bosome, my condemned Lord,
Is doomde a prisoner by proud Bullingbrooke.
                    H2   Heere

The Tragedie of

Oh if you rayse this house against his house,
It will the wofullest diuision proue,
That euer fell vpon this cursed earth:
Preuent it, resist it, and let it not be so,
Least child, childes children crie against you woe.
  North. Well haue you argued sir, and for your paynes,
Of Capitall treason, we arrest you here:
My Lord of Westminster, be it your charge,
To keepe him safely till his day of triall.
May it please you Lords, to graunt the common suite,
Fetch hither *Richard*, that in common view
He may surrender, so we shall proceed without suspicion.
  Yorke. I will be his conduct.
  Bull. Lords, you that are heere, are vnder our arest,
Procure your Sureties for your dayes of answere,
Litle are we beholding to your loue,
And litle looke for at your helping hands.
       Enter king Richard.
  Rich. Alacke why am I sent for to a King,
Before I haue shooke off the regall thoughts
Wherewith I raignd; I hardly yet haue learnt
To insinuate, flatter, bow, and bend my limbes?
Giue Sorrow leaue a while to tutor me to this submission:
Yet I well remember the fauours of these men,
Were they not mine? did they not sometimes cry all hayle
To me? so *Iudas* did to *Christ*; but he in twelue,
Found trueth in all but one, I in twelue thousand none:
God saue the King, will no man say Amen:
Am I both Priest and Clarke; well then, Amen,
God saue the King, although I be not hee,
And yet Amen, if heauen do thinke him mee:
To doe what seruice am I sent for hither?
  Yorke. To doe that office of thine owne good will,
Which tired maiestie did make thee offer,
The resignation of thy State and Crowne
To *Harry Bulingbrooke*.
  Rich. Scale the Crowne.
                                          Heere

King Richard the Second.

Heere Coosin, on this side my hand, and on that side yours:
Now is this golden Crowne like a deepe Well,
That owes two Buckets filling one an other,
The emptier euer dauncing in the ayre,
The other downe vnseene, and full of Water:
That Bucket downe, and full of teares, am I,
Drinking my griefe, whilst you mount vp on high.
  Bull. I thought you had beene willing to resigne?
  Rich. My Crowne I am, but still my Griefes are mine:
You may my Glories and my State depose,
But not my Griefes, still am I King of those.
  Bull. Part of your Cares you giue me with your Crowne.
  Rich. Your cares set vp, do not plucke my cares downe,
My care is losse of care, by old care don,
Your care is game of care by new care won:
The cares I giue, I haue, though giuen away,
They tend the Crowne, yet still with me they stay:
  Bull. Are you contented to resigne the Crowne?
  Rich. I, no no I; for, I must nothing bee:
Therefore no no, for I resigne to thee.
Now marke me how I will vndoe my selfe:
I giue this heauie waight from off my head,
And this vnweildie Scepter from my hand,
The pride of kingly sway from out my heart:
With mine owne teares I wash away my balme,
With mine owne hands I giue away my Crowne,
With mine owne tongue deny my sacred state,
With mine owne breath release all duties rites,
All pompe and maiestie I do forsweare,
My Manners, Rentes, Reuenewes I forgoe,
My Actes, Decrees, and Statutes I denie:
God pardon all Oathes that are broke to me,
God keepe all Vowes vnbroke that sweare to thee:
Make me that nothing haue, with nothing grieud,
And thou with all pleasd, that hast all archieud:
Long mayst thou liue in *Richards* seat to sit,
And soone lie *Richard* in an earthy pit:
                    H2   God

When the first quarto edition of Richard II *was printed in 1597, the crucial passage in which King Richard surrenders the crown to Henry Bolingbroke was cut, probably because the censors saw it as a threat to the sovereignty of Elizabeth I. On the page from IV.i in this edition shown at top some 160 lines of text are omitted between the fifteenth and sixteenth lines (Trinity College, Cambridge). The passage was not restored until 1608 when it appeared in the fourth quarto edition of the play, as shown at the bottom of this page and on the next (Bodleian Library).*

The Tragedie of

God saue King *Harry*, vnkingd *Richard* sayes,
And send him many yeeres of Sun-shine dayes.
What more remaines?

  North. No more, but that you read
These accusations, and these greeuous crimes,
Committed by your person, and your followers,
Against the State and profit of this Land,
That by confessing them, the soules of men
May deeme that you are worthily deposde.

  Rich. Must I doe so? and must I rauell out
My weaud vp Folly, gentle *Northumberland?*
If thy offences were vpon record,
Would it not shame thee in so faire a troope,
To read a lecture of them, if thou wouldst,
There shouldst thou finde one haynous article,
Contayning the deposing of a King,
And cracking the strong warrant of an Oath,
Markt with a blot, damd in the booke of heauen:
Nay of you that stand and looke vpon,
Whilst that my wretchednesse doth bate my selfe,
Though some of you (with *Pilat*) wash your hands,
Shewing an outward pittie, yet you *Pilates,*
Haue heere deliuer me to my sowre Crosse,
And water can not wash away your sinne.

  North. My Lord dispatch, read ore these Articles.

  Rich. Mine eyes are full of teares, I cannot see:
And yet salt water blindes them not so much,
But they can see a sort of Traytors heere:
Nay, if I turne mine eyes vpon my selfe,
I find my selfe a Traytor with the rest,
For I haue giuen heere my soules consent
To vndecke the pompous body of a King,
Made Glory base, and Soueraigntie a slaue,
Proud Maiestie a subiect, State a peasant.

  North. My Lord.

  Rich. No Lord of thine, thou haught insulting man,
Nor no mans Lord, I haue no name, no title,

H   No

King Richard the Second.

No not that name was giuen me at the Font,
But tis vsurpt: alacke the heauie day,
That I haue worne so many Winters out,
And know not now, what name to call my selfe.
O that I were a mockerie King of Snow,
Standing before the sunne of *Bullingbrooke,*
To melt my selfe away in water drops.
Good King, great King, and yet not greatly good,
And if my name be sterling, yet in England
Let it command a mirrour hether strayte
That it may shew me what a face I haue,
Since it is banckrout of his Maiestie.

  Bull. Goe some of you and fetch a Looking-glasse.

  North. Read ore this paper while the Glasse doth come.

  Rich. Feind, thou torments me ere I come to Hell.

  Bull. Vrge it no more my Lord Northumberland.

  North. The Commons will not then be satisfied.

  Rich. They shall be satisfied, Ile read enough,
When I doe see the very Booke indeed,
Where all my sinnes are writ, and that's my selfe.
Giue me the Glasse: no deeper wrinckles yet?
Hath Sorrow stroke so many blowes vpon this
Face of mine, and made no deeper wounds?
Oh flattering Glasse, like to my followers in prosperitie,
Was this the face that euery day vnder his
Houshould roofe did keepe ten thousand men?
Was this the face that faast so many follies,
And was at last outfaast by *Bullingbrooke?*
A brittle Glorie shineth in this face,
As brittle as the Glorie is the face,
For there it is crackt in a hundred shiuers,
Marke silent King the morall of this sport,
How soone my sorrow hath destroyde my face.

  Bull. The shadow of your sorrow hath destroyd
The shadow of your face.

  Rich. Say that againe: the shadow of my sorrow?
Ha, let's see, tis very true, my griefe

H 3.   Lies

The Tragedie of

Lies all within, and these externall manners
Of laments are meerely shadowes to the vnseene,
Griefe that swelles with silence in the tortured soule,
And I thanke thee King that not onely giuest
Me cause to wayle, but teachest me the way
How to lament the cause: Ile begge one boone,
And then be gone, and trouble you no more.

  Bull. Name it faire Coosin.

  Rich. Faire Coose, why? I am greater then a King:
For when I was a king, my flatterers were then but subiects,
Being now a subiect, I haue a King heere,
To my flatterer, being so great, I haue no need to beg.

  Bul. Yet aske.

  Rich. And shall I haue it?

  Bul. You shall.

  Rich. Why then giue me leaue to goe.

  Bull. Whither?

  Rich. Whither you will, so I were from your sights.

  Bull. Goe some of you conuey him to the Tower.

  Rich. O good conuey, conueyers are you all,
That rise thus nimbly by a true Kings fall.

  Bull. On Wednesday next we solemnely set downe
Our Coronation, Lords prepare your selues.

  Exeunt. Manet West, Carleil, Aumerle.

  Abbot. A wofull Pageant haue we heere beheld.

  Carl. The woe's to come, the children yet vnborne,
Shall feele this day as sharpe to them as thorne.

  Aum. You holy Clergie men, is there no plot,
To rid the Realme of this pernitious blot?

  Abbot. Before I freely speake my minde herein,
You shall not onely take the Sacrament,
To bury mine intents, but also to effect,
What euer I shall happen to deuise:
I see your browes are full of discontent,
Your heart of sorrow, and your eyes of teares,
Come home with me to supper, Ile lay a plot,
Shall shew vs all a merry day.

  Exeunt. Enter

H

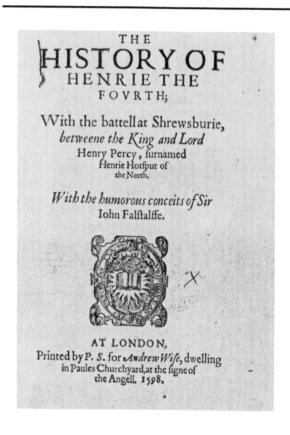

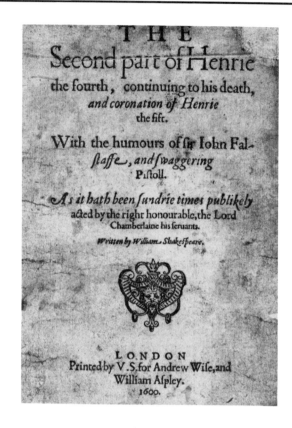

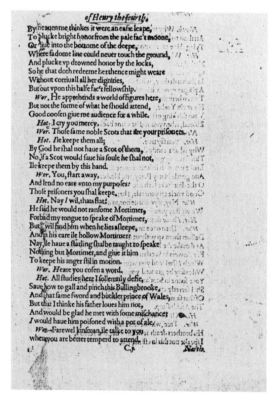

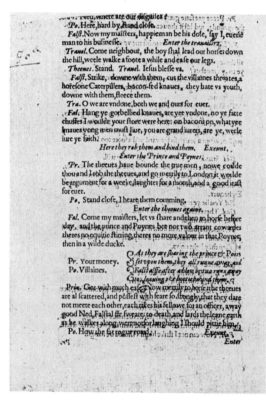

Title pages for 1598 and 1600 quarto editions of Shakespeare's examination of the reign of Henry Bolingbroke after his usurpation of the English crown (top left, Trinity College, Cambridge; top right, Henry E. Huntington Library and Art Gallery) and the first and last pages of an eight-leaf fragment from an earlier 1598 quarto edition, now preserved at the Folger Shakespeare Library.

as a play about the evils of anti-Semitism (as critical of the Christian society that has persecuted the Jew as it is of the vengeance he vents in response), its central trial scene is profoundly disturbing for an audience that has difficulty viewing Shylock's forced conversion as a manifestation of mercy. Shylock's "hath not a Jew eyes" speech impels us to see him as a fellow human being—notwithstanding the rapacious demand for "justice" that all but yields him Antonio's life before Portia's clever manipulations of the law strip the usurer of his own life's fortune—so that even if we feel that the Jew's punishment is less severe than what strict "justice" might have meted out to him, his grim exit nevertheless casts a pall over the festivities of the final act in Belmont.

By contrast with *A Midsummer Night's Dream*, a play in which the disparate components of the action are resolved in a brilliantly satisfying synthesis, *The Merchant of Venice* remains, for many of us, a prototype of those later Shakespearean works that twentieth-century critics have labeled "problem comedies." Even its fairy-tale elements, such as the casket scenes in which three would-be husbands try to divine the "will" of Portia's father, seem discordant to a modern audience that is asked to admire a heroine who dismisses one of her suitors with a slur on his Moroccan "complexion." Though it seems to have been written in late 1596 or early 1597 and, like *A Midsummer Night's Dream*, was first published in a good quarto in 1600, *The Merchant of Venice* feels closer in mood to *Measure for Measure*—which also pivots on a conflict between justice and mercy—than to most of the other "romantic comedies" of the mid to late 1590s.

But if *The Merchant of Venice* strikes us now as a play that looks forward to a later phase of Shakespearean dramaturgy, the plays he worked on next were a return to his beginnings. Possibly as early as 1595, and certainly no later than 1597, Shakespeare began a fresh exploration of the "matter" of English history with a play focusing on the events that precipitated the Wars of the Roses. It is impossible to say whether Shakespeare knew, when he began composing *Richard II*, that he would go on to write the two parts of *Henry IV* and the drama on *Henry V* that would furnish the link between *Richard II* and the *Henry VI* trilogy with which he had begun his career as a playwright. But complete the cycle he did, and the four English history plays Shakespeare wrote between 1595 and 1599 were even more impressive in their epic sweep than the four plays he

THE CRONICLE

History of Henry the fift,

With his battell fought at *Agin Court* in France. Togither with *Auntient Pistoll*.

As it hath bene sundry times playd by the Right honorable the Lord Chamberlaine his seruants.

LONDON

Printed by *Thomas Creede,* for Tho. Millington, and Iohn Busby. And are to be sold at his house in Carter Lane, next the Powle head. 1600.

Title page for one of the first, if not the first, of Shakespeare's plays to be performed at the Globe theater, which opened in 1599 (Anderson Galleries, sale number 1405, 4-5 March 1919)

had completed prior to the theatrical hiatus of 1593-1594.

Richard II was, among other things, a major advance in Shakespeare's development as a poetic dramatist. Not only does the play contain the dying John of Gaunt's paean to "This royal throne of kings, this sceptred isle, . . . This other Eden, demi-paradise," it also affords us a telling contrast between the laconic bluntness of Henry Bolingbroke, a man of action who is not quick to speak, and the self-indulgent lyricism of Richard II, a man of words who is, finally and fatally, not quick to act.

At the beginning of the play Richard's security in his presumption that God's deputy is above the law leads him to disregard the principles of primogeniture that are the basis of the King's own position as head of state. He disregards the counsel of his elders, seizes the estates of John of Gaunt and other nobles, banishes in Bolingbroke a former ally who has maintained a discreet silence about crimes that would taint the monarch himself, and sets in motion the rebellion that will eventually render his throne untenable. By the climax of the play Richard is forced to surrender his crown in a deposition scene that neatly counterpoises the declining King's complicity for his own downfall with the rising King's usurpation of a throne to which he has no legitimate title. And by the end of the play Richard's pastoral musings in the Tower transform him into a quasi-martyr whose meditations on "the death of kings" are as deeply moving as anything that Shakespeare had written up to this point in his career. As Richard prophesies, his murder at the hands of Henry IV's henchmen releases a tide of bloodshed that will not be stemmed until another legitimate monarch ascends the throne nearly a century in the future.

When *Richard II* was published in a good quarto in 1597 it lacked the crucial deposition scene, owing almost certainly to the censor's awareness that it would seem threatening to the aging Queen Elizabeth. That such apprehensions were justified was borne out four years later when the play was performed on the eve of the abortive rebellion of the Earl of Essex. The deposition scene's first appearance in print was in the fourth quarto of 1608.

As with the earlier English history plays, *Richard II* and the three *Henry* plays that followed derived in large measure from the 1587 second edition of Holinshed's *Chronicles*. But in all probability, they were also influenced by, and possibly even inspired by, the 1595 publication of Samuel Daniel's *Civil Wars*. In any event, it seems more likely that within a year of the completion of *Richard II* Shakespeare began work on its sequel, the first part of *Henry IV*. Taken together, parts 1 and 2 of *Henry IV* focus our attention on the immediate consequences of Henry Bolingbroke's usurpation of the crown. The first consequence is signaled by the opening lines of the first part, where the new King, "shaken" and "wan with care," announces his desire to lead a crusade to the Holy Land, both as a means of expiating his guilt and as a means of unifying a "giddy-minded" nation that is now divided into warring factions. Unfortunately, rest is not to be attained by this tainted monarch. His claim to the throne is immediately challenged by his former allies, the Percies, and thereafter his reign is disturbed

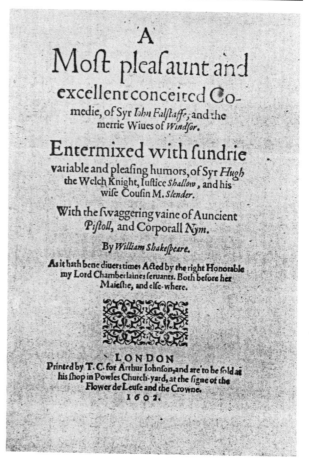

Title page for the 1602 quarto edition of the play that was probably first produced before Queen Elizabeth and George Carey, Lord Hunsdon, patron of the Lord Chamberlain's Men, at Windsor Castle on 23 April 1597, in honor of the awarding of the Order of the Garter to Hunsdon (British Library)

by one threat after another. The King does eventually arrive at "Jerusalem" near the end of *Henry IV, part 2*, but ironically this destination turns out to be a room in the castle, and the setting for his deathbed scene, rather than the city he had hoped to wrest from pagan occupation at the birthplace of Christendom.

The price that Henry IV pays for his usurpation turns out to be a nagging consciousness that "uneasy lies the head that wears the crown." And as significant as any other cause of the King's uneasiness is his fear that God has chosen to punish him with a wayward son whose "loose behavior" will forfeit the throne his father has expended so much anguish to mount and maintain. For all the King and his rivals can tell, the "nimble-footed madcap Prince of Wales" is squandering his royal inheritance in the dissolute company of "that villainous abominable misleader of youth, Falstaff," and a low-life lot of tavern keepers, thieves, and prostitutes. But as we learn early in *Henry IV*, part 1, Prince Hal is actually "redeeming time" in ways that surpass the political sagacity of even so Machiavellian a ruler as his father. Hal is acquiring firsthand knowledge of his nation's ordinary citizens, and the benefit he anticipates is that once he is King of England he will be able to "command all the good lads in Eastcheap." As he prepares himself for the military trials with which he must be tested, moreover, he does so in the awareness that once he throws off the "base contagious clouds" that "smother up his beauty from the world," he will emerge as England's true "sun," rather than the flawed monarch he knows his father to be.

And so he does. In the battle of Shrewsbury at the end of *Henry IV*, part 1, the valiant Hal defeats the fiery warrior the King would have preferred for a son. By winning Hotspur's honors, Hal finally earns, at least for a moment, the respect and gratitude of a father whose life and kingdom he has saved. But it is not enough for Hal to have demonstrated the courage and prudence required of an heir apparent. In part 2 Shakespeare has him back at the Boar's Head tavern once again, and it is only after he has demonstrated the remaining kingly virtues of temperance and justice–by casting off the influence of Falstaff and claiming as his second surrogate father the Lord Chief Justice–that Hal is finally granted the crown for which he has been so thoroughly educated.

His epic reaches its apogee in *Henry V*, a play described by its Chorus as a pageant in honor of "the mirror of all Christian kings." Whether or not we are to feel that the new King has dismissed some of his humanity in his rejection of the "old fat man" at his coronation, and whether or not we are to regard with suspicion the ambiguous "Salic Law" that the Bishops invoke to justify the King's invasion of France, and whether or not we are to see the King as cruel in his threat to allow the maidens and children of Harfleur to be raped and slaughtered if the town refuses to surrender, the dominant impression that *Henry V* has made on most readers and producers is one of heroic celebration. The King proves firm and resourceful in battle, mingling with his men in disguise on the eve of the engagement and exhorting them to noble valor in his famous St. Crispin's Day address. And once his "happy few," his "band of brothers," have triumphed against all odds and won the day, the King gives the glory to God. He thus illustrates

those qualities of the nurturing mother pelican– piety, self-sacrifice, humility, and magnanimity– that "Christian kings" were to display in addition to the monarchial attributes that Machiavelli and other political theorists had long associated with the lion and the fox. And in his wooing of his French bride, Katherine, at the end of the play, the King also exhibits the wit and charm that had endeared the historical Henry V to his admiring countrymen.

It is possible that the "wooden O" referred to in the Chorus's opening prologue was the Globe, newly opened on Bankside in 1599, and hence that *Henry V* was one of the first, if not *the* first, of Shakespeare's plays to be performed in that now-famous playhouse. Be that as it may, the play was probably completed in 1599, a year after *Henry IV*, part 2, and two years after *Henry IV*, part 1. All three plays had made their first appearances in print by 1600, the two parts of *Henry IV* in good quartos and *Henry V* in a bad quarto. The first reliable text of *Henry V* was that published in the First Folio in 1623.

The first good text of a related play, *The Merry Wives of Windsor*, also appeared in the Folio, but it too was initially published in a bad quarto, this one a memorial reconstruction dated 1602. Just when *Merry Wives* was written, and why, has been vigorously debated for decades. According to one legend, no doubt apocryphal but not totally lacking in plausibility, Shakespeare was commissioned to write the play because the Queen wanted to see Falstaff in love. If so, it seems likely that the play was also produced as an occasional piece in honor of the award of the Order of the Garter to Lord Hunsdon, the patron of the Lord Chamberlain's Men, on 23 April 1597. There are references to a Garter ceremony at Windsor Castle in act five of *The Merry Wives of Windsor*, and Leslie Hotson has argued that even though the play may well have been performed later at the Globe, its first presentation was before Queen Elizabeth and Lord Hunsdon at Windsor on St. George's Day 1597.

The Merry Wives of Windsor is unique among Shakespeare's comedies in having an English town for its setting. Its bourgeois characters have delighted audiences not only in the playhouse but also on the operatic stage, in what many critics consider the most successful of Verdi's numerous achievements in Shakespearean opera. Despite its obvious charms, however, the play has never been a favorite among Shakespeare's readers and literary interpreters. The reason is that the Falstaff we see in *The Merry Wives of Windsor* is a Falstaff largely lacking in the vitality and appeal of the character we come to love in the first part of *Henry IV*. Without Prince Hal and the wit combats afforded by his jokes at Falstaff's expense, the Falstaff of *Merry Wives* is merely conniving and crude. We may laugh at the comeuppances he receives at the hands of the merry wives he tries to seduce—the buck-basket baptism he gets as his reward for the first encounter, the beatings and pinchings he suffers in his later encounters—but we see nothing of the inventiveness that makes Falstaff such a supreme escape artist in part 1 of *Henry IV*. So attenuated is the Falstaff of *The Merry Wives of Windsor* that many interpreters have argued that it is simply a mistake to approach him as the same character. In any case, we never see him in love. His is a profit mo-

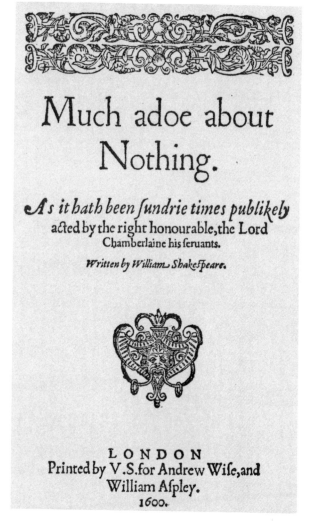

Title page for the 1600 quarto edition of one of Shakespeare's most popular comedies (Anderson Galleries, sale number 2078, 24-25 May 1926)

tive without honor, and it is much more difficult for us to feel any pity for his plight in *Merry Wives* than it is in the three Henry plays that depict the pratfalls and decline of the young heir-apparent's genial lord of misrule.

The play does have the clever Mistress Ford and Mistress Page. And in the jealous Master Ford and the tyrannical Master Page it also has a pair of comic gulls whose sufferings can be amusing in the theater. But it is doubtful that *The Merry Wives of Windsor* will ever be among our favorite Shakespearean comedies, particularly when we examine it alongside such contemporary achievements as *Much Ado About Nothing* and *As You Like It*.

Much Ado About Nothing and *As You Like It* were probably written in late 1598 and 1599, respectively, with the former first published in a good quarto in 1600 and the latter making its initial appearance in the 1623 First Folio. Both are mature romantic comedies, and both have enjoyed considerable success in the theater.

"Nothing" is a word of potent ambiguity in Shakespeare (the playwright was later to explore its potential most profoundly in the "nothing will come of nothing" that constitutes the essence of *King Lear*), and in *Much Ado About Nothing* its implications include the possibilities inherent in the wordplay on the Elizabethan homonym "noting." Through the machinations of the surly Don John, who gulls the superficial Claudio into believing that he "notes" his betrothed Hero in the act of giving herself to another lover, an innocent girl is rejected at the altar by a young man who believes himself to have been dishonored. Fortunately, Don John and his companions have themselves been noted by the most incompetent watch who ever policed a city; and, despite their asinine constable, Dogberry, these well-meaning but clownish servants of the Governor of Messina succeed in bringing the crafty villains to justice. In doing so, they set in motion a process whereby Hero's chastity is eventually vindicated and she reappears as if resurrected from the grave. Meanwhile, another pair of "notings" have been staged by the friends of Benedick and Beatrice, with the result that these two sarcastic enemies to love and to each other are each tricked into believing that the other is secretly in love. At least as much ado is made of Benedick and Beatrice's notings as of the others, and by the time the play ends these acerbic critics of amorous folly, grudgingly acknowledging that "the world must be peopled," have been brought to

This portrait of Shakespeare was once attributed to Richard Burbage and said to have belonged to Sir William Davenant, but it is now believed to have been painted in the eighteenth century (by permission of the National Portrait Gallery, London)

the altar with Claudio and Hero for a double wedding that concludes the play with feasting and merriment.

Shakespeare could have drawn from a number of antecedents for the story of Hero and Claudio, among them cantos from Ariosto's *Orlando Furioso* and Spenser's *Faerie Queene*. But the nearest thing to a "source" for Beatrice and Benedick may well have been his own *The Taming of the Shrew*, where another pair of unconventional would-be lovers struggle their way to a relationship that is all the more vital for the aggressive resistance that has to be channeled into harmony to bring it about. In any event, if there is some doubt about where Benedick and Beatrice came from, there is no doubt about the direction in

which they point—to such gallant and witty Restoration lovers as Mirabell and Millamant in William Congreve's *The Way of the World*.

With *As You Like It* Shakespeare achieved what many commentators consider to be the finest exemplar of a mode of romantic comedy based on escape to and return from what Northrop Frye has termed the "green world." As in *A Midsummer Night's Dream* (where the young lovers flee to the woods to evade an Athens ruled by the edicts of tyrannical fathers) and *The Merchant of Venice* (where Belmont serves as the antidote to all the venom that threatens life in Venice), in *As You Like It* the well-disposed characters who find themselves in the Forest of Arden think of it as an environment where even "adver-

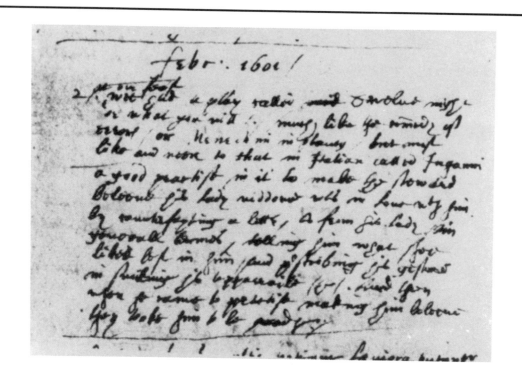

Top: passage from the diary of law student John Manningham, who reports having seen a performance of Twelfth Night *on 2 February 1602 (1601 according to the calendar then in use) at a feast in the hall of the Middle Temple (British Library, MS. Harley 5353, f. 12; by permission of the British Library Board). Bottom: the hall in which the play was performed. Manningham compares the play to* The Comedy of Errors, *Plautus's* Menaechmi, *and the Italian comedy "called 'Ingannati'" (Gl'Ingannati, which may in fact have been one of Shakespeare's sources for* Twelfth Night*), and he praises the scene in which Malvolio the steward, having been tricked into believing the Countess Olivia loves him, dresses and acts in a way that convinces the lady he is mad.*

sity" is "sweet" and restorative.

Duke Senior has been banished from his dukedom by a usurping younger brother, Duke Frederick. As the play opens, Duke Senior and his party are joined by Orlando and his aged servant Adam (who are running away from Orlando's cruel older brother Oliver), and later they in turn are joined by Duke Senior's daughter Rosalind and her cousin Celia (who have come to the forest, disguised as men, because the wicked Duke Frederick can no longer bear to have Rosalind in his daughter's company at court). The scenes in the forest are punctuated by a number of reflections on the relative merits of courtly pomp and pastoral simplicity, with the cynical Touchstone and the melancholy Jaques countering any sentimental suggestion that the Forest of Arden is a "golden world" of Edenic perfection, and her sojourn in the forest allows the wise and witty Rosalind to use male disguise as a means of testing the affections of her lovesick wooer Orlando. Eventually Orlando proves a worthy match for Rosalind, in large measure because he shows himself to be his brother's keeper. By driving off a lioness poised to devour the sleeping Oliver, Orlando incurs a wound that prevents him from appearing for an appointment with the disguised Rosalind; but his act of unmerited self-sacrifice transforms his brother into a "new man" who arrives on the scene in Orlando's stead and eventually proves a suitable match for Celia. Meanwhile, as the play nears its end, we learn that a visit to the forest has had a similarly regenerative effect on Duke Frederick, who enters a monastery and returns the dukedom to its rightful ruler, Duke Senior.

As You Like It derives in large measure from Thomas Lodge's romance *Rosalynde or Euphues' Golden Legacy,* a prose classic dating from 1590. But in his treatment of the "strange events" that draw the play to a conclusion presided over by Hymen, the god of marriage, Shakespeare hints at the kind of miraculous transformation that will be given major emphasis in the late romances.

The last of the great romantic comedies of Shakespeare's mid career, probably composed and performed in 1601 though not published until the 1623 First Folio, was *Twelfth Night.* Possibly based, in part, on an Italian comedy of the 1530s called *Gl'Ingannati, Twelfth Night* is another play with implicit theological overtones. Its title comes from the name traditionally associated with the Feast of Epiphany (6 January, the twelfth day of the Christmas season), and much

of its roistering would have seemed appropriate to an occasion when Folly was allowed to reign supreme under the guise of a Feast of Fools presided over by a Lord of Misrule. In Shakespeare's play, the character who represents Misrule is Sir Toby Belch, the carousing uncle of a humorless countess named Olivia. Together with such companions as Sir Andrew Aguecheek, the jester Feste, and a clever gentlewoman named Maria, Sir Toby makes life difficult not only for Olivia but also for her puritan steward Malvolio, whose name means "bad will" and whose function in the play, ultimately, is to be ostracized so that "good will" may prevail. In what many consider to be the most hilarious gulling scene in all of Shakespeare, Malvolio is tricked into thinking that his Lady is in love with him and persuaded to wear cross-gartered yellow stockings in her presence–attire that he believes will allure her, but attire that persuades her instead that he is deranged. The "treatment" that follows is a mock exercise in exorcism, and when Malvolio is finally released from his tormentors at the end of the play, he exits vowing revenge "on the whole pack" of them.

As with the dismissal of Shylock in *The Merchant of Venice,* the punishment of Malvolio's presumption in *Twelfth Night* has seemed too harsh to many modern viewers and readers. But that should not prevent us from seeing that *Twelfth Night* is also a play about other forms of self-indulgence (Count Orsino's infatuation with the pose of a courtly lover, and Olivia's excessively long period of mourning for her deceased brother) and the means by which characters "sick of self-love" or self-deception are eventually restored to mental and emotional sanity. Through the ministrations of the wise fool, Feste, and the providential Viola, who arrives in Illyria after a shipwreck in which she mistakenly believes her brother Sebastian to have died, we witness a sequence of coincidences and interventions that seems too nearly miraculous to have been brought about by blind chance. By taking another series of potentially tragic situations and turning them to comic ends, Shakespeare reminds us once again that harmony and romantic fulfillment are at the root of what Northrop Frye calls the "argument of comedy."

If Shakespeare's middle years are notable for sophisticated achievements in the genre we now refer to as romantic comedy, they are equally notable for the playwright's unprecedented strides in the development of two other

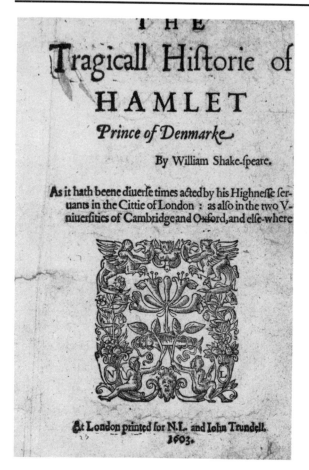 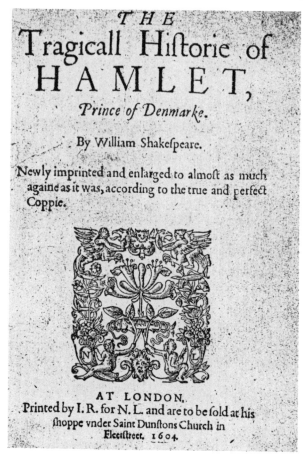

Title pages for the 1603 corrupt quarto edition (Henry E. Huntington Library and Art Gallery) and the 1604 good quarto edition (Library of the Earl of Verulam) of Shakespeare's first great tragedy

genres: tragedy and tragicomedy. In 1599, probably at the Globe, the Lord Chamberlain's Men offered the earliest recorded performance of *Julius Caesar* (the first of three mature tragedies, now grouped as "the Roman Plays," which all saw print for the first time in the 1623 Folio). Two years later, in late 1600 or early 1601, the company probably added to its repertory *Hamlet* (a play whose immediate and sustained popularity was attested to by its 1603 publication in an unauthorized bad quarto, succeeded a year later by a good quarto that most textual scholars still rely upon for all but a few passages, in preference to the slightly revised text in the 1623 Folio, which was set principally from a copy of the promptbook). Then in late 1601 or early 1602–once again drawing on the "classical" matter that had been the basis for the action of *Julius Caesar* and for many of the allusions in *Hamlet*–Shakespeare completed *Troilus and Cressida,* a play so uncompromisingly "intellectual" in its insistence that the audience "by indirections find directions out" that

critics from the seventeenth century to the present have found it all but impossible to classify. If *Troilus and Cressida* is a comedy, as the epistle prefacing the 1609 First Quarto would indicate, it is at best a specimen of black humor very different in tone and treatment from Shakespeare's other efforts in tragicomedy. If it is a tragedy, as its equivocal placement (occupying a no-man's-land between the Histories and the Tragedies) in the First Folio has led some scholars to argue, it is unique to the genre in the way its language and action undercut the dignity of its heroic protagonists. *Troilus and Cressida* was followed, in 1602-1603 and 1604 respectively, by two other plays, again ambiguous in tone, that are also frequently discussed today as "problem plays." *All's Well That Ends Well* and *Measure for Measure* (both of which made their initial appearances in print in the First Folio) are tragicomedies that turn on "bed tricks," and in their preoccupation with the seamier aspects of sexuality they can be viewed as links between *Hamlet,* the first of Shakespeare's

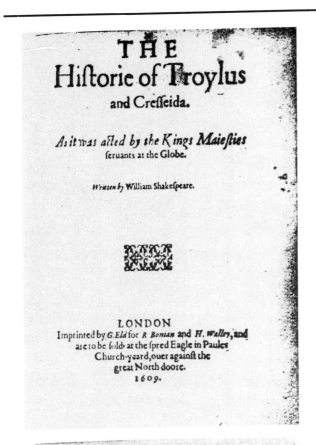

THE
Hiſtorie of Troylus
and Creſſeida.

As it was acted by the Kings Maieſties
ſeruants at the Globe.

Written by William Shakeſpeare.

LONDON
Imprinted by G. Eld for R Bonian and H. Walley, and
are to be ſold, at the ſpred Eagle in Paules
Church-yeard, ouer againſt the
great North doore.
1609.

THE
Famous Hiſtorie of
Troylus and Creſſeid.

Excellently expreſſing the beginning
of their loues, with the conceited wooing
of Pandarus Prince of Licia.

Written by William Shakeſpeare.

LONDON
Imprinted by G. Eld for R. Bonian and H. Walley, and
are to be ſold, at the ſpred Eagle in Paules
Church-yeard, ouer againſt the
great North doore.
1609.

A neuer writer, to an euer
reader. Newes.

Eternall reader, you haue heere a new
play, neuer ſtal'd with the Stage,
neuer clapper-clawd with the palmes
of the vulger, and yet paſſing full of
the palme comicall; for it is a birth of
your braine, that neuer vnder-tooke
any thing comicall, vainely: And
were but the vaine names of comedies changde for the
titles of Commodities, or of Playes for Pleas; you ſhould
ſee all thoſe grand cenſors, that now ſtile them ſuch
vanities, flock to them for the maine grace of their
grauities: eſpecially this authors Commedies, that are
ſo fram'd to the life, that they ſerue for the moſt common Commentaries, of all the actions of our liues, ſhew-
ing ſuch a dexteritie, and power of witte, that the moſt
diſpleaſed with Playes, are pleaſd with his Commedies.
And all ſuch dull and heauy-witted worldlings, as were
neuer capable of the witte of a Commedie, comming by
report of them to his repreſentations, haue found that
witte there, that they neuer found in them-ſelues, and
haue parted better wittied then they came: feeling an
edge of witte ſet vpon them, more then euer they
dreamd they had braine to grinde it on. So much and
ſuch ſauored ſalt of witte is in his Commedies, that they
ſeeme (for their height of pleaſure) to be borne in that
ſea that brought forth Venus. Amongſt all there is
none more witty then this: And had I time I would
comment vpon it, though I know it needs not, (for ſo
much

THE EPISTLE.
much as will make you thinke your teſterne well be-
ſtowd) but for ſo much worth, as euen poore I know to be
ſtuft in it. It deſerues ſuch a labour, as well as the beſt
Commedy in Terence or Plautus. And beleeue this,
that when hee is gone, and his Commedies out of ſale,
you will ſcramble for them, and ſet vp a new Engliſh
Inquiſition. Take this for a warning, and at the perrill
of your pleaſures loſſe, and Iudgements, refuſe not, nor
like this the leſſe, for not being ſullied, with the ſmoaky
breath of the multitude; but thinke fortune for, the
ſcape it hath made amongſt you. Since by the grand
poſſeſſors wills I beleeue you ſhould haue prayd for them
rather then beene prayd. And ſo I leaue all ſuch to bee
prayd for (for the ſtates of their wits healths)
that will not praiſe it.
Vale.

*Variant title pages for the 1609 quarto edition of the play that has been variously classified as comedy, tragedy, and tragicomedy;
and the epistle to the reader in the second state, which contradicts the statement on the title page of the first that the play had been performed (top left: Elizabethan Club, Yale University; top right and bottom: British Library)*

"great tragedies," and *Othello*, the second (which seems to have been composed in 1604, when there is a record of performance at Court).

Julius Caesar—a play that may owe something to sources as seemingly remote as St. Augustine's *City of God* and Erasmus's *Praise of Folly* in addition to such obvious classical antecedents as Plutarch's *Lives* and Tacitus's *Annals*—is now regarded as a dramatic work of considerable complexity. On the one hand, the play captures with remarkable fidelity the ethos and rhetorical style of late-republican Rome—so much so, indeed, that it may be said that Shakespeare's portraits of Caesar and his contemporaries have largely formed our own impressions of how the ancient Romans thought and talked and conducted their civic affairs. Recent studies of the play's references to "philosophy" indicate, moreover, that Shakespeare knew a good deal about Roman Stoicism and perceived it as one of the characterizing traits that differentiated Brutus from Cassius, an Epicurean continually nonplussed by his companion's mental rigidity and emotional aloofness.

But if Shakespeare brought to his dramatic art a historical imagination capable of reconstructing a self-consistent Roman world—and one that was distinct in significant ways from his own Elizabethan England—he was also capable of embodying in his representation of that world a perspective that amounted, in effect, to a Renaissance humanist critique of pre-Christian civilization. Thus it was quite possible for Shakespeare to portray the conspirators and their cause, as it were, "sympathetically"—so much so, indeed, that a twentieth-century audience, unwittingly misreading the play, finds it almost impossible not to hear in such exclamations as "peace, freedom, and liberty!" the precursors of America's own founding fathers. At the same time, however, Shakespeare would have known that he could rely on his Elizabethan contemporaries to regard as foredoomed any attempt to achieve social harmony through what they would have seen on the stage as bloody butchery and regicide. By the same token, of course, Shakespeare could encourage his audience to "identify" with Brutus through participation in his soliloquies, while simultaneously assuming that alert members of that audience would recognize that Brutus's thought processes are often misguided and self-deceptive.

In the late 1930s Mark Van Doren observed that, whatever Brutus's positive qualities as a high-minded patriot, he tends to come across in the play as a self-righteous, almost pharisaical prig, particularly in the quarrel scene with Cassius. In recent years a number of scholars have confirmed the validity of Van Doren's perception by showing that it is consistent with the hypothesis that in his portrayal of Brutus Shakespeare was drawing on a widely held Christian tradition that regarded Stoicism as a philosophy that rendered its adherents hard-hearted, arrogant, and so assured of their own virtue as to be largely incapable of recognizing or repenting of their faults. If this reading of Brutus is closer to Shakespeare's intention than the more sentimental view that approaches everything in the play from the retrospective vantage-point of Mark Antony's eulogy for "the noblest Roman of them all," it tends to cast much of *Julius Caesar* in an ironic light—and by implication to require an audience alert to clues that are not always so self-evident as a twentieth-century reader or viewer might expect.

Such an audience seems called for by *Hamlet* as well, at least if we are going to take seriously Hamlet's admonition that the players address their performance to "the judicious," to those who are capable of viewing all the action, including that involving the most engaging of protagonists, with a critical eye. This is difficult for us, because we have long been accustomed to thinking of Hamlet as the "sweet prince" who epitomizes the ideal Renaissance courtier.

There is no danger, to be sure, that Hamlet will ever lose his appeal as an articulate and ardent existentialist—as the prototype of modern man in spiritual crisis. But recent critical studies and productions of the play have raised questions about the "matter" of *Hamlet* in Elizabethan terms that suggest a somewhat less admirable protagonist than most of us would like to believe the play presents. It is no longer universally assumed, for example, that the play within the play, by proving the Ghost "honest" in his testimony about Claudius's guilt, is sufficient to prove the Ghost "honest" in Hamlet's more fundamental sense. Enough evidence remains in the play to suggest that the Ghost may yet be a "devil" intent on "abusing" the melancholic Hamlet by exhorting him to the kind of vengeance that Elizabethan Christians believed to belong only to God or to his deputed magistrates. And Hamlet's disinclination to "try" the spirit earlier in the play is but one of many indications in the text that he fails to put to proper use what he elsewhere describes as "godlike reason." A close exam-

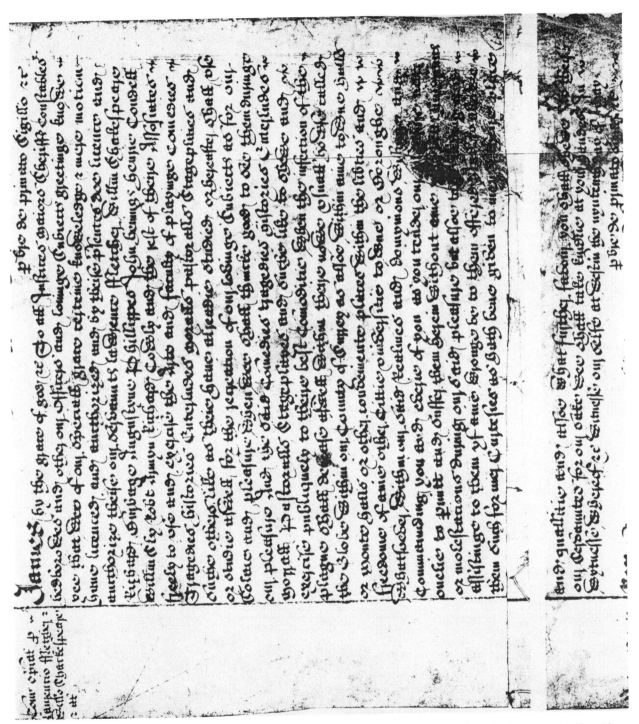

Shakespeare's company becomes the King's Men: Letters Patent under the Great Seal, 19 May 1603 (Public Record Office, Chancery, Patent Rolls, C.66/1608, m. 4; by permission of the Controller of Her Majesty's Stationery Office)

Pages from the account book of Sir Edmund Tilney, Master of the Revels, in which a scribe listed eleven court performances by the King's Men from 1 November 1604 to 31 October 1605. Seven of the plays were by Shakespeare: Othello *(first recorded performance),* The Merry Wives of Windsor, Measure for Measure *(first recorded performance),* The Comedy of Errors, Love's Labor's Lost, Henry V, *and* The Merchant of Venice, *which was performed on two occasions. Though the authenticity of these records was once challenged, they are now generally accepted as genuine (Public Record Office, Audit Office, Accounts, Various, A.O. 3/908/13; by permission of the Controller of Her Majesty's Stationery Office).*

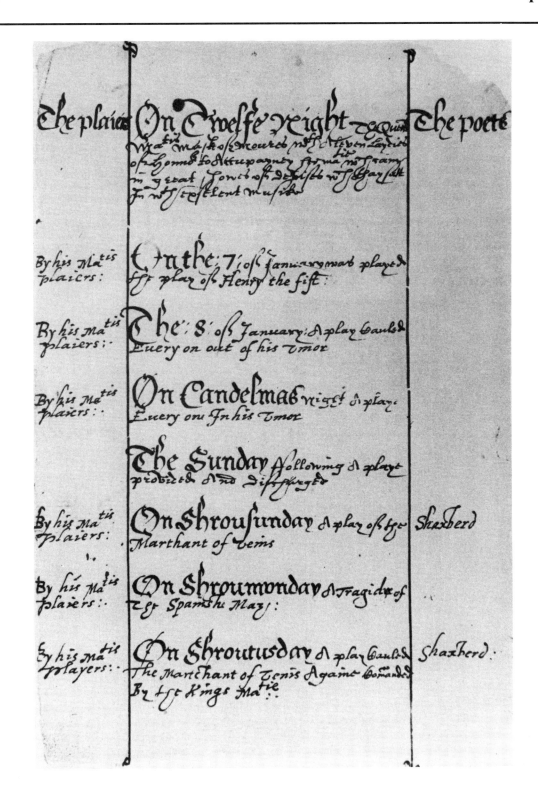

ination of many of Hamlet's reflective speeches, including his celebrated "To be nor not to be" soliloquy, will show that they serve functions similar to those of Brutus in *Julius Caesar*. By bringing the audience into the protagonist's confidence, they endear him to us and incline us to see everything and everyone else in the action through his eyes. But if we pay careful attention to the nuances of thought in these reflections, we will notice that many of them tend to be irrational—peppered with non sequiturs and disclosing the kind of emotional stress that renders a man prone to error.

A dispassionate scrutiny of the roles of Rosencrantz and Guildenstern will reveal that, however conventionally ambitious these young courtiers may be, they mean Hamlet well and are anything but the "adders fanged" that Hamlet regards them as having become. The play provides no evidence that they deserve the "sudden death, not shriving time allowed" that Hamlet gleefully bequeaths them; and it is arguable that Shakespeare expected his audience to feel that they *should* be "near Hamlet's conscience" when he assures Horatio that they are not. And near the end of the play, when Hamlet disregards the "gaingiving" that warns him not to accept the "wager" proffered by the treacherous Claudius—when he dismisses Horatio's prudence and disdains the kind of premonition that "would perhaps trouble a woman"—he allows himself to be seduced (and in a way that parallels Julius Caesar's being led to the Capitol) into a trap that means certain death. Far from being guided by providence, as his New Testament allusions would suggest at this point in the action, Hamlet is being lured by pride into an ambush that he might have avoided by heeding his "godlike reason." As Claudius had predicted, Hamlet shows himself to be "remiss."

None of which in any way diminishes the attractiveness of Hamlet's wit and fervor, or suggests that he is not infinitely to be preferred to the "mighty opposite" whose regicide and usurpation he puts to scourge. No, there is no doubt that Hamlet uncovers and "sets right" much that is "rotten in the state of Denmark." The only question is whether the play invites us to consider a set of "might have beens" that would have permitted us to approve of the protagonist even more unreservedly than we do. If the findings of recent commentators are to be credited, it would seem likely that our identification with Hamlet's cause should be qualified by an awareness that he did not completely find the way "rightly to be great."

"The whole argument is a whore and a cuckold." So the acid-tongued Thersites sums up the "matter of Troy" and the occasion of *Troilus and Cressida*. We may not wish to see our legendary forebears reduced so unceremoniously to the base matter of lust and dishonor, but there is little in the plot or dialogue of Shakespeare's play to cite in refutation. The Trojan War is in fact a conflict over the ravishingly beautiful but thoughtless Helen (the "whore" whom Paris has stolen away from the "cuckold" Menelaus), and one would have to search hard to find anything to admire in most of the principals who figure in the inconsequential council scenes, squalid intrigues, and interrupted combats that dominate the action. Because what *Troilus and Cressida* is largely "about" is a ludicrously unheroic siege to determine whether the Trojans return Helen to the Greeks or see their city fall in defense of a cause that even the greatest Trojan warrior considers unworthy of their "several honors."

As Hector points out, the Trojans can appeal to neither justice nor reason in support of their determination to keep Helen; the best that anyone can say of her is that, quite apart from what she may be in and of herself, "she is a theme of honor and renown,/A spur to valiant and magnanimous deeds." But when we look for such deeds in the play, what we find on both sides are acts of questionable valor at best (as when Hector, having challenged the Greeks to find a combatant to uphold their honor as lovers, breaks off a hand-to-hand duel with Ajax on the grounds that they are cousins) and downright cowardice at worst (as when Achilles, having come upon Hector at a moment when he has removed his armor to rest, merely summons his Myrmidons to slaughter the champion of the Trojans). In the meantime we are treated to the voyeurism of Pandarus, an impotent and diseased bawd whose only pleasure in life is to serve as go-between for Troilus and Cressida, and the homoerotic indulgence of Achilles and Patroclus, who have withdrawn from combat because of a slight the prima donna Achilles thinks he has suffered at the hands of the Greek general, Agamemnon. Small wonder that Ulysses should observe that "degree is shak'd." And little wonder that director Jonathan Miller, in his 1982 BBC television production of *Troilus and Cressida,* hit upon *M*A*S*H* as the most apt twentieth-century analogue for a satiric seventeenth-century depiction of war as the triumph of unreason, ennui, and depravity.

THE
Tragœdy of Othello,
The Moore of Venice.

As it hath beene diuerse times acted at the
Globe, and at the Black-Friers, by
his Maiesties Seruants.

Written by VVilliam Shakespeare.

LONDON,
Printed by *N. O.* for *Thomas Walkley,* and are to be sold at his
shop, at the Eagle and Child, in Brittans Burse.
1622.

Title page for the 1622 quarto edition of the second of Shakespeare's four major tragedies (Elizabethan Club, Yale University)

There is, to be sure, some momentary relief in the scenes depicting the wooing of Troilus and Cressida. And when Cressida is eventually delivered back to the Greek camp at the request of her father, one feels that her surrender to Diomede is more a result of her feminine helplessness in a male-controlled world than a manifestation of some prior proclivity to infidelity. But despite the lyricism of Troilus and Cressida's lovemaking, and the agony both lovers feel upon parting, one emerges from this play moved less by the pathos of the love story than by Shakespeare's presentation of what T. S. Eliot, writing three centuries later about another literary work deriving ultimately from Homer, praised as a reflection of "the immense panamora of futility and anarchy which is contemporary history." It may well be that *Troilus and Cressida* seemed just as "modern" and puzzling in the early seventeenth century as Joyce's *Ulysses*

seemed when it appeared in the early twentieth.

Modern in another sense may be a good way to describe *All's Well That Ends Well.* After a long history of neglect, this tragicomedy has recently enjoyed a good deal of success in the theater and on television, and one of the explanations that have been given is that it features a heroine who, refusing to accept a preordained place in a hierarchical man's world, does what she has to do to win her own way.

Orphaned at an early age and reared as a waiting-gentlewoman to the elegant and sensitive Countess of Rossillion, Helena presumes to fall in love with the Countess's snobbish son Bertram. Using a cure she learned from her dead father, who had been a prominent physician, Helena saves the life of the ailing King of France, whereupon she is rewarded with marriage to the man of her choice among all the eligible bachelors in the land. She astonishes Bertram by selecting him. Reluctantly, Bertram consents to matrimony, but before the marriage can be consummated he leaves the country with his disreputable friend Parolles, telling Helena in a note that he will be hers only when she has fulfilled two presumably impossible conditions: won back the ring from his finger, and borne a child to him. Disguised as a pilgrim, Helena follows Bertram to Florence. There she substitutes herself for a woman named Diana, with whom Bertram has made an assignation, and satisfies the despicable Bertram's demands.

One of the "problems" that have troubled critics of *All's Well That Ends Well* is the device of the "bed trick." But we now know that Shakespeare had biblical precedent for such a plot (Genesis 35), and that it was associated in the Old Testament with providential intervention. Which may be of some value to us in dealing with the other major issues: why should Helena want so vain and selfish a man as Bertram in the first place, and how can we accept at face value his reformation at the end? If we suspend our disbelief enough to grant the fairy-tale premises of the plot (which derived from a story in Boccaccio's *Decameron*), we should be able to grant as well that in a providentially ordered world, the end may not only justify the means but sanctify them. And if the end that Helena has in view is not only to win Bertram but to make him "love her dearly ever, ever dearly," we must grant the playwright the final miracle of a Bertram who can be brought to see his evil ways for what they are and repent of them.

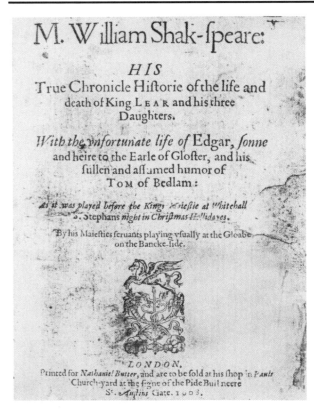

M. William Shak-fpeare:

HIS
True Chronicle Hiftorie of the life and
death of King LEAR and his three
Daughters.

With the unfortunate life of Edgar, fonne
and heire to the Earle of Glofter, and his
fullen and affumed humor of
TOM of Bedlam:

As it was played before the Kings Maieftie at Whitehall
vpo. Stephans night in Chriftmas Hollidayes.

By his Maiefties feruants playing vfually at the Gloabe
on the Bancke-fide.

LONDON,
Printed for Nathaniel Butter, and are to be fold at his fhop in Pauls
Church-yard at the figne of the Pide Bull neere
St. Auftins Gate. 1608.

Title page for the 1608 quarto edition of what many scholars now regard as a memorial reconstruction of an earlier version of King Lear *than the text published in the 1623 First Folio (Bodleian Library, Oxford)*

A similar miracle would seem to be the final cause of *Measure for Measure*. At the beginning of the play, Duke Vincentio, noting that he has been too lenient in his administration of the laws of Venice, appoints as deputy an icy-veined puritan named Angelo, whom he expects to be more severe for a season of much-needed civic discipline. Almost immediately upon the Duke's departure, Angelo finds himself confronted with a novitiate, Isabella, who, in pleading for the life of a brother condemned for fornication, unwittingly arouses the new deputy's lust. Angelo offers her an exchange: her brother's life for her chastity. Astonished by the deputy's disregard for both God's laws and man's, Isabella refuses. Later, as she tries to prepare Claudio for his execution and discovers that he is less shocked by the deputy's offer than his sister had been, Isabella upbraids him, too, as a reprobate.

At this point the Duke, who has been disguised as a friar, persuades Isabella to "accept" Angelo's offer on the understanding that his former betrothed, Mariana, will sleep with him instead. Once again the bed trick proves effectual

and "providential." In the "trial" that takes place at the entrance to the city upon the Duke's return, Isabella accuses Angelo of having corrupted his office and executed her brother despite an agreement to spare him (an order of the deputy's that, unknown to Isabella, has been forestalled by the "friar"). But then, in response to Mariana's pleas for her assistance, she decides not to press her claim for justice and instead kneels before the Duke to beg that Angelo's life be spared. The Duke grants her request, and Angelo—illustrating Mariana's statement that "best men are molded out of faults"—repents and accepts the Duke's mercy.

Measure for Measure qualifies as a tragicomedy because the questions it raises are serious (how to balance law and grace, justice and mercy, in human society) and the issue (whether or not Angelo will be executed for his evil intentions with respect to Claudio) is in doubt until the moment when, by kneeling beside Mariana, Isabella prevents what might have been a kind of revenge tragedy. (The Duke tells Mariana, "Against all sense you do importune her./Should she kneel down in mercy of this fact,/Her brother's ghost his paved bed would break,/And take her hence in horror.") In Shakespearean comedy, of course, all's well that ends well. Revenge gives way to forgiveness or repentance, and characters who might have died in self-deception or guilt are given a second chance. As for Isabella, she too gains insight and sensitivity as a consequence of her trials, and at the conclusion of the play she finds herself the recipient of a marriage proposal from her previously disguised counselor, the Duke. Whether she accepts it, and if so how, has become one of the chief "problems" to be solved by directors and actors in modern productions.

After *Measure for Measure*, so far as we can tell, Shakespeare turned his attention entirely to tragedy for three or four years. By 1604, apparently, he completed *Othello*, the second of the four major tragedies. By 1605 he seems to have completed *King Lear*, the third and, in the estimation of many, the greatest of the tragedies. And by 1606 he had evidently written the last of the "big four," *Macbeth*. During the next two to three years Shakespeare turned once more to classical sources, completing *Antony and Cleopatra* and *Coriolanus*, respectively, in 1606-1607 and 1607-1608, and abandoning *Timon of Athens* (if we are correct in thinking that it was left unfinished and unacted) sometime around 1607 or 1608. Only two of these plays appeared in quarto printings, *King*

Macbeth and the Witches *from the first illustrated edition of Shakespeare's works, edited by Nicholas Rowe in 1709 (Maggs Bros., catalogue number 550, 1931)*

Lear in 1608 in what many scholars now regard as a memorial reconstruction of an early version of the play, and *Othello* in 1622 in a text of uncertain provenance. Most modern editions of *King Lear* and *Othello* follow the First Folio texts as their prime authorities, supplementing those texts where appropriate with readings or passages from the quartos (although, particularly with *King Lear*, where the two printings of the play are thought by some to derive from discrete and self-consistent earlier and later scripts of the play, there is now a school of thought that op-

poses conflating the Folio and quarto versions). The other three tragedies all appeared for the first time in the 1623 Folio.

When we come to *Othello* fresh from a reading of either *Hamlet* or *Measure for Measure*, we can see links with the earlier plays in *Othello's* treatment of sexual love and in the play's preoccupation with ethical questions that turn, ultimately, on revenge versus forgiveness. For whatever else *Othello* is, it is a species of revenge tragedy. To the extent that Iago is impelled by something more specific than what Coleridge termed

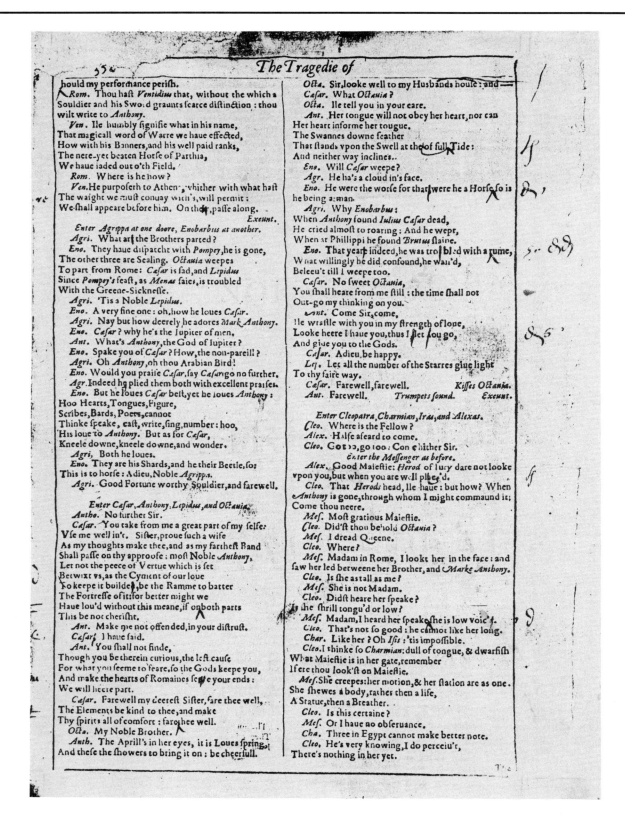

Proof, with corrections in an unknown hand, for Antony and Cleopatra *in the 1623 First Folio (by permission of the Folger Shakespeare Library)*

"motiveless malignity," he is motivated by a determination to prove Othello "egregiously an ass" for promoting Michael Cassio rather than Iago to the lieutenancy. And Iago's vengeance extends to Cassio as well as to Othello. But more to the point, once Iago convinces Othello that Desdemona has slept with Cassio, he transforms Othello into the principal tool as well as the prime object of his revenge.

Iago's "poison" is administered in two doses. First he provides enough circumstantial "proof" to make plausible his insinuation that Desdemona has been unfaithful to Othello. But second and far more crucial, he works Othello into such a frenzy that he is unable to give serious consideration to any response to his "knowledge" other than revenge. Once Othello becomes persuaded that Desdemona is indeed guilty of infidelity, his instinctive reaction is to exclaim "But yet the pity of it, Iago! O Iago, the pity of it, Iago!" To which Iago replies "If you are so fond over her iniquity, give her patent to offend, for if it touch not you, it comes near nobody." Here as elsewhere Iago's method is to get Othello to focus, not on Desdemona, but on himself. By constantly reiterating such terms as "reputation," "good name," and "honor," Iago plays upon Othello's insecurity as a Moorish alien and implies that his wife's behavior will make him the laughingstock of Venetian society.

It is a mark of his worthiness as a tragic hero that, to the end, Othello retains the "free and open nature" that made him vulnerable to Iago in the beginning. Iago may manipulate Othello into committing a rash and terrible murder, but he cannot reduce Othello entirely to a blunt instrument of the ensign's vengeance. Before Othello can bring himself to suffocate Desdemona, he must first delude himself into believing that he is an agent of divine justice. And even in that role his innate compassion leads him to offer his wife a moment to prepare her soul for heaven. It is true that Othello becomes angry again when Desdemona fails to confess to a crime that would have been inconceivable to her, but one of the things that makes his act pathetic rather than malicious is the fact that he continues to express his devotion for Desdemona even as he forces himself to snuff out her life. In that sense as well as in Iago's more cynical sense, then, Othello becomes "an honorable murderer." And no matter how we judge Othello's final speech and "bloody period," we have to agree with Cassio's assessment that "he was great of heart."

With *King Lear* we come to a tragedy whose pattern is without parallel in the Shakespearean canon. In all the other tragedies, despite the beauty of the benedictions that convey the protagonists to their eternal destinies, we are left at the end with a nagging sense of "purposes mistook" that might have been averted or deflected. The basic movement of the plot has been downward, and we come away feeling that we as audience have perceived something that the tragic protagonists themselves have been unable or unwilling to see. In those tragedies in which the protagonists have committed suicide, we are shown that in so doing they are wittingly or unwittingly admitting failure or surrendering to despair, notwithstanding their best efforts to keep their spirits up and evade the full consequences of the choices that have brought them to their present pass. But this is not the pattern we find in *King Lear*. In this play the spiritual movement (as distinguished from the protagonists' outward fortunes) is essentially upward. To be sure, there are terrible errors and terrifying consequences; in this play, however, we are led to believe that at least some of the pain is cathartic. There can be little doubt that both Lear and Gloucester are in some sense "better" men at the end of their lives than they were at the beginning of the action. And if the play is performed in such a way as to emphasize the degree to which the protagonists have been able to learn and grow through the endurance of tragic suffering, the audience is likely to emerge with a sense of uplift rather than with the weight of unmitigated pity and fear.

This is not to suggest, of course, that there is any less agony and tragic loss in *King Lear* than in Shakespeare's other works in the same genre. Indeed, given the play's cosmic resonance—the honored place it now holds in the tradition represented by such theodicies as the Book of Job—*King Lear* has been thought by many to evoke more existential terror than all of Shakespeare's other tragedies combined.

Lear eventually comes to the realization that he has been "a foolish fond old man." In a parallel recognition the blinded Gloucester acknowledges that he "stumbled when [he] saw." But first both fathers must feel the brunt of the savagery their earlier misdeeds have unleashed upon the world. Having abdicated his throne and divided his kingdom, Lear soon discovers that he is powerless to prevent his "pelican daughters" from joining with Gloucester's bastard son in an all-out

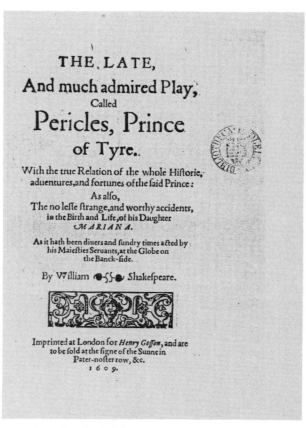

THE, LATE,
And much admired Play,
Called
Pericles, Prince
of Tyre..

With the true Relation of the whole Hiſtorie,·
aduentures,and fortunes ofthe ſaid Prince:
As alſo,
The no leſſe ſtrange,and worthy accidents,
in the Birth and Life,of his Daughter
MARIANA.

As it hath been diuers and ſundry times aɛted by·
his Maieſties Seruants,at the Globe on
the Banck-ſide.

By William ❦ Shakeſpeare.

Imprinted at London for *Henry Goſſon*,and are
to be ſold at the ſigne of the Sunne in
Pater-noſter row, &c.
1 6 0 9.

*Title page for the 1609 quarto edition of the late romance
that was omitted from the 1623 First Folio and not included
in a collection of Shakespeare's works until 1664
(Bodleian Library)*

effort to devour it—and each other. Lear's faithful Fool wastes away. The loyal Kent and Edgar are reduced to "wretches." And, most insupportable of all, at the end of the play the innocent Cordelia is hanged. For Lear as he enters cradling his beloved daughter in his arms, this is the ultimate punishment for the arrogance and folly that had led him, at the beginning, to spurn and disinherit her.

But as heartrending as this concluding pietà is for any of the play's audiences, it can represent "a chance which does redeem all sorrows" if it is staged in harmony with the psychological and spiritual undulations of Lear's dying moments. Just before he says "Pray you undo this button," Lear believes that, as Kent puts it, "all's cheerless, dark, and deadly." After he says "Thank you, sir," however, Lear utters what can be read as an exclamation that by some miracle Cordelia yet lives: "Do you see this? Look on her! Look, her lips,/Look there, look there!" In our time these words have most often been interpreted as expres-

sions of bleak despair. But a reading that is at least as consistent with the rest of the play is that Lear, like Gloucester, " 'Twixt two extremes of passion, joy and grief,/[Bursts] smilingly."

We know, of course, that Cordelia is "dead as earth." But it seems fitting that as he dies Lear should see her as alive. If so, it may be nothing more than a merciful hallucination. It may be a desperate man's last grasp at something to sustain a flicker of faith. But it may also register an experience comparable to that of another long-suffering king, the protagonist in Sophocles' *Oedipus at Colonus.* In short, it may be that Lear is here granted a last epiphany that takes him out of this "tough world" to a glimpse of something better beyond: because by the end of his long pilgrimage, in the words of T. S. Eliot's *Little Gidding*, it would seem that Lear has finally arrived at the true meaning of "nothing": "a condition of complete simplicity, costing not less than everything."

Near the end of Macbeth's bloody reign, as he braces for the closing in of his adversaries, he too would like to achieve a kind of simplicity: "I gin to be aweary of the sun,/And wish th' estate o' th' world were now undone." But in Macbeth's case the goal to be obtained is "mere oblivion," not the brief but beatific vision of a broken old man for whom at last something has come of nothing. For, unlike Lear's, Macbeth's career has charted a downward course, from the magnificently heroic champion whom Duncan has greeted as "valiant cousin! worthy gentleman!" to the desperate tyrant whose acts of regicide and wanton slaughter have "tied [him] to a stake" as the "fiend" who must be executed to set the time "free."

As a tragic action, *Macbeth* is almost the polar opposite of *King Lear.* Whereas in *Lear* we may be inclined to feel that "death is swallowed up in victory," in *Macbeth* we feel that the protagonist's defeat is merely the prelude to final judgment and damnation. Lear's is the kind of "fortunate fall" that results from a miscalculation born of habitual self-indulgence; it forces the King to contemplate "unaccommodated man" in all his vulnerability, and it subjects him to a refining "wheel of fire" that purifies him spiritually. Macbeth's, on the other hand, is the kind of fall that results from premeditated murder in the service of "vaulting ambition." As he himself acknowledges, there are no extenuating circumstances behind which he can shield his crime, and the only change it brings about in Macbeth is tempo-

Dr. Simon Forman's description of a performance of Cymbeline *that he saw at the Globe, perhaps in 1611 (Bodleian Library, MS Ashmole 208, f. 206; by permission of the Curators)*

rarily to rob him of sleep and security until, "supp'd full with horrors," he eventually loses all capacity for "the taste of fears" or any other humanizing emotion or sensation. By the final act, life for Macbeth is "but a walking shadow," "a tale/ Told by an idiot, full of sound and fury,/ Signifying nothing."

And yet, despite his infamy, we still find it possible to participate in, and even in some fashion to identify with, Macbeth's descent into hell. In part this results from our awareness of his auspicious beginnings—our recollection of that period at the outset when we see Macbeth tempted but nevertheless resisting the promptings of the Witches and Lady Macbeth. Because Macbeth himself is aware of the heinousness of the deed he is on the verge of committing, we can sympathize with him as a man like one of us. And then, once he has taken the fatal plunge, we become parties to his inner turmoil. By means of the soliloquies and meditations that Shakespeare allows us to "overhear," we share Macbeth's torment and anxiety, his feverish desire to put out of mind that which he cannot bear to dwell upon. And thus, even though what he and Lady Macbeth do is beyond the pale of thinkable human behavior, we can still bring pity and fear to both their stories—recalling, in the words of a famous prayer, that "there, but for the grace of God, go I."

Moving from *Macbeth*'s Scotland to the Mediterranean ambience of *Antony and Cleopatra* is a culture shock so disorienting as almost to make us lose our bearings. Can the same author who gave us Macbeth and Lady Macbeth, two potent personalities who seize power and then degenerate into tremulous tyrants, so soon thereafter have created Antony and Cleopatra, two mercurial rulers who seem, at least in their grandiloquent gestures, to become increasingly engaging as their fortunes wane and they almost willfully throw their power away? And how do we graph the movement of the action in a play where at least part of the problem is to assess the relative merits of a "Roman" way of looking at things (which judges both lovers as failures because they have declined to elevate civic and military duty above all other human concerns) as opposed to an "Egyptian" way of looking at things (which is based on the premise that one should be willing, in Dryden's later phrase, to sacrifice "all for love")? Is it likely that Shakespeare expected his audience to bring a coherent "Elizabethan" perspective to bear on both ancient cultures? And if so, what would an audience viewing the play from that perspective

have thought about Antony and Cleopatra?

These are the kinds of questions a reading of *Antony and Cleopatra* elicits, and the majority of its interpreters during the last three centuries have answered them in such a way as to place this second "Roman play" in a category largely its own. Noting that the "Roman" characters are bloodless and coldly calculating–particularly Octavius and his sister Octavia, whose hand Octavius gives to Antony in an effort to resolve the political differences he has been having with his slothful counterpart in Egypt–most critics and theater professionals have found them much less appealing than they do the two lovers. The consequence has been that readers and viewers have tended to see Antony and Cleopatra as the characters see themselves and thus to regard the play primarily as a dramatization of what John Donne termed "the canonization of love."

The main problem with this interpretation of the action is that it requires us to ignore the many indications, throughout the play, that both lovers are impulsive and escapist. A sentimental approach to *Antony and Cleopatra* blinds us to clues that the "new heaven and new earth" to which the lovers direct their suicides is little more than a fantasyland that they have created as a way of palliating their defeat and impending capture. We may be stirred by the magic of Enobarbus's descriptions of Cleopatra's transcendent charms, and we cannot help but admire the eloquence with which Antony and Cleopatra prepare themselves for death. But we should remember at the same time that it is relatively simple to count the world well lost if through neglect one has already handed it over to one's enemies. An apt Elizabethan gloss on *Antony and Cleopatra* might well be borrowed from Shakespeare's Sonnet 129: "All this the world well knows, yet none knows well/To shun the heaven that leads men to this hell."

Because of the vividness of its central figures and the exoticism and luxuriousness of its language, *Antony and Cleopatra* has long been one of Shakespeare's most popular plays. But nothing could be farther from the case with its successor. *Coriolanus*, the third and last of Shakespeare's mature "Roman plays," is sparing and harsh in its diction and spartan in its spectacle. And only rarely–but usually with distinction–has it been performed, even in our own production-rich century.

The hero of the play is one of the least endearing of Shakespeare's major characters. God-like in battle, where his feats of valor and

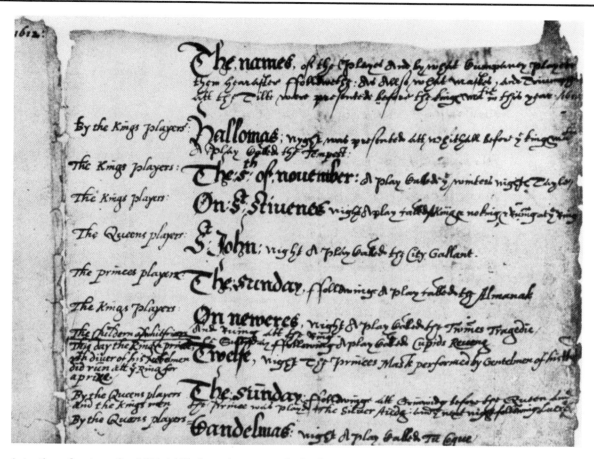

A portion of a page for 1611-1612 from the account book of Sir George Buc, Master of the Revels, in which a scribe listed a performance of The Tempest *at Court on Hallomas (1 November) 1611 (Public Record Office, Audit Office, Accounts, Various; by permission of the Controller of Her Majesty's Stationery Office)*

leadership are so extraordinary as to seem Herculean, Coriolanus becomes a veritable beast when called upon to participate in the civic affairs of early republican Rome. His contempt for the moblike plebeians is exceeded only by his hatred of the tribunes and senators who play the soldier-general and the common people off against one another. Coriolanus refuses to flatter anyone for any reason, and he lashes out at the hypocrisy required of him when he is told that he must bare his wounds and beg for the "voices" of the citizens in order to be elected tribune, an office he has not sought and a responsibility he makes clear he does not want. Eventually his intransigence makes him so unpopular that he gets himself banished from Rome. To which he offers an arch retort that is perfectly in character: "I banish you!"

Confident that "there is a world elsewhere," Coriolanus departs from the city as "a lonely dragon." But soon, to the astonishment and terror of his former fellows, he joins forces with Rome's arch-enemies, the Volscians. In the final movement of the play we see him lead an army to the gates of Rome that threatens to destroy the Empire in its infancy. But at this point Coriolanus's mother, Volumnia, intervenes and pleads with the hero to spare his native city for her sake. Reluctantly, and with a premonition that his decision will prove fatal to him, Coriolanus accedes to his mother's request. Then, cunningly provoked to one last intemperate outburst by the foxlike Volscian general Aufidius, who calls him a "boy of tears," Coriolanus brings down upon himself the wrathful hordes of the Volscians he has just betrayed.

Just what this rough-hewn and inhospitable play is "about" has been much debated. But critics as varied as T. S. Eliot and Frank Kermode, and actors as distinguished as Laurence Olivier and Alan Howard, have shown that it can be a challenging and at times a thrilling dramatic achievement. In all likelihood it will receive more attention—and admiration—in the future than it

John Lowin, who joined Shakespeare's company in 1603 and became shareholder in the King's Men in 1604 (Dulwich College, by permission of the Governors). By tradition Lowin was the first actor to play Henry VIII and took over the role of Falstaff in the Henry IV plays.

has tended to receive in the past.

Whether this will be true of Shakespeare's final experiment in tragedy, *Timon of Athens*, is less certain. Derived, like the three major Roman plays, primarily from Plutarch's *Lives, Timon of Athens* is generally regarded as a play that the author left unfinished. There is no record of its having been performed in Shakespeare's lifetime, and it has only appeared sporadically (and seldom notably) in the centuries since.

As a character, Timon has affinities with Lear and Coriolanus. Like Lear, he comes to think of himself as a victim of ingratitude, a man "more sinned against than sinning." And, like Coriolanus, he responds to his mistreatment by "banishing" all society from his presence. Unlike either character, however, Timon is incapable of growth or compromise. Once he has spurned the

"friends" who have refused to help him with the creditors his excessive generosity has brought to the door, Timon retreats to a cave and disregards every entreaty to concern himself with his fellow man. His foil, Alcibiades, can forgive Athens its injustices and return to save the city from ruin. But Timon elects to spend the rest of his life in solitude, cursing all of humanity with an invective that eventually becomes tedious in the extreme.

Critics such as G. Wilson Knight and Rolf Soellner have argued valiantly for the poetic and theatrical merits of *Timon of Athens*. But thus far their adherents have proven only slightly more numerous than the followers of Timon himself. Original the play may be; but few have come to praise it as a fully realized work of dramatic art.

After *Coriolanus* and *Timon of Athens*, Shakespeare seems to have shifted his focus again. He wrote no more tragedies, so far as we know, and the single "history play" that appeared was so different from his previous efforts in that genre that it seems to belong to the realm of romance rather than to the world of ordinary political and social interaction. And indeed "romance" is now the generic term most frequently applied to the mature tragicomedies that critics once referred to somewhat loosely as "the Late Plays." If we include *Henry VIII* in their number, there are six surviving works that qualify as late romances. One of them, *The Two Noble Kinsmen,* we know to have been written by Shakespeare in collaboration with his fellow dramatist John Fletcher. Two others, *Pericles* and *Henry VIII,* are also regarded by many scholars as likely to have resulted from joint authorship–as was evidently the case, too, with the lost *Cardenio,* attributed to Shakespeare and Fletcher in a Stationers' Register entry of 1753. Which leaves us with three plays–*Cymbeline, The Winter's Tale,* and *The Tempest*–that are unanimously accepted as works entirely by Shakespeare.

Since all but one of the Late Plays (*Pericles,* which seems to have been completed in 1606-1608) appeared after Shakespeare's company added the Blackfriars as a venue for performance–and since even that work may have been written with indoor staging in view (we know that *Pericles* was presented at Court sometime between January 1606 and November 1608)–it seems eminently possible, as Gerald Eades Bentley has suggested, that Shakespeare's modifications in dramaturigcal style resulted, at least in part, from changes in emphasis by the King's Men. If Shakespeare and his colleagues were easing away from total dependence on the comparatively broad-based audiences they had long attracted to the Globe and were beginning to cast their fortunes more confidently with the aristocratic clientele they served at Court or would be able to cultivate at the private Blackfriars theater, they may well have begun to rethink their dramatic repertory. Under these circumstances, Shakespeare and his fellow shareholders could readily have arrived at a determination to concentrate on offerings such as their more well-to-do audiences had grown accustomed to seeing: masquelike entertainments of the sort that Court patronage encouraged, and mythological and fanciful diversions of the type that the children's companies had made their specialty in indoor halls like the Blackfriars.

In any event, the sequence of dramatic works initiated by *Pericles* is strikingly different in many respects from the sequence that preceded it. Relying as many of them do on such devices as a choral "presenter" (Gower in *Pericles,* or Time in *The Winter's Tale*) to narrate background incidents, the romances tend to be rambling and panoramic by comparison with the earlier plays (the salient exception being *The Tempest,* which is unusually focused in time, place, and action). Frequently, they contain incidents that are wildly implausible (as when Antigonus exits "pursued by a bear" in *The Winter's Tale*), and most of them draw heavily on storms, shipwrecks, and other violently disruptive "acts of God" to move the action forward. Families are separated at sea, left to wander for years in adversity, and then miraculously reunited at the close. Symbolically named children (Marina in *Pericles,* Perdita in *The Winter's Tale,* Miranda in *The Tempest*) function dramatically as instruments of special grace, restoring faith and vision to parents who have temporarily

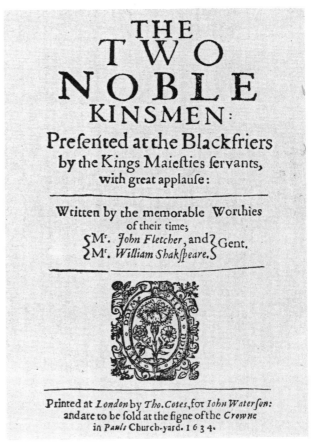

Title page for the 1634 quarto edition of a play that Shakespeare wrote with the playwright who succeeded him as chief dramatist for the King's Men (Maggs Bros., catalogue number 493, 1927)

To the Reader.

This Figure, that thou here feeſt put,
　It vvas for gentle Shakeſpeare cut;
Wherein the Grauer had a ſtrife
　with Nature, to out-doo the life :
O, could he but haue dravvne his vvit
　As vvell in braſſe, as he hath hit
His face ; the Print vvould then ſurpaſſe
　All, that vvas euer vvrit in braſſe.
But, ſince he cannot, Reader, looke
　Not on his Picture, but his Booke.

　　　　　　　　　　　　　B. I.

Mr. WILLIAM
SHAKESPEARES
COMEDIES,
HISTORIES, &
TRAGEDIES.

Publiſhed according to the True Originall Copies.

LONDON
Printed by Iſaac Iaggard, and Ed. Blount. 1623.

Note to the reader by Ben Jonson and title page for the First Folio (Folger Shakespeare Library). The engraved portrait is by Martin Droeshout the younger, who was fifteen when Shakespeare died and twenty-two when this volume was published. Droeshout is unlikely to have drawn Shakespeare from life and probably worked from a drawing given to him. It has been pointed out that the volume's editors, John Heminge and Henry Condell—both shareholders in Shakespeare's company—accepted the portrait for inclusion in the volume, though the fact that it was twice revised during the printing of the First Folio indicates that it was considered to be less than perfect.

lost their way. Terrible calamities are but narrowly averted, and then only because of sudden reversals that depend either upon some character's astonishing change of heart or upon an inexplicable visitation from above. Rather than conceal their artifice, the romances tend to display it openly, on the one hand reminding the audience that what it is witnessing is only make-believe, on the other hand manipulating viewers' responses so as to prepare the audience for some climactic "wonder" toward which the entire sequence has been directed.

　　The first three acts of *Pericles* seem so naive dramaturgically that many scholars consider them to be by a playwright other than Shakespeare. Among the contemporaries whose names

have been proposed for the dubious honor of collaborator in accordance with this hypothesis is George Wilkins, whose novel *The Painful Adventures of Pericles Prince of Tyre* appeared in the same year (1608) as the entry for *Pericles* in the Stationers' Register. All we know for certain is that the play was first published in 1609 in a relatively crude quarto that was reprinted several times before *Pericles* made its initial folio entry when it was added to the second issue of the Third Folio in 1664. Just why *Pericles* was not included in the First Folio has never been determined. Its omission may have had something to do with the poor condition of the only available text. Or it may have stemmed from the assumption that the play was not completely by Shakespeare. The sec-

A CATALOGVE

of the feuerall Comedies, Hiſtories, and Tragedies contained in this Volume.

COMEDIES.

He Tempeſt.	Folio 1.
The two Gentlemen of Verona.	20
The Merry Wiues of Windſor.	38
Meaſure for Meaſure.	61
The Comedy of Errours.	85
Much adoo about Nothing.	101
Loues Labour loſt.	122
Midſommer Nights Dreame.	145
The Merchant of Venice.	163
As you Like it.	185
The Taming of the Shrew.	208
All is well, that Ends well.	230
Twelfe-Night, or what you will.	255
The Winters Tale.	304

HISTORIES.

The Life and Death of King John.	Fol. 1.
The Life & death of Richard the ſecond.	23
The Firſt part of King Henry the fourth.	46
The Second part of K. Henry the fourth.	74
The Life of King Henry the Fift.	69
The Firſt part of King Henry the Sixt.	96
The Second part of King Hen. the Sixt.	120
The Third part of King Henry the Sixt.	147
The Life & Death of Richard the Third.	173
The Life of King Henry the Eight.	205

TRAGEDIES.

The Tragedy of Coriolanus.	Fol. 1.
Titus Andronicus.	31
Romeo and Juliet.	53
Timon of Athens.	80
The Life and death of Julius Ceſar.	109
The Tragedy of Macbeth.	131
The Tragedy of Hamlet.	152
King Lear.	283
Othello, the Moore of Venice.	310
Anthony and Cleopater.	346
Cymbeline King of Britaine.	369

Table of contents for the First Folio (Folger Shakespeare Library). In addition to the plays listed here the volume contains
Troilus and Cressida.

ond of these hypotheses would also explain the exclusion of *The Two Noble Kinsmen* (though of course it would not explain the *inclusion* of *Henry VIII* if, as many scholars believe, that too was a play that Shakespeare wrote in collaboration with another playwright).

Whatever the case, *Pericles* is immediately recognizable as a point of departure. Drawing from a fifth-century romantic narrative by Apollonius of Tyre as retold in the *Confessio Amantis* of the fourteenth-century English poet John Gower, the play is studiously "antique" in its apparently unsophisticated presentational style. Old Gower himself is resurrected to serve as the barnacled chorus, and the singsong tetrameters that serve as the metrical vehicle for his medieval diction remove the play's events from the present to a dreamlike past more suited to fairy lore than to realistic fiction. In such an atmosphere the audience is more readily induced to suspend its disbelief–with the consequence that we become vicarious participants in episode after episode as the hero's adventures convey him from youth (when he solves the riddle of Antiochus and is immediately forced to flee for his life upon disclosing his knowledge of the wicked King's incestuous relationship with his daughter) through old age (when, having been reduced almost to despair by decades of wandering and loss, Pericles is miraculously rejoined with his radiant daughter, Marina). As we allow ourselves to be hypnotized into accepting the premises of such a providential universe, we fall under the spell of a "moldy tale" peopled by such characters as a wicked stepmother (Dionyza), a Bawd, and a Governor (Lysimachus) who becomes so enraptured by Marina's innocence that he forswears a life bedimmed by vice.

Pericles' final "awakening" has often been compared to Lear's reunion with Cordelia. And a lovely lyric ("Marina") by T. S. Eliot is eloquent in its testimony that twentieth-century audiences can still be moved by a beloved child's power to regenerate her father and renew his faith in life. Until recently *Pericles* has rarely been performed, but as the magic of its marvels becomes more widely appreciated it may one day find its way to a more secure footing in the repertory.

Such may also be the case with *Cymbeline*. First printed in the 1623 Folio, it probably enjoyed its initial performances in 1609-1610, either at Blackfriars or at the Globe (where the physician Dr. Simon Forman saw it, probably in 1611). Its historical frame, featuring a pre-Christian monarch from approximately the same era as King Lear, Shakespeare derived primarily from Holinshed's *Chronicles*. In this portion of the play, wherein Cymbeline at first refuses and then later volunteers Britain's annual tribute to Emperor Augustus Caesar, Shakespeare adumbrates the commingling of British and Roman traits that Renaissance Englishmen believed to be at the root of their nation's greatness. Shakespeare combined with this theme a number of other romantic motifs, his sources varying from Boccaccio's *Decameron* to a pair of anonymous plays of the 1580s, *The Rare Triumphs of Love and Fortune* and *Sir Cloyomon and Sir Clamydes*. The result is a romantic tragicomedy unusually episodic in structure and so bewildering in the rapidity and complexity of its concluding disclosures as to leave an audience wondering how any agency other than providence could possibly have untangled the various strands of the plot.

At the heart of the play is Imogen, a woman of exemplary chastity whose foolhardy husband Posthumus allows himself to be tricked into thinking that she has been seduced by a braggart named Iachimo. Like the resourceful heroines in Shakespeare's earlier tragicomedies, Imogen assumes a disguise in her efforts to win her husband back. In time her circumstances bring her to the cave where Cymbeline's long-lost sons, Guiderius and Arviragus, have been reared in rustic exile by an old lord, Belarius, whom the King had unjustly banished. She casts her lot with them and becomes a participant in Britain's war against Rome. Once the conflict is over, the King and his sons are reunited in the same denouement in which Posthumus recognizes Imogen as his "most constant wife." And in a reconciliation scene that carries overtones of the Augustan "pax Romana" under which Christ was born, Cymbeline announces that "Pardon's the word to all." Evil has been exorcised (Cymbeline's "bad angels," his wicked Queen and her doltish son Cloten, have died), and the wayward characters who survive have all experienced enlightenment and contrition.

Enlightenment and contrition are prerequisite to the happy ending of *The Winter's Tale*, too. Here again a husband falls victim to vengeful jealousy, and here again the plot builds up to the moment when he can be forgiven the folly that, so far as he knows, has brought about his innocent wife's death. Based primarily on Robert Greene's *Pandosto: The Triumph of Time*, a prose romance first published in 1588 and reprinted under a new title in 1607, *The Winter's Tale* was probably completed in 1610 or 1611. Its initial appearance in print was in the 1623 Folio.

The action begins when Leontes, King of Sicilia, is seized with the "humour" that his wife Hermione has committed adultery with his childhood friend Polixenes. It is abundantly clear to everyone else, most notably Hermione's lady-in-waiting Paulina, that Leontes' suspicions are irrational. But he refuses to listen either to the counsel of his advisers or to the oracle at Delphi–persisting with this "trial" of Hermione until he has completely devastated his court. He drives Polixenes away with the faithful Sicilian lord Camillo; he frightens to death his son Mamilius; and he pursues Hermione so unrelentingly that she finally wilts into what Paulina declares to be a fatal swoon. At this point, suddenly recognizing that he has been acting like a madman, Leontes vows to do penance for the remainder of his life.

Years later, after Perdita (the "lost" child whom the raging Leontes has instructed Paulina's husband Antigonus to expose to the elements) has grown up and fallen in love with Florizel, the heir to Polixenes' throne in Bohemia, the major characters are providentially regathered in Leontes' court. Leontes is reunited with his daughter. And then, in one of the most stirring and unexpected moments in all of Shakespeare's works, a statue of Hermione that Paulina unveils turns out to be the living–and forgiving–Queen whom Leontes had "killed" some sixteen years previously. In a speech that might well serve to epitomize the import of all the late romances, Paulina tells the King "It is requir'd/You do awake your faith." The regenerated Leontes embraces his long-lamented wife, bestows the widowed Paulina on the newly returned Camillo, and blesses the forthcoming marriage of Perdita to the son of his old friend Polixenes, the object of the jealousy with which the whole agonizing story has begun.

The circle that is completed in *The Winter's Tale* has its counterpart in *The Tempest*, which concludes with the marriage of Prospero's daughter Miranda to Ferdinand, the son of the Neapolitan king who had helped Prospero's wicked brother Antonio remove Prospero from his dukedom in Milan a dozen years previously.

Like *The Winter's Tale*, *The Tempest* was completed by 1611 and printed for the first time in the 1623 Folio. Because it refers to the "still-vext Bermoothes" and derives in part from three accounts of the 1609 wreck of a Virginia-bound ship called the *Sea Adventure*, the play has long been scrutinized for its supposed commentary on the colonial exploitation of the New World. But if the brute Caliban is not the noble savage of Montaigne's essay on cannibals, he is probably not intended to be an instance of Third World victimization by European imperialism either. And Prospero's island is at least as Mediterranean as it is Caribbean. More plausible, but also too speculative for uncritical acceptance, is the time-honored supposition that the magician's staff with which Prospero wields his power is meant to be interpreted as an analogy for Shakespeare's own magical gifts–with the corollary that the protagonist's abjuration of his "potent art" is the dramatist's own way of saying farewell to the theater. Were it not that at least two plays were almost certainly completed later than *The Tempest*, this latter hypothesis might win more credence.

But be that as it may, there can be no doubt that Prospero cuts a magnificent figure on the Shakespearean stage. At times, when he is recalling the usurpation that has placed him and his daughter on the island they have shared with Caliban for a dozen lonely years, Prospero is reminiscent of Lear, another angry ruler who, despite his earlier indiscretions, has cause to feel more sinned against than sinning. At other times, when Prospero is using the spirit Ariel to manipulate the comings and goings of the enemies whose ship he has brought aground in a tempest, the once and future Duke of Milan reminds us of the Duke of Vienna in *Measure for Measure*. But though his influence on the lives of others turns out in the end to have been "providential," Prospero arrives at that beneficent consummation only through a psychological and spiritual process that turns on his forswearing "vengeance" in favor of the "rarer action" of forgiveness. Such dramatic tension as the play possesses is to be found in the audience's suspense over whether the protagonist will use his Neoplatonic magic for good or for ill. And when in fact Prospero has brought the "men of sin" to a point where they must confront themselves as they are and beg forgiveness for their crimes, it is paradoxically Ariel who reminds his master that to be truly human is finally to be humane.

Uniquely among the late tragicomic romances, *The Tempest* has long been a favorite with both readers and audiences. Its ardent young lovers have always held their charm, as has the effervescent Ariel, and its treatment of the temptations afforded by access to transcendent power gives it a political and religious resonance com-

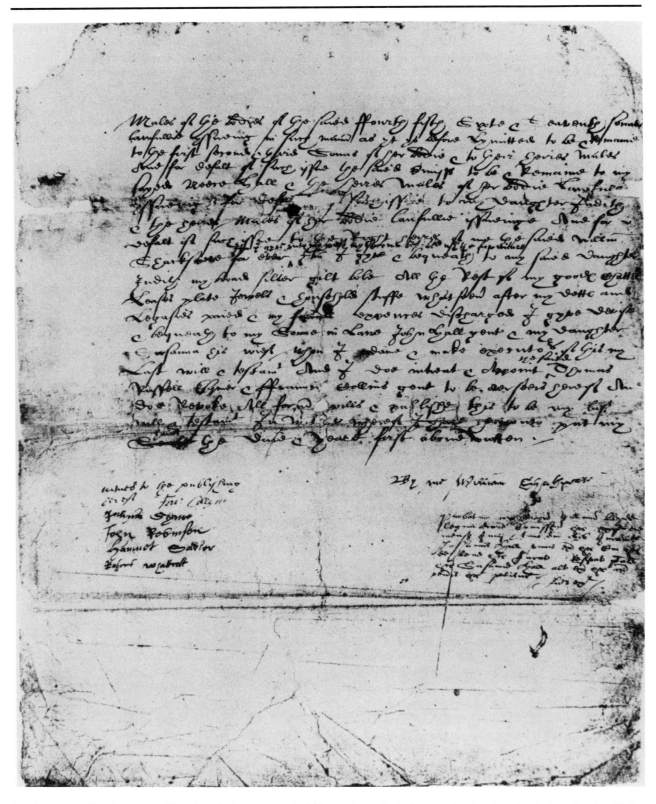

The last page of Shakespeare's will, written by lawyer Francis Collins or his scribe in January 1616 and revised in March, when Shakespeare signed each of the three pages (Public Record Office, Principal Probate Registry, Selected Wills, Prob. ¼ ; by permission of the Controller of Her Majesty's Stationery Office)

mensurate with the profundity of its exploration of the depths of poetic and dramatic art. In the end its burden seems to be that an acknowledgment of the limits imposed by the human condition is the beginning of wisdom.

The last of the plays attributed wholly to Shakespeare by its inclusion in the First Folio, where it first achieved print, is *Henry VIII*. Modern stylistic analyses have called Shakespeare's sole authorship into question, of course, but since the case for collaboration has never been definitively proven we may do just as well to proceed on the assumption that *Henry VIII* was mostly if not entirely a play for which the playwright was responsible. Its theatrical history has had more ups and downs than is true of many of Shakespeare's other dramatic works (the most notable occurrence on the down side being the accident during its earliest recorded performance, on 29 June 1613, that burned the Globe to the ground), and its critical reception, like that of *Troilus and Cressida*, has been complicated by debates about the play's genre.

In many respects *Henry VIII* seems to be the capstone to Shakespeare's nine earlier English history plays. It focuses on kingship as the key to a nation's political and social stability, and it glorifies the Tudor dynasty as God's means of bringing peace, prosperity, and empire to an England whose greatness had reached new heights during the reigns of the two monarchs under whom Shakespeare had served. Fittingly, the play's "final cause" is the birth of Elizabeth, the "royal infant" whose advent, according to the prophecy uttered by Archbishop Cranmer at the end of the play, "promises/Upon this land a thousand thousand blessings." But, as is so often true in Shakespeare, it also offers the audience a topical glance at an event of contemporary significance, the February 1613 wedding of Princess Elizabeth, daughter of King James I and his Queen, to Frederick, the Elector of Palatine.

Like the earlier English history plays, *Henry VIII* is epic in its scope and in its patriotic impulse. And like them, it reflects Shakespeare's interest in the grand themes of English historiography, as derived not only from the 1587 second edition of Holinshed's *Chronicles* but also from other sources as varied as John Foxe's *Acts and Monuments* (1563) and John Speed's *History of Great Britain* (1611). In its earliest performances the play even seems to have had an alternate title, *All is True*, to assert its fidelity to the essence of its historical subject matter. But a close examination of its

way of treating that matter will indicate that *Henry VIII* is more "cosmic" than the history plays that preceded it–a play that presents the events it dramatizes almost solely in the light of eternity.

Though the King is not without his faults, he is portrayed more positively in Shakespeare than he had usually been depicted by historians prior to *Henry VIII*. During the first half of the play the bluff Henry may be misled by his "bad angel" Cardinal Wolsey; but the King's intentions are noble, and after Wolsey's discomfiture he evolves into a creditable exemplar of God's deputy. Meanwhile, there is an unmistakable emphasis on providential design throughout the play. The action is structured around a succession of "trials," each of which serves to test a character's mettle and to induce in him or her a new degree of self-knowledge, humility, faith, and compassion. Buckingham is framed by Wolsey's machinations, but as he proceeds to his execution he forgives his enemies and blesses the King who has condemned him. Katherine, another of Wolsey's victims, pleads eloquently and forcibly in her own defense; but once her fate is settled, she resigns herself with patience to the destiny prepared for her and goes so far as to express pity for her archenemy Wolsey. And once he recognizes that there is no escape from the noose he has unwittingly prepared for himself, Wolsey himself dies penitent and "never so happy." In each instance death is swallowed up in a victory of sorts, and the sequence as a whole reinforces the audience's sense that even in the often-brutal arena of English history all's well that ends well.

Perhaps the best way to describe *Henry VIII* is to call it a tragicomic historical romance. But whatever it is generically, it is a play that offers a plenitude of majestic pageantry. As the 1979 BBC television production reminded us, it is Shakespeare's version of *Masterpiece Theatre*.

Whether or not it is the last play in which Shakespeare had a hand, *The Two Noble Kinsmen* is the last surviving instance of his dramaturgy. With but a handful of exceptions, modern scholars regard the play as a collaborative effort in which the guiding hand may have been John Fletcher's rather than William Shakespeare's. It was probably completed in 1613, and its first appearance in print was in a quarto edition of 1634 that attributed it to both playwrights. It was reprinted in the Beaumont and Fletcher second folio of 1679, but it never appeared in any of the

The Shakespeare Monument (top) and grave (bottom) in Holy Trinity Church, Stratford-upon-Avon. The monument was made by Gheerart Janssen, a stonemason from Amsterdam whose name was anglicized to Gerard Johnson and who may have been acquainted with Shakespeare.

seventeenth-century folios of Shakespeare's dramatic works.

The play is a dramatization of Geoffrey Chaucer's "Knight's Tale" about two cousins, Palamon and Arcite, who come to blows as a consequence of their both having fallen in love with the same damsel, Emilia. Like the other late romances of Shakespeare, it has a remote Mediterranean setting (ancient Thebes and Athens), it invokes the gods for intervention in human affairs, and it depends for its effects on scenes of grand pageantry such as the wedding procession of Theseus and Hippolyta. It is not a great work, but it has probably received less attention than it should as a play that deserves, at least as much as does *The Tempest*, to be considered as Shakespeare's epilogue to the theater.

Tradition holds that Shakespeare returned to Stratford for his declining years, and three years after the burning of the Globe his own flame went out. Following his death on 23 April 1616, he was laid to rest where fifty-two years earlier he had been christened. Shortly thereafter, a monument to his memory was erected above the tomb in Holy Trinity, and that monument is still in place for Shakespeare admirers to see today. But an even greater monument to his memory appeared seven years later, when his theatrical colleagues, John Heminge and Henry Condell (both of whom had been mentioned in the playwright's will) assembled a large volume of his collected plays. The 1623 First Folio was a labor of love, compiled as "an office to the dead, to procure his orphans guardians" and "to keep the memory of so worthy a friend and fellow alive as was our Shakespeare."

Our Shakespeare. It is not without exaggeration that the book that preserves what is probably his most reliable portrait and the most authoritative versions of the majority of his dramatic texts (indeed the *only* surviving versions of half of them) has been called "incomparably the most important work in the English language." In the words and actions that fill his poems and plays, in the performances that enrich our theaters and silver screens, in the countless offshoots to be found in other works of art, and in the influence the playwright continues to have on virtually every aspect of popular culture throughout the world, now as much as in the age of Elizabeth and James, Shakespeare lives.

Bibliographies:

William Jaggard, *Shakespeare Bibliography: A Dictio-*

nary of Every Known Issue of the Writings of Our National Poet and of Recorded Opinion Thereon in the English Language (Stratford-upon-Avon: Shakespeare Press, 1911);

Walter Ebish and Levin L. Schucking, *A Shakespeare Bibliography* (Oxford: Clarendon Press, 1931);

Gordon Ross Smith, *A Classified Shakespeare Bibliography, 1936-1958* (University Park: Pennsylvania State University Press, 1963);

Ronald Berman, *A Reader's Guide to Shakespeare's Plays*, revised edition (Glenview, Ill.: Scott Foresman, 1973);

David Bevington, *Shakespeare* (Arlington Heights, Ill.: AHM Publishing, 1978);

Larry S. Champion, *The Essential Shakespeare: An Annotated Bibliography of Major Modern Studies* (Boston: G. K. Hall, 1986).

See also the annual bibliographies in *Shakespeare Quarterly*, plus the reviews of current scholarship, criticism, and performance in two annuals, *Shakespeare Survey* and *The Year's Work in English Studies*.

Handbooks and Study Guides:

Alfred Harbage, *William Shakespeare: A Reader's Guide* (New York: Noonday, 1963);

F. E. Halliday, *A Shakespeare Companion, 1564-1964* (London: Duckworth/Harmondsworth: Penguin, 1964);

O. J. Campbell and Edward G. Quinn, *The Reader's Encyclopedia of Shakespeare* (New York: Crowell, 1966);

John W. Velz, *Shakespeare and the Classical Tradition: A Critical Guide to Commentary, 1660-1960* (Minneapolis: University of Minnesota Press, 1968);

Kenneth Muir and S. Schoenbaum, eds., *A New Companion to Shakespeare Studies* (Cambridge: Cambridge University Press, 1971);

David M. Bergeron, *Shakespeare: A Study and Research Guide* (New York: St. Martin's, 1975);

David M. Zesmer, *Guide to Shakespeare* (New York: Barnes & Noble, 1976);

Stanley Wells and Gary Taylor, *William Shakespeare: A Textual Companion* [to the Complete Oxford Shakespeare] (Oxford: Clarendon Press, 1987).

Biographical Studies:

E. K. Chambers, *William Shakespeare: A Study of Facts and Problems*, 2 volumes (Oxford: Clarendon Press, 1930);

M. M. Reese, *Shakespeare: His World and His Work* (London: Arnold, 1953);

Gerald Eades Bentley, *Shakespeare: A Biographical*

Handbook (New Haven: Yale University Press, 1961);

A. L. Rowse, *William Shakespeare: A Biography* (London: Macmillan, 1963);

Anthony Burgess, *Shakespeare* (Harmondsworth: Penguin, 1970);

S. Schoenbaum, *Shakespeare's Lives* (New York: Oxford University Press, 1970);

Schoenbaum, *William Shakespeare: A Documentary Life* (London: Oxford University Press/ Scolar Press, 1975);

Schoenbaum, *William Shakespeare: Records and Images* (London: Oxford University Press/ Scolar Press, 1981);

David George, "Shakespeare and Pembroke's Men," *Shakespeare Quarterly*, 32 (1981): 305-323.

Periodicals:

Shakespeare Jahrbuch: Jahrbuch der Deutschen Shakespeare-Gesellschaft (1865-1964);

Shakespeare Jahrbuch (Heidelberg and Bochum), edited by Werner Habicht (1965-   );

Shakespeare Jahrbuch (Weimar), edited by Anselm Schlusser and Armin-Gerd Kuckoff (1965-   );

Shakespeare Newsletter, edited by Louis Marder (1951-   );

Shakespeare Quarterly, edited by James G. McManaway, Richard J. Schoeck, John F. Andrews, Barbara A. Mowat (1950-   );

Shakespeare Studies, edited by J. Leeds Barroll (1965-   );

Shakespeare Studies (Tokyo), edited by Jiro Ozu (1962-   );

Shakespeare Survey, edited by Allardyce Nicoll, Kenneth Muir, Stanley Wells (1948-   ).

References:

BACKGROUND, MILIEU, SOURCE, AND
INFLUENCE STUDIES

E. A. Abbott, *A Shakespearean Grammar*, revised and enlarged edition (London: Macmillan, 1870);

John Cranford Adams, *The Globe Playhouse* (Cambridge: Harvard University Press, 1942);

John F. Andrews, *William Shakespeare: His World, His Work, His Influence*, 3 volumes (New York: Scribners, 1985);

T. W. Baldwin, *William Shakspere's Small Latine & Lesse Greeke* (Urbana: University of Illinois Press, 1943);

Bernard Beckerman, *Shakespeare at the Globe, 1599-1609* (New York: Macmillan, 1962);

Gerald Eades Bentley, *The Profession of Dramatist in Shakespeare's Time, 1590-1642* (Princeton: Princeton University Press, 1971);

Bentley, *The Profession of Player in Shakespeare's Time* (Princeton: Princeton University Press, 1984);

Bentley, "Shakespeare and the Blackfriars Theatre," *Shakespeare Survey*, 1 (1948): 38-50;

Fredson Bowers, *Bibliography and Textual Criticism* (Oxford: Clarendon Press, 1964);

Bowers, *On Editing Shakespeare* (Charlottesville: University Press of Virginia, 1966);

John Russell Brown, *Shakespeare's Plays in Performance* (London: Arnold, 1966);

Geoffrey Bullough, ed., *Narrative and Dramatic Sources of Shakespeare*, 8 volumes (London: Routledge & Kegan Paul, 1957-1975);

Fausto Cercignani, *Shakespeare's Works and Elizabethan Pronunciation* (Oxford: Clarendon Press, 1981);

E. K. Chambers, *The Elizabethan Stage*, 4 volumes (Oxford: Clarendon Press, 1923), III: 479-490;

Wolfgang Clemen, *The Development of Shakespeare's Imagery* (Cambridge: Harvard University Press, 1951);

Ruby Cohn, *Modern Shakespeare Offshoots* (Princeton: Princeton University Press, 1976);

Ann Jennalie Cook, *The Privileged Playgoers of Shakespeare's London: 1576-1642* (Princeton: Princeton University Press, 1981);

Richard David, *Shakespeare in the Theatre* (Cambridge: Cambridge University Press, 1978);

Madeleine Doran, *Endeavors of Art: A Study of Form in Elizabethan Drama* (Madison: University of Wisconsin Press, 1954);

G. R. Elton, *The Tudor Revolution in Government* (Cambridge: Cambridge University Press, 1953);

Roland M. Frye, *Shakespeare and Christian Doctrine* (Princeton: Princeton University Press, 1963);

W. W. Greg, *The Editorial Problem in Shakespeare: A Survey of the Foundations of the Text* (Oxford: Clarendon Press, 1954);

Greg, ed., *Dramatic Documents from the Elizabethan Playhouses: Stage Plots; Actors' Parts; Prompt Books*, 2 volumes (Oxford: Clarendon Press, 1931);

Andrew Gurr, *Playgoing in Shakespeare's London* (Cambridge: Cambridge University Press, 1987);

Gurr, *The Shakespearean Stage, 1574-1642* (Cambridge: Cambridge University Press, 1970);

Alfred Harbage, *Shakespeare's Audience* (New York: Columbia University Press, 1941);

Christopher Hill, *The Century of Revolution, 1603-1714* (New York: Norton, 1961);

Charlton Hinman, *The Printing and Proof-Reading of the First Folio of Shakespeare*, 2 volumes (Oxford: Clarendon Press, 1963);

C. Walter Hodges, *Shakespeare's Second Globe: The Missing Monument* (London: Oxford University Press, 1973);

Richard Hosley, "The Discovery-Space in Shakespeare's Globe," *Shakespeare Survey*, 12 (1959): 35-46;

Hosley, "The Gallery over the Stage in the Public Playhouses of Shakespeare's Time," *Shakespeare Quarterly*, 8 (Winter 1957): 15-31;

Hosley, ed., *Shakespeare's Holinshed* (New York: Putnam's, 1968);

Jack Jorgens, *Shakespeare on Film* (Bloomington: Indiana University Press, 1977);

Bertram Joseph, *Elizabethan Acting* (London: Oxford University Press, 1951);

George R. Kernodle, *From Art to Theatre: Form and Convention in the Renaissance* (Chicago: University of Chicago Press, 1944);

Helge Kökeritz, *Shakespeare's Pronunciation* (New Haven: Yale University Press, 1953);

Wallace T. MacCaffrey, *The Shaping of the Elizabethan Regime* (Princeton: Princeton University Press, 1968);

Scott McMillin, *The Elizabethan Theatre & The Book of Sir Thomas More* (Ithaca: Cornell University Press, 1987);

W. Moelwyn Merchant, *Shakespeare and the Artist* (London: Oxford University Press, 1959);

Sister Miriam Joseph, *Shakespeare's Use of the Arts of Language* (New York: Columbia University Press, 1947);

Kenneth Muir, *Shakespeare's Sources*, 2 volumes (London: Methuen, 1961);

Richmond Noble, *Shakespeare's Biblical Knowledge and Use of the Book of Common Prayer* (New York: Macmillan, 1935);

C. T. Onions, *A Shakespeare Glossary*, revised edition (Oxford: Clarendon Press, 1919);

John Orrell, *The Quest for Shakespeare's Globe* (Cambridge: Cambridge University Press, 1983);

Eric Partridge, *Shakespeare's Bawdy*, revised edition (London: Routledge & Kegan Paul, 1969);

Alfred W. Pollard, *Shakespeare's Folios and Quartos: A Study in the Bibliography of Shakespeare's Plays, 1594-1685* (London: Methuen, 1909);

Alexander Schmidt, *Shakespeare-Lexicon*, revised and enlarged by Gregor Sarrazin, 2 volumes (Berlin: de Gruyter, 1962);

S. Schoenbaum, *Shakespeare: The Globe and the World* (New York: Oxford University Press, 1979);

Peter J. Seng, *The Vocal Songs in the Plays of Shakespeare: A Critical History* (London: Oxford University Press, 1967);

Charles H. Shattuck, *Shakespeare on the American Stage: From the Hallams to Edwin Booth* (Washington: Folger Shakespeare Library, 1976);

Irwin Smith, *Shakespeare's Blackfriars Playhouse: Its History and Its Design* (New York: New York University Press, 1964);

Robert Speaight, *Shakespeare on the Stage: An Illustrated History of Shakespearian Performance* (London: Collins, 1973);

T. J. B. Spencer, ed., *Shakespeare's Plutarch* (Harmondsworth: Penguin, 1964);

Marvin Spevack, *The Harvard Concordance to Shakespeare* (Cambridge: Harvard University Press, 1973);

Arthur Colby Sprague, *Shakespearian Players and Performances* (Cambridge: Harvard University Press, 1954);

Lawrence Stone, *The Crisis of the Aristocracy, 1558-1641* (Oxford: Oxford University Press, 1965);

Stone, *The Family, Sex, and Marriage in England, 1500-1800* (New York: Harper & Row, 1977);

J. L. Styan, *The Shakespeare Revolution: Criticism and Performance in the Twentieth Century* (Cambridge: Cambridge University Press, 1979);

J. A. K. Thomson, *Shakespeare and the Classics* (London: Allen & Unwin, 1952);

E. M. W. Tillyard, *The Elizabethan World Picture* (London: Chatto & Windus, 1943);

J. C. Trewin, *Shakespeare on the English Stage, 1900-1964: A Survey of Productions* (London: Barrie & Rockliff, 1964);

Virgil K. Whitaker, *Shakespeare's Use of Learning* (San Marino, Cal.: Huntington Library, 1953);

Glynne Wickham, *Early English Stages, 1300-1600*, 2 volumes (London: Routledge & Kegan Paul, 1959-1972).

GENERAL CRITICAL STUDIES

W. H. Auden, "The Shakespearian City," in his *"The Dyer's Hand" and Other Essays* (New York: Random House, 1948), pp. 171-172;

Gerald Eades Bentley, *Shakespeare and Jonson: Their Reputations in the Seventeenth Century*

Compared, 2 volumes (Chicago: University of Chicago Press, 1945);

David Bevington and Jay L. Halio, eds., *Shakespeare: Pattern of Excelling Nature*, essays from the 1976 Washington Congress of the International Shakespeare Association (Newark: University of Delaware Press, 1978);

M. C. Bradbrook, *The Living Monument: Shakespeare and the Theatre of His Time* (New York: Barnes & Noble, 1969);

Philip Brockbank, ed., *Players of Shakespeare* (Cambridge: Cambridge University Press, 1985);

Sigurd Burkhardt, *Shakespearean Meanings* (Princeton: Princeton University Press, 1968);

James L. Calderwood, *Shakespearean Metadrama* (Minneapolis: University of Minnesota Press, 1971);

Nevill Coghill, *Shakespeare's Professional Skills* (Cambridge: Cambridge University Press, 1964);

Walter Clyde Curry, *Shakespeare's Philosophical Patterns* (Baton Rouge: Louisiana State University Press, 1937);

Leonard F. Dean, ed., *Shakespeare: Modern Essays in Criticism,* revised edition (New York: Oxford University Press, 1967);

Alan C. Dessen, *Elizabethan Drama and the Viewer's Eye* (Chapel Hill: University of North Carolina Press, 1977);

Dessen, *Elizabethan Stage Conventions and Modern Interpreters* (Cambridge: Cambridge University Press, 1984);

John Drakakis, *Alternative Shakespeares* (London: Methuen, 1985);

Juliet Dusinberre, *Shakespeare and the Nature of Women* (London: Macmillan, 1975);

Arthur M. Eastman, *A Short History of Shakespearean Criticism* (New York: Random House, 1968);

Philip Edwards, *Shakespeare and the Confines of Art* (London: Methuen, 1968);

G. Blakemore Evans, *Shakespeare: Aspects of Influence* (Cambridge: Harvard University Press, 1976);

Michael Goldman, *Shakespeare and the Energies of Drama* (Princeton: Princeton University Press, 1972);

Harley Granville-Barker, *Prefaces to Shakespeare*, 2 volumes (Princeton: Princeton University Press, 1946-1947);

Alfred Harbage, *Shakespeare and the Rival Traditions* (New York: Macmillan, 1952);

Terence Hawkes, *That Shakespeherean Rag* (London: Methuen, 1986);

Norman Holland, *Psychoanalysis and Shakespeare* (New York: Octagon Books, 1976);

Robert G. Hunter, *Shakespeare and the Mystery of God's Judgments* (Athens: University of Georgia Press, 1976);

Emrys Jones, *The Origins of Shakespeare* (Oxford: Clarendon Press, 1977);

Jones, *Scenic Form in Shakespeare* (Oxford: Clarendon Press, 1971);

Coppelia Kahn, *Man's Estate: Masculine Identity in Shakespeare* (Berkeley: University of California Press, 1981);

Alvin B. Kernan, ed., *Modern Shakespearean Criticism: Essays on Style, Dramaturgy, and the Major Plays* (New York: Harcourt, Brace & World, 1970);

Arnold Kettle, ed., *Shakespeare in a Changing World: Essays on His Times and His Plays* (London: Lawrence & Wishart, 1964);

Arthur C. Kirsch, *Shakespeare and the Experience of Love* (Cambridge: Cambridge University Press, 1981);

G. Wilson Knight, *Shakespeare and Religion: Essays of Forty Years* (London: Routledge & Kegan Paul, 1967);

L. C. Knights, *Some Shakespearean Themes* (London: Chatto & Windus, 1959);

Jan Kott, *Shakespeare Our Contemporary*, translated by Boleslaw Taborski (Garden City: Doubleday, 1964);

Clifford Leech and J. M. R. Margeson, eds., *Shakespeare 1971: Proceedings of the World Shakespeare Congress, Vancouver, August 1971* (Toronto: University of Toronto Press, 1972);

Harry Levin, "The Primacy of Shakespeare," *Shakespeare Quarterly*, 26 (Spring 1975): 99-112;

Richard Levin, *New Readings vs. Old Plays: Recent Trends in the Reinterpretation of English Renaissance Drama* (Chicago: University of Chicago Press, 1979);

James G. McManaway, ed., *Shakespeare 400: Essays by American Scholars on the Anniversary of the Poet's Birth* (New York: Holt, Rinehart & Winston, 1964);

John Munro, ed., *The Shakespeare Allusion Book: A Collection of Allusions to Shakespeare from 1591 to 1700*, 2 volumes (London: Chatto & Windus, 1909);

Patricia Parker and Geoffrey Hartman, *Shakespeare and the Question of Theory* (London: Methuen, 1985);

Hereward T. Price, *Construction in Shakespeare* (Ann Arbor: University of Michigan Press, 1951);

Norman Rabkin, *Shakespeare and the Common Understanding* (New York: Free Press, 1967);

Rabkin, *Shakespeare and the Problem of Meaning* (Chicago: University of Chicago Press, 1981);

Rabkin, ed., *Approaches to Shakespeare* (New York: McGraw-Hill, 1964);

Thomas M. Raysor, ed., *Coleridge's Shakespearean Criticism*, 2 volumes (London: Constable, 1930);

Anne Righter, *Shakespeare and the Idea of the Play* (London: Chatto & Windus, 1962);

A. P. Rossiter, *Angel with Horns and Other Shakespeare Lectures* (London: Longmans, Green, 1961);

Wilbur Sanders, *The Dramatist and the Received Idea* (Cambridge: Cambridge University Press, 1968);

Murray M. Schwartz and Coppelia Kahn, eds., *Representing Shakespeare: New Psychoanalytic Essays* (Baltimore: Johns Hopkins University Press, 1980);

Arthur Sherbo, ed., *Johnson on Shakespeare*, volumes 7 and 8 of *The Yale Edition of the Works of Samuel Johnson* (New Haven: Yale University Press, 1968);

Theodore Spencer, *Shakespeare and the Nature of Man* (New York: Macmillan, 1942);

Derek Traversi, *An Approach to Shakespeare*, revised and enlarged edition (Garden City: Doubleday, 1956);

Robert Y. Turner, *Shakespeare's Apprenticeship* (Chicago: University of Chicago Press, 1974);

Mark Van Doren, *Shakespeare* (New York: Holt, 1939);

Brian Vickers, ed., *Shakespeare: The Critical Heritage*, 6 volumes (London: Routledge & Kegan Paul, 1973-1981);

Enid Welsford, *The Fool: His Social and Literary History* (London: Faber & Faber, 1935);

Robert H. West, *Shakespeare and the Outer Mystery* (Lexington: University of Kentucky Press, 1968).

STUDIES OF THE NONDRAMATIC POEMS

Stephen Booth, *An Essay on Shakespeare's Sonnets* (New Haven: Yale University Press, 1969);

Edward Hubler, *The Sense of Shakespeare's Sonnets* (Princeton: Princeton University Press, 1952);

Hubler, Northrop Frye, Stephen Spender, and R. P. Blackmur, *The Riddle of Shakespeare's Sonnets* (New York: Basic Books, 1962);

Murray Krieger, *A Window to Criticism: Shakespeare's "Sonnets" and Modern Poetics* (Prince-

ton: Princeton University Press, 1964);

J. B. Leishman, *Themes and Variations in Shakespeare's Sonnets* (London: Hutchinson, 1961);

J. W. Lever, *The Elizabethan Love Sonnet* (London: Methuen, 1956);

Giorgio Melchiori, *Shakespeare's Dramatic Meditations: An Experiment in Criticism* (Oxford: Clarendon Press, 1976);

Hallett Smith, *Elizabethan Poetry* (Cambridge: Harvard University Press, 1952).

STUDIES OF THE COMEDIES, TRAGICOMEDIES, AND ROMANCES

C. L. Barber, *Shakespeare's Festive Comedy: A Study of Dramatic Form and Its Relation to Social Custom* (Princeton: Princeton University Press, 1959);

Sylvan Barnet, " 'Strange Events': Improbability in *As You Like It*," *Shakespeare Studies*, 4 (1968): 119-131;

Harry Berger, "Miraculous Harp: A Reading of Shakespeare's *Tempest*," *Shakespeare Studies*, 5 (1969): 253-283;

Ralph Berry, *Shakespeare's Comedies: Explorations in Form* (Princeton: Princeton University Press, 1972);

M. C. Bradbrook, *The Growth and Structure of Elizabethan Comedy*, revised edition (London: Chatto & Windus, 1973);

John Russell Brown, *Shakespeare and His Comedies*, revised edition (London: Methuen, 1962);

O. J. Campbell, *Comicall Satyre and Shakespeare's "Troilus and Cressida"* (San Marino, Cal.: Huntington Library, 1938);

H. B. Charlton, *Shakespearian Comedy* (London: Methuen, 1938);

Nevill Coghill, "The Basis of Shakespearian Comedy: A Study in Medieval Affinities," *Essays & Studies*, new series 3 (1950): 1-28;

Jackson I. Cope, *The Theater and the Dream: From Metaphor to Form in Renaissance Drama* (Baltimore: Johns Hopkins University Press, 1973);

Bertrand Evans, *Shakespeare's Comedies* (Oxford: Clarendon Press, 1960);

Howard Felperin, *Shakespearean Romance* (Princeton: Princeton University Press, 1972);

Northrop Frye, "The Argument of Comedy," in *English Institute Essays 1948* (New York: Columbia University Press, 1949), pp. 58-73;

Frye, *A Natural Perspective: The Development of Shakespearean Comedy and Romance* (New York: Columbia University Press, 1965);

Frye, *The Secular Scripture: A Study of the Structure*

of Romance (Cambridge: Harvard University Press, 1976);

Darryl J. Gless, *"Measure for Measure," the Law, and the Covenant* (Princeton: Princeton University Press, 1979);

William Green, *Shakespeare's "Merry Wives of Windsor"* (Princeton: Princeton University Press, 1962);

Joan Hartwig, *Shakespeare's Tragicomic Vision* (Baton Rouge: Louisiana State University Press, 1972);

Sherman H. Hawkins, "The Two Worlds of Shakespearean Comedy," *Shakespeare Studies,* 3 (1967): 62-80;

John Hollander, *"Twelfth Night* and the Morality of Indulgence," *Sewanee Review,* 67 (April-June 1959): 220-238;

G. K. Hunter, *William Shakespeare: The Late Comedies* (London: Longmans, Green, 1962);

Robert G. Hunter, *Shakespeare and the Comedy of Forgiveness* (New York: Columbia University Press, 1965);

Frank Kermode, "What is Shakespeare's *Henry VIII* About?," *Durham University Journal,* 40 (Spring 1948): 48-55;

Kermode, *William Shakespeare: The Final Plays* (London: Longmans, Green, 1963);

Alvin B. Kernan, *The Cankered Muse: Satire of the English Renaissance* (New Haven: Yale University Press, 1959);

Arthur C. Kirsch, "The Integrity of *Measure for Measure,*" *Shakespeare Survey,* 28 (1975): 89-105;

G. Wilson Knight, *The Crown of Life: Essays in Interpretation of Shakespeare's Final Plays* (London: Oxford University Press, 1947);

W. W. Lawrence, *Shakespeare's Problem Comedies* (New York: Macmillan, 1931);

Clifford Leech, *"Twelfth Night" and Shakespearian Comedy* (Toronto: University of Toronto Press, 1965);

Alexander Leggatt, *Citizen Comedy in the Age of Shakespeare* (Toronto: University of Toronto Press, 1973);

Leggatt, *Shakespeare's Comedy of Love* (London: Methuen, 1974);

Barbara Lewalski, "Biblical Allusion and Allegory in *The Merchant of Venice,*" *Shakespeare Quarterly,* 13 (Summer 1962): 327-343;

Barbara Mowat, *The Dramaturgy of Shakespeare's Romances* (Athens: University of Georgia Press, 1976);

Kenneth Muir, ed., *Shakespeare, The Comedies: A Collection of Critical Essays* (Englewood Cliffs,

N.J.: Prentice-Hall, 1965);

A. D. Nuttall, *Two Concepts of Allegory: A Study of Shakespeare's "The Tempest" and the Logic of Allegorical Expression* (London: Routledge & Kegan Paul, 1967);

Stephen Orgel, *The Illusion of Power: Political Theater in the English Renaissance* (Berkeley: University of California Press, 1975);

Douglas L. Peterson, *Time, Tide, and Tempest: A Study of Shakespeare's Romances* (San Marino, Cal.: Huntington Library, 1973);

E. C. Pettet, *Shakespeare and the Romance Tradition* (London: Staples, 1949);

Hugh M. Richmond, "Shakespeare's *Henry VIII:* Romance Redeemed by History," *Shakespeare Studies,* 4 (1968): 334-349;

Jeanne Addison Roberts, *Shakespeare's English Comedy: "The Merry Wives of Windsor" in Context* (Lincoln: University of Nebraska Press, 1979);

Leo Salinger, *Shakespeare and the Traditions of Comedy* (Cambridge: Cambridge University Press, 1974);

Ernest Schanzer, *The Problem Plays of Shakespeare: A Study of "Julius Caesar," "Measure for Measure," and "Antony and Cleopatra"* (London: Routledge & Kegan Paul, 1963);

David L. Stevenson, *The Achievement of Shakespeare's "Measure for Measure"* (Ithaca: Cornell University Press, 1966);

Joseph H. Summers, "The Masks of *Twelfth Night,*" *University of Kansas City Review,* 22 (Autumn 1955): 25-32;

E. M. W. Tillyard, *Shakespeare's Last Plays* (London: Chatto & Windus, 1938);

Tillyard, *Shakespeare's Problem Plays* (Toronto: University of Toronto Press, 1949);

Derek Traversi, *Shakespeare: The Last Phase* (London: Hollis & Carter, 1954);

Glynne Wickham, *"Love's Labor's Lost* and *The Four Foster Children of Desire,* 1581," *Shakespeare Quarterly,* 36 (Spring 1985): 49-55;

David Young, *The Heart's Forest: A Study of Shakespeare's Pastoral Plays* (New Haven: Yale University Press, 1972);

Young, *Something of Great Constancy: The Art of "A Midsummer Night's Dream"* (New Haven: Yale University Press, 1966).

STUDIES OF THE ENGLISH HISTORY PLAYS

Edward I. Berry, *Patterns of Decay: Shakespeare's Early Histories* (Charlottesville: University Press of Virginia, 1975);

Lily B. Campbell, *Shakespeare's "Histories": Mirrors*

of Elizabethan Policy (San Marino, Cal.: Huntington Library, 1947);

Larry S. Champion, "The Function of Mowbray: Shakespeare's Maturing Artistry in *Richard II*," *Shakespeare Quarterly*, 26 (Winter 1975): 3-7;

Alan C. Dessen, "The Intemperate Knight and the Politic Prince: Late Morality Structure in *1 Henry IV*," *Shakespeare Studies*, 7 (1974): 147-171;

Donna B. Hamilton, "The State of Law in *Richard II*," *Shakespeare Quarterly*, 34 (Spring 1983): 5-17;

Sherman H. Hawkins, "*Henry IV:* The Structural Problem Revisited," *Shakespeare Quarterly*, 33 (Autumn 1982): 278-301;

Hawkins, "Virtue and Kingship in Shakespeare's *Henry IV*," *English Literary Renaissance*, 5 (Autumn 1975): 313-343;

G. K. Hunter, "Shakespeare's Politics and the Rejection of Falstaff," *Critical Quarterly*, 1 (Autumn 1959): 229-236;

Harold Jenkins, *The Structural Problem in Shakespeare's "Henry the Fourth"* (London: Methuen, 1956);

Ernst H. Kantorowicz, *The King's Two Bodies: A Study in Mediaeval Political Theology* (Princeton: Princeton University Press, 1957);

Robert Ornstein, *A Kingdom for a Stage: The Achievement of Shakespeare's History Plays* (Cambridge: Harvard University Press, 1972);

Robert B. Pierce, *Shakespeare's History Plays: The Family and the State* (Columbus: Ohio State University Press, 1971);

Moody E. Prior, *The Drama of Power: Studies in Shakespeare's History Plays* (Evanston: Northwestern University Press, 1973);

M. M. Reese, *The Cease of Majesty: A Study of Shakespeare's History Plays* (London: Arnold, 1961);

Irving Ribner, *The English History Play in the Age of Shakespeare* (Princeton: Princeton University Press, 1965);

David Riggs, *Shakespeare's Heroical Histories: "Henry VI" and Its Literary Tradition* (Cambridge: Harvard University Press, 1971);

Peter Saccio, *Shakespeare's English Kings: History, Chronicle, and Drama* (New York: Oxford University Press, 1977);

E. M. W. Tillyard, *Shakespeare's History Plays* (London: Chatto & Windus, 1944);

Harold E. Toliver, "Falstaff, the Prince, and the History Play," *Shakespeare Quarterly*, 16 (Winter 1965): 63-80;

Eugene M. Waith, ed., *Shakespeare, The Histories:*

A Collection of Critical Essays (Englewood Cliffs, N.J.: Prentice-Hall, 1965);

Karl P. Wentersdorf, "The Conspiracy of Silence in *Henry V*," *Shakespeare Quarterly*, 27 (Summer 1976): 264-287;

Richard P. Wheeler, *Shakespeare's Development and the Problem Comedies* (Berkeley: University of California Press, 1979);

J. Dover Wilson, *The Fortunes of Falstaff* (Cambridge: Cambridge University Press, 1943).

STUDIES OF THE TRAGEDIES, INCLUDING
THE ROMAN PLAYS

Janet Adelman, *The Common Liar: An Essay on "Antony and Cleopatra"* (New Haven: Yale University Press, 1973);

John F. Andrews, "The Catharsis of *Romeo and Juliet*," in *Contributi dell' Istituto di filologia moderna*, Serie inglesi, 1, edited by Sergio Rossi (Milan: Unversita Cattolica del Sacro Cuore, 1974), pp. 142-175;

Andrews, " 'Dearly Bought Revenge,': *Hamlet, Samson Agonistes*, and Elizabethan Revenge Tragedy," *Milton Studies*, 13 (1979): 81-108;

John S. Anson, "*Julius Caesar:* The Politics of the Hardened Heart," *Shakespeare Studies*, 2 (1966): 11-33;

Howard Baker, *Induction to Tragedy: A Study in a Development of Form in "Gorboduc," "The Spanish Tragedy," and "Titus Andronicus"* (Baton Rouge: Louisiana State University Press, 1939);

J. Leeds Barroll, *Artificial Persons: The Formation of Character in the Tragedies of Shakespeare* (Columbia: University of South Carolina Press, 1974);

Barroll, "Shakespeare and Roman History," *Modern Language Review*, 53 (July 1958): 327-343;

Roy W. Battenhouse, *Shakespearean Tragedy: Its Art and Its Christian Premises* (Bloomington: Indiana University Press, 1969);

Adrien Bonjour, *The Structure of "Julius Caesar"* (Liverpool: Liverpool University Press, 1958);

Stephen Booth, *"King Lear," "Macbeth," Indefinition, and Tragedy* (New Haven: Yale University Press, 1983);

Fredson Bowers, *Elizabethan Revenge Tragedy, 1587-1642* (Princeton: Princeton University Press, 1940);

Bowers, "Hamlet as Minister and Scourge," *PMLA*, 70 (September 1955): 740-749;

M. C. Bradbrook, *Themes and Conventions of Elizabe-*

than Tragedy (Cambridge: Cambridge University Press, 1935);

A. C. Bradley, *Shakespearean Tragedy: Lectures on "Hamlet," "Othello," "King Lear," and "Macbeth"* (London: Macmillan, 1904);

Nicholas Brooke, *Shakespeare's Early Tragedies* (London: Methuen, 1968);

Cleanth Brooks, "The Naked Babe and the Cloak of Manliness," in his *The Well-Wrought Urn* (New York: Reynal & Hitchcock, 1947), pp. 21-46;

Reuben A. Brower, *Hero and Saint: Shakespeare and the Graeco-Roman Heroic Tradition* (New York: Oxford University Press, 1971);

Lily B. Campbell, *Shakespeare's Tragic Heroes: Slaves of Passion* (Cambridge: Cambridge University Press, 1930);

Paul A. Cantor, *Shakespeare's Rome: Republic and Empire* (Ithaca: Cornell University Press, 1976);

Larry S. Champion, *Shakespeare's Tragic Perspective: The Development of His Dramatic Technique* (Athens: University of Georgia Press, 1976);

H. B. Charlton, *Shakespearian Tragedy* (Cambridge: Cambridge University Press, 1948);

Maurice Charney, *Shakespeare's Roman Plays: The Function of Imagery in the Drama* (Cambridge: Harvard University Press, 1961);

Charney, *Style in "Hamlet"* (Princeton: Princeton University Press, 1969);

Dolora G. Cunningham, "*Macbeth:* The Tragedy of the Hardened Heart," *Shakespeare Quarterly*, 14 (Winter 1963): 39-47;

J. V. Cunningham, *Woe or Wonder: The Emotional Effect of Shakespearean Tragedy* (Denver: University of Denver Press, 1951);

John F. Danby, *Shakespeare's Doctrine of Nature: A Study of "King Lear"* (London: Faber & Faber, 1949);

Alan C. Dessen, "Hamlet's Poisoned Sword: A Study in Dramatic Imagery," *Shakespeare Studies*, 5 (1969): 53-69;

Franklin M. Dickey, *Not Wisely But Too Well: Shakespeare's Love Tragedies* (San Marino, Cal.: Huntington Library, 1957);

T. S. Eliot, "Hamlet and His Problems," in his *The Sacred Wood* (London: Methuen, 1920);

William R. Elton, *"King Lear" and the Gods* (San Marino, Cal.: Huntington Library, 1966);

Willard Farnham, *The Medieval Heritage of Elizabethan Tragedy* (Berkeley: University of California Press, 1936);

Farnham, *Shakespeare's Tragic Frontier: The World of His Final Tragedies* (Berkeley: University of California Press, 1950);

Francis Fergusson, "*Macbeth* as the Imitation of an Action," in *English Institute Essays 1951*, edited by A. S. Downer (New York: Columbia University Press, 1952), pp. 31-43;

Northrop Frye, *Fools of Time: Studies in Shakespearean Tragedy* (Toronto: University of Toronto Press, 1967);

S. L. Goldberg, *An Essay on "King Lear"* (Cambridge: Cambridge University Press, 1974);

O. B. Hardison, Jr., "Myth and History in *King Lear*," *Shakespeare Quarterly*, 26 (Summer 1975): 227-242;

Robert B. Heilman, *Magic in the Web: Action and Language in "Othello"* (Lexington: University of Kentucky Press, 1956);

Heilman, *This Great Stage: Image and Structure in "King Lear"* (Baton Rouge: Louisiana State University Press, 1948);

Heilman, "'Twere Best Not Know Myself: *Othello, Lear, Macbeth*," *Shakespeare Quarterly*, 15 (Spring 1964): 89-98;

John Holloway, *The Story of the Night: Studies in Shakespeare's Major Tragedies* (London: Routledge & Kegan Paul, 1961);

David L. Jeffrey and Patrick Grant, "Reputation in *Othello*," *Shakespeare Studies*, 6 (1970): 197-208;

Paul A. Jorgensen, *Lear's Self-Discovery* (Berkeley: University of California Press, 1967);

Jorgensen, *Our Naked Frailties: Sensational Art and Meaning in "Macbeth"* (Berkeley: University of California Press, 1971);

G. Wilson Knight, *The Wheel of Fire: Interpretation of Shakespeare's Tragedy* (London: Methuen, 1949);

L. C. Knights, "How Many Children Had Lady Macbeth?," in his *Explorations: Essays in Criticism* (London: Chatto & Windus, 1946);

Clifford Leech, ed., *Shakespeare, The Tragedies: A Collection of Critical Essays* (Chicago: University of Chicago Press, 1965);

Harry Levin, *The Question of "Hamlet"* (New York: Oxford University Press, 1959);

Maynard Mack, "The Jacobean Shakespeare: Some Observations on the Construction of the Tragedies," in *Jacobean Theatre*, edited by John Russell Brown and Bernard Harris, Stratford-upon-Avon Studies, 1 (London: Arnold, 1960);

Mack, *"King Lear" in Our Time* (Berkeley: University of California Press, 1965);

Mack, "The World of *Hamlet*," *Yale Review*, 41 (June 1952): 502-523;

J. M. R. Margeson, *The Origins of English Tragedy* (Oxford: Clarendon Press, 1967);

Bernard McElroy, *Shakespeare's Mature Tragedies* (Princeton: Princeton University Press, 1973);

Kenneth Muir, *Shakespeare's Tragic Sequence* (London: Hutchinson, 1972);

Matthew N. Proser, *The Heroic Image in Five Shakespearean Tragedies* (Princeton: Princeton University Press, 1965);

Eleanor Prosser, *Hamlet and Revenge*, revised edition (Stanford: Stanford University Press, 1971);

William Rosen, *Shakespeare and the Craft of Tragedy* (Cambridge: Harvard University Press, 1960);

Marvin Rosenberg, *The Masks of "King Lear"* (Berkeley: University of California Press, 1972);

J. L. Simmons, *Shakespeare's Pagan World: The Roman Tragedies* (Charlottesville: University Press of Virginia, 1973);

Susan Snyder, *The Comic Matrix of Shakespeare's Tragedies* (Princeton: Princeton University Press, 1979);

Snyder, "*King Lear* and the Psychology of Dying," *Shakespeare Quarterly*, 33 (Winter 1982): 449-460;

Rolf Soellner, *"Timon of Athens," Shakespeare's Pessimistic Tragedy, With a Stage History by Gary Jay Williams* (Columbus: Ohio State University Press, 1979);

Robert Speaight, *Nature in Shakespearian Tragedy* (London: Hollis & Carter, 1955);

Bernard Spivack, *Shakespeare and the Allegory of Evil: The History of a Metaphor in Relation to His Major Villains* (New York: Columbia University Press, 1958);

Brents Stirling, *Unity in Shakespearian Tragedy: The Interplay of Theme and Character* (New York: Columbia University Press, 1956);

Elmer E. Stoll, *Art and Artifice in Shakespeare* (Cambridge: Cambridge University Press, 1933);

Gary Taylor and Michael Warren, *The Division of the Kingdoms: Shakespeare's Two Versions of "King Lear"* (Oxford: Clarendon Press, 1983);

Marvin L. Vawter, " 'Division 'tween Our Souls': Shakespeare's Stoic Brutus," *Shakespeare Studies*, 7 (1974): 173-195;

Eugene M. Waith, *The Herculean Hero in Marlowe, Chapman, Shakespeare, and Dryden* (New York: Columbia University Press, 1962);

Waith, "The Metamorphosis of Violence in *Titus Andronicus*," *Shakespeare Survey*, 10 (1957): 39-49;

Virgil K. Whitaker, *The Mirror up to Nature: The Technique of Shakespeare's Tragedies* (San Marino, Cal.: Huntington Library, 1965);

Harold S. Wilson, *On the Design of Shakespearian Tragedy* (Toronto: University of Toronto Press, 1957).

Papers:

The Booke of Sir Thomas More (a play probably written principally by Anthony Munday, with revisions by Thomas Dekker, Henry Chettle, William Shakespeare, and possibly Thomas Heywood) survives in a manuscript now at the British Library (Harleian MS. 7368). Most scholars now believe that two brief passages are Shakespeare's work, circa 1594-1595, and that one of them represents the only surviving example of a literary or dramatic manuscript in Shakespeare's own hand. For a convenient summary of *Sir Thomas More* and the evidence linking it with Shakespeare, see G. Blakemore Evans's discussion of the play in *The Riverside Shakespeare* (Boston: Houghton Mifflin, 1974), pp. 1683-1700; and Scott McMillin's *The Elizabethan Theatre & The Book of Sir Thomas More*.

Nicholas Udall
(December 1504-December 1556)

Marie Axton
Cambridge University

PLAY PRODUCTIONS: Pageant verses made at the Coronation of Queen Anne, by Udall and John Leland, streets of London (Cornhill, Leaden Hall, Cheapside), 31 May 1533;

Thersites, attributed to Udall, unknown hall (?), between 12 and 22 October 1537;

Jacob and Esau, attributed to Udall, unknown hall, circa 1547-1557;

Jack Juggler, attributed to Udall, unknown hall, circa 1547-1557;

Ralph Roister Doister, possibly at Windsor, September 1552;

Respublica, attributed to Udall, at Court (?), Christmas season circa 1553-1555;

Ezechias, King's College, Cambridge, 8 August 1564.

BOOKS: *Floures for Latine Spekynge Selected and Gathered Oute of Terence*, Latin textbook, compiled, with English translations, by Udall (London: Printed by Thomas Berthelet, 1534);

Apophthegmes, That Is to Saie, Prompte, Quicke, Wittie Saiynges. First Gathered by Erasmus, translated by Udall (London: Printed by Richard Grafton, 1542);

The First Tome or Volume of the Paraphrase of Erasmus vpon the Newe Testamente, translated by Udall, Princess Mary Tudor (with the help of Francis Malet), and Thomas Key; edited by Udall (London: Printed by E. Whitchurche, 1548);

A Discourse or Traictise of Petur Martyr Vermill a Florētine, Wherein He Declared His Iudgemente Concernynge the Sacrament of the Lordes Supper, translated by Udall (London: Printed by R. Stoughton [E. Whitchurche] for N. Udall, 1550);

Compendiosa Totius Anatomie Delineatio, by Thomas Geminus, translated by Udall (London: Printed by N. Hyll for T. Geminus, 1553);

A New Enterlude Called Thersytes, attributed to

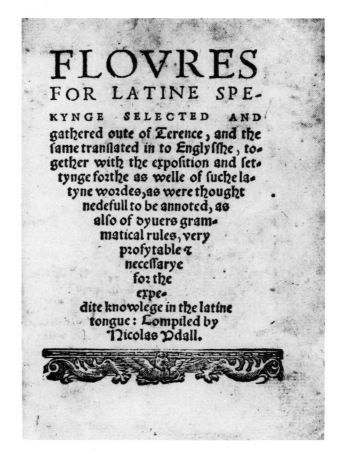

Title page for the 1534 octavo edition of Udall's influential Latin textbook (Henry E. Huntington Library and Art Gallery)

Udall (London: Printed by J. Tysdale, 1562?);

A New Enterlued for Chyldren to Playe, Named Jacke Jugeler, attributed to Udall (London: Printed by William Copland, 1562?);

Ralph Roister Doister (London: Printed by H. Denham for Thomas Hackett?, 1566?);

A Newe Mery and Wittie Comedie or Enterlude, Newely Imprinted, Treating vpon the Historie of Jacob and Esau (London: Printed by Henry Bynneman, 1568).

Editions: *Respublica*, attributed to Udall, edited

by W. W. Greg, Early English Text Society, Publication no. 226 (London: Oxford University Press, 1952);

Jacob and Esau, attributed to Udall, edited by John Crow and F. P. Wilson (London: Malone Society, 1956);

Thersites, attributed to Udall, in *Three Tudor Classical Interludes,* edited by Marie Axton (Woodbridge, U.K.: D. S. Brewer, 1982), pp. 37-63;

Ralph Roister Doister, in *Four Tudor Comedies,* edited by William Tydeman (New York & Harmondsworth: Penguin, 1984), pp. 95-205;

Jacke Jugeler, anonymous, in *Four Tudor Comedies,* pp. 43-94.

OTHER: "Verses and dities made at the coronation of Queen Anne [Boleyn]," by Udall and John Leland, in *The Progresses, and Public Processions of Queen Elizabeth,* by John Nichols, volume 1 (London: Privately printed, 1788), pp. i-xx.

An Oxford-trained classical scholar, Nicholas Udall belongs to the second generation of English humanists. His works consistently reflect his trust in English as a language rich and flexible enough to transmit the subtleties of the classics and truth of the Bible to a modern reader. Although his fame in his own century rested securely on sensitive and accurate translations of Terence and Erasmus, he is known today chiefly as the "father of English comedy." Typical of his century, Udall acknowledged his hand in his Latin translations, writing prefaces for them and carefully superintending their publication; but his surviving plays were printed posthumously and anonymously. It is therefore perhaps inevitable that the playwright whose one legitimate comedy, *Ralph Roister Doister,* brought the Roman five-act structure to the English stage should in the twentieth century have accumulated a little family of unattributed "classical" interludes. John Bale, writing in 1557, praised Udall's *"Comœdias plures"* but did not name them. Udall's authorship of *Ralph Roister Doister* was attested by his pupil Thomas Wilson, fixing its likely date of composition at 1552. In the third edition of his *The Rule of Reason* (1553) Wilson, who was later principal secretary to Elizabeth I, praised his former teacher as a master of double meanings and quoted the verse letter from *Ralph Roister Doister,* which may be read, according to its punctuation or its line endings, either as an amorous epistle or a gross insult (an innovation Shakespeare may have imitated in his prologue to "Pyramus and Thisbe" in *A Midsummer Night's Dream*). Those who believe Udall to be author of the interlude *Thersites,* the Plautine imitation *Jack Juggler,* the five-act comedy *Jacob and Esau,* and the five-act morality *Respublica* point to an evident mastery of native as well as classical comic forms and confirm Bale's judgment of Udall's importance to English literature. He stands with John Heywood, John Skelton, and Sir David Lyndsay.

Southampton was his birthplace. Conflicting information about his age comes from the records of his schooling at Winchester and Corpus Christi College, Oxford, but he is believed to have been born sometime in December 1504. He entered Oxford as an undergraduate in 1520, received his B.A. on 30 May 1524, and was elected a full fellow of his college in 1526. Studying first under Thomas Lupset and Vivés, he later became a lecturer in logic and in Greek. The first hint of his Protestantism came in 1528 (according to John Foxe) when Udall was named as one of the Oxford scholars receiving illicit books, which included Tyndale's English translation of the New Testament. He left Oxford in 1529. His first surviving entertainment, written in collaboration with the antiquary John Leland (31 May 1533), celebrates that watershed of the English Reformation, the coronation of Anne Boleyn, with pageants about Apollo and the Muses, St. Anne, the Three Graces, and the Judgment of Paris.

The next year, 1534, marked a turning point in Udall's career. He published the text which influenced school Latin for the rest of the century, teaching its grammar through excerpts from three Terentian comedies. *Flowers for Latin Speaking* is based upon *Flosculi,* the 1530 collection by Grapheus, and is amplified by Udall's own wide scholarship. Oxford University opposed Udall's popularization of Terence, stipulating in the supplication for the master's degree which Udall received in 1534 that he translate no more Latin books into English. The seeds had been released, however, and *Flowers for Latin Speaking* went into eight more editions during the Tudor period. From this textbook and from Udall's own English comedies the influence of the Roman dramatist passed into the language and structure of Tudor drama. Udall's appointment as headmaster of Eton followed in the same year. He continued to be active in theatricals at Eton and at Court, as is attested by a payment made on 2 February 1538 by Thomas Cromwell to Udall "scolem[aster] of Eton . . . for playing before him." The considerable sum of £5 (Lord Cobham's players received 20 shillings in the same season) suggests an elaborate show, more appropriate to Udall's lost *Ezechias* (later performed before Elizabeth I in 1564 at King's College) than to the often-attributed interlude *Thersites* (whose epilogue does, nevertheless, record a performance between 12 and 22 October 1537).

Udall left Eton in March 1541 under a cloud of disgrace, for what his biographers have explained variously as "burglary" or "buggery." He was briefly imprisoned and tried by the Privy Council. Details of his defense have not been recovered but in a letter to his patron Sir Thomas Wriothesley, Udall acknowledged some culpability in his personal conduct. The indictment charged him with disposal of Eton chapel ornaments, which suggests that he may have sympathized with the policy of removing church images, at a time when Henry VIII backed a more conservative position. The charge is close in time to the reforming Cromwell's own fall from favor. Whatever interpretation one puts upon these shadowy events, Udall's reputation as a scholar and translator did not ultimately suffer. His translation of Erasmus's *Apophthegmes* (published in September 1542) and his patronage by the sympathetic Queen Catherine Parr show him at the height of his powers by 1543. The Queen chose Udall to translate the Book of Luke in Erasmus's *Paraphrase of the New Testament;* the first volume (1548) was largely Udall's work although Thomas Key is credited with Mark and Princess Mary began translating John, assisted by her chaplain.

Under Edward VI Udall is credited with a reply to insurgents of Cornwall and Devon who objected to the reformed prayer book of 1549. The year 1550 saw the publication of Udall's translation of a work which was strongly to influence the doctrine of the Communion finally acceptable to the Edwardian and Elizabethan church: Peter Martyr Vermigli's *Discourse . . . concerning the Sacrament of Our Lord's Supper.* Udall's commitment to other branches of the New Learning is apparent in his 1553 translation of Thomas Geminus's medical treatise (1545), an adaptation of two continental works by Vesalius and Vicary. The book, complete with copperplate engravings, is a landmark in English medical and printing history. By age forty-eight he had published a series of books which influenced the classical education, not only of his better-known pupils—Thomas Tus-

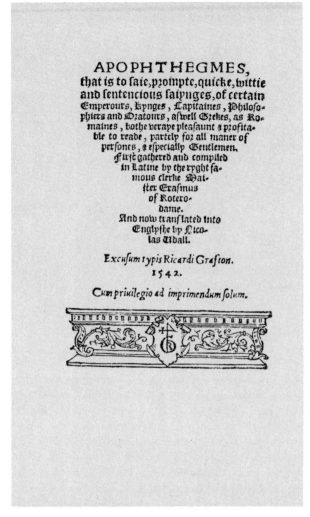

Title page for the 1542 octavo edition of Udall's first translation of a work by Erasmus (Bodleian Library, Oxford)

ser, Richard Mulcaster, Thomas Wilson, and John Parkhurst (Bishop of Norwich)—but generations of English schoolchildren. His books were equally important to the Protestant cause. He was rewarded in the last year of Edward's reign with the Rectorship of Calbourn (Isle of Wight). Together with the canonry of St. George's Chapel, Windsor (which had come to him in 1551), this appointment would have brought an end to financial worry. But his faith lost him those benefices, though not the friendship of Mary Tudor. During her reign he may have been instrumental in founding Westminster School; he was appointed headmaster of St. Peter's Grammar School, Westminster, on 16 December 1555. He died a year later and was buried at St. Margaret's, Westminster, on 23 December 1556.

All the printed interludes attributed to Udall survive in Elizabethan editions. Of these, *Thersites*, printed circa 1562, was probably written in the late 1530s, a plausible period too for Udall's lost play *Ezechias*. *Jacob and Esau* with its insistence on election and reprobation is Calvinistic in tone and has often been cited as Edwardian in its outspoken Protestantism. It was, however, registered for posthumous publication in 1557, the last year of Mary's reign. One printed sheet from this edition was found by Paul Morgan in 1967 at New College, Oxford, but no complete copy is extant.

The most serious attempts to construct and to date a Udall canon have focused on *Ralph Roister Doister*, *Jack Juggler*, and *Respublica*. Udall's attitude to the Marian counterreformation is crucial to any such attempt and has been variously represented. Was he apostate or mole? There is no critical consensus. Udall's prefaces to his translations show him to have been sympathetic to a Bible and prayer book in English and to a reduction in the number of sacraments, all policies of the boy king, Edward VI. Nevertheless the revels accounts for the Christmas season 1553-1554 show that Udall presented "certen plaies . . . Dialogues and Enterludes" for the Catholic Queen Mary. W. W. Greg, in his edition of *Respublica*, has made a good case for Udall's authorship of this dramatic allegory; the manuscript play is dated 1553 and was probably performed within a year of that date. *Respublica* heralds the new reign while analyzing the misgovernment of the previous one. Udall's authorship has also been argued by J. E. Bernard and Leicester Bradner on the rather sketchy evidence of metrical tests showing a predominance of tetrameter couplets (the staple of early Tudor drama). Opinions vary about how far Udall compromised his beliefs. The most favorable interpretation of *Respublica* points to the author's analysis of mistaken financial rather than religious policies during the reign of Edward VI. By this interpretation Udall appears clearly loyal to the new Catholic Queen, critical of royal counselors, and prudently silent on the question of religious belief. *Jack Juggler* (printed about 1562), an interlude based on Plautus's *Amphitruo*, provides a witty paradigm (with its comedy of impersonation and consequent mistaken identities) for a crisis of identity common to those who lived through the reversals of Henrican, Edwardian, and Marian religious belief. Dating its composition is consequently difficult and is further complicated by critics, such as David M. Bevington, who believe the bitter epilogue to be a later Elizabethan addition.

Udall's authorship of *Ralph Roister Doister* is securely established although the dates of composition and performance are still debatable. According to William L. Edgerton the first performance occurred at Windsor in September 1552 during a visit of the ailing Edward VI. Udall, as canon, was resident there in the summer of 1552. Here he would have had a cast of well-trained choristers for the song-filled comedy. Further support for composition in the year 1552 comes from T. W. Baldwin, who shows that Udall's comedy is the first in English to be shaped with five acts according to the Terentian design of *protasis*, *epitasis*, and *catastrophe*. An English translation of Terence's *Andria*, in five acts, was printed in London in 1530. Baldwin, however, argues that the theoretical and analytical materials necessary for a formal vernacular experiment were available for the first time in the Roigny folio edition of Terence's works printed in Paris in 1552. Moreover, in that same year in Paris the first regular French five-act comedy appeared. Udall's work in 1552 was thus avant-garde, experimental theater. There had, indeed, been five-act plays by John Bale in English and in Latin by Nicholas Grimald. But Bale's *Three Laws*, printed circa 1548, is divided into acts according to a didactic plan by which each act is devoted to its own subject matter: act one, divine law; act two, natural law corrupted; and so on. Udall was consciously innovative, constructing in English a continuous classical action. Adapting the subplot of Terence's *Eunuchus*, Udall devotes two acts to the protasis or exposition: the boaster Ralph, egged on by the parasite-vice, Merrygreek, desires the widow Christian Custance, who, recently engaged to the merchant Gawyne Goodlucke, will admit no suit. In act two Ralph and Merrygreek overcome the widow's servants through comic byplay with Custance's old nurse Mumblecrust, and the protasis ends with their successful delivery of the braggart's love letter. The epitasis or complication begins in act three and continues through act four. In act three Ralph's love pangs are burlesqued in a mock funeral as Merrygreek intones the Latin tropes. The wooer's mercenary motives are then revealed through his mispunctuated letter, read aloud to the heroine by Merrygreek in III.iv:

> Sweete mistress where as I love you nothing at all,
> Regarding your substance and richesse chiefe of all,
> For your personage, beautie, demeanour and wit,
> I commende me unto you never a whit.

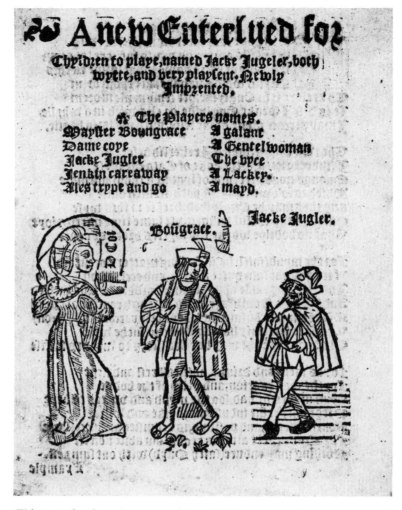

Title page for the unique copy of the 1565(?) quarto edition of an interlude that has often been attributed to Udall (Henry E. Huntington Library and Art Gallery)

Act four introduces Gawyne's best friend, who arrives and, hearing Ralph's boasts, assumes Custance's infidelity. Merrygreek (like Sir Toby Belch in Shakespeare's *Twelfth Night*) convinces Ralph that he must finally win Custance by a display of martial valor. Helmeted in an old pot, the roister besieges the heroine's house; Custance and her maids defend themselves vigorously. Act five, the catastrophe, sees the arrival of Gawyne, his accusation of Custance, her vindication through the testimony of true friends, and the reconciliation of all parties. The classicism (echoes of Terence and of boasting by Pyrgopolinices from Plautus's *Miles Gloriousus*) is lightened by the addition of songs and by vernacular literary references and recollections: Custance, the long-suffering heroine of Chaucer's *Man of Law's Tale;* Sir Thopas, Chaucer's mock-heroic knight; Hen-

ry Medwall's late-fifteenth-century interlude *Fulgens and Lucres* (in which a servant destroys his master's love suit by his garbled transmission of messages). The blend of these traditional elements results in a play of remarkable originality.

The word *roister* seems to have entered the English language about the time Udall wrote the play. Thersites, in the earlier interlude attributed to Udall, fits such a description, but he is simply called a "boaster." The word *roister* may derive from the French *rustre; Le Rustre* is a character in *Le mistère du Prodigue* (1504). The cowardly braggart turned wooer in Udall's five-act comedy seems to have been well-enough known as a type in that Gabriel Harvey and Thomas Nashe use his name as a term of abuse in their slanging correspondence forty years after *Ralph Roister Doister* was written; they even coined *roister-doisterdome,* *roister doisterly* vanity, and *roister doistering* jests.

Ralph Roister Doister was revived at University College, London, on 27 May 1920 and enjoyed a short flurry of performances in the next decade culminating in a successful short run at the Malvern Festival with Ralph Richardson as the parasite-vice, Merrygreek. The play's theatrical resilience has been demonstrated more recently by productions in 1964 at Bristol (where it ran in repertory with *Respublica)* and in 1986 at the Edinburgh Festival.

If the canon of five plays—so different in form—were to be firmly established, Udall's claim to critical attention would be equal to that of John Heywood and greater than that of Medwall, whose experiments with classical story remained in native interlude. Udall's imaginative adaptation of classical forms underpins the work of Lyly and Shakespeare, and his experiments with language deserve more critical attention than they have hitherto received.

Udall's life and work have been most thoughtfully evaluated by William Edgerton. W. W. Greg's introduction to *Respublica* is the best example of balanced argument in favor of Udall's authorship of an anonymous work. David M. Bevington places Udall in the native traditions of dramaturgy and sixteenth-century politics, while Joel B. Altman offers a rhetorical analysis of *Ralph Roister Doister.* John N. King, while ignoring the problem of *Respublica,* gives a powerful assessment of Udall as penman of Edwardian reform; he sees *Ralph Roister Doister* as a turning of the homiletic attacks of Hugh Latimer and Thomas Cranmer into courtly comedy, and a transformation of Custance, Chaucer's passive Roman heroine, into an English woman fit for the struggle to establish the Protestant ideal of married love as the best basis for a Christian commonwealth. There remain important interpretative disagreements about the political and religious implications of Udall's dramatic works, but it is clear that he had a spark of genius for reformation in both senses.

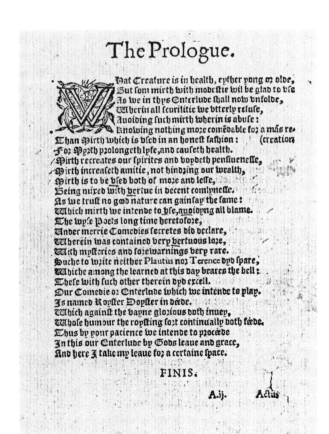

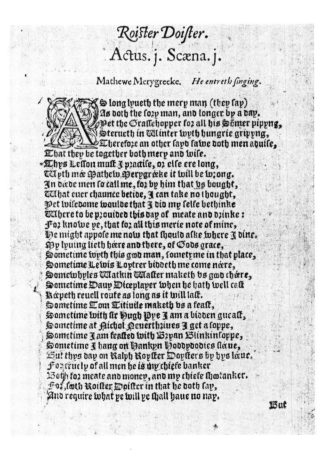

The first surviving pages from the unique copy of the 1566(?) quarto edition of the play that earned Udall the title "father of English Comedy" (Eton College Library)

Bibliography:

Phillip Dust and William D. Wolf, "Recent Studies in Early Tudor drama: *Gorboduc, Ralph Roister Doister, Gammer Gurton's Needle* and *Cambises,*" *English Literary Renaissance,* 8 (1978): 107-119.

References:

Joel B. Altman, *The Tudor Play of Mind* (Berkeley: University of California Press, 1978), pp. 149-151;

T. W. Baldwin, *Shakspere's Five-Act Structure* (Urbana: University of Illinois Press, 1963), pp. 375-401;

J. E. Bernard, *Prosody of the Tudor Interlude* (New Haven: Yale University Press, 1939), pp. 78-80, 93-94, 112-113, 125-126, 215-216;

David M. Bevington, *From Mankind to Marlowe* (Cambridge: Harvard University Press, 1962), pp. 28, 30-33;

Bevington, *Tudor Drama and Politics* (Cambridge: Harvard University Press, 1968), pp. 109-126;

David W. Blewitt, "Records of Drama at Winchester and Eton 1397-1576," *Theatre Notebook,* 38, no. 2 (1984): 88-95; 38, no. 3 (1984): 135-145;

Leicester Bradner, "A Test for Udall's Authorship," *Modern Language Notes,* 42 (June 1927): 378-380;

William L. Edgerton, *Nicholas Udall* (New York: Twayne, 1966);

John N. King, *English Reformation Literature* (Princeton: Princeton University Press, 1982), pp. 130-131, 301-309;

Paul Morgan, "Fragments of three lost works from the Stationers' Registers recently found in bindings in college libraries," *Bodleian Library Record,* 7 (1969): 300-302, 304;

G. Scheurweghs, Introduction to *Nicholas Udall's Roister Doister,* edited by Scheurweghs (Louvain: Librairie Universitaire, C. Uystpruyst, 1939), pp. xi-lxxix;

Robert F. Willson, Jr., *Their Form Confounded* (The Hague: Mouton, 1975), pp. 1-26;

F. P. Wilson, *The English Drama 1485-1585* (Oxford: Oxford University Press, 1969), pp. 90, 93-95, 103-109, 226-227.

Papers:

The Harry Ransom Humanities Research Center at the University of Texas, Austin, holds the manuscript of *Respublica.* The British Library has Udall's autograph letter to Sir Thomas Wriothesley (Cotton MS Titus B. VIII, fols. 386-388), his autograph Latin and English verses made at the Coronation of Queen Anne (Royal MS 18.A. LXIV fols. 1-16), and an answer to the articles of the commoners of Devonsheir and Cornewall (Royal MS 18.B. XI fols. 3-40). A manuscript transcription of Ralph Roister Doister's letter from the 1553 edition of Wilson's *Rule of Reason* is at the Bodleian Library, Oxford (Rawlinson MS poet. 26, fol. 16ᵛ).

Arden of Faversham

Robert F. Fleissner
Central State University, Ohio

PRODUCTION: London, unknown theater, circa 1587-1592.

FIRST PUBLICATION: *The Lamentable and True Tragedie of M. Arden of Feversham* (London: Printed by E. Allde for E. White, 1592).

Editions: *Arden of Faversham,* in *Three Elizabethan Domestic Tragedies,* edited by Keith Sturgess (Baltimore: Penguin, 1969), pp. 55-148;
The Lamentable and True Tragedy of M. Arden of Feversham 1592 (Menston: Scolar Press, 1971);
The Tragedy of Master Arden of Faversham, edited by M. L. Wine, The Revels Plays (London: Methuen, 1973);
Arden of Faversham, edited by Martin White, New Mermaids (New York: Norton, 1982).

Called a *"Lamentable and True Tragedie"* when it was published anonymously in 1592, *Arden of Faversham* is a well-developed early Elizabethan melodrama and realistic satire which has earned the title of the first English domestic tragedy. Composed possibly as early as 1587, it has gained the status of the best of the Shakespearean apocryphal plays. Relatively few scholars today consider the Stratford genius as the probable author, but some continue to present internal evidence on behalf of Shakespeare's authorship of the play.

Concerned with a cunning wife, Mistress Arden, who, because of her love for Mosby, hires assassins, Shakebag and Black Will, to do away with her husband, it mixes Senecan horror with comical effects. For example, the assassins are thwarted five times before they succeed at killing Arden while he plays backgammon. It has been suggested that the plot is related to the Clytemnestra-Agamemnon story, but the play seems closer to domestic concerns than foreign influence, Alice Arden–a prototype of Lady Macbeth in her cold-blooded instigation of murder–being a triumph in realistic portraiture. The popularity of the play, written some forty years after the actual historical events on which it

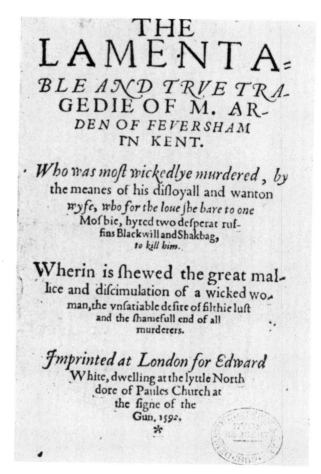

Title page for the 1592 quarto edition of the play that has been called the first English domestic tragedy (Victoria and Albert Museum)

is based, relates to its being a kind of early detective mystery. Thomas Arden was murdered in 1551, the fourth year of Edward VI's reign and a period of great social unrest. Taking advantage of the dissolution of English monasteries in 1538 and the subsequent dispersal of church property, Arden became wealthy and the leading citizen of Faversham through his acquisition of lands that had been held by Faversham Abbey, in effect taking the property from the lower classes. The epilogue, spoken by Arden's friend Franklin, does not have the moral meaning that would be ex-

A modern photograph of Thomas Arden's house in Faversham

pected from the title page, for it leaves the reader with the feeling that Arden has gotten his comeuppance because he failed to treat the lower classes right. (His villainy, however, is much more pronounced in the chief source, Holinshed's *Chronicles*.) As Martin White states, "The playwright is concerned to show that in both public and private life–though their objectives may be different–men and women are driven to commit immoral acts by similar covetous urges, and the structure of the play is designed to establish the affinity between *all* these actions." The play has also been credited for its treatment of psychology as well as social issues. A central concern is whether the emphasis is truly on Master Arden, as the title implies, or his wife, Mistress Alice, who is the subject of a later anonymous ballad, *The Complaint and Lamentation of Mistresse Arden of Feversham in Kent* (1633?).

Ascription to Shakespeare is usually traced to Edward Jacob's 1770 edition of the play and Ludwig Tieck's German translation. Goethe accepted this attribution as did several later critics. In his *Internal Evidence and Elizabethan Dramatic Authorship* (1966) Samuel Schoenbaum, a noted au-

thority, suggested that "conjecturists appear to have given up" their attempts to attribute the play to Shakespeare, but he neglected MacDonald P. Jackson's Oxford B.Litt. thesis (1963), which presents an extensive case for Shakespeare's authorship. More recently M. L. Wine's Revels edition (1973) has resuscitated interest, especially after his study of the problem was prominently published on the front page of the *Shakespeare Newsletter*. Wine's work demonstrates that the popular ascription to Thomas Kyd can no longer be countenanced. Numerous parallels to the play have been found in the works of Christopher Marlowe, but few Marlovians now entertain his possible authorship, alone or with either Shakespeare or Kyd (though Marlowe would have been more likely to have worked with Kyd if there was a collaboration). Parallels to *Arden of Faversham* have been found in *Macbeth*, and many more can be detected in Shakespeare's earlier plays. Accepting the assumption that the extant text of the play is based on the reports of an actor or scribe and hence presumably inferior, Wine has suggested that parallels with other authors are automatically in doubt; however, this memorial reconstruction theory–advanced by Peter Alexander and others–is itself in doubt among some scholars today. Yet in 1945 W. W. Greg presented external evidence–which he called "plausible at least if not conclusive"–that *Arden of Faversham* was attributed to Shakespeare before 1770. Greg has cogently argued that Edward Archer's 1656 catalogue of printed plays incorrectly ascribes the play because of a printing-house error and that Archer intended to list Shakespeare as the play's author. Archer is not always trustworthy, but the negative evidence that *Arden of Faversham* is not included in the early folio editions of Shakespeare's works means little, if the drama was a collaboration, because Shakespeare's early editors are known to have omitted at least two plays that Shakespeare wrote with another dramatist. Nowadays, critics have preferred to think that *Arden of Faversham* was written by a single author. However, the possibility remains that the young Shakespeare, who is believed to have joined the Queen's Men sometime between 1587 and 1592, may have had a hand in the play. Common sense suggests that a play involving possibly an apprentice hand among others was likely to have been published anonymously, especially if it was a so-called actors' play (that is, an actors' "showcase"). Because of Shakespeare's early association with the Queen's Men, he may have at least acted in it. (One of its leading rogues, Black Will, is recalled by name in *The True Tragedie of Richard III*, a play in the repertory of the Queen's

Men and one in which Shakespeare could also have had a hand, part of its title–"*With a lamentable ende of Shore's wife, an example for all wicked women*"–harking back to Mistress Arden's villainy.)

Although modern critics such as Kenneth Muir have raised a question as to whether the style of *Arden of Faversham* is at all Shakespearean, certainly the penchant also for punning and lowlife, sometimes expressed in a grandiose manner, looks ahead to works such as *Macbeth* and the Falstaff dramas. The rascal Shakebag's name is strikingly linked with Will's throughout. The name Shakebag is like Falstaff, that is, if the bag shakes like a spear, so the staff falls. Although the historical name for Shakebag was Loosebag, the shift was already made in the play's main source, Holinshed (albeit only once). Shakebag's role is considerably enlarged in the play, but Will is even more dominant.

The argument over the play's authorship continues. Alexander Leggatt's contribution in *Shakespeare Survey* is a valuable treatment with new insights, and S. F. X. Dean (pen name of Francis Smith) has composed a mystery novel, *It Can't Be My Grave* (1983), which argues that it was written by a woman.

In addition to Holinshed, another notable source has been shown to be Chaucer; for example, some of the names are reverberations of ones not only in Holinshed but in the *Canterbury Tales* (Franklin, Clark), the play taking place on the pilgrimage route. The tragedy has inspired

Frontispiece for a 1633 quarto edition of Arden of Faversham *showing the murder of Arden at the backgammon table (British Library)*

later dramas such as the anonymous play *A Warning for Fair Women* (published in 1599), and its productions have been well received, notably a German version called *Arden Muss Sterben* and the recent one by Terry Hands for the Royal Shakespeare Company (1982).

References:

Percy Allen, "*Arden of Feversham* and *Macbeth*," in his *Shakespeare, Jonson, and Wilkins as Borrowers: A Study in Elizabethan Dramatic Origins and Imitations* (London: Palmer, 1928);

Max Bluestone, "The Imagery of Tragic Melodrama in *Arden of Feversham*," *Drama Survey*, 5 (1966): 171-181; republished in *Shakespeare's Contemporaries: Modern Studies in English Renaissance Drama*, edited by Bluestone and N. C. Rabkin (Englewood Cliffs, N.J.: Prentice-Hall, 1970), pp. 173-183;

A. H. Bullen, Introduction to *Arden of Feversham, a Tragedy: Reprinted from the Edition of 1592*, edited by Bullen (London: Jarvis, 1887);

Raymond Chapman, "*Arden of Faversham*: Its Interest Today," *English*, 11 (1956): 15-17;

Henry Collyer, *A Short Account of Lord Cheyne, Lord Shorland, and Mr. Thomas Arden* (Canterbury: Privately printed, 1739);

Hardin Craig, *The Literature of the English Renaissance, 1485-1660* (New York: Collier, 1962);

C. E. Donne, *An Essay on the Tragedy of "Arden of Feversham"* (London: Russell Smith, 1873);

R. F. Fleissner, "'The Secret'st Man of Blood': Foreshadowings of *Macbeth* in *Arden of Feversham*," *University of Dayton Review*, Proceedings of the 1978 Ohio Shakespeare Conference, 14 (Winter 1979/1980): 7-13;

W. W. Greg, "Shakespeare and *Arden of Feversham*," *Review of English Studies*, 21 (April 1945): 134-136;

Anita Holt, "*Arden of Feversham*: A Study of the Play First Published in 1592," *Faversham Papers*, no. 7 (1970);

A. F. Hopkinson, ed., *Arden of Feversham* (London: Sims, 1898);

Charles Knight, Introduction to *Arden of Faversham*, in volume 8 of *The Pictorial Edition of the Works of Shakespeare*, 8 volumes, edited by Knight (London: C. Knight, 1839-1843);

Alexander Leggatt, "*Arden of Faversham*," *Shakespeare Survey*, 36 (1983): 121-133;

Michael T. Marsden, "The Otherworld of *Arden of Feversham*," *Southern Folklore Quarterly*, 36 (March 1972): 36-42;

Ian and Heather Dubrow Ousby, "Art and Language in *Arden of Faversham*," *Durham University Journal*, 37 (1976): 47-54;

Karl Warnke and Ludwig Proescholdt, Introduction to *Arden of Feversham*, edited by Warnke and Proescholdt (Halle: Niemeyer, 1888);

Karl P. Wentersdorf, "The 'Fence of Trouble' Crux in *Arden of Feversham*," *Notes and Queries*, new series 4 (April 1957): 160-161;

Sarah Youngblood, "Theme and Imagery in *Arden of Feversham*," *Studies in English Literature*, 3 (Spring 1963): 207-218.

Gammer Gurton's Needle

Stanley J. Kozikowski
Bryant College

PRODUCTION: Christ's College, Cambridge, 1559-1560?.

FIRST PUBLICATION: *A Ryght Pithy, Pleasaunt and Merie Comedie: Intytuled Gammer Gurtons Nedle*, attributed to William Stevenson (London: Printed by T. Colwell, 1575).

Edition: *Gammer Gurton's Needle*, in *Representative English Comedies*, volume 1, edited by Charles Mills Gayley (New York: Macmillan, 1903).

Gammer Gurton's Needle is regarded as one of the first regular comedies of the English stage. Combining formal elements of classical comedy with raucous and farcical ingredients of English country life, the play, very likely written by an academician interested in church matters, proves to be artfully funny, even ingenious. The play's characters, its setting, its tone, and its allusions are English; but its dramatic structure, its conventions of plot, and its observance of the classical "unities" of time, place, and action stamp it as unmistakably classical in form. The play's assimilation of rowdy domestic comedy with its fine classical restraint and order creates a special comic effect beyond the obvious humor of its farce and the aesthetic pleasure of its formal comedy.

The play's authorship has been attributed, circumstantially, to William Stevenson, who was a fellow and playwright at Christ's College, Cambridge University, during 1551-1554 and 1559-1561. The play's only extant early edition, which is dated 1575, makes reference to its having been "Played on Stage, not longe ago in Christes Colledge in Cambridge" and that it was "Made by Mr. S. Mr. of Art." The play, very likely however, was written a number of years previously and is no doubt substantially the same play identified as "Dyccon of Bedlam,&c," which was licensed in 1563. An entry in the bursar's books of Christ's College, moreover, makes reference to a sum "Spent at Mr. Stevenson's plaie, 5s." This entry, dated 1559-1560, coincides with

a period of Stevenson's fellowship; and it renders all the more probable the case for Stevenson's authorship.

The biography of William Stevenson is much less an account of a man of the theater than a man of the church. He was born at Hunwick in Durham, matriculated at Cambridge as a sizar in November 1546, received his B.A. in 1550, M.A. in 1553, and B.D. in 1560. He was ordained a deacon in London in 1552, appointed prebendary of Durham in January of 1561, and died in 1575. Whether or not Stevenson wrote the play, and there is some evidence that he did, there are clear indications in *Gammer Gurton's Needle* of the kind of comedy which has more depth and range than farce–a type of comedy that only a university-trained wit, sensitive to issues concerning the Anglican church, could have written. Although the play's farcical plot and characters dominate with their crude humor, other comic purposes appear to be at hand.

Gammer Gurton's Needle humorously portrays the dailiness of sixteenth-century English rustic life, focusing initially upon the petty anxieties, jealousies, and mean quarrels of Gammer Gurton, the countrywoman who is the play's main character; Hodge, Gammer Gurton's bungling handyman; Dame Chat, a village gossip of sorts; Tib, Gurton's maid; Doctor Rat, the village curate; and Master Bailiff, the presiding village official. Perhaps the most interesting character of the play, whose machinations generate its plot and whose name was the play's early title, is Diccon of Bedlam. Diccon, a harebrained but foxlike fellow, has arrived upon the scene, having traveled, as he reports, "Many a myle . . . diuers and sundry waies" and having been provided for at "many a good mans house." Diccon connives against virtually everyone else in the play and seemingly represents a personification of Mischief. Scholars have found in Diccon, particularly in the theatrical delight with intrigue that he so readily exhibits, the quality of the Vice figure popularized earlier in English morality drama. He certainly helps us to appreciate an unusually interesting contrast in characterization which this play establishes. The townfolk, including the learned Doctor Rat, who is "esteemed full wyse," plod through their ludicrous ways all too willingly; while Diccon, the breezy outsider and shrewd conniver, ranges about freely and playfully. In several wonderful instances, Diccon amusingly soliloquizes, appearing to delight more in sharing his smugness with the audience than in manipulating his promised intrigues. He demonstrates an exuberant affection for his own plottings, which in their management parallel the well-organized plot of the play itself. Diccon's keen, aggressive comedy contrasts sharply with the dull musings, superstitions, and gullibilities of the townfolk, whose pressing concerns are typified by their devotion to Tom Tankard's cow, a mischievous cat, Tom Simpson's maid, Hob Filcher's ale, Dame Chat's poultry, and a lost needle.

The plot of the play is admirably simple: Gammer Gurton, while mending Hodge's breeches, looses her needle. The townspeople, Hodge in particular, are in an uproar over the matter, when Diccon arrives on the scene. While they comically thrash about in search of the needle, Diccon gets Hodge to swear—on Diccon's breeches—an oath of fealty to him. That done, he frightens Hodge away with a comic prank, as he pretends to conjure up the devil. Diccon then moves to set Gammer Gurton and Dame Chat against each other; and he pulls the greatest prank against Doctor Rat, the poor curate, whose attempt to remedy things between the two village ladies winds up in rowdy farce. Confusion is resolved when Master Bailiff appears and proceeds to pass judgment upon the villagers, singling out Diccon for special attention. Diccon, in a scenic reversal, is himself now required to swear upon Hodge's breeches that he will make amends to Gammer Gurton, Dame Chat, and Doctor Rat. He proceeds to smack Hodge's breech and dislodges the lost needle, much to Hodge's immediately very painful, but eventually very pleasurable, surprise. The play thus ends on this triumphant note, with its plot sewed up by the restoration of the all-precious needle.

There is evidence, whether or not Stevenson did in fact write the play, that a churchman-author's hand lies at the core of *Gammer Gurton's Needle*. Immediately with the prologue, instances of churchly humor appear: Dame Chat, we are told, knows no more of the lost needle "Than knoeth Tom, our clarke, what the priest saith at masse." This mild poke at the layman who led in

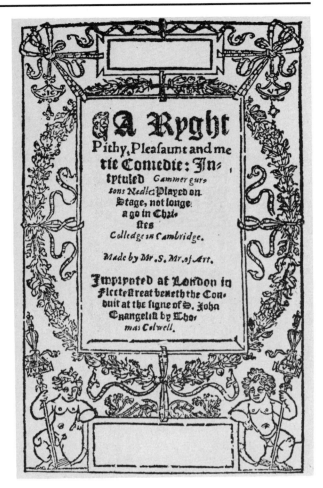

Title page for the 1575 quarto edition of the comedy that has been circumstantially attributed to William Stevenson, a fellow at Christ's Church College, Cambridge, in 1551-1554 and 1559-1561 (Anderson Galleries, sale number 1375, 2-3 December 1918)

reading the responses helps set the play's comic tone. No doubt much of the thrust of the play's comedy is directed against the incompetence, unruliness, and scandal which concerned the Anglican church with regard to the ministry, especially in the country. Doctor Rat's failure to resolve a country squabble is played off against Master Bailiff's administrative expertise. Rat's parishioners, likewise, carry on religious customs and traditions, exaggerated for comic effect, from pre-Elizabethan Catholicism, which were clearly targeted during the Reformation. Such articles of religious belief as Hodge's superstitions, the villagers' extraordinary invocations of saints and their elaborate blessings of themselves and others, and their curious notion that a "blessing" is equally a sign of good will or a punch to the head—all of these—are made fun of, particularly by Diccon.

Even Gammer Gurton is not above the special barb of such satire in that she appears to have nothing of Queen Elizabeth's famous (and furious) objections to lighting candles in church; for she promises one to God and another to Saint Anne (provided, of course, that her needle is found). Undoubtedly the play was written from the perspective of someone who was sympathetic to the emerging Church of England. Finally, although the author no doubt shared a churchman's irritation with unseemly references to the divine in the curses and oaths of railers, he must also have appreciated the comic value of the villagers' unpretentious, imaginative exclamations as they proceed with the business of dealing with life's daily exasperations and discomforts. As a result, a number of exceptionally funny and clever oaths issue from the mouths of the characters in *Gammer Gurton's Needle.*

Exuberant in wit and in will, Diccon of Bedlam is the primary vehicle for releasing some of the play's sharpest ecclesiastical humor; and Diccon delivers his most telling gibes in the zany oath-swearing rituals with Hodge, which are at the very core of the play. Once he has persuaded Hodge that he must swear an oath, Diccon asks the rustic if he has a Bible. When Hodge replies that he does not, Diccon observes, "Then needes must force us both,/Upon my breech to lay thine hand, and there to take thine oathe." The oath-swearing on the breeches is repeated in the final act at the suggestion of Master Bailiff, who assumes the deus ex machina role after the curate's incompetence is evident. But most important, the author's comic ingenuity is evident when we regard both oath swearings as parodies upon the "Breeches Bible" or the Geneva Bible of 1560. The "Breeches Bible" became known as such because of its translation of Genesis 3:7, which read that Adam and Eve "knewe that they were naked, and they sewed figtree leaues together, and made them selues breeches."

The thrust of the comic satire in these scenes, although certainly aimed at the unfortunate translation, was probably also directed at the reception given to the "Breeches Bible," which, although never authorized for church use, remained the most popular English Bible for some fifty years. No doubt there was also humor found in the ridicule of a countryman, very likely a Catholic, whose use for a holy book, as some might have it, was either very limited or nonexistent. The parody appears even more relevant when we learn that the "Breeches Bible," unlike most of its predecessors, was published in quartos, much handier and cheaper than folio translations, but especially that it was the first English Bible to have been printed in roman type. Its handy comprehensiveness thus made it the first household Bible of the English people. Therefore, Diccon's question of Hodge, "Hast no booke?," was not entirely farfetched; it coincided with the publication of the first English common Bible.

Hence, although most amusing as farce, *Gammer Gurton's Needle* betrays a distinctive and artful arrangement of special comic effects which alluded to some of its audience's concerns as churchmen—parish misrule, clerical incompetence, loose behavior and language, careless laying of oaths, and indifference toward the Bible. The play treats these issues, as well as matters which touch upon the pre-Anglican church, in a freewheeling, spirited fashion, resorting to ingenious parody in the case of the "Breeches Bible." The sharpness of some of the comedy is particularly evident in the verbal barbs of Diccon, the amusingly ironic naiveté of Doctor Rat, the theatrical officiousness of Master Bailiff, the very blunt but never dull tongues of Gammer Gurton and Dame Chat, and the reductive and parodic effects achieved by certain juxtaposed scenes. The play's exceptionally well-managed comic devices help to accentuate the spectacle of a humanity oblivious to its bodily folly, resisting its powers of reason, and running away from, or avoiding stupidly, the terms of its salvation. And perhaps not the least of the comedy's fascination lies with recognizing how its playful manner is extended to tease its own genre, as a classical comedy, with delightful parody worthy of contemporary fiction making.

The play's comic vision excludes little, including the proprieties of its classical form. In presenting the three unities, the playwright gives us one night instead of one day; one place but within another place: a country setting (of all places) at Cambridge; and the one action, consisting of the immensely reductive plot to obtain a lost needle. This sense of comic inversion is evident throughout the play. The *nuntius* or messenger, a country lad named Cock, fulsomely recites offstaged maneuvers between Hodge and Tib the cat, as both threaten to clash by night. Stichomythia—in classical drama the alternating lines of dialogue in a dispute between two actors—is physically enacted, and reduced, in the quid pro quo slamming-to-the-floor between Dame Chat and Gammer Gurton, while Hodge—in an amusing choriclike exhibition—outrageously threatens doom to his mistress's aggressor as he dashes away in fright. And struck with wonder and mortal fear during Diccon's comic invocation of the devil, Hodge experiences a catharsis of sorts by uncontrollably, and embarrassingly, purging himself in his terror. All matters are concluded by a deus ex machina: the slap to the rump which dislodges the lost needle. And the overbearing Doctor Rat, whose recognition of how to change his ways is exceeded by his fear of amending them, conducts a humorous variation upon an anagnorisis, or recognition scene. Thus the play's most typifying features, no less than its earthy content, are enveloped by a comic spirit every bit as worthy of the Cambridge audience which has been associated with the play. Unquestionably, the play's comic appeal thus gained greatly in having been conceived by a learned, witty churchman for his audience at Christ's College.

And so may the matter of the lost needle be understood. The plot of Gammer Gurton's lost needle and the subsequent frantic search, with candle in hand, a search leading to a jubilant recovery, would have been readily identifiable to the play's original ecclesiastical audience at Christ's College, as a slightly modified allusion to Luke 15:8-10, the parable of the lost coin, set forth as follows in the 1559 *Book of Common Prayer:* "Either what woman having ten groats, if she lose one, doth not light a candle and sweep the house, and seek diligently till she find it? And when she hath found it, she calleth her lovers and her neighbors together saying, Rejoice with me, for I have found the groat I lost. Likewise, I say unto you, shall there be joy in the presence of the angels of God over one sinner that repenteth." The loss of Gammer Gurton's needle, like that of the woman's groat, recalls that loss which is the unrepentant sinner's lot. Accordingly, it is only when the play's characters express their willingness to amend their ways that Gammer Gurton's needle is recovered. And the needle's unlooked-for recovery, for which both Master Bailiff and the curate Doctor Rat do "rejoyce," symbolizes the unsearchable mystery of God's redemption of man.

The spur of this needle, which makes itself felt in Hodge's breeches while the trickster Diccon forswears roguery, also recalls the proverbial "prick" of Christian truth mentioned in Acts 9:5: "It is hard for thee to kick against the prick." These words, Christ's apocryphal warning to Saul on the road to Damascus, suggest how even one who is indifferent to Christ may yet be saved by him. Consequently, "the neele Hodge found by the prickynge" is deservingly acclaimed by Gammer Gurton, who says joyously, and undoubtedly ironically, to the foolish Hodge, "Christs blessing light on thee, hast made me for ever!" *Gammer Gurton's Needle,* in the low comic exertion of its most high theme, presses forth ingeniously, with most extraordinary art, the special order of its comic effects.

References:

R. W. Ingram, *"Gammer Gurton's Needle:* Comedy Not Quite of the Lowest Order?," *Studies in English Literature,* 7 (Spring 1967): 257-268;

Stanley J. Kozikowski, "Comedy Ecclesiastical and Otherwise in *Gammer Gurton's Needle,*" *Greyfriar,* 18 (1977): 5-18;

Kozikowski, "Stevenson's *Gammer Gurton's Needle,*" *Explicator,* 38 (Spring 1980): 17-18;

Charles W. Roberts, "The Authorship of *Gammer Gurton's Needle,*" *Philological Quarterly,* 19 (April 1940): 97-105;

William B. Toole, "The Aesthetics of Scatology in *Gammer Gurton's Needle,*" *English Language Notes,* 10 (June 1973): 252-258;

Homer A. Watt, "The Staging of *Gammer Gurton's Needle,*" in *Elizabethan Studies and Other Essays in Honor of George F. Reynolds,* edited by E. J. West (Boulder: University of Colorado, 1945), pp. 85-92.

Locrine and *Selimus*

Peter Berek
Williams College

PRODUCTIONS: *Locrine,* London, unknown theater, circa 1591-1594;
Selimus, London, The Theatre, circa 1591-1594.

FIRST PUBLICATIONS: *The First Part of the Tragicall Raigne of Selimus* (London: Printed by T. Creede, 1594);
The Lamentable Tragedy of Locrine (London: Printed by T. Creede, 1595).
Editions: *Locrine,* in *The Shakespeare Apocrypha,* edited by C. F. Tucker Brooke (Oxford: Clarendon Press, 1908), pp. 37-65;
The Tragedy of Locrine, 1595, edited by Ronald B. McKerrow (Oxford: Printed for the Malone Society at Oxford University Press, 1908);
The Tragical Reign of Selimus, 1594, edited by W. Bang (London: Printed for the Malone Society at Chiswick Press, 1909).

Locrine and *Selimus* are anonymous plays more interesting for the light they can shed on the English theater in the 1580s and 1590s than for any particular artistic merit. They have both been attributed, not convincingly, to authors of some renown: *Selimus* to Robert Greene (see also the Greene entry) and *Locrine* to Greene and to Shakespeare. Because there are many virtually identical passages in both plays, they clearly have some connection to each other.

Locrine, almost certainly the earlier of the two plays, was printed in London by Thomas Creede in 1595. The title page describes the play as "Newly set forth, overseene and corrected, by W. S." The initials proved irresistible to the printers of the third collected edition of Shakespeare's works, the so-called Third Folio of 1664, and they included *Locrine* in their volume. Thus the play joined fourteen other minor Elizabethan works as part of a group now known as the Shakespeare apocrypha, a group which also includes such anonymous plays as *Arden of Faversham, Edward III, Mucedorus,* and *A Yorkshire Tragedy.* Though the title page of the 1595 quarto gives no indication of performance, *Locrine* probably belonged to the Queen's Men.

Locrine derives from the legendary British history compiled by Geoffrey of Monmouth in his *History of the Kings of Britain* (written circa 1138-1139). The play first recounts the story of the war between Locrine, king of Britain (and son of Brutus, the Trojan founder of Britain), and the invading king of the Huns, Humber. In this war Humber kills Locrine's brother, Albanact. The war against Humber then becomes a battle for revenge, with the Britons spurred on by Albanact's ghost. After defeating Humber, Locrine takes as his concubine Humber's former mate, Estrild—to the consternation of his own lawful wife, Guendolin. The remainder of the play dramatizes Guendolin's war of revenge against Locrine, which culminates in the deaths by suicide of Locrine, Estrild, and their daughter, Sabren. In the course of the story, the audience learns the source of some celebrated British names: Humber drowns in the river which afterward bears his name, and Sabren in drowning gives her name to the river Severn. Though the plot is based on Geoffrey of Monmouth, the story of Locrine, Guendolin, and Estrild was available nearer to hand in Raphael Holinshed's *Chronicles* (1578, enlarged 1587) and John Higgins's enormously popular *Mirror for Magistrates,* first printed in 1574. The story also appears in book three of Edmund Spenser's *Faerie Queene* (1590) and Thomas Lodge's *The Complaint of Elstred* (1593).

Much of the style and dramaturgy of *Locrine* seem archaic for a play of 1595–the year of such Shakespeare plays as *Romeo and Juliet* and *Richard II.* Its blank verse is workmanlike but undistinguished, and some of its Senecan bombast, dumb shows, and choruses seem characteristic of the 1580s. But the play also renders the warriors Humber and Albanact as vaunting heroes whose rhetoric seems to imitate that of the hero of Christopher Marlowe's first play for the public theater, *Tamburlaine* (produced circa 1587). The mixed

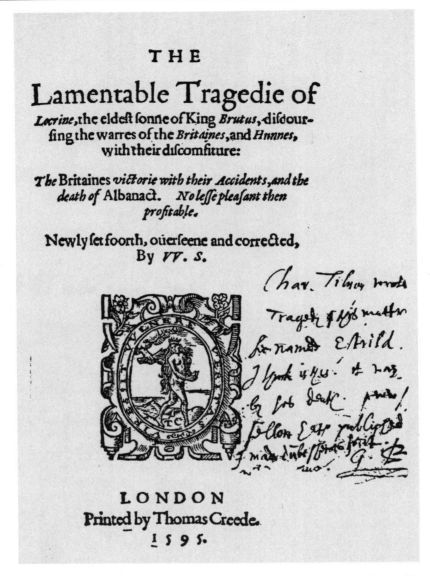

Title page for the 1595 quarto edition of the anonymous play Locrine, *with a note by Sir George Buc, Master of the Revels under James I, claiming that this play is Charles Tilney's "Estrild," for which Buc wrote dumb shows (Anderson Galleries, sale number 2078, 24-25 May 1926). Modern scholars believe that* Locrine *is another playwright's revision of Tilney's play.*

quality of *Locrine* may be explained by the likely circumstances of its composition. One of the surviving copies of the 1595 quarto contains a handwritten note on the title page asserting that the play was written by Charles Tilney (1561-1586). The note is signed "G. B.," and the modern scholars Sir Walter Greg and R. C. Bald agree that the handwriting is that of Sir George Buc, Master of the Revels under King James and a man well placed to have knowledge of the theatrical traditions of the 1580s and 1590s. According to the note, Tilney wrote the play under the title "Estrild," and Buc himself wrote dumb shows for it. The play was lost, and "now some fellow hath published it." But the play in its present form cannot be entirely the work of Charles Tilney. It contains many echoes of poems by Edmund Spenser that almost surely were not written until the early 1590s. By piecing together both external and internal evidence, one can show that some parts of *Locrine*—especially the fifth act—appear to reflect "Estrild" as Charles Tilney wrote it in the mid 1580s, while other parts of the play must have been revised by someone much influenced by

Marlowe's innovations in the theater in the years following 1587.

It seems plausible that an unidentified playwright came upon Charles Tilney's "Estrild" and decided to update it in accord with the theatrical fashions of the early 1590s. Doing so, he turned Albanact and Humber into vaunters of overreaching ambition, fit colleagues of Marlowe's Tamburlaine and Faustus. But they remain embedded in an old-fashioned tale of revenge. Moreover, although the Tamburlainean figures in *Locrine* echo Marlowe's hero in asserting their domination of Fortune, the choruses in the play assert a most unMarlovian belief in the vanity of all human aspirations. The revisions of *Locrine* introduce Marlovian rhetoric and stage spectacle, both of which seem to have held great appeal for audiences in the early 1590s, but they show no coherent interest in Marlowe's radical ideas. The play reveals how a minor writer tries to accommodate genuine theatrical innovation without giving up old, comfortable ideas—even if those ideas are incompatible with the innovations he tries to embrace.

Selimus was printed by Thomas Creede in 1594; the title page says it was played by the Queen's Men. There is no indication of authorship, though the anthology *England's Parnassus* (1600) prints excerpts from the play and ascribes them to Robert Greene. But this evidence is inconclusive; some passages ascribed to Greene in *England's Parnassus* are known to have other authors. The play is based on Turkish history as reported in the Turkish Chronicles of Paulus Jovius. *Selimus* dramatizes the struggle to succeed the Turkish Emperor Bajazet among his three sons, Acomat, Corcut, and Selimus. Bajazet initially favors Acomat as his heir, though the warrior Selimus has greater popular support. After Bajazet puts down a rebellion led by Selimus, Acomat rebels against his father, and Selimus takes command of his father's armies against his brother. Acomat behaves with extraordinary brutality. He tosses one victim to his death on a forest of spear points, and he puts out the eyes and cuts off the hands of his father's aged emissary, Aga. After defeating Acomat, Selimus forces Bajazet to abdicate, poisons both him and Aga with the help of a Jew named Abraham, and exterminates his brother Corcut and all other potential rivals to the throne.

Selimus is even richer than *Locrine* in echoes of other works, including Marlowe's *Tamburlaine* and *The Massacre at Paris*, *The Faerie Queene*, and

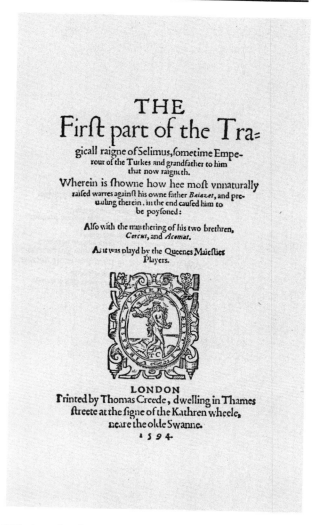

Title page for the 1594 quarto edition of the play that is believed to have been written by the author of Locrine *(Anderson Galleries, sale number 2077, 20-21 May 1926)*

Sidney's *Astrophil and Stella* and *Arcadia*. Several times it imitates Spenser's *Complaints* (1591). Each of the passages from Spenser is also imitated in *Locrine*, and it can be shown that the line of transmission runs from the *Complaints* to *Locrine* to *Selimus*. Moreover, *Selimus* includes a clown, Bullithrumble, whose role is clearly based on the clown in *Locrine*, Strumbo. This peculiar pattern of imitation, a pattern bordering on plagiarism, suggests that the author who revised "Estrild" into *Locrine* then went on to write *Selimus*.

The Tamburlainean qualities of *Selimus* are integral to the play and not, as in *Locrine*, novel trappings added to an old story. In that sense, *Selimus* is very much a part of the vogue for conqueror plays which followed Marlowe's great success in the public theater of the late 1580s. The mutilation of Aga parallels similar acts in Shakespeare's notorious early tragedy *Titus Andronicus,* and his blinding anticipates the blinding of Gloucester in *King Lear.* But like *Locrine,* *Selimus* does not endorse the religious unorthodoxy or radical notions of self-creation implicit in *Tamburlaine.* The conquering Selimus by the end of the play is clearly defined as a villain; the audience can enjoy the thrill of entertaining shocking possibilities while ultimately remaining safe from ethical challenge.

The title page of *Selimus* announces the play as *The First Part of the Tragicall Raigne of Selimus,* implying that, like Marlowe's *Tamburlaine,* the play will be followed by part two. No such second part is known. Perhaps the play was not enough of a success to make a second part commercially attractive.

References:
R. C. Bald, "The *Locrine* and *George-a-Greene* Title Page Inscriptions," *Library,* fourth series 15 (December 1934): 295-305;

T. W. Baldwin, *On the Literary Genetics of Shakespeare's Plays, 1592-1594* (Urbana: University of Illinois Press, 1959);

Peter Berek, "*Locrine* Revised, *Selimus,* and Early Responses to *Tamburlaine,*" *Research Opportunities in Renaissance Drama,* 23 (1980): 33-54;

W. W. Greg, "Three Manuscript Notes by Sir George Buc," *Library,* fourth series 12 (December 1931): 307-321;

Terence P. Logan and Denzell S. Smith, *The Predecessors of Shakespeare* (Lincoln: University of Nebraska Press, 1973);

Baldwin Maxwell, *Studies in the Shakespeare Apocrypha* (New York: King's Crown Press, 1956);

Kenneth Muir, "Who Wrote *Selimus*?," *Proceedings of the Leeds Philosophical and Literary Society,* Literary and Historical Section, 6, no. 6 (February 1949): 373-376;

Irving Ribner, *The English History Play in the Age of Shakespeare,* revised edition (London: Methuen, 1965).

Mucedorus

Paul G. Kreuzer
Lehman College, City University of New York

PRODUCTIONS: London, unknown theater, circa 1590-1598; London, at Court, 1610.

FIRST PUBLICATION: *A Most Pleasant Comedie of Mucedorus* (London: Printed for W. Jones, 1598).

Editions: *Mucedorus*, in *The Shakespeare Apocrypha*, edited by C. F. Tucker Brooke (Oxford: Clarendon Press, 1908), pp. 103-127;

Mucedorus, in *Elizabethan Plays*, edited by Arthur H. Nethercot, Charles R. Baskerville, and Virgil B. Hetzel, revised edition (New York: Holt, Rinehart & Winston, 1971), pp. 577-604.

First published in 1598, the anonymous play *Mucedorus* went through at least sixteen editions by 1668, fourteen of them after 1610. This fact may baffle the modern reader; the play does not seem good enough to warrant so many more editions than any other popular Elizabethan play. Value judgments aside, the number of editions does suggest that the play enjoyed considerable popularity, at least after it was performed before King James I in 1610. Although the evidence is not ironclad, it is generally accepted that the King's Men, Shakespeare's own company, was responsible for this revival of what must have seemed a creaking antique of a play. Such revivals were popular at the time, and the edition of 1610 gives evidence of some revision for the changed tastes of the Jacobean audience. The prologue addressed to the King is one obvious addition; among others are expanded scenes for Mouse, the clown, and some satirical lines directed at the nobility. Such changes suggest a Jacobean interest in modernizing or improving the work. The 1610 edition may also be taken as the most polished text. The earlier publications, as Leo Kirschbaum has shown, are most likely reconstructions based on the memory of an actor. The 1610 edition, however, seems to have been prepared from a written script.

Perhaps because of the 1610 performance by the King's Men, perhaps because of the occasionally extraordinary, fanciful flights of Mouse, or perhaps because of the apparent popularity of the work, an early attribution to Shakespeare stuck for many years despite the clear lack of the bard's genius in the play. Critics have posited other authors including George Peele, Robert Greene, and Thomas Lodge, but C. F. Tucker Brooke's suggestion that the play was written by an obscure, moderately talented disciple of the University Wits is the generally accepted twentieth-century solution to the problem of authorship. Yet by accepting the anonymity of the play's author, modern readers need neither revile the play, as Brooke does, to demonstrate that Shakespeare could not possibly be responsible for it, nor search for previously unnoticed beauties to justify an attribution to a major figure. Instead the modern reader can approach the play without preconception to discover what *Mucedorus* offered to the Jacobean audience, whose interest in the play continued long after 1610, as well as what it offers to the twentieth-century reader, whose interest in the play is most likely inspired by a general curiosity about Elizabethan and Jacobean drama.

The general plot of the work is derived from Sir Philip Sidney's *Arcadia*. Like the Arcadian Musidorus, the hero of the play disguises himself as a shepherd, falls in love with a princess, saves her from a bear, alternately finds favor and disfavor at court, plans an elopement, owes his life to the intercession of the princess, and lives happily ever after in the arms of his lady love. There are, of course, differences: the characters of Segasto, Tremelio, and Bremo are original with the play's author, and the addition of Mouse, a clever but foolish clown, demonstrates a rejection of Sidney's principles of decorum. Although Sidney would have completely disapproved of allowing a foolish clown to appear so close to a king's throne, the large number of editions in which Mouse is mentioned prominently in the complete title of the play suggests that his character accounts for much of the play's Jacobean popularity. Curiously enough, Mouse's foolishness also accounts for some of the modern critics' scorn for the play.

Modern distaste for the work appears in many guises. From some critics we hear sarcastic laughter at the very idea that someone could ever have attributed this play to Shakespeare. From others we discover that popularity and value are unrelated because the taste of vulgar audiences is always questionable. As George Reynolds suggests, *Mucedorus* is the Elizabethan equivalent of a third-rate movie. Since recent scholarship suggests that many accepted ideas about the largely lower-class composition of the popular audiences are questionable, the argument that *Mucedorus* appealed to only the illeducated, vulgar mob seems specious at best.

To understand why the play was popular the modern reader must investigate both its weaknesses and its virtues. Even in the vastly improved 1610 edition, the text of the play is not without flaws. Some of these–a lack of richness in the poetry, an occasional extraneous scene, even a certain lack of unity–are flaws recognized primarily by a reading scholar. The language, which pales in comparison to that of John Lyly or Christopher Marlowe, is neither doggerel nor nonsense, and the alliterative repetitions and puns are responsible for some of the play's humor. The most clearly extraneous scene, Mouse's encounter with the Old Woman, is a momentary showcase for the clown. A unity problem such as the unresolved subplot of the Catalonian prisoner is likely to go unnoticed by the viewing audience, whose enjoyment of the play may even be enhanced by such seeming flaws as the clown's extra scenes.

This is not to suggest that the viewer of *Mucedorus* would leave the theater without recognizing some of the major problems. Certainly one might wonder how Tremelio, within a span of five minutes, can change from a hero in the King's war to an unmitigated, mercenary villain hired by Segasto to murder Mucedorus. One might even wonder what happens to Collen and the Catalonian prisoner. The viewer is also likely to be confused by Mucedorus's reputation at court. When Segasto–whom the King has named his successor and future son-in-law–reveals his jealousy of the disguised prince's reception, the audience understands that the tale of Mucedorus's exploit with the bear is known; but several scenes later when Segasto attempts to have the hero exe-

cuted for the murder of Tremelio, Princess Amadine amazes the court by disclosing Mucedorus's heroic slaying of the beast. A similar confusion is caused by the use of the hero's name. Amadine knows Mucedorus to be the name of the prince of Valencia. She, like the rest of the court, is astonished when he finally reveals himself at the end of the work, and yet she calls him by name throughout the Bremo scenes, in which she supposedly believes that he is a shepherd. Whereas the reader has time to dwell on such compositional errors, the viewer's momentary confusion is likely to be forgotten with the next entrance of the clown.

Perhaps a more serious problem for most modern readers is the general flatness of the characters, a flaw of which most viewers would be aware. Mucedorus and Amadine are notably dull. A dull hero and heroine, however, are not necessarily grounds for criticism. Such characters are common enough in Elizabethan romances. While their poetry is more lovely than that of Mucedorus and Amadine, Ferdinand and Miranda in *The Tempest* hardly excite Prospero's isle with complex personalities. Shakespeare's play, however, is hardly a common romance, and it offers richness of characterization elsewhere. In *Mucedorus* even simple motivation is lost at times. At the beginning of the play Mucedorus, choosing to see for himself if Amadine lives up to her reputation for beauty, insists on going to Aragon in disguise without ever suggesting a reason. Segasto behaves at one moment like a coward, at another like a villain, and at the end like a noble courtier. There is little in the play to suggest the source of such character changes.

If the play offers so little in beauty of language, clarity of plot, and interesting characters, what does it have to make it worth considering? Quite simply, the play offers a wealth of conventions; it is, indeed, a friendly play. As each character trots upon the stage, as each new situation appears, the Elizabethan or Jacobean viewer must have smiled with recognition, and the modern reader learns a bit more about the conventions with which those audiences were familiar.

Mucedorus contains conventional characters of many different types. Some are obviously recognizable today; others are more peculiar to the Renaissance. Certainly any modern reader or viewer would recognize Mucedorus as the standard hero-prince of comedy. Like a boy scout, he is thoughtful, brave, and courteous. Similarly, Amadine is a standard heroine-princess of comedy. She is beautiful, promised to a man not her equal, and prone to being in distress. Although his character varies greatly, Segasto is still recognizable as the undeserving fiancé of the princess and as the villain of the piece. Anselmo is recognizable as the loyal friend of the hero, and the kings are clearly wise leaders.

More peculiar to the Renaissance are the bear, the wild man, and the fool. The bear has received more attention from modern critics than he deserves because no clear statement of who plays the role appears in the dramatis personae. This gap has enabled scholars to suggest, with no specific evidence, the possibility of a live bear having been used at least once and to attribute the play's popularity to the notoriety of such a performance. The Elizabethan and Jacobean audiences would have recognized in the bear a powerful threat to the hero and heroine. One of the great monsters of northern Europe, the bear is the form taken most often by the shape changers of fantastic legend. In this context the popularity of the spectacle of bearbaiting in Renaissance England is hardly surprising. It offered evidence of the triumph of humans over this mysterious, threatening creature, which, able to raise himself on two legs like a man, was capable of using powerful arms and massive teeth to maul his enemy. A man wearing a bear costume in a comedy such as *Mucedorus* offers a dramatic, if comic, equivalent. Despite all the threatening associations, real danger is not present, and the imitation enables the audience to laugh, to celebrate Mucedorus's slaying of the "bear" as man's victory over an accepted menace.

More interesting than the bear, both within the play itself and as a literary convention, is the wild man. Wild men, savages, and cannibals appear frequently in Renaissance literature: folktales abound with legends of wodewoses; Spenser includes "salvages" in books four and six of *The Faerie Queen;* both George Gascoigne and Lyly introduce speaking wild men into dramatic works; and Caliban animates much of *The Tempest.* The proliferation of literary wild men during the Renaissance reflects a natural fascination with the tales of the explorers. Accounts of strange savages with odd dress and odder customs circulated freely, and stories of cannibals from all corners of the globe fascinated Europe. The explorers seemed to bring verification, no matter how unlikely, for the folktales that had amused people for centuries. That their stories were often exaggerations or fabrications is unimportant. Wild men became part of the public consciousness.

The traditional wild men of European folklore can be classified into two types, as R. H. Goldsmith has shown. In northern Europe the wodewose, the wild man of the woods, is the prominent type. Characterized by a wild visage and a raging disposition, he resembles the berserkers of the Anglo-Saxons. In the Mediterranean regions the prominent type of wild man is the satyr. Characterized primarily by unchastity and related to classical myth, this wild man is less human than the wodewose. To varying degrees the two share conventions of behavior. The satyr is more likely to be governed by uncontrollable lust and to occupy a position on the moral scale between men and beasts than the wodewose, who is more likely to be governed by rage and to be of noble blood. Yet these characteristics are sometimes mixed, and cannibalism and monstrous shape, as well as the ability to be tamed by a lady, are conventions associated with wild men in general. Whereas the "salvage man" of book four of *The Faerie Queene* is more of a satyr–he is a creature representing lust, the "salvage man" of book six is more of a wodewose–he is recognizably of noble descent. Like Bremo in *Mucedorus*, Lyly's wild man, and even Caliban to some extent, Spenser's wodewose is frightening to behold, clearly dangerous, and yet, characteristically, tamed by a noble lady.

Caliban, of course, is more than a simple wild man. Transformed from convention, as Shakespeare in his maturity transformed nearly everything he touched, Caliban is, as Frank Kermode has shown in the introduction to his edition of *The Tempest*, the natural man against whom the cultivated man is measured. Lustful enough to attempt a rape of Miranda, Caliban is also capable of being taught by her to be human, to speak. Tamed by Prospero and human enough to desire freedom, he seeks release by offering himself as a slave to Stephano. Morally damnable and yet pitiable, Caliban challenges the reader and viewer. Rather than smiling with recognition at a conventional type, the audience is faced with complexity.

Bremo, on the other hand, combining attributes of the satyr and the wodewose, is recognizably conventional at his entrance. Indeed within his opening scene Bremo reveals rage, cannibalism, and susceptibility to Amadine's taming influence. Encountering the princess, who is waiting in the forest for Mucedorus, he reveals his character with his first speech:

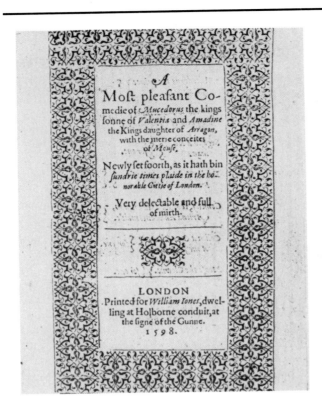

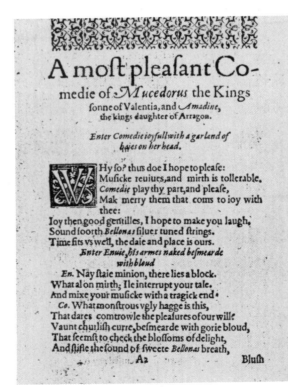

Title page, dramatis personae, and first and last pages of text from the 1598 quarto edition of the Elizabethan play that became popular with Jacobean audiences after the 1610 performance of a revised version before James I (British Library)

A happy prey! Now Bremo, feed on flesh!
Dainties, Bremo, dainties, thy hungry panch to fill!
Now glut thy greedy guts with lukewarm blood!
Come fight with me; I long to see thee dead.

Bremo is clearly the conventional cannibalistic wild man, and yet his appearance as flesh eater is mitigated by his humorously alliterative speech pattern:

No pity I; I'll feed upon thy flesh;
I'll tear thy body piecemeal joint from joint.
....
I'll crush thy bones betwixt two oaken trees.

I'll suck the sweetness from thy marrowbones.
....
With this bat will I beat out thy brains!

Such lines—establishing the conventional type and also defining the comic version—are too funny to be truly threatening.

Later in the scene Bremo is transformed by Amadine's beauty. Although he is hardly metamorphosed into a prince, he discovers that he cannot strike her, that she holds some sexual power over him:

How now, what sudden chance is this?
My limbs do tremble and my sinews shake;
My unweakened arms hath lost their former force.
....
Some newcome spirit, abiding in my breast,
Saith, "Spare her," which never spared any.
To it, Bremo, to it! Say again.—
I cannot wield my weapons in my hand;
Methinks I should not strike so fair a one.
I think her beauty hath bewitched my force
Or else within me altered nature's course.
Ay woman, wilt thou live in woods with me?

Although Bremo does not embody the convention of the nobly borne wild man, he conceives of himself as a prince of the wood; and in lines that come close to those which a viewer would expect from a nobleman, he offers Amadine a crown. He is, of course, unaware of the irony of making such an offer to a princess:

If thou wilt love me, thou shalt be my queen;
I will crown thee with a chaplet made of ivory,
And make the rose and lily wait on thee.
I'll rend the burly branches from the oak,
To shadow thee from burning sun.
The trees shall spread themselves where thou
    dost go,
And as they spread, I'll trace along with thee.

Because of the convention that the wild man, noble or not, may be tamed by the sight of a beautiful lady, a Renaissance audience would not have been surprised by Bremo's gentle speech.

Also aware that the wild man may fall prey to his sexual urges, the audience would not have been shocked at Bremo's more urgent speeches:

The day I'll spend to recreate my love
With all the pleasures that I can devise,
And in the night I'll be thy bedfellow,
And lovingly embrace thee in mine arms.
....
The satyrs and the wood-nymphs shall attend on thee
And lull thee asleep with music's sound,
And in the morning when thou dost awake,
The lark shall sing good morrow to my queen,
And whilst he sings, I'll kiss my Amadine.
....
When thou art up, the wood lanes shall be strowed
With violets, cowslips, and sweet marigolds
For thee to trample and to trace upon,
And I will teach thee how to kill the deer
To chase the hart and how to rouse the roe,
If thou wilt live to love and honor me.

In these speeches Bremo both separates himself from the satyrs of the forest and shows his derivation, at least in part, from the satyr type, the lustful wild man.

Before Bremo has a chance to work himself into an uncontrollable sexual passion, Mucedorus appears, and the savage reverts to his cannibalistic character. Mucedorus, with no weapon, tries to tame Bremo with reason. In his long, remarkable speech he alludes to Greek myth, reminding the audience of the classical wild man who is a reversion to a form that existed previous to Orpheus's taming of the species. Mucedorus's words suggest that noble men, deprived of reason, can become like the satyrs of old:

In times of yore, when men like brutish beasts
Did lead their lives in loathsome cells and woods
And wholly gave themselves to witless will,
A rude, unruly rout, then man to man
Became a present prey; then might prevailed;
The weakest went to walls.
Right was unknown; for wrong was all in all.
As men thus lived in their great outrage,
Behold, one Orpheus came, as poets tell,
And them from rudeness unto reason brought,
Who, led by reason, some forsook the woods.
Instead of caves they built them castles strong;
Cities and towns were founded by them then.

Glad they were, they found such ease, and in
The end they grew to perfect amity.
Weighing their former wickedness,
They termed the time wherin they lived then
A golden age, a goodly golden age.
Now Bremo, for so I hear thee called,
If men which live to fore, as thou dost now,
Wild in wood, addicted all to spoil,
Returned were by worthy Orpheus' means,
Let me like Orpheus cause thee to return
From murther, bloodshed, and like cruelty.

This speech helps to define Bremo for the audience. Though Mucedorus fails to convince the wild man and is saved only by Amadine's intervention, his words make it clear that Bremo, like the wild men whom Orpheus calmed, is capable of being tamed.

Mouse, the clown in *Mucedorus,* is, like Bremo, an amalgamation of two conventional types. The first of these is a descendant of the medieval court jester, whose humor is likely to be a series of jokes, tricks, and puns performed with the energy of a gymnast. A familiar character in the tradition of the commedia del l'arte, he brings laughter to the audience but has little effect on the outcome of the plot. The second type of fool, of which Feste in Shakespeare's *Twelfth Night* is an example, is a clear-sighted commentator whose humor is not that of the jokester but that of the satirist. He can find a home in a tragedy such as *King Lear* as well as in traditional comedy.

The combining of these two types of clowns is hardly unique to *Mucedorus.* Certainly most of Shakespeare's clowns, despite all of their satire, bear some resemblance to the jesters as well. Mouse, however, plays the jester so well that his occasional moments of wisdom may go unnoticed. In his opening scene, an addition in the 1610 edition, Mouse demonstrates the various aspects of his character:

> O, horrible, terrible! Was ever poor gentlemen so scared out of his seven senses? A bear? Nay, for sure it cannot be a bear, but some devil in a bear's doublet, for a bear could never have had that agility to have frighted me. Well, I'll see my father hanged before I'll serve his horse any more. Well, I'll carry home my bottle of hay, and for once make my father's horse turn Puritan and observe fasting days, for he gets not a bit. But soft! This way she followed me; and therefore I'll take the other path; and because I'll be sure to have an

eye on him, I will take hands with some foolish creditor, and make every step backward.

At the end of the scene Mouse tumbles backward over the bear and runs away; the tradition of slapstick is built into his character. The choice to walk backward and the assertion that no real bear could scare him demonstrate his use of nonsense. And yet juxtaposed with these remarks are a topical and satirical reference to the Puritans, an ironic comment on creditors and debt, and the clear-sighted recognition that the bear is only a performer in a bear's suit. Mouse shows more complexity, perhaps, than any of the other characters in the play.

Mouse's foolish attributes appear throughout the play. One of these is his ability to use language in a nonsensical or illogical way. In describing his encounter with the bear to Segasto, for example, he suggests that he saw a beast while completely blindfolded:

> I tell you what, sir, as I was going afield to serve my father's great horse, and carried a bottle of hay upon my head—now do you see, sir—I, fast hoodwinked that I could see nothing, I perceiving the bear coming, I threw my hay into the hedge and ran away.

Such a lack of logic is one means for creating humor through language. At the beginning of the scene in which Mouse encounters the Old Woman, he uses rhyme as another device for evoking laughter: "But I care not; I'll face her out, and call her old rusty, dusty, musty, fusty, crusty firebrand, and worse than all that, and so face her out of her pot." The language devices are simple, but they work.

Mouse also evokes laughter through slapstick. Not only does he tumble over the bear in his first scene, but in his show-stealing scene with the Old Woman he drinks the beer he has stolen from her while she searches him. The sight gag ends as they tumble in battle. Though hardly essential to the plot, the scene does make the audience laugh, and—by its placement directly after the scene in which Bremo abducts Amadine—it may help to assure the viewer of a comic outcome.

Mouse's relationship to the knowing fools of Renaissance drama is not as clear at first as his relationship to the jesters. Certainly his malapropisms, mispronounciations, and deliberate misunderstandings seem more foolish than clever, although his language transformations become more sophisticated as the play progresses. Yet there are scenes in which his truth speaking guides the audience. Having established himself as a knowing fool, by identifying the bear as a costumed man in his opening speech, Mouse prepares the audience to give credence to his occasional commentary on the action.

In the scene in which Segasto accuses Mucedorus of the murder of Tremelio (whom Mucedorus has killed in self-defense), Mouse, in two asides, comments on the action and keeps the audience informed. In the first of these, he reminds the viewer of Segasto's cowardice in running away from the bear that Mucedorus killed:

> SEGASTO. The slaughter of a man deserves great blame.
> KING. Indeed, occasion oftentimes so falls out.
> SEGASTO. Tremelio in the wars, O king, preserved thee.
> AMADINE. The shepherd in the woods, O king, preserved me.
> SEGASTO. Tremelio fought when many men did yield.
> AMADINE. So would the shepherd, had he been in field.
> CLOWN. [Aside.] So would my master, had he not run away.

By making the audience laugh at Segasto's cowardice at the very moment when he is most dangerous to Mucedorus, Mouse reassures the audience of the eventual comic outcome.

At the end of the scene, after the King has spared Mucedorus, Mouse again provides commentary for the audience:

> CLOWN. . . . Faith, master, now I cannot hang the shepherd, I pray you, let me take the pains to hang you–it is but half an hour's exercise.
> SEGASTO. You are still in your knavery, but sith, I cannot have his life, I will procure his banishment forever. Come on, sirrah.
> CLOWN. Yes, forsooth, I come.–[To audience.] Laugh at him, I pray you.

Mouse's offer to hang Segasto elicits laughter from the viewer and confirms his sense that Segasto, more than Mucedorus, deserves punishment. But it is the aside at the end of the scene that demonstrates most clearly how Mouse guides the audience's response. Because banishment, like death, would prevent the marriage of hero and heroine, it is a threat to the traditional ending of comedy, but the possibility of Mucedorus's banishment cannot be taken seriously once Mouse has made his aside. Segasto

is to be laughed at, not feared.

Mouse's clearest moment of vision comes in a subtle distinction he makes in response to Segasto's order to find Amadine and Mucedorus when her disappearance is discovered: "How? Is the shepherd run away with the king's daughter, / or is the king's daughter run away with shepherd?" By distinguishing between abduction and elopement, Mouse suggests the possibility that Amadine may have made the choice, and thus attempts to awaken Segasto to the possibility that she has bestowed her love on Mucedorus. Although Segasto remains blind to his own hopelessness, Mouse and the audience can laugh together at his foolishness. The villain has been foiled.

Although the individual actions of the play's conventional characters vary to suit this particular plot, there are no real surprises, except perhaps for Segasto's sudden willingness to relinquish his claims to Amadine once he discovers that Mucedorus is a prince. The Elizabethan and Jacobean audiences would enjoy seeing such familiar characters just as children enjoy hearing fairy tales.

As there are no real surprises among the characters, so also are there no real surprises among the events of the plot or in the structure of the play. *Mucedorus* is clearly a standard comedy in which the young prince and princess fall in love, struggle against obstacles in the way of their marriage, and finally marry. This is conservative comedy: the old order is not overthrown; the blocking characters are not mercenary, insensitive parents; and the hero and heroine are not really rebels. The closest *Mucedorus* comes to making a political statement is in presenting the idea that a shepherd has a chance to win the love of a real princess; but Mucedorus is really a prince; Segasto is noble enough by birth to qualify as a suitor to Amadine; and the order established by the joining of two royal families in marriage reflects a basic belief in the rightness of monarchy and faith in the innate nobility of the aristocracy.

Although the basic plot outline of the play is extremely traditional, the use of disguise, the incorporation of pastoral elements, and the framing of the main action are aspects of interest to the modern reader. Disguise, of course, is an ancient literary convention. Familiar in the Greek and Roman traditions as well as in the literature of the Middle Ages, disguise is used in Elizabethan drama primarily to launch the plots of comedies. As Leo Salingar has shown, the outcomes of

Shakespeare's comedies depend in large part on mistakes of identity caused by the disguises of major characters. One need think only of Viola in *Twelfth Night* or of the servants and masters in *The Comedy of Errors* to see how disguise can create complex plots.

The use of disguise in *Mucedorus* launches the plot proper. Except for his encounter with the bear, all of Mucedorus's tribulations, all the real threats to the marriage of the hero and heroine, derive from his initial decision to visit Aragon in disguise. From that moment the audience expects his identity to be mistaken, his purpose to be thwarted, and his unmasking to mark the resolution of the plot. Furthermore the audience recognizes the test of love that the use of disguise allows. As Mucedorus says in the very moment before he reveals himself:

> And, Amadine, why wilt thou none but me?
> I cannot keep thee as thy father did;
> I have no lands for to maintain thy state.
> Moreover, if thou mean to be my wife,
> Commonly this must be thy use:
> To bed at midnight, up at four,
> Drudge all day and trudge from place to place,
> Whereby our daily victual for to win;
> And last of all, which is the worst of all
> No princess then, but plain a shepherd's wife.

Amadine insists she will have no one except her shepherd, but she also indicates that she will use her fortune and position to make Mucedorus a prince. This line of reasoning is odd since Amadine has already proved her willingness to give up her noble position by agreeing to leave Aragon:

> Well, shepherd, sith thou suff'rest this for my sake,
> With thee in exile also let me live—
> On this condition, shepherd, thou canst love.
> ....
> Well, shepherd, hark what I shall say:
> I will return unto my father's court,
> There for to provide me of such necessaries
> As for my journey I shall think most fit;
> This being done, I will return to thee.

Mucedorus's disguise serves all of its purposes: it enables him to woo Amadine anonymously, to test and prove her love, and to set up a conventional structure of comedy; the expectations of the audience are fulfilled.

Mucedorus as a shepherd brings to mind the hope for a new golden age, an age in which shepherds live together in peace and harmony.

Alive and well in Elizabethan England, the pastoral tradition found expressions in the works of poets such as Sidney and Edmund Spenser. Partly a response to court intrigue, the pastoral offers simplicity and satisfies the democratic yearnings of a prosperous public. Ironically, works in the tradition tend to be populated with princes and courtiers; the real shepherds are often loutish. Pure Arcadia, like the golden age itself, is mythical.

As in Sidney's *Arcadia*, the work that gives *Mucedorus* its bare bones, the country is hardly idyllic. Characters exhibit vices of all sorts. Peace and good humor are constantly threatened. Segasto's insistence that Mucedorus be banished leads not only to the elopement but to Bremo's abduction of Amadine. Even the King's agreement to the banishment of the hero suggests that all is not heavenly in the imaginary Spain of the play. Such threats to the idyllic world of the pastoral, however, were expected by the Elizabethan and Jacobean audiences. Certainly the heroes in Sidney's work are perpetually threatened by intrigue, and jealousy abounds in the works of Spenser. As Mucedorus makes clear in his speech to Bremo, the golden age is past; the present contains a mixture of virtue and vice.

Used conventionally the pastoral tradition in *Mucedorus* has raised questions for both the modern and Elizabethan audiences. The tradition does suggest the value of simplicity and the destructiveness of intrigue, but it also suggests that the grace of the court, indeed even the wealth of princes, should not really be snubbed. Comfort can be appreciated when discomfort is known. Freedom can be treasured when bondage has been experienced. Pure bliss cannot exist in a vacuum. The mixture of vice and virtue, suspense and relief is at the heart of *Mucedorus*. Because of this very mixture, comedy, it seems, is not necessarily pure laughter and happiness. Elizabethan audiences, like modern audiences are forced to define the nature of dramatic comedy itself.

The play proper is framed by scenes between the goddesses, Comedy and Envy. This device, both structurally and thematically, is one of the most interesting features of the play to the modern reader, partly because the question of the nature of comedy is raised explicitly. The tradition of framing dates back at least as far as the Middle Ages; the induction is a common narrative device in medieval literature. An older, and perhaps related device, is the deus ex machina. The god who enters the play to resolve the plot suggests a world external but necessarily related to the play.

In English drama the induction is often used as a means for the author to discuss the nature of his work. As Jacqueline Pearson has shown, the induction allows the author to use characters external or unimportant to the play proper to comment on the action. In the romantic plays of the Elizabethans, the inductions are populated by allegorical or supernatural figures. *Mucedorus*, appearing as early as 1590, followed such plays as *The Rare Triumphs of Love and Fortune, The Spanish Tragedy,* and *Alphonsus King of Aragon*—all of which employ this device.

The frame of *Mucedorus* consists of two parts, the induction and the epilogue. In the induction the goddess Envy threatens to mar the play of the goddess Comedy with treble death, and Comedy responds that she will triumph over any obstacles Envy can throw in her path. In the epilogue, the bickering continues despite Comedy's triumph in the play proper. In a lovely parallel to the scene in which Amadine tames Bremo, the playwright varies the tradition of the deus ex machina by taming Envy with the presence of the King. Framed by a debate between Comedy and Envy, the story of Mucedorus is even further removed from the actual beginning and end of the play by the prologue of praise for the King and the final hymn in praise of the monarch that ends the epilogue. This kind of play-within-a-play structure was familiar to the Elizabethans, and it provides a solid sense of closure for the audience.

The frame is important thematically because it introduces the idea of genre, which, in itself, leads to questions about the nature of drama. Comedy introduces the theme in her opening speech:

> Why so! Thus do I hope to please.
> Music revives, and mirth is tolerable.
> Comedy, play thy part and please;
> Make merry them that come to joy with thee.
> Joy, then, good gentles; I hope to make you laugh.

The nature of comedy is to please with joy and laughter. That most naive definition is challenged, however, by Envy's immediate threat to "mix" Comedy's "music with a tragic end." As the argument continues, Comedy learns that her triumph comes not just from mirth or lovely tales, but from the transformation of tragic events into mirth and pleasure. She can, in the middle of the argument, still define herself as a goddess who:

> . . . is mild, gentle, willing for to please,
> And seeks to gain the love of all estates,
> Delighting in mirth, mixed all with lovely tales
> And bringeth things with treble joy to pass.

By the end of the scene, she can answer Envy's threat of treble death with a statement of strength against adversity:

> Then ugly monster, do thy worst;
> I will defend them in despite of thee.
> And, though thou think'st with tragic fumes
> To prove my play unto my deep disgrace,
> I force it not; I scorn what thou canst do;
> I'll grace it so thyself shall it confess
> From tragic stuff to be a pleasant comedy.

By responding in this manner to Envy's threat, Comedy establishes the basic structure of the play: the hero and heroine will be threatened by death three times and will triumph three times. And indeed, Mucedorus must engage in deadly battle against the bear, Tremelio, and Bremo. Not surprisingly, the dramatis personae suggests that the actor who plays Envy would also play Tremelio and Bremo. By the end of the induction the audience understands that Comedy, by definition, is a genre in which love and order triumph over threats of death and disorder.

The English Renaissance was a period of great dramatic experimentation. Despite the flourishing of cycle and morality plays in the Middle Ages, Western civilization had not seen such dramatic outpouring since Greek and Roman times. It is hardly surprising that the plays of the period were consciously concerned with defining the genre, the nature of representation, the taking on of roles, and the process of transformation. *Mucedorus*, a basically simple play, deals explicitly with such ideas.

Occasionally in the play, the author refers to dramatic forms or the taking on of roles to represent ideas or character types. Such references are momentary reminders to the viewer that he is watching drama, that what he sees is a representation of events. Mucedorus is able to disguise himself as a shepherd because his friend, Anselmo, still has a shepherd's costume from playing the role in a masque. Bremo in his attempt to feed on Amadine, tells himself to "play thy part"; the author complicates the issue by having an actor play a wild man telling himself to play a wild man. The clown has an ironic line in which he suggests that Segasto in his encounter with the bear "played the man and ran away." Like the frame, such language keeps the audience aware that they are seeing a play.

One reason that has been suggested for the number of editions of *Mucedorus* is that the distribution of parts listed in the dramatis personae enables small groups of players to present the work. Indeed some editions actually specify that one actor play the Aragonian King and Rumbelo, that another play Comedy, a Boy, an Old Woman, and Ariena, and that still another play Envy, Tremelio, and Bremo. Such casting, which perpetually reminds the viewer that he is seeing actors taking on roles, does not necessarily undermine the credibility of the production but rather adds complexity and texture to the experience of drama. The viewer sees the same actor play different types of people, a device that emphasizes the idea of actors representing character types. Rumbelo, a drunken sailor, is a vastly different character from the noble King, but the actor is the same. Comedy in the role of the Old Woman, who is herself a comic character, threatens Mouse, the play's most purely comic figure.

Envy's roles, rather than providing contrasts, are remarkably similar, and would, in a well-designed production, draw attention in a different way to the transformations through which the actor must go. Although the dramatis personae does not provide an actor for the bear, it is reasonable that the part, like Tremelio and Bremo, would be played by the Envy actor. The bear is, after all, the first of the three death threats that Envy promises to send to destroy Comedy's play. As the actor appears in successive roles, the audience is reminded of the triumph of comedy, the genre to which the play conforms, and of the fact that a play is a representation of life, not life itself.

The use of a single actor in successive roles becomes central to the comedy of the play if in each of Envy's roles, the actor appears in a more battered condition than before. Thus as the roles increase in the danger that they pose to the hero, the actor would appear weaker. Envy is Mucedorus's weakest opponent as the bear simply because he is a weaponless beast. The actor, however, is unbattered at this point in the play. Tremelio, a great warrior, has a weapon and is an equal to Mucedorus, who is also a warrior with a weapon. The actor, however, has already had to die once as the bear and ought to appear

slightly the worse for his first encounter with the hero. Bremo, a creature of rage, has a weapon, while Mucedorus, with none, must rely first on Amadine's ability to tame the brute and then on his own cleverness. If Bremo bears the scars of the two earlier battles, the audience laughs at the incongruity of a battered actor presenting great danger to the hero. Against the weakest threat, which ought to be the strongest, the hero is actually faced with the greatest difficulty. The audience observes at first hand the kinds of complex patterns drama allows.

The use of disguise and the playing of several roles are all part of a larger pattern of transformation that runs through the play. Drama, by its very nature, is a transformation of actors into characters, stages into countries, and everyday language into art. By drawing attention to the idea of transformation, the author stresses further the thematic question of the nature of drama. Comedy's determination to change Envy's threats into pleasantness introduces the idea in the induction. The first bit of action in the play proper transforms Mucedorus into a shepherd, and the pattern of transformation would become fully fixed in the minds of the audience if the bear appears clearly as Envy in a new costume.

The language of the play emphasizes the idea of transformation as well. Much of Mouse's humor involves transforming the language of other characters. The most simple form of this is the obvious substitution of one word for another. By perpetually performing such substitutions in the presence of Mucedorus, Mouse builds, both for the hero and for the audience, a pattern of transformation and a set of expectations that he can undercut at will. Mouse performs for the first time directly after Tremelio is killed:

> SEGASTO. Come, help: away with my friend!
> CLOWN. Why, is he drunk? Cannot he stand on his feet?
> SEGASTO. No, he is not drunk; he is slain.
> CLOWN. Flain? no, by Lady; he is not flain.

The transformation of "slain" to "flain" is simple and helps to turn the death of a villain into a comic rather than horrific event.

Later in the play, Mouse transforms the language of a messenger by taking advantage of a homonym to make a joke:

> MESSENGER. All hail, worthy shepherd!
> CLOWN. All rain, lousy shepherd!

The comic effect of the line is obvious, but Mucedorus, like the audience, is becoming sensitive to the games Mouse plays with language.

Toward the end of the play when Mucedorus has chosen to transform himself from a shepherd into a hermit rather than revealing his true, noble nature, Mouse manages to transform "hermit" into "emmet." Mucedorus and the viewer now know how Mouse's games work; and because they expect such language transformations, they actively try to outthink the clown. Mucedorus tries his luck immediately:

> MUCEDORUS. O, Master Mouse, I pray you, what office might you bear in the court?
> CLOWN. Marry, sir, I am a rusher of the stable.
> MUCEDORUS. O, usher of the table!
> CLOWN. Nay, I say 'rusher,' and I'll prove mine office good; for look, sir, when any comes from under the sea or so, and a dog chance to blow his nose backward, then with a whip I give him the good time of the day and strow rushes presently. Therefore, I am, a rusher, a high office, I promise ye.

The pattern is completed; once language transformations become expected through repetition, Mouse undercuts those expectations by refusing to be consistent. The changes of Envy into his successive roles and even the transformations of Mucedorus by disguise follow a similar undercutting. The least threatening figure is the enemy Mucedorus has the most difficulty defeating. When the hero is faced with disaster, the viewer would expect him to reveal his true identity, but he does not, choosing rather to accept his fate or, when all seems lost, to change his disguise.

By forcing the viewers to think about transformation of character and language, the author confronts them with the very idea of drama. *Mucedorus* defines the genre of comedy as a representation of life in which love and order triumph over death and disorder, and it consciously plays with the concept of drama as a representation of real life in which actors, stages, and language are transformed to reveal characters, places, and art. At the heart of this simple, flawed play are the conventions of the age. *Mucedorus* satisfied its original audience by addressing their concerns simply and conventionally; it can satisfy a modern reader by revealing much about the Renaissance as well as by providing an amusing, if unpretentious and uncomplicated, evening of theater.

References:

M. C. Bradbrook, *The Growth and Structure of Elizabethan Comedy* (London: Chatto & Windus, 1956);

R. H. Goldsmith, "The Wild Man on the English Stage," *Modern Language Review*, 53 (October 1958): 481-491;

Leo Kirschbaum, "The Texts of *Mucedorus*," *Modern Language Review*, 50 (January 1955): 1-5;

Paul G. Kreuzer, "*Mucedorus*: A Comedy of Transformation," *Thoth*, 16 (Fall 1976): 33-42;

Jacqueline Pearson, *Tragedy and Tragicomedy in the Plays of John Webster* (Totowa, N.J.: Barnes & Noble, 1980), pp. 7-13;

George F. Reynolds, "*Mucedorus*, Most Popular Elizabethan Play?," in *Studies in the English Renaissance Drama in Memory of Karl Julius Holzknecht*, edited by Josephine W. Bennett, Oscar Cargill, and Vernon Hall, Jr. (New York: New York University Press, 1959), pp. 248-268.

Appendices

The Theater in Shakespeare's Time

The Publication of English Renaissance Plays

Sources for the Study of Tudor and Stuart Drama

The Theater in Shakespeare's Time

Andrew Gurr
University of Reading

I. The Society

The plays written in London during Shakespeare's lifetime were the most brilliant exploitations of language any culture has ever known. The conditions which brought about this achievement were unique. By 1642, the year when all the playhouses were closed at the outbreak of England's civil war, London was the fastest-growing and largest city in Europe, with a population of four hundred thousand. Before then for nearly a century it had been attracting all the wealthiest and most ambitious people in the country to what it could offer. It was the seat of government and the stronghold of commerce. In order to get to London landowners sold their land and converted it into the gold which Francis Drake had captured from the Spanish bullion ships. Gold demanded none of the responsibilities for which land called and could be spent on the pleasures that London alone offered. This flood of gold and pleasure hunters into London created the market for entertainment which Shakespeare and his fellow playwrights supplied.

Early in the sixteenth century the Reformation brought about a gradual displacement of Latin by the ordinary language of the country. This change gave a strong spur to the growth of a vernacular literature in England. English was a new and fertile language, ripe for exploitation as it grew and changed under the pressure of changing social conditions. The new nation-states needed an educated class of administrators, and the government promoted the development of schools and universities to cater for this need. By the end of the sixteenth century England's schools were producing large numbers of highly trained students who could not always manage to secure, or who did not always rest content with, the secretarial service which the government and great magnates demanded of them. They turned to creative writing. The English language was fresh, flexible, and easy, and it had a rapidly growing audience. Some of the new generation of educated writers made a living by writing for the stage. In the late 1580s Christopher Marlowe, the son of a Canterbury shoemaker, William Shakespeare, the son of a Stratford merchant, and a few years later Ben Jonson, the son of a Westminster bricklayer, began to provide the plays which the London market now demanded.

The commercial playhouses and acting companies for which Marlowe, Shakespeare, and Jonson wrote had been operating in London for twenty or more years by the time Marlowe's *Tamburlaine*, the first great hit of the period, came to the stage. Professional acting companies had existed for centuries, making a living by traveling around the country performing in marketplaces and town halls, or working as servants to a great lord who would use them to entertain his guests on feast days. The first commercial playhouse to be built for paying customers appeared in London in 1567. It was a large open-air amphitheater, rather like a bullring, with three tiers of galleries and a yard containing a large platform stage. Two more were built in 1576 and 1577, one of which later was pulled down to make the framework for Shakespeare's Globe, the playhouse for which he wrote his greatest plays. At the same time a second type of playhouse, a much smaller indoor or "hall" theater, was developed to accommodate companies of boy actors formed in the chorister schools where the boys who sang at St. Paul's Cathedral and the Chapel Royal were trained. The boy companies catered to much smaller and wealthier groups of people than the adult companies who played in the amphitheaters. John Lyly, who wrote plays for the boy companies in the 1580s, aimed specifically at courtiers, gentlemen, and ladies and packed his plays not only with material based on the classical reading of his courtly audience but with in-jokes about the royal Court and thinly veiled allegories about Queen Elizabeth and state affairs. The boy companies, however, performed much less often than the adult players and were a less profitable concern. They ran for fifteen years from 1575 until they were closed down by the government

Public entertainment in 1635, from Adriaen van de Venne's Tafereel van de Belacchende Werelt, *published in Holland (courtesy of the Folger Shakespeare Library). In* Early English Stages *Glynne Wickham writes, "Few pictures can give a more vivid impression of the general conditions prevailing in public playhouses than this engraving. Rope-dancers, gymnasts, musicians and performing monkeys jostle with the spectators for attention in a large barn equipped with a raised trestle-stage, a* frons scenae *of curtains strung from side to side at the back of the stage, and a splendid pavilion in the centre: the focal point of the picture is the vaulting horse of the sort demanded by Webster in Act II scene ii of* The White Devil. *Scenic trees are visible above the curtain screen to left and right of the pavilion: spectators appear to be sitting on the stage on the left and musicians on the right."*

in 1590, and for another ten from 1599. After that Shakespeare's company of adult players took over the best of the hall playhouses. From 1609 until the playhouses were closed in 1642 almost all the playing companies were composed of adult players, who performed in both the popular open-air amphitheaters and the more exclusive hall theaters.

Between the time when Marlowe started to write for the stage and the general closure in 1642, playgoing changed from being the casual product of a casual impulse, shared by numbers of idle Londoners wanting something more gripping than bearbaiting or displays of swordfighting for their entertainment, into the predominant feature of London's cultural life. King Charles himself not only enjoyed plays put on for his pleasure at Court but bought playbooks, wrote comments on them in their margins, and engaged in serious discussion of their literary merits with his courtiers. This rise in the

valuation put on plays was the result of the tremendously rapid and intense development in the early years, when Marlowe and Shakespeare were writing. This rapid development makes it important to trace the historical changes which took place between the first performances of Marlowe's *Tamburlaine* circa 1587 and the plays written after 1616, when the growth began to slow down. The changes show themselves most distinctly in the plays themselves, but the changes also appear in the companies which performed the plays and the playhouses where they were staged.

II. The Playhouses

Seven amphitheater playhouses were built in London in the sixteenth century: the Red Lion in 1567, the Theatre in 1576, the Curtain in 1577, the Rose in 1587, the Swan in 1595, the Globe in 1599, and the Fortune in 1600. Of these only the Globe and Fortune remained important in the seventeenth century, though the Swan and the Curtain remained in occasional use. Two other playhouses, the Boar's Head and the Red Bull, opened early in the new century, and a third, the Hope, was used for a short time as a playhouse before it reverted to its alternative function as a bearbaiting arena. Through most of the early seventeenth century three amphitheaters, the Globe, the Fortune, and the Red Bull, were used regularly, except that after 1609 the Globe was only used for the summer months when the light and the weather were most favorable to open-air performances. In the seventeenth century on the whole the amphitheaters lost ground to the hall theaters.

The design of the open-air amphitheaters reflects the "popular" origin of commercial playgoing in London. Following the model of the marketplaces where most of the adult players learned their trade, each of these theaters consisted of a large open space in which stood a wooden platform. At the back of this stage was a curtained "booth" or room where the players waited for their cues to enter. The audience was expected to stand around the platform for the duration of the performance. This body of "understanders," as they were sarcastically called by the more educated and wealthy playgoers seated in other parts of the playhouse, was the center of attention and the players' main concern, clustered as it was close to the stage platform, restless since everybody was on foot throughout the play, and noisy as people are always likely to be when standing in the open air. Admission to this basic viewing place, the "yard," cost only one penny, the smallest price one could pay to see a play anywhere. Behind the understanders were three rings of galleries, one above the other, each nine or ten feet high, where the people who were prepared to pay a little more for a seat and some shelter from the weather could position themselves. These places cost a second penny. For a third penny you could get the best seats and a cushion as well. For the really wealthy or extravagant playgoers there were special rooms, known, perhaps flatteringly, as "lords' rooms," where there was space for three or four customers, each prepared to pay sixpence for the privilege. These rooms were on the balcony over the stage doors, at the back of the stage platform,

A section from Wenceslas Hollar's "Long View" of London, engraved in 1644 from drawings made in the 1630s (courtesy of the Folger Shakespeare Library). Hollar made his careful drawings from the tower of St. Mary Overies (now Southwark Cathedral), looking north across the Thames. This section is from the western (lefthand) portion of the view. On the south bank of the river it shows the Globe (labeled "beere bayting h.") and the Hope or Bear Garden (labeled "the Globe"). In the city the roof of the Blackfriars playhouse is visible as a long ridge with a central lantern below and to the right of the tall tower of St. Bride's church, which stands up slightly to the right of Baynards Castle.

and allowed the occupants to be seen better than they could see, which is probably what they wanted. Even if they were not deeply interested in the play, though, their presence behind the stage completed the circle of the audience, which completely surrounded the players. The "picture-frame" or "proscenium-arch" stage, which puts the scene into a pictorial frame keeping the audience separate and in front of it, did not exist until the Restoration theaters came into existence in 1660. The picture-frame stage is the basis of most modern staging and certainly the model for all cinema and television screens.

The "popular" character of the first playhouse amphitheaters is perhaps most clearly indicated by the number of customers they expected to cram in to see a performance: three thousand people at the Globe and the Swan, and not many fewer at the others. This number, in an arena only one-hundred feet in outside diameter, must have created a fearsome crush when a playhouse was full. Playgoing at the Globe was anything but an activity for the solitary and pensive.

By contrast with the amphitheaters the hall playhouses were much more like modern cinemas. Roofed halls lit by candelabra, they could hold only six- or seven-hundred people. They provided seats for everyone, and unlike the amphitheaters the more one paid the closer one could sit to the stage. They were usually rectangular halls with the stage at the end of one of the shorter sides. The cheapest seats, which cost sixpence, secured a place in the topmost gallery at the end of the hall furthest from the stage and the players. A bench on the floor of the playhouse, the "pit," cost three times that amount, and the "boxes" flanking the stage itself cost five times the minimum. The gallants and gentleman who wanted to be seen positioned themselves on stools on the stage itself. When the playhouses reopened at the Restoration in 1660 the Cockpit in Drury Lane, which had been built as a hall playhouse in 1616, was made into a proscenium-arch playhouse by cutting out the boxes on the flanks of the stage and using them as wings for scenery, creating a picture-frame stage. The ampitheaters look back to the early sixteenth-century tradition of performing plays in market places. The hall playhouses look forward to the operatic and proscenium-arch theaters of the eighteenth and nineteenth centuries.

Although the auditoriums of the two types of playhouse in use before 1642 were so different, the stages and the staging of plays on them were strikingly similar. At both types the chief apparatus and the chief focus of attention was the stage itself. Thrusting out from the rear wall into the middle of the yard in the amphitheaters, it measured more than forty-five feet across and twenty-three feet from front to rear. In the much smaller hall theaters it might be half that size, though even then it still provided ample space by modern standards. Unlike the halls, the amphitheater stages had to suffer the impediment of two large pillars rising from the middle of the stage to support the "shadow" or "heavens," a painted ceiling over the stage which protected the players from rain and in later years allowed them to fly boys playing gods down on wires or ropes from a ceiling trapdoor. The pillars of course could become trees or places of concealment, or posts to tie people to when needed. Both halls and amphitheaters usually had a trapdoor in the stage platform itself, for devils and ghosts to appear through, or for such uses as Ophelia's grave in *Hamlet*. At the back of the stage platform was the curtained wall through which the players entered and left the stage, behind which was their dressing room or "tiring house." The tiring-house wall usually had two doors and a central alcove or "discovery space" which could be used to show static scenes—a scholar studying, a lady sick in bed, a heap of treasure, or the statue of a dead queen, as in the final scene of *The Winter's Tale*. Over the stage-entry doors was the balcony, most of the rooms on which were occupied by the lords and gallants. One of these lords' rooms might sometimes be reserved for the players if a play called for a balcony scene, as in *Romeo and Juliet*. In the halls the central balcony room was normally set aside for the musicians, who entertained the audience during the short intervals between the acts while the candles were being trimmed, and who often provided music for the plays. After 1609, when the players started to perform at the Globe during the summer and at the Blackfriars hall for the rest of the year, they adapted one of the Globe's balcony rooms into a musicians' gallery, where it no doubt doubled as Juliet's balcony whenever necessary.

III. The Players

In the early years players were close to being social outcasts. At a time of rapid population growth and massive unemployment a talent for making money by entertaining one's fellows was a valuable commodity. Nonetheless it was not considered a respectable occupation. There was no formal training, no seven-year apprenticeship of the kind the craft guilds enforced, and certainly no institution to teach men how to act. It was an insecure, traveling life, even for the outstanding players who were able to settle themselves at a base in the new London playhouses. Until the seventeenth century there was no security even in London, since the London authorities were the players' enemies and closed the playhouses whenever they could. According to most of the Lord Mayors of London the plays only distracted idle men who should be working. Plays encouraged large assemblies of people who might spread diseases such as the plague, which reached epidemic proportions at times throughout the period. And the players who put on such dangerous shows were themselves vagrants and seducers of good people. The Lord Mayors never stopped trying to have plays banned, and through most of the sixteenth century they largely succeeded in fending off the players and preventing them from performing inside the City of London itself. All the amphitheaters had to be built in the suburbs outside the city walls, because the Lord Mayor's authority did not extend there. For many years players were regarded as little better than what the government called "rogues and vagabonds," the homeless poor and unemployed of Elizabethan England. They traveled the country, entertaining whomever they could attract to watch them and getting their income by passing a hat around the audience. Not until early in the seventeenth century did stage playing start to become a respectable occupation.

Companies of players in the middle of the sixteenth century, before the first London playhouses were built, usually formed themselves into groups claiming to be the servants of a great lord, their "patron." The masters of the great country houses would often employ a band of entertainers to perform for the amusement of their guests, and these entertainers traveled the country using their lord's name as their patron and protector. When the government began to regulate stage playing in 1574, it issued patents to the best companies under such titles as "the Earl of Leicester's Men" or "the Lord Berkeley's Men." The lord so named would ultimately be held responsible for the company since technically the players were his servants. These patents authorized the players to perform and exempted them from the persecution which travelers otherwise suffered as "sturdy vagabonds" and beggars. A

company would show their patent to the mayor of the town they were visiting as a token of their professional status. Usually they were their patron's servants in reality as well as in name and had to perform for him whenever he wanted them to. They also performed at Court, especially through the long season of festivities over the Christmas period. By the early 1580s, in fact, the choice of a particular company to perform at Court became a measure of the importance of the company's patron. This came to be regarded as potentially dangerous, and as a result in 1583 the Queen's chief secretary, Francis Walsingham, destroyed the competition by picking out the best players from all the existing companies and using them to form a new and distinctive troupe of players. This new company was graced with the title of the supreme patron, the Queen herself. It was the first major step toward respectability for players. The Queen's authority could be used to counter the hostility of the Lord Mayor. From 1583 until 1589, when Tarlton, the company's leading clown, died, the Queen's Men dominated playing in London and at Court.

The Queen's Men was a tightly organized troupe of highly skilled men. It had two famous players of tragic and serious parts, William Knell and John Bentley. It had two famous clowns, Robert Wilson, who also wrote plays, and the greatest clown of them all, Richard Tarlton. Altogether it had eight experienced players, who took most of the speaking parts and who formed the "sharers" of the company, dividing the expenses and the profits equally among them. Most of the sharers had attached to them a boy apprentice, who was learning to become a player and who performed the women's roles, since before 1660 it was not regarded as respectable to have women onstage. The sharers also employed a few extras in walk-on parts, calling them "hired men" to distinguish them from the company sharers. Some of these men also did the backstage chores of prompting and carrying the few properties used in the performances on and offstage.

Altogether a traveling company in the 1580s might consist of ten or eleven men and boys. The companies lucky and skilled enough to stay in London for any length of time usually assembled a larger number of players than the traveling companies needed, since they had a much more secure source of income. They also, however, had much higher costs. They had not only to pay the rent for their playhouse and employ extra helpers, but they had to provide a far

A facsimile of the title page for the 1600 quarto edition of Kemps Nine Daies Wonder, *an account of Will Kempe's marathon dance from London to Norwich, with an engraving of Kempe dancing a morris (courtesy of the Folger Shakespeare Library)*

greater number of plays than were needed for touring. In the country the same play would do for each town, so the same few properties and costumes would do for the whole tour. In London on the other hand they had to provide a new play every day, for six days a week, with few repeats. Each play might need new costumes and possibly new properties, quite apart from the cost of the playbook itself and the scribe who had to copy out everyone's part before the play could be brought to the stage. Residence in London was the biggest possible stimulus to the players, and the biggest incentive to the composition of new plays. London's appetite was enormous.

Through most of the 1590s two companies played regularly in London, one in Shoreditch, a suburb just north of the City walls, and one on the Bankside, just across the Thames to the south of the City. The first was led by Richard Burbage, the first player of Hamlet, and included the clown Will Kempe and, as writer and player of king's parts, Shakespeare. The second company was led by Edward Alleyn, the first man to play Tamburlaine and Faustus. Alleyn became the wealthiest player of the time, a churchwarden and a pillar of society who founded the College of God's Gift, which still survives as Dulwich College in south London.

The story of the playing companies reflects most clearly the rapid growth of the market for plays in London, the equally rapid rise in the social status of players and playgoing, and the growth in reputation of the plays that they staged. When the Queen's company was formed in 1583 there were several companies of adult players and two companies of boys all trying to secure places in London. The Queen's Men had a better basis for growth than any company before them. They secured a near monopoly, as well as the rise in status which came from the Queen's patronage. That did not prevent other companies competing with them, of course, and by the early 1590s several companies were again struggling to secure the prime positions in London. In 1594 the Lord Chamberlain, the member of the Queen's chief governing body, the Privy Council, who had direct charge of entertainments and similar matters, began to control the companies more tightly. He gave orders that only two adult companies could perform regularly in London and specified which playhouses might be used. In a time of such rapid change that order lasted no longer than the supremacy of the Queen's Men, and by 1601 the two adult companies had been joined by a third, and two boy companies had also started up again. There was also some shifting of playhouses. From 1600 two adult companies settled in amphitheaters in the northern suburbs, and a third, Shakespeare's company, was fixed at the Globe on the south bank of the river. Two boy companies, free from the constrictions imposed on the adult companies, played once a week in the center of the City of London itself. This pattern ran for nearly ten years, until the boy companies collapsed and Shakespeare's company moved into the hall playhouse the boys had vacated in the center of the city, in Blackfriars.

From 1609 Shakespeare's company became by far the strongest and best company in London. It was so well equipped, with all of Shakespeare's plays and two playhouses, the Globe amphitheater and the Blackfriars hall, that it ran in unrivaled prosperity right through to the general closure in 1642. No other company lasted more than ten years without breaking up. In 1616 Christopher Beeston, once a player with Shakespeare, set up a hall in Drury Lane, known as the Cockpit or Phoenix, to rival Blackfriars. Few of its companies lasted more than three years, though. The only one that did ran for ten years (from 1626 to 1636), between two very severe epidemics of the plague, each of which kept the playhouses closed for a whole year and broke up all the companies except the King's Men. The King's Men were Shakespeare's fellows, gaining that ultimate title when James came to the throne in 1603. Only Beeston's Cockpit company ever rivaled them in fame and prosperity, and then only for a few years around 1630.

Shakespeare's company, followed in later years by the few other companies who managed to secure hall playhouses in the City of London, became the company which performed for the gentry. The high cost of admission to the hall playhouses and the smaller numbers they could accommodate made them the favorite playhouses of the wealthy. The socially privileged went to the hall playhouses while the citizens and their wives, the artisans and apprentices, house servants, the self-employed and the unemployed all went to the amphitheaters. Curiously though, Shakespeare's company, for all that it started the practice of adult companies' using hall playhouses, always insisted on catering for both kinds of customer. In 1609 after ten years of performing for citizens at the Globe, they had the chance to abandon them and turn to the wealthy at the Blackfriars. They chose not to do so and started a practice they held to for the next thirty-three years without a change. They deliberately catered to both ends of the market by using both their playhouses alternately. Instead of selling one of them, they chose to continue performing at the Globe through the summer months and to use the Blackfriars only in the winter. Even when the Globe was accidentally burned down in 1613 they did not abandon it. They rebuilt it more expensively than ever, so that they could carry on with their evidently satisfactory new practice of alternating between the wealthy in the winter and the citizenry in the summer. No other company could ever afford the luxury of leaving one playhouse empty while they performed in the other. They were unique in choosing to satisfy the whole range of London's playgoing population. It was a policy they maintained at considerable cost to themselves when they had to rebuild the Globe.

The other companies had to choose narrower sections of the community. The companies which used the two other hall playhouses (the third was built in the West End in 1629) played only to the wealthy. The rest played in the northern suburbs for citizens. Once King James gave his name to Shakespeare's company the players were made fairly safe from anything other than the routine government censorship and the troubles which followed closures because of the plague. By the time Shakespeare died, in 1616, it had become normal to have four companies playing regularly. Two performed for the citizens and two—at least through the winter when most of the courtiers, lawyers, and gentry were in London—played in the enclosed halls to the wealthy. From this time on the rate of growth slowed. The companies needed a smaller number of new plays each year. Plays became much less of a novelty, and the radical experimentation of the earlier playwrights faded away. Playgoers knew what to expect and knew what they wanted. By the 1630s playgoing was a feature of the life of London's high society, whether for the ladies of the Court and the wives of great city magnates to be seen in the boxes at the hall playhouses or for the gallants and gentlemen exercising their wits at composing plays themselves or in criticizing what they went to see. Discussion of the quality of new plays became a feature of high-society gossip.

At the same time the "citizen" playhouses were still catering for the tastes fixed when the only playhouses open were amphitheaters, in the 1590s. Plays such as Christopher Marlowe's *Tamburlaine* and *Faustus* and Thomas Kyd's *The Spanish Tragedy* remained popular for more than fifty years at the Red Bull and Fortune playhouses in the northern suburbs. The Red Bull in particular became famous for plays with spectacular battles in them. It would not, however, be true to say that the tastes which were established in the 1590s were popular only at the amphitheaters. The Cockpit had close links with the Red Bull, and several plays which began their life at the Red Bull later found their way to the Cockpit, where they were unhesitatingly served up to the gentry. Marlowe's *The Jew of Malta* and Thomas Heywood's *The Rape of Lucrece*, which was written for the Red Bull circa 1608, were popular at the Cockpit in its heyday in the early 1630s.

IV. The Company System and Staging

The player Edward Alleyn, who founded Dulwich College in 1619, left a great deal more to posterity than a school. The College of God's Gift has carefully preserved his papers from his playing days, and they comprise a unique and remarkable record of how the companies were organized and financed in Shakespeare's day.

Alleyn's company performed on the Bankside up to 1600 and in the northern suburbs thereafter, always in amphitheater playhouses. Alleyn's papers, and especially the "diary" of his father-in-law, Philip Henslowe, a notebook of his business affairs and playing accounts, show that the company performed as many as thirty-five plays a year, every afternoon of the year except Sundays and Lent. A new play would be read and approved by the sharers of the company, who

Edward Alleyn as Tamburlaine, an engraving published in the 1603 folio edition of Richard Knolles's The Generall Historie of the Turkes, *largely a translation of a French history (courtesy of the Folger Shakespeare Library). Most of the engravings of Turkish sultans, all turbaned and dressed in long white gowns, are copied from the French text, but Knolles's picture of Tamburlaine has no original there, and his dress, which looks Elizabethan, indicates that the engraver used Alleyn's stage costume as his model. Henslowe's inventory of costumes includes a copper-laced coat for Tamburlaine, which may well be the one he wears in this picture.*

would then commission a scribe to copy out the parts and prepare a "plot" of the play to hang in the tiring house for the prompter and the offstage players, so that they could keep a check on the progress of the play on stage. The players would learn their parts and rehearse the play in the course of three weeks before the first performance. They studied their parts and rehearsed in the mornings and performed whatever play was scheduled for that day in the afternoon. If the new play was not liked on its first performance (for which the admission charges were doubled) it would be dropped and never appear again.

Even the most popular plays were staged no more than four or five times a month, and none appeared much more than twenty times a year. Evidently London developed a huge appetite for new plays through the 1580s and 1590s, and the players had to work desperately hard to provide for it. There were usually only two, and never more than four, companies performing in London at any one time, and many playgoers went so frequently to the playhouses demanding new plays that the players had to develop a staggeringly high-speed system to satisfy their hunger. No repertory system has ever supplied so many plays so quickly to the stage as the London companies of the 1590s. The leading players might have as many as eight-hundred lines of verse to learn for each play. With six plays to be staged each week, every one different and one of them very likely new, these players' memories were required to hold something like four-thousand lines of verse ready for use each week, and at frequent intervals to add another eight-hundred lines.

This process was so rapid that there was little time for refinement in the delivery, or for elaborate staging. Casting was fairly standardized, with the chief tragedian, the chief villain, the clown, the junior or romantic lead, the player of comic old men, the player of stately roles, kings and judges, and the women's parts all easily allocated. The acting must have been similarly standardized, given the short time for rehearsal and the speed at which the plays were performed. Relatively few properties were required, though, and most of the preparation went into costumes and the attendant items such as swords, banners, scrolls of paper, or similarly portable properties which helped to clarify the function of a particular character or to assist the action of the plot. The players had evolved their traditions in the days when they traveled from town to town with their plays and had no use for set scenery or large and troublesome furniture. Their stage properties had to be as portable as themselves. Their spectacle was displayed in their costumes and their acting. Throughout the seventy-five years in London before the playhouses were closed in 1642 no playhouse developed the practice of mounting a play with scenery.

Scenery, whether it remains the same throughout the performance or is changed from scene to scene to denote changes of locality, slows a play down. It also requires a patient audience, waiting for the changes and willing for a while to look at cloth and cardboard instead of the actors. The Elizabethan tradition, especially in the amphitheaters, where half the audience was on its feet and probably standing in the rain, wanted none

of that. Plays swept on rapidly, with no pause for scenery to be changed or even for an interval. Not until after 1609, when a hall playhouse was first occupied by an adult company, was there even any call for pauses between the acts. This novelty was prompted in fact more by the need for pauses to allow the candles which lit the stage and auditorium to be trimmed than for the comfort of the audience or scene changing. The norm throughout the period was for a play to run without a break from beginning to end, and to do so much faster than modern productions. The standard time allowed for a performance was, in Shakespeare's words, the "two hours' traffic of the stage." This is probably a rather economical estimate of the full playing time, since the amphitheaters usually sent on their clown to perform a jig or comic rhyming playlet at the end of the main performance, which lengthened the full performance time by several minutes. Nonetheless it seems from contemporary testimony that the audience would begin to gather at the playhouse between one and two o'clock in the afternoon, and that the play started at two and was finished by about five o'clock.

Modern performances of Elizabethan plays—even when done for the radio or records, where no scene changing is needed—never take less than three hours. The Elizabethan players must have delivered their lines markedly faster than modern actors. Such high-speed playing could be expected in front of an impatient and leg-weary audience out of doors in London. Holding a restless audience's attention calls for loud and rapid speech and attendant noise and bustle. There were enough comments on the "stalking-stamping player, that will raise a tempest with his tongue, and thunder with his heels" to justify the conclusion that Elizabethan playing was noisy and on the whole unsubtle in its emphasis.

Costumes were colorful, as all the Elizabethan clothing worn by the wealthy, especially the men, tended to be. The players invested as much capital in costumes as in playbooks, buying discarded cloaks or doublets of noblemen which had been passed on to their servants. The servants, being unable to wear such finery themselves because of their humble social status, sold them to the players, who could wear them, at least on stage. Costumes were valuable and durable properties, often more so than the playbooks for which the costumes were bought. The Henslowe company paid more for the costume of the boy playing the heroine in *A Woman Killed with*

Frontispiece for Francis Kirkman's The Wits, or Sport upon Sport *(1662), a collection of "drolls," brief extracts from the plays of the Shakespearean period which were performed illegally while the playhouses were officially closed between 1642 and 1660 (courtesy of the Folger Shakespeare Library). This first published picture of early Shakespearean characters onstage features Falstaff and the Hostess of the Boar's Head, from part two of* Henry IV, *and characters from Middleton's* The Changeling *and other plays. The stage depicted is in a hall playhouse, judging by the candelabra hanging from the ceiling. The figures on the balcony on each side of the curtained music room are members of the audience.*

Kindness than they paid Thomas Heywood for the text of the play itself. Sometimes costumes were made especially for certain leading parts in historical dramas or plays requiring supernatural figures to appear. Commonly, however, there was little concern for historical accuracy. Henslowe's papers include a list of costumes, one of which is an Elizabethan doublet for Alleyn to play Tamburlaine in. The original Tamburlaine was a shepherd from fourteenth-century Scythia, who would have worn a white gown and turban when he was not in his military armor. The engraving of him printed in Richard Knolles's translation of a history of the Turkish empire makes him look like an Elizabethan gentleman. On the other hand a drawing of a scene from Shakespeare's *Titus Andronicus* made in about 1595 shows Titus in Roman costume, while his warriors are carrying the pikes of Elizabethan foot soldiers and wearing the standard military costumes of the time. On the whole, no great efforts were put in to make special costumes for new plays, an economy which is hardly surprising when we remember that a play might not last beyond its first performance. Not that we should underrate the importance of costume: it made the greatest visual impact, and it could often tell more than was put into words. It could even signify a particular locality. A hunting party or a group of travelers would appear in riding boots with muddy cloaks, for instance. A bedroom scene would be signaled by the entry of a character in nightcap and white nightgown, as readily as a night scene would be marked by torches and candles or a battle would be signaled by trumpet calls and the entry of characters with drawn swords.

Some larger properties were used on the London stages to signify locations or special kinds of scene. A chair and table, usually revealed in the "discovery space" by drawing back a curtain, would denote a study. Similarly a bed might be revealed behind the curtain, or a "spectacle" set up, such as the shop in the opening of *Eastward Ho!* or the horde of gold treasure which is "discovered" at the opening of Ben Jonson's *Volpone*. The most important property of all, one which appeared in a majority of the plays written between 1570 and 1640, was a throne. Scenes at the royal Court, or trial scenes in a law court, always took place with a large throne or "chair of state" occupying the center of the stage. The "chair of state," or "state" as it was commonly called, was placed on a dais three or four steps high, with a "cloth of estate" hung behind and a canopy over the top. The cloth of estate signified the "presence" of royalty, and courtiers always took off their hats to it. Sir Thomas Smith, in *De Republica Anglorum* (1583), noted that it was normal for respect to the king to extend to his emblem behind the chair of state. "No man speaketh to the prince . . . but in adoration and

Illustration from the title page for the 1605 quarto edition of part one of Thomas Heywood's If You Know Not Me, You Know Nobody, *a Red Bull play (courtesy of the Folger Shakespeare Library). Its depiction of Queen Elizabeth on her chair of state was copied from a famous engraving of her opening Parliament in 1586. Some such canopied throne would have stood onstage for the performance of the play, which includes several ceremonial uses of the "state," and one comic use when a character is presumptuous enough to sit on it while taking off his boots and is punished by having it pulled away from under him.*

kneeling, all persons of the realm be bareheaded before him, insomuch that in the chamber of presence, where the cloth of estate is set, yea though the prince be not there, no man dare tarry there but bareheaded." Thrones with their daises and canopies were a feature of all plays which involved kings, whether a play nostalgic for the reign of Elizabeth, such as Thomas Heywood's *If You Know Not Me, You Know Nobody* (produced circa 1604), or a play about the deposition of kings, such as Shakespeare's *Richard II*, where the empty throne is an important symbol of the

A woodcut from the title page for the 1620 quarto edition of Swetnam the Woman Hater, *a Red Bull play (courtesy of the Folger Shakespeare Library). The female judge sits in judgment on Swetnam in a chair very like a royal throne. This picture may not be a precise reproduction of the scene as presented onstage, if the windows at the rear are any indication. The tiring-house front at the Red Bull had no windows in it.*

power vacuum. In *Hamlet,* the "state," meaning not only the realm and the chair of state but its occupant, proves to be as "rotten" as Marcellus says, in that famous and much misunderstood diagnosis, "Something is rotten in the state of Denmark." The throne was the central icon or symbol of authority in all plays concerned with affairs of state. It dominated the scene, positioned squarely in the center of the stage and elevating its occupant above the pedestrians around him, all of whom would automatically stand bareheaded in his presence and kneel when they spoke.

Tangible properties such as thrones, beds, or banquet tables were signals giving the location of specific scenes. They were portable and emblematic. There was no attempt to make significant use of sets or scenery for realism, even though in many respects the tiring-house front at the back of the stage platform looked like the face of an Elizabethan house and might be used as one. The balcony, for instance, which was used most famously in *Romeo and Juliet* and its many imitators of the 1590s, might be used as a house balcony but was more often used simply for any kind of elevated position. It might become the wall of a besieged city, for instance, as in Shakespeare's *Henry V,* or the ramparts of a castle, as in *Richard II.* In any case it was hardly practical to build elaborate and special sets for plays

which were not going to be performed more than once in any one week. Nothing that could not be erected in a morning and taken down the next morning made sense under the repertory system that prevailed throughout the earlier part of the period. Anything either elaborate or very heavy would make it difficult to transport the play to the Court or to a nobleman's house in London, let alone carry it on tour around the country. Unlocalized, emblematic staging was the primary characteristic of staging in the Shakespearean period.

The absence of elaborate fixed sets and painted scenery was a major difference of the Shakespearean stage from modern stages. The absence of lighting was another. The amphitheaters used the afternoon light, an evenly distributed glow of indirect sunlight, with players onstage and spectators in the auditorium equally sheltered from the direct glare of whatever sunlight London could offer. The halls used candlelight and windows, which illuminated both the stage and the audience. Without the focus which modern spotlights supply and the control of the environment which the other devices of electric lighting give, the whole mood of an Elizabethan performance was different. It was a community experience, not the solitary thrill that a film seen in the seclusion of a modern darkened cinema can be.

This complete absence of what on modern stages gives the stage manager his greatest technical control meant that several things were done differently on the early stages. There were no curtains or lights to reveal any spectacle at the opening of the play. It started with a player or a group of players coming onstage and speaking. Words were the chief means of holding the audience's attention, not spectacle. As the play went on it was never possible for the audience to lose itself in the story as easily as people can do in modern cinemas, since there were no soft armchairs to ease personal discomfort and no darkness to conceal members of the audience from one another. An audience which can watch itself as well as the play is likely to be much more conscious of where reality is, that the theater is a theater, that the stage illusion is a trick, a "play" or game.

These differences do not mean that spectacle was missing from Elizabethan performances, of course. The resources for the display of technical ingenuity were different, but not necessarily wholly inferior. There were not only the symbolic flaming torches and candles carried onstage whenever a night scene was to be signaled, but cannon and smaller firearms might be set off, sometimes quite dangerously. A report of the performance of a play, probably part 2 of Marlowe's *Tamburlaine*, in 1587, tells how one of the guns fired at a player turned out to be loaded and killed a child and a pregnant woman in the audience. Shakespeare's *Henry VIII* at the Globe in 1613 required a cannon to be fired for a ceremonial triumph. The wadding from the shot lodged in the thatch covering the gallery roof, and the result was the complete destruction of the playhouse by fire. Fireworks were always used in early plays such as Marlowe's *Dr. Faustus*, where devils would appear, leaping out of the stage trapdoor with fireworks spouting from their mouths and their trousers. A reference in 1620 to *Faustus* at the Fortune spoke of how "shagge-haired devils" would "run roaring over the stage with squibs in their mouths, while drummers make thunder in the tiring-house, and the twelve-penny hirelings make artificial lightning in their heavens." One spectacular and rather comic entry with fireworks was set up by Shakespeare in *Cymbeline* IV.ii. He made the Roman god Jupiter descend from the trap in the cover or "heavens" over the stage, riding an eagle and throwing out fireworks. The stage direction reads, "*Jupiter*

descends in thunder and lightning, sitting upon an eagle. He throws a thunderbolt." When he disappears one character makes sure that anybody in the audience so clogged with London's cold that they cannot sense the main effect of the fireworks is reminded of it verbally, commenting, "He came in thunder; his celestial breath/Was sulphurous to smell." Some of the pyrotechnics in Thomas Heywood's plays for the Red Bull in about 1611 seem deliberately designed to outdo Shakespeare's at the Globe. In *The Silver Age*, for instance, various stage directions tell a spectacular story: "*Enter* Pluto *with a club of fire, a burning crown . . . and a guard of devils, all with burning weapons.*" Copying *Cymbeline*, Heywood even has Jupiter appearing under a rainbow and descending in a similar tumult: "*Thunder, lightnings,* Jupiter *descends in his majesty, his thunderbolt burning.*" One stage direction in this play concludes, "*fireworks all over the house.*" It is rather a wonder that no more than two playhouses were destroyed by fire.

It is never easy to visualize the differences between one way of doing something and another. It is not easy, for instance, to think of the staging of a famous scene like the shipwreck which opens Shakespeare's *The Tempest* without assuming that it contains some of the scenic effects we would expect when a storm at sea is supposed to be taking place. Ever since the first introduction of scenic staging in London, when the theaters started up again in 1660 after their eighteen-year closure, *The Tempest* has always opened with a spectacular storm scene. The more ambitious nineteenth-century productions actually showed a ship crossing the stage and sinking amid heaving waves, with a background uproar of thunder and flashes of lightning. A close scrutiny of the text of the play as it was first published in 1623, however, shows that Shakespeare wrote it expecting little more than some hurried movements on and offstage by his players, some thunder in the tiring house, and a lot of offstage cries and whistles. He did not even demand the lightning that his players could have supplied, partly no doubt because the play was composed to be staged at the indoor Blackfriars, where the sulphurous stink of fireworks took longer to disperse and was consequently less welcome. No production since Shakespeare's own time has been so economical with its stage effects. Most, in fact, have cut the dialogue heavily in order to give more time for scenic effects. This is the reverse of the Shakespearean principle in staging.

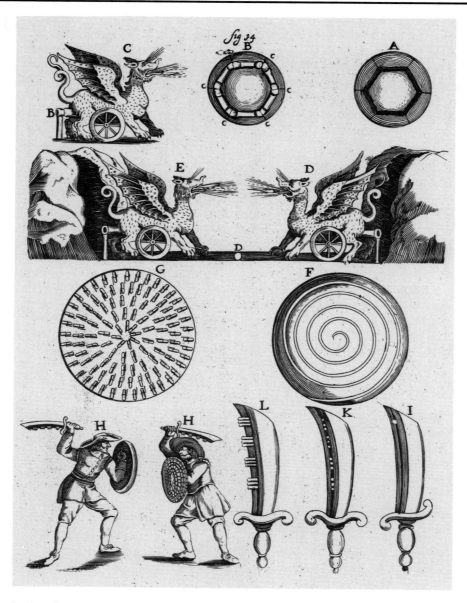

Devices designed for displays of fireworks, an illustration from the 1635 folio edition of John Babington's Pyrotechnia, or, A Discourse of Artificiall Fire-works *(courtesy of the Folger Shakespeare Library). The top half of the picture shows fire-breathing dragons emerging from rocks, a kind of spectacle which was more usual in the set pieces of masques than onstage, though such constructions were not unknown in the theaters. The lower illustration shows swordsmen fighting with fiery swords and shields, the squibs (known as "fisgigs") emitting sparks as the swords were swung. Spectacles in Thomas Heywood's plays of the Four Ages at the Red Bull used this kind of device.*

V. The Audiences

Across the eighty or more years that preceded the closing of the theaters in 1642, the characteristics of the audiences that attended the plays were in constant change. In the earliest days the amphitheaters were crowded with a range of social types, from the poorest handicraft apprentices, through the young gentry studying law at the Inns of Court, to the Court ladies and wealthy citizens' wives who had more of both money and leisure than anyone else in London. In the middle years, especially the 1590s when only two amphitheaters were open to provide London with its daily entertainment, representatives from a full cross section of society seem to have gathered there, excepting only the more puritanical members of the church and their followers. But in 1600 a split began, which grew wider and wider through the following years, until in the 1630s different playhouses were catering for quite distinct segments of the population. Since plays written for different playing companies at different playhouses reflect these different kinds of audiences, it is necessary to sketch the changes in the audience each playhouse catered to with some precision.

The first differences appear in 1575, when the two types of playhouse, amphitheater and hall, first began to compete in London. So far as we can tell, the amphitheaters then catered to everyone. They offered plays every day, while the hall playhouses opened only once a week, and they could accommodate much greater numbers than the halls, with a much wider range of prices. The halls on the other hand catered to the wealthier few. John Lyly, the chief playwright for the boy companies who performed in the hall playhouses in this period, often addressed the ladies and gentry in his audience. His plays are crammed with delicate and witty allusions to affairs of state and the kind of matter which was Court gossip in those years. Such direct comment on sensitive political matters proved in the end more hazardous than the plainer matters of the amphitheater plays. The boy companies were suppressed in 1590, and for the next decade, while Shakespeare and Marlowe were delighting playgoers at the amphitheaters, only two adult companies were allowed to entertain the crowds.

The major change in this pattern started in 1599 and 1600, when two boy companies were revived and began playing in the two hall playhouses inside the City of London. From this time on the hall playhouses, and especially the Blackfriars, catered to the more extravagant tastes, offering satire and "railing" plays aimed precisely at the avant-garde, the courtiers, law students, and wealthy and idle gentry. While the amphitheaters could stage great outdoor scenes including battles with cannons and swordplay, the halls always preferred wit combats to combats with swords. Partly this was tradition: the boy companies were not expert swordsmen as the adult players were. Partly it was natural caution. A duel in a dimly lit hall is far more hazardous than one in the open air. Verbal dexterity was

A vignette from the 1632 octavo edition of Roxana, *a play by William Alabaster (courtesy of the Folger Shakespeare Library). It shows a scene in a hall playhouse, with the audience on benches in front of the stage and in the gallery behind.*

the chief feature of hall plays, from Lyly in the 1580s to Massinger and Ford in the 1620s and 1630s.

In contrast and possibly in reaction to the narrowing of their audience range in 1600, the amphitheater companies, especially those in the northern suburbs, started to perform "citizen" plays, such as Thomas Dekker's *The Shoemakers' Holiday*, a play warmly celebrating London's artisan life. Nostalgia for Queen Elizabeth produced a run of plays about her reign after she died in 1603, and plays which upheld citizen values—financial prudence (largely presented in the "prodigal son" plays), the marital virtues of chaste wives, and the romantic and heroic adventures of apprentices, usually noblemen's sons in disguise—dominated the northern playhouses, the Fortune and Red Bull. The same playhouses also kept the plays which were successful in the 1590s, especially Marlowe's *Faustus* and *Tamburlaine*, and *The Spanish Tragedy*, and ran an increasingly old-fashioned type of "drum and trumpet" play right through to the closure.

While the boy companies in the city hall playhouses went after one kind of audience and the adult companies in the northern amphitheaters went after another, Shakespeare's company, occupying their new Globe amphitheater on the South Bank, did neither. They seem to have occupied a middle position, attracting both the gentry who went weekly to the Blackfriars and the apprentices who went to the northern suburbs. The company's repertoire of Shakespeare's plays attracted everyone. But even their middle-of-the-road policy became difficult to sustain after 1608, when the chief boy company gave up the Blackfriars hall and it fell into the hands of Shakespeare's leading player, Richard Burbage, and his brother. The Burbages had previously found it necessary to cut in the players of the company as shareholders in the Globe when it was first built. Now they cut them into a share of the Blackfriars as well. Thus from 1609 onward the company had two playhouses. For the next thirty-three years the system whereby they performed daily at the Globe through the summer and retreated to the Blackfriars hall in the winter gradually focused their attention more and more on the privileged among London's playgoers.

The Blackfriars was not the only hall available for the gentry to sit and see plays in. Christopher Beeston, a fellow player with Shakespeare in 1599, opened a second hall playhouse in Drury Lane, just outside the city walls but in the wealthy West End close to the Inns of Court, in 1616. In 1629 Richard Gunnell opened a third in Whitefriars, also in the West End. This was clearly the more profitable end of the market. Through the 1620s and 1630s all the hall playhouses performed to the more exclusive audiences at the upper end of the spectrum of wealth. In many ways as a result the plays written for the halls differed from the more traditional fare offered to the citizens and apprentices in the suburbs. Their concerns were the concerns of the gentry, and they followed the changes of courtly taste. It is easy to overstate this division between the citizen repertoire and the gentry tastes, though. As time went on more and more popular plays were added to the available range, and so fewer new plays were needed. And fewer new plays meant that there was less new material to reflect new fashions in plays. In the 1630s, for instance, Beeston's playhouse made regular use of plays originally written for the Red Bull or even older playhouses. Just as Marlowe's *Jew of Malta,* written in 1589 for the Rose amphitheater, was regularly performed at the Cockpit, so Shakespeare's *The Taming of the Shrew* was revived at the Blackfriars. In some ways the

audiences in the later years changed and diversified more drastically than the plays.

VI. The Playwrights

The huge appetite for new plays in these eighty or so years produced well over a thousand play texts. Many of them did not survive beyond their first performance, and relatively few have survived in print or manuscript. A playwright would sell his script to the company which was prepared to stage it, and after that it was the company's business what to do with it. Few companies were prepared to allow their plays to get into print, since that allowed other companies access to their property. Only the greatest playwrights slipped easily into print, and even then it was usually long after their plays had made a hit on the stage. Fewer than twenty of Shakespeare's thirty-seven extant plays appeared in print in his lifetime. Thomas Heywood, who claimed late in his life that he had had a hand or at least "a main finger" in the writing of two hundred and twenty plays in all, probably saw fewer than a dozen reach print before he died. Ben Jonson, who had a higher opinion of his own writing and of plays generally than any of his contemporaries, saw his early plays into print himself in 1616, calling them his *"Workes,"* and was attacked scathingly for his presumption in doing so. Nobody followed his lead, and the only two other collections of plays published in imitation of the Jonson *Workes* were both published after their authors were dead: Shakespeare's plays in 1623, and folio editions of the many Beaumont and Fletcher plays in 1647 and 1679.

One reason why playwrights and players were so modest about the plays they staged was that they were seen as works of business rather than art. Particularly in the early years, when the public appetite for plays was at its peak, writing was a hurried exercise, often involving up to five writers working together on one text. Plays were written for money, and the faster the plays appeared the quicker came the means to feed hungry dependents. The Henslowe papers contain several begging letters from impoverished writers asking for an advance on their next play, as they mortgaged their future with promises of a speedy delivery of their completed play manuscripts. Henslowe kept a team of writers, Chettle, Day, Heywood, Porter, Webster, Dekker, Munday, and others, sometimes working in teams and sometimes separately. Some of the writers were also players and kept the money coming in

John Fletcher, an engraving from the first folio edition of the plays of Beaumont and Fletcher, published in 1647 (courtesy of the Folger Shakespeare Library)

by working as sharers while they augmented it in the evenings with their pens. Besides Shakespeare, Heywood, Will Rowley, Robert Armin, Nathan Field, and several others adopted this double role. Shakespeare and probably Heywood seem to have been the only early writers to have had a regular contractual arrangement to supply their playing company with plays. Shakespeare seems to have written roughly two plays every year from about 1589 until 1610, one serious and one comic each year. Later playwrights such as Richard Brome certainly had contracts—Brome got into trouble because he

could not produce his agreed quota of three plays a year in the late 1630s.

The business of play writing was complicated by many factors, the low level of pay being only one of them. Companies were not often very wealthy themselves and were utterly at the mercy of the invasions of plague or other troubles which attacked their profession with distressing frequency throughout the period. Few companies ever afforded the relative luxury of a contracted playwright who was not also doubling duty as a player, and few writers worked with companies that remained wealthy long enough to make it profitable. Only Shakespeare's company stayed strong for long enough to have resident playwrights who could feel secure in their employment. Shakespeare himself was the first of them and of course contributed massively by means of his supremely popular plays to the security and continuity which kept the company at the top of its profession for nearly fifty years. He was followed by John Fletcher, who seems to have joined the company when Shakespeare went back to Stratford in 1609, and who remained as their resident writer until his death in 1625.

The great success story among playwrights of the Shakespearean period after Shakespeare himself was not Ben Jonson, but the team of Beaumont and Fletcher. Jonson's plays were, like Marlowe's, great successes in his own time, but for popular esteem and the respect of the gentry they were outdone by the mass of plays generated under the names of his two younger protegés. The two men teamed up to write at least one play for the Blackfriars boy company before that enterprise collapsed in 1608 and the playhouse was taken over by Shakespeare's company. Their next plays were taken over along with the playhouse, and, performed by the adult company, they were an instant success. The reputation of the two writers in fact grew so splendidly that even after Beaumont left London for a comfortable marriage and a home in Leicestershire (and an early death, in 1616), the plays in which Fletcher but not Beaumont had a hand were still ascribed to the two of them. Fletcher was a constant contributor to the repertoire of the Shakespeare company until he died, sometimes writing alone but more often in partnership with Nathan Field or Philip Massinger, who eventually took over from him as the company's chief supplier.

From the whole period rather more than six hundred plays have survived, probably less than half the total written and put onstage. Since almost every play written in the period was composed with a detailed and often intimate knowledge of the other plays then being staged, our evidence for the circumstances of composition is rather restricted. Certainly the playwrights expected their audiences to be familiar with the other plays of their time. Much of Jonson's *The Alchemist* makes little sense to anyone who cannot recognize its jokes about Kyd's *The Spanish Tragedy*. Shakespeare's *Merchant of Venice* assumes that its audience will be familiar with Marlowe's *Jew of Malta*. Much of the Beaumont and Fletcher

Francis Beaumont (by permission of Hugh Sackville West, agent for Knowle Estates)

canon assumes that audiences know their Shakespeare intimately and will recognize an echo of a situation in *Hamlet* or *Othello*. Often such echoes were used as a kind of shorthand, to signal a particular set of emotions or complications to the plot. The whole body of plays of the Shakespearean period is full of echoes and often parodies of *Romeo and Juliet* and the Falstaff plays, as well as *Tamburlaine* and *The Spanish Tragedy*. They might be open burlesques, like Ancient Pistol's and Bottom's use of Marlowe's "mighty line," or they might be more subtle examples of intertextual echoes designed to amplify the scope of the later text. One such example is Beaumont and Fletcher's *The Maid's Tragedy*, where Hamlet's problem of choice about killing the king is split into two, with one character choosing to remain loyal to the point of death and the other taking revenge and being destroyed for it. Without a memory of *Hamlet* in the background, the play's presentation of the irreconcilable choices which personal honor lays on the two main characters would hardly be comprehensible.

Between the writing of *Tamburlaine* in the 1580s and a play such as Ford's *'Tis Pity She's a Whore* in about 1630, many things changed.

Marlowe's play was written for the outdoor stage. Its hero speaks better verse than his rivals, defeating them with the bravado he trumpets through the "mighty line" of striking and strident verse which made Marlowe famous. Alleyn delivered his lines strongly, "stalking and roaring" in a forceful manner quite alien to modern verse speaking. By the time Ford came to write his poignant verses for the incestuous brother and sister of his play, forty years further on, restraint had become the norm. The smaller indoor playhouses made possible a quieter style of delivery, at the same time as their smaller stages reduced the opportunities for noisy battles or duels and scenes with devils sprouting fireworks from every orifice. Shakespeare's use of the stage's possibilities in his plays changed from the early battles in the Wars of the Roses of the first English history plays to the sex-war combats of Antony with Cleopatra. By the end of the 1590s militancy onstage evidently paid fewer and fewer dividends for the Shakespearean company. From *Henry V* to *Antony and Cleopatra* Shakespeare's battles largely happen offstage. The language of human interplay and personal debate was winning over the language of large-scale action and superhuman conflict. The frenetic pace of the drama, and the pace of its innovations, was beginning to slow down. The novelty of the idea of commercial playgoing was wearing off. It began to settle into a quieter, more sedate, and less aggressive style. The history of the Shakespearean drama is the history of a new social institution and its gradual establishment as a pillar of respectable London life.

The Publication of English Renaissance Plays

Fredson Bowers
University of Virginia

An old tradition has it that the theatrical company would gather in a tavern to hear an author read his new play and then would decide on the spot whether to accept or to reject it. Doubtless the facts were not quite so simple, but it is known that when a company accepted a play the author was required to furnish a fair copy, whether made by himself or a scribe. A dramatist like Shakespeare, who was an actor-owner of the King's Men and was under an informal contract to write plays only for them, might well furnish instead his final draft or working papers, hard to read in places because of the hurried handwriting, the deletions, interlineations, and all sorts of changes, and the company's bookholder or a paid scribe could make the fair copy that was necessary before the company would discuss whatever cuts or theatrical changes seemed necessary for the actual staging of the play. The actors' parts would then be copied out and the final promptbook (a script of the play with stage directions for the use of the prompter) made up. We do know, however, that Shakespeare's company preserved the "foul papers" (as they were called) of various of his plays, presumably as insurance against loss of or damage to the promptbook or a predecessor fair copy. Sometimes an authorial or scribal fair copy could itself be marked up and made into the promptbook, with all its notations, used to regulate the rehearsals and performance on stage. Other times, it would appear, such prepared copies were recopied into official promptbook form, complete with marginal memoranda about properties to be on hand, actors to be warned to be ready for entrances, and sometimes notes about how to perform the action on the stage.

It must be understood that the publication of plays differed markedly from that of other books. Unless there was a special agreement such as Ben Jonson insisted on, as well as some later Court dramatists tender of their literary reputations, the professional playwright gave up all rights to his play when he sold it to the company. Thus the company controlled and profited from publication when the play had lost its drawing power and they would not lose attendance to readers. Or if the play continued to be popular, the company could withhold publication entirely in order to maintain the curiosity of the public.

Plays were profitable to print, and thus there was considerable competition among booksellers to secure play manuscripts. Companies were often plagued by unauthorized manuscripts being leaked, sometimes by authors who had kept some form of their copy but others by surreptitious copying of the theater's manuscripts or else simple theft. When a company failed, its stock of plays was likely to come on the market unless it promptly merged with another. At other times when the theatrical companies were hard up owing to the prohibition against acting during serious plague visitations when congregations were forbidden and actors had a difficult time making both ends meet, the companies themselves might sell some manuscripts for whatever gain was possible. After the Commonwealth authorities closed the theaters in 1640, more plays came on the market.

Under such varying circumstances the manuscripts that publishers secured were of every possible kind and degree of authority according to the sources from which they were purchased. Since copy that had gone through the printer's shop would be so stained by inky fingers and wear and tear that it would be useless thereafter and would be destroyed, the seller of a play manuscript, if it were a company, would never release its precious promptbook, which had written in it the irreplaceable official license that it could be acted. But this promptbook could be copied, or—more often—the company was able to sell off the earlier forms it had preserved, such as the authorial "foul papers" or a fair copy made from them at the time before the promptbook. If by some subterfuge or bribery a bookseller was able to secure copy from private hands, it could be a manuscript in any state of preparation except for the promptbook itself. Occasionally, and especially in the later period, an influential company would be able to stop unauthorized publication by persuading the authorities to issue an order, title by title, against any publication of the company's plays; or else a friendly

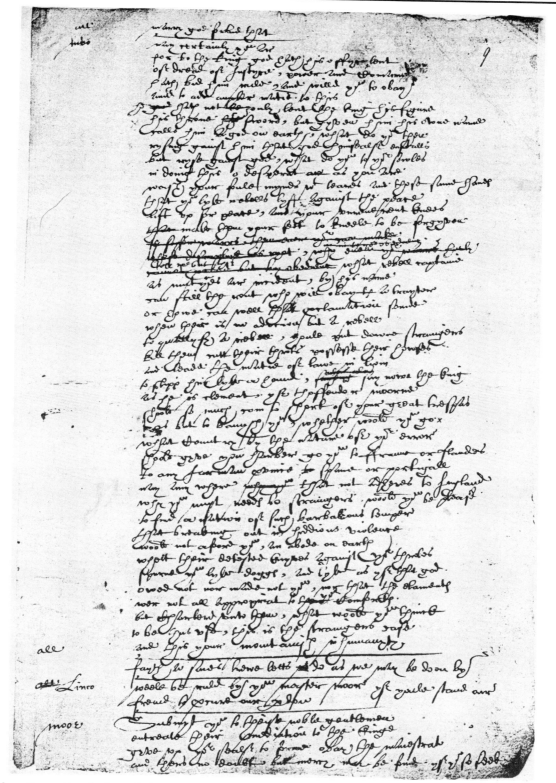

A page from the working draft or "foul papers" for Sir Thomas More. *After the Master of the Revels found the original version (probably by Anthony Munday) politically objectionable and refused to license it for production, four dramatists—Thomas Dekker, Henry Chettle, probably William Shakespeare, and possibly Thomas Heywood—were hired to revise the play. The page shown above is thought to be in Shakespeare's hand (Harleian MS 7368, fol. 9ᵃ; by permission of the British Library).*

A page from the fair-copy promptbook for Philip Massinger's Believe as You List, *in the author's hand and annotated with stage directions by Edward Knight, bookkeeper for the King's Men (MS Egerton 2828, fol. 20ᵃ; by permission of the British Library)*

bookseller, conscious of future favors, might copyright the play in the official Stationers' Register but never publish it himself, the copyright entry keeping anyone else from infringing on his rights without severe penalty.

Technically, a play published without the theater's permission from copy secured from private sources could be called piracy, but at this distance it is very difficult to establish what publication was or was not approved by the owners of the plays (the companies). Once a copy was available to a stationer the company would have no recourse. The Stationers' guild, which registered manuscripts for publication, had no interest in the origin of the copy and its true ownership so long as the rights of another publisher were not involved and so long as the manuscript had gone through the formality of being approved by the representative of the Bishop of London as being free from political or personal content against the public interest.

The theatrical companies, of course, would regard as piracy any play that was acted or printed without their permission; but for printing their case had no legal basis no matter how keenly they might feel the harm that resulted by unauthorized publication of what they considered their legitimate property. In contrast, the Stationers' Company, which was legally in control of publication, would regard as a pirate only a bookseller who published a play without first paying his fee and registering it for copyright, or one who printed a play as his own that in fact belonged to another. But because of the rigid control exercised by the Company there seems to have been little piracy of this nature, that is, surreptitious and unauthorized reprinting. The most extraordinary piracy was the special case of the so-called Pavier Quartos, a collection of nine Shakespeare plays (two of these falsely attributed) printed and bound together in 1619 for the bookseller Thomas Pavier but with their original dates and imprints carefully reprinted so as to give the illusion that these were the same 1600 or 1608 editions. No records are preserved whether the King's Men or the Stationers' Company objected to this fraudulent reprinting, but it is clear that Pavier's piratical intention to produce a collected edition of Shakespeare was stopped.

Another special class of plays can also properly be called piracy. These are labeled as "bad quartos" because of the corrupt nature of their texts. Marlowe's *Massacre at Paris* is known only from such a "bad quarto" but the majority were of Shakespeare's most popular plays. Some of these were adequate representations if one did not know

the originals, such as we find in *Richard III*; others like *Romeo and Juliet* and *Henry V* were generally inadequate; *Hamlet* and *The Merry Wives of Windsor* were atrocious. The way in which these bad texts came into existence must have varied considerably but all have a theatrical origin and have been reconstructed from memory of the original performances. The usual explanation involves some struggling companies which acted only on tour in the provinces without the money to pay for plays to be written for them and so relied chiefly on those that had been printed. But a popular new London play would be a drawing card in the provinces and so invited piracy. Some plays may have been deliberately memorized, as much as possible, from attending the London performances. Others seem to have been reconstructed by a minor London actor who had joined the group and knew his part and could recollect something of the rest. A classic example comes in *Hamlet* where in the bad quarto of 1603 it has been observed that whenever Marcellus is on the stage the report is fairly good but that it degenerates markedly when he is off. Moreover, this actor seems to have doubled the part of Voltimand, whose speeches are almost letter perfect. But after the ambassadors are dispatched to England the play goes to pieces. For example, this is the (modernized) beginning of the famous "To Be or Not to Be" soliloquy:

> To be, or not to be—ay, there's the point:
> To die, to sleep—is that all? ay, all. No;
> To sleep, to dream—ay marry, there it goes
> For in that dream of death, when we awake,
> And borne before an everlasting judge,
> From whence no passenger ever return'd,
> The undiscovered country, at whose sight
> The happy smile, and the accursed damn'd. . . .

And so on. A few times the theater company may have thought that such dreadful pirated texts might be taken as what was acted on the stage and would turn off customers. That may have been the reason for the company's release of a good text of *Hamlet* later in the same year; but for *King Lear, The Merry Wives,* and the other pirated Shakespearean texts the true version was not printed until the collection of all his plays in the First Folio of 1623.

The manuscripts secured by play publishers run the gamut from the author's own originals, whether in draft or in his fair copy, through various stages of scribal transcription, including perhaps copies of promptbooks but not the books themselves except when a company went out of business

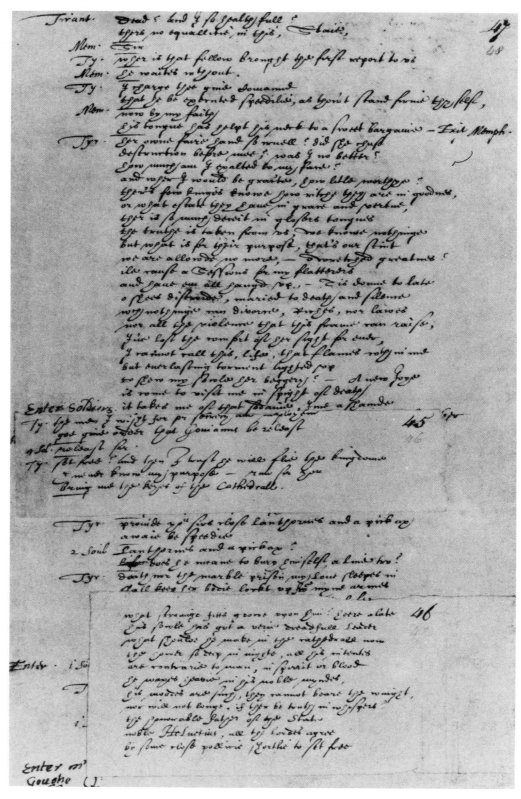

A page from the promptbook, prepared by a professional scribe, for The Second Maid's Tragedy, *sometimes attributed to Thomas Middleton. The scribe wrote revisions required by the censor on strips of paper and pasted them on the page. Stage directions were added in another hand (MS Lansdowne 807, fol. 48ᵃ with fols. 46ᵃ, 47ᵃ; by permission of the British Library).*

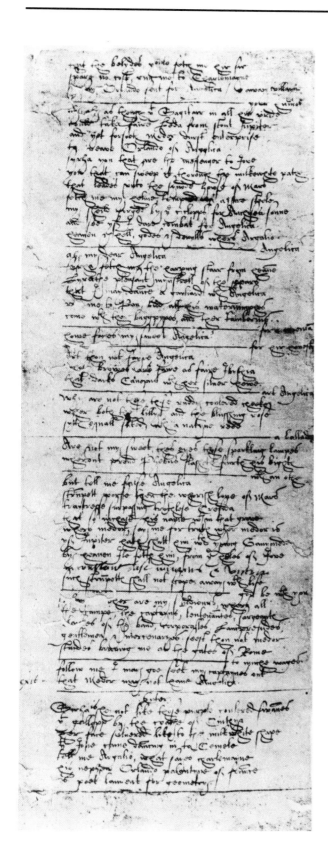

A portion of an actor's part for the title role in Robert Greene's Orlando Furioso, *written in the hand of a scribe. Edward Alleyn may have used this manuscript when he played Orlando in a 1591 production (MS I, item 138, fol. 264, strip 8; by permission of Dulwich College, London).*

Ham. O that this too much grieu'd and sallied flesh
Would melt to nothing, or that the vniuersall
Globe of heauen would turne al to a Chaos!
O God, within two months; no not two : married,
Mine vncle : O let me not thinke of it,
My fathers brother : but no more like
My father, then I to *Hercules.*
Within two months, ere yet the salt of most
Vnrighteous teares had left their flushing
In her galled eyes : she married, O God, a beast
Deuoyd of reason would not haue made
Such speede: Frailtie, thy name is Woman,
Why she would hang on him, as if increase
Of appetite had growne by what it looked on.
O wicked wicked speede, to make such
Dexteritie to incestuous sheetes,
Ere yet the shooes were olde,
The which she followed my dead fathers corse
Like *Nyobe,* all teares : married, well it is not,
Nor it cannot come to good:
But breake my heart, for I must holde my tongue.

Ham. O that this too too sallied flesh would melt,   but
Thaw and resolue it selfe into a dewe,
Or that the euerlasting had not fixt
His cannon gainst seale slaughter, ô God, God,
How wary, stale, flat, and vnprofitable
Seeme to me all the vses of this world ?
Fie on't, ah fie, tis an vnweeded garden
That growes to seede, things rancke and grose in nature,
Possesse it meerely that it should come thus

But two months dead, nay not so much, not two,
So excellent a King, that was to this
Hiperion to a satire, so louing to my mother,
That he might not beteeme the winds of heauen
Visite her face too roughly, heauen and earth
Must I remember, why she should hang on him
As if increase of appetite had growne
By what it fed on, and yet within a month,
Let me not thinke on't ; frailty thy name is woman
A little month or ere those shooes were old
With which she followed my poore fathers bodie
Like *Nube* all teares, why she
O God, a beast that wants discourse of reason
Would haue mourn'd longer, married with my Vncle,
My fathers brother, but no more like my father
Then I to *Hercules,* within a month,
Ere yet the salt of most vnrighteous teares,
Had left the flushing in her gauled eyes
She married, ô most wicked speede, to post
With such dexteritie to incestious sheets,
It is not, nor it cannot come to good,
But breake my hart, for I must hold my tongue.

Hamlet's soliloquy as it appeared in the 1603 "bad" quarto edition of Hamlet *(above left; British Library), in the 1604-1605 "good" quarto (above right; Bodleian Library, Oxford), and in the 1623 First Folio edition of Shakespeare's plays (next page; Folger Shakespeare Library)*

Ham. Oh that this too too folid Flefh, would melt,
Thaw, and refolue it felfe into a Dew:
Or that the Euerlafting had not fixt
His Cannon 'gainft Selfe-flaughter. O God, O God!
How weary, ftale, flat, and vnprofitable
Seemes to me all the vfes of this world?
Fie on't? Oh fie, fie, 'tis an vnweeded Garden
That growes to Seed: Things rank, and groffe in Nature
Poffeffe it meerely. That it fhould come to this:
But two months dead: Nay, not fo much; not two,
So excellent a King, that was to this
Hiperion to a Satyre: fo louing to my Mother,
That he might not beteene the windes of heauen
Vifit her face too roughly. Heauen and Earth
Muft I remember: why fhe would hang on him,
As if encreafe of Appetite had growne
By what it fed on; and yet within a month?
Let me not thinke on't: Frailty, thy name is woman.
A little Month, or ere thofe fhooes were old,
With which fhe followed my poore Fathers body
Like *Niobe*, all teares. Why fhe, euen fhe.
(O Heauen! A beaft that wants difcourfe of Reafon
Would haue mourn'd longer) married with mine Vnkle,
My Fathers Brother: but no more like my Father,
Then I to *Hercules.* Within a Moneth?
Ere yet the falt of moft vnrighteous Teares
Had left the flufhing of her gauled eyes,
She married. O moft wicked fpeed, to poft
With fuch dexterity to Inceftuous fheets:
It is not, nor it cannot come to good.
But breake my heart, for I muft hold my tongue.

and its stock came on the market. Moreover, there was practically no authorial revision in later editions. Several reasons exist for this situation. First, plays were not regarded as "literature" but as relatively ephemeral entertainment reading on no higher plane than, say, a novel made from the script of a popular moving picture. Then, since the author himself seldom sold the copy to the bookseller, he had no personal or financial interest in his play's aftercareer except on the stage, the more especially since he did not believe that in a play he was writing in a medium that would bring him literary fame.

Shakespeare is a perfectly normal example. He supervised the printing of his "literary" works *Venus and Adonis* and *The Rape of Lucrece*; however, there is no evidence that he ever lifted a finger to see that his plays were published during his lifetime or when they got into print to correct or revise them or to provide another manuscript for a better text. Except for substitutes for bad quartos, or for a slipshod version corrected by the second edition of Beaumont and Fletcher's *Philaster*, the only time that better texts were made available was in such posthumous collections as Shakespeare's *Comedies, Histories and Tragedies*, the First Folio of 1623 edited by two actors in his company, or in the 1679 Beaumont and Fletcher *Comedies and Tragedies*, in which the publisher took a personal interest in securing different manuscripts and comparing them with the texts already printed in the folio of 1647. In Shakespeare's Folio the selection of different manuscripts in the company's stock from those used for some earlier printings provides us with the only evidence we have for considerable variation in the texts like *King Lear, Hamlet, Othello, Richard III*, and *Troilus and Cressida*. Moreover, although for many plays the Folio editors were content merely to hand over to the printer a copy of some earlier edition instead of using a new manuscript, yet some slight attention was paid in most to minor correction by comparing the prints with the theater's promptbooks. In a few plays like *Richard II* a number of marginal changes were made so that the play much more resembled the promptbook.

No record is preserved of any publisher ever paying for a play to be written just for printing. Booksellers bought up play manuscripts from whatever source they could find. No royalty system was known. A cash payment transferred complete ownership to the stationer with all rights to publish as many editions as the market would allow, or to sell the copyright to another stationer if he chose. Plays were cheaply and not always carefully printed

and proofread since they were speculative profit-making ventures only, without prestige, and, for purchasers, not to be kept in a library but to be read and discarded. They cost sixpence. Makework regulations limited an edition to 1,000 copies, later raised to 1,200, without a resetting of the type. The format was standard, what is known as a quarto. That is, after printing, a full sheet of paper was folded once across the short side, bringing the two ends of the rectangle together. It would then be folded once more across its new short side to form a quarto of four leaves or eight pages. For cheapness's sake play quartos were not bound by sewing but would be "stabbed" (the equivalent of stapling). There was no cover, and so they would quickly become dog-eared from use and perhaps lose their front or back leaves. Not precisely throwaways, these play quartos were not intended to be preserved for very long and were treated accordingly.

In contrast, a folio edition (a full sheet folded once to form two leaves or four pages) was printed for permanent possession and was what would now be called a deluxe edition. The large size required binding. Rough forms of publishers' binding were available but most purchasers would have had folios privately bound to their specifications. Except for a few plays by Court dramatists who may have subsidized the expensive printing, plays were printed in folios only in large collections, like the Shakespeare, Jonson, or Beaumont and Fletcher. Copies of these survive in larger numbers than the cheaper popular quartos.

Probably the majority of plays that saw print have survived in one or more copies: sometimes as many as twenty or thirty quarto copies have been preserved, but the average is much less. A reference in 1598 suggests that Shakespeare wrote a play called *Loves Labours Won* and that it might have been printed, but if so no copy has survived. Another Shakespeare play called *Cardenio* is referred to in the eighteenth century but only in manuscript. Only one gathering of eight pages is known of the first edition of *1 Henry IV*, and the *Titus Andronicus* first edition exists in a single copy found in a castle in Scandinavia.

The majority of play quartos were not popular enough to warrant reprinting, and in fact when a large number of copies are preserved the reason is very likely that they never had been sold. A few very popular plays, mostly by Shakespeare or Beaumont and Fletcher, were frequently reprinted, *1 Henry IV* going through six editions before the Folio and *Richard III* through eight. In contrast, no second edition for *2 Henry IV* was ever called for. The later the date of these reprinted plays, the commoner they grow, but a great many dramatists in single editions were still available and advertised during the Restoration period (1660-1700) when plays grew even more popular as reading matter and began to be collected. But the Great Fire of 1666 in London must have destroyed a number of books. The Elizabethan theater acted a constantly changing repertory of plays so long as they drew audiences. Revivals were not uncommon after a lapse of even ten or more years, especially for Court performance. Often a reprinted edition followed a revival with its renewal of interest in a play.

Contrary to our present attitude that places these plays as the outstanding literary genre of the period, the key to understanding their original status is the recognition that in their own day they were not highly regarded except as entertainment, without literary value, and that strongly religious and moral persons regarded reading them as a waste of time that should have been devoted to better purposes. Thus the printing was likely to be careless, and it was not in the nature of the time to be at all concerned with the textual purity of whatever manuscripts a publisher could acquire. The earlier the printing followed the performance the more likely it is that we have the play in something like its original form. But as the years passed and the play grew old-fashioned, a revival was often marked by the company hiring some currently popular playwright to freshen up the text or even substantially to rewrite it. Thus if the first printing came years after the initial acting, the text would almost inevitably reflect the loss of the original in the refashioned play according to later tastes. For example, Christopher Marlowe's *Jew of Malta* was first produced about 1592, was copyrighted by a publisher in 1594 but apparently never printed, and when in 1633 it first saw the light of day in a quarto, it had been thoroughly reworked by the dramatist Thomas Heywood for a revival the preceding year. We shall never know the play as Marlowe originally wrote it. The popular Beaumont and Fletcher plays were likely to suffer the same fate, and a number of these when first printed in the folio of 1647 had been rewritten in part or in whole by popular dramatists like Massinger or Shirley. In our only known text of *Macbeth* in the folio, some of the witches' scenes were revised by Thomas Middleton.

Modern editions of the drama of the period, then, are faced with correcting the early printed texts from the corruption of careless printers, with estimating the kind of manuscript copy from which the printer worked and its near or distant relation to the author or to the theater, and in the special case of plays printed long after initial production of sorting out the refurbishing efforts of other writers brought in to bring the play up to date for a revival. More skill is needed for editing these texts owing to their complex textual history than is usual for nondramatic works of the period. Most nondramatic books were published with the consent and assistance of the author, who would provide the manuscript. On the contrary, Renaissance plays from the popular stage were brought into print through intermediaries and a variety of sources of mixed authority. The dramatist himself seldom participated in preparing printer's copy and might never know ahead of time that one of his plays was about to be printed.

There are exceptions, of course, and not alone with playwrights like Jonson with literary pretensions, since a few professional dramatists might profit from their own sale of plays and so would provide the copy but not often any supervision of the printing. Jonson was unique in demanding proofs before printing. Otherwise the custom for any author who took an interest in the printing of his plays was to come to the printer's shop every day, read whatever was printing on the press, mark what he wanted, and the press would be stopped while the required changes were made in the type before printing resumed. This practice resulted in some early sheets being printed and bound without corrections and some with authorial or the shop's proofreader's alterations. But the irregular printing schedule made it difficult for even a conscientious author (and they were few) to be present for every sheet run through the press, and the workman assigned to read proof never seems to have compared the play's proof with the manuscript and so was more intent on marking printing defects than with the careful reproduction of the text. Compositors would memorize several lines of the play before turning to their cases and setting the type; as a consequence their memory could easily fail them—especially toward the end of the memorized set of lines—and unconsciously they could substitute their own words for the author's, mistakes which the usual printing house proofreading of the time was not geared to catch and correct unless the result was utter nonsense. Sometimes even this passed muster, the more especially since the shop's proofreader may have trusted the compositors to have looked over the typesetting for

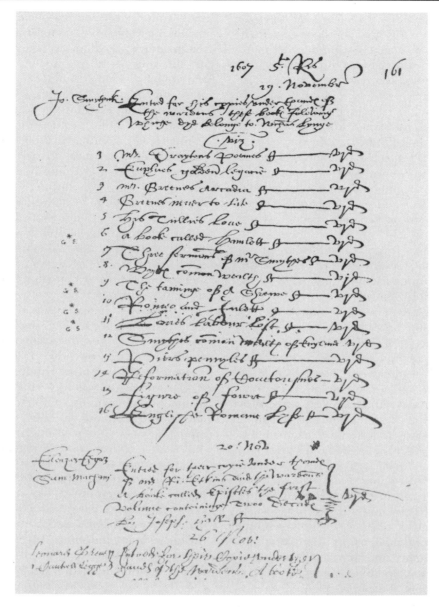

An entry in the Stationers' Register transferring the copyrights for sixteen plays—including Hamlet *(number 6),* The Taming of the Shrew *(number 9),* Romeo and Juliet *(number 10), and* Love's Labor's Lost *(number 11)—from bookseller Nicholas Ling to bookseller John Smethwick (Register C, f. 161, Stationers' Hall, London)*

technical faults before printing and so did not himself proofread every sheet.

It is easy to exaggerate the sometimes suspect authority of the play manuscripts that were printed and the comparative carelessness with which most were produced without authorial supervision. Nevertheless, the drama—now thought to be one of the period's chief literary achievements—was likely to see the light of day in print under circumstances that at the time scarcely did it justice.

Sources for the Study of Tudor and Stuart Drama

Albert H. Tricomi

State University of New York at Binghamton

The following selected bibliography supplements the lists of references that follow the entries. It consists of multiple author studies as well as reference works and background studies related to Tudor and Stuart drama from approximately 1485 to 1642. Annotations are primarily descriptive and, when evaluative, are intended to reflect a widely held or current view of the work cited. Books whose titles are self-explanatory sometimes receive no further annotation.

I. Primary Sources

Adams, Joseph Quincy, ed. *The Dramatic Records of Sir Henry Herbert.* New Haven: Yale University Press, 1917.

The office book of the Master of the Revels. During the reign of Charles I (1625-1649), Herbert licensed plays for performance and frequently recorded Charles's prescriptions for their censorship or "reformation."

Arber, Edward, ed. *A Transcript of the Registers of the Company of Stationers of London: 1554-1640,* 5 volumes. Volumes 1-4, London: Privately printed, 1875-1877; volume 5, Birmingham: Privately printed, 1894.

In England booksellers were required to register books for publication, in effect securing the copyrights on them. This transcript is invaluable for identifying authors and printers, and especially for piecing out the composition dates for many works. A volume to be used in conjunction with Arber's work is *A Companion to Arber: Being a Calendar of Documents in Edward Arber's "Transcript of the Registers of the Company of Stationers of London 1554-1640," with Text and Calendar of Supplementary Documents* (Oxford: Clarendon Press, 1967), edited by W. W. Greg, with the assistance of C. P. Blagden and I. G. Philip.

Cunningham, Peter. *Extracts from the Accounts of the Revels at Court, in the Reigns of Queen Elizabeth and James I, from the Original Office Books of the Masters and Yeoman.* Shakespeare Society Publications, no. 7. London: Printed for the Shakespeare Society, 1842.

Eyre, G. E. Briscoe, ed. *A Transcript of the Registers of the Worshipful Company of Stationers: From 1640-1708 A.D.,* transcribed by H. R. Plomer, 3 volumes. London: Privately printed, 1913-1914.

A continuation of Arber.

Feuillerat, Albert, ed. *Documents Relating to the Office of the Revels in the Time of Queen Elizabeth.* Materialien zur Kunde des alteren Englischen Dramas, no. 21. Louvain: Uystpruyst, 1908.

Scholarly, detailed presentation of primary source materials on the Elizabethan drama and its regulation.

Feuillerat, ed. *Documents Relating to the Revels at Court in the Time of King Edward VI and Queen Mary.* Materialien zur Kunde des alteren Englischen Dramas, no. 44. Louvain: Uystpruyst, 1914.

Scholarly, detailed presentation of primary source materials on the early Tudor drama and its regulation.

Greg, W. W., ed. *Dramatic Documents from the Elizabethan Playhouses: Stage Plots, Actors' Parts; Prompt Books,* 2 volumes. Oxford: Clarendon Press, 1931.

Greg and E. Boswell, eds. *Records of the Court of the Stationers' Company 1576 to 1602—From Register B.* London: Oxford University Press for the Bibliographical Society, 1930.

Supplements Arber with records to which he was not given access.

Henslowe, Philip. *Henslowe's Diary,* edited, with supplementary material, introduction, and notes by R. A. Foakes and R. T. Rickert. Cambridge: Cambridge University Press, 1961.

Now frequently read in place of Greg's older edition (see below), Foakes and Rickert's edition includes an introduction intended "to reconsider the meaning of Henslowe's entries and Greg's detailed interpretation of them."

Henslowe. *Henslowe's Diary*, 2 volumes, edited by W. W. Greg. London: Bullen, 1904, 1908.

The first part contains Greg's painstakingly edited transcript of the diary kept by the manager and owner of the Lord Admiral's Men during the years 1594-1600. This precious document is a primary source for information about dates of performances, payments, and receipts for plays, authorship and revisions of plays, costumes, props, and other theatrical matters. Part two, a monumental piece of scholarship, contains Greg's scrupulous commentary.

Henslowe. *Henslowe's Papers, Being Documents Supplementary to Henslowe's Diary*, edited by Greg. London: Bullen, 1907.

A lesser-known but invaluable addition to our knowledge of Henslowe as theater manager.

Sabol, Andrew J., ed. *Songs and Dances for the Stuart Masque: An Edition of 63 Items of Music for the English Court Masque from 1604 to 1641*. Providence: Brown University Press, 1959.

II. Bibliographies

Primary Bibliographies

Greg, W. W. *A Bibliography of the English Printed Drama to the Restoration*, 4 volumes. London: Printed for the Bibliographical Society at Oxford University Press, 1939-1959.

A complete listing of printings and editions of plays written before the end of 1642 or printed before the beginning of 1660, with transcriptions of title pages and, wherever possible, dates and names of printers and booksellers that do not appear on title pages.

Pollard, A. W., and G. W. Redgrave. *A Short-Title Catalogue of Books Printed in England, Scotland & Ireland, and of English Books Printed Abroad, 1475-1640*, revised and enlarged edition, begun by W. A. Jackson and F. S. Ferguson, completed by Katherine F. Pantier, 2 volumes. London: The Bibliographical Society, 1976, 1986.

An indispensable research tool. Entries include pertinent data from original title pages, supplying additional publication information whenever possible. Numbers assigned to items in these volumes are employed to index the University Microfilms International facsimiles of works from this period.

Stratman, Carl J. *Bibliography of English Printed Drama, 1565-1900*. Carbondale: Southern Illinois University Press, 1967.

A comprehensive guide.

Wing, Donald. *A Short-Title Catalogue of Books Printed in England, Scotland, Ireland, Wales and British America and of English Books Printed in Other Countries, 1641-1700*, revised and enlarged edition, 3 volumes. New York: Modern Language Association of America, 1972- .

Similar to Pollard and Redgrave (above), these volumes complete the cataloguing of English books published in the seventeenth century. Nearly all the extant works listed have been microfilmed and catalogued according to the numbers assigned by Wing.

Secondary Bibliographies

Logan, Terence P., and Denzell S. Smith, eds. *The Later Jacobean and Caroline Dramatists: A Survey and Bibliography of Recent Studies in English Renaissance Drama*. Lincoln & London: University of Nebraska Press, 1978.

All volumes of *A Survey and Bibliography of Recent Studies in English Renaissance Drama* offer eminently useful, annotated bibliographies on the major dramatists and their plays, as well as sections on anonymous plays and on minor dramatists. This volume treats Beaumont and Fletcher, Massinger, Ford, Shirley, Brome, and Davenant.

Logan and Smith, eds. *The New Intellectuals: A Survey and Bibliography of Recent Studies in English Renaissance Drama*. Lincoln & London: University of Nebraska Press, 1977.

This volume treats Jonson, Chapman, Marston, Tourneur, and Daniel.

Logan and Smith, eds. *The Popular School: A Survey and Bibliography of Recent Studies in English Renaissance Drama*. Lincoln: University of Nebraska Press, 1975.

This volume treats Dekker, Middleton, Webster, Heywood, Munday, and Drayton.

Logan and Smith, eds. *The Predecessors of Shakespeare: A Survey and Bibliography of Recent Studies in English Renaissance Drama*. Lincoln: University of Nebraska Press, 1973.

This volume treats Marlowe, Greene, Kyd, Nashe, Lyly, Peele, and Lodge.

Pennel, Charles A., and W. P. Williams, eds. *Francis Beaumont, John Fletcher, Philip Massinger, 1937-1965; John Ford, 1940-1965; James Shirley, 1955-1965*. Elizabethan Biographies Supplements, no. 8. London: Nether Press, 1968.

Penninger, Frieda Elaine. *English Drama to 1660 (Excluding Shakespeare): A Guide to Information Sources.* Detroit: Gale Research, 1976.

Ribner, Irving. *Tudor and Stuart Drama,* updated by Clifford C. Huffman. Arlington Heights, Ill.: AHM, 1978.

A fine, eminently usable, selected bibliography for students of English Renaissance drama. Categories include works on the major dramatists as well as critical, historical, and theatrical studies.

Salomon, Brownell. *Critical Analyses of Renaissance Drama, A Bibliographical Guide,* updated edition. New York & London: Garland, 1985.

Selected, concisely annotated, descriptive entries.

Studies in English Literature 1500-1900. 1961- .

This quarterly journal publishes an annual review of critical books and essays on the Elizabethan-Jacobean drama.

Wells, Stanley, ed. *English Drama (excluding Shakespeare): Select Bibliographical Guides.* Oxford: Oxford University Press, 1975.

Surveys by established scholars of studies on dramatic theory, theater history and prac-

Textual Studies

Bowers, Fredson. *Bibliography and Textual Criticism.* Oxford: Clarendon Press, 1964.

Bowers. *On Editing Shakespeare and the Elizabethan Dramatists.* Richmond, Va.: William Byrd Press for the Philip H. and A. S. Rosenbach Foundation of the University of Pennsylvania Library, 1955. Revised and enlarged as *On Editing Shakespeare.* Charlottesville: University Press of Virginia, 1966.

The principles of editing by one of the foremost authorities on bibliographical criticism.

Bowers. *Principles of Bibliographical Description.* Princeton: Princeton University Press, 1949.

Bowers. *Textual and Literary Criticism.* Cambridge: Cambridge University Press, 1959.

McKerrow, R. B. *An Introduction to Bibliography for Literary Students.* Oxford: Clarendon Press, 1927.

A handy guide for students.

Schoenbaum, S. *Internal Evidence and Elizabethan Dramatic Authorship: An Essay in Literature, History, and Method.* Evanston: Northwestern University Press, 1966.

Sets forth the rules for sifting evidence on dates and authorship using colorful examples from the tradition.

III. Glossaries, Dictionaries, and Word Studies

Campbell, Oscar James, and E. G. Quinn, eds. *The Reader's Encyclopedia of Shakespeare.* New York: Crowell, 1966.

The emphasis is on Shakespeare from the Elizabethan age to the present, but the entries, which are of moderate length, listed alphabetically, touch all aspects of the drama, including printers' names, theatrical companies, critics, classical influences, contemporaries, and a great deal more.

Dent, R. W. *Proverbial Language in English Drama Exclusive of Shakespeare, 1495-1616: An Index.* Berkeley: University of California Press, 1984.

Dent. *Shakespeare's Proverbial Language: An Index.* Berkeley: University of California Press, 1981.

Expands enormously and revises the "Shakespeare Index," appended to Morris Tilley's *The Proverbs of England* (cited below).

Fischer, Sandra K. *Econolingua: A Glossary of Coins and Economic Language in Renaissance Drama.* Newark: University of Delaware Press, 1985.

Halliday, F. E. *A Shakespeare Companion 1564-1964,* revised edition. Baltimore: Penguin, 1964.

A guide, with brief entries organized alphabetically, not only to Shakespeare, but to his contemporaries and to the Elizabethan-Jacobean theatrical milieu.

Kökeritz, Helge. *Shakespeare's Pronunciation.* New Haven: Yale University Press, 1953.

The standard work, useful in studies of the prosody and rhyme of Shakespeare and his contemporaries.

Partridge, Astley C. *Orthography in Shakespeare and Elizabethan Drama: A Study of Colloquial Contractions, Elision, Prosody, and Punctuation.* Lincoln: University of Nebraska Press, 1964.

Partridge, Eric H. *Shakespeare's Bawdy: A Literary and Psychological Essay and a Comprehensive Glossary,* revised and enlarged edition. New York: Dutton, 1969.

A glossary with appropriate examples and explanations of the Elizabethans' seemingly inexhaustible love of double entendre and sexual cant. As appropriate to the study of Shakespeare's contemporaries as to Shakespeare.

Schmidt, Alexander. *Shakespeare-Lexicon,* 2 volumes, revised and enlarged by Gregor Sarrazin. Berlin: G. Reimer, 1902.

Skeat, Walter W. *A Glossary of Stuart and Tudor Words, Especially from the Dramatists,* edited, with additions, by Anthony L. Mayhew. Oxford: Clarendon Press, 1914.

Stagg, Louis Charles. *The Figurative Language of the Tragedies of Shakespeare's Chief 16th-Century Contemporaries, An Index.* New York & London: Garland, 1984.

Sugden, Edward H. *A Topographical Dictionary to the Works of Shakespeare and His Fellow Dramatists.* Manchester: University of Manchester Press/London: Longmans, Green, 1925.

Tilley, Morris P. *A Dictionary of the Proverbs in England in the Sixteenth and Seventeenth Centuries.* Ann Arbor: University of Michigan Press, 1950.

An important research tool for exploring the fund of shared attitudes expressed proverbially in English Renaissance drama.

IV. Theater History

Adams, John Cranford. *The Globe Playhouse: Its Design and Equipment,* enlarged edition. New York: Barnes & Noble, 1961.

A once-influential study whose reconstruction of the Globe theater, along with its evidence and methodology, has been repeatedly challenged.

Adams, Joseph Quincy. *Shakespearean Playhouses: A History of English Theatres from the Beginning to the Restoration.* Boston & New York: Houghton Mifflin, 1917.

A still serviceable examination of the playhouses in Shakespeare's age.

Armstrong, William A. *The Elizabethan Private Theatres: Facts and Problems.* London: Society for Theatre Research, 1958.

A study by a noted authority on the boys' companies that performed in indoor theaters and catered to more well-to-do audiences, competing with adult companies such as Shakespeare's the King's Men, which until 1608 performed only in open-air theaters.

Barroll, J. Leeds, Alexander Leggatt, Richard Hosley, and Alvin Kernan, eds. *The Revels History of Drama in English, Volume III: 1576-1613.* London: Methuen, 1974.

An ambitious work, especially fine in tracing Elizabethan-Jacobean conditions of performance and the development of the

major theaters. Profuse illustrations and reproductions of theatrical documents and drawings.

Beckerman, Bernard. *Shakespeare at the Globe, 1599-1609.* New York: Macmillan, 1962.

An illuminating, careful study of the repertory, acting techniques, stage, and staging at London's most famous theater.

Bentley, Gerald Eades. *The Jacobean and Caroline Stage,* 7 volumes. Oxford: Clarendon Press, 1941-1968.

Arguably the most important of the multivolume works on the known facts of early Stuart drama. A continuation of E. K. Chambers's *The Elizabethan Stage,* Bentley's volumes present exhaustive materials on actors, companies, and individual plays.

Bentley. *The Profession of Dramatist in Shakespeare's Time, 1590-1642.* Princeton: Princeton University Press, 1971.

Bentley. *The Profession of Player in Shakespeare's Time.* Princeton: Princeton University Press, 1984.

Bentley, ed. *The Seventeenth Century Stage: A Collection of Critical Essays.* Chicago: Chicago University Press, 1968.

Valuable essays on actors and acting, theaters and production, by such respected critics as Michael Jamieson, Marvin Rosenberg, Charles Sisson, and William Armstrong.

Bradbrook, M. C. *Elizabethan Stage Conditions: A Study of Their Place in the Interpretation of Shakespeare's Plays.* Cambridge: Cambridge University Press, 1932.

Bradbrook. *The Living Monument: Shakespeare and the Theatre of His Time.* New York: Barnes & Noble, 1969.

Bradbrook. *The Rise of the Common Player: A Study of Actor and Society in Shakespeare's England.* London: Chatto & Windus, 1962.

A respected study of the evolving social status of professional actors.

Chambers, E. K. *The Elizabethan Stage,* 4 volumes. Oxford: Clarendon Press, 1923.

For students of Renaissance drama, one of the monumental works on the period. A comprehensive rendering of the social-theatrical background, the known facts concerning the composition of individual plays, their dates, authorship, and conditions of performance.

Cook, Ann J. *The Privileged Playgoers of Shakespeare's London, 1576-1642.* Princeton: Princeton University Press, 1981.

A sociological, cultural study advancing the notion, which has not yet entirely been accepted, that the privileged audiences of London became increasingly important and were, in fact, the predominant audience for most of the age.

Craik, T. W. *The Tudor Interlude: Stage, Costume, and Acting*. Leicester: Leicester University Press, 1958.

The standard study.

Dessen, Alan C. *Elizabethan Stage Conventions and Modern Interpreters*. Cambridge: Cambridge University Press, 1984.

An astute examination of meaning as conveyed through performance. Intended to bridge the gap between spectators, directors, and scholars.

Foakes, R. A. "Tragedy of the Children's Theatres after 1600: A Challenge to the Adult Stage." In *Elizabethan Theatre II*, edited by David Galloway. Toronto: Macmillan of Canada, 1970, pp. 37-59.

A highly respected study of the repertories and acting style of the Children of the Queen's Revels and the Children of Paul's during their last decade of influence. Although these companies were primarily known for their satires, Foakes discerns four phases in the kinds of tragedy they presented.

Gair, Reavley. *The Children of Paul's: The Story of a Theatre Company, 1553-1608*. Cambridge: Cambridge University Press, 1985.

With recourse to the documentary evidence, Gair treats this prominent company of child actors in the context of the business of court and city. He also examines the children's distinctive acting style.

Gildersleeve, V. C. *Government Regulation of the Elizabethan Drama*. New York: Columbia University Press, 1908.

Although the liberal, Whiggish overview of this study is evident, Gildersleeve provides what remains a valuable narrative of the way that official dramatic regulation and censorship worked.

Gurr, A. J. *The Shakespearean Stage 1574-1642*, revised and enlarged edition. Cambridge & New York: Cambridge University Press, 1980.

The most accessible, readable, and informative of the single-volume surveys of English Renaissance theater. Numerous pictures, drawings, and plates.

Harbage, Alfred B. *Annals of English Drama, 975-1700*, revised by S. Schoenbaum. London: Methuen, 1964.

This handy, single-volume work offers a chronological list of all English plays and dramatic and quasidramatic entertainments, extant and lost, from the time of the first recorded play to year of the death of John Dryden. For each play it includes whatever information is known about author, auspices of production, genre, earliest texts, and the most recent editions. See also Schoenbaum's supplement and second supplement to this edition, published by Northwestern University Press (1966, 1970).

Harbage. *Shakespeare and the Rival Traditions*. New York: Macmillan, 1952.

A work whose scholarship has won plaudits while its contentious argument has gained few converts. Harbage argues not only that there existed two dramatic traditions with distinctive repertories, but that the tradition of the "public" theaters represented the interests of a nation, while the rival tradition at the indoor, "private," theaters catered to a decadent coterie.

Harrison, G. B. *Elizabethan Plays and Players*. London: Routledge, 1940.

An engaging historical narrative beginning with the building of London's first permanent theater in 1576 and ending with the death of Elizabeth in 1603. Notable for its biographical accounts of playwrights such as Robert Greene, Christopher Marlowe, and Ben Jonson and actor Edward Alleyn.

Hattaway, Michael. *Elizabethan Popular Theatre: Plays in Performance*. London: Routledge & Kegan Paul, 1982.

An impressively informed treatment of the playhouses, of the city and court audiences, and of the staging of numerous selected plays.

Hillebrand, H. N. *The Child Actors: A Chapter in Elizabethan Stage History*. Urbana: University of Illinois Press, 1926.

This highly regarded study examines original documents to provide a reliable account of the history of the indoor theaters—primarily Paul's and the First Blackfriars theaters—with their child actors in the Elizabethan and early-Jacobean periods.

Hodges, C. Walter. *The Globe Restored: A Study of the Elizabethan Theater*, revised edition. London & Toronto: Oxford University Press, 1968.

Attempts to reconstruct the Globe theater. Provides colorful chapters on the use of the tiring house, scaffolds, and other scenic devices. Ample presentation of plates, diagrams, historical drawings, and maps.

Hodges. *Shakespeare's Second Globe: The Missing Monument.* New York: Oxford University Press, 1973.

Introduces new evidence modifying Hodges's original views about the nature of the Globe theater.

Joseph, Bertram. *Elizabethan Acting.* Oxford: Oxford University Press, 1951.

Styles of acting with attention to rhetoric, delivery, decorum, and characterization.

Joseph. *The Tragic Actor.* London: Routledge & Kegan Paul, 1959.

A serviceable account of the great Shakespearean actors through the centuries.

Kernodle, George R. *From Art to Theatre: Form and Convention in the Renaissance.* Chicago: University of Chicago Press, 1944.

Lawrence, W. J. *The Elizabethan Playhouse and Other Studies.* Stratford-upon-Avon: Shakespeare Head Press, 1912.

The Elizabethan playhouse as a physical structure, with attention as well to music, song, and the masque.

Murray, John Tucker. *English Dramatic Companies, 1558-1642,* 2 volumes. Boston: Houghton Mifflin, 1910.

Full of records and accounts, especially useful for its data on provincial companies.

Orrell, John. *The Quest for Shakespeare's Globe.* Cambridge: Cambridge University Press, 1968.

Penniman, Josiah H. *The War of the Theatres.* University of Pennsylvania Series in Philology, Literature, and Archaeology, 4, no. 3. Boston: Ginn, 1897.

An account of the several dramatists, including Ben Jonson, Thomas Dekker, and John Marston, who at the turn of the seventeenth century alluded in their plays to rival dramatists and theaters. The notion of a "war of the theaters" has been accepted but identification of the topical allusions and historical personages aimed at is frequently speculative and hazardous.

Reynolds, George F. *The Staging of Elizabethan Plays at the Red Bull Theater, 1605-1625.* New York: Modern Language Association of America/London: Oxford University Press, 1940.

An excellent, much-needed study of performance at one of London's less reputable, outdoor public theaters.

Sanders, Norman, Richard Southern, J. W. Craik, and Lois Potter, eds. *The Revels History of Drama in English, Volume II: 1500-1576.* London & New York: Methuen, 1980.

Offers an account of the conditions of performance, companies, plays, playwrights, as well as the social-historical context, including the Tudor suppression of the cycle drama.

Shapiro, Michael. *Children of the Revels: The Boy Companies of Shakespeare's Time and Their Plays.* New York: Columbia University Press, 1977.

A solid study of the acting styles, repertory, and history of London's companies of boy actors.

Sharpe, Robert B. *The Real War of the Theaters: Shakespeare's Fellows in the Rivalry with the Admiral's Men, 1594-1603.* Modern Language Association of America, Monograph Series 5. Boston: Heath/London: Oxford University Press, 1935.

Sibley, Gertrude M. *The Lost Plays and Masques, 1500-1642.* Ithaca: Cornell University Press, 1933.

Sisson, C. J. *The Boar's Head Theatre: An Inn-Yard Theatre of the Elizabethan Age,* revised and edited by Stanley Wells. London & Boston: Routledge & Kegan Paul, 1972.

Small, Roscoe A. *The Stage-Quarrel Between Jonson and the So-called Poetasters.* Breslau: M. & H. Marcus, 1899.

Really a study of the "war of the theaters" with emphasis on Jonson and his contemporary playwrights. A useful account of a difficult, speculative subject.

Smith, Irwin. *Shakespeare's Blackfriars Playhouse: Its History and Its Design.* New York: New York University Press, 1964.

A well-researched, thorough, frequently cited examination.

Southern, Richard. *The Staging of Plays before Shakespeare.* London: Faber & Faber, 1973.

A much-needed examination of the staging of individual plays, treated chronologically from the Tudor morality play *Mankind.*

Steele, Mary. *Plays and Masques at Court During the Reigns of Elizabeth, James, and Charles.* New Haven: Yale University Press, 1926.

Attempts a complete chronological listing of performances by event along with frequent, concise, contemporary reactions and notations.

Wallace, Charles W. *The Evolution of English Drama up to Shakespeare; with a History of the First Blackfriars Theatre: A Survey Based upon Original Records Now for the First Time Collected and Published.* Berlin: G. Reimer, 1912.

A respected work, still cited for its scholarly presentation of pertinent contemporary documents.

V. Critical and Historical Studies

Adams, H. H. *English Domestic or Homiletic Tragedy 1575-1642.* New York: Columbia University Press, 1943.

Establishes unexceptionably the presence of this didactic tradition in the Elizabethan drama.

Agnew, Jean-Christophe. *Worlds Apart: The Market and the Theater in Anglo American Thought: 1550-1750.* Cambridge: Cambridge University Press, 1986.

Treats the English theater in relation to the commercial imperatives that helped to direct its development.

Albright, Evelyn May. *Dramatic Publication in England, 1580-1640: A Study of Conditions Affecting Content and Form of Drama.* Modern Language Association of America, Monograph series 2. New York: Heath/London: Oxford University Press, 1927.

Despite its dated Whiggish perspective, Albright's book is still an essential study, full and complex, of the various overlapping agencies and authorities that regulated dramatic publication.

Altman, Joel B. *The Tudor Play of Mind: Rhetorical Inquiry and the Development of Elizabethan Drama.* Berkeley: University of California Press, 1978.

A fine scholarly study of "wonder" as expressed by the rhetoric of drama.

Anglo, Sydney. *Spectacle, Pageantry, and Early Tudor Policy.* Oxford: Clarendon Press, 1969.

An excellent study of pageantry as an instrument of Tudor policy, diplomacy, and aggrandizement.

Baker, Howard. *Induction to Tragedy: A Study in a Development of Form in "Gorboduc," "The Spanish Tragedy" and "Titus Andronicus."* Baton Rouge: Louisiana State University Press, 1939.

Barber, C. L. *The Idea of Honour in the English Drama, 1591-1700.* Gothenburg Studies in English, no. 6. Göteborg, 1957.

A thorough examination of the evolution of this concept, which initially signified one's virtue but later came to denote one's reputation.

Belsey, Catherine. *The Subject of Tragedy: Identity and Difference in Renaissance Drama.* London & New York: Methuen, 1985.

An insightful feminist study of gender conceptions.

Bentley, Gerald Eades. *Shakespeare and Jonson: Their Reputations in the Seventeenth Century Compared,* 2 volumes. Chicago: University of Chicago Press, 1945.

Bergeron, David M. *English Civic Pageantry 1558-1642.* Columbia: University of South Carolina Press, 1971.

A lucid account of progresses, royal entries, Lord Mayors' shows, and pageants. Later chapters are devoted to the major composers.

Bergeron, ed. *Twentieth Century Criticism of English Masques, Pageants and Entertainments: 1558-1642: With a Supplement on Folk-Play and Related Forms by H. B. Caldwell.* San Antonio: Trinity University Press, 1972.

Bernard, J. E., Jr. *The Prosody of the Tudor Interlude.* New Haven: Yale University Press/London: Oxford University Press, 1939.

An important but neglected subject. The "art" of the Tudor interlude is frequently devalued without sufficient examination.

Bethell, Samuel L. *Shakespeare and the Popular Dramatic Tradition.* Westminster: King & Staples, 1944.

Still a widely read, respected work.

Bevington, David M. *From Mankind to Marlowe: Growth of Structure in the Popular Drama of Tudor England.* Cambridge: Harvard University Press, 1962.

A pioneering historical-theatrical examination of dramatic structure with special attention to casting and staging.

Bevington. *Tudor Drama and Politics: A Critical Approach to Topical Meaning.* Cambridge: Harvard University Press, 1968.

The definitive study in a play-by-play analysis of political topicality in the pre-Shakespearean drama.

Bluestone, Max, and Norman Rabkin, eds. *Shakespeare's Contemporaries: Modern Studies in English Renaissance Drama,* enlarged edition. Englewood Cliffs, N.J.: Prentice-Hall, 1970.

An excellent collection, chronologically organized, which begins with an essay on *Gammer Gurton's Needle* (produced circa 1559) and ends with Fredson Bowers's analysis of the revenge motif in James Shirley's *The Cardinal* (produced in 1641).

Boas, F. S. *An Introduction to Stuart Drama.* Oxford: Clarendon Press, 1946.

Boas. *An Introduction to Tudor Drama.* Oxford: Clarendon Press, 1933.

Boughner, Daniel C. *The Braggart in Renaissance Comedy: A Study in Comparative Drama from Aristophanes to Shakespeare.* Minneapolis: University of Minnesota Press, 1954.

Bowers, Fredson. *Elizabethan Revenge Tragedy: 1587-1642.* Princeton: Princeton University Press, 1940.

This original study limns and then traces the development of the tradition of the revenge play as a dramatic form.

Bradbrook, M. C. *English Dramatic Form: A History of its Development.* London: Chatto & Windus, 1965.

Bradbrook. *The Growth and Structure of Elizabethan Comedy.* London: Chatto & Windus, 1955.

Really a history of the development of English Renaissance comedy with attention to traditions, conventions, and forms. Also treats over a dozen comic playwrights in separate sections or chapters.

Bradbrook. *Themes and Conventions of Elizabethan Tragedy.* Cambridge: Cambridge University Press, 1935.

A close analysis and discussion of the conventions of speech and action in the drama. Bradbrook holds more firmly than most that the manner of Elizabethan acting was "formal."

Bristol, Michael D. *Carnival and Theater: Plebeian Culture and the Structure of Authority in Renaissance England.* New York & London: Methuen, 1985.

An original study of the disruptive knowledge of the "other" contained in popular culture and drama.

Brodwin, Leonora L. *Elizabethan Love Tragedy, 1587-1625.* New York: New York University Press, 1971.

Discerns the patterns within this subgenre and treats the plays with a pronounced narrative emphasis.

Brooke, Nicholas. *Horrid Laughter in Jacobean Tragedy.* London: Open Books, 1979.

A discriminating discussion of "serious" laughter in six Jacobean tragedies.

Brooke, Tucker C. F. *The Tudor Drama.* Boston & New York: Houghton Mifflin, 1911.

A survey by genre that includes treatments of the interlude and history play as well as topical drama.

Brown, John Russell, and Bernard Harris, gen. eds. *Elizabethan Theatre.* Stratford-upon-Avon Studies, no. 9. London: Arnold, 1967.

Brown and Harris, gen. eds. *Jacobean Theatre.* Stratford-upon-Avon Studies, no. 1. London: Arnold, 1960.

A well-known volume that includes G. K. Hunter's essay on "English Folly and Italian Vice." Dramatists treated include Jonson, Marston, Middleton, Shakespeare, Fletcher, Webster, and Chapman.

Butler, Martin. *Theatre and Crisis, 1632-1642.* Cambridge: Cambridge University Press, 1984.

Bound to be received as the most revitalizing interpretation of Caroline theater since Alfred Harbage's *Cavalier Drama.* In contrast to Harbage, Butler, revealing an intimate knowledge of the politics of the Stuart court, argues that court drama, even when its plots are romantic, is fundamentally political and frequently oppositionist.

Cardozo, J. L. *The Contemporary Jew in Elizabethan Drama.* Amsterdam: H. J. Paris, 1925.

This respected study establishes the historical context that informed the stereotypical representation of the Jew on the English stage.

Champion, Larry S. *Tragic Patterns in Jacobean and Caroline Drama.* Knoxville: University of Tennessee Press, 1977.

Treating formalistically the works, exclusive of Shakespeare's, that are generally regarded to be the most powerful, Champion directs attention to the ways that early Stuart plays "create the vision of a fragmented and decadent society."

Charlton, H. B. *The Senecan Tradition in Renaissance Tragedy.* Manchester: University of Manchester Press, 1946.

A republication of an essay that first appeared in 1921 as an introduction to the poetical works of Sir William Alexander. Despite the specificity of the original subject, the comprehensive knowledge Charlton brings to bear on it makes this book live up to its ambitious title.

Chute, Marchette. *Shakespeare of London.* New York: Dutton, 1949.

Employing the records left by such prose pamphleteers as Robert Greene, Thomas Nashe, and Robert Peele, Chute, whose brilliant style has been widely acclaimed, vividly re-creates London's theatrical world in the Elizabethan-Jacobean age.

Clemen, Wolfgang. *English Tragedy before Shakespeare: The Development of Dramatic Speech*, translated by Theodor S. Dorsch. London: Methuen, 1961.

An excellent, learned study of the set speech and other formal elements in pre-Shakespearean drama.

Cohen, Walter. *Drama of a Nation: Public Theater in Renaissance England and Spain*. Ithaca & London: Cornell University Press, 1985.

A Marxist-oriented, cultural study that ascribes the decline of popular Renaissance theater in England and Spain to the growing absolutism in the court of each country.

Cope, Jackson I. *The Theatre and the Dream: From Metaphor to Form in Renaissance Drama*. Baltimore: Johns Hopkins University Press, 1973.

A high-powered, insightful, if not always convincing, treatment of master metaphors as an organizing form.

Corrigan, Robert W., ed. *Comedy: Meaning and Form*. San Francisco: Chandler, 1965.

First-rate, diachronic studies of the genre, including several essays that address the features of Shakespearean and Jonsonian comedy.

Corrigan, ed. *Tragedy Vision and Form*. Scranton: Chandler, 1965.

Fine diachronic studies of the genre by renowned authorities, including several essays that address features of Elizabethan and Jacobean tragedy.

Craig, Hardin. *The Enchanted Glass: The Elizabethan Mind in Literature*. New York: Oxford University Press, 1936.

A respected study in the history of ideas.

Cunliffe, John W. *The Influence of Seneca on Elizabethan Tragedy*. London & New York: Macmillan, 1893.

A solid examination of a pervasive dramatic influence.

Danby, John F. *Poets on Fortune's Hill: Studies in Sidney, Shakespeare, Beaumont, and Fletcher*. London: Faber & Faber, 1952.

An influential study whose judgmental view of Beaumont and Fletcher as decadent playwrights has shaped the outlook of a generation of critics.

Dessen, Alan C. *Elizabethan Drama and the Viewer's Eye*. Chapel Hill: University of North Carolina Press, 1977.

An astute, lucidly written study, attentive to the meaning of the play in performance.

Dollimore, Jonathan. *Radical Tragedy: Religion, Ideology and Power in the Drama of Shakespeare and His Contemporaries*. Chicago: University of Chicago Press, 1984.

A hard-hitting polemical study fraught with the ferment of Renaissance ideas which contends that Elizabethan-Jacobean tragedy was radical in its depiction of an antihumanistic vision of decentered man.

Doran, Madeleine. *Endeavors of Art: A Study of Form in Elizabethan Drama*. Madison: University of Wisconsin Press, 1954.

An impressively learned, lucid historical study of the tastes and influences that shaped Elizabethan and Jacobean dramatic genres.

Downer, Alan S. *The British Drama: A Handbook and Brief Chronicle*. New York: Appleton-Century-Crofts, 1950.

The first four chapters treat interludes, miracle plays, morality plays, *de casibus* tragedy, revenge plays, comedy, tragedy, and tragicomedy.

Eliot, T. S. *Elizabethan Essays*. London: Faber & Faber, 1982. Republished, with the omission of three essays and the addition of one, as *Essays on Elizabethan Drama*. New York: Harcourt, Brace, 1932. Republished as *Elizabethan Dramatists*. London: Faber & Faber, 1963.

Known for its influential opinions, to which modern scholars continue to turn, often in rebuttal.

Ellis-Fermor, Una M. *The Jacobean Drama*, fourth edition, revised. London: Methuen, 1958.

A probing, sensitive, atmospherically rich survey that includes one of the first serious examinations of the closet dramatist Fulke Greville.

Farnham, Willard. *The Medieval Heritage of Elizabethan Tragedy*, revised edition. Oxford: Blackwell, 1956.

An excellent historical study of Wheel of Fortune or *de casibus* tragedy as transmitted by such influential works as Lydgate's *Mirror for Magistrates*.

Fluchère, Henri. *Shakespeare and the Elizabethans*. New York: Hill & Wang, 1964.

A useful introductory study whose tripartite organization treats "The Spirit of the Age," "Technique," and "The Themes."

Ford, Boris, ed. *The Age of Shakespeare*. The Pelican Guide to English Literature, volume 2, revised edition. Baltimore: Penguin, 1962.

An overview, with originality and depth, principally of Tudor-Stuart drama, by well-known scholars.

Freer, Coburn. *The Poetics of Jacobean Drama*. Baltimore & London: Johns Hopkins University Press, 1981.

Gibbons, Brian. *Jacobean City Comedy: A Study of Satiric Plays by Jonson, Marston, and Middleton*. Cambridge: Harvard University Press, 1968.

A notable analysis that helped to define the nature and purposes of this genre.

Goldberg, Jonathan. *James I and the Politics of Literature: Jonson, Shakespeare, Donne, and Their Contemporaries*. Baltimore & London: Johns Hopkins University Press, 1983.

Influenced by the French theoretician Michel Foucault, this work examines "the relationships between authority and its representations," with particular emphasis on the power of language.

Greenblatt, Stephen, ed. *The Power of Forms*. Norman: University of Oklahoma Press, 1982.

An important text for studying what is called "the New History" in drama. Takes for its subject not so much the antecedent facts of history, but the total linguistic and cultural inheritance that shapes dramatic attitudes.

Greenfield, Thelma N. *The Induction in Elizabethan Drama*. Eugene: University of Oregon Press, 1969.

The standard work on this specialized subject.

Hallett, Charles A. and Elaine S. *The Revenger's Madness: A Study of Revenge Tragedy Motifs*. Lincoln & London: University of Nebraska Press, 1980.

Halliday, F. E. *Shakespeare in his Age*. London: Duckworth, 1956.

A fine, lively, informative rendering of Shakespeare's age. Includes historical chapters as well as discussions of dramatists, theaters, companies, and the masque.

Harbage, Alfred B. *Cavalier Drama*. New York: Modern Language Association of America/London: Oxford University Press, 1936.

Now much under attack, this detailed survey of mostly little-known court plays depicts the Caroline drama as essentially précieux and effeminate.

Hardison, O. B., Jr. *Christian Rite and Christian Drama in the Middle Ages: Essays in the Origins and Early History of Modern Drama*. Baltimore: Johns Hopkins Press, 1965.

Although the body of the work treats medieval drama, its frequently cited introduction cogently argues against the view that pre-Shakespearean drama is important solely or even primarily because it anticipates Shakespeare's own.

Heilman, Robert B. *Tragedy and Melodrama: Versions of Experience*. Seattle: University of Washington Press, 1969.

Heineman, Margot. *Puritanism and Theatre: Thomas Middleton and The Opposition Drama under the Early Stuarts*. Cambridge: Cambridge University Press, 1980.

An important, scholarly study that draws attention to Puritan "oppositionist" attitudes expressed in the drama by Middleton and many other writers of lesser note.

Herndl, George C. *The High Design: English Renaissance Tragedy and the Natural Law*. Lexington: University Press of Kentucky, 1970.

Herrick, Marvin T. *Comic Theory in the Sixteenth Century*. Urbana: University of Illinois Press, 1950.

A learned examination of the rhetorical tradition, the influence of comic theorists and comic character types.

Herrick. *Tragicomedy: Its Origin and Development in Italy, France, and England*. Urbana: University of Illinois Press, 1955.

Learned, dense, historically oriented.

Honigmann, Ernst, ed. *Shakespeare and his Contemporaries: Essays in Comparison*. Manchester: Manchester University Press, 1986.

Essays by distinguished scholars compare Shakespeare to one or more of his contemporaries. Subjects include, among others, bourgeois comedy, historical English tragedy, and the Roman plays.

Howarth, R. G. *Literature of the Theatre: Marlowe to Shirley*. Sydney, Australia: Halstead Press, 1953.

Hoy, Cyrus. *The Hyacinth Room: An Investigation into the Nature of Comedy, Tragedy, and Tragicomedy*. New York: Knopf, 1964.

Especially fine for its treatment of tragicomedy.

Kantorowicz, Ernest H. *The King's Two Bodies: A Study in Medieval Political Theology*. Princeton: Princeton University Press, 1957.

Essential to an adequate understanding of the English history play, this standard study sets forth the doctrine that the anointed king is a mystical embodiment of the divine will and yet, paradoxically, subject to all the corruptions of the flesh.

Kaufman, R. J., ed. *Elizabethan Drama: Modern Essays in Criticism.* New York: Oxford University Press, 1961.

A strong collection featuring Hereward Price's classic essay on the oxymoronic imagistic patterns in Webster's tragedies.

Kernan, Alvin. *The Cankered Muse: Satire of the English Renaissance.* New Haven: Yale University Press, 1959.

An excellent holistic study of dramatic and nondramatic satire.

Kirsch, Arthur. *Jacobean Dramatic Perspectives.* Charlottesville: University Press of Virginia, 1972.

A lucid, predominantly formalistic study that examines three primary components in the Jacobean drama–tragicomedy, satiric tragedy, and the coterie theaters.

Klein, David. *The Elizabethan Dramatists as Critics.* New York: Philosophical Library, 1963.

Knights, L. C. *Drama and Society in the Age of Jonson.* London: Chatto & Windus, 1937.

A respected Marxist-oriented approach to the drama focusing on such figures as Jonson and Middleton, whose drama probed the spiritual implications of the capitalistic enterprise as it began to displace the older feudal order and its values.

Kogan, Stephen. *The Hieroglyphic King: Wisdom and Idolatry in the Seventeenth-Century Masque.* Rutherford, N.J.: Fairleigh Dickinson University Press, 1986.

An astute, comprehensive, analytic-historical treatment of the composers and their masques.

Kolin, Philip C. *The Elizabethan Stage Doctor as a Dramatic Convention.* Elizabethan & Renaissance Studies, 41. Salzburg: Institut für Englische Sprache und Literatur, Universität Salzburg, 1975.

Kronenberger, Louis. *The Thread of Laughter: Chapters on English Stage Comedy from Jonson to Maugham.* New York: Knopf, 1952.

Leggatt, Alexander. *Citizen Comedy in the Age of Shakespeare.* Toronto: University of Toronto Press, 1973.

Akin to Gibbons's examination of city comedy, Leggatt's thematically organized study views the genre more broadly to treat Thomas Dekker and other lesser-known playwrights along with the major dramatic satirists.

Leinwand, Theodore B. *The City Stage: Jacobean Comedy, 1603-1613.* Madison: University of Wisconsin Press, 1986.

Treats its subject by character type, from the merchant-citizen and gallant to the whore and widow.

Lever, J. W. *The Tragedy of State.* London: Methuen, 1971.

A brief, eminently readable examination of Jacobean drama in its political dimension as "a product of the intellectual ferment and spiritual upheaveal" that preceded the English civil war.

Levin, Richard. *The Multiple Plot in English Renaissance Drama.* Chicago: University of Chicago Press, 1971.

A rigorously organized, comprehensive examination of the subject.

Levin. *New Readings vs. Old Plays: Recent Trends in the Reinterpretation of English Renaissance Drama.* Chicago: University of Chicago Press, 1979.

In this study of methodologies, Levin, a longtime reviewer of journal essays, seeks to expose the excesses resulting from "thematic" and "topical" interpretations, among others, of Tudor-Stuart plays.

Lindabury, R. B. *A Study of Patriotism in the Elizabethan Drama.* Princeton: Princeton University Press, 1931.

A solid work.

Loftis, John. *Renaissance Drama in England and Spain: Topical Allusion and History Plays.* Berkeley: University of California Press, 1986.

One of a growing number of crosscultural studies. Loftis's approach enables him to offer fresh interpretations of works by Marlowe, Middleton, and Massinger, as well as of Jonson's masques and Shakespeare's *King John.*

Lucas, F. L. *Seneca and Elizabethan Tragedy.* Cambridge: Cambridge University Press, 1922.

Along with Cunliffe's *The Influence of Senaca on Elizabethan Tragedy,* Lucas's study traces one of the most important influences in the development of English Renaissance tragedy.

Lyons, Bridget Gellert. *Voices of Melancholy.* London: Routledge & Kegan Paul, 1971.

A study of the Elizabethan humor of melancholy with particular emphasis in the drama on *Hamlet* and on Marston's Antonio plays and *The Malcontent.*

Margeson, John M. R. *The Origins of English Tragedy*. Oxford: Oxford University Press, 1967.

A fine, clear-sighted study seeking to identify Renaissance tragedy in the conflict with or rebellion against the divine order.

McAlindon, T. *English Renaissance Tragedy*. Vancouver: University of British Columbia Press, 1986.

A fresh study of ideas and dramatic influences with notable focus on the contributions of Thomas Kyd and Christopher Marlowe.

McDonald, Charles O. *The Rhetoric of Tragedy: Form in Stuart Drama*. Amherst: University of Massachusetts Press, 1966.

Mehl, Dieter. *The Elizabethan Dumb Show: The History of a Dramatic Convention*. Cambridge: Harvard University Press, 1966.

A classic, specialized study of the convention whereby selected dramatic events were sometimes mimed rather than spoken.

Sister Miriam Joseph. *Rhetoric in Shakespeare's Time*. New York: Harcourt, Brace & World, 1962.

A valuable treatment of the theory and practice of composition in the English Renaissance, including grammar, topics of invention, argumentation, pathos, and ethos.

Nicoll, Allardyce. *Stuart Masques and the Renaissance Stage*. London: Harrap, 1937.

Olson, Elder. *Tragedy and the Theory of Drama*. Detroit: Wayne State University Press, 1961.

An Aristotelian interpretation.

Orgel, Stephen. *The Illusion of Power: Political Theater in the English Renaissance*. Berkeley: University of California Press, 1975.

A brief, powerful demonstration of the political implications of theatrical representation, particularly of "the royal spectacle" of the masque.

Orgel and Roy Strong. *Inigo Jones: The Theater of the Stuart Court*, 2 volumes. Berkeley: University of California Press, 1973.

Large, lavish reproductions of Inigo Jones's drawings of costumes, sets, and stages for Stuart masques, with their texts.

Ornstein, Robert. *The Moral Vision of Jacobean Tragedy*. Madison: University of Wisconsin Press, 1960.

With its many single-author chapters, this work, which searches for the "intrinsic values in experience," has been one of the most widely read books of critical interpretation in the field.

Orr, David. *Italian Renaissance Drama in England before 1625*. Chapel Hill: University of North Carolina Press, 1975.

An erudite examination of Elizabethan-Jacobean tragedy, comedy, and pastoral.

Parrott, Thomas Marc, and Robert Hamilton Ball. *A Short View of Elizabethan Drama*. New York: Scribners, 1958.

One of the handier compendiums, with brief treatments of virtually all the plays by the major and minor playwrights in the Elizabethan age to the closing of the theaters in 1642.

Paster, Gail Kern. *The Idea of the City in the Age of Shakespeare*. Athens: University of Georgia Press, 1985.

Stylistically fine, this study treats, principally, Shakespeare, Jonson, and Middleton.

Patterson, Annabel. *Censorship and Interpretation: The Conditions of Writing and Reading in early Modern England*. Madison: University of Wisconsin Press, 1984.

A valuable study of the complicated interrelationships among censors, authors, and audience, with an important chapter on the hermeneutics of censorship.

Perry, Henry Ten Eyck. *Masters of Dramatic Comedy and Their Social Themes*. Cambridge: Harvard University Press, 1939.

Peter, John. *Complaint and Satire in Early English Literature*. Oxford: Clarendon Press, 1956.

A survey, widely cited for its distinction between "satire" and "complaint." Treats nondramatic as well as dramatic satire through John Marston.

Potter, Robert. *The English Morality Play: Origins, History and Influence of a Dramatic Tradition*. London & Boston: Routledge & Kegan Paul, 1975.

An essential work of scholarship.

Potts, L. J. *Comedy*. London & New York: Hutchinson's University Library, 1948.

Beginning with the premise that comedy must be understood as issuing from the viewer rather than from the form in which it is expressed, Potts draws widely from the entire comic tradition.

Prior, Moody E. *The Language of Tragedy*. New York: Columbia University Press, 1947.

An unsurpassed study of its kind, Prior's formalistic analysis examines the implications of the use of dramatic prose and verse drama from the Elizabethan to the modern age.

Ramsey, P. A., ed. *Rome in the Renaissance, The City and the Myth*. Binghamton, N.Y.: Center for Medieval & Early Renaissance Studies, 1982.

Includes three notable essays treating Jonson's and Shakespeare's use of Roman history in their dramatic work.

Reed, Robert R. *The Occult on the Tudor and Stuart Stage*. London: Christopher, 1965.

Ribner, Irving. *The English History Play in the Age of Shakespeare*, revised and enlarged edition. London: Methuen, 1965.

Among the finest developmental studies of the genre.

Ribner. *Jacobean Tragedy: The Quest for Moral Order*. London: Methuen, 1962.

More historically oriented than Ornstein's *The Moral Vision of Jacobean Tragedy*. Ribner's study concerns itself with the difficulties inherent in a Jacobean affirmation of moral order. Especially noteworthy is the analysis of the problematic moral outlook of Chapman's *Bussy D'Ambois*.

Ricks, Christopher, ed. *English Drama to 1710*. History of Literature in the English Language, volume 3. London: Barrie & Jenkins/Sphere Books, 1971.

A well-organized survey with chapters by acknowledged experts on their subjects.

Riefer, Frederick. *Fortune and Elizabethan Tragedy*. San Marino, Cal.: Huntington Library, 1983.

A wide-ranging, substantial, scholarly examination of the tradition and its dramatists.

Ristine, Frank Humphrey. *English Tragicomedy: Its Origin and History*. New York: Columbia University Press, 1910.

A useful survey still.

Rossiter, A. P. *English Drama from Early Times to the Elizabethans*. London: Hutchinson's University Library, 1950.

A respected work of historical scholarship.

Roston, Murray. *Biblical Drama in England: From the Middle Ages to the Present Day*. Evanston: Northwestern University Press, 1968.

Rozett, Martha Tuck. *The Doctrine of Election and the Emergence of Elizabethan Tragedy*. Princeton: Princeton University Press, 1984.

A fine study of how the doctrine that God has predestined some individuals to salvation and others to damnation affected popular drama.

Salingar, Leo. *Dramatic Form in Shakespeare and the Jacobeans: Essays*. Cambridge: Cambridge University Press, 1986.

Salingar. *Shakespeare and the Traditions of Comedy*. London: Cambridge University Press, 1974.

Sanders, Wilbur. *The Dramatist and the Received Idea: Studies in the Plays of Marlowe and Shakespeare*. Cambridge: Cambridge University Press, 1968.

A closely-argued, illuminating, judgmental reading of the strengths and weaknesses of Marlowe and Shakespeare, often to the detriment of Marlowe.

Schelling, F. E. *Elizabethan Drama, 1558-1642*, 2 volumes. Boston & New York: Houghton Mifflin, 1908.

Although its point of view is no longer current, Schelling's study still offers a reasonable overview of the vast achievement of English Renaissance drama.

Schelling. *Foreign Influences in Elizabethan Plays*. New York & London: Harper, 1923.

An inadequate overview of a neglected subject.

Schucking, Levin L. *The Baroque Character of the Elizabethan Tragic Hero*. Oxford: Oxford University Press, 1938.

Sharpe, Robert B. *Irony in the Drama: An Essay on Interpretation, Shock, and Catharsis*. Chapel Hill: University of North Carolina Press, 1959.

Silvette, Herbert. *The Doctor on the Stage: Medicine and Medical Men in Seventeenth-Century England*, edited by Francelia Butler. Knoxville: University of Tennessee Press, 1967.

Sisson, C. J. *Lost Plays of Shakespeare's Age*. Cambridge: Cambridge University Press, 1936.

Expands our knowledge of plays whose texts have not survived but about which we know something—as for example, through court records that tell in great detail the outlines of George Chapman's topical comedy *The Old Joiner of Aldgate*.

Smith, G. C. *College Plays Performed at the University of Cambridge*. Cambridge: Cambridge University Press, 1923.

Speaight, George. *The History of the English Puppet Theater*. New York: John de Graff, 1955.

Frequently cited in treatments of Jonson's *Bartholomew Fair*, in which a puppet play is enacted.

Spencer, Theodore. *Death and Elizabethan Tragedy: A Study of Convention and Opinion in the Elizabethan Drama*. Cambridge: Harvard University Press, 1936.

A useful treatment of the medieval background and of the language, ideas, and dramatic techniques of tragedy.

Spencer. *Shakespeare and the Nature of Man.* New York: Macmillan, 1942.

A study basic to the understanding of the age. Spencer examines the threat posed to humanistic ideals by such seminal thinkers as Machiavelli, Montaigne, and Copernicus.

Spivack, Bernard. *Shakespeare and the Allegory of Evil.* New York: Columbia University Press, 1958.

A classic study that ranges through the pre-Shakespearean drama to illuminate the mystery of Shakespeare's villains, which culminates in the figure of Iago.

Stilling, Roger. *Love and Death in Renaissance Tragedy.* Baton Rouge: Louisiana State University Press, 1976.

Treats love tragedy as a genre.

Sullivan, Mary Agnes. *Court Masques of James I.* Lincoln: University of Nebraska Press, 1913.

A neglected work that establishes James's use of the occasion of the masque to carry forward his policies, particularly with foreign dignitaries.

Sutherland, Sarah P. *Masques in Jacobean Tragedy.* New York: AMS Press, 1983.

Talbert, Ernest W. *Elizabethan Drama and Shakespeare's Early Plays.* Chapel Hill: University of North Carolina Press, 1963.

The focus falls mainly on Shakespeare's plays.

Thompson, Elbert N. S. *The Controversy between the Puritans and the Stage.* New York: Holt, 1903.

Tokson, Elliot H. *The Popular Image of the Black Man in English Drama, 1550-1688.* Boston: G. K. Hall, 1982.

Tomlinson, Thomas B. *A Study of Elizabethan and Jacobean Tragedy.* London: Cambridge University Press, 1964.

A frequently judgmental study of major dramatists, in which Tourneur, Shakespeare, and Middleton are accorded high praise, while Webster, Chapman, and Ford are denigrated as either decadent or "hollow."

Tricomi, Albert H. *Anti-Court Drama in England, 1603-1642.* Charlottesville: University Press of Virginia, forthcoming 1988.

A comprehensive examination of the varieties of plays that were critical or condemnatory of the court as a political and /or social institution.

Ure, Peter. *Elizabethan and Jacobean Drama,* edited by J. C. Maxwell. Liverpool: Liverpool University Press, 1974.

Eleven essays on Shakespeare and contemporaries by an admired critic.

Waith, Eugene M. *The Herculean Hero in Marlowe, Chapman, Shakespeare, and Dryden.* New York: Columbia University Press, 1962.

With focus on seven plays, this fine study examines the myth of the hero as manifest in the representation of Hercules in the genres of epic and tragedy.

Waith. *The Pattern of Tragicomedy in Beaumont and Fletcher.* New Haven: Yale University Press, 1952.

Among the best studies of its kind, it ranges far beyond Beaumont and Fletcher's work to illuminate the nature of the genre.

Ward, A. W. *A History of English Dramatic Literature to the Death of Queen Anne,* revised edition, 3 volumes. London: Macmillan, 1899.

Less useful now than it once was, Ward's work is still cited for its perspective on plays, playwrights, and movements.

Weld, John S. *Meaning in Comedy: Studies in Elizabethan Romantic Comedy.* Albany: State University of New York Press, 1975.

Begins by emphasizing dramatic metaphor as a means of exemplification in the Tudor morality tradition and concludes with an examination of the romantic comedy of John Lyly and the early Shakespeare.

Welsford, Enid. *The Court Masque: A Study in the Relationship Between Poetry and the Revels.* Cambridge: Cambridge University Press, 1927.

A learned, classic study.

Welsford. *The Fool: His Social and Literary History.* London: Faber & Faber, 1935.

A highly regarded study, frequently cited to address the problems of performing the role of the Fool in *King Lear* and other plays. Welsford also examines the relationships linking the fool to the traditions of licensed satire and the festivities of the Lord of Misrule.

Wickham, Glynne. *Early English Stages 1300-1660,* 3 volumes. New York: Columbia University Press, 1959-1981.

A valuable general study informed by a lifetime of learning. Wickham's third volume, which treats the development of English comedy and tragedy to 1576, displays a keen awareness of the Christian patterns of dramatic representation and symbol that pervade Tudor drama. A fourth volume is planned to include the period from 1576-1660.

Wilson, F. P. *The English Drama: 1485-1585*. New York: Oxford University Press, 1969.

A narrative study by genre of the Tudor morality and interlude and the development of comedy and tragedy from 1540-1584. Includes chronological table of plays and events and a fine, annotated author bibliography.

Contributors

John F. Andrews ....*National Endowment for the Humanities*
Marie Axton ....*Cambridge University*
Philip J. Ayres ....*Monash University*
Peter Berek ....*Williams College*
Fredson Bowers ....*University of Virginia*
Gordon Braden ....*University of Virginia*
Raymond S. Burns ....*Pace University*
Irby B. Cauthen, Jr. ....*University of Virginia*
Peter Davison ....*Westfield College, University of London*
Kevin J. Donovan ....*University of New Hampshire*
Robert F. Fleissner ....*Central State University, Ohio*
Roma Gill ....*Oxford, England*
Andrew Gurr ....*University of Reading*
James L. Harner ....*Bowling Green State University*
Cyrus Hoy ....*University of Rochester*
Daniel Kinney ....*University of Virginia*
Stanley J. Kozikowski ....*Bryant College*
Paul G. Kreuzer ....*Lehman College, City University of New York*
Charles Larson ....*University of Manchester at St. Louis*
Leah Scragg ....*University of Manchester*
Albert H. Tricomi ....*State University of New York at Binghamton*
D. Jerry White ....*Central Missouri State University*
Karen Wood ....*University of California, Berkeley*

Cumulative Index

Dictionary of Literary Biography, Volumes 1-62
Dictionary of Literary Biography Yearbook, 1980-1986
Dictionary of Literary Biography Documentary Series, Volumes 1-4

Cumulative Index

DLB before number: *Dictionary of Literary Biography*, Volumes 1-62
Y before number: *Dictionary of Literary Biography Yearbook*, 1980-1986
DS before number: *Dictionary of Literary Biography Documentary Series*, Volumes 1-4

A

445

D

E

G

I

L

O

P

Q

R

S

U

Y

Satiro-mastix.
OR
The vntrussing of the Humo-
rous Poet.

As it hath bin presented publikely,
by the Right Honorable, the Lord Chamberlaine his Seruants; and privately, by the
Children of Paules.

By Thomas Dekker.

Non recito cuiquam nisi Amicis idq; coactus.

LONDON,
Printed by E. A. for Edward White, and are to
be solde at his shop, neere the little North doore of Paules
Church, at the signe of the Gun. 1602.

The Spanish Tragedie:
OR,
Hieronimo is mad againe.

Containing the lamentable end of Don Horatio, and
Belimperia; with the pittifull death of Hieronimo.

Newly corrected, amended, and enlarged with new
Additions of the Painters part, and others, as
it hath of late been diuers times acted.

LONDON,
W. White, for I. White and T. Langley,
and are to be sold at their Shop ouer against the
Sarazens head without New-gate. 1615.
Printed by W. White, for I. White and T. Langley,

The Iron Age:
Contayning the Rape of Hellen: The siege of Troy:
The Combate betwixt Hector and Aiax: Hector and Troilus
slayne by Achilles: Achilles slaine by Paris: Aiax and Vlisses
contend for the Armour of Achilles: The Death
of Aiax, &c.

Written by THOMAS HEYVVOOD.

Aut prodesse solent aut Delectare.

HECTOR. AIAX.

Printed at London by Nicholas Okes. 1632.

BEN: IONSON
his
VOLPONE
Or
THE FOXE.

—— Simul & iucunda, & idonea dicere vitæ.

Printed for Thomas Thorp.
1607.